The Meanin… …owing

The Meaning of Learning and Knowing

Erik Jan van Rossum
University of Twente, The Netherlands

Rebecca Nicolette Hamer
Utrecht University

SENSE PUBLISHERS
ROTTERDAM/BOSTON/TAIPEI

A C.I.P. record for this book is available from the Library of Congress.

ISBN: 978-94-6091-250-4 (Thesis ed.)
ISBN: 978-94-6091-251-1 (paperback)
ISBN: 978-94-6091-252-8 (hardback)
ISBN: 978-94-6091-253-5 (e-book)

Published by: Sense Publishers,
P.O. Box 21858,
Rotterdam,
The Netherlands
http://www.sensepublishers.com

Printed on acid-free paper

Excerpts Gomes (2004) and Beah (2007) used by kind permission of the authors.

Cover photo: Rebecca Hamer

TABLE OF CONTENTS

Ik ben wie ik ben
Ik ben wie ik zou zijn
Ik ben wie ik wil dat ik ben
Ik ben zoals de wereld mij gemaakt heeft
Ik ben wie ik ben zoals ik wil
Ik ben wie ik ben, zelfs al zou ik dat niet willen
Ik ben niet zomaar iemand
Ik ben dan ook niet iemand anders
Ik ben ook niet wie je denkt dat ik misschien zou kunnen zijn
Want, beste vriend
Ik ben *ik*

En niets of niemand anders
Wat er ook gebeurt

Jij kan zeggen dat ik iemand anders ben geworden, maar eigenlijk ben jij juist anders geworden.

(Veerle van Rossum)

I am who I am
I am who I would be
I am who I want to be
I am the way the world made me
I am the way I want to be
I am who I am, even if I didn't want to be
I am not anybody
I surely am not someone else
I am not who you think I may be
Because, dear friend
I am *me*

And nothing or nobody else
Whatever happens

You may say I have changed, but in fact
it is you who has changed

Acknowledgements

The seed of this study lies with the committee performing the international accreditation for the Hotelschool The Hague in 1993. Their recommendation to move towards a more activating curriculum opened the way for the use of our existing model of students' learning conceptions for curriculum development. This study was in part financially supported by the Mobiliteitsfonds HBO, an institute concerned with promoting research in higher professional education in the Netherlands. The Hotelschool supported this initiative between 2005 and 2007. However first and foremost, our thanks go to all the students who, by freely giving us their time and repeatedly putting their thoughts in writing, provided the meat for this study. This concerns the students from our earlier university and Hotelschool based studies of course, but in particular we are grateful for the easy going and welcoming attitude of the many Hotello's towards their teacher who just would not stop contacting them in all those far away places. Their responses were often heartwarming.

One former student in particular we would like to thank in more ways than one. He was involved at the beginning and at the end: the current study. Jan Vermunt, a psychology student at Tilburg University in the 1980s, contributed to our first study into learning conceptions as a respondent. And again, about a quarter century later he agreed to be the supervisor for our thesis. In the latter role he had full confidence in our abilities, providing us with the freedom to write this book as we had envisioned it. In addition, his insightful questions put us onto new avenues of thought, at the same time forcing us to sharpen our own thoughts and arguments. Thank you Jan for giving us space and support. We look forward to continued cooperation.

While writing we contacted many of the researchers included in the reference list who – with very few exceptions – all responded cordially and provided us with some difficult to obtain articles, often including their newest papers and insights as well. Thank you all. In particular we would like to thank Marcia Baxter Magolda for her fruitful comments in the early stages and for the opportunity to explore self-authorship more fully.

Then of course there are our colleagues and friends who took our lack of social involvement over the recent years in their stride. Many provided us with moral support and some slipped in a useful reference or two.

Finally we would like to apologise to our children who bore the brunt of our distraction. It may not be easy to experience one parent preparing a thesis while you are young, but to lose both to the lure of intellectual engagement for many an evening and weekend must have been frustrating on occasion to say the least. Thank you Tim and Veerle for accommodating us and for loving us still.

Rebecca Hamer and Erik Jan van Rossum
The Hague, March 2010

CHAPTER 1

A MODEL OF STUDENTS' DEVELOPING CONCEPTIONS OF LEARNING AND TEACHING

ό δέ ανεξέταστος βίος ου βιωτός ανθρώπωι

(The unexamined life is not worth living, Socrates,

by Plato in Apology)

To set the stage for this study we will first introduce the model we have spent more than 25 years refining: a model about the different ways students view the meaning of learning (learning conceptions) and how they see good teaching (teaching conceptions). In discussing the views on learning we will draw mainly on Säljö's (1979a) seminal study for the first five learning conceptions, examples from students (and teachers) of the current study are presented in the chapters about Enterprising Learning (chapters 6 through 9). For the sixth learning conception we refer to our own 1984 study where we described this learning conception for the first time, as well as to Marton et al. (1993) and Beaty et al. (1997). The examples used in the section on teaching conceptions are taken from our earlier work with university students and more recent work with students of the Hotelschool The Hague – higher professional education. Following the elaboration of the learning and teaching conceptions, in a third major section of this introduction, we will revisit three early studies where we linked students' learning and teaching conceptions to their conceptions of a number of key concepts in education (van Rossum, Deijkers and Hamer, 1985; van Rossum, 1988; Taylor and van Rossum, 1986), and will discuss in particular students' conceptions of understanding and applying, and students' conceptions of intelligence.

Following this exposé we present our six-stage model of students' learning and teaching conceptions. Finally, at the close of this chapter we propose that the epistemological development described in this study is only the first tier of human cognitive development, linking our model to adult cognitive development. We have fleshed out this thought more thoroughly in Hamer and van Rossum (2008).

Central to our work and the current study are students' conceptions of learning and of good teaching. It is therefore important to try to make clear what we understand 'conceptions' to be. In 1992, Daniel Pratt formulated a description – a definition if you will – which we feel covers our understanding of conceptions well: "Conceptions are specific meanings attached to phenomena which then mediate our response to situations involving those phenomena. We form conceptions of virtually every aspect of our perceived world, and in so doing, use those abstract representations to delimit something from, and relate it to, other aspects of our world" (Pratt, 1992, p. 204).

Students' Conceptions of Learning

> *To all, the teacher is a mirror that shows not only the self but the path and its choices, the task and its demands—the difficulties, the joys. To all and from all, the teacher is a learner, a person—and a prism through which the ordinary continuously reveals itself to be miraculous.*
>
> *Gerald Grow, 1977*

Learning conceptions play an important role in students' study behaviour in higher (tertiary) education, because "we view the world through the lenses of our conceptions, interpreting and acting in accordance with our understanding of the world" (Pratt, 1992, p. 204). In 1979 Roger Säljö found that five categories were sufficient to describe the views on learning prevalent within a heterogeneous group of respondents, selected on age and exposure to formal education. The ages ranged from 15 to 73, and length of attended formal education ranged from 6 to 16/17 years. At the time of the study all participants were students (part time or full time).

In his studies into learning Säljö used the phenomenographic methodology devised by Ference Marton who reported in detail on this method for the first time in 1981 (Marton, 1981; Marton and Booth, 1997). Again we refer to Pratt (1992) for a succinct description of the phenomenographic method: "Phenomenography is a method for describing qualitatively different ways in which people understand or conceptualize an aspect of their world. It moves beyond individual, idiosyncratic understanding of a phenomenon [e.g. learning] to provide a general map of the qualitatively different ways in which the phenomenon is understood" (p. 205). So, phenomenography focuses on "revealing how things look from the point of view of the respondent", taking a second-order perspective (Pratt, 1992, p. 204). Phenomenography and issues of reliability are discussed in the next chapter. This method is based on a repeated review and categorisation of the ideas of individuals about various aspects of reality – in our case learning, teaching, etcetera. Naturally, it is essential that in this type of research the respondents are given a lot of freedom to express their views and ideas. In Säljö's original study interviews were used.

The five learning conceptions described by him are listed below:

1) Learning as the increase of knowledge.
2) Learning as memorising.
3) Learning as the acquisition of facts, procedures etcetera, which can be retained and/or utilised in practice.
4) Learning as the abstraction of meaning.
5) Learning as an interpretative process aimed at the understanding of reality.

These categories have been repeatedly confirmed in our research (van Rossum and Schenk, 1984; van Rossum, Deijkers and Hamer, 1984 and 1985; van Rossum and Hamer, 1985; van Rossum and Taylor, 1987; van Rossum, 1988; van Rossum, Würffel and Hamer, 2002; van Rossum, Hamer and Würffel, 2003 and van Rossum and Hamer, 2004). In our work we base our analysis on written answers to open questions (see chapter 2 and 6). In these studies we have shown that students' conceptions of learning are related to

a) study strategies and learning outcomes;
b) conceptions of significant educational concepts (teaching, understanding, application, etcetera);

and that they

c) develop over time, and
d) do not differ between university and (higher) professional education.

In this type of research the naming of the categories is often not sufficient to infer what kinds of responses belong to each category. Often quotes are used to overcome this problem. We will use the same procedure throughout in the remainder of this book, sometimes quoting other research and sometimes quoting our own respondents.

Learning Conception 1: Learning as the Increase of Knowledge

Responses in this first category are characteristically vague and learning is taken for granted. Learning is not an object of reflection, it is simply something "everybody does", like breathing, and as such the respondent doesn't seem to understand the meaning of the question. As Säljö describes in a fragment of an interview:

> [Interviewer]: What do you actually mean by learning?
> [Subject]: What do you mean by 'What do you mean'?
> [Interviewer]: I just wondered what you mean by that... what's the first thing that strikes you? …
> [Subject]: Learning… It's only a question of … well …
> (Säljö, 1979b, p. 447)

It often seems like they are not answering the question at all, but list activities or synonyms.

> … to learn, it's to learn new things, other things that you did not know before… a lot of things in History and so on, you did not know about that before, and the same thing in Swedish and Grammar and so on… (Säljö, 1979a, p. 12)

> … it's to increase your knowledge … you kind of start with a small bag and there is not much in it, but then the longer you live, the more you fill it up… (Säljö, 1979a, p. 13)

These two quotes address two aspects that are often separated in the answers but in fact are connected, namely the aspect of process (how you go about learning) and product (what you end up with – the outcome). In this stage the process seems to be collecting, and the outcome is fragmentary pieces of knowledge. Learning and knowledge are perceived as parallel tracks leading to the same destination. People "tend to equate knowledge with (…) 'discrete units of information' or simply 'facts', and learning is consequently the transfer of these discrete units into the head of the learner" (Säljö, 1979b, p. 446).

The focus on collecting and possession, picturing the learner as an 'avid collector', who, once in a specialty shop (the classroom), purchases everything the shopkeeper (teacher) has on offer, supports shortening the label to Increasing Knowledge, focusing it on the process.

Learning Conception 2: Learning as Memorising

Learning is equal to memorising and the ability to reproduce what memorised, usually in a school test setting. Reproduction is the product, while the process is memorising. Like the previous conception, learning is seen in quantitative terms: learning more is being able to reproduce more.

> ... To learn... yes, that's... you have to cram up your homework and learn a little bit of this and that by heart... well that's about it ... (Säljö, 1979a, p. 14)

> ... Well, it's to learn what's in the books. In principle it means to learn in order to be able to answer the questions which the teacher gives you ... (Säljö, 1979a, p. 14)

Here learning is seen as banking: "The students are not called upon to know, but to memorize the contents narrated by the teacher. Nor do the students practice any act of cognition, since the object towards which that act should be directed is the property of the teacher" (Freire, 2000, p. 80). The learner is an 'honest Joe' who works hard and puts aside his money (knowledge) to pay the bills (do the test) and perhaps save for a rainy day. There is also an awareness of not having to learn everything, of a selection towards

> ..[starting] to sort out things and you kind of learn what the teachers want, you learn to listen to them during the lessons and then you know more or less what the test will be like... (Säljö, 1979b, p. 448)

Here are the first signs of reflection, if not on the quality of what you learn, at least on the quantity. In banking terms, you don't set aside all of your earnings, only what you need to pay the bills. The concept of putting aside part of what you know for a specific use justifies the distinction between learning conception 1 (saving everything) and learning conception 2. We shortened the label to Memorising.

Learning Conception 3: Learning as the Acquisition of Facts, Procedures, etc, which can be Retained and/or Utilized in Future

Here the process of learning is selecting and memorising those facts, procedures, ideas etcetera which *may* be useful later in life. Respondents value this process over the - in their eyes - inferior process of memorising only for (school) tests. The product is the "feeling" of being able to apply knowledge in practice (later on). Both aspects are present in the following quote.

> ... well I think of learning plain facts which you select from your head more or less that is, as regards studies...., but then it is... I mean you have to be

> able to use it if, let's say if you find yourself in a similar situation to the one you were in earlier or if it reminds you of it, then you should be able to pick our the correct facts so to say or the correct way to proceed ...(Säljö, 1979a, p. 15)

Here as well learning is seen as a quantitative phenomenon and application takes on the character of applying an algorithm or copying. The learner starts to reflect further upon what is learned to decide whether or not it might turn out to be useful in the future. Our metaphor here is 'Rembrandt's apprentice' able to copy the master's (teacher's) brushstrokes, colour choice and composition in such a way that it is difficult to distinguish the apprentice's painting from the real thing. This view on learning has a flavour of not only memorising, but also "practicing until perfect" without changing the knowledge or the procedures. We re-labelled this category to Reproductive understanding/application or Application foreseen.[1]

The three learning conceptions above form by far the most common set of responses found in literature and our studies. About 70% of the 600-plus students participating in our studies over the past quarter of a century could be categorised as functioning at one of these epistemological levels at the beginning of their studies. In the remainder of this manuscript at times we refer to students or respondents using level-x-thinker, with x standing for their dominant learning conception at that time, e.g. "a level-three-thinker" or "some level-two-thinkers". In no way should this convention be interpreted as labelling or fixing the person in a particular category, nor should it be seen as implying that no change is possible. Indeed the crux of our model is that everyone is capable of change: epistemological development is a naturally occurring phenomenon that may be accelerated by formal education.

Learning Conception 4: Learning as the Abstraction of Meaning

This learning conception is the watershed in our model: seemingly a considerable obstacle that only about one in four of our respondents showed to have crossed at any time during our studies. At this level of thinking the focus shifts from taking in ready-made things (facts, procedures) existing 'out there' to constructing *meaning*. Säljö (1979a) describes this shift as follows "Learning is no longer conceived of as an activity of reproducing, but instead as a process of abstracting meaning from what you read or hear" (p. 16). The object of reflection here is understanding the subjects studied.

> ...take the subjects I'm studying, let's say history for example, it means that I should be able to understand a lot more about what development really is, sort of understand the process in a country or among a people in some way ... (Säljö, 1979b, p. 450)

The process within this learning conception is understanding, which is reached through relating ideas within the subject, finding out things, looking at the subject matter in a lot more depth, collecting various viewpoints on the studied material and getting the big picture. By constructing meaning respondents take an active part in the construction of their own view of the world, which still may be strongly dominated by the perspective provided by external experts. The product of this learning conception seems to be the internalisation of a "way of thinking", one of the purposes of higher education with its emphasis on the intellectual ability to think coherently, logically and analytically.

> Yes, to learn ... well it is not just a matter of learning facts. It is also to understand, to see contexts and to be able to use knowledge to draw conclusions, to think independently... I think I learned that at school... well perhaps everyone doesn't learn that, but I think I have... (Säljö, 1979a, p. 17)

> [To] have a process of thought that sort of "sets in motion" when you look at something... looking at something new in a far more logical way, and seeing the steps and the moves towards arriving at some sort of conclusion... learning is thinking clearer... Perhaps it is just the skill you have learned of thinking more coherently. (Beaty et al., 1997, p. 159)

Learning is seen as using a way of thinking (a skill) to arrive at an "informed view" (Beaty et al. 1997, p. 156). The students can perhaps be typified as the "criminal investigator", where the classroom is the crime scene and the product is to think through all the clues and follow up on leads in such a way as to come up with a plausible explanation to present to the judge (teacher). In an educational context this means that the learner must really understand the subject at hand, and we re-labelled this fourth conception to Understanding subject matter.

Learning Conception 5: Learning as an Interpretative Process Aimed at the Understanding of Reality

Säljö found that learning at this level is characterised by the expectation that what you learn should help you interpret the reality you live in, implying an important difference with the previous level: that learning moves outside the limits of the school situation. A second characteristic is that learning acquires personal meaning as opposed to the more technical view on learning in the previous stage. This interpretation is supported by Morgan et al. (1981, as quoted in van Rossum and Taylor, 1987, p. 20) when they say "While to some extent this [fourth] conception involves the student as an active agent in learning, what is to be learnt is still not necessarily of personal significance. The emphasis can be very much on understanding other people's ideas and theories [in 4], rather than on developing one's own [in 5]." Fundamental here is taking other perspectives into account, instead of only one's own, in a sense reintroducing the existence of multiple perspectives, but now including the benefit of evidence and argumentation.

> .. what's most important really, that's the connection between what I read and what I do and see otherwise during the days. I guess I have discovered this in some way, I guess it's the strategy. I've worked a little bit with problems like these in companies... I mean with problems of learning and teaching new

> things and then I have tried to... well if you don't see connections between what you read and your own situation, not very much will happen really. In some way I think I've found out that you learn things twice somehow. The first time could have been at school really, the second time is the connection, I mean it becomes conscious in some way... (Säljö, 1979a, p. 18)

Marton et al. (1993) and Beaty et al. (1997) expanded on Säljö's original interpretation, using more examples to support and clarify the nature of this fifth learning conception. Discussing the process aspect of this conception, they refer to notions such as broadening your outlook on things, opening your mind and widening your horizons. The outcome of this process (the product) is seeing things differently, a different view of the world, a – provisional – personal and contextuated view of reality. In our opinion, this conception of learning, with its truly relativistic flavour, matches Perry's fifth position (Perry, 1970 and below). One of subjects in Beaty et al. (1997) uses the expression "to look at the world with those eyes" (p. 156) to explain the role of the disciplinary framework learnt at university in developing a perspective. The relativeness of the perspective is explained by another subject when she says "You might have seen it in one way before and you sort of see it in a different way now" (p. 161). So looking at the world with eyes coloured by a particular perspective transforms this world to fit this perspective. By subsequently (consciously) changing one's perspective, one transforms the way the world is perceived. The object of reflection here is now personal development.

In metaphor, learning here is seen as a journey, with the learner as 'traveller', accompanied by companions (teachers and peers) who examine and enjoy the local scenery with him along the way. Together, the travellers try to widen their horizon through this journey. In educational terms one could interpret this as the teacher and students seeking new ways to look at things together, finding different perspectives to come to a 'better' understanding of the world around them. The product here is seeing things differently: being able to transform the way of seeing things by changing perspectives. Beaty et al. (1997) – in one of the few studies discussing developments in conceptions of learning – observe about this widening of horizons that it "has important implications for seeing oneself as a participant (rather than only a spectator) in what is happening" (p. 161). Focusing on the process we now re-label this learning conception Widening horizons[2].

While level-four-thinkers are already relatively scarce, less than 5% of all our respondents could at any time be categorised as level-five-thinkers.

Learning Conception 6: Self Realisation

In 1983 we[3] came to realise that there was another, qualitatively unique view on learning and identified this as a sixth learning conception, described in van Rossum, Deijkers and Hamer (1984) as "Self realisation". Some nine years later Marton et al. (1993) published what they thought was the first description of the sixth learning conception and named it "Changing as a person". In a footnote (p. 292) they acknowledged that we found this particular conception earlier and, more importantly, they acknowledged that both conceptions refer to the same view on learning. An important factor here is the rarity of this type of thinking, particularly in the usual age group of 18 to 25 years. In our sample of the 1984 study some relatively older students were included and Marton et al.'s study included adult students as well, which made detection more probable. In all our studies taken together we have found only few level-six-thinkers, slightly more than 1% of all respondents. However, once we recognised the response as belonging to a separate category, each new case encountered was distinct by the typical language used and the type of issues addressed in the response.

Learning conception 6 is characterised by an existential dimension, the self of the learner seems to be the focus of learning.[4] The process aspect of this conception is growing self-awareness, looking for answers to the question "Who am I?" The self has become the ultimate object of reflection. The product is self-realisation: becoming the person you feel you are (van Rossum, Deijkers and Hamer, 1984; van Rossum and Taylor, 1987; van Rossum and Hamer, 2004). Quotes of our own respondents will be presented below, in the discussion of conceptions of good teaching.

Beaty et al. (1997) present two different aspects of learning in this conception: the organic nature of the metaphors used and the feeling of becoming an agent and "being in charge". Both aspects can be seen in the quote below.

> … something personal and it's also something that's continuous, once it starts it carries on and it might lead to other things. It might be like a root that has other branches coming off it… it is for the person before and for the person afterwards sort of thing … Learning is self-realisation … when I've been made aware of something … the effect of learning how I feel … I've got more positive views and more positive ideas and I know which side of the fence I am on. (p. 158.)

> … expanding yourself. It is being more alive, more aware, feeling more in control. You tend to think that life just took hold of you and did what it wanted with you and I think that you come to realise that now you should take hold of life and make it go your way because you know it is possible. (p. 160)

The feeling of "being in charge" of your own life (or destiny) is very similar to having found an Internal Foundation, a concept used by Baxter Magolda (2001) to describe the final stage of her Epistemological Reflection Model (ERM).

The appropriate metaphor for learning here is growing, the self a 'living tree' firmly rooted in a garden (environment), providing shade and protection to and cared for by a number of gardeners (significant others), each with their own speciality. This conception of learning we re-label Growing self-awareness.

In Table 1.1 below we summarise the developing learning conceptions and in analogy to Säljö (1979b) we present the object of reflection central to each level.

Morgan and Beaty (1997) discuss three themes can be recognised in the development of students' learning conceptions: confidence, competence and control. Their Open University students reported that over time they developed confidence in their own ability to learn, to decide what to study, and to question or debate

Table 1.1. Developmental model of students' learning conceptions

	Van Rossum-Hamer Learning Conception	*Object of Reflection*
1	Increasing knowledge	None
2	Memorising	Exam relevancy
3	Reproductive understanding/ application or Application foreseen	Usefulness later on
4	Understanding subject matter	Subject matter meaning
5	Widening horizons	Personal development
6	Growing self awareness	Self

the material. Closely related their students reported increasing competence in studying, based on a larger repertoire of study skills. The third theme of control relates to increasing independence and autonomy.

> ..I suppose it's a process because whatever I am reading now, I'm not absolutely dogmatic about things but I certainly know what my position is. Whatever it is that I'm reading I know which one of the approaches is mine. I'm not thinking "Oh yes, well it could be that or I could think this way about it". My own view jumps out at me first and then I'll consider the others. Studying didn't always seem to be like that. (Morgan and Beaty, 1997)

It is remarkable that in their work with Open University adult students (distance education) Morgan and Beaty found similar stages as Perry (1970) found for college students, in our opinion indicating that Perry's model – and our model for that matter – may prove to be more generally applicable than many researchers feel comfortable to consider. Morgan and Beaty (1997, p. 236) conclude that the development of confidence is "the key step, perhaps a limiting factor or prerequisite, in developing competence in learning."

Students' Conceptions of Good Teaching

> *To the sleeper, the teacher is the wake-up call of birds at sunrise. To clay, the teacher is potter, sculptor, and trainer in self-shaping. To the wanderer, the teacher is a knowing guide. To the developed mind, the teacher is colleague, listener, friend.*
>
> *Gerald Grow, 1977*

In 1984 we included a question on teaching in our essay questionnaire with the purpose to study students' view on 'good teaching'. Initially, we made a distinction in teaching conceptions that was loosely based on the dichotomy between surface level and deep level approaches to learning (e.g. Marton et al., 1997; Chapter 5). These two categories could be characterised as "teacher directed" conceptions and on the other hand more "student directed" conceptions.

This soon proved to be insufficient to cover the full range of views expressed by the students, and we adjusted our approach toward describing a conception of good teaching matching each of the six conceptions of learning. In this way we felt we were listening more closely to what the students actually said, than what theory proposed us to look for. In retrospect, it did not surprise us that we found that these conceptions could be ranked on a dimension teacher-student directedness. As students moved along this dimension, their influence on the teaching-learning process increased while at the same time that of the teacher decreased. A remarkable finding – at that time – was that, within a single student, learning conception and teaching conception would be (logically) congruent. This led us to propose that we could improve our learning conception model by including and linking the conceptions of good teaching. Over the years, new data from other educational contexts helped us to refine the descriptions, focusing on the student-teacher relationship, which culminated in our 2004 model of linked continua of conceptions of learning and good teaching (van Rossum and Hamer, 2004).

Below we will now describe the students' conceptions of good teaching, using this six-stage model as point of departure and using quotes of a few typical students to illustrate each category.

Teaching Conception 1: Imparting Clear/Well Structured Information

This view on teaching is not found very often in higher education (and then only at the beginning of a student's educational career). Its main characteristic is total teacher dependence, as Femke says,

> Good teaching to me is presenting the subject matter to be learnt in such a way that it is not too dry (presented with humour if possible). The subject matter needs to be explained well and presented in a well-organised way. Resulting in a situation where further learning by oneself does not lead to problems due to sometimes disorganised and unintelligible teaching.

This conception of teaching depends upon the transfer of knowledge from the teacher to the student whose role is in the teaching-learning process is minimal.

Teaching conception 2: Transmitting Structured Knowledge, Acknowledging the Receiver

For these students teaching needs to be clear, orderly, efficient, entertaining and include opportunities to ask questions, implying a limited type of student-teacher interaction in a still very teacher dominated environment. Amelie elaborates,

- Good Teaching:
- There are teachers who twaddle on a whole hour about their holiday, or football[5] and ruin every class. It's fun to talk about other things in class once in a while, as an interruption, and then continue with the subject. This makes a class pass more quickly. Further, a teacher needs to be clear, giving concrete examples, so you know what he/she is talking about.

- I detest it when a teacher shows contempt because you just happen to be not that good in this particular subject. A little bit more attention is more useful than remarks such as 'you won't ever learn'.
- I really dislike lectures when there is no opportunity at all for students to say something. I don't always need to say something, but the idea that it is possible is agreeable.
- Having a chat or a bit fun occasionally, and for the rest a decent lecture, consequently not too many disruptions.

While the teacher in this conception is still dominant, students want to be recognised as the recipients of the message, and – e.g. through posing questions – become a little more involved. Students in this category are still very attached to structure and completeness of explanations.

Teaching Conception 3: Interacting and Shaping

The final predominantly teacher-directed view on teaching presented here, is characterised by teacher-dominated discussion, up-to-date examples, cases from practice, and an enthusiastic teacher who shapes and motivates the students using positive and negative feedback. Jeroen's teaching conception shows this clearly:

> [In good teaching] Lectures need to be short and to the point, be more like a discussion group. Furthermore topics need to be current and connected to practice. I found the Promotion Management lectures were best, because there cases from practice were discussed in relationship to the literature. Following this, a short case - related to the topic addressed in the lecture – was given as an assignment to be made in small groups.

> [An ideal teacher is] a teacher who uses a lot of examples from practice and connects these to the literature, and he/she should invite discussions during the lecture so that sufficient interaction takes place. In addition, I feel it is important that a teacher motivates students for his subject using his enthusiasm; I feel humour is very important in lectures. Furthermore it is important that a teacher gives feedback to his students in a positive way. This means not only emphasising the negative, but also evoking the best in his students.

This third teaching conception is characterised by a wide range of elements displaying the student's growing need for involvement in the teaching-learning process and an emergent independence within the student-teacher relationship. Students attach a lot of importance to being heard, and it is also a deeper reason for the emphasis on discussion, giving them the opportunity to express their opinions. These opinions can be related to the subject matter, but may also apply to more organisational aspects of the course, while students do not indicate anywhere that these opinions need to be informed. Petra says about this,

> Most important is – I think – that a teacher and his students have a good contact. The teacher should not be too authoritarian and should not show that

> he thinks that he's superior to the students (which happens a lot!). Then the student wouldn't want to appear interested anymore and everybody will be talking at cross-purposes. Also, I find that a teacher should not only make his own opinion about something clear, but that he should listen to students' opinions as well, so that these can be discussed. Consequently good teaching can only happen in small groups.

Teaching Conception 4: Challenging to Think for Yourself/Developing a Way of Thinking

For the students in this category of thinking about teaching most important in the teaching process are

1) the challenge to (start to) think for yourself or to undertake something,
2) the new, coaching role of the teacher and a less formal contact
3) the realisation of multiple solutions to any problem and multiple ways of reasoning
4) developing a "way of thinking" (logical and analytical).

Oliver catches almost all these aspects in his answer.

> To me, [good] teaching is stimulating the train of thought. Or looking for connections and using these for other purposes as well. To me, the ideal type of teaching would be that connections are well documented and that you're not just taking anything at face value. I feel a trial and error process is the best way to achieve this.
>
> The ideal teacher would be someone who consciously challenges me to think to achieve a goal (a grade). The teacher should then just let me go and not steer me too much. In this way I can find out for myself whether something is or is not possible or true. Assessment should then need to focus on the process and not so much on the end result. An ideal teacher should also have an hour or two a week to interact with students in a different way. Informal conversations in a bar for instance, would be a stimulus for both student and teacher because of the informal nature. The aim of teaching is not such much the knowledge accumulated, but [that it] improves and broadens the way of thinking.

Martijn's answer is much shorter covering most of the same points, while he also addresses specifically the confidence building emphasised by Morgan and Beaty (1997) as essential in the developmental process:

> [Good teaching is] doing projects, a lot of learning and thinking for yourself. There are not right or wrong answers, only many ways of reasoning and many options.
>
> [A good teacher is a] coach and mentor, (…) You must be able to walk in [his door] with problems and questions and not get the impression that you're badgering [the teacher]

> [A good teacher...] gives structure. And makes students feel strong about themselves.

At this stage the student has become an active participant in the teaching-learning process, while the teacher's role lies more in coaching the learning process. Both focus more on understanding and how solutions are found within a particular discipline (building expertise), and less on finding 'the correct answer'.

Teaching Conception 5: Dialogue Teaching

Students at this level of thinking about teaching appreciate a teaching environment based on learning partnerships (Baxter Magolda, 2004); where – in dialogue – teachers and students become equal partners in the mutual construction of knowledge. This emphasis on dialogue is central in the quotes below from Diana and Maria.

> Good teaching is – in my opinion – teaching that involves the students as much as possible in the subject. Consequently not that a teacher reels off his lectures while the students listen quietly – at least that's what you hope. So, I think that dialogue teaching is best, for me too. Then you stay involved in the subject. There's less chance that your thoughts wander. Furthermore I think that a teacher should be open to criticism, especially when it comes from the students: that he remains the teacher without putting himself on a pedestal. (Diana)

> In my opinion good teaching is working through a specific class, chapter or problem together and discussing it (teacher and students together) so that all parties can learn. As student you ought to ...oh well... have the impression that the whole group is on the same level and that you too can come out with a suggestion or solution. I find it very comforting and also in fact necessary, that there is someone (i.e. the teacher) who knows "everything" about a particular subject, to prevent students' hopeless wanderings. Then, the teacher is a guide who stands amongst the students. In secondary education the teacher is still too far away from the pupils, which is not beneficial to a mutual relationship. The latter is, in my opinion, more important for the pupils and students than you would expect at first glance. (Maria)

The importance of relativistic teaching, teaching which addresses for example underlying assumptions is brought into focus in Minka's answer,

> Good teaching explicitly shows its own limitations. [This happens when] one first discusses the assumptions, implicit truths and methods [all] underpinning the discipline and one places the subject matter in a context. The context can be historical, societal, religious, etcetera. Then it makes more sense. ... Furthermore I prefer studying in a group as small as possible, because often lots of questions are raised and to answer them seriously the teacher needs to tell the other side of the story as well...

The juxtaposition of dialogue and a personal perspective in this teaching conception is comparable to the blending of communion and agency that Baxter Magolda sees as the essence of the two highest levels of thinking about knowledge, teaching and learning (see Baxter Magolda, 2004 and chapter 3, Contextual Knowing).

Teaching Conception 6: Mutual Trust and Authentic Relationships: Caring

A good teaching environment, at this level, seems to be defined almost exclusively in language referring to emotion, autonomy and reciprocal relationships and seems to boil down to mutual trust and caring. At its most blunt it almost sounds like 'I'll learn something only when I feel good about it, when I want to and when the teacher is an inspiration to me'. Cora's answer is a good example of this.

> I don't really have an idea of what good teaching is. I do know, that (this refers more to learning from people than to teaching) as soon as some one tells me 'you have to do it this way or that way' I start to bristle. I feel: Just show me what, who, how and why you are, do, feel etc… Live as you think is right and if I can learn from that (what is almost sure to happen) then I can pick that up myself.
>
> I can only become wiser when I want to, you can't make me. I do feel the latter is valid within teaching. Good teaching is presenting the subject matter in such a way that [for] those already interested it stays that way or becomes more so.

The students' view on teaching shows a relative dismissive approach to the teaching technique or method. For good teaching freedom, enthusiasm and inspiration – within an authentic teacher-student relationship – have become essential, as Anna says:

> Good teaching develops in a situation of total understanding between student and teacher. (…) To me [the] teaching method is no longer important. As long as I can see that the man/woman in front of the group is really interested in the subject and in the people before him/her, it doesn't really matter how the subject is communicated. If he/she clearly is not interested in me or the things I want to learn, then I will not open myself up to communication of knowledge.

In these descriptions of good teaching learning has become 'endless' and fickle and it flourishes best in a free environment and with an inspirational teacher. The seemingly minimalist expression of good teaching is formulated by Craig Nelson[6] in summarising Perry (1970) "Eventually, students here have just one question… Are you OK?" "Who the teacher is becomes an essential part of the learning experience in a new and deeper way" (Nelson, 1999). Exploring the kind of teaching that is most appropriate for these students, Perry himself (1970) concludes that to convince students of their care and be worthy of their trust, the teacher

- must have "... a certain openness—a visibility in their own thinking, groping, doubts, and styles of Commitment",
- and have "the duty of confirming the student in his community with them—a membership he achieves (at the very least as an apprentice or colleague-to-be) through his own making of meaning, his daring to take risks, and his courage in committing himself"

These teacher requirements formulated by Perry – we feel – echo perfectly the quotes of Cora and Anna. In Table 1.2, we have completed our base model, including the linked teaching conceptions.

In the chapters 3 and 4 we will describe epistemological models that have strong resemblance to our model. This comparison is made to strengthen the fundament of our model for two reasons: first the observation of different approaches leading to very similar categories underpins the reliability and validity of our own findings, and second, all three types of models (phenomenographic, epistemological and quantitative), in fact describe and refer to the same kind of development. But first we will elaborate on the relationship between learning conceptions and the conceptions of three ubiquitous concepts in education, namely understanding, applying and intelligence. We include these three sets of conceptions because they form an integral part of the outcome space of the models discussed in chapters 3 and 4. Introducing these conceptions here increases the fullness of our comparison. Finally, in chapter 6 these concepts return in descriptions of 'signature' or key features of responses to our learning and teaching questions and so they are used to categorise data. The paragraphs below supply the background for the inclusion of these conceptions in our data analysis and categorisations.

Table 1.2. Developmental model of students' learning and teaching conceptions

	Van Rossum-Hamer Learning Conception	*Object of Reflection*	*Teaching Conception*
1	Increasing knowledge	None	Imparting clear/well structured knowledge
2	Memorising	Exam relevancy	Transmitting structured knowledge (acknowledging receiver)
3	Reproductive understanding/ application or Application foreseen	Usefulness later on	Interacting and Shaping
4	Understanding subject matter	Subject matter meaning	Challenging to think for yourself / developing a way of thinking
5	Widening horizons	Personal development	Dialogue teaching
6	Growing self awareness	Self	Mutual trust and authentic relationships: Caring

Students' Conceptions of Understanding and Applying

> *..it was decided to read* Das Kapital *by Marx... And the torment began. However not because Marx immediately defeated us with complicated constructions or other difficult things. No, on the contrary, already in the first chapter we succumbed to very evident issues, of which [Marx] made ridiculously elaborate points. ... [each of which] I understood perfectly. What then is it really about? The case was that we understood every separate word very well. The words made sentences which we also understood. But when we wanted to integrate these sentences into a whole, everything came tumbling down and we remained – not understanding it at all – amidst the rubble after which, agonised, we started all over again.*
>
> *(Doblaev, 1984)*

In our research, and in other studies into epistemology, we frequently encounter the use of words such as understanding, comprehension, application etcetera when describing learning activities or learning outcomes. Very often this happens without these concepts being further elaborated upon, and without clarity as to what exactly is meant in each instance. Also in students' group discussions we have observed that they use very divergent definitions of concepts as applying (knowledge) and understanding. While conceptions of understanding and application are not central to our developmental model, we feel it is necessary to discuss two of our early studies (van Rossum, Deijkers and Hamer, 1985; van Rossum, 1988) that clarified the qualitative differences in meaning of these important concepts as they relate to learning and teaching.

In van Rossum, Deijkers and Hamer (1985) and van Rossum (1988), we described a study in which 42 university Arts students were asked to fill in an open-ended questionnaire with eight questions, of which the following four are relevant to this study:

1. What do you mean by **learning**? (the learning conception)
2. What do you mean by **(good) teaching?** (the teaching conception)
3. What do you mean by **understanding** a text, **insight** into the subject matter?
4. What do you mean by (being able) **to use/apply** what you have learned?

Other concepts that were analysed in the above mentioned studies were the influence of the type of exam questions (assessment) on study strategy, and the difference between active and passive learning.

Below we will discuss the conceptions of understanding and applying as they were found to be related to learning and teaching conceptions.

Conceptions of understanding and applying 1. In the interpretation of concepts such as understanding and applying, the atomistic view of the first learning conception is expressed in a characteristic detail-directedness. The way the subjects see it, they have 'understood' something when they have "understood everything", every word, every sentence (see quote of Doblaev above). Similarly applying has a very absolute meaning, reminding us of Kuhn's realist level of thinking (chapter 3, section on Kuhn): applying is comparing facts to reality.

> Applying makes me think of comparing what is learned to reality. To see whether *it is really so* (Bert in Van Rossum, Deijkers and Hamer, 1985, p. 624)

Conceptions of understanding and applying 2. Characteristic for learning at this level of thinking is the exam directedness. Understanding and applying still are conceived foremost as reproductive activities, with understanding and applying both meaning being able to reproduce the original information, and to answer exam questions correctly. Two quotes illustrate this.

> I have understood a text when I literally understand what is said and when I can apply this in an exam. For me to understand a "text" and to apply it is something very different from having insight into the subject matter: when I have insight *and* understanding of a text, I'll get the best results. But I can also get good marks when I just understand the text, I only repeat what is said. (unnamed student in van Rossum, 1988, p. 203)

> The ability to apply what is learned is: applying it at an exam, so that the questions are answered correctly and the results coming from this are favourable. (unnamed student in van Rossum, Deijkers and Hamer, 1985, p. 626)

For these students there seems to be no difference between reproduction, understanding and applying: "To me the application of the text is the same as the concept of reproduction that I have used already a few times in my answers" (Henry in van Rossum, Deijkers and Hamer, 1985, p. 626).

Conceptions of understanding and applying 3. At this level of thinking we see the developing ability to separate main issues from issues of lesser importance to the storyline of a text. This distinction is major in the conception of understanding. The criteria for understanding are whether one can reproduce the main issues of a text in general terms (showing selectivity), and whether one can use or discuss it.

> "Understanding", "having insight into the subject matter": by this I don't actually mean the fact that you can literally reproduce all kinds of facts and definitions, etcetera, but more so that you can follow the continuous thread of through the subject matter, that you know what it's about in a broad sense (that you can reproduce it generally in your own words). Besides this I think that, if you understand the subject matter, you then must be able to use it, to apply it to other areas and problems, to discuss it. (Audrey in van Rossum, Deijkers and Hamer, 1985, p. 629)

Application is seen as more complex than before, there may be two expressions of application: 1) answering (exam) questions, doing sums and 2) practical applications, however, where application goes beyond an algorithmic level it is seen as problematic, see Rob's answer to this question.

> Very roughly you can say the "being able to apply what is learned" means that you must be able to solve a given problem, either at an exam, either from practice or otherwise, [using] the knowledge provided. This can be more exactly formulated if you let the applications also depend on the subject or speciality. For instance the application of mathematics is different from the application of sociology of literature. Mathematics you can apply in technical cases, ranging from architectural problems to computer programs; sociology of literature wants to provide an insight into the various views on literature and the application of this is vague and questionable… (Rob in van Rossum, Deijkers and Hamer, 1985, p. 629)

Conceptions of understanding and applying 4. Here we see a qualitative difference emerge in both conceptions of understanding and applying as compared to the previous, more reproduction oriented levels. Understanding is seen as tracking down the theme of a text, finding out the author's intention. Making connections and *constructing* meaning out of the material is mentioned for the first time. Sometimes constructing meaning, when expanding beyond a single text, is seen as having insight into the subject matter, as Emmy says,

> Understanding a text: knowing what the text is about, knowing what the theme of a text is, what the author of the text has tried to get across to the reader.
>
> Insight into the subject matter: if you can see interrelationships between different texts and perhaps the lecture notes and then [you] discover the main lines in them (the entire subject matter) and [you] can maybe connect them to other subjects (Emmy in van Rossum, Deijkers and Hamer, 1985, p. 631)

Application at this level is seen as "use of knowledge" when the situation requires it and is based on "constructed meaning". Use is perceived as more flexible, perhaps heuristic, in nature and there is no mention of a lag in time. Use can be immediate and/or much later in life, important is that it is constructive, and takes place outside test and exam situations. Jane and Emmy have the following to say about applying,

> If you can apply what you have learned, you are also busy with it outside your study, when you're not attending lectures or studying. Things strike you that you can connect with your study, for instance they confirm what you have learned or, on the contrary, evoke questions. You can also explain to others in a comprehensible way why these things strike you. (Jane in van Rossum, Deijkers and Hamer, 1985, p. 632)

> … I can also imagine that you start using the studied subject matter in a small study or the writing of an essay (Emmy in van Rossum, Deijkers and Hamer, 1985, p. 632)

At this level we can see the recurring theme of construction: construction of meaning, focusing on meaningful activity when using knowledge, and being critical and creative while doing so. However, at the same time these descriptions have a clearly rational and somewhat technical flavour to them: creativity is something you can achieve by following (the) rules, thinking the way *they* – the successful professionals in your discipline – want you to think.

Conceptions of understanding and applying 5. Where students at the previous level sometimes express their thoughts in a somewhat technical way, devoid of personal involvement, at this level personal views are more prominently included in interpretations of learning, teaching, understanding and applying. Furthermore, examining the evidence, formulating arguments for or against and internally discussing the value of the content are frequent themes in these answers. During these internal discussions, conceptions of knowledge, learning, understanding, insight and applying sometimes seem to merge to a certain extent. For instance, Roger says

> You probably have understood a text well when you can rephrase the content, the purport of the text rather easily in your own words, when you can support or oppose it with your own examples, when you can give a personal opinion about the clearness, the correctness, etcetera of the text, when you can include the content and the purport in your own argumentations. ……… I think "applying" is the only criterion for have learned something. If you can't apply it (and here applying doesn't mean correctly answering the knowledge questions – in a conventional sense – in an exam), you haven't learned anything. Being able to apply means having understood it well. In that sense applying contains, among other things, that which I spoke of while answering the [question on understanding]. (Roger in van Rossum, Deijkers and Hamer, 1985, p. 634–635)

Vera discusses applying as problem solving and stresses its heuristic nature, while including the importance of evidence, critical thinking and the ability to take on another viewpoint.

> Using your knowledge in a way which is not reproducing, but problem-solving. Using knowledge to clarify things that have no direct connection with the area concerned. You must also be able to use the knowledge, for instance, to relate new views, opinions to what you already know; to discern various viewpoints and to compare them critically. Based on the knowledge you have acquired, you must then be able to look at certain data or situations from a "different" viewpoint; to describe certain things from a viewpoint that is related to the acquired knowledge, even if it isn't specifically your view. (Vera in van Rossum, Deijkers and Hamer, 1985, p. 635)

Here, Vera is formulating the basic requirements for true relativism and interprets understanding and application in a qualitatively distinct way from any previous level of thinking. Applying is not only something you can do *after* you have understood something, it is a necessary step *in* understanding and learning.

In these last three levels we find three distinct conceptions of applying, that are compared to each other in Treffers et al. (1982) discussing understanding and applying arithmetic: application can be seen "not only as *ap-plication-afterwards*, but also as application *integrated* in the formal arithmetic, and even preceding it as *pre-plication*, as point of departure for the development of understanding" (translated in van Rossum, 1988, p. 201).

Conceptions of understanding and applying 6. At this highest level of thinking about learning and teaching, we only found one student whose view on understanding texts reflects the sense of agency we – over the years – have come to expect at this level: "You understand a text when you could have written it yourself" (van Rossum, 1988, p. 205). However, having only one student to go on in this sample and lacking additional responses from other studies we will not include this level in the scheme below.

Summarising Conceptions of Understanding and Applying

In Table 1.3 below we have tried to capture the essence of the conceptions of understanding and applying for the first five levels of thinking. These descriptions are

Table 1.3. Linking learning conceptions to conceptions of understanding and applying

	Van Rossum-Hamer Learning Conception	*Conception of Understanding*	*Conception of Applying*
1	Increasing knowledge	Understanding every word, every sentence	Comparing facts to reality
2	Memorising	Answering exam questions by reproduction	Reproducing at exams
3	Reproductive understanding/ application or Application foreseen	Reproducing the main points (using selectivity); using or discussing what is learned	Answering exam questions; Using knowledge algorithmically in practice
4	Understanding subject matter	Making connections between sources, constructing the author's intention	Using knowledge in flexible ways, within and outside the educational setting; 'creativity' is reached by following disciplinary rules
5	Widening horizons	Formulating arguments for or against, and using what is learned in your own argumentations	Problem solving in a heuristic and relativist way
6	Growing self awareness	-	-

somewhat amended from the earlier work, because – in the years since these analyses (1985 and 1988) – we have come to see a broader picture, recognising more clearly the essential nature of each level of thinking. So, while staying true to our original model, we now occasionally have come to place our emphases slightly different than before, in an attempt to improve understanding.

Students' Conceptions of Intelligence

Intelligence is knowing what to do when you don't know what to do.

(Jean Piaget)

In 1986, Taylor and van Rossum published an internal (Dutch-language) report of the Tilburg University on the relationship between conceptions of learning and conceptions of intelligence.[7] In this exploratory study, 47 first-year psychology students were asked about their views on learning, understanding, their ideal learning situation and intelligence. Only the responses to the learning and intelligence question were discussed in Taylor and van Rossum (1986).

Analysis of the learning conception responses revealed that this sample contained no students with learning conception 1. However, for the learning conceptions 2 through 6 this report contains examples of clearly different conceptions of intelligence. As with the learning conceptions, the development in views on intelligence is from intelligence as an unsophisticated, one-dimensional, and unchangeable type to intelligence seen as complex, changeable and difficult to ascertain. Like before, we will illustrate the different ways of thinking about intelligence with excerpts from responses of the students, beginning from level 2. The students in the report were identified by number.

Conception of intelligence 2. As learning at this level of thinking, intelligence is seen as a one-dimensional, self-evident concept: it says something about how smart you are, how little trouble you have with learning. However, intelligence is something that is not necessarily connected to 'knowing a lot'; it's more an innate talent.

> I think intelligence is the ability to learn easily (in the broadest sense of the word). A person's intelligence quotient reflects I think their intellectual abilities, the measure in which a person can take in information, process it and rephrase it in their own words, and to what extent he can reason logically and has insight.
>
> Intelligence is something you are born with, so it's hereditary, but I think the environment and circumstances you grow up in play a big role in the extent to which that intelligence is developed. (S16, Taylor and van Rossum, 1986, p. 13)
>
> I see intelligence as the innate IQ. Intelligence cannot be increased. You can't increase your IQ through studying, that only leads to becoming more learned.

> I think that the IQ is best measured in children in pre-school [kindergarten]. They haven't learned that much (I mean like reading, arithmetic, etcetera). As soon as children start to learn they increase their learnedness and then the IQ is only measurable with tests. (S6, p. 15)

This second level conception of intelligence can be summarised with the following key words: fixed, innate and testable with the current IQ-tests.

Conception of intelligence 3. Students at this third level of thinking about learning and teaching still feel that intelligence (IQ) is fixed and innate, but that intelligent behaviour is something that can be learned. The focus at this level is on applying or using one's innate intelligence, the more one uses it, the more intelligent one's behaviour.

> I think IQ is innate, but that intelligence (or displaying intelligent behaviour) is learned. Someone – with a lower IQ - who is stimulated by the environment, can attain better results than someone with a higher IQ who is not stimulated. The former shows more intelligent behaviour than the latter. I think everyone can reach a certain level of intelligence (the one perhaps with more difficulty than the other) by using specific approaches to studying and problem solving.

> … I think that you can't talk about intelligence as having a high IQ. People with a high IQ can fail to use it and then they don't show intelligent behaviour. People with a lower IQ can, with more effort, still show pretty intelligent behaviour. So, I think, there is actually no relationship between IQ and intelligent behaviour. (S2, Taylor and van Rossum, 1986, p. 16–17)

At this level students separate innate IQ from intelligent behaviour, where intelligent behaviour refers to the use you make of your innate intelligence.

Conception of intelligence 4. By students that see learning as understanding - and applying what is learned based on this understanding, both in academic areas and in everyday life – intelligence is viewed in a logically coherent way, as the ability to function well and independently in everyday life: as one student puts it, intelligence is "a way of life" (p. 19). Intelligence is also something that can be developed. It loses its absolutist interpretation and it leads to reflection about many things.

> I think intelligence is the ability to learn everyday things in a relatively short time, such as filling in cheques. And being able to follow the classes at school, without needing continuous repetition of the meaning of something. Being able to act independently in situations in a way that there are no unpleasant or weird consequences. (S31, Taylor and van Rossum, 1986, p. 19–20)

> I don't think I'm that intelligent, but I think that is something that grows. It is important to develop yourself well, and I think that is a form of intelligence too.

> It is not only learning (I notice this in my own environment) that makes someone intelligent, but also life experience and thinking about the meaning of it all, thinking about life etcetera now and then is also intelligence. I think you don't really need to be intelligent to go to college or learn. If you are really interested, than you are willing to study things, to put in some effort. What then is intelligent behaviour? …
>
> What is intelligent? I think everyone is intelligent, depending on the criterion you use. (S4, p. 21)

At this level intelligence is no longer a fixed personal aspect; it is something you can develop through thinking and learning (both from school and life). Being intelligent is expressed in everyday behaviour, including independently solving everyday problems and situations with relative ease.

Conception of intelligence 5. At his level, intelligence is sometimes seen as problem solving in the broadest sense. It includes a view on which (problem solving) skills are most necessary in society for it to function well, and intelligence is clearly seen as something that can be developed, and needs to be developed when society needs it.

> One option is to define intelligence as problem solving ability and to specify this for a variety of problem areas that need to be addressed. (S7, Taylor and van Rossum, 1986, p. 22)
>
> … Once you have made an inventory of the widest variety of skills, you would need to establish which skills are necessary in the society you want. Once you've made that choice (in the larger sense that society knows where it wants to go) then you can determine how people, who lack certain necessary skills, can be helped to acquire these skills (in much the same way dyslectic children are helped in learning to read). (S11, p. 23)

Here we see the signs of 'widening horizons' the associated learning conception is named after. The horizon of intelligence is now outside the individual, it includes society as a whole. A second aspect of intelligence that emerges at this level is personal development, taking one's own route, and understanding the relativity of what one observes in everyday life.

> I think an intelligent person pays attention to what happens around him in everyday reality, and is able to put things in perspective so he can continue to go his own way. An intelligent person will want to develop himself further and further, and tries to learn from his experiences, both positive and negative. This kind of intelligence is not easy to establish. (S20, p. 24)

Conception of intelligence 6. At this level, views on intelligence include cognitive and affective aspects, seeing it as a comprehensive, intellectual and non-intellectual phenomenon. Where at the previous level intelligence was seen as problem solving, here it is seen as a creative process. Perhaps the distinction is between problem solving (5) and problem posing (6).

> Intelligence occurs in many areas. Social-emotional intelligence for instance (where in particular mentally handicapped people show an enormous richness). So, intelligence is not only intellect. ... You should have a comprehensive conversation with someone, about social, emotional, relational, cultural and intellectual issues. And then you would be missing quite some issues still, such as the areas of art, ethics, creativity of people etcetera. But I do think a one-on-one conversation is the best way to find out about all of it. (S28, Taylor and van Rossum, 1986, p. 25)

> Intelligence is 'something' that is difficult to describe, but that, I feel, can express itself in a variety of ways such as (...) creativity. ... With creativity I mean playing with the knowledge you have and creating new or adapted theories, so not parroting what other people say, but adapting what you do to your own norms and rules. (S26, p. 29)[8]

Comparing the two extremes found in this study we can see a development from intelligence seen as an innate, fixed IQ, towards a comprehensive conception of intelligence, including a variety of non-cognitive aspects. The study this section is based on was limited in scope and exploratory in nature, with some learning conceptions comprising of only a few respondents. Although these conceptions of intelligence show striking consistency with the associated learning conceptions, and have some resemblance with more quantitative epistemological belief dimensions (e.g. Schommer, 1990, see chapter 4), we would suggest further studies to properly define the (six) conceptions of intelligence.

Below in Table 1.4 we have summarised the found conceptions of intelligence and linked them to their associated learning conception.

Table 1.4. Developmental model of students' learning and intelligence conceptions

	Van Rossum-Hamer Learning Conception	*Object of Reflection*	*Conception of intelligence*
1	Increasing knowledge	None	-
2	Memorising	Exam relevancy	Innate and fixed IQ
3	Reproductive understanding/ application or Application foreseen	Usefulness later on	Innate and fixed IQ versus intelligent behaviour
4	Understanding subject matter	Subject matter meaning	Not fixed anymore Independently thinking and solving everyday problems with ease
5	Widening horizons	Personal development	Personal development Problem solving skills, as needed in society
6	Growing self awareness	Self	Creativity Intelligence is intellect and affect

A Developmental Model of Students' Learning and Teaching Conceptions

In the remainder of this study we will refer frequently to our learning-teaching conception model as presented in Table 1.2 (and repeated in the first three columns of Table 1.5 below). However as summary of this chapter in table 1.5 we have linked all the conceptions treated above in one model.

Table 1.5. Summary model of learning-teaching conceptions and related conceptions of some relevant educational concepts

	Van Rossum-Hamer					
	Learning Conception	*Object of Reflection*	*Teaching Conception*	*Conception of Understanding*	*Conception of Applying*	*Conception of Intelligence*
1	Increasing knowledge	None	Imparting clear/ well structured knowledge	Understanding every word, every sentence	Comparing facts to reality	-
2	Memorising	Exam relevancy	Transmitting structured knowledge (acknowledging receiver)	Answering exam questions by reproduction	Reproducing at exams	Innate and fixed IQ
3	Reproductive understanding/ application or Application foreseen	Usefulness later on	Interacting and Shaping	Reproducing the main points (using selectivity); using or discussing what is learned	Answering exam questions; Using knowledge algorithmically in practice	Innate and fixed IQ versus intelligent behaviour
4	Understanding subject matter	Subject matter meaning	Challenging to think for yourself / developing a way of thinking	Making connections between sources, constructing the author's intention	Using knowledge in flexible ways, within and outside the educational setting; creativity is reached by following rules	Not fixed anymore Independently thinking and solving everyday problems with ease
5	Widening horizons	Personal development	Dialogue teaching	Formulating arguments for or against, and using what is learned in your own argumentations	Problem solving in a heuristic and relativist way	Personal development Problem solving skills, as needed in society
6	Growing self awareness	Self	Mutual trust and authentic relationships: Caring			Creativity Intelligence is intellect *and* affect

Possible Development beyond the Sixth Learning-Teaching Conception

After describing the various developmental stages (see especially Table 1.2 before), one might wonder about the logic of why students develop at all. What is the process and what are the questions that may drive development? We feel that it may be a series of cycles of differentiation and integration. Because the majority of students start higher education as level-two-thinkers we start with them, and not the level-one-thinkers who are not aware of the option of reflection.

In traditional secondary education level-two-thinkers have learnt to focus on what is important to pass examinations, addressing the important issue of "How do I pass exams?" So exams define what to learn and know.

After a while, perhaps confronted with the demands of higher education and life, level-two-thinkers may experience discomfort with memorising and passing exams alone, and the need for (reproductive) meaning making and application differentiates out of learning conception 2 into learning conception 3. Learners then become level-three-thinkers trying to answer the issue "What is useful for me to know?" For level-three-thinkers later work or practice define what to learn and know.

The imminent future as a successful professional – or working experiences – may stimulate learners to develop into level-four-thinkers (learning conception 4), where the way of thinking of level-two-thinkers and level-three-thinkers become elements in an integrated system focusing on autonomy and understanding within a context, addressing the issue of "How should I think?" or "How do I make sense of reality?" This is a big change in thinking and we have referred to this shift as the watershed in epistemology within our six-stage model. The learning and knowing of level-four-thinkers is defined by a professional's (disciplinary) way of thinking.

The realisation that there may be more contexts including other autonomous people, leads to the differentiating move into learning conception 5. Level-five-thinkers focus on connection and multiple perspectives: "How do I relate to other people and perspectives?" and their learning and knowing is still defined externally by these perspectives.

These five first tiers of development seem to focus on epistemology: knowledge and knowing. We have referred to this first set of five as a model of "learning to know" (van Rossum and Hamer, 2008), introducing a second shift in focus within our original six-stage developmental model. We have discussed this second shift, and the provisional second tier of development introduced below, which focuses on "learning to be", in more detail in Hamer and van Rossum, 2008.

Learning conception 6 can be seen either as the final stage or the first of a second type of development. Either way it is characterised by the integration of autonomy (level-four-thinkers) and connection (level-five-thinkers) into a new structure addressing more ethical issues such as "Who am I?" Here, *for the first time* the self becomes 'the boss' who defines learning and knowing. Level-six-thinkers have made a step upwards to another, ontological plane which led us before to propose a change of nomenclature: learning to be me or "knowing **me"**.

In response to a query what then would constitute learning to be 2 and beyond [9], we have used both the idea of differentiation and integration used above, as well as the idea of 'stepping out of embeddedness' that Kegan introduced (see chapter 3) to extrapolate a possible developmental trajectory (see Hamer and van Rossum,

2008 for a more elaborate discussion). So if level-six-thinkers ask "Who am I?", level-seven-thinkers might focus on differentiation and finding out "Who are you?", embracing the other in a new way of knowing Parker Palmer might be referring to when he says "a way of knowing and of living that has moved beyond fear of the other into respect for, even *a need for*, its otherness" (Palmer, 1998, p. 56, italics ours). Level-eight-thinkers then – stepping out of 'you-and-I' – might integrate this into the question "What defines humanity (to me)?"[10] Perhaps we see an example of these three levels in John Donne's meditation XVII[11], where he links the self to others and mankind:

> All mankind is of one author, and is one volume; when one man dies, one chapter is not torn out of the book, but translated into a better language; and every chapter must be so translated...
>
> As therefore the bell that rings to a sermon, calls not upon the preacher only, but upon the congregation to come: so this bell calls us all: but how much more me, who am brought so near the door by this sickness....
>
> No man is an island, entire of itself...any man's death diminishes me, because I am involved in mankind; and therefore never send to know for whom the bell tolls; it tolls for thee.

And after considering humanity, in becoming a level-nine-thinker, one might differentiate towards non-human life: "What about all other living things?", perhaps in time progressing towards a new structure. Becoming a level-ten-thinker could mean addressing the issue of "What is humanity's place and responsibility in the system, in and towards the ecology and the planet we live on, in short 'life as we know it'?" Although, this speculation seems to call us "to boldly go where no-one has gone before", we choose to leave the contemplation of "life, *not* as we know it" to another time and place.

This leaves the issue why people ask these questions undecided, although some schools of thought believe that making sense of our environment by asking questions (inquiry) may be "hard wired" into our brain (e.g. Pinker, 1997, 2002). On the other hand, perhaps it is only the beliefs – the results of these inquiries - that get hard wired or at least "hard set" at an early age.

> It begins with the innate need of humans to make meaning out of their experience of the world. So we develop, at quite early ages – as five-year-olds, for example – basic sets of ideas about how the world works, what's dangerous, who's friendly, about right and wrong, what to like and how to behave, and so on. The scary part is that these childhood versions of reality tend to get pretty hardwired into the brain and prove quite resistant to change: Once we think we've figured out some corner of the world, we tend to see what we want to see and hear what we want to hear, bending subsequent experience into confirmation. I say "scary" because the existence of prior beliefs can be a major impediment to subsequent learning: The beliefs, after all, may be objectively wrong, or bigoted, or dysfunctional, and block fair and open encounter with the new or different.

> Very significantly, prior beliefs turn out to be especially impervious to classroom-based instruction, and especially to teaching as telling. (Marchese, 1998. p. 5)

Or it may be the human condition to struggle to balance the paradoxes inherent to the profound truths of life (Palmer, 1998, p. 62–63). As mentioned before, we have treated this further developmental tract more elaborately in Hamer and van Rossum (2008). In chapter 11, Educating the educators, we present a credible example of the seventh learning-teaching conception in discussing the way this could influence teaching.

Returning to terra firma, in the interpretation of such a developmental model as our own, in phenomenography (see also chapter 2) we often encountered views that implicated that when moving from one stage to the next, you lose the skills and advantages of the previous one. This interpretation likens development to buying new clothes to replace old, tattered ones. Perhaps this mindset came from a reticence to label one way of thinking as (inherently) better than another, going only so far as to label the one as more (or less) appropriate than another within a context. We feel that this interpretation ignores the hierarchical inclusiveness of the categories, as many students in higher levels clearly indicate that they have not forgotten - nor have become unable to function at - the lower levels when called for. We would suggest amending the analogy to purchasing new clothes, adding to your wardrobe in order to dress appropriately for a new situation: you may not need a suit when you're at school, but one may prove necessary when applying for a job. In this case you usually don't throw away your jeans. You simply reserve them for occasions when they are appropriate apparel. We speak not only from personal experience, as said above numerous respondents refer to using "old" ways of learning as well as new approaches or strategies (for examples see chapters 7 through 9 below). We also have some corroboration from a respected external source as well: when Blythe Clinchy - in revisiting Women's Ways of Knowing - admits of sometimes growing "impatient with students who behave as Received Knowers" (McVicker Clinchy, 2002, p. 67) and continues

> I can muster some compassion for Received Knowers by recalling how I revert to this position whenever I am faced with something novel, complex, and incomprehensible, like the first time I saw a game of cricket or heard a piece of atonal music. On such occasions I yearn for an expert who will just tell me what it all means. (p. 67)

In addition, keeping less sophisticated approaches alive while they are still useful is not limited to epistemology. It is a well-known aspect of (school or applied) science: Nelson discusses the uses of outmoded conceptions (of physics).

> Consider the brilliance of the flat earth model. The earth is in fact very flat – precisely as flat as the surface of a small pond on a still day. Although the pond is wonderfully flat, it domes imperceptibly up in the middle to exactly

> match the earth's curvature. Moreover, the flat earth model is by far the most widely used quantitative model of the shape of the earth in practical human applications such as architecture and engineering. (We assume that in a square room, opposite vertical walls will be parallel rather than vertically divergent; this assumes that the earth is flat.) Thus, the flat earth model has precisely the same present scientific validity as do Newton's laws of motion. Both capture important pieces of reality. Both are of immense, quantitatively precise, practical importance. And both are quite wrong and wrong in exactly the same sense. Each is a quantitatively quite good local first approximation that fails spectacularly on larger scales. Our current explanatory models in most, if not all, fields are useful in about these same senses, and many (perhaps all) either are now known to be wrong or will likely turn out to be wrong in about the same sense. (Nelson, 1999)

Higher levels of thinking are necessary when one becomes aware that knowledge and learning are more complex than one ever thought possible before. Entwistle and Walker (2000, see chapter 5) interpret models such as Säljö (1979a) and Perry (1970) as models of Expanding Awareness: the expanded awareness of the nature of learning, academic study, knowledge and interpersonal relationships.

We agree with this interpretation and would like to offer as well that such development leads to increasing competence, confidence and feeling of being in control in a complex world. Furthermore, if students' fail to reach higher levels of thinking demanded in higher education – and thus are unable to perform at the level of complexity that is expected – in a very real sense they are *In over their heads* (paraphrasing Kegan, 1994 see chapter 3).

Conclusions

In chapter 1 we introduced our six-stage developmental model of linked learning and teaching conceptions. We found that each learning-teaching conception captures not only students' views on learning and teaching, but that each stage or learning-teaching conception is a complex structure consisting of concepts with meanings specific to each stage. We have discussed the different interpretation of concepts such as understanding, application and intelligence within each of the six learning-teaching conceptions. This means that for important concepts commonly used in the teaching-learning process participants assign meanings to these concepts in a way congruent with their own way of knowing: both teachers and students use the same words to indicate different things. For research this means that

1) researchers can be deceived regarding the epistemological sophistication of respondents when they focus more on the words used than on the meaning that is conveyed;
2) the issues respondents spontaneously use themselves in describing their way of knowing are essential data in the analysis; and

3) because the interpretation of words/concepts varies by developmental stage the validity of typical inventory items is less than straightforward: you never know exactly what the respondent meant with his/her answer (e.g. Perry, 1970).

In daily life when ways of knowing between students or between teacher and students differ greatly, conversations in teaching and learning may consist mainly of miscommunications of which participants are blissfully unaware.

Not only do people mean different things when using the same words or concepts, the interpretations of these concepts have direct and indirect effects on many aspects of learning: motivation, sense of control over what is learned and how, expectations (and thus also the subsequent reaction) towards the learning-teaching environment, study strategies and views on assessment to name but a few. In 1984 we have seen that the complex of beliefs characteristic for each learning-teaching conception has immediate effect on how students learn and the quality of what they have learnt. Learning-teaching conceptions 1 through 3 can be associated with surface-level processing and learning outcomes that are mostly of a reproductive nature. Learning-teaching conceptions 4 through 6 in turn can be associated with deep-level processing and learning outcomes that are mostly of a constructive nature.

In learning-teaching conception 1, learning is not reflected upon: it is simply something "everybody does," like breathing. Learning is described as a list of activities or synonyms. Students with this learning conception view teaching as the transfer of knowledge. The role of the student is minimal and the teaching-learning process is defined entirely by the teacher.

To students with learning-teaching conception 2, learning is equal to memorising and the ability to reproduce what is memorised, usually in a school test setting. Level-two-thinkers see learning in quantitative terms: learning more is being able to reproduce more, but they also have a budding awareness of not having to learn everything, being able to make a selection of the facts to be memorised. For these students teaching needs to be clear, orderly, efficient, entertaining and must include opportunities to ask questions, implying a limited type of student-teacher interaction in a still very teacher-dominated environment.

At learning-teaching conception 3, the process of learning is selecting and memorising those facts, procedures, ideas, etcetera which *may* prove useful later in life. Learning and understanding both are interpreted as being able to apply what is learned in the future. The major focus of learning is still quantitative and reproductive, and neither the learner nor what is learned is changed in any way. Teaching is characterised by teacher-dominated discussion, up-to-date examples, cases from practice, and an enthusiastic teacher who shapes and motivates the students using positive and negative feedback. These students attach a lot of importance to being heard, to giving them the opportunity to express their opinions. They feel any opinion is as good as any other.

About three quarters of all our students could be allocated to one of the three reproduction oriented learning-teaching conceptions described above.

In moving to learning-teaching conception 4, students move across what we call the *watershed*: the focus shifts from taking in ready-made things (facts, procedures) existing 'out there' to actively constructing meaning. Such students prefer teachers who: 1) challenge students to (start to) think for themselves, 2) encourage students to realise that multiple informed approaches and solutions to problems are possible, 3) encourage and coach students to develop "a way of (disciplinary) thinking" through 4) a less formal – confidence building – interpersonal relationship. Level-four-thinkers have become active participants in the teaching-learning process. Student and teacher both focus on understanding and finding evidence-based solutions within a particular discipline. They realise that most knowledge is uncertain and consequently authorities lose the exclusive ownership of it. Everybody may develop a point of view based on a set of arguments using the rules of the discipline. About one in four of our students had crossed this watershed to a way of thinking that is generally accepted as the outcome of higher education, on average about 20% of our students was allocated to this particular way of knowing at any time.

For students functioning at the fifth level of thinking, learning has acquired a more personal meaning as opposed to the relatively technical view on learning in the previous stage. This way of thinking is characterised by notions such as broadening one's outlook on things, opening one's mind, widening horizons, or looking "at the world with those eyes" (Beaty et al., 1997, p. 156). By changing the eyes one sees with, students can transform the way they perceive reality (i.e. self-transformation, Kegan in Debold, 2002). Level-five-thinkers appreciate a teaching environment based on dialogue, where teachers and students become equal partners in the mutual construction of knowledge. About 4% of our students could at any time be allocated to this category of description.

The most sophisticated learning conception that we have found in our student data is characterised by an existential or ontological dimension, the self of the learner seems to have become the focus of learning. This position is extremely rare, only slightly more than 1% of all our students studied over about three decades was identified as making meaning in this way. The process aspect of this conception is growing self-awareness, looking for answers to the question "Who am I?" The self has become the ultimate object of reflection. The product is self-realisation: becoming or defining the person you feel you are (i.e. self-definition, Hamer and van Rossum, 2010). Good teaching to level-six-thinkers seems to be defined almost exclusively in language referring to emotion, autonomy and reciprocal relationships and it boils down to mutual trust and caring while showing an almost dismissive approach to teaching techniques and methods.

Learning-teaching conception 4 can be interpreted as the expression of academic or scientific thinking: the ability to use the full range of rules and assumptions of a discipline or system such as scientific thought. The move from reproductive to constructive thinking, the move from learning-teaching conception 3 to 4, is the largest and most difficult one to effectuate in higher education: we refer to this move as *crossing the watershed*. In the latter part of chapter 1 we proposed that the move from learning-teaching conception 5 to 6 may be a second large move: a shift in focus from learning-to-know towards learning-to-be, from epistemological development to an existential one. We summarised a model of continued development, linking our epistemological model to existing theories of adult cognitive development (see for more details Hamer and van Rossum, 2008).

NOTES

1 This category has been called 'More than Memorising' in some of our more recent studies.

2 In earlier studies we refer to this category as Understanding reality.

3 Rien Deijkers – having an active interest in Zen - initiated the discussions leading up to this discovery.

4 We feel that the change here is sufficiently large to consider a change of context, from learning-teaching conceptions to conceptions of being, with this position being perhaps conception of being 1: learning to be *me* (Hamer and van Rossum, 2008). See also the final section of this chapter.

5 In the US, and increasingly in the UK, this game is known as soccer.

6 Personal communication, 2003.

7 We include this early study in particular because it relates to findings discussed in chapter 4: Quantitative Approaches to Epistemology and Learning. Students' views on intelligence are important within learning contexts – regarding motivation and learning – as discussed by Dweck in a number of publications (e.g. Dweck and Bempechat, 1983; Dweck, 2002).

8 The learning conception of S26, who makes the distinction between knowledge and wisdom, is quoted in Dawn's story, chapter 3, comments on Baxter Magolda.

9 Jan Vermunt, personal communication in 2007.

10 Baxter Magolda, 2007 suggests that as 'Internal Foundation' (see chapter 2) evolves "wisdom" and "realising your own (and other's) humanity" may become new themes. We will revisit this development in chapter 3, comments on Baxter Magolda.

11 Published in Devotions upon Emergent Occasions.

CHAPTER 2

A PRAGMATIC VIEW ON PHENOMENOGRAPHY AND ISSUES OF VALIDITY AND RELIABILITY

I spy with my little eye ………

In the previous chapter we have introduced our six-stage model for epistemological development that has its origins in a phenomenographic research approach to students' views on learning and (good) teaching. We have refined this model over the years by remaining open to new information present in many students' responses to open questions about learning and (good) teaching. In this sense we have remained phenomenographic researchers of student thinking, although more recently, we have also put this theoretical model to a more practical use, e.g. in designing a more activating curriculum (van Rossum and Hamer, 2004; see chapter 6) in order to improve the quality of student learning. In our daily life as well we have used this model to understand why sometimes communication breaks down: when, although objectively all parties are talking the same language, ideas don't seem to pass through an epistemological barrier. For us this model is "real" in a very practical sense, while for many readers it still is mostly of theoretical interest and perhaps even fundamentally flawed because it grew from qualitative and unashamedly subjective seed, i.e. phenomenography.[1]

Taking the issue of subjectivity in research and the assumption that quantitative research by its nature is *less* subjective than qualitative research by the horns, we would like to quote Bowden and Green (in press a).

> Researchers are human beings, researching into human experience and communicating outcomes to other human beings. It is impossible to take the person out of such research and, therefore, impossible for such research to be objective. ... The difference is not between objective, quantitative research and subjective, qualitative research but rather variation among different kinds of subjectivity and the situations in which it arises, in both quantitative and qualitative research. Subjectivity is the natural state of all research involving human participants.
>
> Quantitative ... research is subjective in that the ideas expressed by the researcher are central ....
>
> [E.g. the] processes by which researchers choose what items to include for scoring and what words they use to express them are subjective ......
>
> Where subjectivity comes in [in qualitative research] is in the way that the interview is conducted (whether respondents are encouraged to be open and forthright, whether the interviewer asks leading questions or not, and so on) and how the data are analysed. ....

> It should be acknowledged that all such research, whether quantitative or qualitative, has subjective elements whose negative influence on the quality of research outcomes can be offset by rigorous research practices (in press a, p. 4, 5 and 7).

Obviously, we agree with Bowden and Green, "The time has come to abandon the tribal conflict between quantitative and qualitative research with its spurious claims of objectivity for one but not the other" (p. 7 in press a). This discussion inevitably leads to the conclusion that while both approaches are always susceptible to subjectivity, quantitative and qualitative research differ most in the *moment* that the influence of subjectivity is greatest and the ready *acknowledgement* of this subjectivity. In quantitative research subjectivity is most noticeable in the preparation phase, for instance in choosing dimensions to study, items to include and words to use. Qualitative research is most vulnerable to subjectivity during data collection (e.g. qualitative interviewing) and data analysis.

The main purpose of this study is to introduce a larger public to the background of our model (chapter 1 and 2), the supporting evidence for it (see e.g. chapters 3, 4 and 5), its practical use for educational innovation (chapters 6 through 9) and the resulting consequences for educational policy (chapters 10 and 11). We have chosen to structure our attempt at dissemination around a limited number of fundamental research questions elaborated in the final paragraph of this chapter. However, first we discuss in more detail the roots and practicalities of the phenomenographic method followed by considerations regarding establishing validity and reliability within this interpretative research methodology.

Phenomenography

The first phenomenographic studies emerged from a fundamentally pragmatic research programme undertaken by Ference Marton and his colleagues at the Gothenburg University in Sweden. They had become dissatisfied with the traditional psychological approach to studying learning in formal settings as was common at that time, because they felt that "Mental models, which locate the objects of description in the minds of people, are in line with the 'knowledge interest' of psychology. However, [such] psychological models are not particularly helpful in solving practical pedagogical problems" (Marton, 1986, p. 43). In the early 1970s, the initial Gothenburg group started an alternative approach by collecting respondents' verbal descriptions of their understanding of a particular study text. When reading (and rereading) the transcripts of the interviews the researchers noticed "a striking fact .... Students understood the very same text materials in a number of qualitatively different ways" (Marton, 1986, p. 36). This fundamental finding, the occurrence of a limited number of qualitatively different understandings of a phenomenon, returned in study after study the group undertook. This led the group to assume that "it was reasonable to expect that people in general hold qualitatively different conceptions of all kinds of phenomena" (Marton, 1986, p. 37). In 1979 the group coined the name phenomenography to describe a research method aimed at

> ... mapping the qualitative different ways in which people experience, conceptualize, perceive, and understand various aspects of, and phenomena in, the world around them (Marton, 1986, p. 31) ...
>
> [in order to] describe relations between the individual and various aspects of the world around them, regardless of whether those relationships are manifested in the forms of immediate experience, conceptual thought, or physical behaviour. (p. 41–42)

In the second section of this quote the most important characteristic of phenomenography is verbalised explicitly: the focus on the *relations* that exist between human beings and the world around them. This focus is expressed in the preoccupation of phenomenographers with describing the range of qualitatively different ways people experience reality, and *not* with describing reality as such, an *experiential* perspective. As Marton says,

> ... we try to describe an aspect of the world as it appears to the individual. This means that we adopt an experiential, or what phenomenographers call a "second-order" perspective (Marton, 1981). We do not try to describe things as they are, nor do we discuss whether or not things can be described "as they are"; rather, we try to characterize how things appear to people. (Marton, 1986, p. 33).

Realising that people do not just experience, but that they experience things, results in phenomenography necessarily being *content-oriented*: descriptions of experience are always made in terms of their content, be it learning, teaching or more concrete concepts such as motion, vision or price. Because these descriptions reflect how things are experienced or perceived, according to Marton phenomenography cannot be other than a fundamentally *qualitative* research method.

> To characterize how something is apprehended, thought about, or perceived is, by definition, a qualitative question (1986, p. 33).

In short, phenomenography results in descriptions that are relational, experiential, content-oriented and qualitative in nature. In a sense, the observation that eventually led to the creation of phenomenography – that different people can perceive the same phenomenon in distinctly different ways – was the identical observation that about a quarter of a century earlier put Perry on the road to his model of ethical and intellectual development (see chapter 3).

Phenomenography focuses on the analysis of descriptions of experience: "Phenomenographers categorize their subjects' descriptions, and these categorizations are the primary outcomes of phenomenographic research" (Marton, 1986, p. 33). These categorisations lead to a limited set of *categories of description* referring to a particular phenomenon. To give an example, in our model the phenomena of learning and good teaching are each categorised into six categories of description. In our research *we* have never made any meaningful distinction between the terms categories of description or conceptions: in our perception the nature of a conception is captured in the matching category of description.

The act of forming categories is central to phenomenography, however deriving categories of description from responses to open questions is far from easy (see also below). Relevant categories cannot be reached through applying algorithms and in the initial discovery phase chances are that different researchers may discover different categories. Indeed in many studies researchers have acknowledged this very difficult first phase of phenomenographic research and have developed different ways to deal with this (see e.g. Bowden and Walsh, 2000). In this study, however, the focus was not on the discovery of categories of description. Our existing model (van Rossum and Hamer, 2004) was the point of departure for the current study. We focused on refining elaborate categories of description (i.e. learning-teaching conceptions) by relating our own model to alternative models in chapters 3, 4 and 5, simultaneously enhancing the validity or accuracy of the categories of description (i.e. learning-teaching conceptions) in the model we subsequently used to analyse the empirical data of the current study. In a sense, the chapters 3 through 5 in particular are included as a pragmatic approach to establishing validity (by convergence of outcomes) and reliability.

Once categories have been discovered and defined in detail through what can be interpreted as an iterative procedure (e.g. Bowden and Walsh, 2000; Åkerlind, 2005), "it must be possible to reach a high degree of intersubjective agreement concerning their presence or absence if other researchers are to be able to use them" (Marton, 1986, p. 35). This consideration is the basis of the frequent use of interjudge reliability in the phenomenographic research tradition (e.g. Marton et al., 1993), and we have used it in the same pragmatic way: we applied our system of expanded learning-teaching conceptions to our empirical longitudinal student data discussed in the chapters 7 and 8 using traditional measures to establish reliability. A detailed account on how we performed our analysis can be found in chapter 6. However, there is considerable discussion on issues of validity and reliability within phenomenography from a less traditional and more philosophical perspective, which we will discuss in summary below.

To return to the formulation of categories of description, this involves much more than merely sorting data or counting utterances or words. Categories of description or conceptions need to differ from each other in an essential way: each category of description must represent a structurally distinct way of perceiving reality, i.e. it must describe a distinct way of knowing. As Marton formulated it,

> ... we are looking for structurally significant differences that clarify how people define some specific portion of the world .... we look for the most essential and distinctive structural aspects of the relation between the individual and the phenomenon (Marton, 1986, p. 34).

Furthermore, in phenomenographic research the categories of description do not only describe the relation between an individual and a phenomenon, the set of categories itself forms a logically related set of views on the phenomenon under scrutiny. Categories of description may be the primary outcome of phenomenography, however, we agree with Marton in stating that

> each category is a potential part of a larger structure in which the category is related to other categories of description. It is a goal of phenomenography to discover the structural framework within which various categories of understanding exist. Such structures (a complex of categories of description) should prove useful in understanding other people's understandings (Marton, 1986, p. 34).

And indeed this is exactly how we would like to position our elaborated learning-teaching conception model in this study. While the roots of this model lie firmly within the context of higher education, we have attempted to decontextualise our model by integrating insights from other models on knowing and thinking such as Belenky et al. (1997), Kegan (1994) and Kuhn (1991), see also chapter 3. At this moment in time we have come to believe that our model may provide a window onto the nature and dynamics of human interaction in society. The title of this study, The Meaning of Learning and Knowing, refers not only to its meaning to learning and teaching, but to society as well. From a traditional phenomenographic standpoint we could be criticised for leaving the original ambition of studying internal person-world relationships and taking a more psychological perspective (Säljö, 1997). We have always differed from the Gothenburg interpretation of phenomenography in this sense, and it would seem that Säljö is also referring to our work as well when he states

> … the observant reader can, without too much trouble, find research studies within this [phenomenographic] tradition in which, for instance, people "have" conceptions and in which the borderline between values/attitudes/ conceptions appears far from clear… (1997, p. 176)

In a way, by returning to a more psychological perspective, we clearly deviate from the ideology as expressed at the programmatic level (Säljö, 1997) and therefore we can be best characterised as *pragmatic phenomenographers*: recognising the value of the methodology without adhering strictly to the ideology. Not only this, as we will discuss later we also perceive ourselves as *developmental phenomenographers* (Bowden, 2000).

> The research that I do is developmental in that it is undertaken with the purpose of using the outcomes to help the subjects of the research, usually students, or others like them to *learn*. The insights from the research outcomes can help in the planning of learning experiences which will lead students to a more powerful understanding of the phenomenon under study, and of other similar phenomena. The outcomes from these research studies can also be used to *develop generalisations about ways to organise learning experiences* in the particular field of study. The research outcomes and the way they are obtained can also be used more generally—as an analogy—in *programmes for teachers*, to demonstrate ideas about teaching and learning. (Bowden, 2000, p. 4, italics ours).

Bowden, in fact, formulates exactly our purpose and approach to our learning-teaching conceptions model over the years. We used the model to deepen our own understanding of learning and teaching in higher education in order to be able to provide guidelines and theoretical background for curriculum development and teacher training aimed at furthering students' epistemological development and their more powerful understanding of core concepts of their study (chapter 6). Although in 1986, Marton did not affiliate himself with something like developmental phenomenography—a term introduced in the early 1990s—he did clearly acknowledge the educational value of phenomenographic studies.

> Encouraging teachers to pay attention to students' ways of thinking and to facilitate students' realization that there are different ways of thinking may be the most important pedagogical implications of a phenomenographic view of learning (1986, p. 47).

Data Collection and Analysis

The primary method of **data collection** used in phenomenographic research is interviewing. As Marton discussed, the reason lies in that interviewing makes it possible to use

> questions that are as open-ended as possible in order to let the subjects choose the dimensions of the question they want to answer. The dimensions they choose are an important source of data because they reveal an aspect of the individual's relevance structure. Furthermore, though we have a set of questions at the start of the interview, different interviews may follow somewhat different courses. (1986, p. 42)

In particular the final sentence of this quote refers to the fact that phenomenographic interviewing does not follow a comprehensive fixed protocol, phenomenographic interviews are more a semi-structured or open interview. The protocol in this case consists of one or more start-questions to open the discussion on the issue under study. Furthermore, phenomenographic interviewers are very careful to use only prompts that elicit further elaborations without priming the interviewees towards particular outcomes. Such prompts may look like "What do you mean when you say ……' or "Could you explain that further?" The route of the interview, the sequence of themes discussed, is thus inevitably dependent on the dimensions the respondent chooses. However, it is the responsibility of the interviewer to keep the interview focused on uncovering the particular way the interviewee understands a particular phenomenon or issue. It is also the responsibility of the interviewer to notice when a theme has been treated in depth and either the interview can stop or a new theme may be introduced. So while the interview may seem to wander, it is *not* a conversation in any everyday sense! As Bowden and Green have summarised it, a phenomenographic interview focuses on the voice of the interviewee and they recommend "a consistent opening scenario followed only by neutral questions and no judgmental statements (or body language) … as standard practice for the interviews" (in press b, p. 8). Bowden provides an excellent example of a good phenomenographic interview.

> The phenomenographic interview has a focus—the way in which interviewees understand the chosen concept—and this focus is maintained throughout the interview. Interviewees are encouraged to express their qualitative understanding of the phenomenon under investigation. The researcher may ask interviewees to clarify what they have said, and ask them to explain their meaning further using questions such as 'Could you explain that further?', 'What do you mean by that?', 'Is there anything else you would like to say about this problem?' ... Such questions aim to get interviewees to reflect on what they have expressed, to explain their understanding more fully and to reveal their way of understanding the phenomenon (Bowden, 2000, p. 9–10).

The interviews are then transcribed verbatim to prepare them for analysis. Considering the all important focus on the voice of the interviewee, it is of vital importance that these transcripts are complete and accurate. As Bowden and Green correctly emphasise, these complete and accurate transcripts form the only evidence for the research outcome of phenomenographic research, and therefore need to be of impeccable quality. Ashworth and Lucas (2000, p. 304) remark that transcribing interviews is "much more than a mere clerical task", and recommend to "include anything that is likely to affect the interpretation of meaning." For studies using interviews an approach could be to listen to the recording of the interviews before starting the analysis of the transcripts. Another approach can be to include information about changes in tone of voice, silences and emotional reactions by the respondents by adding such comments in brackets as follows: ... (voice rising) ...., ... (pause) ...., ... (laughing) ..... (see Perry, e.g. in chapter 3).

In our studies (from the early 1980s onwards) we used not interviews but essays. The starting point of an essay-questionnaire is very similar to the start of a phenomenographic interview, namely posing an open-ended question about (in our case) the respondent's view on (real) learning or (good) teaching. Furthermore respondents were given maximum freedom to describe their experience by encouraging them to use as much space/paper as necessary in describing their understanding of learning and teaching (see also Ashworth and Lucas, 2000). For full details on the question formulation for the current study, see chapter 7. Of course, this approach precluded the option of prompts, but facilitated using relatively large samples at low cost. Occasionally it was possible to ask respondents to come back in to elaborate and expand their essay. And with the introduction of email (halfway the 1990s) we were even better able to integrate prompting into our research procedure. This led us to coin the concept of *email conversation* for our internet-interview technique (see chapters 7 and 8). We feel that in this way we were able to combine the logistic and cost advantages of essays as data source with the information advantages of interactive interviews. Our email conversations in turn followed the phenomenographic interview approach, with non-priming prompts, as described above by Bowden, and so fulfilled the requirement of a "conversational partnership" (Ashworth and Lucas, 2000, p. 302). Our data then consist not of verbatim (and accurate) transcripts of interviews, but of complete and unabridged essays and email conversations including any emphases the respondents provided themselves through the use of exclamation marks, underlining, bold or capital lettering, emoticons, etcetera.

As we also noticed (and describe in chapter 7, section on email conversations) Marton indicated that phenomenographic interviewing in itself can have interesting by-products.

> We have found that when fundamental issues are discussed during interviews, the subjects may become conscious of contradictions in their own reasoning and attempt to rid themselves of such contradictions by considering alternative ideas ... [even up to observing students] shifting from an incorrect to an improved conception of reality (Marton, 1986, p. 44).

We expect that such by-products may even be more common when respondents are not interviewed but asked to write down their thoughts, because they can read them back themselves. This would also imply that a good phenomenographic interviewer could use email conversations to construct prompts that bring contradictions to the fore. Indeed it proved easy for us to do by including previous mails into each correspondence: we could simply refer back to earlier answers when asking for elaboration or explanation. This procedure is consistent with good phenomenographic practice, as Bowden says,

> ... pointing out to interviewees and asking them to comment on the apparent inconsistency between ideas they have expressed at different points in the interview is consistent with the principle of interviewing that I have outlined (2000, p. 10).

In the early publications of the Gothenburg group, procedures of **data analysis** were not described in such detail that other researchers could follow these in their own research. As a result, within the phenomenographic research community there is a range of similar, but definitely not identical, procedures for dealing with (mostly) interview transcripts. Åkerlind (2005) provides an overview of concrete descriptions of practice, observing that "there is a dearth of such concrete descriptions of practice in the phenomenographic literature, with only occasional exceptions .... a point on which phenomenography has been critized" (p. 324). However, Marton gives a consideration why such detailed analysis procedures are difficult to supply

> ... we cannot specify exact techniques for phenomenographic research. It takes some discovery to find out the qualitatively different ways in which people experience or conceptualize specific phenomena. There are no algorithms for such discoveries (Marton, 1986, p. 42).

Marton then subsequently explained his own way of proceeding with the task of data analysis. We will quote his description of the procedure in detail in order to contrast it to our own approach.

> The first phase of the analysis is a kind of selection procedure based on criteria of relevance. *Utterances found to be of interest for the question being investigated ... are selected and marked.* The meaning of an utterance

> occasionally lies in the utterance itself, but in general the interpretation must be made in relation to the context from which the utterance was taken. ... The phenomenon in question is narrowed down to and interpreted in terms of *selected quotes* from all the interviews. ... The selected quotes make up the data pool which forms the basis for the next and crucial step in the analysis. *The researcher's attention is now shifted from the individual subjects ... to the meaning embedded [in] the quotes themselves.* (Marton, 1986, p. 42–43, italics ours)

Marton refers to this more or less decontextualised set of quotes as "the pool of meanings" which forms a *new context* for the selected quotes. While Marton himself claims that the interpretation of these quotes within the pool of meanings takes the original (interview) context into account, it is unclear from his following description how he reconciles these two contexts. In fact we feel using the pool of meanings decontextualises the selected utterances.

> A step-by-step differentiation is made within the pool of meanings. As a result of the interpretive work, utterances are brought together into categories on the basis of their similarities. Categories are differentiated from one another in terms of their differences. In concrete terms, the process looks like this: quotes are sorted into piles, borderline cases are examined, and eventually the criterion attributes for each group are made explicit. In this way, the groups of quotes are arranged and rearranged, are narrowed into categories, and finally are defined in terms of core meaning, on the one hand, and borderline cases on the other. Each category is illustrated by quotes from the data. ... [This] kind of analysis is dialectical in the sense that meanings are developed in the process of bringing quotes together and comparing them. As the meanings of categories begin to form, those meanings determine which quotes should be included and which should be excluded from specific categories (Marton, 1986, p. 43)

Marton admits that this phase of the research is hard, in his own words, this "continual sorting and re-sorting of data" (p. 43) is difficult, tedious and time-consuming, but eventually the iterative process will lead to a stable system of meanings. From this description it remains unclear whether utterances taken from one interview may provide input for (the description of) different categories, which only emphasises to us the controversial issue of decontextualising the utterances from their original context: the whole interview. Bowden and Green (in press b, p. 9) refer to this procedure as the "pool of excerpts approach" and set this analysis approach in contrast to their own approach: the "whole of transcript approach".

In the whole of transcript approach researchers choose to deal with the complete data of each interviewee, and not to select and "cut out" specific utterances. The pool of data then is not a pile of selected quotes taken from a number of interviews, *but* a collection of complete interviews. The interviews are then compared and sorted in their entirety. While sorting and re-sorting large transcripts as if they are one data item seems to us a very difficult task, it is probably more in keeping with the original premise of phenomenography, to "look at any particular utterance in the context of what is said in the rest of the transcript" (Bowden and Walsh, 2000, p. 12). And how is this analysis of the whole transcript then performed? In its most bare form, an individual researcher reads and re-reads the transcripts, drafting and redrafting categories of description, until a stable system of categories of description covering all the interviews has been established. In this process any utterance is put into context by the researcher who is constantly moving backwards and forwards through the transcript, seeking clarification of the utterance in context. While utterances are still the major means to come to categories of description, here, instead of sorting utterances separately, utterances are sorted within the whole of the original context, keeping all utterances in one interview together and all the relations between them intact. The categories of description, on the other hand, are the "interpretation of the collective voice derived from the contextualised individual voices" (Bowden and Green, p. 10 in press b). So in the whole of transcript approach the researcher does not perform so much an analysis of each separate interview, but an analysis of all the interviews taken together as a choir with sopranos, altos, baritones etcetera, each group of singers with their own distinct tone of voice to be discovered. Considering the complexity of this particular analytic task, one might rightfully ask whether phenomenographic analysis is an appropriate task to assign to students or novice researchers in a particular field of study. Such a task would seem to us to require at least some expertise in the field of study, and extensive training in the fundamentals of phenomenographic research. Analyses performed by students and novice researchers of course have their value as educational tools, but should not, we feel, be used as basis for scientific publications. In their own analytic work, Bowden and Green (in press b) recognise the complexity of the analysis procedure and prefer to work with a group of researchers in which some researchers can be assigned to perform the role of devil's advocate, continuously asking for justification of the emerging categories of description. To further prove that the task of phenomenographic data analysis is complex and a learning curve all in itself, we refer to the studies by Boulton-Lewis et al. (2000a, 2000b, 2001 and 2004) where she and her various collaborators describe the evolution of the categories of description for the learning experience of a sample of indigenous Australian students.

How does our own analytic approach compare to the "pool of selected quotes" approach and the "whole of transcript" approach? Initially, in the early 1980s we were interested in replicating the findings of Säljö (1979a), and were confronted with a lack of information about the theoretical background and procedural details of phenomenography. Based on what little information we had, we devised our own procedure of data collection (written essays about the meaning of learning) and proceeded to use the categories of description provided in the study by Säljö (1979a) to establish whether similar categories could be found in a sample of Dutch psychology students (van Rossum and Schenk, 1984). This type of study has proved to be common enough to merit a recognised status in the phenomenographic tradition, "much phenomenographic research has been replicatory in nature ..... This is a specific kind of phenomenographic research where the analysis is not a process of discovery, but a means of searching for predetermined categories" (Ashworth and Lucas, 2000, p. 301). It proved that the descriptions of the more reproductive learning conceptions were easily recognised in the data as well as the fourth learning conception. Immediately we experienced that the description of learning conception 5 was not very effective. Using the first four categories, we categorised most of the essays (81%), but a small number remained that did not quite fit well, and sometimes not at all, in Säljö's description of learning conception 5. However, all these essays clearly displayed a more complex view on learning than the others. Coming from a traditional research tradition, we can now, in hindsight, conclude that at that time we were more attentive to Säljö's categories than to the voice of our respondent group.

However, some uneasiness remained particularly with regard to the essays that did not quite fit. In our opinion our first study was too much a traditional replication, and too little an attempt at true phenomenographic research. Furthermore, we had noticed in this first study that specific words (e.g. understanding) were used differently in the different learning conceptions. In a second study (van Rossum, Deijkers and Hamer, 1985) we wanted to improve our analysis procedure and address this issue of word use. This time in the analysis we came much closer to the analysis procedure that we more or less still use today: paying true attention to what the researched are saying, bracketing our knowledge of the learning conceptions model as much as possible, using the whole of the essay and not taking utterances out of context while looking for the specific alternative meanings given to important concepts in the educational environment. As we described then, our analysis procedure was as follows

> First, we repeatedly read, closely and empathically, the answers to the learning conception question. While reading we tried to be open to the unique meaning and substance that the respondents give to the learning phenomenon, to *their* interpretation, definition and elaboration of terms. We granted less importance to the statements or terms used *themselves.* What really is important is the students' way of elaborating and giving substance to them. We feel that in this situation the nature of the intentional relationship between the learner and his/her learning environment, described either implicitly or explicitly, is particularly essential. We read with open minds for the uniqueness of the answer of each respondent, but at the same time tried to transcend the pure individualness by looking for similarities in [and contrasting differences between] the answers of the various respondents. This was done by seeking certain main themes and continuously returning leitmotifs, in the respondents' description of the learning conception. We kept an eye open for new main themes but, of course, we could not ban earlier research results from our thought completely. In this way a number of groups of answers to the learning conception question, which display a stronger similarity to each other than to other answers, were formed: categories of description emerged (Van Rossum et al., 1985, p. 621).

Considering more recent reviews of the phenomenographic analysis procedures (e.g. Åkerlind, 2005; Bowden and Walsh, 2000) we have come to the conclusion that our self-developed analytic procedure regarding the conception of learning is very similar to the more recently described "whole of transcript" approach (Bowden and Walsh, 2000; Bowden and Green, in press b). Considering the nature of our data, in comparison with interview transcripts relatively short written essays, it is perhaps not surprising that we were able to use the "whole of transcript" approach almost immediately. In 1985, we also looked at the relationship between the conception of learning and the interpretation of a number of other educational concepts. Because this study focused on "a much broader slice of the lifeworld" (Ashworth and Lucas, 2000, p. 304), we found that our outcomes were less sets of *categories of description* for each of the concepts studied, but more a set of five *profiles*, one for each conception of learning. In such a profile, central themes within a learning conception were described as they affected the respondent's interpretation of other educational concepts. Ashworth and Lucas discussed that in certain types of phenomenographic research presenting research findings not only as categories of description, but also using profiles and themes can be an enrichment of the phenomenographic analytic process by increasing its validity and accuracy (2000, p. 305),

> ... it may be that an alternative means of presenting findings might be more appropriate, if one wishes to ensure faithfulness to the lifeworlds of the participants.

Following this 1985 study, in our attempt to listen even more closely to the voice of the respondents, one might in hindsight conclude that we went a bit overboard and started to make distinctions within learning conceptions (van Rossum and Taylor, 1987), albeit exclusively within the reproductive learning conceptions. Here we encountered the tension between being faithful to the detail in the data and wanting to create an elegant and preferably parsimonious outcome space (see also Ashworth and Lucas, 2000). In 1987 the parsimony was sacrificed in an attempt towards more faithfulness and accuracy. In later work we discontinued this practice, because the subdivisions made seemed to refer to non-critical variation within particular conceptions (Åkerlind, 2005). In this study we have again looked more closely at conceptions noticing small increases in complexity *within* a particular conception of learning. We have described these findings in chapter 7, where we focus more closely on the possible nature of the transitions between the different conceptions of learning.

Two major results of this more phenomenographic analysis procedure were a significantly improved description of learning conception 5 (van Rossum et al., 1985; van Rossum and Taylor, 1987) and the "discovery" of learning conception 6 (van Rossum, Deijkers and Hamer, 1984; van Rossum and Taylor, 1987), some 9 years before Marton et al. (1993) confirmed this latter finding. The themes that defined the improved learning conception 5 resulting from these early studies remain a central part of the fifth learning conception to this day. The major themes for learning conception 5 were recognised as referring to seeing things differently, from different perspectives or in a more differentiated way. In 1993, Marton et al. also confirmed this particular finding (see chapter 1). Learning conception 6 addresses a number of essentially different issues in learning than any of the earlier, less complex, learning conceptions, namely the realisation and expression of the "true self" as a theme, coupled with a striving for autonomy, wisdom and happiness through a meaningful life (see chapter 1 and 3).

The 1985 study gave rise to expectations that the view on learning was not "just a conception" with little or no relation to conceptions related to other concepts in the learning teaching environment. So we expanded the model to link conceptions of learning to those on teaching and concepts such as understanding, application, insight etcetera (see chapter 1). As early as 1985 we discussed with Ference Marton during his visit to Tilburg, the possibility that learning conceptions were symptomatic for a more fundamental development in thinking. At that time we started to deviate from mainstream phenomenography by proposing a developmental model to replace the fundamentally contextual approach common in the early phenomenographic studies in education, and linking learning conceptions to the epistemological model of Perry (1970). Säljö (1997) recalled this early contextual approach as follows:

> What eventually became codified as phenomenographic research started out as an attempt to scrutinise and understand human learning by focussing on what people are in fact doing in *situated* practices and when studying. In particular, the approach was driven by an attempt to replace the abstract and empirically unverifiable conceptual frameworks such as those that implied that people "process" or "store" information in various processing devices of dubious ontological status. The spirit was one of disregarding preformed categories and largely empty conceptual frameworks derived from unfounded analogies with computers and that could not be verified in any kind of realistic learning situation. The aim was one of reinstating a truly empirical approach to learning as a human an institutional phenomenon with an interest in clarifying *functional* relationships between what people do when they engage in learning activities and the nature of understanding they end up with. In every such attempt, it became evident that *the actor's definition must play a central role* ... The spirit ... was one of adding sensitivity to understanding by showing that *content and context* were essential, and that any attempt to do away with these would lead to abstractions (Säljö, 1997, p. 188, italics ours).

In interpreting our learning-teaching model as one accessing a more fundamental epistemological or perhaps even an existential development, we have taken a more decontextualised theoretical approach to phenomenography, while we remained true to the procedures of data collection and data analysis fundamental to it. We position ourselves as pragmatic phenomenographers in this way. The current study, and in particular the chapters 1, 3 and 4, is the culmination of our journey towards our current thinking about the meaning of conceptions of learning etcetera for education and society.

One issue we have not yet discussed in detail here is the famous *bracketing* that is central in phenomenographic data collection as well as in analysis. Bracketing refers to the "need for the researcher to set aside his or her own assumptions, so far as is possible, in order to register the student's own point of view" (Asworth and Lucas, 2000, p. 297). Ashworth and Lucas list a number of presuppositions that researchers should recognise as potential hazards to the difficult task of careful listening to the respondents' views. A number of these presuppositions that they feel must be firmly bracketed refer to previous findings and theories. We agree that during data collection and analysis a researcher should not impose these presuppositions onto the respondent's experience. But, at the same time we feel, researchers should not take this bracketing too far: only with prior (theoretical or empirical) knowledge can a researcher recognise when to prompt respondents for e.g. much needed clarification. If taken too far bracketing would make interviewing directionless. However, a certain measure of bracketing would seem essential to be able to enter the respondent's experience or lifeworld: empathic listening is only possible with some (or even considerable) bracketing of the researcher's lifeworld.

> Empathy requires a detachment from the researcher's lifeworld and an opening up to the lifeworld of the student. For instance, views and factual claims which the student expresses in an interview may well be regarded by the researcher as quite erroneous. The temptation would be to marginalise such material. But the researcher who adopts an attitude of empathy with the student should find such views and factual claims of *immense interest* ... Empathy in this context involves imaginative engagement with the world that is being described by the student. (Ashworth and Lucas, 2000, p. 299)

As is described above in our portrayal of our data analysis procedure in 1985, we already encountered the necessity of an empathic stance in phenomenographic research in our early studies and it has remained a permanent feature of our research approach. Furthermore, while bracketing our theoretical and empirical knowledge *during the execution* of all our subsequent studies, *not bracketing* this knowledge helped us to refine our data collection and data analysis and finally to improve our model in a complex iterative process over the years.

Validity and Reliability Issues

Considering that phenomenography has its roots in studies in higher education, it may not be surprising that, in 1997, Entwistle discussed the validity of phenomenographic studies in this context. In keeping with the initial pragmatic start of the methodology, Entwistle emphasised a pragmatic interpretation of the concept validity.

> For researchers in higher education, however, the test is generally not [phenomenography's] theoretical purity, but its value in producing useful insights into teaching and learning.
>
> There are good reasons why phenomenography has been taken up enthusiastically. In higher education, we are generally intending to encourage the development of conceptual understanding in students, so a method which so

> vividly portrays differing conceptualisations must have direct relevance to teaching and learning. And so it has proved. ...... phenomenography sees learning as relational—its takes place trough an interaction between the student, the content of learning material, and the overall learning environment ..... This is a conception which offers a powerful insight to many staff in higher education who have not thought about teaching and learning in this way before (Entwistle, 1997, p. 128–129).

This description of validity indicates that within phenomenography other than the more traditional types of validity indicators need to be considered. Åkerlind (2005, p. 330) looked into this issue and observed that

> With the widespread understanding that an interpretive process can never be objective and, in phenomenographic terms, represents the data as experienced by the researcher ..... the focus of research quality shifts to ensuring that the research aims are appropriately reflected in the research methods used.

In Åkerlind (2005), the focus of the two types of phenomenographically appropriate validity checks she discusses is on the research method and practical usefulness of the outcomes: communicative validity and pragmatic validity. We propose to add a third validity check, *convergence of outcomes validity*, focusing on establishing the accuracy of the description of the (experienced) phenomenon by comparing the outcomes of different theoretical approaches to the study of (more or less) the same phenomenon: in casu learning and knowing in (higher) education.

Regarding reliability Åkerlind (2005) recognises two types of reliability checks that are commonly used in qualitative research with answers to open questions: coder reliability (interjudge reliability) and dialogic reliability. Sandberg (1997) objects to coder reliability in particular, and feels that any reliability measure descendent from an objectivistic epistemology is inappropriate for phenomenographic research. He proposed a different type of reliability check which he felt is more in line with the "epistemology of intentionality underlying phenomenography" (Sandberg, 1997, p. 211).

Three Approaches to Validity

Communicative validity

The core of communicative validity is the persuasiveness of researchers regarding the appropriateness of their research methods and final interpretations as judged by the relevant research community. In a strict sense, this could mean that communicative validity is most relevant to other phenomenographers. As another measure of the communicative validity of phenomenographic research one can look at the relative ease and frequency with which it appears in peer-reviewed journals, and at the acceptance by intended audiences.

Pragmatic validity

This pragmatic approach to validity can be recognised in Entwistle's remarks above and is a type of validity favoured by many phenomenographic researchers (ourselves included) as the most important test for their research results: "the extent to which the research outcomes are seen as useful ... and ... are meaningful to their intended audience" (Åkerlind, 2005, p. 331). In essence, research outcomes are pragmatically valid if e.g. an interested party can use the insights gained to improve teaching in higher education or when staff in higher education is supported in understanding and implementing curriculum innovations.

Convergence of outcomes validity

As Åkerlind says, "Validity is widely regarded as the extent to which a study is seen as investigating what it aimed to investigate, or the degree to which the research findings actually reflect the phenomenon being studied" (2005, p. 330). The phenomenon studied in the current study is the experience of learning and knowing in higher education, and we would prefer to check whether our description of this experience is similar to the descriptions derived from other research approaches than phenomenography. In this sense, convergence of outcomes validity lies closer to more traditional conceptions of validity, than the two types of validity commonly practiced in the phenomenographic community. Indeed, looking at validity in terms of convergence of outcomes can only be successful if, as Entwistle (1997) remarked

> the categories [are] treated as provisional descriptions. They will remain open to some extent subjective interpretations, which further research will challenge and modify. It is important to recognise that qualitative research is necessarily interpretative, developing like historical research as much from contested interpretations as from definitive findings (p. 133).

We would like to add that, for us, this "further research" need *not* be only phenomenographic, but may come from unexpected fields of study. Of course, convergence of outcomes validity presupposes an empathic attitude to other research approaches and fields, the willingness to look for communalities without disregarding possible differences, and the open-mindedness to accept possible enrichments to one's own work from other sources. In particular the latter aspect can help to improve the understanding – and the description – of rare conceptions, such as for instance learning-teaching conceptions 1 and 6.

The chapters 3, 4 and 5 of the current study are our attempt at exactly this validity check: a check that we feel aims at a more fundamental type of validity than communicative and pragmatic validity. This means that for our purposes chapters 3, 4 and 5 are more than merely a literature review and theoretical background, they are an essential part of our methodology. In addition these chapters are important for the message we want to communicate with this study: the meaning of learning and knowing is not a static phenomenon, people change and formal education should challenge its students to develop those skills and conceptions necessary to function well in today's complex society.

Three Approaches to Reliability

Coder reliability

Coder reliability is more commonly known as interjudge or interrater reliability and it is the reliability measure used most often in phenomenographic research. In principle it is an indicator of the agreement between independent judges, usually two. Indeed it is the reliability check we have used in the current study (see chapters 7 and 9). The procedure is to allocate categories to the transcripts independently after which the categorisations of the two judges are compared, and the level of agreement is usually presented as a percentage. In phenomenographic research the norm is to resolve disagreements between judges by discussion, resulting in all transcripts being allocated to one, and only one category. Not uncommon is the choice to allocate transcripts to the highest (i.e. most complex) conception for which evidence was found in the transcript and we have always complied with this convention.

In contrast to the criticism that detailed accounts of the data analysis procedures are often missing (Åkerlind, 2005), the issue of interjudge reliability was clearly described by Marton et al. (1993),

> ... two judges who had discussed a number of cases together, independently classified the remaining 16 cases. ... On the basis of the description of the conceptions .... there was agreement in 10 of the 16 cases (62.5%). ... When comparing the judgements, one of the judges came to the conclusion that the difference in all six cases was due to the fact that he failed to focus on some aspect of [the] student's answer that was crucial for making a correct judgement. There was thus in the end a total agreement between judges. ....
>
> The interjudge reliability of 62.5% can, however, hardly be considered "reasonably high" (p. 295).

Marton et al. proceeded to argue that this low level of agreement was due to the fact that these 16 cases belonged to the least obvious transcripts to categorise.

The logical question to pose here would be about when one can say that the level of agreement is acceptable. In general, levels of agreement above 75% are deemed acceptable or good in phenomenographic research. An obvious critique on this measure is that it does not take into account the number of agreements due to chance. It is possible to correct interjudge reliability measurements for this chance agreement, by using another indicator, Cohen's kappa (K) (Van de Sande, 1999). Obviously correcting for chance agreement results in lower levels or percentages of agreement. Cohen's kappa values above 0.60 (60% or more agreement) are seen as indicating sufficient interjudge reliability. Nowhere in the phenomenographic literature (up to 2009) have we come across the use of Cohen's kappa and our interjudge reliabilities are well within the accepted range. However, Cohen's kappa is becoming more common in the literature on qualitative studies in general and so we have included this measure in chapters 7 and 9.

Dialogic reliability

Dialogic reliability is not common in phenomenographic research (Åkerlind, 2005). It is a measure of agreement between researchers "reached through discussion and mutual critique of the data and of each researcher's interpretive hypotheses" (Åkerlind, 2005, p. 331). Bowden uses this measure of reliability in his approach to phenomenographic data analysis, where he works within a group of researchers who together reach a stable set of categories of description through an iterative process of proposing draft versions, criticising these draft versions (playing devil's advocate), amending them, re-reading transcripts, etcetera (Bowden and Walsh, 2000). We propose that our iterative process of refinement of and continuous discussion about the nature of each conception (since the early 80s) together with our attempt at convergence of outcomes validity, form a longitudinal and cross-methodological expression of dialogic reliability.

Reliability as the researcher's interpretative awareness

In particular the common use of interjudge reliability as a measure of reliability in phenomenographic research has been severely criticised by Sandberg (1997). Issues regarding the quality of the researcher's procedures and the quality of the data may remain unexamined when focusing on interjudge reliability alone. The researcher's procedures in phenomenography should be appropriate to achieve a faithful description of, or fidelity to, the individuals' conceptions of reality (Sandberg, 1997). A researcher may arrive at categories of description while these outcomes are heavily influenced by the researcher's own preconceptions, a case of insufficient bracketing. However, if these descriptions are easily recognisable for co-judges, high interjudge agreement is the logical result, while meaningless. Considering that we have refined our research procedures over the decades aimed at increasing our empathic approach to data collection and data analysis (see above), and our singular preoccupation with improving the fidelity of the categories of description (introducing convergence of outcomes validity), we feel that there is no reason to reject interjudge reliability in the current study.

Sandberg's other argument to reject interjudge reliability in phenomenographic research is more fundamental. He feels that because interjudge reliability is derived from an objectivistic epistemology and phenomenography is based *not* on an objectivistic epistemology, *but* on a phenomenological "epistemology of intentionality" (Sandberg, 1997, p. 211), phenomenography requires a different approach to reliability: reliability as interpretative awareness. This implies

> first and foremost that the researcher must demonstrate how he/she has dealt with his/her intentional relation to the individuals' conceptions being investigated. That is, in order to be as faithful as possible to the individuals' conceptions of reality, the researcher must demonstrate how he/she has controlled and checked his/her interpretations throughout the research process: from formulating the research question, selecting individuals to be investigated, obtaining data from those individuals, analysing the data

obtained, and reporting the results. Hence, based on the epistemology of intentionality, establishing reliability of the researcher's interpretation is crucial; ....*To maintain an interpretative awareness means to acknowledge and explicitly deal with our subjectivity throughout the research process instead of overlooking it.* (Sandberg, 1997, p. 209, italics ours)

Sandberg (1997) proposes to use the phenomenological reduction as a means to maintain interpretative awareness, which involves that "the researcher should strive to hold back his/her known theories and prejudice in order to be fully and freshly present to the individuals' conceptions under investigation" (p. 209). Sandberg (1997) gives five steps as a set of guidelines towards maintaining interpretative awareness – explicating and documenting how researchers ideally can deal with their subjectivity in the research process: 1) maintaining a clear focus throughout the study, 2) a conscious orientation towards describing rather than explaining, 3) treating all aspects of the lived experience under investigation as equally important, 4) searching for the basic meaning structure of the outcome space, and 5) using an intentional analysis to explicate the variation in the conceptions identified (see for example Marton et al., 1993).

Regarding these guidelines we feel that throughout this study we have described clearly how we dealt with our subjectivity, and therefore that in this study we have complied with this criterion of reliability as interpretative awareness. The research questions are listed below and at the end of each chapter we have addressed these questions. In this chapter and the empirical chapters (7, 8 and 9) we have described our aim towards achieving maximum fidelity to the experience of the individuals being investigated. In data collection and data analysis we have attempted to clarify the students' and teachers' learning and teaching conceptions from an empathic standpoint. However, this need not mean that all words, sentences or issues in a particular essay are treated as equally important to the focus of the study. For instance, when in discussing learning a student referred to a particular instance of exam fraud, we interpreted this as interesting background information, but not immediately relevant to establishing the student's conception of learning, the main focus of the study. Some issues that came up with some regularity in the essays were not directly related to this main focus. When these issues were considered relevant to the experience of learning at the Hotelschool (e.g. the prominence of group work) they were included in this study (see chapter 8). In this way we feel we have complied with the issue of treating all aspects of the experience with equal respect. For further details on the data analysis, see chapter 6.

Research Questions

After introducing our six-stage developmental model of linked learning and teaching conceptions, and making a short extrapolation towards adult cognitive development, the remaining chapters can be grouped as addressing specific research questions that drove the current study.

In chapters 3 and 4 we address what we have called convergence of outcomes validity through a comparative study using the following questions:

- Are there similar models, originating from different schools of thought and research approaches that describe the same epistemological or intellectual development underlying our six-stage model of student thinking about learning and teaching?
- Do these models enrich our understanding of the categories of description we have identified through our own research?
- In what way can the metaphor of an ecology provide additional insight in the plethora of education innovation strategies leading to sometimes disappointing results?

In chapter 5 we address the issue of matching student and teacher thinking. We have discussed this earlier in van Rossum and Hamer (2004), but here we have attempted to expand on the findings reported there. The leading questions in chapter 5 are:

- Is it possible to find additional evidence from literature that underpins the linking of our model of student thinking to teacher thinking on learning and teaching? In short is Yero (2002) correct in assuming that teachers are 'merely' students grown up?
- If so, does this exercise help to understand differences in teachers' teaching practice?
- Do these differences in teacher thinking and teaching practice influence students' learning?

In chapters 6 we introduce the empirical part of the study and in chapters 7, 8 and 9 we address the following questions:

- How did Enterprising Learning – as implemented at the Hotelschool The Hague between 1997 and 2007 – affect students' epistemological development?
- In what way may teachers' views on learning and teaching have affected the implementation of Enterprising Learning?
- What happens when students and teachers have widely different views on learning and good teaching?

In chapters 7 and 8 we have also discussed less central issues regarding for instance the influence of culture on epistemological development, retrospective questioning and the use and by-products of email conversations.

In chapters 10 and 11, we address the issue of practical consequences flowing from our model

- What are the consequences of applying our developmental model of conceptions of learning and teaching to existing educational systems? How can it help to change learning and teaching in higher education?
- How can our developmental model be applied to staff development? How can we educate our educators?

In the final chapter, chapter 12, we summarise the main results of this study and also we discuss important issues that seem to follow from or are related to these results. Such issues are among others a deeper analysis of the influence of culture, discipline or gender on epistemology and its development. The final chapter closes with a number of suggestions regarding new avenues of research.

NOTES

[1] Phenomenography as discussed here is restricted to the state of the art at the time of the inception of this study, the late 1990s. We do not discuss in any great detail more recent developments within the phenomenographic research community.

CHAPTER 3

MODELS OF EPISTEMOLOGICAL DEVELOPMENT

...it is possible to learn how to learn, to learn how to see, to learn how to be, in ways that make one more self-directing in many areas of life

(Grow, 1991, p. 147)

It has become tradition when describing models of epistemological development to start with William Perry's seminal work on college students. We have decided to take a different tack in this study and take Marcia Baxter Magolda's model as the starting point of our discussion. The reasoning underpinning the decision focuses on three arguments

- the fact that her work is based on a mixed gender group of college students, which is true for our own studies as well,
- even though in Perry's work much attention is given to educational aspects of epistemological development, the model of Baxter Magolda is more explicit in this regard and more consistent, which make the link to our own work on the development of students' learning conceptions (see chapter 1) more self evident, and
- while many researchers in the field (e.g. Hofer and Pintrich 1997) purposefully make the distinction between conceptions of knowledge/knowing (epistemological beliefs) and conceptions of learning/teaching wider, Baxter Magolda increasingly treats these two approaches as interchangeable and in our opinion ultimately as identical.

In her work Baxter Magolda refers to Robert Kegan (1982 and 1994), in particular she discusses the similarities between his Orders of Consciousness model and her Ways of Knowing (see below, e.g. Baxter Magolda, 1992a, p. 201). We will include Kegan's model as well as in our opinion there is a clear correspondence between our conceptions of teaching and his model. In discussing the later work of both Baxter Magolda and Kegan we will expand upon the concept of self-authorship: a concept that is increasingly important in Baxter Magolda's work in later years. So much so, that she feels that her more recent work is no longer a continuation of her ERM in the stricter sense (personal communication, 2008).

Belenky et al.'s model of Women's Ways of Knowing (1986, edition 1997) was a major inspiration for Baxter Magolda's work on gender differences in epistemology. Although we ourselves, never included possible gender differences in conceptions of learning, as these differences were never obvious in our data, we will discuss this model here because it has been influential in epistemological research and its categories show great similarity to our learning conceptions including an unrecognised sixth way of knowing. In addition we propose a measure of rehabilitation for Silence, a somewhat controversial category of description in later years, as an epistemological strategy well worthy of further exploration.

Evidently, Perry was a major influence on our earlier work – in the nineteen eighties– and we will include his model (Perry, 1970, 1981) later in this chapter. We were lucky to be able to correspond directly with William Perry about our findings at that time – and meet in Lancaster, UK in 1985. Both Perry and Bill Moore supported us in our developmental perspective on conceptions of learning at a time when many researchers in the field explicitly disagreed. In a book review in the Harvard Educational Review of The Experience of Learning (Marton, et al., 1984) Perry criticised Marton and Säljö for not recognising the developmental character of our work (Perry, 1986).

In this book review Perry discusses a reissued publication of Marton's and Säljö's 1976 experiment in which they attempted to change students' study strategy through cueing them with either atomistic factual questions, or questions about main idea and supporting argument. Marton and Säljö found that it was relatively easy to influence students towards learning focused on factual information. However, it proved very difficult to influence all students towards learning aimed at meaning and understanding. The authors experienced great confusion about these unexpected results within their contextual – and not developmental – approach to study strategies. Perry, on the other hand, had no difficulty to interpret the results from a developmental perspective. In such a perspective – where higher levels of thinking evolve from, but still incorporate, lower levels – it is consistent that students at lower levels usually fail to grasp the demands linked to higher levels. Perry, in turn, was confused because in this very chapter of this book Marton and Säljö referred to our work (van Rossum and Schenk, 1984) in which in his opinion such a hierarchical developmental stance is present. In this review he refers to our work as follows: "[it] describes a developmental sequence of five coherent constellations of students' conceptions of learning, teaching, examinations, understanding, application and activity/passivity in learning. But [Marton and Säljö] limit the reference to van Rossum and Schenk's *classifications*, omitting their "point": that the constellations are hierarchical and also persuasively developmental when viewed in parallel with a model of development derived from a longitudinal study by the staff of the Bureau of Study Counsel at Harvard University (Perry, 1970)" (Perry, 1986, p. 191). In retrospect Perry mis-referenced van Rossum and Schenk (1984) while describing van Rossum, Deijkers and Hamer (1985), but the quote makes clear that developmental thinking within the European school of thought on learning at that time was not standard.

The final epistemological model discussed in this chapter will be the model of Epistemological Theories by Deanna Kuhn (Kuhn, 1991). Her work is interesting in the context of learning and epistemology because she addresses the issue of argumentation and reasoning with regard to everyday topics. In addition, her subjects are average people, from all walks of life, which is, in our opinion, an enrichment of the models because the major studies in the field of education and epistemology are based on college or university students. Furthermore, her approach appeals to us because it has the same informal research attitude we were looking for when we started our study on conceptions of learning: if you really want to know how people view something, why don't you start by just asking them and really listen to what *they* say?

The central question in this chapter is whether models relating to how people (learn to) to know and think in and outside the educational context describe a similar outcome space as our learning-teaching conception model. Especially when these models have been derived from a different research perspective, we feel that if we can establish a persuasive argument affirming fundamental similarities between models, we may propose to see this as a form of confirmation of our findings. In a sense this chapter can be interpreted to address the issue of the positivist reproducibility of results that is philosophically and methodologically problematic to link to interpretative methods such as phenomenography as well as the approaches used to arrive at the models discussed below.

A second question that is addressed here concerns whether the models discussed below, if compatible with our own learning-teaching conception model, also enrich our understanding of each epistemological position and that insights gained from these models complement the descriptions of each level.

Baxter Magolda

> *You are so the master of your own destiny at college. It's such a time of stretching and growing all the way around. You test the ground and see how it feels in a lot of different areas. And you are trying to fly off cliffs, and you crash a few times, and you soar a few times.*
>
> *Gwen (Baxter Magolda, 2004)*

Intrigued by the similarities between the epistemological development model developed by Perry (1970, 1981, 1988), the model described by Belenky and her associates (Belenky et al., 1986 edition 1997 see below), and by the difficulties that some researchers experienced applying the Perry scheme to the experiences of women, in 1986 Baxter Magolda decided to embark on a longitudinal study of a mixed gender group of college students. She "specifically planned to reveal gender similarities and differences in order to create a more comprehensive picture of students' ways of knowing" (Baxter Magolda, 1992a, p. 8). Her initial study covers five years in which her respondents talked about their experiences during their college years at the Miami University (Oxford, Ohio) and - for some - their first work related experiences after graduation.

The approach to data collection used is similar to Perry's open interview method, namely a yearly interview with students based on the Measure of Epistemological Reflection (a short-essay questionnaire). The six aspects of the college experience addressed in the interviews are the role of

1. the learner
2. the instructor

3. peers
4. evaluation in learning as well as
5. the nature of knowledge and
6. decision making.

In all these interviews she asked students specifically about their "learning experience", the role they prefer to play to make learning more effective and the role they expect the teacher to play to accomplish this same goal (e.g. Baxter Magolda, 1992a, p. 412). These questions address the same issues and sometimes use the same words as our own essay questions about learning and 'good' teaching (e.g. van Rossum, Deijkers and Hamer, 1985; van Rossum and Taylor, 1987; van Rossum and Hamer, 2004). In our opinion this underlines our third argument to begin our discussion on epistemological development with Baxter Magolda's work. The first wave of respondents consisted of 101 freshmen students balanced by gender, on average about 18 years old. The gender balance was preserved during the study while attrition was low, with 80 students in year 4 and 70 students participating in the fifth year interview.

In Making Their Own Way (Baxter Magolda, 2001), Baxter Magolda analysed annual conversations about life after college with 39 of her original participants. By the time of their final conversations, the participants were in their late twenties to thirty years old. Of these 39 participants, Baxter Magolda collected 14 yearly interviews. In this later work she has adjusted her research approach, under the influence of the work of Kegan (1982, 1994), focusing less on ways of knowing and more on self-authoring one's life. In this section we try connect both approaches to come up with one model of student development that relates to our work on learning and teaching conceptions.

Epistemological Reflection Model

Baxter Magolda's first study, published in 1992, presents evidence for a four stage model of epistemological development – ways of knowing – which indeed paints a picture of increasing complexity in student thinking about issues related to learning, teaching, evaluation and knowledge. Epistemological reflection refers to assumptions about the nature, limits and certainty of knowledge (Baxter Magolda, 2004a). She sees these assumptions as the core of personal epistemology. In relationship with our work, most interesting is that she sees beliefs about learning and instruction as part of the personal epistemology and closely intertwined with the assumptions about the nature of knowledge given above.

Below we will present these four ways knowing, discuss their main characteristics and show – through examples (taken from Baxter Magolda, 1992a) – the essence of the students' thinking within each stage. Here we will focus on examples that emphasise the similarities between her work and our own developmental model of student thinking.

Stage 1: Absolute Knowing

Absolute Knowers view all knowledge as certain, and absolute answers exist in all areas of knowledge. Authorities (i.e. teachers) are the custodians of this knowledge and of the (right) answers. The role of learners is to obtain knowledge from the instructors. Important in relation to our own work on teaching is the assertion that "This point of view translates into learning methods that focus on acquiring and remembering information" (Baxter Magolda, 1992a, p. 37). This description fits seamlessly to the main focus of learning conception 2 students (van Rossum and Hamer, 2004 and chapter 1).

For these students the *teacher* is responsible for transferring the certain knowledge to them. And so the students are extremely dependent on the teacher to provide the correct clues, correct explanation, and the correct environment to learn. Here as well, the expectations described echo the view on good teaching described by learning conception 2 students (van Rossum and Hamer, 2004 and chapter 1).

Taking the view on knowledge, learning and teaching together, it is not surprising that these students would perceive evaluation as an opportunity to reproduce what they have they have learned in order to see whether their knowledge is correct, i.e. is it the right answer?

All these aspects are present in two quotes from students, presented by Baxter Magolda (1992a) as Jim and Toni.

> I like to listen – just sit and take notes from an overhead. The material is right there. And if you have a problem, you can ask him, and he can explain it to you. You hear it, you see it, and then you write it down (Toni, p. 73)

> The information is cut and dried. It is either right or wrong. If you know the information, you can do well. It is easy because you just read or listen to a lecture about the ideas, then present it back to the teacher. (Jim, p. xi)

It is clear to us that Absolute Knowers have not developed a voice of their own, they "echo authority" (Baxter Magolda, 1992a, p. 193) in all aspects of learning and teaching. In our opinion to echo authority is the first expression of "following external formulas", which Baxter Magolda introduces in her 2001 book on post-college development. To develop their own voice, participants seem to start with patterning their voice on the voices of important others, in this case teachers. College students and graduates developing their own distinctive voice is a main storyline in Baxter Magolda's body of work (story line "emergence of voice" 1992a; 2001).

We feel that in our work the development of "voice" is captured in the description of students developing learning conceptions. Without a distinctive voice of their own, Absolute Knowers view authority as all-knowing and we feel this second storyline "relationship with authority" in her work (1992a) runs parallel to the focus on the teacher-student relationship prevalent in our descriptions of conceptions of good teaching.

Stage 2: Transitional Knowing

The change that occurs when students move to Transitional Knowing is the discovery of their own voice, a voice that they may use to express personal opinion. The voice is not strong as yet, and Baxter Magolda characterises it as "the emerging voice". This discovery leads to an increase in (or return of) self confidence – especially in a supportive environment – students feel the first cracks in the Authorities monopoly on knowledge.

> I'm trying to speak up because I've always admired people who could do that in class. I'm working on self-confidence, which I think I had a lot of when I was younger, but I started to lose it somewhere along the way. And I think being able to speak helps me. (Anita, p. 122)

The cracks in the monopoly are caused by the discovery that authorities disagree, so perhaps not all knowledge is certain. Some disciplines, such as the humanities, are more prone to this type of disagreement and open about the uncertainty of facts and knowledge. Technical or more science-oriented disciplines may prove more able to preserve the myth of certain knowledge for a much longer period of time, and subsequently the epistemological development may proceed at different speeds for different disciplines. We feel that this difference in myth maintenance may be at the core of the view that epistemological beliefs are only context specific.

If knowledge is no longer absolutely certain, than learning cannot consist solely of acquiring and remembering information, but starts to include an aspect of understanding. Understanding at this level is strongly related to the application of knowledge, as it is in learning conception 3 (see chapter 1). When Megan (quoted in Baxter Magolda, 1992a) talks about measuring 'understanding' she says,

> You have to know the rules to apply them. If you've applied them correctly and you know them, you're going to get a good grade. I mean, it's not just like memorize this and write it down. You have to know how to be able to use it, ... (p. 111)

We feel that at this level not only the voice emerges for the first time, but also the concept of understanding. To understand the development of the students' conception of understanding we refer to van Rossum (1988) and chapter 1.

It follows that for 'understanding' to develop the students feel the need for increased interaction in the classroom, such as working in groups (peer-peer interaction) or group discussions (teacher-student interaction). The students become more involved, but the teacher remains responsible for the learning process and learning outcome. Gwen (quoted in Baxter Magolda, 1992a) describes her French teacher's effective approach as

> ... So she's started getting us into group discussions using our reading, but she corrects our tenses and sentence structure. It's much more real, much more practical, and I think that's what we need. ... (p. 39)

In this quote one can recognise not only the interaction, but also the shaping aspect of teaching that is preferred by these students. It is precisely these two components of the teacher-student relationship that are emphasised in our third teaching conception (chapter 1). Another student quoted by Baxter Magolda, Kris, describes the development she has experienced and so shows that firstly there is indeed a development that even students themselves recognise.

> We're working in groups, whereas other professors just lecture. This is weird – because I can hear myself saying this, and I used to live for lectures. All through high school and into my freshman year, lectures were it. I learned best from lectures. They told me what I needed to know, and I could just put it right down. And now it seems where I'm internalizing – this is good! – internalizing and making this stuff my own. I'm growing up, I guess. I don't know. (p. 117)

This quote also shows that it is possible to ask students to describe how they felt about learning and teaching at an earlier moment in time. This opens the possibility of retrospective inquiry into the epistemological development. In the work of Perry and Baxter Magolda many instances of retrospection are included to support the developmental phenomena discussed. We will use this retrospective method to reconstruct the developments for a subgroup of our research participants (chapter 7). In many quotes the students indicate that discussion and involvement helps them to "remember more" and "remember longer". In this sense learning is more effective as well as more than memorising (for the short term).

If learning is more than remembering, evaluation will need to address more than reproduction. It will need to include some form of testing the students' 'understanding': can they manipulate the rules (or formulas) and – confronted with questions – do they think. Discussing a physics test based predominantly on formulas, Tony says,

> … Because if I just had memorized the original formula and not really understood why it worked, I could have never thought how to manipulate it to use it [in] the way he wanted us to. (Baxter Magolda, 1992a, p. 126)

The importance of essay tests lies in the option to use their emerging voice to formulate answers in their own way. Derek's thoughts on essay testing show this clearly

> … Essay tests make you sit down and analyze the question more. It makes you think through it. I think the biggest thing is being able to write your thoughts in words, just comprehension. I prepare more for essays; it make me not just memorize the material. It helps me develop the kind of thinking for when you're into the real world. I mean, your aren't going to have many tests after you get out of here. (Baxter Magolda, 1992a, p. 132)

These quotes are characterised by four main themes:

1) learning is more than memorising
2) understanding equals being able to apply or manipulate
3) the teacher remains firmly in control
4) what you learn should be useful later when you are in the real world

These four aspects are the defining values of our third learning and teaching conception. Although Derek already uses "big words" such as analysing and thinking through, we need to realise that, as with understanding, there are levels within the concept of analysis and thinking through. Students will use these same words in the next stages, but their use will show that the meaning of these words evolves.

The aspect of teacher control is particularly interesting when comparing – again – Baxter Magolda's Ways of Knowing to her evolved model described in Making Their Own Way (Baxter Magolda, 2001). Her category of "following external formula" takes on a different form for Transitional Knowers as the following two students explain.

Amy would prefer to pattern her voice more on the external formula of the teacher providing more structure and specific guidelines to help her formulate her ideas.

> ... That's one of my problems I have with writing things, you know, writing papers is actually showing my own ideas. I'm kind of scared of being completely off, and so I think I play the line very straight and I don't really take a lot of chances (...) I'm always worried that what I say is not right (...) when something's in front of me and I have complete rein to do whatever I want, whether it's in a paper or doing a project or doing something, that kind of scares me because I feel like I can do better when I have specific guidelines... (Baxter Magolda, 1992a, p. 86–87)

The same need for clear guidance and structure is expressed by Al.

> ... When we analyze a case [in marketing], there're different ways to go about it. At least from the classes I've had, there's a process you go through to analyze the case. In one class, he gave us a process, but we don't know what to do with it because he never gives us a concrete [idea of] what you should do. There have to be more guidelines or structure I think. (Baxter Magolda, 1992a, p. 106–108)

The external formula characteristic for Transitional Knowing seems to focus on providing structure with regard to using (or applying) knowledge.

Stage 3: Independent Knowing

In this stage students begin "to think for themselves" and discover the validity of their own distinctive voice. This shift in student thinking is caused by the realisation that most knowledge is uncertain and consequently authorities lose the exclusive ownership of it. Anybody may develop a point of view based on a set of arguments using the rules of the discipline. In the context of reading texts, the uncertain nature of knowledge is described by Gwen

> .. It's funny. You read the same thing, and yet people see three different stories or three different meanings or interpretations. And although you might have grounded yours, it's very easy to see how they might have come up with that reading. ...

> It's amazing how much different it is when you really are interested and involved. Before, I could read the material and say okay. Now I read the material, and I think about it. There's the difference, because before you would read the material and be familiar with it and they'd tell you what to think, as opposed to know, when they say, "What do you think?" and you [say to yourself], "Oh, I'd better think of something" (Baxter Magolda, 1992a, p. 50–52).

The change in study approach that Gwen describes retrospectively here is reminiscent of the step from surface level approach to studying in a deep level way (Marton and Säljö, 1984; van Rossum and Schenk, 1984). Deep level study strategies are typically associated with at minimum the fourth learning conception (chapter 1; van Rossum and Schenk, 1984).

Independent Knowers construct knowledge by interpreting things they read or hear themselves as opposed to accepting the interpretation the teacher presents as true. This is the way that teachers tell them it works in the senior year of college. Max is quite clear about this in the context of effective evaluation,

> Most professors, if you can support what you say with evidence and show it – and you're trying to say it's this and they say it's that – if you can support what you say, then they'll generally give you a good grade because they can't really tell you it's wrong. But if you just say something and don't support it, and it's not what they believe, then it's wrong. Or maybe not wrong, but it's not supported, so it's not so credible. (Baxter Magolda, 1992a, p. 162)

Mark in his senior interview, makes a similar observation when comparing the contribution of his peers to the contribution of the instructor:

> ... the interchanges that really stimulate my brain come from the teacher; they don't come from other classmates. (...) I understand people more. But I don't want to get in one of those situations in the classroom where everyone's voice is validated; you know, everybody gives everybody a hug, either. Everybody needs to be interrogated; I do, too. But when I learn something from what's said in class, it's the teacher [the supposed expert] interrogating my voice, not so much other students, although occasionally that will happen. (Baxter Magolda, 1992a, p. 63)

Gwen and Max both express that they are somewhat pressured into thinking for themselves, and that (some) professors provide opportunity and encouragement. This implies that the development of Independent Knowing is *still* dependent on external formulas (or voices of important others, Baxter Magolda, 2001), but compared to Transitional Knowing, the nature of the formula [read the role of the teacher] has changed considerably. Lowell describes the instructor's role in his favourite senior class.

> [The instructor's role is] Largely secondary. It was just kind of a guidance. And if we needed, if we were trying to find something, he'd have his experiences to draw on and say, "Well, you can look here, and they might be

> able to help you." Guidance and kind of setting deadlines. Just kind of pushing us. We learned how to push ourselves from that. (Baxter Magolda, 1992a, p. 160)

The teacher is perceived more as a coach, providing advice and cues when asked, but not as a source of all the answers.

In studying the post-college development of her participants the fact that Transitional as well as Independent Knowers seemed to follow external formulas, confused Baxter Magolda in interpreting the data for her book Making Their Own Way (Baxter Magolda, 2001). In our opinion the qualitative difference between Transitional and Independent Knowing is not the fact whether or not the students follow external formulas, but the type of external formulas that they follow. As we see it, the external formulas of Transitional Knowers refer to good structure and specific guidelines to be able to use knowledge correctly. Whereas the formulas of Independent Knowers refer to being able to support opinions or ideas with arguments, and implying that some opinions are more valid than others because the underpinning arguments are better (or just there! See Max and Mark above). Such formulas help students to construct knowledge and the peculiarity lies in that through "echoing" these formulas, a student develops a distinctive voice.

In the context of the fourth learning conception, students would call the latter formula e.g. "a way of thinking" or "thinking like a .... [architect, historian, etcetera]". Almost exactly these same words were used by students in Perry's study (see below in the section on Perry). In our model as well, thinking at this level implies that there are experts and that thinking like a professional is better than the "multiplistic" (everybody is entitled to their own opinion, Perry, 1970) thinking of Transitional Knowers. This means that the end point of the storyline relationship with authority – becoming an expert in a given context (Baxter Magolda, 1992a, p. 193) – is in fact an aspect of Independent Knowing, while Contextual Knowing (the next stage in her ERM, see below) is characterized *not* by becoming an expert, but by *partnership in knowing*. This implies as well that Independent Knowers will be more judgemental than Contextual Knowers, as the latter are aware of the contextual nature, and so the relativeness, of knowledge. In her 2001 study, Baxter Magolda subscribes to this shift in interpretation "Participants made the best decisions possible in particular contexts, but were aware of the on-going uncertainty in a contextual world" (Baxter Magolda, 2001, p. 149).

The introduction of the concept of "the crossroads" as the watershed between following external formulas and self-authorship (see below, Baxter Magolda, 2001) at first presented us with some difficulty in interpretation. We felt that as she was describing in both books the journey from young impressionable people towards self-realisation (learning conception 6), our difficulty was in establishing where in the journey this concept would express itself. The realisation that the crossroads represented the struggle within the learner between the external formulas and the internal voice, together with the realisation that she specifically refers to "the crossroads to self-authorship", brought us to closely rereading the passages about Independent Knowing in Baxter Magolda 1992a. We found two clear references that could imply that – at least in 1992 – Baxter Magolda viewed Independent Knowing as the crossroads to the next stage – then called Contextual Knowing. Self-authorship, a concept introduced by Kegan (1994) to describe a state of being necessary to cope with the current complex modern society, becomes the central theme in Baxter Magolda's later work (e.g. 2007, 2008). In this later work Independent Knowing is seen as the first stage of self-authorship. We have discussed the link between self-authorship and our own model explicitly in Hamer and van Rossum (2010) and summarize our standpoint below in a comment on Baxter Magolda.

On page 258, Baxter Magolda (1992a) describes the view on evaluation of Independent Knowers and the struggle between the internal voice and the external formulas (voice of authority). "[these students] all valued opportunities to express themselves. In most cases, freedom to voice ideas helped in the struggle to develop personal perspectives. Phrases like 'support what you said,' 'back it up,' and 'come up with some reasoning' show the beginning of justifying personal opinions." Two pages later she discusses the qualitative difference in the student-teacher relationship between independent and Contextual Knowers. In this quote we recognise support for our interpretation that Independent Knowing *itself* is the crossroads. "Support to take chances and relationships in which students or employees felt like partners in learning and working provided the freedom that Contextual Knowers preferred. Although Independent Knowers also described wanting to be treated like adults, collegial relationships for Contextual Knowers extended beyond an attitude to concrete interactions in which the distinction between teacher and student was diminished" (Baxter Magolda, 1992a, pp. 260–262). If Independent Knowing is indeed the crossroads, as we feel it must be[1], then the ERM again fits perfectly with our own learning conception model. In this model learning conception 4 is the watershed between the first three reproductive learning conceptions and learning conception 5 which focuses on creating personal perspectives.

Stage 4: Contextual Knowing

Contextual Knowing is the end point of the story line emergence of voice, the starting point being echoing authority by Absolute Knowers (Baxter Magolda, 1992a, p. 193). The voice of Contextual Knowers is characterised as constructing their own perspective from a multitude of options or constructing their own approach to solving problems. Creating one's own perspective (or approach to solving problems) means to define internally what one believes, which is the epistemological expression of self-authorship (Baxter Magolda, 2001) and in this sense Contextual Knowing represents learning conception 5. We will try to portrait this aspect of Contextual Knowing using quotes from Baxter Magolda 1992a. Deirdre describes the literary criticism course in her senior year

> I took literary criticism, where we were introduced to all these new ways of looking at literature that no one ever talked about in high school. You know, it was always formal and always had to do with the things that were in the text.

> Nothing was taken out, nothing cultural or historical, no other perspective, no Marxism or communism or anything like that. Those tools were never yours to use… (p. 169)

She describes her discovery of the influence of context, or the perspective of the author, on the possible interpretations of a text, and comments that this "made me re-evaluate just about everything I had learned, right down to my choice of major. Everything kind of just got reworked" (Baxter Magolda, 1992a, p. 170). She is clearly trying to find a new perspective (in life) and realises that almost everything is relative to the context. In this we recognise the fifth position of Perry's epistemological model (Perry, 1970, further discussed below). The new perspective includes an open view on knowing – knowledge evolves and is by definition uncertain: the optimal solution depends on the context taken. Sean describes this while discussing his approach to reading study material

> … Just sit and run it over in your mind, think about different perspectives, intentionally bringing up things that you know are wrong and just go with it to see where it's going to end up. And just try to analyze it through enough different viewpoints, if you can get them, to see if you feel in your own judgment that it's solid all the way around or if it's got some flaws. But it's much more sit back and reflect on it. You can work through it back and forth until you come up with some kind of conclusions, hopefully, satisfactory conclusions. (p. 172)

Jim is very clear about the temporary nature of conclusions, which opens up the way to the dialogue characteristic of Contextual Knowing (see below).

> … There's not a certain way to say, "Well, that's right" or "that's wrong." It's based on what you have learned, what you believe in, and what kind of supporting arguments they have. (p. 173)

As mentioned before Baxter Magolda's second story line – relationship with authority – has strong similarities to our students' conceptions of teaching, in the sense that teaching conceptions discuss the student teacher relationship equalling the interpersonal aspect of self-authorship. The second story line starts with viewing authority as all knowing (Absolute Knowing) and ends with "… authorities, whether formal educators or peers, become partners in the process of sorting through knowledge claims…" (Baxter Magolda, 1992a, p. 198). This description indicates that Contextual Knowers while engaging in relationships with teachers or peers stress interdependency, characterized by equality and ongoing dialogue. At this level Baxter Magolda claims that agency (constructing one's own perspective) and communion (interdependency) are more in balance and the gender related differences in reasoning she found at earlier stages of knowing start to fade. While Mark is clearly dissatisfied with the teaching he encountered at law school after college, he gives insight into the importance that Contextual Knowers attach to partnerships in teaching.

> For instance – and none of my professors did this the first day, but I thought they should have – if they had said something like, "*We're engaged.*" And

> I think people could do this at the undergraduate level, too, to make it clear to the student that the teacher's also a student and that we're all in the classroom engaged in kind of a joint venture. "I can learn from you, you can learn from me" approach. Say something to the extent, "If you answer a question and it later proves to be wrong or questionable, don't be embarrassed." It's a little different [here] because it's a totally new discipline, and the professor does have all the answers. But I think it's more admirable for a student to stick to her guns than just say "oh, okay." Unfortunately, the professor's approach sometimes will deter the student from saying anything else. (p. 167)

These types of comments arise when students' level of epistemological thinking is not in line with the epistemological level of the teaching they encounter. We have found similar experiences in our research on learning and teaching conceptions and have coined the phrase disenchantment to describe it (van Rossum, Würffel and Hamer, 2002), and we will discuss this further in chapter 8, When Worlds Collide. Vermunt and Verloop refer to such experiences in their discussion of friction (Vermunt and Verloop, 1999).

Considering that in our analysis, Contextual Knowing revolves around 1) constructing – or authoring – one's own perspective among other perspectives and 2) student-teacher interdependency (and dialogue), we propose to rename this stage Self-authored Knowing. To avoid confusion between the interpretation of Baxter Magolda and our own, we will refer to this stage as such in the remainder of this chapter. In Self-authored Knowing, individuals 'author' personal perspectives, whereas in Independent Knowing individuals 'author' their own interpretations of situations/ problems according to the rules of a discipline. Obviously, our interpretation of Contextual Knowing and self-authorship differs from that of Baxter Magolda in three important aspects:

1. the notion that "some ideas are more valid than others" is in our opinion already present in Independent Knowing (see Max and Mark above) and
2. *what* is 'authored' by the self depends on the student's epistemological stage, and
3. the intrapersonal dimension of self-authorship (Who am I?) is an aspect more appropriate to Internal Foundation, the final stage of Baxter Magolda's models discussed in this section.

In later work Baxter Magolda seems to have struggled with the same issues and inconsistencies, coming to the conclusion that self-authorship must be "an incremental, cyclical" process (Baxter Magolda, 2008, p. 272) moving across Independent Knowing (where one first encounters the internal voice) through Self-authored Knowing (learning to trust the internal voice) and culminating in full self-authorship in Internal Foundation (where one is living one's convictions). We prefer to see self-authorship as a state consistent with learning conception 4, a position that is in line with the elaboration that Kegan provided in chapter 8 of his 1994 book (Hamer and van Rossum, 2010). We return to this issue shortly in the comments below.

In discussing the epistemological dimension of self-authorship Baxter Magolda (2001) gives a number of examples that show that in Self-authored Knowing, knowledge and knowing are subject to continuous re-evaluation. The ability to hold different systems up to evaluation is typical for the fifth order of consciousness, trans-system structures (Kegan, 1994, p. 291), placing Self-authored Knowing separate from self-authorship itself, underpinning our discussion above. Barry discusses his difficulty creating a perspective about ethical questions in a relativistic world.

> The way things are done [in China], it's basically going a hundred years back – into a time machine. Ethically, you separate yourself – it is a different culture, they have different needs than our country has. (…) You walk into factories, thousands of mostly young women have certificates saying they are over 16, the legal working age. Looking at that and saying my God (…) [but] If you went back [in time] into Northeastern US, we had child labor, rough conditions, no infrastructure, a huge immigrant workforce. (…) The ethics in that is a test: what am I doing here? Yes, I rationalized it; thought about our country and what CNN would say 100 years ago about the exploitation of America. If we didn't do that, where would we be today? You have to look at all this in the context of the growth curve. (Baxter Magolda, 2001, p. 147)

In this stage of thinking, Barry feels the need to accept situations he does not really agree with. We would argue that even at this stage of Contextual Knowing and relativistic thinking, in a certain way Barry is a victim of his own level of thinking. One wonders if he will choose to make a commitment to himself in the next stage of development – Internal Foundation – that will resolve his conflict and answer the fundamental questions: "Who am I?" and "Do I want to be involved in this?"

Stage 5: Internal Foundation

This stage of thinking people wrestle with fundamental questions such as

- Who am I?
- Do I want to be involved in this? and
- Have I become the person I feel I am?

These questions not only emphasise intellectual knowing – as is central in the previously described stages – but also the role of intuitive knowing, feeling good about decisions not only in a rational way. In 1984 we encountered this type of thinking when developing the sixth learning conception: Learning as Self Realisation (Van Rossum, Deijkers and Hamer, 1984). Students express this level of thinking in "[a]nswers like 'learning is living and living is learning" and 'learning is growing and growing is a condition for a meaningful existence'" (Van Rossum, Deijkers and Hamer, 1984, p. 42). At that time we already concluded that their focus on feeling, intuition and their own self was unique to this level and a radical turning point in their development. From now on, each choice you make contributes and affirms the evolving sense of self, the person you feel you are. In our opinion, here each commitment or decision to live according to one's convictions adds to the definition of the authentic self, confirming that in learning conception 6 the focus shifts from learning to *know* to learning to *be*, supporting our proposal to rename it to "conception of being 1" implying – in principle – infinite developments in this vain, both matching Perry's expectation of ongoing commitments after position 6 and Baxter Magolda's expectation of an incremental, cyclical process of "building an Internal Foundation" (2008).

We quote Mark, Sandra and Dawn (Baxter Magolda, 2001) in an attempt to illustrate this level of thinking and feeling, in short living.

> I have a clearer vision of what I really want to do. I have a stronger image of who I am. I'm not so wrapped up in being a counselor, I'm being Sandra. I have a clearer vision of Sandra and the different things that make up who I am. I went from "I am a counselor" to "I do some social work". I'm not afraid to say what I believe in and stand for it. I don't make reckless decisions that hurt my lifestyle or self – like quitting my job – but I am able to say, "this is how it is." (...) To help others, you have to maintain self. Now that I'm out of my old job, I recognize the point where I began to lose myself. If it happens again, I see it and don't do it. I don't worry much. I'm confident that I do a good job; I know this. If others disagree, they can find someone else. (...) It sounds nonchalant, but that is how I feel. Some of that was blurry in my old job. I knew some things I wouldn't do, but as we were speeding towards them, I couldn't tell how many I would do. Now I can see the line, and know what I won't do. (Sandra, p. 166 and 168)

Sandra has taken the step that still eludes Barry (above), has taken control over her life and can answer the question: Do I want to be involved in this? This is, we feel, the first stage where external authorities are no longer influencing decision-making. Some participants on this level describe a feeling of "coming home". After backpacking around in Australia for two months and experiencing many new aspects of herself, Dawn says,

> I noticed that if you listen to the world around you, you can learn a great deal about where you are and what you are doing. It gave me a chance to develop my intuitive nature; I never planned ahead for anything – just wake up and decide each day. It was a tremendous feeling of freedom, a sense of doing it on my own. I came back, felt more self confident, at peace with who I was and reasons why I did things. I had a much clearer sense of self. (...) When you take yourself way from [every day life] you realize your existence is all that matters. There is a clarity that almost instantly happens. (p. 162–163)

Returning to education, Mark connects his new found perspective to the level of contextual thinking he held previously during college and law school.

> In college I believed you had to analyze it. I [now] believe there is a truer way to understand than through analysis. Forms of meditation. Turning your mind off. Then gaining understanding of who you are and what this is around you, the world, without mental effort. I could read a text at college or law school, and could say this is a feminist critique of this text, then whip on the other pair of

glasses. I found conservative lenses in law school. I could figure out what various kinds of people would think. With Taoist philosophy, I've gotten closer to understanding what my own pair of eyes internally and externally are seeing. (...) getting to what it means to be a human being with a soul. (p. 65)

On the interpersonal aspect, Internal Foundation is also different from Self-authored Knowing, and shows clear similarity with the sixth teaching conception. In this aspect we recognise "a sense of communion (...) evident in the ability to connect meaningfully and mutually with others while maintaining an authentic self" (Baxter Magolda, 2001, p. 184) as an expression of the need for authentic relationships often mentioned in the sixth teaching conception.

Considering that for a number of participants their age is included in the quotes from the conversations, and they say for instance "I felt by 27, I would know what I wanted to do with my life" (Amy in a holding pattern within the crossroads, Baxter Magolda, 2001, p. 108) it seems safe to assume that not all participants reached the stage of Internal Foundation around 30 years of age. This supports the experience that not all people develop at the same speed, nor that all people reach the highest level. This is consistent with Perry's model, where he explicitly discusses non-developmental forms: "Temporizing", "Retreat" and "Escape" (Perry, 1970, p. 177 and below).

Comments on Baxter Magolda

Epistemological developments at Miami University

In Baxter Magolda (1992a) a graph (Figure 3.1, replicated below) was included that showed the rate of epistemological development in the sample of students during college and a fifth year. One can see clearly that absolutism is declining over the years, to disappear in the fifth year, while Transitional Knowing is on the rise

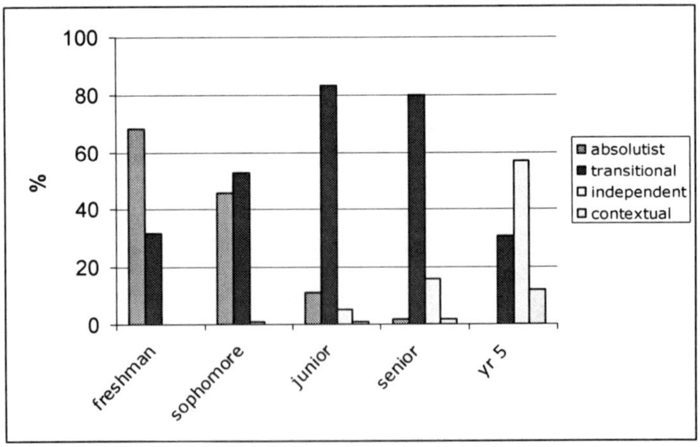

Figure 3.1. Ways of knowing by year (Baxter Magolda, 1992a, p. 71).

during college, stabilising around an incidence of eighty percent in the final years. Only after college does Independent Knowing come to the fore as the way of knowing of the majority. This means that in four years of college most students develop only one stage upwards, to Transitional Knowers, which is – we feel and many others with us – not in line with the aims of higher education.

We assume that the mainly traditional learning environment, and the famous 'Miami Bubble' protected the students from sufficiently 'shocking' epistemological experiences necessary for rapid development—and which they do seem to have encountered in the years after college (Baxter Magolda, 2001).

This interpretation is supported by Gavin where he explains the difference between failure in college and failure in life after college.

> In college, if you had a bad class, you got a bad grade. That was just something that happened because you lived with all your friends and there were always things to put that aside. But when you deal with real-life situations, like you've got rent to pay or you bought a house, ups and downs are much, much more emotionally felt because it has a direct impact on how you live. In college you can't really see that. It's a lot more emotional learning once you get out [of college] because before you always knew you could always just give up and go home. Now you can't give up and you can't go home. (Gavin, Baxter Magolda, 2001, p. 285)

Baxter Magolda acknowledges Gavin's story and argues for an educational environment, a learning partnership, that encourages reflection on real challenges, students' responsibility and autonomy in learning and educators providing guidance in processing (positive and negative) experiences (Baxter Magolda, 2007).

Self-authorship within Epistemological Development

Kegan is somewhat unclear about the nature of self-authorship. On the one hand, Kegan's definition of self-authorship includes a number of characteristics that seem to stem from different orders of consciousness, or at least from various stages in our and many other models. Kegan defined self-authorship as the ability of a 'self' to "coordinate, integrate, act upon, or invent values, beliefs, convictions, generalizations, ideals, abstractions, interpersonal loyalties, and intrapersonal states" (Kegan, 1994, p. 185) and the self "is no longer *authored by* them, it *authors them* and thereby achieves a personal authority" (p. 185). This seems to indicate that self-authoring refers to a self, no longer authored by traditions but able to author an identity capable of observing and evaluating systems, but Kegan fails to define the frame around these systems. On the other hand, Kegan himself linked this mindset (self-authorship) firmly to the fourth order of consciousness, the framework of a discipline when he stated that self-authored learners see a discipline or ideology as "a method, procedure or system of interpretation for reflecting on hypotheses, evaluating values and validating knowledge" (1994, p. 286). In our analysis, self-authorship refers to learning teaching conception 4 (Hamer and van Rossum, 2010) and to Independent Knowing. In other research however, the concept has undergone a considerable evolution from a state to a process to encompass the various aspects listed in Kegan's original definition above (e.g. most clearly in Baxter Magolda, 2008). In addition, in studying self-authorship Baxter Magolda has pulled into the limelight two dimensions of development that may have been underexposed in her earlier work: the interpersonal dimension dealing with relationships, and the intrapersonal dimension important in understanding identity issues. To be fair, in our opinion the ERM did include all three aspects (epistemology, interpersonal and intrapersonal) as does our own model, be it that the more affective dimensions were perhaps cloaked in other characteristics. For instance we feel that the interpersonal dimension is central in our teaching conception, while the epistemological dimension is caught in the learning conception. The identity development dimension (intrapersonal) influences both. In the table below, from Hamer and van Rossum (2008), we link the three dimensional approach to our learning-teaching conception model. In her more recent work Baxter Magolda proposes that each of these three dimensions can be the trigger of development.

Table 3.1. Learning and teaching conceptions in relation to epistemology, relationships (interpersonal dimension) and identity or sense of self (intrapersonal dimension)

	Hamer and van Rossum (2010)				
	Learning Conception	*Teaching conception*	*Epistemology (knowing)*	*Relationships (interpersonal)*	*Sense of self (intrapersonal)*
1	Increasing knowledge	Imparting clear/well structured knowledge	-	Obedience	-
2	Memorising	Transmitting structured knowledge (acknowledging receiver)	(selecting for) Memorisation	Asking questions, subservient	Seen through the eyes of others
3	Reproductive understanding/ application or Application foreseen	Interacting and Shaping	(Reproductive) Applying	Interacting and discussing	Having a personal opinion
4	Understanding subject matter	Challenging to think for yourself / developing a way of thinking	The way of thinking within a discipline	Actively participating	Thinking for yourself, personal authority
5	Widening horizons	Dialogue teaching	Relativism or Realisation of multiple perspectives	Engaging in true dialogue	Constructing a personal perspective
6	Growing self-awareness	Mutual trust and authentic relationships: Caring	Paradoxical thinking and emergence of wisdom	Compassion and caring	Coming home (to yourself)

Concluding we feel that self-authorship as interpreted by among others Baxter Magolda (e.g. 2007 and 2008) covers at least three epistemological stages:

1. Independent Knowing/learning conception 4: here the notion that one opinion is more valid than another is realised and new values, abstractions, generalisations are constructed (or authored) using the rules of a system, a discipline;
2. Contextual Knowing/learning conception 5: here one realises that there are more ways to look at a problem, more theories to explain a phenomenon, and at this level one is able to hold multiple systems in the mind in order to evaluate them. Different perspectives show 'different' realities and by moving from one perspective to another one can "transform" (or author) the perception of reality; and
3. Internal Foundation/learning conception 6: here a growing set of commitments or convictions form the fundament for the realisation of the authentic self with personal values, beliefs, convictions, ideals, interpersonal loyalties, and intra-personal states.

In Hamer en van Rossum (2010) we have further argued that Kegan himself links the term 'self-transforming' to the fifth order of consciousness characterised by the ability to evaluate multiple systems without necessarily choosing one above another (see Kegan, 1994, p. 292), indicating a mindset that is more amendable to relativity, contradiction, perhaps even paradox. Learning conception 6 and Internal Foundation then are quite a long way beyond self-authorship. To describe this latter epistemological position we have proposed to add a new term to the chain started by Kegan: self-defining (Hamer and van Rossum, 2010).

Research to further uncover the nature of higher levels of thinking

Most epistemological research focuses on high school, college or university students, and in these studies students with higher levels of thinking about learning and knowledge (Contextual Knowing and higher) are fairly rare. Even Perry's position nine is not an empirically based position, but an argued extrapolation (Perry, 1970). As age and epistemological sophistication seem to have a certain co-variation, 'super-longitudinal' studies are probably necessary to better describe the nature of these higher levels of epistemological thinking. We were, therefore, happy to receive Marcia Baxter Magolda's 2007 AERA presentation, where she reported results from her already twenty-year longitudinal study. We will treat the development of Dawn, one of Baxter Magolda's original students whom she has interviewed annually during these twenty years and who has been quoted in most of the publications since 1992 (Baxter Magolda, 1992a, 2001, 2004 and 2007). In this way we can try to trace the speed and the nature of Dawn's epistemological development, in as far as her interviews are included in the publications. Our aim here is to support our premise that – as the lower levels of thinking have been treated in detail (e.g. Baxter Magolda, 1992a) – in future epistemological research would need to focus on following students over much longer periods than usual. Either that, or studies are needed with more mature subjects (e.g. ages over forty) who have sufficient experience of formal education and life to make a higher level of thinking probable. In Hamer and van Rossum (2008) we have proposed avenues of research using bibliographic or literary sources (such as elder tales, Chinen, 1997).

Dawn's story. During her college years, Dawn developed no further than Transitional Knowing, which we will illustrate with a few quotes from Baxter Magolda (1992a). In discussing disagreements and interaction in class, Dawn said,

> There are oftentimes disagreements. That's kind of an education in and of itself, to know that not everybody's opinion counts. Or, yes, they all count, but what you take in is what you choose to take in. I suppose it depends on the validity of what they're saying. And I suppose that you're going to ask me "How do you judge the validity of what they're saying?" And I don't know if I know the answer to that question. (1992a, p. 158)
>
> Any person we come in contact with has a lot to teach us and we them; interaction is a good way to learn. (1992a, p. 242)

In these two quotes Dawn showed the typical non-judgemental respect that learning-teaching conception 3 students have for other people's opinions, and the appreciation of interaction in teaching.
During her twenties, after college, Dawn slowly discovered a new way of knowing, Independent Knowing. In Baxter Magolda (2007) this level is seen as the first step in achieving full self-authorship and it is renamed to 'initial self-authorship'. In Baxter Magolda, 2004, this position of 'initial self-authorship' seemed to be preceded, in Dawn's case, by her choice of theatre as major, a choice in her junior year driven by personal interest alone. As Dawn says,

> "What the heck. If it's what I want to do, why be unhappy doing something else?" It seems so much easier for me to get the grades doing something that I like to do. (2004, p. 21)

Shortly after graduation Dawn (then in her early twenties) elaborated on her satisfaction with this choice:

> I mean, this is all just a wonderful, wonderful life experience to be having. Fortunately, it's in what I want to be doing. It's like for the first time in my life, I know I'm in the career vein that I have always wanted to be in and should be in. I think there's a lot of floundering that goes on while you're in school, "What's my major? What am I going to do with my life?" And I think I've found where I need to be and want to be. (2004, p. 22)

As said before, Dawn developed into *'initial self-authorship'* during her twenties, a level of knowing that is equal to our learning-teaching conception 4. This development was driven – as Baxter Magolda indicates in 2004 and 2007 – by her theatre work.

> I'm more willing to express my ideas and take chances expressing my ideas. "Who cares what people think?" sort of thing. When you're not as self-confident, you're afraid that people are going to laugh at what you think or you're afraid that they're going to think you're stupid—it's all those petty, little things that inhibit us. Whereas when you're confident, you are more willing to say, "This is my opinion; this is why I hold this opinion. You may agree with it or not, but this is what –with my mind I have formulated this opinion and that's how I think and feel." ... You can think and formulate ideas for yourself and ultimately that's what's important. *You have a mind and you can use it.* That's probably the most important thing, regardless of the content of what your thoughts and opinions are. ... It's the fact that you can form an opinion that's more important than the opinion itself. (2004, p. 22–23, italics ours)

Here, Dawn could answer the question about how to establish the validity of an opinion. An answer she had no idea of when leaving college. In addition, Dawn emphasised the importance of procedure above content and in this she seemed to prefer a form of separate knowing (Belenky et al., 1997, see below). After entering the phase of 'initial self-authorship', one can expect that self-authorship develops further, and the next phase Dawn described is '*listening to her inner voice'*. A phase where she tried to shut out the noises of daily life and find herself, reminding us of Erica (Belenky et al., 1997, p.132) who uses the phrase "turning back on myself" to describe the transition to Constructed Knowledge, or our fifth learning conception. At this stage in her life, Dawn needed solitude –finding it in going into the outback of Australia and in mountain climbing in Africa – and acceptance of her sexual orientation, to be able to listen to her inner voice. Around thirty, Dawn arrived in this next stage, and in describing her state of mind she discussed intuition and listening to her inner voice,

> ... I believe that there are forces in this world that are more powerful than we are, and there are some we can readily acknowledge and others that I think we cultivate over time. It's, I mean, I would say one of those [that we cultivate] would be intuition – well actually it could fall into both [categories]. It is readily available, but it takes time to cultivate as far as trusting your intuition and trusting that voice that says, "This is where I need to be." ... It all ties in, coming back to that intuition thing and listening to the voice inside of you. ... Your intuition is the central processing unit. ... I don't think the linear mind, the brain cannot process that on a linear level, but the heart and soul can, because it knows what's going on. That is the big clarity that happens when I travel. (2001, p. 178–179)

> It wasn't that I couldn't talk about [being gay]... Now I am at that point that I am comfortable—it doesn't bother me. ... That has contributed a great deal to how I see things and how I think. Getting to where I am now, the confidence thing; you know you have the inner strength to stand apart from the mainstream. (2004, p. 23)

Now that Dawn had learned to hear her inner voice when travelling, she needed to learn how to hear it even through the noise of daily life. To reach the next level, she had to learn to '*cultivate and trust her inner voice*'. The diagnosis of multiple sclerosis (MS), at age 33, hastened this development.

> The whole thought process of just taking stock of where you are in life. It's like putting your life through a sieve, getting the big awkward chunks out of your life, getting the nice finely sifted residue – it is kind of sorting it all out. What is *the essence of you* and what isn't? What is important to the essence of you and what isn't? … You have to decide what it is that you want and don't want. Little by little, things take a much more specific shape. … I think I'll be on this path for a while until it is time to go in another direction. (2004, p. 19, italics ours)

Indeed, Dawn proved to be right, she would be on this path, with all its multiple ups and downs, for a while (Baxter Magolda, 2007). The focus on defining her essence, her identity, and cultivating and trusting her inner voice, led to a new type of relationship with 'the world',

> … If you respect yourself, if you have confidence in your ability, that changes your whole perspective. If you respect yourself, it is pretty much a given that you will respect others. Treating others with compassion and understanding can only happen when you've achieved a certain level of that yourself. … Stepping into the realm of not judging people, treating them with compassion, acting in my life without judging and with compassion. … It is a simpler, more peaceful way of living. ... It contributes to you as an individual being a better person and getting more out of life. (2004, p. 20)

The caring attitude Dawn showed for other people is typical of teaching conception 6 (see chapter 1). That life at this level is neither really simple nor peaceful comes from the fact that one has to understand the art of "controlling without controlling" (2007, p. 9),

> Knowing how to make things happen en let things happen. When you find the balance between those things, life is spectacular. … That is a constant process for me. To be able to say this is my life and it's on my terms: I love that. (2004, p. xxi)

During the following interviews it became clear that it is anything but easy to keep your balance. And when you lose it – e.g. as Dawn did when she lost *herself* in a relationship - you can tumble down into 'the shadow lands', where the inner voice seems to have faded because you are not paying enough attention (to yourself), and you lose your way. To recover the feeling of centeredness is hard work.

> I felt very lost… I always felt like I was fighting to get back on track and I just couldn't and that lasted for a couple of months where I just felt like I was just tumbling around in space with no sense of direction or anything to cling to and I was just out there lost. And I don't know if I can pull it to one defining

> moment where everything came right back together for me. I think probably sometime in the early spring it started to gel again, and now I feel like I'm at the complete opposite end of the spectrum because I know, have such a clarity over what I think, what I believe, spiritual purpose, which is kind of an interesting journey. You don't stay in the light all the time. I mean there are times when you go to the shadow lands ... (2007, p. 10)

Over the years, Dawn dipped in and out of the shadow lands, changing careers and life partner, learning to accept herself, her talents, more clearly and finally arriving at a place where she felt she is finally "settling into herself", experiencing a feeling of 'coming home to herself' for the first time at age 36.

> ... I just feel such a complete sense of settling into myself and everything about me. This is the most peaceful I have felt, I think, in a very, very long time, if ever, you know? And I just feel like I'm landing in who I am and what it is I'm meant to do, and where, all these things that I can do and all these tools that I have available to me, and I know how to use them. And it's like OK, the extraordinary life has begun. I mean it has always been so, but it's just like now you're completely aware of it. I opened this door, and there is no going back...So there's been a big shift in that approach to myself and my life. (2007, p. 12)

Baxter Magolda feels this level – Internal Foundation – is the end of the process of *developing* self-authorship. In this article (2007), and throughout Baxter Magolda's other work to date, the question whether self-authorship can be associated with a particular epistemological level whether it is a process spanning levels is ongoing. As noted before, Baxter Magolda herself leans towards the process interpretation, as she says "The key element in developing self-authorship is gaining confidence in one's inner voice. Educators create contexts for students to gain confidence when they validate students' ability to explore their inner voices and structure that exploration in ways that enable students to engage it" (2007, p. 22). In 2008 Baxter Magolda takes this position even further, claiming full self-authorship in the position Internal Foundation and Securing Internal Commitments (2008).

At this end of the process Baxter Magolda refers to as developing self-authorship – in our model the journey from learning-teaching conception 4 to 6 – Baxter Magolda reports that creativity and one's own vision become more important, while 'knowledge' takes on a new character, it becomes 'wisdom' and no longer 'just knowing'.

> I started to look at what I'm good at and how to take those things, and particularly with the cooking, it's just like, "No, I am tired of working for somebody else's vision." I have my own ideas. I have my creativity. I have my own style in the kitchen. Why can't I start working for my own vision and make that a success, and make a living off that? (2007, p. 11–12)

> It's starting to feel – more like wisdom than knowledge. To me knowledge is an awareness of when you know things. You know them as facts; they are there in front of you. When you possess the wisdom, you've lived those facts,

> that information so fully that it takes on a whole different aspect than just knowing. It is like you absorbed that information into your entire being. Not just that you know things. It is something deeper. Knowledge is brain – wisdom comes from a different place I feel like. Something deeper connecting with our brain so that you have something different to draw from. A point where knowing you are going to do something – the knowledge has a deeper level – internal, intuitive, centered in entire being, the essential part of you that just – makes the basic knowledge pale by comparison. (2007, p. 13–14)

> … You start to shift over into information or feelings or intuitions or senses that you don't … that aren't necessarily tangible, but you almost pick them up by osmosis. When it starts to become that sort of a thing, that to me is crossing over into wisdom. (2007, p. 15)

We would like to compare Dawn's introduction of wisdom with a learning conception 6 example taken from Taylor and van Rossum, 1986: "Learning is consciously acquiring wisdom and/or knowledge (where I see the latter as referring to what you get out of books or transfer, while wisdom comes from personal experience). The most important activity is the process of awareness … I strive after a feeling, an emotion, a yearning I call happiness. What that is exactly, I cannot describe, or to put it more strongly, I don't even know. It is indefinable. It is something like seeking peace and tranquillity … I feel I have learned something when I "feel happy" after becoming aware of a change in my thinking or acting that I am personally responsible for" (S26, Taylor and van Rossum, 1986, p. 24–25). The change of view on knowledge described here may prove –we feel– that epistemological development is still possible even *after* learning-teaching conception 5.

In her example on her cooking, where she now relied so much on her intuitive wisdom that she seemed to be able to think "about other things while [cooking]" (2007, p. 14), Dawn reminds us of descriptions of expert thinking in expert-novice literature (e.g. in van Rossum and Hamer, 1985).

Wisdom gave Dawn a greater sense of certainty, a feeling that, as Baxter Magolda interpreted it, "she can do what she sets her mind to and adjust to unknowns that the next day brings" (Baxter Magolda, 2007, p. 16). In Dawn's own words this greater sense of certainty means

> Well, it kinda goes back to that whole superhero thing I was telling you about, … it's in that confidence … This is just … it's just a certainty … as certain as I was when I got on my bike to ride 150 miles … Now it's just like, well, lemme do this, and then I'm gonna watch what happens. It's more engaged and OK, now I'm gonna do this, and I'm gonna watch what happens. That's a very conscious way of expressing it, but you know, I think it does become more unconscious when you're actually proceeding through each day. (2007, p. 15–16)

We see this sense of certainty as the other, more optimistic face of Internal Foundation, where the pessimistic face is 'tumbling around in the shadow lands'. Baxter Magolda seems to see it in a similar way, when she says, "With wisdom came the certainty of knowing that self, of being grounded, centered, and connected to self and others. Yet being able to exist in that space, to navigate it in everyday life, remained a challenge." (p. 19). The sense of certainty described here reminds us of the sense of agency, of being in control, we spoke of as an important characteristic of learning conception 6 (see chapter 1).

In this sixth position, Dawn was mostly focused on finding herself. In the interviews that followed, Dawn seemed to start to apply the sense of self, her wisdom, in her relationships, looking outside herself more. She opened herself up to the scrutiny of others and their reactions. '*Opening yourself (or your self) to the world'* – perhaps swinging back to seeking communion (Kegan, 1994, see below) - after having found your self, *may be* a new level of thinking and it is accompanied by struggle, and increase in uncertainty:

> … I've never been one to be really open and vulnerable. I'm feeling like currently that's what's getting the most immediate attention and response is that it's like, OK, to get what you want there's gonna have to be a certain element of that, so yes, that has been something that I've never dealt with really head on is like being really open and being really honest emotionally and accessible emotionally. … I feel like I'm more ready to take on that challenge now than I ever have been before. Maybe having more inner strength and more courage to say OK, this part of me can be exposed. …
>
> … a lot is going on right now around the whole MS disclosure, not with [my partner] but with some other people. I got a little fearful, um how are you gonna handle this? What are you gonna think about all this? Because this is huge. I means this is a big part of who I am and … did I wait too long? Probably. But it was all fine and it really opened up a lot of communication with us, but … I felt like in a sense I kind of stepped back a few steps 'cause I was so bound and determined to do everything differently this time and, you know, new resolve. Everything's coming together, like we had talked about. And it's like I feel strong. I feel powerful, and then I got to that and it's like [moan]. And I just took like three steps back and I'm like, "no, you can't take three steps back. You have to stay with this. You have to be open and honest and pursue this". (2007, p. 17–18)

The exploration of opening yourself back onto the world, onto the others, may lead to an even deeper examination of the self. And attempting to answer the question, *What does it mean to be human?*, may be the first sign of yet another way of thinking, influencing every aspect of life.

> I'm on a mission to bring back the humanity to myself, you know what? You are human. You don't have to be Hercules about the issues that come up in your world and how well you can handle them and how much weight you can carry on your shoulders. … That pursuit of wisdom, that pursuit of something deeper, knowing yourself. That's always been prevalent with me and I think I'm entering a very big new phase of all of that and at the core of my being I'm like, well, this is what you want. This is part of your mission in life is to

> plumb the depths, seeking something more and seeking that wisdom. So this is just a whole new way of doing that. I just didn't know it was gonna happen *in every facet of my life*, but that's how it happened, so … (2007, p. 18–19, italics ours)

These excerpts from Dawn's interviews seem to point towards the conclusion that the developmental focus shifts after epistemological level 5. In the first five stages of Baxter Magolda's ERM and our own learning-teaching conception model, the focus of development is 'views on knowledge and learning'. We have already proposed that the sixth level seems to point in a new direction, coining the phrase "conception of being 1" (see chapter 1). In Dawn's interviews we see signs that the focus of development from level 6 onwards may not be life, but the exploration of self. We feel that the '*essential self*' discovered in level 6 may be the base line for the development towards '*opening your self to others*' which in turn perhaps is followed by '*acknowledging your own humanity*'. Perhaps a better term for the stages in this second tier of development is not 'conceptions of being' but '*learning to be*'.

Linking Baxter Magolda to Van Rossum-Hamer

Table 3.2. Relating students' developing learning/teaching conceptions to the ERM

	Van Rossum-Hamer Learning Conception	*Teaching Conception*	*Baxter Magolda 1992a, 2001 ERM*
1	Increasing knowledge	Imparting clear/well structured knowledge	Absolute Knowing
2	Memorising	Transmitting structured knowledge (acknowledging receiver)	
3	Reproductive understanding/ application or Application foreseen	Interacting and Shaping	Transitional Knowing
4	Understanding subject matter	Challenging to think for yourself/developing a way of thinking	Independent Knowing
5	Widening horizons	Dialogue teaching	Self-authored Knowing
6	Growing self awareness	Mutual trust and authentic relationships: Caring	Internal Foundation

In Table 3.2 we summarise the relationship between our model of student thinking described in chapter 1 to Baxter Magolda's Epistemological Reflection Model.

Belenky, Clinchy, Goldberger and Tarule

> *...educators can help women develop their own authentic voices if they emphasize connection over separation, understanding and acceptance over assessment, and collaboration over debate; if they accord respect to and*

> *allow time for the knowledge that emerges from firsthand experience; if instead of imposing their own expectations and arbitrary requirements, they encourage students to evolve their own patterns of work based on the problems they are pursuing. These are the lessons we have learned in listening to women's voices*
>
> *(Belenky et al., 1986 edition 1997, p. 229)*

A major goal for Baxter Magolda's initial study (1992a) was the search for gender related similarities and differences in reasoning patterns within ways of knowing. The gender issue entered the area of epistemological research when Belenky, Clinchy, Goldberger and Tarule (1986 edition 1997) addressed women's ways of knowing in reaction to the almost exclusively male sample used to derive the Perry Scheme (see next section on Perry). Belenky et al. felt that their "work focuses on what else women might have to say about the development of their minds and on alternative routes that are sketchy or missing in Perry's version" (1997, p. 9). Not only did their sample comprise only women, it contained also subjects not usually included in this type of research. The sample consisted of 135 women of diverse ages. The majority, 90, were mostly college students but included also some high school students. The remaining 45 women represented the "invisible colleges" and were clients of three family agencies providing them with parenting information and assistance. The latter group of 45 fell into three categories, rurally located and isolated teenage mothers, parents in self-help groups for people with a history of abuse, and mothers in a rural children's health programme. Belenky et al. interviewed the women in much the same way as Perry, focusing retrospectively on "self-image, relationships of importance, education and learning, real-life decision-making and moral dilemmas, accounts of personal changes and growth, perceived catalysts for change and impediments to growth, and visions of the future" (1997, p. 11).

Women's Ways of Knowing

This study resulted in five – actually we feel they described six – epistemological *perspectives*. Belenky et al. felt that these ways of knowing were not necessarily stages in a clear sequential ordering: "We leave it to future work to determine whether these perspectives have any stagelike qualities" (1997, p. 15). However, this last assertion is not strictly kept to in the discussion of the various perspectives, in part because the women themselves indicated at several points in the study that they developed from one perspective to another. We will now discuss the – in our eyes – six positions in short and indicate where we feel that they merge with our data on learning and teaching. A major metaphor Belenky et al. used to differentiate among the different ways of knowing is *voice* because many of their subjects used metaphors of speaking and listening as opposed to the visual metaphors usually used in the – in their eyes (or would it be ears?) – male dominated science (e.g. equalling 'knowing' with seeing and 'truth' with light): "By telling us about their voice and silences, by revealing to us how much they could hear and learn from the ordinary and everyday … women told us about their views of the world and their place in it" (1997, p. 19).

Silence: the Women Describing Themselves in this Position are Characterised by Feeling Voiceless.

Belenky et al. found only a few of the women in this position at the time of the interviews. All of the women describing this perspective, either at the time of the study or in retrospect, were among the youngest and most deprived (socially, economically and educationally) of the sample of 45 women from the "invisible colleges", and their environments were characterised by extreme gender stereotypes, with silent women obeying 'powerful' men. In general, this epistemological perspective represented "an extreme in denial of self and in dependence on external authority for direction" (Belenky et al., 1997, p. 24). Metaphorically, the way of knowing of these women is typified as "deaf and dumb": "[t]hey felt 'deaf' because they assumed they could not learn from the words of others, 'dumb' because they felt so voiceless" (p. 24). In their responses there is no indication of any reflection: "[t]here were no words that suggested an awareness of mental acts, consciousness or introspection" (p. 25), and describing the self[2] was almost impossible. Retrospectively these women described themselves "in terms of their own movements in and around the geographic space that surrounded them." (1997, p. 31): as Cindy said "Before I got pregnant I used to go and come as I wanted. …I used to describe myself as not being home" (p. 31). This reminds us of one of our students quoted in van Rossum et al. (2003), who, in looking back – at the end of his studies – on his performance in the first year at the Hotelschool, said "Then, it was only seldom that I prepared well for an exam. I lived too much on improvisation and luck" (van Rossum et al., 2003, p. 92) and as such described the non-reflective stance typical of learning conception 1.

Silent women experienced disconnection: in their way of knowing these women seemed to be limited to the present, the actual, the concrete and the specific. There is no dimension in their thinking. In this sense, their way of knowing represents a single point in the epistemological space, much like Kegan described his first order of consciousness (see section on Kegan below, Kegan, 1994, p. 33). They do not trust their own mind to remember or know anything. Authorities are seen as all-powerful and overpowering, leading to blind obedience to and utter dependence on others in order to survive. As Belenky et al. illustrated "Even if the authorities [e.g. teachers] explained their reasoning, there is little evidence that the silent women could imagine themselves actively listening to the authorities' ideas, understanding what they were saying, and then choosing to obey. The commands and the actions are undifferentiated – like puppets moving with the jiggle of a thread. To hear is to obey" (1997, p. 28).

As said above, we surely recognise some of these issues – be it usually in a less severe form – in our learning-teaching conception 1. In its purest form, silence is not to be found often in first-year higher education students. Furthermore, one may wonder if young, powerless men, when treated as these silenced women, would not also turn out to be equally silent. Or, if indeed men are more prone to use visual metaphors, perhaps the male partners of the women in Belenky et al.'s portraits may not be silenced, but blinded. Blinded to any other way of life, any prospect or future. In that sense they are in as dire straights epistemologically as the women portrayed, even if they seem to have the power[3]. We will return to this issue in our comments – discussing descriptions of a young girl and a young boy both it seems Silent, but leave it to other researchers to examine this issue in detail. In the end we feel that, however grim this position is described in Belenky et al., it is (only) a stage in the epistemological development. As such it holds in itself that people – if intrinsically motivated and provided with the right support - *can* indeed move beyond this ultimately powerless and selfless state. And indeed Clinchy admits as much where she says that although "[t]he muting of the profoundly Silent women pervades their entire lives and is much less tractable, ... it is not irreversible" (McVicker Clinchy, 2002, p. 66).

Received Knowledge: Listening to the Voices of Others.

For the deprived women in Silence, parenthood frequently led to an epistemological revolution: the move to Received Knowledge. Listening to the voices of others was exemplified by women who believed that the experts of the family agency knew everything.

> They were wonderful. It just seems that they know all the answers to everything that has to do with children. They have been just everything to me. They've been like a security blanket. You know, I can call anytime something happens—even at night time. They are always friendly and cheerful. You don't have to be afraid. ... When you need them, they take the time to explain things. You know, they are all very patient; they spell it all out –'cause I'm not too smart.' (Ann in Belenky et al., 1997, p. 36)

Here, Belenky et al. felt that women in this position *begin* to see themselves as learners, through the realisation that they "could hear, understand and remember the things [the experts from the agency] taught [them]" (p. 36).

This same position, listening to the voices of others, was also expressed by young, first-year college students. Belenky et al. related this way of knowing to Perry's dualism (Perry, 1970, see also below) where things are either right or wrong, and teachers, as sources of truth, know the (only) right answer to each question. Learning is seen here as 'receiving, retaining and returning' the words of teachers or experts (including books). Women in Received Knowledge are confused when teachers see learning differently, do not provide them with the 'right answer' and use the 'wrong' teaching method: "How could [they] learn if the teacher refused to pass along his knowledge?" (p. 40).

> He would make you feel stupid. He would make you find the answers on your own. And he wouldn't even give you any hints on what the right answers were. (Angela in Belenky et al., 1997, p. 40)

These women hate ambiguity, cannot read between the lines, and fail to really understand: they only collect facts. As Belenky et al. said "Unlike the silent women, who do not see themselves as learners at all, these women feel confident about their ability to absorb and to store the truths received from others" (p. 42–43). We feel that Received Knowledge is identical to our learning-teaching conception 2, with its emphasis on memorising and reproduction, and its emphasis on the teacher explaining everything clearly.

In contrast to women in Silence, these women can describe themselves in a limited way: they described the self as "mirrored in the eyes of others", as other people see them. A college freshman said "Everything I say about myself is what other people tell me I am. You get a pretty good idea of yourself from the comments that other people are saying about you" (Belenky et al., 1997, p. 48). The narratives of other people seem to define the self in this way of knowing. Self-descriptions are also very static, and women find it difficult to describe possible development, growth, change or a possible future self. "Passing grades in academic or corporate structures seem to give these women rather literal rungs on a ladder for providing firm benchmarks for gauging their own progress" (Belenky et al., 1997, p. 50).

With self, knowledge, teaching and learning all essentially defined by others, this way of knowing is a prime example of the consistency and coherence in thinking within a 'way of knowing', a learning-teaching conception or order of consciousness (see Kegan below).

Subjective Knowledge: Listening to the Inner Voice.

Listening to the voices of others is still present at this level, but it is made subordinate to listening to one's inner voice: women listening to their intuition, their gut or 'still small voice'. Belenky et al. remarked that Subjective Knowledge was the way of knowing of about half of their sample, and it "appeared in every educational and agency setting included in the study. [It cuts] across class, ethnic, age, and educational boundaries" (p. 55). Subjective Knowledge was found for adult women escaping from bad relationships, and for the 'hidden multiplists'– young college students from 'good' traditional backgrounds who, once exposed to the diversity in college, dreamt of escape and release in diaries and poetry.

> It seems like there are some things I want to do and I feel I'm going to disappoint [my parents]. Just like I might want to disappear for a year, or join the Peace Corps, or something. Maybe just go off and climb a mountain sometime. My parents have always given so much to my life that I would feel guilty not giving it back. … I think I mean a lot more to them than I want to right now. (Erica in Belenky et al., 1997, p. 65)

Regardless of their background, eventually all these subjectivist women stopped to listen only to the voices of others (experts, teachers, etcetera). In their new way of knowing a common theme is that "[t]hey insist on the value of personal, firsthand experience; and, … if they listen at all to others, it is to those who are most like themselves, in terms of life experiences" (Belenky et al., 1997, p. 68). Belenky et al. explained the transition to the third way of knowing for the clients of family agencies: "By sharing reactions and solutions, whether about childrearing, domestic problems, or weight reduction, by being given the opportunity to talk things over with a sympathetic nonjudgmental person with similar experiences, a women can begin to hear that maybe she is not such an incompetent, a dummy, or an oddity. She has *experience* that may be valuable to others; she, too, can know things. The discovery that firsthand experience is a valuable source of knowledge emerges again and again in the stories of subjectivist women. ...Although they have not yet realized the power of their own minds and are reluctant to generalize from their experience to advise others, they begin to feel that they can rely on their experience and 'what feels right' to them as an important asset in making decisions for themselves" (Belenky et al., 1997, p. 60–61). As a young mother described her new way of knowing,

> When my daughter was first born, there wasn't anybody that really had the right knowledge, the right answers. I would worry about it ... Do I raise her the way I want to? But I'd have questions, and if there wasn't any answer, I'd sit there and worry about it. And six more problems would come up and there was no one there to answer them. But it's changed a lot in the last year because Marcia, my counselor, was there, a sounding board. It made me realize that I'm all right. And sometimes now I think of something before somebody else thinks of it. (p. 61)

For these women, their view on 'truth' takes on a similar cast. Truth is private and unique to each person: an intuitive reaction, something experienced or felt (a gut feeling), and the result of personal history.

> Every person has her own unique body of knowledge that's been given to them through their life's experiences. And realizing that mine is as valid as the next person's, whether or not that person has gone through six or seven years of college, I feel that my knowledge is as important and real and valuable as theirs is. (p. 69)

These women do not seem to see themselves as constructing knowledge yet, they see themselves as "conduits through which truth emerges" (p. 69), and for them the criterion for truth is what feels comfortable, or works best. Furthermore, because everyone has their own personal history and experience, no-one has the right to judge one another's truths or opinions.

Subjectivist knowers trust their inner voice and Belenky et al. saw this as proof of their emerging "sense of self and sense of agency and control" (1997, p. 68). Subjectivists distrust logic, analysis or abstraction (e.g. science) as an approach to 'truth'. For the mothers in the sample this is expressed in standing up to doctors (experts) with regard to the proper treatment of their child, or the proper place for childbirth. As Anna Jean described

> I always thought doctors were like God and knew the answers to everything. But now I'm glad I know it myself. I can figure things out for myself and I don't need them. I ended up learning that it was *me* that knew it all and they didn't. (p. 73)

Learning and teaching are no longer seen as primarily memorising and listening to the voices of teachers. Learning and knowledge must now have an "intuitive, experiential base" (p. 73) and direct sensory experience or personal involvement with the subject matter are preferred to books, memorising and listening: "Reading books is not enough. I really want to talk to people and watch them" (Anna Jean in Belenky et al., 1997, p. 74).

Teachers – especially when they themselves have a constructive view on knowing and learning[4] – may be frustrated when confronted with subjectivists who reject 'classic texts' or 'winning arguments' saying "You can't learn things from teachers and books like you can from experience" or, "What people who are experts say is always general, never specific. And each situation is different" (Belenky et al. 1997, p. 74). Belenky et al. explicitly linked this way of knowing to Perry's multiplicity (Perry, 1970, see below). When describing subjectivists' views on learning and teaching, they emphasised their preference for learning from direct experience, and for personal involvement with the subject matter, which we feel fits seamlessly with our learning-teaching conception 3, where experiential learning, simple application and sharing personal opinions are the major recurring themes.

Self-descriptions in this third way of knowing are no longer dependent on "other people's eyes." The relative newness of the inner voice, and the unstable sense of self, make it hard for these women to describe themselves. Sometimes they use an incoherent string of metaphors

> The easiest way for me to see myself is in images. Images of flowers, in Winnie the Pooh, seagulls. I don't know if I could ever do it using words. (Belenky et al. 1997, p. 82),

or they use a metaphor of birth

> I've never had a personality. I've always been someone's daughter, someone's wife, someone's mother. Right now I'm so busy being born, discovering who I am, that I don't know who I am. And I don't know where I'm going. And everything is going to be fine. (p. 82)

In this third way of knowing, these women experienced the birth of the self, and, as Belenky et al. remarked, this sense of being 'newly born' can occur at any age and is usually accompanied by forward-looking and optimism. In this, the third way of knowing resembles Kegan's third order of consciousness, where he finds that, for the first time in the present, one can see the future as real and possibly different from the present or past (Kegan, 1994, p. 27 and the section on Kegan).

Procedural Knowledge: the Voice of Reason.

In procedural knowledge Belenky et al. discerned two ways of knowing, separate and connected knowing. While both ways were present in their sample, they felt connected knowing was more common among women and separate knowing more common for men, a view supported by Baxter Magolda (1992a), but not at all obvious in our own data. We do know of some tentative quantitative support for differences in ways of *learning* between men and women: “Few indications were found for typical male and female ways of learning. The biggest difference between the sexes was in female preference for, and male dislike of, cooperative learning. On average, female students turned out to be more social and male students more individualistic in their way of learning” (Vermunt, 2005, p. 229).

Separate knowing is characterised by e.g. challenging other people’s views as a way to understanding, while connected knowing aims at understanding other people’s views by following their way of thinking. We feel that both these ways of knowing focus on understanding, whether this refers to connecting to the intention of the author or following the (separate) disciplinary way of thinking. In other words, we see both ways as *related and not distinct* expressions of learning-teaching conception 4.

Most women in this way of knowing attended or were recent graduates from prestigious colleges, they were typically young (between 18 and 25), privileged, white and bright. Belenky et al. remarked that most of these women reached this stage of reasoned reflection after abandoning absolutism (Received Knowledge) and subjectivism (Subjective Knowledge), clearly indicating that Belenky et al. *had come to see* these ways of knowing as steps in a model of epistemological development (1997, p. 88). We use the story of Naomi – a separate knower and one of the women discussed in detail – to elaborate on Belenky et al.’s appreciation of the signs of development in their subjects’ stories.

Naomi, a student of an elite women’s college, experienced a shock in her first-year introductory art history class. According to Belenky et al., her then subjectivist way of knowing had led her to believe that “in a subjective course like art history, there are certain questions that you have to answer for yourself, where there isn’t just a right and wrong. You can like a piece that someone else doesn’t like, and you have to decide for yourself” (p. 89). But simply saying “Wow” when seeing a painting of Van Gogh, definitely does not make a good paper! Naomi experienced that her teachers had a different view on knowing and on what comprised ‘looking’ at paintings: “They give us a [five-page guide] to analyze paintings. Then we analyze the painting and come to a conclusion. There are certain criteria that you judge your evaluation on—the composition, texture, color, lighting, how the artist expresses his feelings, what the medium is” (p. 89). For students like Naomi, who only recently have found their inner voice, these instructions, words of the teacher, are initially total ‘garbage’. Realising that such an attitude doesn’t get you very far in college, and wanting to succeed, ‘nice girls’ like Naomi need to accept that these teacher guidelines are *aids to understanding* paintings and *not* arbitrary difficult things teachers want you to do. The typical strategy, also described in Perry (1970) and which Naomi followed, is to “[f]ind out what the guy wants and give it to him. Composition and texture and ‘all that garbage’ seemed meaningless and unreal to her; but if that was what he wanted, that was what she would try to deliver” (Belenky et al., 1997, p. 91).

> But you’re the one who’s placing the judgment on it and as long as you’re substantiating your argument they can’t—they’re not going to disagree with—They can’t—It’s not a matter of disagreeing, as long as you substantiate

> what you're saying. They're teaching you a method and you're applying it for yourself. (Naomi, p. 91–92)

In this last quote we recognise elements of learning-teaching conception 4 – the way they want you to think – and elements of self-authorship (Kegan, 1994, and below). Initially Naomi will use this new 'way of knowing' only within the academic setting, as public, substantiated interpretations or reasonable arguments, keeping the 'wow'-response for herself as her equally valid private opinion or gut feeling. Moving fully from Subjective Knowing to Procedural Knowing is not easy and usually takes some time. In this it reminds us of the major 'leap' across the watershed we place between our learning-teaching conceptions 3 and 4. It also matches Baxter Magolda's finding that the road to self-authorship, however defined, is often fraught with windings and turns, occasional detours and the danger of losing one's bearings and wandering a while in 'the shadow lands' (2009).

Naomi was interviewed again in her senior year, when she seemed to have developed into a full separate knower: "Naomi gave credit to the art history handout for first 'forcing' her to 'look closely' and showing her 'how to be thorough … Those basic underlying principles have worked their way *into the way I look at other things.'* She reads literary passages 'closely and intensely,' and she gets 'a lot of satisfaction' from writing short papers analyzing in specific detail brief passages of Latin text." (Belenky et al., 1997, p. 94, italics ours). By doing what 'the guy wants', by following his formula in Baxter Magolda's terminology, Naomi has developed a new way of thinking that she *herself* has (slowly) generalised outside the discipline of art history.

Belenky et al. proceeded to describe a number of features of Procedural Knowledge that can very easily be linked to our fourth learning-teaching conception or Kegan's self-authorship. In Procedural Knowledge students know that

- truth is to be found by careful systematic analysis, because it "lies hidden beneath the surface, and you must ferret it out" (p. 94) reminding us of the surface level-deep level distinction made in studies into learning, e.g. van Rossum and Schenk (1984);
- some truths or opinions are (demonstrably) better than others;
- things, once thought simple, such as reading a text, now appear complex and problematic;
- they need to think before they speak, leading to speaking "in measured tones" (Belenky et al, 1997, p. 93);
- form tends to become more important than content: "I couldn't tell you right now the philosophies of most of the people we studied, but I can tell you how you would set about criticizing their arguments and what types of things you should look for" (Faith, p. 95);
- they are acquiring an increased sense of control: "I don't have to think that somebody out there has to figure these things out for me anymore, because if I want to, I can" (p. 96);
- opinions "as the static residue of experience" (p. 97), are – as products – epistemologically less strong than the results of processes such as 'ways of looking', 'ways of thinking', or 'ways of understanding'; and

- they need to be objective: good interpretations really are attentive to the object of interpretation (e.g. a poem), while bad interpretations tell us too much about the interpreter and too little about the object of interpretation. Faith gives an example:

> We were discussing a Robert Frost poem. The title was "A Dust of Snow"—something about a crow sitting in a hemlock tree shaking down the snow. And one of the students said, "Well, you know, this poem has very, very evil connotations to it." And the teacher said, "What are you *talking* about?" And the student said, "Well, a crow is a bird of evil, and hemlock is what Socrates drank." And the teacher was so flabbergasted that for a couple of minutes she couldn't say anything. (Faith, p. 98)

In previous articles and in chapter 1 we have discussed the rather 'technical' nature of learning-teaching conception 4 as compared to the fifth level. At least some, if not all, of the above listed points clearly underpin this position. Belenky et al. seemed to take a similar view when they described Procedural Knowers as "practical, pragmatic problem solvers ... [with] their feet ... planted firmly on the ground. ... [Taking] control of their lives in a planned, deliberate fashion" (1997, p. 99).

Constructed Knowledge: Integrating the Voices, Women Develop a Voice of their Own.

Belenky et al. typify Procedural Knowers as "systematic thinkers in more than one sense of the term. Their thinking is encapsulated within systems" (1997, p. 127) and who "feel like chameleons; they cannot help but take on the color of any structure they inhabit" (p. 129). This, in principle still selfless way of thinking, is possible within separate knowing in particular, through extricating the self. By focusing on pure reason and independent thought these women experience a sense of authority and control. What then is required to reach the next way of knowing? Belenky et al. felt that women need to return to some form of 'selfishness' to strengthen the still fragile sense of self: women need to revisit intuition (or feeling) with the power of reason, not to return to subjectivism, but to gain their own authentic voice.

In Constructed Knowledge the self is reclaimed. Women "must 'jump outside' the frames and systems authorities provide and create their own frame" (p. 134), and they need to feel the "impetus to allow the self back into the process of knowing, to confront the pieces of the self that may be experienced as fragmented and contradictory" (p. 136). Once able to place themselves outside a system or discipline, women can put such a system to their own uses, which creates an enormous feeling of control and agency. Constructed knowledge is clearly linked to the fifth order of consciousness (Kegan, 1994), where stepping out of the frame or disciplinary system adopted in Procedural knowing is the step necessary to observe this system critically.

> I am starting to *care* about academics. I'm beginning to feel that my courses have been connected. It's much more interesting once one discipline starts to

> interconnect with others. You can go through your own courses, pull together your own connections, figure out connections yourself. (p. 140)

However, reclaiming the self, after keeping this door more or less shut during Procedural Knowledge, is not an easy task. It requires a period of intense self-reflection and self-questioning, during which women try "to get to know the self and to reflect on the contexts that confined and defined them" (p. 135). Expressions characteristic for Constructed Knowledge are e.g.

> I have come to see things in my own way. (Adele, Belenky et al. 1997, p. 133)
> You let the inside out and the outside in. (Adele, p. 135)
> ... turning back on myself (Erica, p. 132)
> If I could learn how to see with my own eyes. (Alice Koller, p. 135)

> I think it's important to see why I think the way I do. Some people seem to think that their ideas belong to them, but a lot of things people believe have a long tradition of belief. It helps you to understand your beliefs if you understand where they come from. And it helps you to examine them and say, "Well, do I really agree with this?" (Cecily, p. 137)

In this last quote we find the almost identical question that students at the end of Self-authored Knowing ask themselves (Do I want to be involved in this?, see the section on Baxter Magolda before). This quote is also an almost perfect formulation of the quintessence of the fifth order of consciousness and it paints how crucial living this new way of knowing is before one can start to truly choose which convictions to live by.

In an epistemological sense, these women often ask themselves in what way *they* are going to approach the world as a learner, and they have to decide how *they* want to think. In Constructed Knowledge a woman's own voice – "her own way of expressing what she knew and cared about" (p. 133) – is the integration of the voices of others, intuition and reason: here women integrate Received, Subjective and Procedural Knowledge. For constructivists, one's own frame of reference matters because truth *has become* context dependent (i.e. *just* a perspective), all knowledge is relative and constructed, theories are *just* models, and neither simple questions, nor simple answers exist. Although constructivists have reclaimed the self as source of voice, they can also display a certain detachment towards issues: "Constructivists can take, and often insist upon taking, a position outside a particular context or frame of reference and look back on 'who' is asking the question, 'why' the question is asked at all, and 'how' answers are arrived at" (Belenky et al., 1997, p. 139). If taken too far this detachment can evolve into Perry's 'gamesmanship' (1970, p. 191) or deconstructive postmodernism (Kegan, 1994, p. 329, and below).

Inquiry at this level, takes on the form of question posing and problem posing, and in this it resembles Freire's 'problem-posing education', which, Freire feels, focuses on joint responsibility and true dialogue: "the teacher-of-the-students and the students-of-the-teacher cease to exist and a new term emerges: teacher-student with students-teachers. The teacher is no longer merely the-one-who-teaches, but one who is himself taught in dialogue with the students, who in turn while being taught also teach. They become jointly responsible for a process in which all grow" (Freire, 2000, p. 80). Similarly, Constructive Knowers prefer 'real talk' with its emphasis on sharing, reciprocity and cooperation—community instead of domination. They are 'passionate knowers': "knowers who enter into a union with that which is to be known" (p.141), who have the capacity "to attend to another person and to feel related to that person in spite of what may be enormous differences" (p. 143). Belenky et al. saw this passion as an elaborated form of connected knowing. The emphasis on communion results in a language of intimacy to describe the relationship between the knower and the known, e.g. Jessica, while reading.

> It's a sense of communicating with an author and having rapport with the reading matter. And a lovely feeling of "Oh! I have somebody to communicate with. Somebody has had this experience, too." It's a nurturing reaction. (Jessica, p. 143)

Returning shortly to Naomi, the previously quoted Procedural Knower, who – after a crisis – seemed to have discovered reciprocity in teaching at the end of her studies. Describing her collegial relationship with one teacher:

> One learns a lot with and from her. She knows so much herself, but she still has lots of respect for whatever we have to offer in class. And she has a very special way of sort of elevating what a student says. It seems like a really reciprocal process. She gets a lot out of teaching us and learning from us, and we learn from her. (Naomi, p. 127)

Naomi's way of knowing seemed to have changed as well. Where before she had always known her destination she now found "to her 'total surprise' [that] she had no idea what she would do after college. Earlier not knowing was frightening. Now, she welcomed it, 'because I've always felt so directed. Right know I have little direction. I feel like I'm at a point where I want to become awfully *selfish*. I kind of look forward to living alone and not answering to anyone and not being judged by anyone" (p. 128, italics ours).

The emphasis Belenky et al. placed in this way of knowing on 'relativism', 'moving beyond systems' and 'personal frames of reference', is clearly similar to the central themes in our learning-teaching conception 5, Perry's position 5 or Kegan's fifth order of consciousness (see sections on Perry and Kegan below). On the other hand, there are instances where Belenky et al. used phrases such as "attentive caring" (p. 143), "opening of the mind *and* the heart to embrace the *world*" (p. 141), and "language of intimacy" (p. 143). Such expressions are more often found in the next level of thinking, learning-teaching conception 6, and indeed their discussion of Constructed Knowledge seems to end with a description of a new way of knowing (constructing a meaningful life), much in the same way as Kegan 'introduced' reconstructive postmodernism at the end of his discussion of postmodernism (see section on Kegan, below). A situation not unknown to ourselves as we "overlooked" the very rare sixth level ourselves in the early eighties.

Constructing a Meaningful Life: a Life Foreseen.

This perspective is *not* one Belenky et al. themselves explicitly discuss as a distinct way of knowing. They only refer to it – almost in passing – at the end of the chapter on Constructed Knowledge *(Belenky et al., 1997, p. 150–151)*. However, we feel that it is the (unrecognised) finale of the women's journey to find their own voice.

When some women constructivists discussed the definition of a 'good opinion', Belenky et al. felt they indicated that such an opinion is more like a commitment, something to live by: "The only good opinion is a humanistic one, one that shows an immense respect for the world and the people in it and for those you are going to affect .... [and] ..... I don't take on an opinion as my own unless I have really thought about it and believe in it. Once I do, I really would fight for something I believe in" (Belenky et al., 1997 p. 149). Belenky et al. identified 'caring for the world' as driving the formation of women's commitments and actions, implying that the commitments women make are fundamentally different from the commitments men make, as defined in Perry's developmental model (1970, see below). The commitments of women make up their 'life foreseen' (regarding friendships, work, family etcetera) instead of 'a single commitment foreseen' as Belenky et al. interpret Perry's commitments (in positions 6 and beyond). In this sense 'life foreseen' fits our sixth learning-teaching conception—also introduced as the first 'conception of being' (chapter 1). Beverly gives a good example of this level of thinking.

> I was reading Becker, and he talks a lot about heroic tasks and how we can find things important to us and other people, and by doing these tasks, we gain our own self-importance, self-meaning. And I think, "What is my heroic task?" If I don't have one, I don't really have anything to kind of center my life around. (Beverly, p. 151)

The remainder of Belenky et al.'s discussion of Beverly's efforts to balance her commitments to herself and others – we feel – is no different than the juggling act Perry uses as illustration for his positions eight and nine. Even more, the remark Belenky et al. make that the women at this level "speak and live their lives [in the] moral conviction that ideas and values, like children, must be nurtured, cared for, placed in environments that help them grow" (p. 152) is in our eyes not very different from the basic premise fundamental to our own teaching conception 6.

Comments on Belenky et al.

The position of Silence in epistemology

We feel that the 'ways of knowing' that Belenky et al. (1997) described in Women's Ways of Knowing display more similarities to than differences with our own learning-teaching conceptions, and we acknowledge that they have made significant contributions to the field of epistemology. The first important contribution lies in the inclusion of an unusual sample of women and uncovering the most severe version of learning-teaching conception 1 (Silence). Although Clinchy more recently felt that Silence, on closer reflection, may not be the first phase of epistemological development, but more a description of the failure to develop (McVicker Clinchy, 2002), we still feel the detailed exploration of this way of knowing (or lack thereof) facilitated a more clear view on the nature of the development from level 1 to level 2: the discovery of the mind capable of storing and retrieving received knowledge. Furthermore, we feel that Silence or silence – the capital indicating the epistemological position and the lower case 's' referring to the temporary use of Silence as a strategy – deserves more recognition, as it may be far more common than most of our readers would wish to contemplate (see below).

Connected knowing and separate knowing: two tones of voice?

The second important contribution made by Belenky et al. is the elaboration of the two "tones of voice" that all teachers should (probably) be able to use to encourage learning and epistemological development in all, male and female, students. In our view, connected knowing and separate knowing are *not* really different ways of knowing, but refer each to an approach, a "tone of voice" to be used (by learners as well as teachers) when looking for understanding. The empathic voice of connected knowing is probably appropriate to use when e.g. first exploring an area of knowledge yourself: it's always smart to get the lay of the land, to understand how people before you have come to their points of view. The challenging voice of separate knowing, its questioning stance, seems to us to be essential to further encourage reasoned thought. Clinchy has come to see separate knowing and connected knowing in much the same way: "One voice is more effective in one context, the other in the other. ... Students need to develop skill in both modes, so that they can deploy whichever is appropriate for a given occasion" (McVicker Clinchy, 2002, p. 80). A mix of both would – we feel – be necessary to create an ideal learning environment, giving both challenge and support, as is the hallmark of developmental instruction (see comments on Perry below).

Revisiting silence in extreme situations.

The grim picture Belenky et al. painted of the women in Silence has some resemblance to descriptions found in literature of survivors of extreme cruelty or war situations. To illustrate we will quote Paula Gomes, a survivor of one of the worst Japanese internment camps in Indonesia during the Second World War. She entered this camp when she was ten, lost her mother there to starvation, and after the war saw terrible cruelties during the Indonesian independence war, including her father being taken away never to return, only hours after being reunited with him. When – at the age of thirteen - being finally evacuated to Singapore she describes (as an adult) the mood – the passivity – of the evacuees.

> At the harbour British officers awaited us. "Welcome ladies, you are safe now. On British territory."

> British territory! Did it matter? I walked the gangway. I looked down at the brackish water between quay and the ship. The sun was setting. It would be dark soon; just as well that it would be dark, then I wouldn't see. My country in the dusky gloom, in a while only a line, and then nothing.
>
> Soup was served out with slices of white bread and butter. Families had been torn apart. A mother who did not know where her two young boys were. And many women who didn't know where their husbands were, like I did not know what had happened to my father. Nobody seemed to take any notice. All drank their soup and ate their bread. No-one asked anything. Nobody wondered. … And I didn't answer to any of the questions asked me. (Gomes, 2004, p. 79, translation ours)

And later when repatriated to the Netherlands, she seemed even to have lost knowledge, or at least the belief she could ever learn to read again.

> "She needs to go to school", I heard my Uncle and Aunt say.
>
> "No! No!"
>
> They were startled by my violent reaction. And I didn't dare tell them that I couldn't read any more. I had tried time and time again, but the words would not become sentences anymore.
>
> My Uncle and Aunt did not press me any further. They asked the doctor, a family friend, to write a letter, that I needed more time to recuperate. So I remained apparently doing nothing. In truth, I didn't want to do anything other than sit and stare. (p. 197–198, translation ours)

And somewhat later again, when asked to write about living in her new country.

> "You should write something for our personnel-magazine", said Reyer.
> "What then?"
> "How you feel being here in Holland."
> "Nothing."
> "You don't like it here?"
> "That's not what I mean. I don't feel anything. I'm just here."
> (p. 202, translation ours)

So it seems that Silence indeed – as the women in the interviews indicated – may be a coping mechanism: by losing yourself, you can survive situations of uncommon abuse and totally unpredictable cruelty.

That (young) men can suffer as deeply from Silence becomes obvious when reading similar accounts of experiences of extreme situations. Ishmael Beah (2007) wrote a compelling account of his slide into Silence (or would it be silence), his time there and his slow climb out of it, in his book "A long way gone – Memoirs of a boy soldier". From his account it becomes clear that men, violence being more acceptable for males, may have two ways of expressing Silence: lack of action and extreme violence.

Ishmael Beah was thirteen when he became embroiled in the fighting in his country, Sierra Leone. In the confusion of a guerrilla war, he lost contact with his family and ended up in a boys group walking the land in search of safety. The populace was scared of these boys, fearing them to be dangerous and often running them off violently. Beah described his slide into desperation and Silence.

> To survive each passing day was my goal in life. At villages where we managed to find some happiness by being treated to food or fresh water, I knew that it was temporary and that we were only passing through. So I couldn't bring myself to be completely happy. It was much easier to be sad than to go back and forth between emotions ... I was never disappointed, since I always expected the worst to happen. (Beah, 2007, p. 69)

Following a raid on the village where he and his band of boys had found some refuge, Beah was recruited into the army. After his first raid and kill he displayed signs of shock and Silence.

> We arrived in the village ...... It was quiet, and as if we were afraid of silence, we began cleaning the blood off our guns and the ones we had brought with us ... I went for supper that night, but was unable to eat. I only drank water and felt nothing. As I walked back to my tent, I stumbled into a cement wall. My knee bled, but I didn't feel a thing. I lay on my back in the tent with my AK-47 on my chest and the G3 I had brought with me leaning on the peg of the tent. Nothing happened in my head. It was void, and I stared at the roof of the tent until I was miraculously able to doze off. (p. 120)

During his years as a boy soldier, violence became unremarkable, nothing to discuss or reflect upon.

> A lot of things were done with no reason or explanation. Sometimes we were asked to leave for war in the middle of a movie. We would come back hours later after killing many people and continue the movie as if we had just returned from intermission. (p. 124)

> I ... picked up my gun, and followed my squad to ambush the attackers before they got anywhere near our village. We killed most of them and captured a few whom we brought back to base. "These are the men responsible for the bullet holes in your foot. It's time to make sure they never shoot at you or your comrades."... I am not sure if one of the captives was the shooter, but any captive would do at that time. So they were all lined up, six of them, with their hands tied. I shot them on their feet and watched them suffer for an entire day before finally shooting them in the head so that hey would stop crying. Before I shot each man, I looked at him and saw how his eyes gave up hope and steadied before I pulled the trigger. I found their somber eyes irritating. (p. 159)

Beah was rescued by a UNICEF mission when he was fifteen and entered a rehabilitation camp for boy soldiers. When the boys discovered that a group of rebel boy soldiers was also in the same camp, a fight ensued

> A boy without a bayonet grabbed my neck from behind. He was squeezing for the kill ... so I elbowed him with al my might ... I turned around. I stabbed him in his foot ... As I went to deliver the final blow with my bayonet, someone came from behind me and sliced my hand with his knife. It was a rebel boy ... he fell on his face. Alhaji had stabbed him in the back ..... we continued kicking the boy until he stopped moving. I wasn't sure whether he was unconscious or dead. I didn't care. No one screamed or cried during the fight. After all, we had been doing such things for years ... (p. 135)

The groups were separated and slowly Beah recovered from his trauma. The UN found his uncle and Beah lived with him until a new coup brought the war back to him. His determination not to slide back into Silence and violence made him flee. This account shows, we feel, clearly that the unfeeling cruelty that the Silenced women described as experiencing from the powerful men around them, may indeed be a form of Silence as well. Of course we do not wish to belittle the grim and traumatic experiences of these women in any way, we only feel that the power attributed to their men may actually be a myth in an intellectual or epistemological sense. Without proper incentive and guidance these men are probably as unable as the women to escape Silence on their own.

Over the years, Clinchy seems to have come to a similar conclusion, namely that Silence (in one form or another) may be a coping strategy (McVicker Clinchy, 2002) and there is reason to believe that in less severe conditions, even very articulate people can be (temporarily) silenced.

Only recently, since our own growing acquaintance with Silence, we seem to run into descriptions of Silenced people in less physically abusive environments as well. People living as if only seen with 'other people's eyes', describing themselves as 'being somewhere and then going elsewhere' reminiscent of Cindy (Belenky et al., 1997, p. 31 and before). As an example we would like to quote here Bentz van den Berg, a columnist of a quality newspaper in the Netherlands.

> Of all things it was at a party, somebody's birthday. I had been mingling at such a high speed that I ended up in a group of people all unknown to me. One of them, a woman with green earrings and an exalted way of speech, was recounting of all her far travels, the absolutely wonderful people she had met on those travels and the exciting plans a well-known movie maker had of adapting her life story for the silver screen. When, suddenly in mid-sentence, she sailed away to embrace a new arrival on the other side of the room, the man next to me said "That's quite a different world she is living in". "That's about half right" said the woman across from him, "her world is indeed a different kind of world, but she's not in it herself."
>
> On the way home the line kept singing around in my head: a deadly comment really, with an echo powerful enough to follow the victim far into the underworld. In my mind's eye I saw how the woman, once passed away, would react at the premiere of the movie showing her life without her in it. She would see her parents, the house she grew up in, the schools she attended, friends, holidays, profits and losses, one pivotal moment after another, but she is

nowhere to be found, invisible, deleted. What she must feel then – and for all eternity – is the most profound desolation. (NRC Handelsblad, Cultural Supplement, p. 6, 7 December 2007, translation ours)

From this description it seems the green-earringed woman, living a life of luxury and travel, may be in almost as severe epistemological isolation as any of the Silenced women described by Belenky et al.

Linking Belenky et al. to Van Rossum-Hamer and Baxter Magolda

In table 3.3 we summarise the relationship between our model of student thinking described in chapter 1 to the ERM (Baxter Magolda, 1992a, 2001) and Belenky et al.'s Women's Ways of Knowing (1997).

Table 3.3. Relating students' developing learning/teaching conceptions to the ERM and Women's Ways of Knowing

	Van Rossum-Hamer		*Baxter Magolda 1992a, 2001*	*Belenky et al. (1997)*
	Learning Conception	*Teaching Conception*	*ERM*	*Women's Ways of Knowing*
1	Increasing knowledge	Imparting clear/well structured knowledge		Silence
2	Memorising	Transmitting structured knowledge (acknowledging receiver)	Absolute Knowing	Received knowledge
3	Reproductive understanding/ application or Application foreseen	Interacting and Shaping	Transitional Knowing	Subjective knowledge
4	Understanding subject matter	Challenging to think for yourself / developing a way of thinking	Independent Knowing	Procedural knowledge
5	Widening horizons	Dialogue teaching	Self-authored Knowing	Constructed knowledge
6	Growing self awareness	Mutual trust and authentic relationships: Caring	Internal Foundation	Constructed meaningful life

We will include Belenky et al.'s ways of knowing only in the table below, but not in the other summary tables of this chapter. We feel that the difference between Belenky et al. vis-à-vis the information in the ERM and the Perry Scheme (see below) is fairly small and to keep the table legible we have omitted Women's Ways of Knowing from the later comparisons.

Perry

> *This is how life will be. I must be wholehearted while tentative, fight for my values yet respect others, believe my deepest values right yet be ready to learn. I see that I shall be retracing this whole journey over and over – but, I hope, more wisely.*
>
> *Position 9 (Perry, 1988)*

Perry is generally accepted as the author of the first, seminal study on epistemological development: in his words the development of assumptions about the nature of knowledge and values.

Confronted with the puzzling observation that different students evaluated the same course or teacher in completely, often contradictory ways, he and his colleagues at Harvard University and Radcliffe College (Massachusetts, U.S.A.) decided to study the meaning of these 'differences in personality' in a longitudinal study. His 1970 publication is based on 84 complete four-year sequences of yearly, end-of-the-year interviews covering students' experiences from freshman year to senior year. To evoke the full expression of their 'personality' he decided to use an open interview technique, starting with the following question: "Why don't you start with whatever stands out for you about the year?" (Perry, 1970, p. 19). Interviewers were trained to let the interview flow naturally, only intervening e.g. if students fell still or to ask for clarification. The focus was looking back at their current year at college and as such he uses retrospection to uncover the students' meaning making. The researchers were surprised to find that most students seemed to change their 'personalities' – and their interpretation of their experiences – year by year. The changes progressed in a more or less orderly pattern, and Perry and his colleagues felt it necessary to propose a developmental model to describe this personality (later epistemological) development.

Before discussing the model, it is necessary to describe the context and the sample of the study. The study is based on interviews of students enrolled in Harvard and Radcliffe in the fifties and sixties of the previous century. Only 2 of the 84 students who completed the four year study were female. The large majority of male participants has often been cited as the major weakness of this model and led e.g. Baxter Magolda (1992a; 2001) and Belenky et al. (1997) to look for gender differences in epistemological development.

Secondly, a distinctive feature of Perry's data seems to be

- the relative infrequency of lower (i.e. reproductive) levels of thinking found for entering students (Perry, 1988, p. 149), fully a quarter of these students – when asked to grade two answers to an essay question – prefers the answer crowded with facts, utterly devoid of relevance to the question. Such answers are characterised by 'a lot of knowledge' and so fit the lower level quantitative criterion of 'more = better', and
- the relatively high level of epistemological thinking already found at the end of the first year, translated to learning conceptions (chapter 1) the students characteristically had reached conceptions 3, 4 and 5 by the end of the freshman year.

This picture is – we feel – different from our findings in 1984, where in a sample of freshmen in their first semester:

- 42 percent of the students expressed learning conceptions 1 and 2, and
- a full half start their studies with a surface level approach to studying (i.e. 'memorising' and 'getting the facts')

Our students (van Rossum and Schenk, 1984) start from a lower level and considering the nature of teaching at that time, we would expect a much slower development, had we followed them through the year. Subsequent studies showed that epistemological development at college level can be relatively slow (e.g. van Rossum, Hamer and Würffel, 2003; Baxter Magolda, 1992a), and so Perry's findings seem to be indicative of a particular student population in a particular educational context[5]. Perry says about higher liberal education at Harvard and Radcliffe at that time "…the liberally educated man (…) is one who has learned to think about even his own thoughts, to examine the way he orders his data and the assumptions he is making, and to compare these with other thoughts that other men might have. If he has gone the whole way, as most [75 percent] of our students have done, he has realized that he thinks this way not because his teachers ask him to but because this is how the world "really is", this is man's present relation to the universe. From this position he can take responsibility for his own stand and negotiate – with respect – with other men" (Perry, 1970, p. 39–40). This description, we feel, embraces the three highest learning conceptions discussed in chapter 1 and we recognise herein three important (gender free) goals of higher education:

1. learning to think: being able to argue and use evidence to come to an informed conclusion,
2. recognising relativism and context: comparing perspectives within oneself or between people, cultures etcetera, and
3. taking a stand: defining your position, with respect for others and their choices.

Perry's Model: The Pilgrim's Progress

Perry's model of intellectual and ethical (or epistemological and identity) development consists of nine stages or positions, which number, viewed from a higher level of abstraction can be reduced to (at most) six positions (Perry, 1970, p. 47). We concur, as we have recognised clear similarities between our six categories model of conceptions of learning (and teaching) and Perry's nine positions model. Below we will discuss his model from this higher abstraction level.

Perry views his positions as structures with a certain internal logic or coherence in interpreting the world (Perry, 1970 and 1981), or as 'temporary constellations of perceived relations' (Perry 1988, p. 150). He uses the word 'structure' as referring to "the formal properties of the assumptions and expectancies a person holds at a given time in regard to the nature and origins of knowledge and value" (Perry, 1970, p. 42). Furthermore, he explains that the structures can be characterized by "the quality relationships among content elements, for example, the "authoritarian" or "equalitarian" relations of teacher-learner, parent-child, society-individual. In these relations among content element a structure extends its logic and forms into the forms of action appropriate to it. For example, structurally different epistemological assumptions imply different forms of teaching and learning congruent with them" (Perry, 1970, p. 43). We interpret this as a clear indication that he sees views on many aspects within a structure, such as for instance teaching, learning, knowledge and knowing, and motivation etcetera as being closely linked in an internally logical and coherent way. This means that it is unnecessary and maybe even undesirable to propose any hierarchy between the above mentioned views within each structure and structures can be seen as 'conceptual ecologies'[6]. This is in direct contradiction to the approach taken by a number of other researchers who perceive views on knowledge and knowing as more central than other views, which are considered 'more peripheral'. Perry even carries this so far as to use a short essay on 'How I learn best' as an indicator of the student's epistemological position. We feel we have come full circle now, with our question 'What do you mean by learning?', and Perry seems to have felt the same way, when he spoke about our work at a conference in Lancaster in 1985. We propose a metaphor to end the discourse, all the views within a structure should be seen as facets of a diamond, each one contributing to the lustre, and none more important than any other.

Basic dualism (Position 1)

In his 1970 book Perry indicates that only three or four of the 84 students he followed and discusses, seem to have come to college with this view on knowledge and learning. In this view there are Right Answers and Wrong Answers. The difference is known to Authority (the teacher, parent, etcetera) whose role it is to mediate this, and the role of the learner consists of simple obedience. "Knowledge and goodness are perceived as [committing to memory] quantitative accretions of discrete rightnesses to be collected by hard work and *obedience* (including the requirement to read *all* assigned books word by word from the beginning)" (Perry, 1981, p. 80–81). A certain type of innocence speaks from this position, an innocence based on "its lack of any alternative or vantage point from which a person may observe it.... A person cannot explicitly describe such an outlook while embedded in it" (Perry, 1970, p. 62). These two aspects, simple obedience and being embedded, are identical to the aspects of the first conception of learning, total teacher dependency and lack of reflection on learning. The quotes below typify this position, each referring in turn to simple obedience, embeddedness and collecting just the facts.

> When I went to my first lecture, what the man said was just like God's word, you know. I believed everything he said, because he was a professor, and he's a Harvard professor, and this was, this was a respected position. And-ah, ah, people said, "Well, so what?"… And I began to-ah realize" (Perry, 1970, p. 61)
>
> I certainly couldn't—before I was, you know, I wouldn't ask. … I wouldn't have—I wouldn't be able to *talk* on this subject at *all*… that what I had just—well, was *there* you know. (Perry, 1981, p. 81)

One student, in reaction to one item on Perry's Checklist[7] (If teachers would stick more to the facts and do less theorizing one could get more out of their classes), says in agreement,

> A certain amount of theory is good but it should not be dominant in a course. … I mean theory might be convenient for them, but it's nonetheless—the facts are what's *there.* And I think that *should* be, that should be the main thing. (Perry, 1970, p. 67)

Dualism (Position 2 and 3)

In these positions there is still a clear view on the world in terms of Right and Wrong known by Authority, but there is a budding realisation that one "should not lean on [the teachers] too much … *some* complexity, *some* groping in uncertainty has been given a place" (Perry, 1970, p. 87). The emphasis Perry places on 'some' parallels the emphasis on 'some interaction', 'some involvement' we found in the second teaching conceptions of our students. We view position 3 more as a transition stage, where the seeds for Multiplicity (position 4) are sown. This is the reason why we have taken these two positions together and have linked them to our learning-teaching conception 2.

The students prefer the teacher to teach them 'the facts' – without reading between the lines or interpretation – or, when the teacher persists in confronting them with complexity – by giving them problems to solve – they see this as a teacher's game so that they learn "to find The Answer" for themselves.

> I found that you've got to find out for yourself. You get to a point where you, ah, see this guy go through this rigmarole and everything and you've got to find out for yourself what he's talking about and think it out for yourself: Then try to get to think on your own. And that's something I never had to do, think things out by myself, I mean. In high school two and two was four; there's nothing to think out there. In here they try to make your mind work, … [The answer] wasn't in the *book.* And that's what confused me a lot. *Now* I know it isn't in the book for a purpose. We're supposed to think about it and come *up* with the answer! (Perry, 1981, p. 82)

In addition, the students realise a small change in the teacher-student relationship. While the Authority (teacher) is still there to help you [the learner] and to tell you what to do/know, *you* need to take the responsibility for seeking them out.

> I mean, you, you, you accept things as they are. You, I mean everything here, everything you do, you do on your own. I mean, if you, if you feel that you're in trouble in a course, or anything, it's up to you to see the professor and see the section man, the grader and find out if he can help you out, make you understand what you're not understanding. (Perry, 1970, p. 85)

> I just realized that it's a more mature way of teaching. It puts responsibility right on your own shoulders. I mean-ah, if you're going to go in a lecture hall and sit down and sleep there, you're not going to get anything out of it. So, I realized I'd better keep awake and listen. … At first it scared me, and … it seemed like you were in a shooting gallery. And they were shooting at you. As I say, it's more of a mature way of teaching, and-ah… I think it teaches a

> person to become dependent upon himself, more than it would in high school, where somebody's holding a whip over your head, and sending you down to the office if you don't do anything right. (Perry, 1970, p. 84)

Position 3 has the same quality or structure as position 2, now more accepting of *temporary* uncertainty. It can be seen as a transition to the next stage, Multiplicity, where the students have discovered that uncertainty can last a long time.

> I'd feel rather insecure thinking about these philosophical things all the time and not coming up with any definite answers. And definite answers are, well, they, they're sort of my foundation point. In physics you get definite answers to a point. Beyond that point you know there *are* definite answers, but you can't reach them [yet]. (Perry, 1981, p. 82)

At this position, the criteria for grading become a problem for students, with Authority sometimes grading answers to problems where the Right Answer is (still) unknown. While in the previous position one could trust that hard work and amount of rightnesses would lead to a good grade, this standard vanishes, being replaced by what?

> If I present it in the right manner, it is well received. Or it is received...I don't know, I still haven't exactly caught onto what, what they want. (Perry, 1981, p. 83)

The experiences of getting unexpectedly low marks, not related to the amount of work put in, make the students realise that there *may* be other criteria for judgement.

Multiplicity (Position 4a)

The nucleus of this position is best phrased as a question: "... [If] Authority doesn't know the answer yet, is not any answer as good as another?" (Perry, 1970, p. 89), which, for the moment, takes care of the question of grading criteria. In areas where Authority doesn't know the Right Answer yet, any opinion is as good as any other. In a sense Multiplicity is Dualism doubled: first there is the dualism of Right/Wrong, second is the dualism of Right/Wrong vs. Anything Goes, with the emphasis in this structure shifting to Anything Goes. Further, such an opinion is related to nothing whatsoever "... evidence, reason, experience, expert judgment, context, principle, or purpose – except to the person who holds it" (Perry, 1981, p. 85). This latter atomistic view is one of the reasons we see this structure as unique but *subordinate* to position 4b – contrary to Perry's own interpretation – and we link it to our learning/teaching conceptions 3.

The insistence on everybody's right to their own opinion is defended by a student from Patricia King's dissertation (King, 1977), quoted by Perry (1981). Underlying this passionate defence is the failure to differentiate the person from the opinion, and disqualifying an opinion is perceived as disqualifying the person itself.

Interviewer: Can you say that one point of view is better and another worse?
Student: No, I really can't on this issue [creation versus evolution of man]. It depends on your beliefs. Since there's no way of proving either one.
Interviewer: Can you say that one is more accurate than the other?
Student: No, I can't, I believe they're both the same as far as accuracy.
Interviewer: Would you go so far as to say your opinion is the right one?
Student: No.
Interviewer: But yet you believe so strongly in it; that's why I asking....
Student: I'm the type of person who would never tell someone that their idea is wrong—even if they have searched, well, even if they haven't searched, even if they just believe it—that's cool for them.
Interviewer: Can you say that one opinion is better and one opinion is worse?
Student: No, not at all. It's better for them and like their opinion would probably be worse for me. (Perry, 1981, p. 84)

The freedom found in Multiplicity, that all opinions are equally valid and that one can rebel against Authority in areas of uncertainty, opens the way to more discussion[8] and so to more interaction-rich types of teaching. At the same time the "egalitarian spirit [in Multiplicity discussions] provides a haven of ultimate peace at the end of dormitory bull sessions. At a deeper level, it expresses a respect for others through a respect for their views" (Perry, 1981, p. 85). The expressed 'love' of – basically uninformed – discussion either with peers or with teachers, we feel, supports our linking of this position to our third learning-teaching conception.

The limits of this position become clear to students, when confronted with teachers grading their opinions, and they start to wonder: "How do you *know* one opinion is better than the other?" They are informed that there is something called "an educated opinion" and this must be something else than a right or a wrong answer and different also from 'any old opinion'. Students are still looking to the teacher to tell them what they want them to do – they are looking for a new external formula to follow (Baxter Magolda, 2001). If it isn't more they want, then it must be something different, but what?

The way they want you to think (Position 4b)

In this position, for the first time, learning and knowledge are thought of in terms of better or worse (quality), instead of more or less (quantity). Deciding on the quality of thought or approach, causes students to think about thinking and so discover meta-thought and independent thought. This discovery often stands out vividly in their mind, as a revelation.

> Another thing I've noticed about this more concrete and complex approach—you can get away without ... trying to think about what they want—ah, think about things the *way* they want you to think about them. But if you try to use

> the approach the course outlines, then you find yourself thinking in *complex terms*: weighing more than one factor in trying to develop your own opinion… Somehow, what I think about things seems to be more—ah—it's hard to say it right or wrong—but it seems (pause) more *sensible*. ([Student A], Perry, 1970, p. 100)

> ... my grades got consistently *higher* as I understood their approach. Finally I came to realize about the middle of the second term that they were trying to get you to look at something in a complex *way* and to try to weigh more factors than one, and talk about things in a concrete manner. That is, with words that have some meaning and some relevance to the material you were studying. And all of a sudden my grade just *shot right up* and stayed right up. [I: This was a lift] It was. It really was… (voice rises) … for *that* to happen. To understand all of a sudden. I mean, to realize… the *realization* of the understanding was what was quick…just what the club [Harvard] was driving at and then to use that in the course and suddenly see the grade go right up. That was really a great *lift*, a matter of extreme personal satisfaction! (Perry, 1970, p. 101)

Here students explicitly discuss that they need to learn to think in a particular way, to learn to think for themselves. This is exactly the terminology that characterises the fourth learning-teaching conception. In the area of learning and teaching conceptions, the shift of focus from quantity to quality is seen as the watershed in thinking about learning and teaching. Perry, however, has placed his watershed at the next position, 5. We feel the excitement that speaks from these quotes above indicates that the students are aware of making an *important discovery*: thinking about thinking. As such we feel that the transition between 4a and 4b (or between learning-teaching conception 3 and 4) is the 'leap of faith' towards the unknown. It is a risk students feel they must face, and once successful, their courage is a source of personal satisfaction, increased confidence and feelings of responsibility.

> … I think in the long run it's, it's high time I did begin to think for myself and, ah, I really think it would be better than getting a recipe for the course. I resented it—it's frustrating because, well, shucks, you do like to pass exams and know what to say on papers, but that isn't the real thing, that's not what it is. I mean I have visions sometimes of perhaps not being able to come back here because I didn't, wasn't able to think clearly enough. But I will know then that if I won't be able to come back it will be because it isn't in me to do the kind of work that's to be done, and not just because I didn't happen to remember the formula.

> I think it's just perhaps becoming a little bit more aware of what's inside. If I find that I haven't measured up to the standards expected it won't be because I haven't tried… (Perry, 1970, 106)

If indeed the greatest change occurs here (in 4b), this would go far to explain the odd 'quietness' Perry found at position 5. Then again, the quietness is not strange if you interpret position 5 as the position where the discovery of position 4b has become "habitual" (Perry, 1970, p. 111).

Relativism (Position 5)

It is not completely unexpected that occasionally confusion has arisen about the difference in meaning of Multiplicity and Relativism. These concepts run together somewhat in the eyes of certain researchers, because students in both positions seem to have a high tolerance for differing opinions. The difference, however, is that in multiplicity the opinions are not restrained by evidence or logic, whereas in true relativism views and approaches need to be supported. Students' thinking at this level seems to come back to the more personal quality that also characterises Multiplicity. Now the person is not embedded in his opinions, but has become a creator of perspectives, perhaps even a transformer of perceived reality (Kegan see below). In this sense position 5 can be seen as the coordination of Multiplicity and 'The way they want you to think', e.g. the coordination of the subjective with the objective (Kuhn's 1991 Evaluative theories).

Perry does not refer to his students by name or any other designation, but we have quoted a student we have called Student A in the previous paragraph on 'The way they want you to think'. Perry returns to this student later in his 1970 book when describing the transition to position 5. At position 4b (our learning-teaching conception 4) Student A says,

> I don't know if complexity itself is always necessary. I'm not sure. But if complexity is *not* necessary, at least you have to find that it *is* not necessary before you can decide, "Well, this particular problem needs only the simple approach." (Perry, 1970, p. 113)

This quote, Perry proposes, is not exemplary for position 5 because here the "simple" right-or-wrong is still there as an independent state, and is not (yet) seen as a special case, a derivative of complexity. This means that for these students there are *still* simple absolute truths out there, while *other* things are complex and relative. While, in position 5, simplicity is complexity made simple by using assumptions or underlying methods (e.g. placing it in a context). So, the - for position 4b – simple equation 2+2 *equals* 4 is true, but from position 5 this is true *only* because we assume a particular numeric system.[9]

Our Student A, when confronted with this remark about the simple approach in a later interview, speaking from position 5, says,

> ...You can't even *talk* about taking a simple approach to something, you just kind of, I mean it's just a way of looking at things which *is* complex and therefore you can't talk about being complex as, as a *conscious policy*. I mean it's *not* a conscious policy, it's, it's just something that's been absorbed into you. And this, and that's why this seemed kind of superficial conversation, or seemed just to lack intelligence, because I don't think you can say, well, I'm going to take a simple approach to *this* problem and a complex approach to *that* one, I mean, looking at things, if it's just the way you *do* something. (Perry, 1970, p. 114)

The complex approach has now become the only approach, the habitual approach to use. Perry lists three prominent aspects students report regarding their experience in this position

1. the dissolution of the old structures, balanced by the realisation of growth and competence
2. a changed relation to authority
3. a level of detachment

The following quotes – from Perry, 1970 – illustrate these points in order.

> I think the main thing that was interesting this year was questioning basic assumptions... That is a frightening thought to say it didn't occur to me to question [the assumptions]. Sounds like '1984' or something. Well, it didn't feel *out,* or anything, before. So I'm sure there are things that I'm not questioning now that I should be. Whatever "should be" is ... (p. 117)

> But, sure your way of thinking pretty definitely changes. You work and I think out of your courses, as applied to life in general ... You have to have *some* degree of order to things, as you look at them, but I think it's more accepting, it's a little more accepting things as they come... Be open to a little, say, more tolerant viewpoint ... Not this narrow one. (p. 117)

> I got along fine with the teachers, with, with all the faculty. And even when they disagreed with me, it wasn't a matter of ah, "I disagree with you, therefore you are stupid," it's "I disagree with you, but you might be right". [In high school] it was very personalistic. I could never get in a philosophical debate without it ending up in a debate over whether I was a bum or not... (p. 125)

> To me, it seems to me that the more I-ah...go through this place, the more I work here, the more I feel that what I'm trying to do is-ah become what you might call a detached observer of various situations, of any type of situation that you go into. And by that I mean—ah, one who can, to the utmost of his ability, detach himself-ah emotionally from the problems and look at the various sides of the problem, in an objective, empirical type of way—look at the pros and cons of a situation and then try to ... analyze and formulate a, a judgment—a value judgment it could be on your part... (p. 126)

The changed relationship with authority and the widening of their perspectives to include e.g. life in general (i.e. widening of horizons) described in these remarks, show great similarity to two major aspects of our learning-teaching conception 5, while the sense of detachment of the person, the learner, is also present in the fifth learning conception. Alternating perspectives or 'Ways of seeing' can become a game and when taken too far, can lead to Escape (Perry, 1970, 128) which deflects the learner from further development.

Finally, Perry observes that students in this position sometimes experience a sense of drifting and disorder, which they feel might vanish as long as e.g. one knew "what one wanted to be". The next position is the culmination of this unease, where successive commitments will lead to an, often temporary, reduction of unease.

Commitment (Position 6 and beyond)

The task set for everyone passing from position 5 to position 6 and beyond – or in our research learning-teaching conception 6 – is to find a way to stop drifting and make "my own decisions in an uncertain world with no one to tell me I'm Right" (Perry, 1981, p. 79). As one of Perry's students says,

> [We] just have to sort of make the most of it, as it comes, and I say that's one thing you learn out of college that life is, is not one set narrow little plain. You just have to sort of, it's a very big thing, you just sort of have to make your way through it as best you can after you've, experience of course is always the best teacher. That's just a question of, well, say, broadening your outlook [learning teaching conception 5] and learning to be yourself [learning teaching conception 6].
>
> Everybody they say as they get older tends to get more set in their ways, but we hope not. If, if we can stay flexible as much as you can, it's better. It's not good to get too narrow-minded or set in your ways ... as a child. That of course comes if you're dominated too much by your parents or by older people. (p. 145–146)

Perry refers to the choices students need to make as Commitments through which a person affirms and/or establishes the self. In this sense commitments can be seen as manifestations of Self-realisation (learning conception 6) and Internal Foundation (Baxter Magolda, 2001). While before, up to and including position 5, doubts were mainly epistemological, in this position doubt is "reflected back upon the individual. Can he[10] claim to be who he thinks he is. He must, if he is to live heartily, but with how much certainty? Having reached the limits of reason, 'faith is all you have left.' But faith, in view of the investment, requires courage" (Perry, 1970, p. 176). This exact same point is made by Baxter Magolda (2001) in her discussion of Internal Foundation. In this stage of life, rationality and intuition increasingly interweave when making (life)decisions and choosing to live one's convictions.

When making a commitment, a person becomes an "agent and chooser [of] aspects of his life in which he invests his energies, his care and his identity" (Perry, 1970, p. 135). These choices can be recognised by the following qualities:

1. it is an act typical of an 'examined life' and not of an 'un-examined life', it is a choice that is reached after doubts and (fully) exploring alternatives,
2. it requires coming-to-terms with one's past, in the respect that one considers the degree in which one will continue or break with the values of one's past,
3. it is most often thought of in terms of its content, e.g. career, marriage, political choices,
4. it refers to finding a balance, a point on a scale between extremes (e.g. narrowness vs. breadth , self-centred vs. other-centred, stability vs. flexibility, maintenance vs. growth, etcetera) where one feels one can 'stand' and be oneself; this Perry refers to as the stylistic aspect,

5. it defines one's identity, using both content and form (or stylistic) aspects. Perry feels the stylistic aspects of commitments are often closer to the self than the content aspects. Stylistic aspects say more about the person one thinks one is, e.g. the decision to become a doctor says less about the self, than the decisions regarding how one wants to live 'the doctor's life': the choice between a detached professional and the deeply caring physician.

To illustrate this stage in life, which has proven to be difficult to understand for many people, we will quote a number of students at positions 7 and 8, because 6 is defined as a transitional stage and position 9 is a thought construct and an interpolation of position 8. In position 7 one has taken responsibility and made the first commitment regarding who one is – or will be – for example, by deciding on a profession. By the next position (8) one has experienced the need and the necessity to make further commitments, which may conflict and requires balancing e.g. through adjustments.

> I've always had a lot of doctors in my family, and my father meant to be a doctor and then, ah, quit during the depression. And he'd always wanted me to be a doctor, at which I had rebelled. And well, I had a board and room job this year, taking care of kids, and, well, it just came slowly to me that this is really what I want, and for the first time I had a little direction. Right now I'd like to go into pediatrics; I'm really set on this deal. (Perry, 1970, p. 157)

> I'd rather do something than just sit around and … brood about it. Sometimes I … I'm just about … sometimes you do hasty things … it's a certain amount of relief to … just … just to do something. But … now the only … the only broodiness is sort of an inward broodiness … about whether … whether … whether I'm on the right tack … the right field. There are all kinds of pulls, pressures and so forth … parents… this thing and that thing … but there comes a time when you just have to say, "Well … I've got a life to live… I want to live it this way. I welcome suggestions, I'll listen to them. But when I make up my mind, it's going to be me. I'll take the consequences". (Perry, 1970, 161)

> What you have to do is set up a set of rules for yourself that you're going to live by, and that you're going to, that you've got to, to-ah, you can't lose your self-respect! (…) You still have to recognize that all these things that you learn, all these odd things about yourself and other people are potential tools for destruction or construction, and that you've got to be very careful in the way you utilize each one of them. They are things that you, that's one way of perceiving them, that you are, you are capable of using them. You don't go around turning on compassion and turning it off like a water faucet. You, you can use it. People … people just aren't conscious enough of their roles, that's all. They don't, don't try. There's such a thing as being too self-conscious, but, but you've got to be able to see the effects you're having on other people, and the effect other people have on you. And you've got to be careful about how you use all these things you've developed. And most people

> aren't. I'm certainly not careful about how I use things, but a recognition of your own qualities and what effect they can have on other people is very important.... (Perry, 1970, p. 161–162)
>
> ... [The] ability to ah, to be able to have a sense of myself without, without feeling that the sense is based on other people, which has been very important, very, very important. Ah, of course, it's still based on other people in many, many ways, but it's, it's a little different now. (Perry, 1970, p. 163)

These quotes reflect the sense of agency and communion characteristic for position 6 (and beyond). The higher positions are seen, by us and by Perry, as evolving in content, but not in structure, and as such they can be seen – from a higher level of abstraction – as one position. Position 9 is thought to be the realisation of who one is, and how life will be: an ongoing struggle to balance one's commitments while reaffirming oneself through new choices (see quote at the beginning of this section).

On page 211 where Perry discusses the educational implications of his model of intellectual development, he integrates epistemological perspectives with roles for learners and teachers, in a sense linking our (later) work directly to his own model. "Where knowledge consisted of facts in a single frame of reference, the teacher's primary duties were to make the facts clear and to so correct his students in respect to the right or wrong of each fact as to allow of no error. The student, in turn, collected correct facts and procedures. Where knowledge is contextual and relative, the teacher's task is less atomistic as the student's is more integrational. The good teacher becomes one who supports in his students a more sustained groping, exploration and synthesis. His acts of evaluation must subtend more than discrete rights and wrongs, and extend through time to assist discrimination among complex patterns of interpretation" (Perry, 1970). One may wonder if there exists a more convincing argument of the indivisible-ness of conceptions of learning, teaching and knowledge.

In 1981, Perry reflects on the type of teaching appropriate to support students in dealing with life's paradoxes. He feels that educational institutes should introduce dialectical thinking to students: "... that is, to introduce our students, as our greatest teachers have introduced us, not only to the orderly certainties of our subject matter but to its unresolved dilemmas [as well]" (Perry, 1981, p. 109). This approach is exemplified in the work of Alan Schoenfeld: using titles such as "When good teaching leads to bad results: the disasters of 'well-taught' mathematics courses" and "In fostering communities of inquiry, must it matter that the teacher knows 'the answer'?" (Schoenfeld, 1988 and 1996).

Comments on Perry

Perry's legacy[11]

William Moore at the Center for the Study of Intellectual Development (Olympia, Washington, USA) can be considered as "one of several key custodians" of Perry's legacy, and one of the leading experts in Perry Scheme research and assessment issues.[12] In Moore (2002) the relevance of the Perry Scheme in the 'postmodern' world around the turn of the century is reflected upon, and Moore draws the conclusion that "even after thirty years of extensive and varied scholarship, the Perry scheme continues to reflect the most critical dimension to educators' understanding of learning and students' approaches to learning" (2002, p. 18). Moore disagrees with Hofer and Pintrich (1997) who – while accepting the interrelatedness of the concepts – still propose to conceptually separate epistemological beliefs from beliefs about learning and teaching. Moore is quite outspoken about this and states that "pursuing the kind of 'clarity' Hofer and Pintrich suggest would seem to come at the price of contextual authenticity. After all, the focus of the Perry scheme is on understanding epistemology in the situated context of learning, not studying epistemological beliefs per se. Thus understanding the individual's sense of learning (as well as sense of self-as-learner) and the broader framework of the sociocultural context of the learning are essential to the process" (p. 30). Supporting our premise in this study, linking conceptions of knowledge firmly to conceptions of learning and teaching, Perry and Moore were the first to recognise the relationship between our learning-teaching conceptions model (at that time they referred to van Rossum, Deijkers and Hamer, 1985) and the Perry Scheme, with Moore discussing European developments "There are other intriguing current issues—for instance, I know Bill Perry has mentioned Marton's research in this newsletter, and there is some fascinating related work, describing Perry-like phenomena with other labels and some interesting new twists, being done in the Netherlands by van Rossum—suggesting that the scheme may well be more broadly applicable than some of us had thought!" (Moore, 1988, p. 13–14).

In his 2002 review of the Perry Scheme, Moore discriminates – as has become tradition in the Perry school of research – four major categories of Perry positions: dualism (1, 2), multiplicity (3, 4, or 'pseudorelativism', p. 21), contextual relativism (5) and commitment within relativism (6 and beyond). In this review we have found a number of notable issues which we feel need to be made more explicit to facilitate further debate.

1. The twofold nature of position 4 with sub-positions 4a and 4b.

Traditionally in Perry research the oddity in the scheme of position 4, with its sub-positions, is ignored. It has always intrigued us, why so few people[13] questioned this clearly 'abnormal' position within an otherwise 'elegant' model. Bill Moore is no exception to this because in 2002 he still described position 4 as "Self-processing and a sense of idea ownership increases, but frequently in Position 4 the stance taken is that there is no non-arbitrary basis for determining what's right …; hence an attitude of 'do your own thing' or 'anything goes' tends to prevail in this position" (Moore, 2002, p. 20). In doing this Moore equates position 4 with position 4a, ignoring the qualitative difference between 4a and 4b – the difference between 'being' an opinion and 'having' an opinion - almost entirely. In the current study we have tried to 'iron out this wrinkle' by linking position 4a to learning-teaching conception 3 and 4b to learning-teaching conception 4. We have discussed this issue in chapter 1 and will be revisiting it when appropriate throughout the current study.

2. How many times does development cycle through "diversity in the form of multiples" (Moore, 2002, p. 22)?

In chapter 1 we introduced the concept of cycles of differentiation and integration in epistemological development. Moore proposed a similar system of cycles, focusing on differentiation as multiples: "multiple opinions about a given subject or issue ... multiple contexts/perspectives from which to understand or analyze issues or arguments ... multiple Commitments through which one defines his or her values and identity" (Moore, 2002, p. 22). In seeing and including position 4b and learning conception 4 as a separate position, this leads us to propose an amendment resulting in a fourfold cycle of multiples from learning conception 3 through 6:

- multiple opinions (level-three-thinkers),
- multiple informed interpretations within a context (level-four-thinkers), multiple perspectives across contexts (level-five-thinkers),
- multiple Commitments in life (level-six-thinkers).

While proposing this amendment, this extension does not influence the validity of Moore's conclusion regarding the consequences for learning and teaching "This central epistemology about knowledge and learning triggers parallel shifts in the learner's views about the role of the teacher—moving from an Authority as the source of 'Truth' to an authority as a resource with specific expertise to share, as well as the role of the student—moving from a passive receptor of facts to an active agent in defining arguments and creating new knowledge" (Moore, 2002, p. 22).

3. Turning a corner: the qualitative difference of the development from position 1 through 5 and that of position 6 and beyond.

As we tried to illustrate in chapter 1, making Commitments (positions 6 and 7) brings a new focus into epistemological development, moving from intellectual epistemological development into a new type, 'conceptions of being'. Moore (2002) has recognised this paradigm shift within the Perry Scheme as well. Identifying the development through positions 1 to 5 as "systematic, structural change toward increasing differentiation and complexity" (p. 19), he proposed that the new plane of development focused on "Commitments ... [defining] one's identity in a contextually relativistic world" (p. 21). The question whether the development on this new plane will also imply structural changes is not clear at the moment. We feel that this is in part due to the fact that researchers have – until now – focused mainly on undergraduates who according to Moore "rarely [reflect] post-contextual-relativistic thinking" (2002, p. 21) or – even worse – on graduation rarely "reason consistently from a contextually relativistic perspective" (p. 23). For a more extensive treatment of this issue we refer our readers to Hamer and van Rossum, 2008, obtainable from the authors on request.

4. Interpreting similarity and dissimilarity between various developmental stage models.

The models of epistemological development proposed by Baxter Magolda (1992a) and Belenky et al. (1997) Moore feels are more similar to – and an enrichment of – the Perry Scheme than the authors would like to acknowledge: “there is no compelling evidence that these frameworks in fact define distinct theories. All of these efforts represent important areas of scholarship with respect to intellectual development, but rather than being separate theoretical models they extend and expand descriptions of the same fundamental journey described by Perry’s framework” (p. 23–24). We would like to suggest, as we do in the current chapter, that this assertion holds as well for our own learning-teaching conceptions model and Kegan’s ‘Orders of Consciousness’ model (Kegan, 1994, see further in this chapter).

5. How many Perry Scheme’s are there?

Following Lee Knefelkamp’s proposal, Bill Moore also separates three types of Perry:
- a general Perry: “the original overall perspective”,
- a contextual Perry: “the varying ways in which learners make sense of particular contexts (e.g., different disciplines)”, and
- a functional Perry: “the way the model can be used to understand how people recycle through earlier perspectives in confronting new and unfamiliar learning situations” (Moore, 2002, p. 23).

We have discussed the general Perry above and will not repeat this here. However, we feel that the contextual Perry addresses issues such as domain dependence of epistemological views – separating general development from the influence of specific contexts, where contexts refer not only to academic disciplines but also to e.g. teaching and assessment practices. An example of a study using a contextual Perry-like approach is Palmer and Marra (2004), who found evidence of inconsistency in students’ epistemologies across domains, as well as in the development of students’ epistemologies across domains (sciences versus social sciences/humanities). We will treat this issue in more detail in the sections on Schommer and Vermunt in chapter 4 and in the chapter Changing Teaching and Learning. We discuss the consequences of the functional Perry in various sections, where appropriate. Examples are found in the section on Vermunt (chapter 4) where we discuss the influence of the transition from secondary to higher education, and in chapter 8, When Worlds Collide. In a sense we feel that the contextual and functional Perry together are the response Moore can give to the question Schommer and Vermunt pose – Is epistemological development consistent (and general) or context specific? – namely it is *not* an issue of ‘either-or’ but ‘both’ (see the relevant sections in chapter 4).

6. The Perry Scheme describes more than intellectual development.

Some researchers interpret – in our opinion clearly incorrectly – Perry as uni-dimensional (e.g. Schommer, see our discussion on this issue in chapter 4). Others feel that the scheme focuses too much on modes of reasoning as the primary mover of intellectual development, and too little on the interpersonal and affective skills associated with each position (e.g. Widick, 1977 and below). Moore on the other hand, disagrees with both these views: "the Perry model reflects the critical intertwining of cognitive and affective perspectives at the heart of a college education – a difficult journey toward more complex forms of thought about the world, one's discipline/area of study and one's self" (Moore, 2002, p. 19). Moore performed factor analyses on the LEP (Learning Environment Preferences, Moore, 1989, 1991, 1994) – an objective measure of the Perry Scheme – that resulted in a solution with three main factors, indicating quantitative support for the multi-dimensionality of the Perry Scheme.[14]

7. How general (or universal) is the Perry Scheme?

The issue of the universal nature of the Perry Scheme has never been an assumption made by Perry nor by any of his major interpreters. On the contrary, Perry has always been very clear on the fact that "the scheme has always been clearly grounded in Western higher education" (Moore, 2002, p. 25). Concerning our own learning and teaching conceptions, we started this study feeling that these reflect more the educational practices in (Dutch, and so definitely Western) secondary and higher education or sociocultural influences (Moore, 2002), than being 'natural' characteristics of pupils or students. On the other hand, the amount of agreement found between the various developmental models (see throughout this study and chapter 12) is remarkable, considering that they were developed in contrasting (although as far as we know predominantly Western oriented) educational contexts, indicating some measure of universality. Recaping the complete study, we will discuss this issue in more depth in chapter 12. Future research could shed some more light on this issue if it broadens the base of Perry research to include very cultures with less formal educational systems (e.g. Paupa see also chapter 8) and people of more advanced age (e.g. as Baxter Magolda, 2007, who has been following some of her initial undergraduate subjects for 20 years now).

Some Perry-research on development and interventions: initial and more recent.

Shortly following publication the Perry Scheme (1970), Carole Widick (1977) [15] discussed the usefulness of the Perry Scheme as a guide for educational programming in higher education. While Perry's scheme is a model for intellectual development in the college years, students' intellectual development is neither an automatism nor plain sailing. As Widick succinctly puts it "students do not simply move through the stages with clockwork precision and arrive at position nine two weeks prior to graduation. In fact [in Perry's study], most students' developmental progress occurred in spurts and jerks and many showed definite 'lags' in growth. Some of these lags seemed a necessary pause for integration of new learnings; others seemed to result from excessive environmental pressures. In some instances, Perry found students who were so overwhelmed by the college experience that they appeared fixated in dualism. Development is perceived to be an interactive process; thus, a college environment can either help or hinder the student in his/her growth" (Widick, 1977, p. 36).

Widick sees the Perry Scheme as an excellent guide for formulating educational goals: once one knows 'where the student is' one can plan a route to the next stop on the journey towards position nine, a journey that "seems a perfect operational definition of the 'examined life' and is imminently relevant to the collegiate context" (Widick, 1977, p. 36). However, Widick feels that Perry overemphasises changes in modes of reasoning as the primary mover of intellectual development, and 'underexposes' the interpersonal and affective skills associated with each position and as such the Perry Scheme "does not prescribe the universe of potential developmental goals" (Widick, 1977, p. 37). Since then, in her work Baxter Magolda has addressed this particular omission (1992a, 1999a, 2001). Related to formulating educational goals are diagnosis of 'where the student is' and interventions fostering epistemological development. In 1977, Widick felt that Perry's Scheme gave hints, but did "not provide a sufficiently comprehensive and detailed description of the developmental sequence to guide a diagnosis/intervention methodology" (p. 37). Now, some 30 years and much research later, we feel that throughout this chapter we address this issue and by pulling together different perspectives and research approaches into one coherent scheme (at the end of this chapter) we provide more detail on the precise characteristics of the different developmental positions.

Of the questions Widick formulated for further investigation, in particular the third and fourth are still relevant. Her third question pertained to processes of developmental change, using the term 'disequilibrium' - a common concept at that time – to explain developmental change. At the present time, in the discussion of developmental change the terminology used *can* be quite different: including terms such as 'constructive frictions' or 'process-oriented instruction' (see the section on Vermunt in chapter 4), or 'a process model of epistemic belief change' (Bendixen, 2002). Over the years, it has been established that students can change (during higher education), but questions about what the underlying processes are or what causes development are still not answered satisfactorily, and Widick's remark that "the specific conditions for progressive position change need to be clarified and experimentally tested" (1977, p. 37) is still valid. Her fourth comment concerned the general applicability of the Perry Scheme and is relevant to the current study. She stated that the relevance of the Perry Scheme needs to be investigated also at "community colleges, vocational-technical schools, and professional schools" (p. 37). Our study is, we feel, an application of a Perry-like model in higher professional education and while it deals with Widick's remark, it remains one of the few examples[16] of the use of a Perry-like Scheme outside the university context.

Widick, Knefelkamp and Parker (1975)[17] developed a curriculum intervention promoting personal growth and intellectual development for freshman students because they expected that the optimal time to accomplish epistemological development was at the beginning of higher education. In designing the course, Perry's Scheme and the role of the developmental instructor – "one who understands the student's developmental stage and knows how he or she might be changed and what the college might do to bring about desirable development" (p. 287) – were both fundamental to developing integrative instructional methods. When designing the developmental course examined here, Widick et al. chose to focus on the 'resolution of identity' in the course 'Themes in Human Identity', in fact building two courses or approaches around the same content – four identity themes based on material from the fields of literature and psychology that provided conflicting viewpoints within and between books. One approach aimed at students with a dualist view on knowledge, the other at relativist students and each approach was built around tailored and aligned challenges and support. To establish which course students would follow, Widick et al. performed a pre-assessment[18] on 31 freshman students, resulting in a division into 32% dualists, 48% multiplists (transition) and 20% relativists. The 'dualist course' challenged students by introducing ambiguity (e.g. instructional procedures aimed at formulating alternative perspectives and class discussion), and providing experiences (experiential learning, e.g. role playing in class and interviewing people about their identity out-of-class to have concrete experience with the abstract concept of identity). To make sure that these students were not overwhelmed by these challenges, the course was moderately structured - clear planning and expectations - and a personal support atmosphere was created in the classroom so that students would feel safe to express themselves. The 'relativist course' was designed with the same emphasis on personal support, but was less structured and students were challenged to make personal choices and commitments. Overall, the initial dominant stages (3 and 4) had – after the course – increased by one stage to 4 and 5, with the share of dualists decreasing to 3%, multiplists decreasing to 29% and relativists increasing to 68%, with no student reaching commitment.[19] Widick et al. concluded that "movement was more easily affected from certain stages than from others. We had success in moving dualistic students up the scale towards relativism. The [dualistic] students were receptive to our efforts to provide them with a wide variety of legitimate perspectives about the major identity issues. ... However, we had little success in moving relativistic students to the point of making commitments" (1975, p. 294).

Bud Stephenson and Christine Hunt (1977) attempted to replicate part of the study of Widick et al. described above, limiting themselves to the dualist intervention for two groups of freshman students (in total n=42 enrolling in the course 'Themes in Human Identity'), but expanding the study by including two control groups of freshman students: one group (n=15) enrolling in a humanities course 'Life of the Mind', the other (n=19) enrolling in an English class 'Contemporary Novel'. The dualist intervention course was identical in instructional set-up as above, but limited to an 11-week course focusing on only two of the four original identity themes. The two control groups differed in instructional atmosphere. The humanities class was characterised by some understanding of, and an alertness to dualist and relativist modes of thinking and a "warm, flexible class atmosphere" (p. 41). The English class was the most traditional in set-up, with an emphasis on lectures and some discussion, and the teacher having no knowledge of individual differences in student thinking. In this way the experimental and control groups formed a set of three different (developmental) learning environments, and Stephenson and Hunt could examine the differential effects of these courses. The authors used pre and post assessment of Perry positions based on short essays (or paragraph completion items of the KneWi). On average, the students in the dualist intervention course progressed 0.85 position in 11 weeks, while the students of the 'warm' humanities course progressed 0.42 position and the students in the 'cold' English course progressed only 0.12 position. Stephenson and Hunt concluded that "the two courses using developmental instruction produced more upward movement on the Perry Scheme, than did two comparison courses using similar content and themes" (1977, p. 41–42). We would like to add that the dissimilarity in results between the two control groups would seem to be indicative of the difference an involved, student-oriented instructor makes – with regard to fostering epistemological development – compared to a traditional, distant and teacher-oriented one. And so, besides the need for a methodology for developmentally oriented instruction, the type of teacher matters a great deal (see also chapter 5, Teachers' Epistemological beliefs and conceptions of teaching).

In the same year, Joanne Kurfiss investigated the sequential and structural aspects of 8 positions of the Perry Scheme. Sequential aspects refer to the assumption that "higher levels of the sequence, if they are indeed more differentiated and complex than lower levels, should be more difficult to comprehend" (Kurfiss, 1977, p. 566) and Kurfiss used scalogram analysis to examine the hierarchical aspects of the Perry Scheme. Structural coherence within a Perry position was examined by studying the correlations between 'scaletypes'[20] on five theoretically related tasks, assuming that high correlations indicate coherence within a Perry position. And finally, she examined whether more advanced positions elicited more favourable responses than lower levels, by asking respondents to indicate their preferred level by rating and ranking statements referring to the 8 Perry positions per task. The respondents in this study were 28 freshman and junior psychology university students, who were asked (in interviews and in writing) to react to randomly presented statements – one for each of the 8 Perry positions – regarding 5 tasks (40 statements in total). Student reactions – reformulations of the presented statements – were scored as 'hits' by raters if they accurately reflected the Perry position in question, indicating comprehension of that position. The sequentiality of the Perry positions was confirmed by the master scaletype analysis, but less so by the scaletype analysis for the individual topics. On the basis of these results Kurfiss concluded that "Perry's positions form a sequence of increasingly complex ideas" (p. 569). Evidence for structural coherence of the Perry positions was relatively poor, leading Kurfiss to suggest that "had all the topics used in the present study centered exclusively on educational concerns, stronger (though perhaps misleading) evidence of an underlying 'structure' might have been obtained" (p. 569). To what extent these results are worrying for a developmental stage model may prove to be a matter of interpretation: e.g. a student in Perry position 5 might, when confronted with a task he/she finds particularly *un*interesting, choose to perform this task at a considerably lower level without violating the structural coherence of his/her position. The opposite, with students at a lower epistemological level (lower Perry position) compensating their lack of epistemological sophistication with topic interest, would violate structural coherence and be more worrying for a stage model, but to our knowledge this has not (yet) been found (e.g. Mason and Boscolo, 2004, see the section on Kuhn in this chapter).

Kurfiss' study also did not decisively point towards a student preference for higher levels of thinking or positions. However, the additional finding that "it is the case that lower-order thinking, even when fully understood, is systematically rejected" (Kurfiss, 1977, p. 569) may point towards quantitative confirmation of Kegan's assertion that people prefer to function at their highest 'order of consciousness' (Kegan, 1994, p. 372, see also the section on Kegan in this chapter). Kurfiss closes with the remark that "Perry's articulation of the fundamental cognitive tasks of late adolescent–early adult development is a potentially powerful tool in educational planning" (p. 570), but sadly in our experience her call has found too little response since, with some notable exceptions (e.g. Mentkowski and Associates, 2000).

Making a jump in time – for brevity sake – without implying that no studies of interest were performed in the interval[21], we will now discuss a number of more recent, Perry inspired studies. In 2004, Felder and Brent, while reviewing stage models of epistemological development and providing instructional suggestions for promoting intellectual development, referred to two studies, one cross-sectional (Pavelich and Moore, 1996) and one longitudinal (Wise et al., 2004), using the Perry Scheme to measure epistemological development. The latter study is in fact one of a series of studies at the Engineering Department of Pennsylvania State University which we will also discuss below.

With a cross-sectional design Michael Pavelich and William Moore studied the epistemological development of undergraduate engineering students at the Colorado School of Mines (CSM) who participated in 'projects courses' in six of the eight semesters of their studies. In the cliented-projects program - consisting of a number of projects courses - students work in teams on "an open-ended problem given to them by an industrial or government agency client" (Pavelich and Moore, 1996, p. 287). Perry's Scheme was used to measure the growth of epistemological development over the duration of the college years, and to examine whether at the end of their senior year students have at their disposal the understandings needed for open-ended problem solving in professional life. Three cohorts of students were interviewed, early freshmen (n=45), late sophomores (n=34) and late seniors (n=46), focusing on two main questions: 1) What is your view of an ideal college education?[22] and 2) In a situation where information is not clear-cut, how do you go about making a decision? Responses were scored using a three-digit rating method: for transitional ratings the middle digit refers to the dominant position, the first digit to the trailing position and the last digit to the opening to the next position. An example would be 3,3,4 where the dominant position is 3 with an opening to position 4. A stable position 4 student would have the rating 4, 4, 4. For statistical purposes these scores were converted to decimal scores by taking the mean: so 3, 3, 4 becomes 3.33 and a score 3, 4, 4 becomes 3.67 etcetera. This system which is quite commonly used in Perry studies, "extends the Perry scale to more of a continuum for scoring purposes" (Pavelich and Moore, 1996, p. 289). After four semesters of projects courses, the students had improved their Perry position by 0.44 position, from 3.27 (freshmen) to 3.71 (late sophomores). After six semesters of projects courses the improvement was 1.01 positions, with the late senior students on average having a Perry position of 4.28. Pavelich and Moore had somewhat mixed feelings about the results in the senior year. While the improvement of one whole Perry position over four years is comparatively substantial, the fact that even after six semesters of projects courses, about one third of the seniors tested below position 4 was disappointing. The senior group seemed to fall into two contrasting sub-groups, the one mentioned above, and another (about one quarter) reaching at least position 5. The latter group was considered to have the quality of thought necessary for professional life.

> College is supposed to teach you how to learn, give you the ability to take information, synthesise it and come up with a decision ... especially in engineering, given a problem that you may never have done anything with ... the challenge you have to meet is to gather information and make your own decision ... you learn that things aren't black and white; there are an awful lot of shades of gray... (student M, Pavelich and Moore, 1996, p. 291)

These students were also very enthusiastic about the projects courses. From a learning conception point of view, student M would be interpreted as at least at learning conception 4. The below-expectation group, exemplified by student R (rating 3.7 in senior year) in response to a question about the existence of shades of gray in mechanical engineering, is characterised by the search for certainty (one good solution).

> It really shouldn't ... given all those courses ... but normally it seems there is ... There should be one best solution, but usually there is not enough difference between that solution and another, so you can make a choice between economics, ease of manufacture, strength. (Student R, p. 291)

And while they liked the multiple solutions that projects courses offered, they were less happy with the responsibility for taking decisions, portraying themselves more as (multiplist) technicians than professionals.

> You tell me what to optimize and I'll optimize it for you. (unknown student, p. 291)

In response to these results Pavelich and Moore suggest that in addition to curriculum development, CSM should invest more in teaching methods by developing forms of high-quality *mentoring*: creating "formats that encourage students to reveal their perceptions about project work and ... developing specific suggestions for responding to student misperceptions and problems." (1996, p. 291). An example of high quality mentoring is given below.

> A freshman team, when asked by the Prof if they were having any difficulties, responded: "Things are in a mess. We talked to the client last week and he says that [solution X] is the way to go. Thus we have to scrap all the information we've gathered on [solutions Y and Z]. All that work is down the drain." This misperceptions arises from the Position 3 students seeing the client as the authority, having the right to dictate the problem's solution. The team sees its role as acceding to that authority. The Prof began by saying: "I understand

> your frustration. Situations like this often arise in consulting, especially when the client has some knowledge of the field. You have done good work to this point and need not throw it out. Let's discuss what you might do by focusing on what value you can be to such a client."
>
> The Prof then asked what the team thought about all three possible solutions. They said that all seemed viable to them. The Prof complimented them on their work and then pointed out that their value to this client, in fact their responsibility to him, was to help him break out of his mindset, to get him to look seriously at alternatives. The team should continue developing Y and Z, but must be aware that they will need stronger evidence to convince the client than if they were to propose solution X. The team bought into this approach, but were sceptical. Twice more in the semester they wanted to talk it through again with the professor, to voice their concerns. (Pavelich and Moore, 1996, p. 291)

Pavelich and Moore's suggestions – and the example of good mentoring cited above – show that developmental instruction rests not only on curriculum development but as strongly on the quality of the student-teacher relationship. This is consistent with our findings regarding the changing role of teachers within students' developing conceptions of good teaching (chapter 1). And this just goes to show (again) that 'good developmental education' is maybe not so much characterised by 'independent learning' – a common misconception – but by the quality of the student-teacher learning partnership (Baxter Magolda, 2004). Perhaps the term 'mentored learning' instead of independent learning would prove to lead to fewer misconceptions in faculty, students and society at large.

In 1996, a longitudinal study on the epistemological development of engineering students was initiated at the College of Engineering, Pennsylvania State University. The first results of this study were reported in Marra et al. (2000), Wise et al. (2004) and Marra and Palmer (2004). Marra et al. (2000) discussed the effects of changes in a first-year design course, Engineering Design and Graphics (ED&G) 100. These changes included an emphasis on an engineering approach for solving open-ended design problems, communication and collaboration skills, critical thinking (data collection, analysis and interpretation) and a changed role of the teacher to coach instead of lecturer: introducing "students to design *process* skills in addition to traditional engineering *content* " (Marra et al., 2000, p. 41). Of the sample of freshman students that participated in the spring of 1997 (cohort A), at the end of their first year, Marra et al. included 52 rated interviews.[23] The semi-structured interviews focused on a number of topics, the three most relevant to the current study were (the role of faculty, students in) an ideal college education, the meaning of learning, and definitions of knowledge[24]. Within the sample, there were students who had completed the first year ED&G course, those who were currently enrolled in ED&G and students who had not taken the design course in their first year. The average Perry rating for the whole group was 3.17 and multiplists formed the largest subgroup (77%), with the students who had completed the course scoring 0.39 Perry position higher than the students who had not taken the course. Analysis of covariance showed that the Perry ratings were not related to gender or honours status, but were significantly and positively related to the first-year design experience[25], although this effect was not significant in subsequent cohorts (Wise et al., 2004). Marra et al. interpreted the effect of the design course as showing that "the average non-design student would be rated as just moving into Perry position three, while students who had completed the design course would typically be rated at position three, opening to position four" (2000, p. 43). Although the research design lacked a Perry pre-test, the authors concluded that "the challenges inherent in a project and team-based curriculum may provide the type of intellectual environment that stimulates students' natural progression toward more complex thinking" (Marra et al., 2000, p. 43).

In the fall of 1998, at the beginning of their third year, 32 second-wave interviews of cohort A students of the above study were rated. About two years later, in the spring of 2000, cohort A students were interviewed for the third time at the end of their senior year, resulting in a final sample of 21 students with three interviews each. Per wave the main interview topics remained the same as in Marra et al. (2000), but there were adaptations in the protocol to accommodate the experiences of the students during their studies. This sample of 21 students is the basis of the four-year longitudinal study reported by Wise et al. (2004). The authors reported that during the study data-collection methods varied (video, audio and written transcripts) and ten interviewers were involved over the four-year period, illustrating additional problems related to longitudinal designs over several years.[26] Explanatory variables included in the design were participation in the first-year design course (see Marra et al. 2000 above), participation in the cooperative education programme (co-op) and experience in the university undergraduate honours programme. The co-op programme "allows students to work in industry for a semester during their undergraduate years" (Wise et al., 2004, p. 105). The honours programme is highly selective and requires writing an undergraduate thesis. The group of 21 students had the following average Perry positions: 3.27 at the end of their first year, 3.33 one and a half year later and, after three years in total, 4.21 at the end of their senior year. The lack of difference between the first and the second wave – indicating that the effect of the design course had disappeared in the second wave[27] – Wise et al. attributed to "the type of environment that presents the professor as 'Authority' …. the holder of knowledge whose job it is to dispense, while it is the student's job to absorb and repeat" (2004, p. 109). The significant increase in the final wave was explained by "the student's entry into the major, where teamwork and project-based learning is more likely to occur" (Wise et al., 2004, p. 109). A similar growth spurt in the final year of a mostly traditional curriculum was found by van Rossum, Hamer and Würffel (2003), and students attributed this change to experiencing more project-like activities. Looking at the frequency distributions of the Perry ratings, the freshmen and early juniors had almost identical (multiplist) distributions, but – as found in Pavelich and Moore – the seniors fell into two subgroups. About one-third remained multiplist, and two-thirds were at least at positions 4 opening to 5. Only one student reached a full position 5, the position Wise et al. considered necessary to be able to solve ill-structured real-life engineering problems. Participation in the co-op programme, gender and participation in the honours programme were not significantly related to Perry ratings. Wise et al. concluded that "curricular changes such as active learning classrooms with team projects can have a positive effect on this [intellectual] development, but the advantage does not last without further experiences that support the new modes of thinking" (2004, p. 109). We cannot but agree with this finding, curriculum change is not the same as isolated incidents of challenging education in a further traditional environment. It should be based on a model of student learning – such as our model – underpinning a curriculum consisting of a coherent series of 'holding environments'[28] (Kegan, 1994, see the section on Kegan in this chapter) or constructive frictions (Vermunt and Verloop, 1999, see Changing Teaching and Learning). These environments or frictions increasing in epistemological complexity and encouraging students to move forward and grow into a level of thinking required by their future professional life.

Taking the perspective that higher education should stimulate or develop students' ability to think complexly about ill-structured problems, Marra and Palmer (2004) examined the experiences and profiles of two groups of graduating senior students. One group of nine multiplist students (Perry rating 3, 4, 4) was designated as Perry Low (PL), and the other group designated as Perry High (PH) consisting of ten students with Perry ratings of 4, 5, 5 or higher. The students had been interviewed in the spring of 1997 and they were part of cohort B (Wise et al., 2004). A major demographic difference between the two groups was the high participation of PH students in the honours programme. For the current study the more interesting section of the study was the qualitative comparison of the views and experiences of the two groups, focusing on four themes. In two of these themes Marra and Palmer found no differences, Teaching and Learning and Group Work. Below we will show that – in our opinion – they missed essential differences between the two groups.

Teaching and Learning:

Initially Marra and Palmer concluded that PL and PH students did not differ in their experiences and views on teaching and learning. However, reading their examples, we *do* see clear differences: the PL students showed obvious signs of learning-teaching conception 3 and the PH students can be identified as at least learning-teaching conception 4. We feel that this initial oversight may be a result of the oddity of Perry position 4 (see Perry's legacy, bullet 1, above). We will quote two students from Marra and Palmer (2004), one PL and one PH to illustrate our position.

> … freshman year learning was going to class, taking notes, studying hard, memorizing all he facts of the exam, go into the exam write it down…Now my classes aren't like that. Like the class[es] have gradually changed to more like applicable situations where there's no more multiple choice tests. It's like write it out. And so you have to start learning a different way instead of memorizing… (PL student Ryan, p. 114)

From our perspective Ryan describes the development from learning conception 2 to 3. David – a PH student – on the other hand describes a point of view typical for learning conception 4, contrasting a laboratory experience at level 2 to one at level 4 and finishing with the observation that one needs to be able to support one's choices with arguments (and evidence).

> [Physics lab] is not really a laboratory experience. There's nothing to prove. It's just an exercise. You do Mulligan's oil drip experiment ... An ideal lab, in my opinion would be like "Demonstrate this principle somehow. Here's all this junk in lab. Do it." And you could pick the, you identify like, what you want to do, and then pick the apparatus. There may be several ways of doing it. And then you would accomplish one way or another and try to justify why your way's the best. (PH student David, p. 115)

In their discussion, Marra and Palmer comment on their initial interpretation, saying that, although both groups indicated that they preferred situations where faculty guided them in problem solving above delivering (only) content, "it may be that these groups value the 'facilitator' role for faculty for different reasons."(p. 119). PL students "still rely on authority ... for guidance to the Truth. This 'on the fence' stand is borne out by PL students' comments such [as] 'you could ask the teacher what they want you to assume', indicating [their] need for more guidance in these ambiguous activities" (Marra and Palmer, 2004, p. 119). On the other hand, PH students "...accept the transitory nature of knowledge [and] value faculty facilitation as one of many resources in their own construction of knowledge" (Marra and Palmer, 2004, p. 119). This latter interpretation we feel confirms our findings of van Rossum, Deijkers and Hamer (1985), where students at different levels of thinking about learning and teaching, use the same words with quite different and distinctive meanings, unintentionally misleading researchers to see similarity where there is none.

Group work:
Both PH and PL students were divided in their appreciation of group work. On the negative side, both groups mentioned the issues of 'some students not pulling their weight' and 'finding times to meet'. In the positive views on group work we do recognise differences that Marra and Palmer did not. PH students welcomed group work as it simulated future work environments and provided opportunities to hear and explore multiple perspectives. In discussing her experiences with comparing assignments, Lisa (PH) says,

> Almost inevitably we have the same answer and have done it two different ways, because we have very different thought processes. And I think it's very good to see... that there are many different roads that can get you to the same spot. So working with groups really helps that, because you've got not just the way I would think about doing it, but the way many people would. (p. 117)

PL students seemed to welcome group work for somewhat different reasons (helping their learning and the opportunities for work division in handling large projects), but felt that the benefits of group work would be larger when structured properly.

> We learn from each other. I learn by like something I might not understand... and then in the process of explaining it [a question] to them I learn about it and then I need to know it. It's just much better (Ryan, PL , p. 117)

> ... for one person to do that it would've been a nightmare. It would've been too difficult to do (Jennifer, PL, p. 117)

We feel that appreciation of multiple perspectives is of a totally different order than asking questions and dividing tasks. So we would say that PH and PL students differ in their appreciation of group work as well. In this we disagree with Marra and Palmer again.

Marra and Palmer found clear differences between PL and PH students on the following two themes

Problem-solving processes:
All PH students proved to be able to describe their own typical problem solving approach to realistic ill-structured problems, in Kevin's words,

> I learned that there's no right way to design an airplane. You can design 30 different airplanes and each one's going to have its benefits and there's going to be problems with each one. So you have to have just use your best idea of what the final situation is going to be. To sort of work backwards and say okay, well this is what I should start at ... And we had four groups—each given the same exact goals, and all the groups came up with something just completely different, just ridiculously different, and all of them were vaguely valid. (p. 116)

The majority of PL students did not seem to have reflected on their problem solving approach, discussing it "only in a surface-level manner—for instance describing it simply as something they had to do frequently" (Marra and Palmer, 2004, p. 116). The PL students who could describe their problem solving, made distinctions between well and ill-defined problems, indicating that they found the latter far more difficult, and they tended to focus more on the practical aspects of solving ill-structured problems. This is illustrated by Sam (PL) quoted below.

> Yeah, I think it's the hardest when you got to come up with your own project. Like design something that pertains to this class...I don't know everything about this class and sometimes I would like to have a goal...I'll actually look it up and study it but for me [to] come up with the idea to design something that I don't know exists, I think that is kind of impossible. .... Let's introduce maybe the project and introduce to you several different ways to do it... how you want to research the different ways. You'll find one and your only goal is like I got to get a grade in this class. I need to get this project done. (Sam, p. 116)

We would interpret this quote as a typical example of learning conception 3 thinking, being able to 'solve' a difficult problem, as long as the teacher *provides* alternative approaches to solving it—making it a well-defined problem. It reminds us of the student in the Pavelich and Moore study who said "You tell me what to optimize and I'll optimize it for you" (1996, p. 291). The PL students clearly do not have real problem solving skills as they "don't know what to do, when they don't know what to do". [29]

'Whole' college experience:
This theme includes experiences outside engineering, such as general education requirements, learning outside the classroom (living independently), and work experiences. The two groups differed in their appreciation of general education and their participation in the co-op programme and professional internships. In general, PH students valued general education as a means to expand their horizon, while PL students mostly saw these requirements as "nothing more than a pleasant diversion from their 'real' learning" (p. 118).

> I think one thing that I really regret is not having more room in my schedule for gen. eds. ... I'm in Art History right now. It's one of my favorite classes. I think it is important for engineers not to be narrowly focused... (Janet, PH, p. 118)
>
> I mean it's one thing to become a more broad person but you also have to keep in mind that you're here for a reason—to learn your future work. And I think sometimes a little too much time is spent becoming a broad person than it is on focusing on what you're supposed to be doing. (Jack, PL, p. 118)

PH students were far more likely to have worked in industry (through co-op and/or internships) and they appreciated these 'real life' experiences as extremely educative and personally motivating (intrinsic).

> ... but that's why I encourage absolutely everyone to seek out internships in the field. That is really what solidified to me 'yes I want to do this.' And there may be a course that I don't like and I'm going to get through it because ultimately this is what I want to do, and I understand how it all gets applied. .... But it's unbelievable to me, people that don't take advantage of everything that's here. At no other point in our lives are we exposed to so many opportunities. (Lisa, PH, p. 118–119)

Where for PH students the 'whole' college experience benefited "their commitment and understanding of their disciplines, and also [broadened] their perspectives" (p. 118–119), the PL students focused more strongly on "learning the nuts and bolts of their major as preparation for future work" (Marra and Palmer, 2004, p. 119). We have difficulty to imagine a more clear example of the difference between learning conceptions 4 and higher (PH) vis-à-vis learning conception 3 (PL).

In addition to the aspect of broadening your mind, Lisa touched on the motivational side of epistemological development. Entwistle et al. (2001) discussed this issue of motivation in comparing the differing development of two students in their first year. In this study one student took full advantage of all the opportunities offered to improve herself and her learning, while the other student basically ignored these opportunities, procrastinated and drifted through the year. Entwistle et al. interpreted the development of the former student as indicative for "development toward a deep approach [epistemological development] stemming from an opportunity, during the process of learning, that the student both recognizes and seizes as a way of improving her ways of studying. This combination of alertness to opportunity and readiness to change suggests important facets of studying not found previously ....It was, however, found in only a small proportion of students. Most of the students showed little general improvement in their studying during the first year and yet saw no need for serious reflection on their studying. Indeed, few even recognized their inadequacies" (Entwistle et al., 2001, p. 121). Perhaps this difference in motivation refers to the different types of motivation referred to as 'mastery-goal orientation' and 'performance-approach/ avoidance orientation' (see the section 'Further research with the EBQ' in chapter 4, in particular Qian and Pan, 2002; Paulsen and Feldman, 1999a and Bråten and Strømsø, 2004).

In discussing the implications for curriculum design, Marra and Palmer recommended "distributing ... challenging and realistic problem solving activities more consistently throughout the curriculum....[while providing] some structure within these ambiguous learning activities so that the discomfort of PL students is somewhat alleviated ... [and making sure that] such structure, or 'scaffolding' [is] used prudently... and gradually 'fade[s]' so students learn to manage their own problem solving processes" (2004, p. 120). Providing 'scaffolding' as described here is we feel the same as creating a 'holding environment' (Kegan, 1994, and later in this chapter) or a constructive friction (Vermunt and Verloop, 1999, chapter 11). In their remark that PL students (a substantial part of the college graduates) "are still likely to see problem solving activities in terms of a procedure previously defined by an authority figure—rather than a creative process that may necessarily involve totally new methods, and unorthodox sources of evidence" (Marra and Palmer, 2004, p. 121) they in fact answer the question "Are college seniors ready for work?" – a question addressed in this study as well (see chapters 8 through 10) – partly negative: some are and some are not.[30]

Linking Perry to Van Rossum-Hamer and Baxter Magolda

In table 3.4 we summarise this section and extend table 3.1 to include Perry's model, here dubbed "Pilgrim's Progress" to illustrate the coherence of these three epistemological approaches.

Table 3.4. Relating students' developing learning/teaching conceptions to the ERM and Perry's model

	Van Rossum-Hamer		*Baxter Magolda 1992a, 2001*	*Perry 1970, 1981, 1988*
	Learning Conception	*Teaching Conception*	*ERM*	*Pilgrim's Progress*
1	Increasing knowledge	Imparting clear/well structured knowledge	Absolute Knowing	Basic Dualism (position 1)
2	Memorising	Transmitting structured knowledge (acknowledging receiver)		Dualism (position 2,3)
3	Reproductive understanding/ application or Application foreseen	Interacting and Shaping	Transitional Knowing	Multiplicity (position 4a)
4	Understanding subject matter	Challenging to think for yourself / developing a way of thinking	Independent Knowing	The way they want you to think (position 4b)
5	Widening horizons	Dialogue teaching	Self-authored Knowing	Relativism (position 5)
6	Growing self awareness	Mutual trust and authentic relationships: Caring	Internal Foundation	Commitment (position 6 and beyond)

Kuhn

How do People Know? (Kuhn, 2001)

Deanna Kuhn's work is interesting in this review of epistemological models because she looks into the thinking of average people about everyday problems. The two models above, and our own for that matter, focus on students in higher education. Not a level all people will attain. It is interesting to know in which different ways people of varied educational and life experience think, Kuhn's subjects varied by age from 14 to 69. In particular, it is interesting to see that here also one can distinguish recognisable epistemological structures (stages or positions).

Kuhn's interest (1991) lies in studying argumentive thinking, defined in her book as thinking that takes on the form of an internal argument: the thinker, in a sense, holds a (rhetorical) internal dialogue to establish and justify an opinion. She feels (as we do) that "[t]he ability not just to think, but to think well is, or at the very least should be, essential to fulfilled adult life" (Kuhn, 1991, p. 1). Based on the studies discussed in the current review, one can question whether the thinking of average people – or even students in higher education for that matter – has the quality that democratic society assumes without question.

Her subjects – 160 in total – were asked to discuss three ill-structured problems, problems with no definite solution or a well defined, correct answer. The problems were chosen "as ones people are likely to have occasion to think and talk about and ones about which people are able and willing to make causal inferences without a large base of technical knowledge. They nevertheless involve phenomena the true causal structure of which is complex and uncertain" (Kuhn, 1991, p. 16). The subjects were interviewed about the following three societal questions:

- What causes prisoners to return to crime after they're released?
- What causes children to fail in school?
- What causes unemployment?

The problems posed varied in expected familiarity, Kuhn expected that the school question would be most familiar and the crime question least familiar. This assumption was corroborated by the subjects.

At the end of the discussion of each problem, the interviewees were asked a number of epistemological questions about

- how sure they were regarding the causes they mentioned,
- whether they felt experts would know the causes for sure (now or after long and careful study),
- how they rated the sureness of their own view compared to the expert,
- whether more points of view regarding the causes were possible, and finally (*if yes*)
- could more than one point of view be right (Kuhn, 1991, p. 300).

Analysis of these questions lead to a model with three levels of epistemological thinking that according to Kuhn (1991) broadly resemble those of Perry (1970). In later articles (e.g. Kuhn et al. 2000; Kuhn and Weinstock, 2002; Weinstock and Cronin, 2003; Kuhn, 2005) the model comprises four or five levels. At the same time Kuhn (2001) and other researchers (Mason and Boscolo, 2004) seem to follow the three level model. This is somewhat confusing, and we will discuss below first the four level model (Kuhn et al., 2000; Kuhn 2005) using as well the elaboration of the three level model (Kuhn 1991). Then we will discuss the distinction made within Evaluativist theories proposed by Kuhn and Weinstock (2002) and Weinstock and Cronin (2003).

Epistemological Theories

In Kuhn et al. (2000 and Kuhn, 2005) a four level model of epistemological thinking is proposed. Kuhn (1991) calls these levels epistemological theories and we will continue tot use this term. Kuhn views people's epistemologies as "what they take it to mean to know something" (Kuhn, 2001, p 1) and she sees the effects of these epistemologies on people's behaviour and thinking in

- the use of different criteria for justifying knowledge claims (assertions),
- a difference in disposition to use their intellectual skills, and
- varying likelihood of belief revision and conceptual change.

Kuhn also assumes a process of epistemological development, extending into the adult years. Mature epistemological understanding – according to Kuhn et al. (2000) – is seen as "the coordination of the subjective and objective dimensions of knowing" (p. 310). At the highest – evaluativist – level of thinking two people can have legitimate positions or both 'be right', but "one position can have more merit ('be more right') than the other to the extent that position is better supported by argument and evidence" (p. 311–312), where the argument and evidence are 'objective' and the position is 'subjective'.

Realist theories: Assertions are copies

This first level of epistemological thinking is not present in Kuhn's 1991 model, and therefore we cannot illustrate this theory with an example from her work. In later work Kuhn sees this first level, Realist theories, as a stage to be overcome by pre-school age (Kuhn et al. 2000, Kuhn and Weinstock, 2002 and Kuhn, 2005). But at the same time realist thinking is found in the epistemological thinking of adult subjects (ranging in age from 19–73 years, Weinstock and Cronin, 2003). We will return to this contradiction – that is also valid for the next two levels of thinking – after presenting the four level model.

At this level knowledge, what one knows, is a copy of an external reality (Kuhn, 2005, p. 31). Kuhn and Weinstock (2002) describe this level of thinking as "simple, unconscious, unreflective knowing about the world" (p. 126). This lack of reflection is characteristic of our learning teaching conception 1 (chapter 1) and Perry's position 1 (Perry, 1970 and see Basic Dualism above). In addition, in the first conception of applying, application is perceived as copying reality. We feel that Realist theory can be placed at the same epistemological level.

Absolutist theories: Assertions are facts

In Kuhn's 1991 study half of her subjects (49%) fell into this category of thinking. People at this level see knowledge as an objective entity, located in the external world which – once apprehended – yields only one valid conclusion, knowable with certainty. Knowledge is regarded in quantitative terms, as accumulating large numbers of certain facts. False beliefs are possible, and have their source in incorrect or incomplete facts about reality. Especially subjects' responses pertaining to expertise provide the basis for categorisation into this level of thinking. Absolutists claim that "experts either *do*, or *can* with sufficient study, know with certainty the causes of the phenomenon in question" (Kuhn, 1991, p. 173–174).

Interviewer: Do experts know for sure what causes school failure?
Subject: If they're experts, they know. (p. 174)
Interviewer: Do experts know for sure what causes prisoners to return to crime?
Subject: Possibly. They have an enormous bunch of facts. (p. 174)

This quantitative view on knowledge places both Realist as Absolutist theories firmly in the lower levels of epistemological thinking, and we equate them to respectively levels 1 and 2 in the scheme of epistemological models (Table 3.5).

Multiplist theories: Assertions are opinions

Almost a third of the subjects (29%) were categorised as multiplists. Two criteria were used to define this category: 1) in a complete reversal from the previous position, multiplists deny the possibility of expert certainty and 2) multiplists claim their own certainty as equal to or greater than that of experts.

Interviewer: Do experts know for sure what causes prisoners to return to crime?
Subject: No. They study, they think they know, and all that, but … they interview and all … but they really don't know. (p. 178)
Interviewer: How sure are you of your view, compared to an expert?
Subject: You know, I found out that the very simple person walking the street has more common sense than some of these experts. (p. 180)

The latter quote contrasts the worth of academic (book) knowledge and "real life" (first-hand) knowledge and stresses the worth of one's own experience. This emphasis on experiential learning is typical of learning teaching conception 3. The basis of facts, characteristic of the previous positions, is now replaced by more subjective entities such as "ideas" and "emotions" expressed as opinions not amenable to proof.

Interviewer: Would you be able to prove this person wrong?
Subject: No.
Interviewer: Why not?
Subject: Because you can't prove an opinion to be wrong, I don't think.
Interviewer: Why not?
Subject: Because an opinion is something which somebody holds for themselves. You can't change their opinion or alter it. They have their own opinion. (p. 182)

At this level respondents do not distinguish between the belief and the person holding the belief: "what is true to me is what is true of me" (Kuhn, 1991, p. 183) and echo Perry's position 4a. An opinion is a personal possession which no one has the right to interfere with. Consequently all opinions are equally legitimate, there is no real need to reconcile divergent views and discussions can lead only to further development or enrichment of the own view.

Kuhn remarks upon the "danger" of this position: "If one's theories are completely tied to one's own personal experience, not only is there a total fusion of the experiential and reflective levels of explanation …, but the possibility of any inductive generalisation across multiple cases is foregone" (Kuhn, 1991, p. 183) This observation supports our interpretation that the transition from multiplist theories to the next level of thinking is the actual watershed in epistemological development: the transition from "anything goes" to "one opinion is better (supported) than another".

Evaluativist theories: Assertions are judgments

Of Kuhn's subjects a little more than one fifth (22%) fell into this highest level found. Evaluativists, as multiplists, also deny the possibility of certain knowledge, but recognise that non-experts such as themselves are less certain about causes of problems than an expert. In comparing views or opinions, one can evaluate the relative merit of an opinion in light of evidence instead of personal experience. The divorce of person and opinion opens the way to disagreement and real discussion, resulting in amendment of opinions: an impossibility in the previous position. Responding to the question "How sure are you of your view, compared to an expert?" two subjects illustrate these points:

> Not as sure. I don't really have that much experience. I haven't seen that many. I would say that if you have more information … if you have more cases to look at, then you're going to have a better idea of what the general trend is.
>
> (Kuhn, 1991, p. 189)

I'm speaking from personal experience. An expert is speaking from years of objective experience. At the moment I think my opinion is justified, but if an expert were to prove me wrong in a way that I would find acceptable, then maybe my opinion could be swayed. (Kuhn, 1991, p. 190)

Although experts may come closer to discovering (plausible) causal structures, more important in this level of thinking are evaluation and judgment of opinions, and an appreciation of the complexity of (convincing) argumentation.

> Interviewer: Would you be able to prove this other person wrong?
>
> Subject: Perhaps to my satisfaction, not necessarily to his. He may not like my statistics and figures anymore than I might like his. I don't think I could flat out prove anyone is wrong. This type of subject is very difficult to say "here you are and here's the proof." Like I said, I think it's more a matter of convincing by arguments, and whatever, than it is by any indisputable proof that you are wrong. (Kuhn, 1991, p. 191)

Comments on Kuhn

Contradictions in Kuhn's Work

As we have discussed before in the section on Realist theories, Kuhn is not very consistent with regard to the timeline of the development of epistemological thinking. Kuhn frequently refers to the fact that most people will have reached the multiplist level by their teens (e.g. Kuhn, 2005, p. 32), while in her research on skills of argument she finds that irrespective of age, about half (49%) of the subjects could be categorised as absolutist (Kuhn, 1991, p. 192), and another 29 percent as multiplist. The contradiction is clear: on the one hand there is the feeling that epistemological development up to multiplist level is quite rapid, leading to predominantly multiplist thinking in adolescence (e.g. Kuhn, 2005), while Baxter Magolda (1992a) found that absolutist thinking is most frequent in the first year of college (68%, Baxter Magolda, 1992a, p. 70). Considering our work on learning teaching conceptions, Perry and Baxter Magolda's work on epistemological development as well as Kuhn's research on skills of argument (1991), in our opinion multiplicity as a level of epistemological thinking generally develops later than adolescence and that – without higher education – even realist and absolutist thinking can persist well into advanced adulthood. Kuhn's own research supports this assertion: education – and not age or gender – was found to increase the likelihood of higher levels of epistemological theories (Kuhn, 1991, p. 192).

Skills versus Values

According to Kuhn (1991, 2001, 2005) in argumentive thinking and inquiry the described epistemological development is important to the development of intellectual values, the valuing of intellectual engagement. To engage in e.g. argumentive thinking "Individuals must also hold the implicit epistemological theory that treats argument as worthwhile, as a fundamental path to knowing. In other words, people must *see the point* of argument, if they are to engage in it" (Kuhn, 1991, p. 201, italicised by us). When knowledge is seen as an accumulation of certain facts, true or false, argumentation about these facts is *pointless*. Additionally, when knowledge is seen as subjective or an opinion, then argumentation about the merit of this opinion is *undesirable* because everyone has a right to his own opinion. Only when knowledge is seen as based on evidence and some opinions can be evaluated as better than others, does argument become "the foundation upon which knowing rests" (Kuhn, 1991, p. 202). This implies that education of skills for thinking (argument and inquiry in Kuhn's later work) can only succeed once students have reached at least evaluativist level. This means that the focus of higher education should be first and foremost on epistemological development and not on skills alone.

Kuhn proposed a model of intellectual performance which acknowledges the difference between skill development – more procedural – and value/ epistemological development – more declarative (Kuhn, 2001, p. 4; 2005, p. 188). Procedural metacognition leads to competencies to establish when and how to apply knowing strategies (inquiry, analysis, inference and argument), and declarative metacognition (epistemological thinking) underlies the valuing and disposition to apply the knowing strategies. While discussing the scarcity of evaluativist epistemological thinking in the adult population, Kuhn feels that "we need to foster individual growth by providing frequent opportunities for the exercise of judgment, but we also need to work toward creating the kind of society [or higher education for that matter] in which thinking and judgment are widely regarded as worth the effort they entail" (Kuhn and Weinstock, 2002, p. 139).

Further Detailing in Evaluativist Theories

In Kuhn and Weinstock (2002) and Weinstock and Cronin (2003) a further sub-division is proposed within the evaluativist theories: Objective evaluativist and Conceptual evaluativist theories.[31] While both use evidence to support their judgments or assertions, the difference between these two evaluativist theories lies in the way discrepancies between accounts of a particular event are treated.

In Objective theories these discrepancies are attributed to different emphases on evidence made in the accounts, in essence weighing evidence differently. In Conceptual theories discrepancies are attributed to differing frames of reference or perspectives of the narrator[32], so for conceptual evaluativists no single true account exists. Where objective evaluativists still have the expectation that one can approach objectivity, conceptual evaluativists have accepted relativism. This distinction parallels the divide between learning teaching conception 4 and 5. Interpreted in this way we reject the note below Table 1 of Weinstock and Cronin

(2003) where they state that there "is no assumption that the evaluativist levels 4 [objective] and 5 [conceptual] are so ordered" (p. 167). We argue that they are ordered as discussed above and as such are typical of distinct ways of knowing and not "alternate paths to resolving multiplist, radical relativism" (p. 167).

Instruments

Through the years, Kuhn has used different methods and instruments to measure epistemological thinking. In the study reported in The Skills of Argument (1991) she used a number of interview questions within a study on argumentive reasoning. A second method used is an interview regarding evaluating the "Livia Problem". The Livia Problem consists of two conflicting historical accounts of a fictitious war (Kuhn and Weinstock, 2002). Relevant to her epistemological model are the questions subjects were asked to answer about

a) whether the two accounts were different, and
b) if so, could only one or could both accounts be correct and
c) if both can be correct, can one be more true than the other.

The third instrument used is based on presenting 15 pairs of contrasting assertions that subjects then are asked to evaluate with regard to the two latter questions. Such as

> Robin believes one book's explanation of what atoms are made up of.
> Chris believes another book's explanation of what atoms are made up of.
>
> (Kuhn and Weinstock, 2002, p. 128)

The first question (Is only one, or could both accounts be correct?) splits absolutists from multiplists, and the second question (If both can be correct, can one be more true than the other?) then splits multiplists from evaluativists. While this instrument is exceedingly simplistic as compared to the time and energy consuming interviews usually applied in epistemological research, and so can be used to measure larger samples, its validity is demonstrated in Weinstock (1998, as reported in Kuhn and Weinstock 2002, p. 130) by showing a highly statistically significant association between this instrument and the Livia Problem.

Mason and Boscolo (2004) used Kuhn's 15-item instrument to measure the epistemological understanding of sixty-five pupils in the 10th and 11th grade. In evaluating an inconclusive dual-position expository text on genetically modified food, pupils' epistemological understanding and topic interest were related to a number of dependent variables: among these writing a conclusion to the dual-position text, answering open-ended questions about the two positions, and topic-specific belief change. The design of this study reminds us of our first attempt to relate learning conceptions to study outcomes (van Rossum and Schenk, 1984) in the sense that learning conceptions played the role that in this study by Mason and Boscolo is played by epistemological understanding. They found, among others, that more advanced epistemological understanding leads to

- higher quality conclusions (conclusions that better reflect the inconclusive nature of the debate),
- more complete and correct answers to open-ended questions, and
- greater belief change.

If one sees the first of these two results as measures of learning outcome, these results support the findings of our 1984 study, and this study proves that Kuhn's simple instrument works surprisingly well. The hypothesis that high topic interest would compensate for less advanced levels of epistemological understanding, was not borne out in this study. Considering the models described above, one would not expect such an interaction between epistemological thinking and interest.

Juror Reasoning

The societal value of Kuhn's epistemological theories has been demonstrated in a number of studies. In 1991 she established that especially the evaluativist level of epistemological thinking is related to the successful use of basic skills of argument (Kuhn, 1991). Weinstock and Cronin (2003) extended this finding when they also studied the relation between epistemological understanding and the skills of juror reasoning. For this study subjects – ranging in age from 19 to 73 – who were serving jury duty, participated as a juror in abridged re-enactments of two criminal cases. The task was to present and discuss – in an interview – the verdict each juror reached after hearing each trial. Aspects discussed where a) use of evidence, b) ability to discount alternative verdict choices, c) ability to generate counterarguments against the verdict choice, d) ability to explain how each of the verdict choices other than their own might be justified and e) the degree of certainty about their own verdict choice, resulting in eight dimensions of juror reasoning that could be clustered into 1) representation of verdict criteria, 2) use of evidence and 3) relation of evidence to verdict. Epistemological understanding was measured using the above mentioned Livia problem. Overall, just less of one half (47%) of the 173 jurors were classified as absolutists, another 39% were classified as multiplists, and only 14% of the jurors were capable of thinking on an evaluativist level, which shows (again) that lower levels of epistemological thinking appear frequently in an adult population. This study showed furthermore that the outcome of the Livia problem – the level of epistemological thinking – could predict the performance on seven of the eight dimensions of juror reasoning. Weinstock and Kuhn (2002) concluded that individuals with higher levels of epistemological thinking were more likely to exhibit higher levels of juror reasoning. Together with the finding that a significant number of people in research on juror reasoning uses a satisficing "make-sense epistemology", in which "the construction of a plausible narrative is sufficient to dictate the corresponding verdict choice, testimony inconsistent with this narrative is disregarded, and alternatives are not considered" (Kuhn, 2001, p. 1), this application of Kuhn's work shows that epistemological thinking plays an important role in everyday informal reasoning about ill-structured problems. More importantly, it shows that there might be something terribly wrong with the current practice of trial by jury. On the other hand, Weinstock is correct in noting that the studies did not take juror-interaction into account: it is possible that interaction with other, perhaps epistemologically more sophisticated jurors might counteract the influence of "make-sense epistemology" in reasoning (Micheal Weinstock, personal communication, 2008). Something akin to this improvement-by-interaction was described by Marton (1986, p. 46), "in group discussions revolving around different ways of thinking, students may become conscious of the fact that there are different ways of thinking. This is a very fundamental insight, *a step on the way to adopting a qualitatively better way of thinking*" (italics ours). In the instance that society is interested in the quality and validity of trial-by-jury, further research that would include juror-interaction would seem an essential next step.

Linking Kuhn to Van Rossum-Hamer, Baxter Magolda and Perry

In Table 3.5 we have again expanded our review of epistemological models to include Kuhn's epistemological theories. This is relevant because Kuhn's work is based on a broader range of subjects and their thinking on everyday problems. It is interesting to see that here as well, we find very similar (if not identical) stages in thinking and ways of knowing. This finding underpins our proposition that developmental epistemological models have meaning in everyday life, and are more than an exercise in scientific or fundamental curiosity.

Table 3.5. Relating students' developing learning/teaching conceptions to the ERM and Perry's model and Kuhn's Epistmological Theories

	Van Rossum-Hamer		*Baxter Magolda 1992a, 2001*	*Perry 1970, 1981, 1988*	*Kuhn 1991, 2000, 2005*
	Learning Conception	*Teaching conception*	*ERM*	*Pilgrim's Progress*	*Epistemo-logical Theories*
1	Increasing knowledge	Imparting clear/well structured knowledge		Basic Dualism (position 1)	Realist
2	Memorising	Transmitting structured knowledge (acknowledging receiver)	Absolute Knowing	Dualism (position 2, 3)	Absolutist
3	Reproductive understanding/ application or Application foreseen	Interacting and Shaping	Transitional Knowing	Multiplicity (position 4a)	Multiplist
*					
4	Understanding subject matter	Challenging to think for yourself / developing a way of thinking	Independent Knowing	The way they want you to think (position 4b)	Objective Evaluativist
5	Widening horizons	Dialogue teaching	Self-authored knowing	Relativism (position 5)	Conceptual Evaluativist
6	Growing self awareness	Mutual trust and authentic relationships: Caring	Internal Foundation	Commitment (position 6 and beyond)	

*) Watershed in epistemological development (van Rossum and Hamer)

Kegan

Experience is not what happens to you, it's what you do *with what happens to you.*

Aldous Huxley (1972, quoted in Kegan, 1982)

Robert Kegan (1994) has developed a five stage model of "Orders of Consciousness" tracing the evolving self responding to the mental demands of life (Kegan, 1982). In this regard this model is interesting because it pulls the study of epistemological development out of the educational context alone. By elaborating the application of the model to many areas of life – e.g. parenting, partnering, working and (psychological) healing – his approach underscores our belief that developing conceptions of learning and teaching are only one manifestation of a deeper and more fundamental development influencing the way people understand and approach the world around them: what they *do* with what happens to them.

In Kegan's model five premises underlie the (development of the) Orders of Consciousness. The first premise refers to orders of consciousness as not being about *what* you know, but being about *the way* you know. This means that the orders focus on people's meaning making, in this sense Kegan's model is a close relation to Perry's model (1970). Kegan sees people as active organisers of their experience. The orders of consciousness differ in the kind of organising principle a person applies to interpret experience in the most general sense, e.g. one's thinking, feeling and social relating.

The second premise refers to the complexity regarding the organising principle of each order of consciousness in contrast to the content. Kegan (1994) sees psychological growth or the evolvement of self as "the unselfconscious development of successively more complex principles for organising experience" (p. 29).

The third premise focuses on the principle of internal logic within each order of consciousness. Kegan (1994) phrases this as that "[the] 'deep structure' of any principle of mental organisation is the subject-object relationship" (p. 32). Object in this sense refers to that aspect of our knowing we can reflect upon, while subject refers to that aspect of our knowing we are (still) embedded in and cannot reflect upon yet. So at each level, we *have* object and *are* subject, e.g. the difference between

- "*that* I am" (I is subject and cannot be reflected upon, reflection is upon being or not being: First order of consciousness) and
- "*what* I am" (I is object and reflection is possible upon the self: Second order of consciousness, Kegan, 1982, p. 89).

The fourth premise is that orders of consciousness are related to each other in a hierarchical sense. This means that each higher order encompasses the prior order(s) and transforms it(/them). Each higher order is more complex, more inclusive and it makes the prior principle(s) into an element or tool within the new system. In this sense every transition is a move where what was once subject now becomes object, a move out of embeddedness to a position where one can observe one's own previous position and the self becomes able to reflect upon one's previous way of knowing.

The final premise follows from the fourth, namely that orders of consciousness are not a fixed personality trait. People, and consequently their order of consciousness, can change. "In fact, transforming our epistemologies, liberating ourself from that in which we were embedded, making what was subject into object so that we can 'have it' rather than 'be had' by it – this is the most powerful way I know to conceptualize the growth of the mind" (Kegan, 1994, p. 34).

Orders of Consciousness

Where Kegan's 1994 model refers to development as going through orders of consciousness, his earlier model (Kegan, 1982) refers to development as finding a new balance between subject and object. In our discussion we will follow the nomenclature of the later model, but will refer to the matching stages from the earlier model when appropriate. Furthermore we feel that Kegan (1994) discusses a sixth order of consciousness when differentiating reconstructive postmodernism as a special case of postmodernism (the fifth order of consciousness).

First order of consciousness

In this first level, thinking is guided by the principle of "independent elements", the underlying structure is characterised by an atomistic view – elements are separate and dimensionless (single points) – and egocentrism in social relating. Within the first learning teaching conception one can also recognise such an atomistic view on learning and knowledge, with reading a text being described as "reading every word", and the teacher is expected to discuss and explain *literally everything* clearly. The latter expresses, we feel, an egocentric attitude towards the teacher, see also pages 2 and 8 before. Children at a young age typically respond in this order of consciousness. When asked to explain a movie, e.g. Star Wars, they will demonstrate "no sense of a story [line] or of a logical connection between one part of the movie and another. Instead, they talk about a single point in time in the movie, or they talk about a single character with no indication that they understand his importance to the story" (Kegan, 1994, p. 33). A response can be

> I loved Chewbaka; he was so big and hairy. (Kegan, 1994, p. 33)

When asked about learning students at this level will also not make connections between aspects, but can respond by listing various activities associated with learning and synonyms of learning (see chapter 1), an arbitrary response much like picking a character out of a story because it comes to mind. As such, this first order of consciousness can also be linked to Biggs' uni-structural level of learning outcomes (1979).

Second order of consciousness

The increased complexity at this level is demonstrated in that independent elements now become part of a set of related elements—a durable category. The single point has now become an object, while the set of points, the line, becomes subject. Explaining Star Wars at this level becomes a linear narrative of the movie, a recounting of a string of events (what happened) at a concrete level. In illustration, Kegan calls to mind the exasperation of any parent when confronted with such a (often long winded) recounting of the entire movie. In our own work with university freshmen(!) (van Rossum and Schenk, 1984), learning outcomes related to surface level processing were characterised as multi-structural (Biggs, 1979). One expression of such a multi-structural outcome is that a student, in attempting to show his 'understanding' of a recently read text, tries to recount the text as completely as possible. In Biggs (1979) this type of answer is described as a catalogue of conclusions "it shows ... it also ... it also" which sounds suspiciously similar to the well-known "then ... and then ... and then ..." format of children's recountings. Kegan (1994) illustrates this level by referring to history teaching. In his model respondents at this level see history as "the story of history" comprising of concrete facts and a narrative line such as "how the world went to war" (p. 291).

Learners are not the only people in the educational context embedded in the world of facts, narratives and memorising. Some teachers perceive the world in the same way. Kegan illustrates this with a story about one teacher teaching the concept of irony, Teacher A.

[Teacher A] asks for a definition [of irony], and the first student responds, "Like when the husband sold his watch to get his wife the combs for her hair, but then she had sold her hair to get him a chain for his watch—that's irony" ... [Teacher A responds] "Well that's not really a *definition* of anything. That's an *example*. Depending on what you think that example means, it might even be a correct example of irony, but it's certainly not a definition. Now, can someone give me a definition of irony, not an example?"

Kegan then continues with a scenario he feels is consistent with this second order of consciousness

(1) Students volunteer a few more examples of irony, which the teacher does not accept as definitions of irony; (2) there is eventual silence on the part of the class; (3) the teacher, having stumped the class, defines the term irony, possibly writing the definition on the blackboard for the students to copy into their notebooks, memorize, and file away for the exam (p. 52)

While the aim of the class was to exceed the second order of consciousness in the mental demand "to define" (inferring the general from the specific), teacher A in fact reduces this class to the second order of consciousness, with his emphasis on rote learning of the given correct definition, and increasing the number of correct facts known with this fact. The quantitative view on knowledge as facts (right or wrong), stored for short term use (at a test or exam), fits the banking analogy for learning we proposed earlier (chapter 1, learning teaching conception 2).

Third order of consciousness: Traditionalism

At this level of thinking, following – as Kegan calls it – the cross-categorical principle people have learnt to subordinate their self-interest to the needs and values of a mutual relationship. Here people are no longer seen as means to an end, or tools to meet your immediate needs, but as others in relationship with you. People – with their separate minds, separate intentions and needs – have become object, embedded in their relationship, the latter is subject and as such closed to reflection. Socialisation, becoming a good citizen, family or community member etcetera is one of the main themes of this order of consciousness. However, because one is embedded, one is unable to be critical of the type of socialisation: you are socialised to the group you are in and you are "had" by this group, you do not "have" the group. You are "had" by the folklore and traditions of your group and you cannot examine these rituals. The third teaching conception's preference for interaction and group discussion fits nicely with this third order of consciousness. In addition, the shaping aspect of the third teaching conception is consistent with this order: education seen as socialisation into a discourse community may amount to an "education for inauthenticity, since one learns the right moves and the right words but accomplishes no "inside out" [fourth order] mastery of the locality's discipline" (Kegan, 1994, p. 289).

At the same time the capacity to think abstractly, to define or infer the general from the particulars, emerges and people are more able to see the future as "something one lives with as real in the present" instead of as "the-present-that-hasn't-happened-yet" (Kegan, 1994, p. 27). The category of datum or fact has become object, and the person is able to e.g. reflect on them to infer something which in turn becomes subject. The fact that people see the future as real in the present implies that people can plan (learn) for the long term – their future life – something that was beyond their scope at a lower order of consciousness. Learning for application later (e.g. in your later profession) is typical for the third learning conception, linking it to the third order of consciousness. The ability to form an opinion, based on abstraction, is also typical of this learning conception. However, people at this level have difficulty differentiating opinions from the holder of the opinions. As described before (see Kuhn, Multiplist theories) at this level one is (embedded in) one's opinion and to deny an opinion's validity is to deny the person. When asked to "think for yourself", students at this level feel they only need to express their own opinions, which need not be grounded in inquiry and evidence. Kegan (1994, p. 40) summarises the difference between this order of consciousness and the previous one: "Concrete thinking, governed by the durable category [second order], is simultaneously capable of holding several pieces of information together and incapable of subordinating the category of the actual to the cross-categorical realm [third order] of the possible, which is required for the construction of long-range plans, patterns, or generalisations".

What would a movie goer in this order of consciousness say about Star Wars? Kegan thinks that such a person could say "the movie might be 'about' the battle between good and evil or some such thematic abstraction in which the *line* of the story's plot is subordinated to a larger field or *plane* of consideration" (Kegan, 1994, p. 33, italics ours). The story's plot lines are now elements in the two dimensional plane of the larger theme: good against evil. What does a student at the third order of consciousness have to say about learning and teaching history? How history is written reflects a subjective perspective, e.g. the values and aims of the narrator: each account is only an opinion about what happened and is as valid as any other.

What would the lesson on irony (discussed above) be like when taught by a third order teacher: Teacher A'? In response to the first student's example (about the husband buying combs for his wife, and the wife selling her hair), teacher A' would say

"Well, that's a terrific example of irony, all right. Let's put that one up on the blackboard and circle it. Okay, can someone give me another example of irony? It doesn't have to be from the story [read in preparation for this lesson], it can be anything"

A possible scenario here is then

(1) the students will offer many more *examples* of irony (...). Teacher A' salutes each example, puts it up on the board, and draws a circle around it; (2) the teacher says, "Let's stop and take a look at all these great examples of irony." He then draws one big circle enclosing all the separate circles. "Now can anyone tell me what *irony* is in a way that would be true for all these examples?"; (3) at this point, the students collectively struggle toward a generalization that can be checked against all the particulars" (Kegan, 1994, p. 52–53)

Teacher A' has created an epistemological stretch for his students, by inviting students to see the examples as objects to reflect upon. By exercising the students' capacity to *define*, one aspect of abstract thinking, in addition to the capacity to *exemplify*, which they have already shown to master, he creates a bridge to the third order of consciousness. As such this teacher provides an ideal *holding environment* for these students: acknowledging who the students are right now, and fostering the students' epistemological evolution to the next order of consciousness. The concept of holding environment is a central element in Kegan's model of orders of consciousness: "[A] holding environment is a tricky transitional culture, an evolutionary bridge, a context for crossing over. It fosters developmental transformation, or the process by which the whole ('how I am') becomes gradually a part ('how I was') of a new whole ('how I am now')" (Kegan, 1994, p. 43).

Fourth order of consciousness: Modernism

In modern democratic society the needs and desires of many groups are considered and balanced to reach a way of living that does (a measure of) justice to all. To understand modern society it is necessary to be able to reflect upon the needs and desires of different, possibly opposing groups, so one needs to be able to rise above one's group, see the needs of one's own and other groups and the relationships between the needs and desires. Modern society is seen as a conglomerate of systems, e.g. "legal, societal, normative system" (Kegan, 1982, p. 101). Systemic thinking, thinking in terms of systems, disciplines, ideologies, etcetera which contain rules and methods for generating, judging and relating its parts (abstractions, inferences of the third order), is an important aspect of the fourth order of consciousness.

In his book *In over our heads* (Kegan, 1994), Kegan says that in areas of public and private life (work, family, relationships, education etcetera), the modern world makes demands on the self, socialisation and the third order of consciousness cannot meet. He calls these demands on the self "the curriculum of the modern world" and he demonstrates that in all these areas, the modern world requires that one develops the capacity to think for oneself, in other words that one develops personal authority or self-authorship. Self-authorship is a key term in his 1994 model of orders of consciousness and it is described as follows "a *self-authorship* that can coordinate, integrate, act upon, or invent values, beliefs, convictions, generalizations, ideals, abstractions, interpersonal loyalties, and intrapersonal states. It is no longer *authored by* them, it *authors them* and thereby achieves a personal authority" (Kegan, 1994, p. 185). To acquire this self-authorship one needs to rise above (or look from the outside into) one's original group, changing the relationship one has to this group. Kegan refers to this as changing the relationship to one's "natural religion" (e.g. your class, ethnic background or religious creed).

Kegan applies this notion of fourth order of consciousness to the concept of self-directed learning in higher (adult) education, learning to be self-directed. In addition to the demand on self-authorship, self-directed learning makes a second demand on the self, namely that one has acquired the cognitive sophistication to take charge of an intellectual discipline and to construct complex systems. On this level disciplines are "neither repositories of discovered facts [second order] nor families of related opinions [third order]. They are each –be they in the sciences, social sciences, or humanities – systematic procedures for generating and evaluating ideas, hypotheses, and 'sincere opinions'. They are public procedures for relating to third order constructions" (Kegan, 1994, p. 286). These two requirements of the fourth order of consciousness are identical to the two main aspects given in the fourth learning teaching conception: learning to think for oneself and developing a way of thinking (within a specific discipline). The concept of self-directed learning can be seen as embracing two developments: on the one hand the question is "who, which self, is directing the learning?" and on the other hand "what is the nature of the learning that the self is directing?", linking our learning teaching conception model directly to Kegan's model of orders of consciousness.

Kegan considers the transition from the third level to this fourth level as a difficult, often long and painful journey to the new self and personal authority. He likens it more to teaching people "to unspeak their native tongue" which is much more difficult than teaching people "to speak a foreign language" (Kegan, 1994, p. 289–290). This unlearning of your own tongue to learn a new one feels, to us, as similar to the unlearning of quantitative thinking about learning (learning teaching conceptions 1 to 3) to learning to think about learning in qualitative terms (learning teaching conceptions 4 and beyond). In this sense we feel that we can interpret the transition to the fourth order of consciousness as crossing the same watershed we propose between learning teaching conception 3 and 4.

The profound nature of the transition from the third order to the fourth is supported by a number of studies into the distribution of orders of consciousness in the adult population in the United States. In studies based on a representative sample of the population, Kegan found that 79% of the subjects do not transcend the third order of consciousness, which is consistent with Kuhn's finding (1991) that 78% of her subjects were absolutist or multiplist thinkers – levels of thinking below the fourth order of consciousness. Also consistent with Kuhn's studies, Kegan finds that advanced education (graduate programmes) seems to influence the distribution of orders of consciousness: in a sample of higher educated respondents, "only" around 50% have an order of consciousness below the fourth level. While advanced education seems to make a difference, it may be disappointing that still about half of highly educated people have been unable to make this crossing and move to the fourth order of consciousness Kegan proposes necessary to meet the demands of modern life. With regard to undergraduate education for students of traditional ages (18 to 21), Kegan finds that "almost no one this age has fully constructed the fourth order of consciousness" (1994, p. 292), which is consistent with findings of Baxter Magolda (1992a) where about 80% of senior college students are below the fourth order of consciousness.

Fifth order of consciousness: Postmodernism

Above, in a number of studies, it is shown that the large majority of the population lacks the way of knowing needed to cope with modern society: the curriculum of modern life. The situation may actually be even more worrisome, if one considers that currently we live in a postmodern society, where traditionalism of tribal societies, modernism and postmodernism exist side by side, leading to claims on people that only few are able to meet, and then "never before midlife" (Kegan, 1994, p. 317). According to Kegan, the capacity for self-authorship and systemic knowing aren't enough to meet the demands of this curriculum of contemporary culture. The three ubiquitous features of postmodernism are

- the rejection of absolutes: there is no single rationality, no single morality and no ruling theoretical framework for the analysis of social and political events (e.g. education, justice);
- social and political discourse are perceived as being saturated with power or dominance: recognising the underlying powerplay, and the implicit ruling ideology behind practice; and
- the celebration of difference: because all ideologies (structures and systems) are mere constructions, there is no reason to value one above the other (relativism) (Kegan, 1994, p. 325).

This relativism demands more than the fourth order of consciousness. The cognitive sophistication of taking charge of a discipline, in itself already a considerable epistemological evolution, must now be subordinated to the realisation of the relative nature of intellectual disciplines. Kegan linked the capacity to reflect critically on "the discipline itself, subjecting its prevailing theories to analysis not just from the perspective of another contending theory but from a perspective 'outside ideology'" to the "5th order of consciousness (trans-system structures)" (1994, p. 291). At the fifth order of consciousness people realise "that each way of knowing is a way of not knowing, that each discipline is itself an ideology offering the power of explanation but at the price of inevitably advantaging someone or something and disadvantaging someone or something else" (Kegan, 1994, p. 290). This emphasis on relativism here is consistent with Perry's fifth position and our own fifth learning teaching conception. Kegan described the shift from the fourth order of consciousness to the fifth, as the move "from the self-authoring self to … the self-transforming self" (Debold, 2002, p. 151 quoting Kegan).

In the fifth teaching conception, students see good teaching as a learning partnership (Baxter Magolda, 2004), where – in dialogue – teachers and students become equal partners in the mutual construction of knowledge. We recognise this partnership theme in descriptions of successful postmodern leadership. Where in modern leadership the successful leader forms a vision unilaterally prior to the contact with prospective followers, a successful postmodern leader provides a context where all stakeholders participate together – in partnership – in creating a vision (Heifetz and Sinder, 1988, as quoted in Kegan, 1994).

In Kegan's interpretation, this order of consciousness holds in itself two structures, an ultimate, pure form of relativism, he calls Deconstructive postmodernism, and a brand of postmodernism, Reconstructive postmodernism, where modernist concepts – such as self-determination, reason etcetera – reappear. In deconstructive postmodernism, sometimes called antimodernism, relativism has gone into overdrive. Assuming that any theory or ideology is 'just' a construction, necessarily incomplete, limited and ideologically partial, deconstructive postmodernists have come to the conclusion that "any of our disciplines, theories or scholarly approaches is ultimately *unworthy of our commitment* to it, and, by implication, that ultimately the only intellectual activity that is worthy is deconstruction" (Kegan, 1994, p. 330, italicised by us). This position by its nature has not been instrumental in formulating positive alternatives for the flawed theories or ideologies criticised and describes well, we feel, the gamesmanship Perry sees as Escape in relativism (Perry, 1970, p. 191).

Reconstructive postmodernism, Kegan feels, follows the stage of deconstructive postmodernism, and in a way integrates the differentiated relativism of the fifth order of consciousness. As such, Kegan is of the opinion that postmodernism is only then fully realised after one becomes reconstructive postmodernist. However, he also acknowledges that the move from deconstructive to reconstructive postmodernism cannot be made without "disturbing the self" (Kegan, 1994, p. 332), which in our opinion indicates that this move is in fact a step to a higher order of consciousness.

Sixth order of consciousness: Reconstructive postmodernism

In Reconstructive postmodernism commitment, privileging or prioritising are reinstated in knowing. In the ultimate relativistic way of knowing, one feels that any choice or commitment is backsliding into modernism. In Reconstructive postmodernism, one has the clear need to make a stand, to identify with a theory, without this commitment denying the essential relativism of the chosen stand. In the fourth order one 'is had' by a discipline, theory or stand, here one 'has' one. Where deconstructive postmodernism says that no stand is possible nor desirable, reconstructive postmodernists advocate choosing positions, not only for the self, but also "for the purpose of nourishing the very process of reconstructing the disciplines and their theories. [One] could argue that the purpose of this reconstructing –this creating of better and better theory—is to arrive eventually at the Complete Theory, but a truly reconstructive view would actually be more likely to associate such a 'victory' with death. As long as life goes on, the process will need to go on" (Kegan, 1994, p. 330). In reconstructive postmodernism, one chooses a position on a particular issue, and grounds oneself in the values one feels define the self one is and re-evaluates this again and again – this *is* commitment in relativism (Perry, 1970), Internal Foundation (Baxter Magolda, 2001), self-realisation (van Rossum, Deijkers and Hamer, 1984) and self-defining (Hamer and van Rossum, 2010).

Comments on Kegan

Consistency Hypothesis

This concept refers to the controversial subject of context specificity versus context independence of epistemological development. In simple terms this refers to the question whether people apply the same order of consciousness to all types of domains (e.g. school, parenting, work), or that their order of consciousness varies over domains: one applies the second order in learning languages, but the fourth order in learning science. Kegan holds to the consistency hypothesis, as we do ourselves. This means that people will in principle function at the highest order of consciousness they have reached. However, circumstances can prevent the expression of this highest level and then the pressure felt to "regress" is experienced as unhappiness because "we do not feel 'like ourselves'" (Kegan, 1994, p. 372). In our work we have found similar "unhappiness", or disenchantment, when students with higher levels of thinking about learning and teaching are confronted with "regressed" teaching environments: e.g. lectures from teachers who present facts and do not interact with students in any meaningful way (see chapter 8). This hypothesis is consistent with the position that the characteristics of earlier epistemological ways of knowing can be used as a strategy when required (see the section on revisiting Silence in this chapter) which supports the hierarchical inclusive nature of orders of consciousness. Furthermore, several studies by Schommer-Aikins and colleagues give at least some quantitative support to domain independency of epistemological belief systems such as orders of consciousness (see chapter 4).

Epistemological Development and Learning Skills

In much the same way as Kuhn makes a distinction between values and skills, Kegan sees the evolution of consciousness as more than mastering new mental skills. He holds a developmental perspective on orders of consciousness, meaning that one cannot develop from the second order to the fourth by simply learning (or being taught) the mental skills appropriate for the fourth order. In order to reach the fourth order, people must first "...'outgrow' the second order and, even then, have to pass through the *third* order before they can organize the world in a fourth order way" (Kegan, 1994, p. 187). Kegan quotes a longitudinal study of yearly interviews of 22 adult students, aimed at examining whether, and how, orders of consciousness change over a number of years. As such, this study shows strong likeness to Perry's and Baxter Magolda's longitudinal studies into epistemological development, and the results confirm the developmental perspective. Over the years his subjects move slowly – one order upwards in four years – from one order to the next, displaying a gradual evolution of a mental capacity.

Introducing the Helix as a Picture of Development

The observation that some researchers see little difference between Perry's stage of multiplicity (position 4a) and relativism (position 5) is well known. It is often ascribed to misquoting or misinterpreting these stages. However, we feel that there may be more to this confusion than misinterpretation. In our opinion, there seems to be a swing in focus going on, highlighting similarities between the odd numbered stages and the even numbered stages in our learning teaching conception model. Kegan remarked the same about his model of orders of consciousness. In his 1982 book "The evolving self" he sees each level as a more or less precarious balance between the need for the self to be independent and the need for the self to be a part of a whole, a group. As both yearnings are powerful, each balance is "slightly *im*balanced" (Kegan, 1982, p. 108), so the relative sense of orderliness one experiences at any stage (be it one of Perry's positions, an order of consciousness, or a view on learning and teaching in our own model) is inherently temporary. Thus, development is a dynamic struggle, but there is also progress made. While one seems to revisit certain central themes again and again, there are clear differences in viewpoint, perspective or abstraction level. For instance we can look at the issue of 'opinion':

- in basic dualism (learning-teaching conception 1) one adopts the opinion of Authority without question as this opinion is the "Right" opinion,
- in multiplicity (learning-teaching conception 3) one questions authority's opinion, it becomes important to establish one's own opinion. Here all opinions are equally valid and a person is identified by his opinions,
- in relativism (learning-teaching conception 5) opinions are again important, but now these opinions – although coloured by context – need to be informed, based on evidence and argument, and more importantly a person can have an opinion which can be changed by new evidence.

In this sense development including this swing in focus is in fact better represented by a helix and not a line. Kegan elaborates this and comments that the helix makes "clear the way we revisit old issues but at a whole new level of complexity" (Kegan, 1982, p. 109). In Kegan's model the issues revisited are independence and inclusion, or in more learning oriented and in epistemological terms the more commonly used terms agency and communion. In this sense the first, third and postmodernism order of consciousness focus more on inclusion and communion, and the even numbered orders of consciousness (including reconstructive postmodernism) focus more on agency. In the next chapter, where discussing Schommer's "loose knit" theoretical framework, we see a similar swing in focus between certainty of knowledge and complexity of knowledge (see the second assumption on asynchronous development of epistemological beliefs).

Table 3.6. Relating students' developing learning/teaching conceptions to Baxter Magolda's ERM, Perry's model, Kuhn Epistemological Theories and Kegan's model of orders of consciousness

	Van Rossum-Hamer		*Baxter Magolda 1992a, 2001*	*Perry 1970, 1981, 1988*	*Kuhn 1991, 2000, 2005*	*Kegan 1982, 1994*
	Learning Conception	*Teaching Conception*	*ERM*	*Pilgrim's Progress*	*Epistemological Theories*	*Orders of Consciousness*
1	Increasing knowledge	Imparting clear/well structured knowledge		Basic Dualism (position 1)	Realist	First order
2	Memorising	Transmitting structured knowledge (acknowledging receiver)	Absolute Knowing	Dualism (position 2,3)	Absolutist	Second order
3	Reproductive understanding/ application or Application foreseen	Interacting and Shaping	Transitional Knowing	Multiplicity (position 4a)	Multiplist	Third order Traditionalism
*						
4	Understanding subject matter	Challenging to think for yourself / developing a way of thinking	Independent Knowing	The way they want you to think (position 4b)	Objective Evaluativist	Fourth order Modernism *Self-authorship*
5	Widening horizons	Dialogue teaching	Self-authored knowing	Relativism (position 5)	Conceptual Evaluativist	Fifth order Post-modernism *Self-transforming*
6	Growing self awareness	Mutual trust and authentic relationships: Caring	Internal Foundation	Commitment (position 6 and beyond)		Reconstructive Post-modernism

*) Watershed in epistemological development (van Rossum and Hamer)

Linking Kegan to Van Rossum-Hamer, Baxter Magolda, Perry and Kuhn

In Table 3.6 we have summarised all four epistemological models and linked the stages to those of our revised learning-teaching conception model. In our experience, our reading (and struggle) with Kegan's view on the development of the self has put a new and brighter light on some aspects of our learning-teaching conception model, leading us to a deeper understanding of the different conceptions of learning and teaching. For instance for many years we were puzzled by the seemingly unrelated components of learning-teaching conception 3: how can 'having an opinion' and 'being able to apply later' fit into one constellation of mind? In the third order of consciousness the new capacity to think abstractly links these seemingly disconnected aspects.

Conclusions

In this chapter we have discussed in detail three models that originated from research questions focusing on education, namely the models developed by Baxter Magolda (1992a, 2001, 2004), Belenky et al. (1986/1997) and Perry (1970). In addition we have added two models from outside the educational realm (Kegan, 1982,1994; and Kuhn, 1991). In comparing the outcome categories of these five models we see many more fundamental similarities with our own model than essential differences. To quote William Moore, "there is no compelling evidence that these frameworks in fact define distinct theories. All of these efforts represent important areas of scholarship with respect to intellectual development, but rather than being separate theoretical models they extend and expand descriptions of the same fundamental journey described by Perry's framework" (Moore, 2002, p. 23–24). In underwriting Moore's conclusion about Baxter Magolda's and Belenky et al.'s relationship to Perry's model, we feel it holds as well for our own learning-teaching conceptions model, for Kuhn's epistemological theories and for Kegan's model of orders of consciousness. This seems to point towards the conclusion that our learning-teaching conceptions model has captured an aspect of a more fundamental intellectual development and may have further reaching consequences for society than one would expect at face value. Furthermore, the descriptions of the various outcomes of the other models added aspects to each level or stage, leading to deeper understanding of the fundamental differences between the different epistemological positions and generating thought regarding new avenues of research.

So what does this mean? Firstly, the intellectual development we are referring to is definitely not a development of *what* you know, but about *the way* you know and *how* this influences the perception of reality. Secondly, based on many studies discussed here, we further conclude this development runs through a stepwise increasing of complexity of thinking, where one regularly *revisits* familiar issues perceiving them from an increased level of complexity in *the way* one knows. Furthermore, all stages are assumed to be hierarchically inclusive implying that capabilities of earlier, less complex ways of knowing remain available (to use as a strategy) as development progresses. Skipping a level of complexity, a stage, therefore seems undesirable, which means that if education is used to promote development, it needs to be in an evolutionary fashion (e.g. stepwise introduction of increased complexity) and not a revolutionary fashion (e.g. a shock treatment). The amalgamated model described in Table 3.6 above provides ample diagnostic capabilities to define epistemological entry and exit levels for each step-up in a developmental pedagogy. Thirdly, because changing *the way* you know means disturbing the self (Kegan, 1994) it should be introduced in a teaching-learning environment characterised by sufficient support (to overcome anxiety) and appropriate challenges (to evoke change; Baxter Magolda and King, 2004), preferably distributed throughout the curriculum (e.g. Marra and Palmer, 2004). In this vain, we proposed to substitute the term independent learning – which has been burdened with the impression of student self-sufficiency that has led to so many misunderstandings regarding what to expect of students in a constructivist curriculum – with **mentored learning**, a term addressing both the roles and responsibilities of teacher (mentor) and student (learner) more accurately. There is evidence (reviewed in this chapter and the next) that more sophisticated teaching often does result in a change in students' *way* of knowing – influencing students' learning and study success – but not always in the same degree. One issue seems to be the effect of the nature of instruction/teaching on the success of any developmental curriculum, which means we need to look into teachers' epistemology and its influence on teaching practice, an issue we address in chapter 5. Finally, we suggest that the six-stage model includes the first tier of a second different type of development, namely not focusing on *the way you know* but on *the way to be*: introducing the second development "learning to be" where the focus is existential (chapter 1 and Hamer and van Rossum, 2008). In this second development, of course, knowing is still important, but increasingly how to live *wisely* emerges as a new central theme and rationality and intuition increasingly interweave when making (life) decisions as one chooses to live one's convictions.

Regarding what we learned about each of the six stages through this review we feel that the in-depth description of Silence in particular helped us to understand the non-reflective stance we had noticed before in learning-teaching conception 1. The essential lack of ego-awareness—a retreat into nothingness that goes so far as to "erase" the self—and the lack of any timeline, a future, it all paints a grim picture of existence indeed. Considering the hierarchical inclusiveness of each epistemological position, it is only logical to postulate that silence (as a strategy and often in a less severe form) is not at all uncommon. Furthermore we postulate that silence may have two faces: absolute obedience and power play or violence. Understanding silence and the circumstances that help counter it may prove useful as a theoretical framework for further research into victims of violence or war.

For the second learning-teaching conception the rejection of ambiguity and the inability to read between the lines added to our understanding of miscommunication rife in teaching in higher education and to a deeper understanding of Nostalgia (see chapter 8). For learning-teaching conception 3 the essential issue of socialisation into a culture, a tribe or tradition (third order of consciousness; following a clear external template or formula on how to behave, think and act) clarifies the issue of how students can be taught the discourse of a discipline. An unsatisfactory type of higher education that leads to graduates displaying all outward signs of disciplinary command through the use of correct jargon, without really touching on the type of understanding necessary in order to become truly creative within the discipline.

The two tones of voice within Procedural Knowing clarified the range of approaches to understanding argumentation that make up learning-teaching conception 4. The voice of connected knowing would seem to us essential in teaching to understand the pre- and possibly misconceptions with which students enter the classroom. The challenging and confrontational voice of separate knowing may not create the safe learning environment that emerging Procedural Knowers need to make the full transition from Subjective Knowing to the logic and rational driven perspective characteristic of Procedural Knowing and scientific thought. Our interpretation of the fourth way of knowing differs from that of Baxter Magolda in a few important aspects. We feel that when students admit to feeling pressured into thinking for themselves, it implies that the development of Independent Knowing is *still* dependent on external formulas (or voices of important others, Baxter Magolda, 2001). This means that to us it is only the nature of the formula that has changed in the watershed and that in learning-teaching conception 4 it is not the self that is being authored, but that self-authorship refers to the first time that a conscious self is authoring (i.e. actively participating in) the way it makes sense of reality.

The discussion regarding the nature of self-authorship was particularly helpful in our attempts to delineate the pertinent differences between the higher, constructivist levels of thinking. In order to describe the differences in our own understanding of the concept and that of the research community growing around self-authorship, we needed to delve deeply into the writings of Kegan: self-admittedly not the easiest of authors to understand. In describing the transformations beyond self-authorship, we needed to discuss and rethink our own definitions, at times going back to the original material, and blessing our luck that we had the opportunity of almost 24/7 communication with our co-author. It made this part of our thesis a true learning experience in the separate knowing tradition. Level four thinking refers to thinking about systems of theories within one particular view on reality (for instance within a positivist view of reality with issues such as the nature of truth, replicability and validity). Level five thinking is characterised by keeping more than one system in mind (e.g. mythos and logos or positivist and constructivist views of reality and knowledge) and regarding them in a critical way. Clarity on this essential difference between level 4 and level 5 may do much to understand the current discussion about the nature of self-authoring and when it changes into self-transforming (Kegan in Debold, 2002).

We feel that in discussing in depth the difference between Multiplicity and Relativism we have ironed out an odd wrinkle in the Perry scheme of intellectual development. Relativism is characterised by a rejection of absolutism in all its forms, it thrives on paradox, sharpening one's position through discussion and controversy but it is also characterised by the absence of a true choice between alternative perspectives. It is an openness to the reality of alternative informed views and the option to transform the way you make sense of reality by adopting (even if only temporary) an alternative view (Kegan in Debold, 2002). Multiplicity in turn seems to focus on a personal type of absolutism: all views are real and of equal value because personal experience is absolute. Paradoxes are ignored and discussion is limited to the exchange of personal opinions without amendment. In Multiplicity, adopting another's view is not an option: personal truth rules absolute. Elaborating on the essential difference between these two positions was greatly helped by Kegan's image of a helix-like development. We had noticed ourselves that when moving from odd to even positions, one seemed to be revisiting familiar issues, but seeing them from a new perspective: as Kegan says we view familiar issues from a new level of complexity.

We found it particularly heartening that in at least four of the models discussed here the very rare sixth position was described. As we noted before, we ourselves found only a few handfuls of level-six-thinkers in 25 years. This position is characterised by agency, the decision to stop drifting along and to contribute in some way to progress – be it of the personal self or society. In more recent work, Baxter Magolda would propose this type of thinking as the formal end point of higher education. We feel that this is probably taking the goals of higher education too far. Particularly given the obstacles to fostering student development toward level four thinking and the extreme rarity of this (sixth) type of thinking overall especially within the age group of formal higher education, we would propose to focus on getting all graduates across the watershed and into constructivist thought as ambitious enough for higher education at this time. However, we feel it is certainly necessary to get a better grip on this sixth type of thinking, which may call for a different type of subject to study.

With regard to the goals of higher education it is essential to realise that without higher education even realist and absolutist thinking can persist well into advanced adulthood. This means that the thinking of many people (including even graduates from higher education) does not have the quality that democratic society assumes without question. To change this educational reform needs to choose between focusing on teaching knowledge and skills or promoting epistemological development. Considering that Kuhn found that "Individuals ... must *see the point* of argument, if they are to engage in it." (Kuhn, 1991, p. 201, italicised by us) and that one learns to see the *point* of argument within level four thinking, it would seem that education aiming at learning to think (scientifically) can only succeed once students have crossed the watershed. This means that the focus of education at all levels should be first and foremost on epistemological development and not on knowledge and skills alone.

Finally, the inclusion of two models rooted outside education (Kegan and Kuhn) made connecting the theory with everyday life and society possible. These two latter models not only included very similar (in our opinion identical to our own, although alternatively formulated) systems of epistemological beliefs or ways of knowing, they included clear examples of the ubiquitous demands that the current complex society makes on its participants and that many seem not able to meet. From a societal perspective, it is particularly worrying that so many exit education unable to meet these common demands and that many (around three quarters of the general population) in government and populace alike remain oblivious to this fact.

NOTES

1 Our line of reasoning was confirmed by Marcia Baxter Magolda (personal communication, 2005).

2 Belenky et al. found that within a way of knowing the themes emerging from women's self-descriptions were also present in their descriptions of knowledge, truth, learning and teaching. Many responses give the impression that each new way of knowing is an "epistemological revolution" where many beliefs change more or less simultaneously in a logically coherent direction. This we feel is one way of describing the nature of changes in an epistemological ecology (see chapter 4).

3 Belenky et al. admit to taking on a clearly feminist position in this book, and sometimes this gave a feeling of anachronism (for one of the current authors) and even led to occasional exasperation (for the other).

4 Not all teachers view learning and teaching constructively, see the chapter 5 on Teachers' epistemological beliefs and conceptions of teaching.

5 Heavily selected students in an environment of "teachings which are deliberately founded in a relativistic epistemology" (Perry, 1970, p. 72).

6 In the sense this concept is proposed by Demastes et al., 1995.

7 Checklist of Educational Views (CLEV).

8 Discussion in the sense that opinions are exchanged, without presenting relevant arguments or evidence to support them.

9 Another example is what happens when you have two sticks of chewing gum. If you put them into your mouth one by one, do you then have 2 wads of gum or only 1 (making 1+1=1)?

10 Obviously these considerations are valid for women as well. The masculine pronoun refers to men and women alike in Perry's work, as was customary at the time.

11 William Perry died in January 1998 at the age of 84.

12 Personal communication, 2007. The Perry Network can be reached at www.perrynetwork.org.

13 With the possible exception of e.g. Belenky et al. (1997), who explicitly refer to the difference between positions 3/4a and 4b in discussing Perry's model. "As the student's personal opinion is challenged by a teacher's insistence on evidence and support for opinion, multiplicity yields to *relativism subordinate*, where an analytical evaluative approach to knowledge is consciously and actively cultivated at least in the academic disciplines one is being tutored in, if not in the rest of one's life." (p. 10).

14 Hill (2000) uses these three dimensions in her work: 'dualistic and absolutist thinking', 'sense of personal agency' and 'reflective and critical thinking'.

15 Widick (1977) is an article previously presented at the 1975 APA convention.

16 Päivi Tynjälä, personal communication, 2003.

17 Lee Knefelkamp is "one of the first and most significant translators of Perry's work into educational practice" (Moore, 2002, p. 17).

18 While Widick et al. did not mention their assessment method or instrument, we assume from Stephenson and Hunt (1977) that they used the KneWi. The KneWi later became known as the Measure of Intellectual Development (MID), a production-task measure of epistemological development.

19 From the description in the article it is not clear whether the initial multiplists followed the 'dualist course' or the 'relativist course' and the duration of the course was not mentioned.

20 Each respondent was given a score on a task (scaletype), corresponding to the number of hits for that particular task (a hit meaning that a particular Perry position is comprehended by the subject, see futher in

the text). In addition Kurfiss calculated a 'master' scaletype: per level the summation of hits over tasks. When for a particular level at least 4 our of 5 tasks were 'hits', the level was scored as 'comprehended'.

[21] For a more exhaustive review of applications of the Perry Scheme we would like to refer the reader to Bill Moore at the Center for the Study of Intellectual Development, coordinator of the Perry Network, 1505 Farwell Ct. NW Olympia, WA 98502, USA or to www.perrynetwork.org

[22] The question about the ideal college education was the inspiration for our initial studies into conceptions of 'good teaching' (van Rossum, Deijkers and Hamer, 1985 and van Rossum and Taylor, 1987), and as such correspondence (by 'snail mail') with Bill Moore in the eighties of the previous century lies at the root of our model.

[23] The interviews were rated by Bill Moore.

[24] We feel that this indicates that the authors see learning, teaching and knowledge conceptions as interrelated, as we do ourselves.

[25] The covariate Verbal SAT was also significantly related to the Perry rating.

[26] In the current study similar 'problems' arose and we will discuss these in chapter 7.

[27] This disappearance may be due to sample mortality.

[28] Following Moore (2002), Perry would see such a holding environment as "the student's experience of being *met*..." (p. 32) where development is fostered by 'moments of meeting' or perhaps even the 'meeting of minds'.

[29] Paraphrasing Jean Piaget "Intelligence is knowing what to do, when you don't know what to do."

[30] On the other hand, following the 'glass half-full' perspective, one could conclude that they answer the question partly affirmative.

[31] Three of the categories developed by Kuhn and Weinstock – multiplist, objective evaluativist and conceptual evaluativist – in our opinion show clear similarity to categories developed by Leadbeater (1986) for classifying relativist reasoning – subjective relativist, objective relativist and conceptual relativist.

[32] The person providing the account of the event.

CHAPTER 4

QUANTITATIVE APPROACHES TO EPISTEMOLOGY AND LEARNING

...quantitative assessment of personal epistemology is still in its infancy...

(Schommer-Aikins, 2004)

In this chapter we will discuss the research performed with two internationally well-known and commonly used inventories to measure personal epistemologies and learning styles (or patterns), and a third initially quantitative but increasingly holistic approach. We will focus on the work of Marlene Schommer-Aikins and Jan Vermunt, and discuss also the theory forming of these two researchers who have made large contributions to the body of quantitative research on learning and personal epistemology. Then we discuss Hofer's journey towards a more qualitative and holistic interpretation of her personal theories.The first issue addressed in this chapter touches on reproducibility and validity again. Here we propose that the dimensions of, or positions in, epistemological development identified in our own model and in the five qualitative epistemological models described in the previous chapter are reproduced within these three major more quantitative approaches to personal epistemology and learning. In a sense we are working towards a convergence of outcomes as a form of reproducibility: a primarily pragmatic approach aimed at reconciling the essentially incompatibility of phenomenography with the accepted methodological criteria of mainstream, positivistic research approaches. An integral part of the aim of this chapter is to establish, but now from a quantitative perspective, whether these quantitative models can contribute to our understanding of the epistemological levels of our own model.

Secondly, in the sections following the introduction of each inventory, we discuss a selection of the studies in which each was used. The aim of these sections is to illustrate how the constructs fundamental to the inventories are related to issues important in the teaching-learning process, such as motivation, study strategies, quality of learning outcome, etcetera. Many of these constructs are already part of our learning-teaching model and included with varying emphasis in the models discussed in the previous chapter.

And finally in this chapter, after the qualitative (chapter 3) and quantitative evidence (this chapter) pointing towards the intricate relations between various epistemological beliefs, learning strategies, motivational and affective aspects of learning and consequently the quality of learning outcomes, we introduce the concept of *epistemological ecology*. Firstly this concept, by using the metaphor of the ecology, emphasises the complexity of how epistemology is connected to many other behaviours and approaches relevant to learning and teaching. Secondly, the complexity of an ecology could do much to provide additional insight in the plethora of educational innovation strategies, the multitude of approaches, the many partial or temporary successes and the sometimes disappointing results. We propose that, as in the biological version, an epistemological ecology is often pretty resistant to change and that it is only in relatively fragile ecologies – for instance in the Australian outback – that relatively small-scale changes – such as the introduction of the European rabbit – can lead to considerable and rather abrupt shifts. For more robust ecologies to change it may be necessary to introduce a range of new species or circumstances for a considerable period of time to effectuate any major changes. Furthermore, it is difficult to predict exactly which new species or circumstance will tip the balance towards a new adjusted ecology. It may be much the same for personal epistemology, learning and thus the way we interpret reality.

Schommer

> *If beliefs about knowledge and learning function as filters to the mind, determining what we see, how we interpret the world, which strategies we select to learn, and how long we persist in pursuit of learning, then it would seem critical that we closely examine these filters.*
>
> *Schommer-Aikins, 2004*

Marlene Schommer is probably one of the most influential exponents of quantitative studies into epistemology. Her focus is on epistemological beliefs, beliefs about the nature of knowledge and learning. When she started her research programme, personal epistemology was commonly seen as unidimensional and developing through a fixed progression of stages or positions. Schommer felt that this was a too simplified and narrow view on thinking about the nature of knowledge and learning. Her formulation of personal epistemology as a system consisting of several more or less independent belief dimensions was based primarily on two sources. In 1984 (a) Ryan used a 7-item questionnaire, the Dualism Scale based on Perry's research, to categorise students as dualists or relativists.[1] When asked to describe how they knew that they understood a textbook chapter (comprehension monitoring), dualists described understanding in quantitative terms as being able to recall facts and to recite definitions. Relativists on the other hand, described understanding as being able to paraphrase and to apply text information. Later research was unable to replicate this relationship between epistemology and comprehension monitoring. Schommer interpreted this inconsistency as due to the unidimensional conception of epistemology in Ryan's research approach. We feel another reason his results were not replicated may lie in Ryan's particular interpretation of the students responses in creating the category of comprehension/application. Looking closely at this category one observes that it contains many different levels of comprehension, extremes being "determining the meaning of individual sentences" and "looking for the author's intentions" (Ryan, 1984b, p. 252), implying that it is – to us at least – unclear what type of comprehension is monitored here (van Rossum, Deijkers and Hamer, 1985). A second reason to explore personal epistemology as a more dimensional system, is to be found in Schommer's synthesis of Perry's work with the research of Dweck and Schoenfeld (Schommer, 1990). In Dweck's work she found the differential effects of views on intelligence: it makes quite a difference whether people see intelligence as a fixed ability or as incremental and something that can improved. Schoenfeld's contribution to her thinking was his finding that students believed that mathematical problems were either solvable rather quickly (within 12 minutes) or not at all. The other extreme of the problem solving dimension underlying this latter belief about speed of learning (problem solving), would logically be that problem solving is a gradual process (requiring effort and focus, and sometimes taking a long time). Indeed this is the approach professor Hendrik Lenstra, a leading Dutch mathematician freely admits to: when tackling a difficult problem he breaks it up into smaller ones he feels he can solve in one day. When he fails, he breaks it up again to try again tomorrow (personal communication, November 2008).

Schommer's formulation of a system of epistemological beliefs initially focused on five more or less independent dimensions (each named after the most naïve extreme)[2]:

- Certain Knowledge: the stability of knowledge, conceptions of knowledge run from unchanging to tentative;
- Simple Knowledge: the structure of knowledge, conceptions of knowledge run from isolated "facts" to integrated concepts;
- Omniscient Authority: the source of knowledge, knowledge is handed down by authority as opposed to knowledge is derived from reason and empirical inquiry;
- Quick Learning: the speed of knowledge acquisition, running from quick-all-or-none learning through to gradual learning;
- Innate Ability: the ability to learn, running from fixed at birth through to subject to life-long improvement.

The first three of these dimensions were derived from Perry (e.g. Perry, 1970, contradicting her assertion that Perry's model is uni-dimensional), the fourth from Schoenfeld and the last from Dweck's work. Schommer developed a 63-item questionnaire, where each of the five dimensions was assessed by at least two subsets of items. The dimension Certain Knowledge was assessed with the subsets "avoid ambiguity" and "knowledge is certain" and with items such as "Scientists can ultimately get to the truth". For the dimension Simple Knowledge, two subsets of items were used: "seek single answers" and "avoid integration". An example of one of these items is "When I study I look for specific facts". Omniscient Authority was measured using the two subsets "don't criticise authority" and "depend on authority" with items such as "How much a person gets out of school depends on the quality of the teacher". Innate Ability and Quick Learning were each measured using three subsets: respectively "can't learn how to learn", "success is unrelated to hard work", "ability to learn is innate" and "learning is quick", "learn first time" and "concentrated effort is a waste of time". Examples of the items are (again respectively) "An expert is someone who has a special gift in some area" and "Successful students learn things quickly" (Schommer, 1990).

In her 1990 study she reports that four of the five postulated dimensions were found after factor analysis.[3] The dimension Omniscient Authority – an important concept in Perry's work – was not found as a separate dimension. This analysis supported her multi-dimensional view on personal epistemology, with perhaps four, more or less independent dimensions. Schommer herself in later work acknowledges the limitations of such a quantitative multi-dimensional approach, namely that "unanticipated epistemological dimensions may go undetected" (Duell and Schommer-Aikins, 2001, p. 446).

In the same 1990 study, Schommer further explored possible sources of the epistemological beliefs, such as age, parents' highest level of education, way of upbringing, own level of education, etcetera. She found that these background variables were especially important to two epistemological beliefs: Simple Knowledge and Quick Learning. One of the more interesting findings of this study was that "the more [parents] expect their children to take responsibility in the home and for their own thinking, the more likely children will develop a sophisticated system of epistemological beliefs" (Schommer, 1990, p. 503). This conclusion may be as valid for an (higher) educational environment, where students are not spoon-fed (e.g. Fox, 1983), but are active participants in the teaching learning process. A second, related finding of interest to higher education is that Certain Knowledge was significantly related to the number of classes the students had done in higher education: the more formal higher education completed, the more likely knowledge was seen as tentative.

In 1990, in her second experiment, Schommer studied the relationship between epistemological beliefs and aspects of comprehension. In this study 86 subjects were asked to read one of the following two inconclusive passages: 1) a psychological essay on four plausible theories about aggression with the underlying theme that the 'final' theory would be a synthesis of these first four, or 2) a text about nutrition dealing with controversies regarding the Daily Recommended Allowance (DRA) of Vitamin B-6 and expected health effects. As a measure of interpretation of information, subjects were then required to write a concluding paragraph for the passage that they had read. These concluding paragraphs were scored on

- simplicity-complexity: e.g. giving a single point of view or avoiding drawing a conclusion versus e.g. integration of key points or elaboration on text information, and
- certainty-uncertainty: e.g. people have (or will have) the answer versus uncertainty now or in the future.

As the measure of comprehension, Schommer asked the subjects to complete a 10-item multiple-choice mastery test: questions were on the levels of recognition and application. Finally, she measured comprehension monitoring using confidence ratings: subjects were asked to indicate how confident they were that they had fully comprehended the passage. These ratings were used to derive a 'predicted test score'. By subtracting the actual test score from the predicted test score, an index for 'the illusion of knowing' was constructed, a positive score indicating overestimation of comprehension.

This study resulted in a number of interesting – and to us patently logical – findings, the first of which is that the more subjects believed in quick-all-or-none learning, the more likely they oversimplified conclusions. Secondly, the more students believed in certain knowledge, the more likely they wrote absolute conclusions.

Thirdly, the effects of quick-all-or-none learning and certain knowledge were equally valid for both passage domains, indicating evidence for domain independence. Fourthly, the more subjects believed in quick-all-or-none learning, the lower their performance on the psychology mastery test, indicating low quality comprehension.[4] Finally, quick-all-or-none learning was related to overestimation of comprehension. These results led Schommer to conclude that epistemological beliefs – as social constructions – have clear and distinct effects on comprehension and learning, and that these beliefs explain better *why* people fail to integrate knowledge or fail to monitor comprehension, than 'schema theory' or the concept of metacognition in itself.[5] In conclusion, Schommer makes an important observation here with regard to the role of education in the development of epistemological beliefs "education may be the key to the prevention and intervention of self-defeating epistemological beliefs. ... Indeed, anecdotal evidence suggests that many of the disabling epistemological beliefs that students have by high school have come from the way in which they have been taught.... That the study of epistemological beliefs is important seems undeniable .... With this understanding [of the effects of epistemological beliefs], we can guide students to become students to become thoughtful, persistent and independent learners" (Schommer, 1990, p. 503–504).

In a later study, 1992, Schommer tried to replicate the above presented four-factor structure of her epistemological questionnaire, and – more important for this study – she examined the relationship between epistemological beliefs (in particular Simple Knowledge), the selection of study strategies and aspects of mathematical comprehension. Here we see a strong resemblance to our 1984 study linking learning conceptions with study strategies and learning outcomes (van Rossum and Schenk, 1984). Consistent with our 1984 findings, Schommer's underlying assumption in this study was that "if learners believe that knowledge is simple, that is, that knowledge is best characterized as isolated facts, then learners would engage in study that is consistent with this belief. They would plan to memorize the facts and avoid integrating the facts" (Schommer et al., 1992, p. 435).

In the first 1992 experiment Schommer asked a larger group of higher education students (n=412, in 1990 n=263) to fill in her 63-item questionnaire. The factor analysis based on the mean subset scores, resulted again in a four factor structure that was largely similar to the previous structure (Schommer, 1990). The four factors were generated in the same order, but the first factor was given a different descriptive title because the subset Innate Ability itself did not load highly on this factor: the new name was Externally Controlled Learning. This name we feel indicates a factor that might have a relationship with the teacher dependence aspect of teaching conceptions, this aspect ranging from teacher dependence (and so externally controlled learning) to teacher independence (student controlled learning). The three remaining factors again were Simple Knowledge, Quick Learning and Certain Knowledge.

The second 1992 experiment aimed at examining the relationship between Simple Knowledge, study strategies and (meta)comprehension of statistical texts. Subjects were asked to read a statistical passage on either 1) central tendency and skewed distributions or 2) central tendency and measures of dispersion. This time their comprehension was measured with a 15-item multiple-choice test, with questions on factual knowledge and application. Their comprehension monitoring was measured in the same way as in the 1990 experiment, using the difference between a predicted and an actual test score. Schommer measured study strategy using two categories of learning strategies, 1) an 'information-processing' category emphasising making links and relationships, and 2) an 'test-preparation' category which emphasised memorising and inability to summarise.

Only Simple Knowledge was shown to be related to statistical test performance, the less students believed in Simple Knowledge, the better their performance on the comprehension test. Again only Simple Knowledge was related to comprehension monitoring, the more students believed knowledge to be simple, the greater their confidence in their comprehension (overestimating their performance). These effects remained significant even after the removal of the effects of age and GPA (grade point average). Most important to our study is the role of study strategies in Schommer's 1992 study. Schommer found that Simple Knowledge had direct as well as indirect effects on comprehension: the indirect effect of Simple Knowledge on comprehension was mediated by the learning strategy category 'test-preparation'. Path analysis showed a relation between Simple Knowledge, 'test-preparation' (memorising) and test performance (comprehension), leading Schommer to conclude that "[these] results are consistent with a logical conclusion. If one truly believes that 'knowledge is a mere basket of facts' …, then one would presumably study so as to master lists of facts. Little effort would be made to interrelate these facts" (Schommer et al., 1992, p. 441). In our terminology this is the conclusion that learning seen as memorising is related to a surface level study strategy (van Rossum and Schenk, 1984).

Questions such as "How do these beliefs develop?" or "How do we purposefully influence these beliefs?" are questions Schommer proposed as important, but – at that time – yet unanswered questions relevant to education. In 1993, Schommer proposes that education may influence epistemological beliefs through implementation of a model of epistemological instruction by 1) modelling epistemological outlooks in lectures and discussions, 2) making underpinning epistemological beliefs of a course more explicit by giving clear objectives and using an appropriate type of assessment, and 3) acknowledging incongruent epistemological beliefs as a source of students' failure to perform up to expectation (Schommer, 1993). The study regarding the development of epistemological beliefs is a major theme in her later publications (Schommer et al., 1997; Schommer, 1998). Before discussing these studies we will elaborate upon her 'loose-knit epistemological theory' that represents her stand within the field of epistemological research.

Epistemological Belief System

Schommer (1994, 2002) describes an emerging theory of an epistemological belief system, for which she lists the following underlying assumptions:

1. Personal epistemology is a multi-dimensional system of more or less independent epistemological beliefs, beliefs about the nature of knowledge and learning.

The question automatically following this postulate is pertinent to the number of dimensions or beliefs. Schommer feels that there is sufficient evidence that this number must be more than one, but the exact number is still unclear. Her original expectation of five beliefs has not been confirmed by her own initial research (see above). Jehng et al. (1993) did find five dimensions using a revised and extended version of Schommer's questionnaire. The main difference between Jehng et al. and Schommer's previous expectation lies in the reformulation of Simple Knowledge as Orderly Process.[6] With this reformulation, Jehng et al. seem to focus more on the process of learning and not on knowledge itself. Jehng et al., who see epistemological beliefs shaped by surrounding culture and social contexts, feel that even "these five factors may not cover the entire scope of an individual's beliefs about learning ...[but] appear to reflect the fundamental beliefs individuals may have about learning" (Jehng et al., 1993, p. 26–27). First, we would like to point out that Jehng et al. equal epistemological beliefs to beliefs about learning, as we do. Secondly, the discussion regarding the "right" number of fundamental beliefs might prove to be pointless, especially within a quantitative approach. It is logical that one will not encounter unexpected dimensions using questionnaires specifically designed for an expected (maximum) number of dimensions or beliefs and using items tailored to measure these expected beliefs. To find the unexpected, one needs to explore and one would need a different – more qualitative – approach. We feel that when Jehng at al. remark that quantitative multi-dimensional models provide a better approximation to the structure of epistemological beliefs than qualitative models such as Perry's model, they and Schommer make the mistake of interpreting Perry's model as uni-dimensional. Perry's model is anything but uni-dimensional as each stage or position is described using (in depth and multi-dimensional) self-portraits of subjects in each stage.

2. That epistemological beliefs are more or less independent refers to the fact that these beliefs need not develop in synchrony: people need not be as sophisticated or naïve in all beliefs in the same way concurrently. A well known example Schommer gives is that a person "may strongly believe in complex knowledge ... and simultaneously strongly believe in unchanging knowledge ..." (Schommer, 2002, p. 106).

We have no quarrel with this postulation, as we feel it fits very well with the nature of our fourth learning conception and Perry's position 4b: learning and knowledge are considered as being complex, but still determined by the nature of the discipline. The "way they want you to think" is the fixed external formula (Baxter Magolda, 2001) one must follow to understand the complexity of disciplinary knowledge, the body of which is certain knowledge and not subject to fundamental discussion. A second example Schommer gives for asynchrony, namely people who view knowledge as simple and at the same time uncertain, well describes – we feel – multiplicity or our third learning conception: knowledge is simple in the sense that it is expressed in opinions not based on argument or evidence, but the world must be very uncertain if all opinions – and as such all views on reality – are equally valid. Considering this, Schommer's examples of asychrony have given us new insight into the transitions from learning conceptions 2 through 6: where in learning conception 2, knowledge is simple and certain,

- in the transition to learning conception 3 uncertainty is increased,
- in the transition to learning conception 4 complexity is increased,
- in the transition to learning conception 5 uncertainty is increased again,
- and finally, in the transition to learning conception 6, complexity is increased again.

In this we see a parallel with Kegan's swing from independence to inclusion and back again described in his evolutionary helix (Kegan, 1982, p. 109; and above). From a different perspective one could see this development as "climbing a ladder", keeping a hand on a rung of the ladder (for instance keeping the level of uncertainty more or less constant), while grasping the next, higher rung (increasing the level of complexity) and then keeping complexity more or less constant while increasing the level of uncertainty. In addition we see this as further support for our assertion that qualitative models such as Perry's, Baxter Magolda's and our own are *not* uni-dimensional.

3. Epistemological beliefs are characterised as frequency distributions, rather than as a single point along one dimension.[7] With regard to Certain Knowledge this would mean that a sophisticated subject thinks that most knowledge is uncertain, some is temporarily uncertain, but there are a few certainties in life (such as gravity, and famously death and taxes). A naïve view on certain knowledge would mean most things are certain, and the rest will become certain in time.

Schommer incorporates this assumption in her work by consistently speaking of subjects who "*strongly* believe in" certain knowledge, quick-all-or-none learning, simple knowledge or fixed ability. We do not see a large difference between Schommer's position here and our own interpretation of the development of learning conceptions as expanding awareness of the meaning of learning (Chapter 1). Each transition can be seen as a step out of embeddedness (Kegan, 1994) or can be interpreted as the old foreground becoming background to a new foreground that dominates the new epistemological structure. It is because of this continuous foreground-background reversals that we consciously choose to categorise students' responses at the highest level expressed. We feel supported in this choice by Kegan's observation that people prefer to function at their highest order of consciousness, and being forced to function at lower orders often brings with it feelings of unhappiness and frustration.

4. Epistemological beliefs have direct and indirect effects on (learning) outcomes such as comprehension, metacomprehension, interpretation, persistence and attitude towards learning.

We have discussed this already above in the section about Schommer's studies in 1990 and 1992. Indirect effects may take on a number of forms. For instance, when students view knowledge as simple, this will influence the study strategy students select and their conception of e.g. comprehension. If comprehension is seen as being able to recite facts and definitions, then rehearsing facts and definitions till they are memorised is a logical strategy to follow. If comprehension is seen as being able to integrate evidence and argument, students will need to follow a strategy that will help them be able to meet this standard – in our research we call such a strategy "deep level processing" (van Rossum and Schenk, 1984).

5. Epistemological beliefs are influenced by experience, hypothesised to change over time: Schommer sees teaching and upbringing as the most important influences on possible development of the epistemological belief system.

We have discussed upbringing as a factor above, so we will concentrate on the effects of education (and beyond). In 1993, Schommer reports on a cross-sectional study with high school students where she found that from freshman to senior years, the belief in Simple Knowledge, Certain Knowledge and Quick Learning decreased. Because cross-sectional designs are problematic to truly track developmental processes, Schommer initiated a longitudinal study which she reported in 1997. We will discuss this study in the next section. Jehng et al. (1993) found that graduate students, compared to undergraduate students, believe more strongly that knowledge is uncertain, that students' independent reasoning is crucial for learning and that learning is not an orderly process. Graduate and undergraduate students did not differ with regard to their belief in Innate Ability and Quick Learning. Within the undergraduates, students did not seem to differ at all: for lower cycle undergraduates (freshmen, sophomores) and upper cycle undergraduates (juniors and seniors) no significant differences on any of the five belief dimensions were found. Jehng et al. proposed that the difference between undergraduate and graduate students could be explained by differences in instructional methods. This analysis is supported by Baxter Magolda (2004) where she described the rapid development in epistemological thinking that was brought about by the challenges after the college years, the new experiences in work, personal life and advanced education. The increased speed of development after the college years was in sharp contrast to the extremely gradual transformation in thinking that Baxter Magolda found in her earlier study concerning development in the college years. This brought her to the following conclusion: she "now view[s] existing developmental models as descriptions of how contexts have shaped young adults (in interaction with young adults' current meaning-making) rather than as descriptions of what is possible in terms of developmental growth" (Baxter Magolda, 2004, p. 39). With this she implies that a conscious choice for a different, more constructivist curriculum might indeed speed up the epistemological development of students. In later chapters we will return to this issue.[8]

6. Epistemological beliefs are domain independent.

In contrast to a number of researchers, Schommer believes that epistemological beliefs are strongly domain independent. We have always had this same opinion about conceptions of learning and teaching, as we see their development in our model as inclusive of lower level conceptions. This implies that people with more sophisticated ways of thinking are able to fall back on lower levels of thinking – using them as a strategy – when context appropriate, but that people with more naïve beliefs are restricted in their ways of thinking and acting (van Rossum et al. 2002; Kegan, 1994). In studies trying to influence study strategies to lower or deeper levels of processing, e.g. Marton and Säljö (1984), it is often found that subjects can be easily influenced to function at a lower level (surface level processing), but it is extremely hard to influence all to perform at a more sophisticated level (such as deep level processing).[9] Taking the potential flexibility of students with sophisticated epistemological beliefs into account, these students are in principle able to respond to possible domain differences. For students with naïve beliefs, there is much less potential for domain specific behaviour, they will use mostly the same strategies in all domains.

On the other hand, there are studies (e.g. Jehng et al. 1993) that seem to point towards domain dependence. When for instance students of soft fields (social science or humanities) are compared to students of hard fields (engineering or business), the latter seem to believe more strongly in the certainty of knowledge, are less reliant on their own independent reasoning, and believe more strongly that learning is an orderly process (Jehng et al. 1993). This (type of) finding – in our opinion – may be more an artefact due to differences in teaching than a reflection of epistemological domain differences. In other words, hard fields may emphasise memorising formulas and using them as algorithms in standard situations ignoring conceptual understanding until very late in formal education, while teachers in the soft fields may be more aware of the tentativeness of the knowledge within their field and the ill-structuredness of the problems they present. These differences in teaching methods may be more fundamental to differences in the 'image' of a domain, while – from an expert view – differences in epistemology between domains may actually be small to non-existent.

After proposing her theory in 1994, Schommer published two studies directly addressing the issue of domain (in)dependence of epistemological beliefs (Schommer & Walker, 1995; Schommer-Aikins et al., 2002). In a sense this issue is similar to the recurring question: are epistemological beliefs in principle contextually dependent or are they more like an individual characteristic open to development (our position). In our view the perception of the context is itself influenced by the individual's epistemological beliefs, while at the same time the perceived context may influence the development of an individual's epistemological beliefs. This shows, we feel, that it is not a question of either/or, but both influencing each other in an iterative process. In Schommer and Walker (1995) the research question "Do individuals have similar epistemological beliefs across content domains?" was addressed by comparing the results of college undergraduates who filled in Schommer's questionnaire twice: once with social sciences in mind, and once with mathematics in mind. The domains social sciences and mathematics were chosen because these were perceived (by the authors at that time) as opposites: social sciences being characterised as more ill-structured and mathematics being characterised as more well-structured. To establish the similarity (or dissimilarity) of the students' epistemological beliefs between the two domains, Schommer and Walker used three indicators:

- the inter-domain correlations between corresponding epistemological beliefs: in the case of domain independence these are expected to be high,
- the inter-domain consistency of the level of epistemological sophistication,
- the inter-domain consistency in the prediction of performance on text comprehension.

In their first experiment Schommer and Walker found that corresponding epistemological beliefs predicted each other best: e.g. a student's belief in Simple Knowledge in social sciences was best predicted by his/her belief in Simple Knowledge in mathematics. These results lead Schommer and Walker to conclude that "[t]here appears to be a substantial relationship between corresponding epistemological beliefs across different domains" (p. 427). For the four epistemological beliefs Schommer and Walker found that the majority of the students had a consistent level of epistemological sophistication. The range varied from 68% of the students being consistent between domains in their belief in Certain Knowledge, to 79% being consistent with regard to their belief in Fixed Ability.

In a second experiment the instruction to keep a specific domain in mind while completing the questionnaire was improved, and the design included a control group. The control group filled in the questionnaire twice as well, but kept the same domain (social sciences) in mind both times. In the experimental group again the correlations between corresponding epistemological beliefs were much higher than the correlations between non-corresponding beliefs. However, the correlations between corresponding epistemological beliefs in the control group (test-retest correlations) were sometimes comparable to the correlations in the experimental group (Fixed Ability and Quick Learning) while the test-retest correlations for Simple Knowledge and Certain Knowledge were much higher. Schommer and Walker concluded from this that "it suggests that although students' beliefs are similar across domains, support is not provided for a strong domain-independent hypothesis" (p. 429). In this second experiment as well, a large measure of consistency was found for the level of epistemological sophistication, but lower than in the first experiment. In this second experiment Schommer and Walker explicitly addressed the prediction of test performance based on epistemological beliefs characteristic for the two domains. Test performance on a social science text was best predicted by the belief in Certain Knowledge in the social sciences or the belief in Certain Knowledge in mathematics: the less students believed in Certain Knowledge the better their performance. Test performance on a mathematics text was best predicted by the belief in Simple Knowledge in mathematics or the belief in Simple Knowledge in the social sciences: the less students believed in Simple Knowledge, the better their performance. This result indicated again that epistemological beliefs are predominantly similar across domains.

In the discussion, Schommer and Walker drew a number of conclusions worth mentioning here because of their relevance to our work and for teaching in higher education (1995, p. 430):

1. "For now, it appears that researchers may assume that epistemological beliefs tend to be domain independent among college students in their early years.

2. [T]eachers may well assume that students showing epistemological naiveté in one discipline may *also* be showing similar epistemological naiveté in other disciplines (italics ours).
3. [E]pistemological beliefs are most likely being modified by classroom interactions."

Schommer and Walker concluded their paper saying "If we want students to be thoughtful, independent thinkers and yet we teach them lists of facts as if they are immutable, then we may be instilling philosophical systems in students that resist our own teaching objectives" (p. 430). We concur with all points made here, with one exception: we believe that epistemological beliefs will remain domain independent as college students progress through college and as people progress through life after college (see Chapter 3). Regardless, Schommer's work (Schommer-Aikins et al., 2002 and Schommer-Aikins, 2004) shows that epistemological beliefs are socially constructed, dependent on experiences in various social contexts (school, culture, etcetera). This realisation may be the reason that Schommer proposed the "Embedded Systemic Model" to be discussed below.

Schommer and Walker's conclusion that epistemological beliefs are "moderately domain general" was criticised with regard to the choice of the two domains examined. In Biglan's classification system of academic disciplines (Schommer-Aikins et al., 2002, p. 351), mathematics and social sciences are both similar along the "pure-applied" classification dimension and so are less opposites than assumed in 1995. In Biglan's classification system these disciplines are both seen as pure while they differ only with regard to the classification dimension "hard-soft". To more rigorously test domain (in)dependence of epistemological beliefs, Schommer-Aikins et al. (2002) not only compared mathematics with social sciences, but also compared mathematics with business which is classified as soft and applied. In this way mathematics is compared with a discipline that differs on two dimensions. In the case of the domain business the students were asked to fill in the questionnaire while thinking about business, such as finance and accounting. If the Biglan classification system includes epistemologically significant differences between domains, and business is indeed more different from mathematics than social sciences, then the inter-domain correlations between corresponding epistemological beliefs for mathematics and business would be smaller than the same correlations for mathematics and social sciences. On the other hand, if epistemological beliefs are more or moderately domain independent, then the inter-domain correlations of corresponding epistemological beliefs would be significant and there would be no significant difference between the results for mathematics and social sciences, and the results for mathematics and business. The experiment was based on an identical design as the 1995 study and the results supported the hypothesis that epistemological beliefs are (moderately) domain general or independent. It is interesting to note that the inter-domain correlations between mathematics and business – contrary to the expectation – tended to be stronger than the correlations between mathematics and social sciences. In their discussion, Schommer-Aikins et al. raised the question whether researchers should continue to explore domain (in)dependence, or that they should reframe the research question towards a new perspective: "What is the *breadth of applicability* of epistemological beliefs" (Schommer-Aikins et al. 2002, p. 363). This is precisely the question we raise in chapter 3, and based on the models discussed there we feel that epistemological beliefs have a very broad range of influence on education (learning and teaching) and everyday life.

In addition to domain (in)dependence Schommer-Aikins et al. (2002) raise two issues that link her work to quantitative, questionnaire-based research into learning conceptions and learning strategies done in the Netherlands by Jan Vermunt. We will discuss Vermunt's work in the second section of this chapter. The first link can be made through their description of research showing that more naive epistemological beliefs are related to a lack of self-regulated learning and lack of intrinsic motivation. The second link to Vermunt's work is the reference to discrepancy between epistemological beliefs of faculty members and students, which when large, may affect academic performance negatively, a so-called "destructive friction" (Vermunt and Verloop, 1999). Schommer-Aikins et al. feel that an optimal educational experience is reached when epistemological beliefs of staff and students are in synchrony, thereby disregarding the option that some discrepancies can lead to "constructive frictions" (Vermunt and Verloop, 1999) or "holding environments" (Kegan, 1994) necessary for epistemological development.

Embedded Systemic Model

In 2004 Schommer-Aikins revisited her 1994 model, placing it in a broader perspective. In this article she seemed to be moving away somewhat from her earlier more analytical approach – e.g. examining the character and influences of specific beliefs within the epistemological belief system – towards a more holistic perspective on the place of her epistemological belief system as a "system-among-other-systems". In this sense, her thinking is becoming more aligned with the qualitative holistic approaches characteristic of the original work of Perry (1970), Baxter Magolda (1992a, 2001) and our own work (e.g. 1984, 1985). For instance in our initial work (van Rossum and Schenk,1984) we linked learning conceptions directly to study strategies and learning outcomes, as well as to (conceptions of) a number of concepts significant in the educational environment (van Rossum, Deijkers and Hamer, 1985). In our approach we never perceived a student's learning conception as a separate conception, but always as one aspect of a multitude of related conceptions. In our view (see chapter 1) the learning conception is only one manifestation of a far more complex systemic development.

In 2004, Schommer placed her epistemological belief system in an Embedded Systemic Model (ESM) where as she postulates various interactions between systems occur. At this time she included in the ESM – besides the epistemological belief system - belief systems such as:

- Cultural relational views
- Beliefs about learning
- Beliefs about ways of knowing
- Classroom performance
- Self-regulated learning

The ESM supposes direct and indirect interactions between systems within a particular student. For instance it supposes that there is a relationship between cultural relational views and epistemological beliefs: "Less sophisticated learners assume a strong hierarchical relationship to experts. That is, they assume that knowledge was handed down to them by omniscient authority. More sophisticated learners are able to relate to experts on a more level plane of status. They assume knowledge comes from empirical evidence and reason, activities the they themselves are capable of pursuing" (Schommer-Aikins, 2004, p. 25). In our opinion Schommer here describes the relationship between students' learning and teaching conceptions as we have described in chapter 1. A second example is given by Schommer, where she proposes a relationship between cultural relational views and conceptions of assessment: "... a student whose dominant framework of relationship is that of a level playing field might view as unfair a teacher who assigns grades using a norm-reference system. In contrast this student might view as fair a teacher who uses a criterion-referenced system to determine how much a student knows. On the other hand, a student whose dominant framework of relationships is that of a hierarchy might view a teacher who assigns grades using a norm-referenced system as giving the best graders to those who deserve it based upon a ranking system. In contrast this student might view a unfair a teacher who assigns grades using a criterion-referenced system that fails to distinguish between average and excellent students" (Schommer-Aikins, 2004, p. 24–25). Although this second example includes a new belief not discussed in any of Schommer's ESM systems, namely the belief (or conception) about assessment, we feel this example highlights an interesting link to our ongoing research into linking conceptions of learning, teaching and assessment. Based on these two examples, the main difference between her perspective and our own is that we perceive (and examine) these relationships as logically consistent, representing an underlying systemic development, where Schommer feels the relationships are not self-evident and need to be established by means of for instance path models and structural equation models.

In addition to the presupposed interactions between systems, Schommer discerns possible feedback mechanisms through reciprocal interactions. Such a feedback mechanism could play a role in epistemological development, for instance " ... if the teacher encourages critical thinking and careful evaluation of expert assertions [the teacher's classroom performance system], learners may revise their beliefs about the certainty of knowledge [the learner's beliefs about knowledge system], which in turn my reduce their unquestioning acceptance of an expert's word [the learner's cultural relational view system], which ultimately lessens their passivity as learners [the learner's beliefs about learning system and the learner's classroom performance system]" (Schommer-Aikins, 2004, p. 26). We added the systems involved in this example and in doing this we show that the ESM is even more complex if one discerns the systems of the teacher and the student separately. If then we go even further, as Schommer with her ESM model does, we need to look at the interactions not only within a student, but also at the interactions between various system holders (learner, peers, family and teachers).

This all seems making the study of epistemological beliefs, their antecedents and consequences, increasingly - and perhaps even too - complex to pursue. This conclusion lead Schommer to suggest a coordinated teams approach to the quantitative study of epistemological beliefs.

Schommer-Aikins raises in her discussion of the ESM a number of questions that she feels need yet to be answered. Here, in our opinion she is too pessimistic about the state of the art regarding research on epistemological beliefs and the – we feel strongly linked - conceptions of learning (see chapter 1). The questions about how self-concept is related to beliefs about knowledge and beliefs about learning are discussed at length (but not quantified) in Baxter Magolda's book of 2001. The question whether epistemologically sophisticated students rebel when placed in an instructional situation that demands memorising without meaning has been confirmed in our own work (van Rossum, Würffel and Hamer, 2002). This rebelling we refer to as "disenchantment" and we will discuss this phenomenon (and nostalgia) at length later (chapter 8). Lastly, a question referring to the relationship between epistemological beliefs and other aspects of cognition and affect will be discussed in the sections below on other reserarch using the EBQ and "Comments on Schommer" using the studies of Paulsen and Feldman (Paulsen and Feldman, 1999a, 1999b, 2005, 2007 in press).

Developments in epistemological beliefs. As mentioned above (see assumption 5) developments are best studied using longitudinal designs. In 1997 Schommer reported on a study regarding the epistemological development of 69 high school students who filled in her 63-item questionnaire twice during their high school period, in 1992 and 1995 (Schommer et al., 1997). Her expectation here was to confirm her assumption that epistemological beliefs develop over time. Analyses showed that over time, students became more mature on all four epistemological beliefs. Their belief in Fixed Ability, Simple Knowledge, Certain Knowledge and Quick-all-or-none Learning decreased significantly. An interesting finding was that as girls progress through high school, they were less likely to believe in quick-all-or-none learning than boys, which might indicate that they feel more strongly that effort is a part of learning. The belief in Quick-all-or-none Learning had a direct effect on students' GPA (Grade Point Average): the less students believed in quick-all-or-none learning, the better their grade.

In a second study with an adult sample, Schommer examined the development of epistemological beliefs during adulthood and the separate influences of age and education (Schommer, 1998). The sample of 418 subjects contained adults from all walks of life (170 different occupations) with a mean age of 37.5. The respondents were more or less equally distributed over three education levels (no more than secondary, undergraduate and graduate education). A first result was the confirmation of the four-factor structure that was found for adolescents and college students, with the annotation that the order of the first two factors was reversed. In this study age appeared to be related to Fixed Ability: the older the subjects, the less likely they were to believe that the ability to learn is fixed at birth. Education had an effect on both Simple Knowledge and Certain Knowledge: the more years of formal education, the less likely the subjects were to believe in certain and simple knowledge. According to Schommer, the practical significance of these findings lie in the effects of particular epistemological beliefs on behaviour:

- Should adults persist in their belief that the ability to learn is fixed at birth, confronted with difficulties in school, work or home life, they will give up more quickly and so be less successful in life.
- When adults persist in their belief that knowledge is simple and certain, the less they are able to acknowledge the complexity and tentative nature of everyday issues, and so they will oversimplify and compartmentalise information, limiting their understanding and their performance on complex tasks.[10]

The question regarding how in particular education can be structured to influence the development of epistemological beliefs – Schommer calls this "epistemologically sound instruction" – is discussed by Beers (1988). Beers expects that some development can be reached through two processes: modelling of epistemological attitudes and reinforcing desired epistemological attitudes (and punishing the undesirable attitudes) through grading of academic work. Beers concludes that her analysis suggests that "teachers' educational goals are most likely to be met when the teacher attends closely to the epistemological integrity of his or her courses. Teachers who are aware of their own conceptions of knowledge and who monitor the articulation of those conceptions with the day-to-day activities of the classroom will stand the best chance of influencing students in a manner which is consonant with their primary educational objectives" (Beers, 1988, p. 92). However, Beers' comment about the finding that college teachers – as their students – display the full range of Perry's positions, we feel implicates that not all teachers have the epistemological sophistication to teach at the level necessary to promote epistemological development. We will return to this issue in the chapter on teacher thinking.

Epistemological beliefs and coping with (everyday) controversial issues. Schommer directly examined the way adults cope with contemporary controversial issues following a similar experimental design Kuhn (1992) used in her studies regarding argumentive skills (Schommer-Aikins and Hutter, 2002). Schommer asked 174 adults from all walks of life, ages ranging from 17 to 71, to respond to questions about two controversial and ill-structured issues discussed recently in the local newspaper: gender differences in conversation style and abortion. In contrast to Kuhn, Schommer used her 63-item questionnaire as a truly independent measure of epistemological beliefs, and assessed whether epistemological beliefs predicted (the level of) thinking about everyday controversial issues. Subjects were not only asked to give their opinion, but to explain how they reached it. These essays in answer to – in total six – open-ended questions regarding the two issues were scored with regard to six largely independent[11] "thinking dispositions": 1) taking multiple perspectives, 2) acknowledging the complexity of issues, 3) engaging in flexible thinking, 4) acknowledging the evolving nature of knowledge, 5) questioning omniscient authority, and 6) making decisions in a thoughtful and reflective way (Schommer-Aikins and Hutter, 2002, p. 9). These measures of everyday thinking were significantly correlated only with the epistemological beliefs Certain Knowledge and Simple Knowledge. Both beliefs are related to 'taking multiple perspectives', 'acknowledging the complexity of issues' and 'making decisions in a thoughtful and reflective way': the less subjects believed in simple or certain knowledge, the more likely they were to take on multiple perspectives, acknowledge the complexity of issues and make decisions in a reflective way. Two further logical results were that Certain Knowledge was also negatively correlated to acknowledging the evolving nature of knowledge and that Simple Knowledge was negatively related to engaging in flexible thinking. These results support the expectation that there is a significant and positive relationship between more sophisticated epistemological beliefs and higher order thinking in day-to-day life.

The implication for secondary and undergraduate education is profound: "that controversy in the classroom is not only inevitable but desirable" (Schommer-Aikins and Hutter, 2002, p. 17). Consequently, education should explicitly include major controversies inherent in the disciplines and teachers should not present the curriculum as an orderly narrative of certain facts and fixed procedures.

We agree with Schommer and Hutter that these findings support as well the critical need for further research into the implications of epistemological beliefs for everyday life: "Understanding the implicit presence and influence of epistemological beliefs in everyday life will provide a knowledge base to enhance communication and public education about complex, ill-structured contemporary issues" (Schommer-Aikins and Hutter, 2002, p. 18).

Further Research using the EBQ

In this section we discuss a number of studies that have focused on linking factors such as Certain Knowledge, Simple Knowledge and Fixed Ability to other concepts related to learning. Our aim here is to illustrate through quantitative research the complex interrelations and multi-dimensionality of the epistemological outcome space found through the six qualitative models discussed in chapters 1 and 3.

Research with Schommer's Epistemological Belief Questionnaire (EBQ) using performance measures

In order to examine the effects of epistemological beliefs, the need for cognition (a tendency to engage in and enjoy complex effortful thinking) and the strength of initial beliefs regarding a controversial issue on the interpretation of conflicting information, Carolanne Kardash and Roberta Scholes (1996) designed a study where they asked 96 undergraduates to read an inconclusive dual-positional text on a controversial issue, the relationship between HIV and AIDS. The text consisted of a number of paragraphs either supporting or opposing the view that HIV is the sole cause of AIDS, but lacked a final conclusion paragraph. Based on this text, students were asked to write a conclusion paragraph for a potential reader. In this study, epistemological beliefs were measured using a shorter, 42-item version of Schommer's EBQ, focusing on items related to beliefs about certainty and structure of knowledge and the speed of knowledge acquisition. In this way 11 subsets of Schommer's original EBQ remained and in deviation of the original procedure, students answered the items on a 7-point Likert scale. The conclusion paragraph was rated for degree of certainty exhibited, resulting in the following relevant categories "certain", "tentative" and "ambiguous". In the analysis, Kardash and Scholes used the same procedure as Schommer to factor analyse their shortened EBQ, resulting in four factors: Quick Learning, Certain Knowledge, Innate Ability and Depend on Authority. Kardash and Scholes felt that the shortened EBQ yielded: "a factor structure that fairly closely approximates those obtained by Schommer" (Kardash and Scholes, 1996, p. 264). Based on a simultaneous multiple regression analysis, the scores on the conclusion task proved to be best predicted by Certain Knowledge, the strength of initial HIV-AIDS beliefs and the Need for Cognition score: "... the less that people believed in certain knowledge, the less extreme their initial beliefs regarding the HIV-AIDS relationship, and the more they enjoyed engaging in cognitively challenging tasks, the more likely they were to write conclusions that accurately reflected the inconclusive, tentative nature of the mixed evidence they read" (Kardash and Sholes, 1996, p. 269). With regard to epistemology, this result means the more people believe in certainty of knowledge, the more likely they are to incorrectly interpret, distort or even ignore tentative or contradictory information. This result is fairly consistent with the results of Schommer's second experiment reported in Schommer (1990) and discussed before.

In a second study, Kardash and Karen Howell (2000) studied the effects of epistemological beliefs and topic-specific beliefs (regarding the relationship HIV-AIDS) on the type and frequency of undergraduate students' strategies when reading the same dual-positional text as used in the study discussed above. To examine how epistemological and topic-specific beliefs influence the reading strategies, they asked 40 undergraduate students to "express all thoughts out loud the moment they come to mind" while reading the dual-positional text (a think-aloud procedure; Kardash and Howell, 2000, p. 526). Again epistemological beliefs were measured using the shortened 42-item EBQ in the same way as before. The think-aloud protocols were analysed in terms of 7 categories: developing awareness, accepting ambiguity, establishing intrasentential ties, establishing intersentential ties, using background knowledge, judgment/decision and inaccurate text processing (examples given in Kardash and Howel, 2000, p. 535). In addition, the students delayed free recall of the text was tested one day after the reading task. A four factor analysis of the shortened EBQ based on a larger sample of 288 undergraduates resulted in factors that were quite different from the factors Kardash and Scholes found in 1996 or found by Schommer: Nature of Learning (emphasising that learning is unambiguous and based on passive acceptance of knowledge), Speed of Learning (emphasising that learning is quick), Certain Knowledge (now the third factor, emphasising that knowledge can be known with certainty) and Avoid Integration (emphasising memorising separate facts).[12] Regarding the relationship between epistemological beliefs and strategy use, only

Speed of Learning influenced the overall frequency of the various strategies used: students holding more sophisticated beliefs used more strategies overall. With regard to the relationship between epistemological beliefs and the type of strategy used, Speed of Learning was associated with three main reading strategies (developing awareness, establishing intrasentential ties and inaccurate text processing), Certain Knowledge was associated with two strategies (establishing intersentential ties, inaccurate text processing). Furthermore, Speed of Learning was related to the number of distortions in delayed free-recall: the more students believed in quick learning, the higher the number of distortions in their free recall. Kardash and Howell concluded that "it is primarily one set of beliefs—those related to beliefs about the speed and effort involved in learning—that are clearly related to strategy use, and their effect appears to be more quantitative than qualitative" (Kardash and Howell, 2000, p. 533). In 2004, Sinatra and Kardash studied the influence of students' epistemological beliefs on their openness for *teaching as persuasion* as a metaphor for conceptual change pedagogy (addressing misconceptions, alternative beliefs etcetera).[13] In this study, they used the Epistemological Beliefs Survey (EBS) developed by Wood and Kardash (2002). The EBS is based in part on modified items of Schommer's EBQ. In this section we discuss only studies using (parts of) the EBQ, consequently, we will not discuss this study here.

Gaoyin Qian and Donna Alvermann (1995, 2000) describe their study using Schommer's EBQ to examine the influence of epistemological beliefs and learned helplessness on secondary school students' conceptual change learning. Qian and Alvermann's contribution is interesting because it extends epistemological belief research into the realm of secondary schooling. In their 1995 experiment Qian and Alvermann asked 212 in majority European American high school students from science classes (average age approx. 17) to fill in the 53-item EBQ revised for high school students, a 10-item Learned Helplessness questionnaire addressing students' attributions of failure (to lack of effort) and a Prior Knowledge Test regarding students' existing knowledge about Newton's first law of motion. The latter test was used to classify students into three groups: those only needing to add new information to their existing knowledge (accretion group), those requiring change to some misconceptions (tuning group) and a group of students with considerable misconceptions and lacking knowledge (restructuring group). During the experiment, two weeks later, the students read a refutational expository text on Newton's first law of motion. This text directly confronted misconceptions of Newton's first law of motion, in particular it contradicted the impetus theory. To measure conceptual change learning, after reading the text followed by a short break, students completed an Achievement Test comprising a Conceptual Understanding Test and an Application Reasoning Test.

Factor analysis of the items of the EBQ resulted in the elimination of another 21 items, resulting in a revised 32-item EBQ. This revised EBQ yielded a three factor model: Learning is quick (Quick Learning), Knowledge is simple and certain (Simple-Certain Knowledge), Ability to learn is innate (Innate Ability). A canonical correlation analysis was performed for the whole group as well as for the tuning and restructuring groups separately. The overall analysis indicated that conceptual change learning was mainly influenced by Simple-Certain Knowledge and (somewhat less by) Quick Learning: students believing more strongly that knowledge is simple and certain and learning is quick "are less likely to relinquish their naive theories in conceptual change learning" (Qian and Alvermann, 1995, p. 288). The analogous analysis performed on the tuning and the restructuring groups yielded similar results, indicating that the influence of epistemological beliefs on conceptual change learning is independent from (the accuracy of) prior knowledge. Consequently, Qian and Alvermann suggest that instructional strategies to improve conceptual change learning need to focus on developing more sophisticated epistemological beliefs. In 2000, Qian and Alvermann proposed four teaching strategies they feel could promote epistemological development: criss-crossing the landscape, reflective inquiry, images of scientists' activities and teachers' epistemological objectives. We will return to these teaching strategies where we discuss the ways to changing teaching and learning (chapter 10).

Addressing the remark that most of the research into epistemological beliefs is based on mostly European American students within Western-styled school cultures, Qian and Pan (2002) designed and described a study in which they examined the influence of different cultural backgrounds on the relationship between epistemological beliefs, goal orientations (motivational orientations) and conceptual change learning. While they indicated that they compared a sample of American and Chinese students, in fact they were comparing Chinese students to a mixed sample of predominantly African, Hispanic and Asian Americans.[14] The latter sample contained representatives of three cultural subsets within the American mainstream culture with possible distinct characteristics different from Qian and Alvermann's earlier sample of European Americans. This design made a number of cross-cultural comparisons possible, European (EA) vs. Non-European Americans (NEA), NEA vs. Chinese and implicitly EA vs. Chinese as well. This experiment was almost identical to the 1995 study, the largest difference lying in the substitution of the Learned Helplessness Test with a Goal Orientation Questionnaire, developed from the Motivated Strategies for Learning Questionnaire (MSLQ; García Duncan and McKeachie, 2005). The study showed that Chinese students believed more strongly in Simple-Certain Knowledge and Innate Ability than NEA, while the two groups did not differ with regard to Quick Learning. These differences Qian and Pan suggested could be explained by the influence of the Chinese school culture – relying on authority, lacking in exposure to multiple viewpoints, discouraging assertiveness and asking questions – and the highly selective process within Chinese education – implying that success is only possible when you are born smart. The NEA sample was more performance goal oriented (extrinsic motivation aimed at good grades). In addition, regression analysis showed a moderate relationship between epistemological beliefs and motivational goals: the more naive the epistemological beliefs, the more performance oriented students were, a finding that is consistent with Paulsen and Feldman (1999a, 2005). A third finding of this study referred to the influence of epistemological beliefs and motivational goals on conceptual change learning. For the NEA sample the results of this study affirmed the finding of 1995: the more students had immature beliefs about knowledge, the less likely they were to relinquish their naive theories about Newton's first law of motion, with the difference that in this sample Innate Ability played a more important role than in the 1995 study. The emergence of Innate Ability in this sample may perhaps imply "a different theoretical model of epistemological beliefs for non-white American high school students in conceptual change learning" (Qian and Pan, 2002, p. 381). In this sample performance goal orientation was positively related to conceptual change learning: students committed to performance goals were more likely to overcome their naive theories. The latter finding was somewhat surprising, as literature based on studies with EA students seemed to indicate that the more students were performance goal oriented the less likely they were to experience conceptual change learning. Comparing the NEA sample with the Chinese students, it is interesting to note that for the Chinese students neither epistemological beliefs nor performance goals were related to conceptual change learning. One explanation suggested by Qian and Pan could be the cultural bias in the EBQ, making it an inappropriate measure for Chinese (and perhaps also non-white American) epistemological development. This would mean that the items of the EBQ need to be adapted to address the specific (school) culture the students experience. The effect pattern of the refutational text on conceptual change learning was similar in both samples studied, indicating that this effect was independent of cultural background. Qian and Pan concluded that "this particular kind of [refutational] text facilitates conceptual change learning not only among American students, but also students in China despite their immature beliefs about learning and knowledge" (Qian and Pan, 2002, p. 381).

Epistemological Beliefs and performance: well-structured versus ill-structured problems

The studies above suggest – and even claim – that more sophisticated epistemological beliefs predict better academic performance on a variety of tasks. However, one can wonder whether this is true of *all* kinds of academic tasks. Is it indeed the case that students with very sophisticated beliefs with regard to the certainty or complexity of knowledge are better at memorising foreign words or answering factual multiple choice questions? Or is there a class of problems that are more sensitive to differences in epistemological beliefs? Kitchener (1983) recognises two major classes of problems, well-structured problems or puzzles and ill-structured problems more relevant to everyday life and decision making. A problem is a puzzle when there is one right answer or solution, which always can be found by applying a particular formula or using a specific rule-based procedure/algorithm. An ill-structured problem on the other hand does not have a single right answer or only one clearly appropriate procedure to use. Ill-structured problems characteristically have many possible answers, depending on evidence and perspective, e.g. what is a good solution for one may be the worst solution for another. Examining the way people go about solving problems, Kitchener proposes a three-level model of cognitive processing:

- the first level refers to cognitive strategies such as reading, memorising, etcetera,
- the second level is metacognition referring to

  - selecting an appropriate strategy (Is memorisation sufficient for this task? Do I need formula A or formula B?) and
  - monitoring the progress (How well have I memorised the facts? Have I found the right answer with this formula?),
- the third level is epistemic cognition.

According to Kitchener, in principle the first two levels of cognition are sufficient to solve puzzles. The third level of cognition Kitchener calls 'epistemic cognition' which "has to do with reflections on the limits of knowledge, the certainty of knowledge and the criteria for knowing" (Kitchener, 1983, p. 230) and Kitchener feels this level of cognition is essential to monitor the progress while solving ill-structured problems. As such, epistemic cognition refers to the developmental stage models described in chapter 3. As absolutists (Perry position 2/3) assume that knowledge is certain and truth is absolute, monitoring their progress will focus on finding the right answer to – or *reproducing* the right procedure for – puzzles and ill-structured problems alike, and it is likely that their solutions to ill-structured problems may not always be well thought through and balanced. Put even more strongly, "As long as individuals assume that a single, correct answer exists for all problems, they cannot consider the possibility that no answer may ever be recognized as universally correct for some problems" (Kitchener, 1983, p. 226). On the other hand, relativists (Perry position 5) can differentiate between puzzles and ill-structured problems, because they accept that – for some problems – there may be more than one answer (or even none) depending on evidence and perspective. The possibility of multiple answers implies that the value of all these possible answers should be considered: for these students this "concession [to multiple answers] precludes the mechanical application of a particular strategy and suggests that the individual must develop a strategy to *construct* a solution" (Kitchener, 1983, p. 226, italics ours). Rephrasing the difference between metacognition and epistemic cognition in more simple terms, we feel that metacognition concerns 'the *action* of monitoring progress' and epistemic cognition defines 'the *standards/criteria* for monitoring progress'. So what does this mean for academic performance? Kitchener predicts that epistemic cognition – or epistemological sophistication – will not influence the solving of puzzles (such as factual tests etcetera) because the first two levels are sufficient, but that it will affect the performance on ill-structured problems, because these problems can only be addressed using all three levels of cognition. Three examples of studies supporting Kitchener's expectation are discussed here, but there are many more to be found in literature. Schraw et al. (1995) tested Kitchener's three-level model of cognitive processing by relating students' epistemic beliefs (epistemological sophistication) to their performance on two tasks, one characterised as a puzzle (syllogistic reasoning) and the other as an ill-structured task (answering the question "Is truth unchanging?").[15] Schraw et al. found that epistemic beliefs only marginally explained differences in performance on the puzzle, but Certain Knowledge and Omniscient Authority on the other hand explained roughly 30% of the variation in performance on the ill-structured task over and above the effects of age and education.

From an educational point of view, Phillips' studies (1998, 2001) are even more interesting as they are situated in 'real-life' accounting education, a discipline not always associated with uncertainty. In 1998, Phillips linked the results on a shortened version of Schommer's EBQ (7 subsets) to two measures of accounting performance: a mid-term multiple choice test and an accounting case.[16] The case represented the ill-structured problem, with students being asked to evaluate the relevance of case facts regarding a recommendation that a company should capitalise or expense travel costs. The shortened EBQ resulted in a three-factor structure. Phillips used a nomenclature based on the sophisticated end of the scales, here, for clarity sake we renamed these factors back to the convention introduced by Schommer (1990): Quick Learning, Certain Knowledge and (Concrete) Simple Knowledge.[17] In addition to the separate factor scores, Phillips computed an aggregate measure of epistemological sophistication (Overall Beliefs) by averaging the scores on the individual factors. Regression analysis showed that the multiple choice performance was not related to the Overall Beliefs about knowledge and learning, nor to any of the three separate belief factors, confirming that epistemological sophistication does not affect puzzle performance. Case performance, on the other hand, was affected significantly by either Overall Beliefs or Certain Knowledge, illustrating the role of epistemological sophistication in addressing ill-structured problems. Considering the role that Certain Knowledge plays in case performance, Phillips suggests that accounting education should focus more on methods or materials that present (accounting) knowledge in a less absolute or certain light: presenting 'facts' in a more balanced way and including different perspectives. That this issue is not specific for accounting is illustrated by Ellen Langer, where she says "Most of what we learn in school, at home, from television, and from nonfiction books we may mindlessly accept because it is given to us in an unconditional form. That is, the information is presented from a single perspective as thought it is true, independent of context. It just *is*. Typically, no uncertainty is conveyed. Much of what we know about the world, about other people, and about ourselves is usually processed in this same way" (Langer, 1997, p. 17). We will discuss this (un)certainty issue at length in the chapter on changing teaching and learning).

Phillips (2001) introduced a refinement into this discussion regarding the effects of epistemological beliefs on ill-structured problem solving by emphasising different kinds of ill-structured problems, implying that sometimes some epistemological beliefs are more salient to a particular type of ill-structured problems than others, affecting the criteria used and study strategies chosen. More specifically, when solving an ill-structured problem requiring integration and consolidation, complex thinking, making connections etcetera, the relevance of sophisticated beliefs regarding Simple Knowledge may be greater than that of the other beliefs and using study strategies aimed at integration and consolidation of knowledge may be more appropriate than others. Using ten scales of the original EBQ, Phillips found four epistemological factors, Fixed Ability, Simple Knowledge, Quick Learning and Certain Knowledge.[18] He measured the use of study strategies with two scales of the Learning and Study Strategies Inventory (LASSI) and the ill-structured problem – a decision-oriented accounting case – was part of a final exam. Results showed that the performance on the accounting case, measured with the extent of consolidated analyses, was directly affected by sophisticated views on Simple Knowledge and marginally by the use of a study strategy aimed at consolidating/integrating knowledge[19], while there was a significant relationship between the sophisticated views on Simple Knowledge and the use of the study strategy of consolidating knowledge. In his previous study (Phillips, 1998) he found that the more salient epistemological belief influencing evaluation of case facts - one key component of ill-structured problem solving – was Certain Knowledge. In the case of consolidating analyses – another key component of ill-structured problem solving – it appeared that Simple Knowledge was the more salient epistemological belief, leading Phillips to conclude that "performance on an unstructured accounting case is predicted by epistemological beliefs *that match features required in the case analysis*" (Phillips, 2001, p. 34, italics ours). We feel that this approach, examining the salience of different epistemological beliefs to either problem solving or (level of) expertise in different domains, may help put a new perspective on the discussion regarding domain (in)dependence of epistemological constellations. We will return to this issue in the final chapter.

Research with Schommer's Epistemological Belief Questionnaire using self-reports on use of motivational, (meta) cognitive and resource-management strategies

In reaction to two studies, Hofer (1994)[20] and Schutz et al. in 1993, Michael Paulsen and Kenneth Feldman initiated a series of studies to investigate the relationship between epistemological beliefs on the one hand and motivational, (meta) cognitive and resource-management strategies (Paulsen and Feldman, 1999a, 1999b, 2005, 2007 in press). Hofer and Schutz et al. reported that sophisticated epistemological beliefs were positively related to intrinsic motivation, deep learning and self-regulated learning. While for us, this result in itself is logically satisfying, Paulsen and Feldman were unsatisfied with the instruments used to measure the various constructs: personal epistemology was measured uni-dimensionally (Schutz et al.) or only concerning a particular discipline (mathematics, Hofer) and the range of motivational and (meta) cognitive strategies measured in these studies was too limited. In 1999 Paulsen and Feldman took a more comprehensive multidimensional approach to measurement of both epistemological beliefs and the various strategies examined. In Paulsen and Feldman (1999a) epistemological beliefs of 246 university students were measured using Schommer's original 63-item EBQ and its four dimensions. The students' motivational strategies were measured using six scales of the MSLQ: intrinsic goal orientation, extrinsic goal orientation, task value, control of learning, self-efficacy and text anxiety. We use the term motivational strategy here in a broad sense, including attitudes, feelings or beliefs. The MSLQ is set up so that the items refer to a particular class or course a student is enrolled in, which makes this measure contextually bound. Simple Knowledge and Fixed Ability were both strongly related to various motivational strategies. Quick Learning was somewhat related to two motivational strategies, and Certain Knowledge was not related significantly to any of the motivational strategies measured here. For Simple Knowledge one can say that the more students believed that knowledge is simple, the more they were motivated by extrinsic goals (grades) and the more likely they were to experience test anxiety, while at the same time, they were less motivated intrinsically, they felt less in control of their learning and reported lower self-efficacy. For Fixed Ability the pattern was somewhat different: the more students believed in fixed ability, the lower they scored on the motivation constructs intrinsic goal orientation, task value, control of learning and self-efficacy. To paraphrase one might say that beliefs in simple knowledge lead to the "wrong type of motivation", while beliefs in fixed ability seem to lead to "demotivation". Paulsen and Feldman concluded that if epistemological beliefs affect students' motivation to learn "college teachers can enhance the motivation of their students to learn by promoting 'motivationally productive' epistemological beliefs" (Paulsen and Feldman, 1999a, p. 22).

In their study with Norwegian undergraduate teacher education students Bråten and Strømsø (2004) used a different measure for academic motivation, achievement goal-orientations, and linked this to the EBQ scales. Goal orientations are defined as "the reasons or purposes students have for engaging in academic tasks, with different purposes also implying that students view competence and academic success in different ways" (2004, p. 371). The three types of goal orientation discerned are

- mastery goal-orientation: orientation towards self-improvement and task mastery (e.g. An important reason why I do my work in school, is because I want to get better at it, Bråten and Stømsø, 2004, p. 379);
- performance-approach orientation: outperforming others (e.g. Doing better than other students is important to me, Bråten and Stømsø, 2004, p. 379);
- performance-avoidance orientation: avoiding losing or looking incompetent (e.g. One of my main goals is to avoid looking like I can't do my work, Bråten and Stømsø, 2004, p. 379).

The aim of the study was to examine the relationships between epistemological beliefs (measured in the first year) and students' adoption of particular goals (measured twice: in the first year and one year later). In a related, but later published study (Bråten and Strømsø, 2005), an item-based factor analysis on the Norwegian EBQ resulted in a four-factor structure: 'speed of knowledge acquisition' (9 items, Quick Learning), 'knowledge construction and modification' (7 items, more or less comparable to a combination of Simple and Certain Knowledge), 'certainty of knowledge' (5 items, Certain Knowledge) and 'control of knowledge acquisition' (3 items, Fixed Ability). Regression analyses of the 24-item EBQ on the three achievement goal-orientations measured in both waves showed that 'speed of knowledge acquisition' (Quick Learning) was most consistently (and 'psycho'-logically) related to goal-orientation: the more students believed in quick learning, the less likely they were mastery goal-oriented and the more likely they were performance goal-oriented (both approach and avoidance). The latter result was confirmed in their 2005 study, with teacher education and business administration students: for both groups again quick learning was consistently negatively associated with mastery goal-orientation. This seems to indicate that "beliefs in quick learning may orient students away from mastery goals and towards performance-avoidance goals, with these orientations, in turn, influencing academic cognition and performance" (Bråten and Strømsø, 2004, p. 384). While Bråten and Strømsø acknowledge that the direction of the causal relationship may not necessarily be as stated above, they do stress that "post-secondary instruction should especially target the self-defeating belief that knowledge acquisition is a quick, all-or-none process" (2004, p. 385).

Paulsen and Feldman (1999b) reported on a study related to the previously discussed study (1999a) examining the results from the same survey, but this time linking epistemological beliefs (the EBQ) to the use of eight (meta)cognitive and resource-management strategies as measured with the MSLQ. The MSLQ learning strategies scales used here were: rehearsal, organisation, elaboration, metacognition, time and study environment management, effort regulation, peer learning and help seeking.[21] The influence of epistemological beliefs on the use of the eight learning strategies was consistent with the results of Paulsen and Feldman (1999a): Fixed Ability had a significant negative effect on all of the eight learning strategies, while Simple Knowledge affected the use of rehearsal strategies positively and affected negatively the use of elaboration, metacognition and effort regulation. Quick Learning had a small negative effect on elaboration, and Certain Knowledge affected none of the strategies examined. In other words, the less students feel that they can improve their capacity to learn, the less likely they will invest effort in any learning strategy that may enhance this capacity. In the same way, the more students feel that knowledge is simple, the less they will use deep-learning strategies and the more they will focus on surface-learning strategies. The set of four epistemological beliefs explained a considerable amount of variance regarding the use of elaboration and metacognition strategies (resp. 21.6% and 14.2%): the more naive the epistemological belief constellation, the less likely the use of deep-level strategies such as elaboration and metacognition. This analysis lead to the same conclusion as in their 1999a study: again Paulsen and Feldman suggest that teachers can promote the use of the studied learning strategies by designing education which challenges students' epistemological beliefs. Where McKeachie remarks that "cognition and motivation are interdependent" (McKeachie, 1995, p. 2) emphasising the two-way interaction between deep-learning and intrinsic motivation, we feel that Paulsen and Feldman have shown that the relationship can be extended to the proposition 'epistemic cognition (Kitchener, 1983), (meta)cognition and motivation are interdependent' and this can be viewed as support of Schommer's Embedded Systemic Model and we will discuss this further, proposing a model of Epistemological Ecology (see end of this chapter).

In their 2005 study with Norwegian teacher education and business administration students, Bråten and Strømsø linked the metacognition scale of the MSLQ to their 24-item EBQ (see above). Confirming Paulsen and Feldman's findings (1999b) Bråten and Strømsø found that the more students believed that knowledge is given and stable, and the more ability is seen as fixed, the less likely students were to plan, monitor and/or regulate their cognition.

In 2005 Paulsen and Feldman reported the results of a new survey expanding their existing research line to include a larger sample of students (n=502) from multiple disciplines, studying not only the main effects, but also conditional and interaction effects of epistemological beliefs on the same set of motivational strategies used in their 1999a study. This is the first study, we know, that examines possible interdependencies of the influence of epistemological beliefs, and as such this study addresses possible implications of Schommer's Embedded Systemic Model. Using a two-way interaction product-term model, it is possible to measure interaction effects: "an interaction effect would exist if the effect of a particular epistemological belief on a motivation learning strategy changed or varied according to the values of one or more other epistemological belief variables. In such cases, the 'effect' of one epistemological belief on the motivational strategy is 'moderated' by one or more of the other epistemological belief variables". (Paulsen and Feldman, 2005, p. 740). In such a model, main effects become conditional effects when significant interaction effects exist. The bivariate correlations between epistemological beliefs and motivational strategies showed a predominantly identical pattern as in the 1999a study, leading to the same conclusion as before. More interesting were the results from the regression analyses using the product-term model. These analyses supported the finding that only the epistemological beliefs regarding Fixed Ability and Simple Knowledge affected motivational strategies. More importantly these analyses indicated that there were four significant interaction effects on the motivational strategies Intrinsic Goal Orientation and Task Value. For both motivational strategies, the negative conditional effects of naive beliefs in both Simple Knowledge and Fixed Ability were intensified by the level of naivety regarding Certain Knowledge. In other words for example, the more a student believes that knowledge is certain, the larger the negative effect of the belief in Fixed Ability on the motivational strategy of Intrinsic Goal Orientation, and similarly the larger the negative effect of the belief in Simple Knowledge on the same strategy. The same relationships were found for Task Value. Paulsen and Feldman feel the positive relationships between Simple Knowledge, Extrinsic Goal Orientation (e.g. grade orientation) and Test Anxiety, not only matched their own previous findings (1999a), but also matched results from the European/Australian school of conceptions of (or approaches to) learning (e.g. Entwistle and Ramsden, 1983; Marton and Säljö, 1984), implying that epistemological research and learning conception research differ more in terminology than in research focus. This latter perspective matches our own, as we have discussed in the first three chapters. Paulsen and Feldman conclude that their study "reveal[s] for the first time the important role that beliefs in certain knowledge play in moderating the effects of other types of epistemological beliefs on use by students of motivational strategies in their learning" (Paulsen and Feldman, 2005, p. 758).

In 2007 Paulsen and Feldman published the partner article to the 2005 study described above (Paulsen and Feldman, 2007 in press). As with the two articles published in 1999 (a, b) these two articles refer to the same study, but describe different analyses: in 1999b and in 2007 they discussed the relationship of epistemological beliefs with the use of eight (meta)cognitive and resource-management strategies measured, as before, with the MSLQ. Again Paulsen and Feldman examined conditional and interaction effects of epistemological beliefs using a two-way interaction product-term model. Comparing the results of 2007 with those of 1999b regarding the use of (meta)cognitive strategies one can remark that, again, Fixed Ability and Simple Knowledge are the main predictors of the use of these strategies where Fixed Ability had a negative effect on the use of all the strategies involved. The influence of Simple Knowledge was negative on the use of elaboration strategies and positive on the use of rehearsal strategies. Contrary to the results in 1999b, Certain Knowledge now had a positive effect on the use of organisation strategies, while Quick Learning had no conditional effects at all. Regarding the use of resource-management studies Fixed Ability remained the prime predictor of the (lack of) use of resource-management strategies and Simple Knowledge, as before, was significantly and negatively related to the use of effort regulation. Certain Knowledge and Quick Learning were again not related to the use of any of the resource-management strategies. In general, one can conclude that the pattern of conditional effects is more or less identical to the direct effects reported in 1999b. Of the interaction effects found the majority involved Certain Knowledge as moderator. For all these interactions, the more naive the belief regarding the certainty of knowledge the more negative the conditional effect of Fixed Ability and Simple Knowledge becomes. While Certain Knowledge itself had almost no conditional effects on the use of the studied strategies, the studies of 2005 and 2007 showed that Certain Knowledge did have an indirect effect, and so it is proven to be an important aspect of epistemological beliefs which would need to be addressed as well when attempting to influence students' use of diverse learning strategies. As these studies seem to indicate that naive beliefs in Certain Knowledge have a detrimental indirect effect on the use of motivational and learning strategies, and consequently on academic performance, it may prove important to address the language used in text books. As Ellen Langer has shown in a set of seemingly 'simple' experiments, changing text book language to present facts and theories in a more probabilistic light seems to result almost immediately in more "mindful learning" and more thoughtful answers to open questions (Langer, 1997, see chapter 10).

Compared to the 1999 studies, a remarkable difference was the only conditional (and positive) effect of Certain Knowledge on the use of organisation strategies: "students with more naive beliefs that the nature and structure of knowledge is absolute and unchanging or constant over time (certain knowledge) are more likely to use strategies of organization in their learning" (Paulsen and Feldman, 2007 in press, see their discussion). Paulsen and Feldman interpreted this unexpected result by suggesting that students may employ organisation strategies in a way consistent with rehearsal and memorising. The items used to measure organisation strategies focused on skills such as outlining and finding the most important ideas within the text (García Duncan and McKeachie, 2005, p. 127, 128), which we have found are skills used in both surface level learning and deep level learning (e.g. van Rossum, Deijkers and Hamer, 1985) but in a qualitatively different way and for a qualitatively different purpose. Paulsen and Feldman had similar interpretations regarding some of the interaction effects: suggesting that respondents read and interpret items of the MSLQ in a way consistent with *their* epistemological sophistication level, which may *not* agree with the level of epistemological sophistication the questionnaire developer intended for a particular item. The fact that respondents may read something different in the item than expected is, in our opinion, a major problem when using questionnaires to measure epistemological beliefs, or learning strategies for that matter. Our study reported in 1985 directly addressed this problem: there we showed that educationally significant terms, such as e.g. understanding, applying etcetera, are indeed interpreted in ways consistent with the student's conception of learning (see chapter 1).

From a cross-cultural perspective, the study by Dahl et al. (2005) is interesting because it is a partial replication of the studies by Paulsen and Feldman using a Norwegian sample of 81 undergraduate university students. Using translated versions of Schommer's 63- item EBQ and five scales referring to learning strategies from the MSLQ[22], Dahl et al. focused on exploring "whether the manner in which university students report using learning strategies when *reading* for their courses is influenced by their beliefs about knowledge and learning" (Dahl et al., 2005, p. 263, italics ours). The intercorrelations between epistemological beliefs and reported use of learning strategies showed that the more sophisticated students' beliefs in Simple Knowledge and Fixed Ability, the more likely they reported using (the majority of) the learning strategies. As in the studies of Paulsen and Feldman, Quick Learning and Certain Knowledge were almost uncorrelated to the use of learning strategies. Especially interesting, to us, were the results of the full model regression analyses. The more students believed knowledge to be simple, the less likely they were to use rehearsal, organisation or metacognitive strategies. The more students believed the ability to learn was fixed, the less likely they were to use elaboration, critical thinking or metacognitive strategies. Overall, these results agreed with the conclusions of Paulsen and Feldman, with one big exception, the negative relationship between naive beliefs in Simple Knowledge and the use of rehearsal strategies. In this study, rehearsal was positively correlated to the other four more deep-level oriented learning strategies, perhaps indicating that for this group of Norwegian students rehearsal strategies were an integrated part of studying. Despite the found significant relationships, Dahl et al. concluded that "none of the beliefs accounted for a high degree of variance in reported learning strategy selection" (Dahl et al., 2005, p. 268–269) which is also consistent with the results of Paulsen and Feldman. The fact that Dahl et al. found strong correlations between Fixed Ability and the other three epistemological beliefs led them to conclude that "beliefs about intelligence should *not* be ignored in research devoted to understanding the relationship between beliefs and actions" (Dahl et al., 2005, p. 271, italics ours). In this remark we see support for Schommer's Embedded Systemic Model and our position on an Epistemological Ecology (see also the final section of this chapter). Finally, Dahl and her colleagues concluded that "some beliefs may be more influential than others when selecting effective reading strategies. The exact constellation of those beliefs is not yet resolved, nor is the issue of how much their relationship with strategy selection may be mediated by other factors" (Dahl et al., 2005, p. 271). This conclusion is supported by the results of an earlier study (Garrett-Ingram, 1997) where the full MSLQ was used and Simple Knowledge was found to be the strongest predictor of the use of learning strategies, motivational strategies and college academic achievement. Garrett-Ingram found a different constellation of beliefs: "Overall, it seems that Fixed Ability, Simple Knowledge, and Quick Learning had the greatest impact on strategy use, and Simple Knowledge had the greatest impact on motivation and achievement" (Garrett-Ingram, 1997, in discussion, capitals ours). Whatever the constellation may be, these results regarding the relationships between epistemological beliefs and reported strategy use measured with the MSLQ, all point towards the *non*-existence of a main effect of Certain Knowledge – the epistemological belief that some researchers (e.g. Rozendaal et al., 2001; Hofer and Pintrich, 1997) believe to be one of the few *real* or *core* epistemological beliefs. As such these findings either undermine the discussion about core and peripheral beliefs (or conceptions) or suggest that Certain Knowledge may not be measured adequately using the current EBQ.

The MSLQ is not the only questionnaire used to measure the use of learning and motivational strategies. Schreiber and Shinn (2003) used Schmeck and Geisler-Brenstein's Revised Inventory of Learning Processes (ILP-R).[23] The ILP-R measures three distinct information processing strategies "as routes to achievement" (Schreiber and Shinn, p. 701): Deep Processing (e.g. comparing and contrasting information), Elaborative Processing (e.g. linking to one's prior knowledge) and Agentic Processing (e.g. learning facts and serial processing). Their study, with the less usual group of (North American) community college students examined the relationship between epistemological beliefs (measured with Schommer's EBQ) and these three processing (or learning) strategies. The intercorrelation analysis showed that Fixed Ability was significantly negatively related to all three learning strategies, while Simple Knowledge was significantly positively related to Agentic Processing. In other words, the more students believe that the capacity to learn is fixed, the less they will use any of the three learning strategies and the more students believe that knowledge is simple, the more likely they are to use Agentic Processing, focusing on remembering facts and processing information in a serial fashion. Path analysis indicated that Fixed Ability had direct negative effects on Deep and Agentic Processing. Simple Knowledge had a direct positive effect on Agentic Processing (including rehearsal strategies). As such these results are consistent with the results of Paulsen and Feldman and – regarding the effects of Simple Knowledge – contradictory to the results of Dahl et al. (2005).

A third type of study discussed here, relates Schommer's EBQ to yet another questionnaire aimed at measuring learning strategies (Cantwell and Scevak, 2004; Rodríguez and Cano, 2006, 2007 in press). The first example is a study by Cantwell and Scevak (2004), who linked the responses to a shortened (42-item) EBQ, to Biggs' Study Process Questionnaire (SPQ) and Cantwell and Moore's Strategic Flexibility Questionnaire (SFQ). The original, 42-item SPQ (Biggs, 1987) measures three underlying approaches to learning each reflecting an interaction of motivational and strategic choices: a Deep approach (deep learning with intrinsic motivation), a Surface approach (characterised by surface learning with extrinsic grade or test orientation) and an Achieving approach (competition driven attainment of institutional goals). Cantwell and Moore's SFQ is a 21-item self-report questionnaire which aims to measure the appropriateness of strategy use in dealing with complexity in learning. Some students attempt to cope with complexity by falling back on well-known trusted routines (inflexible strategic control), other students are able to adapt strategies to meet new, more complex, task demands appropriately (adaptive strategic control) and yet another group of students is aware that their strategies need to be revised, but seem unable to formulate an appropriate approach or strategy (irresolute strategic control). Besides the use of an alternative questionnaire to measure learning strategies, this study is interesting because the respondents were mature students with prior industrial work experience and trade qualifications (after secondary education) giving them entry to university in recognition of their prior learning and experience (RPL) in a cognate field. These 33 RPL students were enrolled in a two-year Bachelor of Education course, and Cantwell and Scevak were interested in their adjustment to the demands of university education, because their prior learning and work experience may have primed them to naivety in their beliefs about the nature of knowledge. While their motivation to learn, their learning strategies and their willingness to adapt to task demands were not seen as a source for concern, Cantwell and Scevak expected that their learning "may be restricted in enactment by the enduring but naive 'practical knowledge' emanating from the industry background [leading to epistemological assumptions which] may impose limits on the perceived depth to which it is possible to take 'knowing' " (Cantwell and Scevak, 2004, p. 134). Compared to beginning undergraduate students, the RPL students were clearly more sophisticated with regard to Quick Learning and Innate (Fixed) Ability, reflecting their work experiences where learning usually incurs hard work and retrying, but they were significantly more naive with regard to their belief in the simplicity of knowledge, reflecting their practical industry background.[24] In this sense, this study is the first we know that gives substance to Schommer's postulation that epistemological beliefs may develop asynchronically. It also calls to mind the developmental helix presented in chapter 3 (Kegan, 1994) as well as our image of development as climbing a ladder (see also our comment on postulate 2 of Schommer's emerging theory of an Epistemological Belief System, above).

More germane to the current discussion was the finding that the students' belief in Simple Knowledge was strongly positively correlated with a Surface Approach and with Irresolute and Inflexible Strategic Control, was strongly correlated with rejection of a Deep Approach and Adaptive Strategic Control and correlated negatively with academic achievement (measured with the students' university GPA). These results confirm the relationship between Simple Knowledge and 'Agentic' learning strategies focusing on rehearsal and memorising established above by Schreiber and Shinn, and Paulsen and Feldman. Cantwell and Scevak concluded that when naive beliefs about knowledge endure and seem resistant to change, students may be at risk academically. They suggest that to facilitate epistemological development, two conditions need to be met forming a bridge between the naive student and the complex university demands: the students must be open to change and the new (academic) demands or challenges are presented in a sympathetic and supportive learning environment. To us, such an environment sounds a lot like Kegan's 'holding environment' essential to epistemological development (Kegan, 1994).

In 2006, Rodríguez and Cano reported on their study also examining the relationship between epistemological beliefs and learning approaches. They used Schommer's EBQ to measure the former and four scales of Biggs' SPQ to measure Deep and Surface learning approaches, referring to Biggs et al. (2001) proposing a two-factor structure for a revised SPQ. The 388 Spanish teacher-education students participating in this study were following a "constructive curriculum" based on active learning related to real-life situations, interactive teaching and conceptual understanding.[25] The responses to the EBQ resulted in four factors resembling the factor structure generally found by Schommer: Quick Learning, Simple Knowledge, Fixed Ability and Certain Knowledge. The SPQ yielded two factors, Deep approach and Surface approach. Two pairs of canonical variates demonstrated significant relationships between epistemological beliefs and learning approaches. The first variate-pair illustrated that the Surface approach was related mainly to naive beliefs in Fixed Ability and Quick Learning.[26] The second variate-pair showed that a Deep approach was related to sophisticated beliefs about Simple Knowledge: in other words, the more students believed that knowledge is complex, the more likely they will use a Deep approach. Of these two pairs of canonical variates, only three variates were significantly related to academic performance. Naive beliefs about knowledge and Surface approach contributed negatively to academic performance, while only sophisticated beliefs about knowledge contributed positively to academic performance. Rodríguez and Cano concluded that "epistemological beliefs and learning approaches were not independent but generally consistent and logically interrelated constructs", naive epistemological beliefs were related to superficial learning and sophisticated beliefs were related to deep learning (Rodríguez and Cano, 2006, p. 630). These results confirmed their own earlier research and were consistent with a study by Chan, who also used the SPQ with a sample of teacher-education students (Chan, 2003). Although the relationships between epistemological beliefs and learning approaches were as expected and significant, the two epistemological beliefs-variates explained only 8% of the variance of the two learning approaches and vice versa only 14% of the variance of the epistemological beliefs was explained by the two learning approaches-variates. This led Rodríguez and Cano (2006, p. 630) to conclude that "little overlap exists between them", meaning that epistemological beliefs and learning approaches are related *but distinct* aspects of a student's experience of learning, matching the conclusions of Paulsen and Feldman and Dahl et al. above.

Vermetten et al. (1999b) – who used Jan Vermunt's Inventory of Learning Styles (ILS, see next section) to measure among others the long-term pattern of relationships between processing strategies, regulation strategies, learning orientations and mental learning models – found that the further students progressed in their study, the stronger and more coherent the relationships between most of these four learning 'components' became. This led Rodríguez and Cano (2007 in press) to study possible changes in the pattern of relationships between epistemological beliefs and learning approaches over time comparing a cross sectional and a longitudinal study. Based on the study by Vermetten et al. they expected the pattern to become more coherent and robust over time. Rodríguez and Cano had two further objectives with this study: firstly to establish possible development in epistemological beliefs and learning approaches during higher education, and secondly to see if they could find groups of students with distinct patterns of development. Rodríguez and Cano used the EBQ and SPQ as described above, administering them to a sample of first and third year students for the cross-sectional comparison and to a sub-sample of 81 of the original first-year students in their third year.

The analysis of the epistemological beliefs and learning approaches of the two cross-sectional samples showed that the third-year students entertained significantly more sophisticated beliefs about Fixed Ability and Certain Knowledge, while they also were less Surface approach oriented and more Deep approach oriented. The longitudinal analysis showed that over time the beliefs in Simple and Certain Knowledge had become significantly more sophisticated and these students had become less surface learning oriented. While the changes in epistemological beliefs and learning approaches were in the expected direction, clearly the change patterns were different for both comparisons and the magnitude of the changes (effect size) was small: "tertiary education seems, in general, to induce a small but favourable change (…) in students' learning experience" (Rodríguez and Cano, 2007 in press). Using a number of indices to determine the strength of the interrelationships between epistemological beliefs and learning approaches over time, Rodríguez and Cano found that the cross-sectional study showed a decline in coherence (contrary to expectation) and the longitudinal study showed a clear increase in coherence. They concluded that longitudinal studies are probably preferable when studying changes in (patterns of) learning experience over time and that, longitudinally, "the relationships (canonical correlations) between learning approaches and epistemological beliefs are more consolidated and coherent as students progress through their studies" (Rodríguez and Cano, 2007 in press).

The patterns of within-subject change were assessed using a cluster analysis on change scores. This analysis resulted in six clusters of students with a similar, group-specific change pattern. Two groups exhibited clear changes over time, the most developed group scoring higher on Deep approach and lower on the other five factors, and a 'regressed' group, who "seemed to take a step backwards in the last course year compared to the first year, in the majority of the dependent variables" (Rodríguez and Cano, 2007 in press). The other four groups showed a mixed pattern of growth and regression. For us this study and in particular the section about within-subject change is especially interesting because the data we will discuss in later chapters also derive from students exposed to a constructive learning-teaching environment (Enterprising Learning) based on some of the same principles described by Rodríguez and Cano above. Their results indicate, we feel, that educational innovations may have different effects on different students and lead to mixed results overall. In earlier work we have found similar mixed results, with some students making large strides towards epistemological sophistication, while others make only small steps, are standing still or even seem to regress (van Rossum et al. 2003) and we expect to find such patterns in the current study as well.

Comments on Schommer

Quantitative measurement of epistemological beliefs. Schommer herself is the first to acknowledge the limitations of measuring epistemological beliefs by means of her questionnaire (Schommer-Aikins, 2004) and remarks that "quantitative assessment of personal epistemology is still in its infancy" (p. 23): "[t]he fact that this questionnaire has been used by researchers around the world speaks more to the need and/or desire to measure epistemological beliefs with an efficient and objective method than the illusion of a perfect instrument" (p. 22). An important characteristic of this questionnaire is the emphasis on reading (Schommer and Walker, 1995), which we feel does not tap into the full range of personal epistemology. Furthermore, examining the items used to measure Simple Knowledge and Certain Knowledge many would not be out of place in any questionnaire measuring study strategies (such as surface vs. deep level learning) which fit more closely in our learning and teaching conception approach. Examples of these items are for instance (Schommer, 1998, p. 561–562):

- I try my best to combine information across chapters or even across classes.
- To me studying means getting the big ideas from the text, rather than the details.
- You never know what a books means unless you know the intent of the author.
- Being a good student generally involves memorising facts.
- Learning definitions word-for-word is often necessary to do well on tests.
- If professors would stick more to the facts and do less theorising, one could get more out of college.
- I really appreciate instructors who organise their lecture meticulously and then stick to their plan.

This short selection of items also shows that many items purported to measure the thinking about "knowing" are phrased as statements about "learning" or "good teaching" and contain phrases that seem to come from answers to the questions "What do you mean by learning?" or "What is good teaching to you?" (see chapter 1). We feel that more than half of the items of Schommer's 63-item questionnaire measure views on learning and good teaching, and in this estimate we have not examined the items on Quick Learning and Innate Ability. This leaves us with the question to what extent measurements as performed with this instrument are actually measuring personal epistemology? And what then *is* the meaning of the term personal epistemology?

Hofer and Pintrich also have similar reservations regarding the validity of some items in Schommer's questionnaire, in particular they are critical about the inclusion of Fixed Ability and Quick Learning as epistemological beliefs

(Hofer and Pintrich, 1997). Based on a review of epistemological models (Perry, 1970; Belenky et al., 1997; Baxter Magolda, 1992a; Kuhn, 1991 and King and Kitchener, 1994), most of which we have treated in chapter 3 before, Hofer and Pintrich conclude that only Certain Knowledge and Simple Knowledge are consistent with the existing epistemological tradition. Furthermore the lack of quantitative evidence in Schommer's studies for the belief dimension Omniscient Authority as a dimension referring to Source of Knowledge is an additional weakness, as Source of Knowledge would fit well within the mentioned epistemological tradition (in particular Belenky et al., 1997). Hofer and Pintrich also criticise the vagueness of some items, the phrasing of items, the absence of confirmatory factor analysis on item level (Hofer and Pintrich, 1997, 109–110) and the fact that this type of approach, using questionnaires and Likert scales, often reflects the author's meaning making and not the students' own meaning making (p. 132). Finally, questioning Schommer's emphasis on the independence of the belief dimensions found, Hofer and Pintrich remark that "more evidence is needed to identify the range of dimensions and to test their independence than exists in Schommer's studies to date" (1997, p. 110). In the final section of this chapter we will discuss Hofer's work in more detail.

Vermunt

> *The habit of many teachers in higher education to speak to hundreds of students in order to transfer the learning contents to them, is probably based more on tradition than on learning psychological findings*
>
> *(Vermunt, 1996, p. 48)*

Researchers have developed a number of self-report questionnaires to measure the different ways that Students learn and study. Such questionnaires are often described as study strategy inventories. Entwistle and McCune (2004) have reviewed six inventories widely-used in higher education, and compared the conceptual bases of the inventories and their scales. Four of the inventories examined originated in the seventies and early eighties of the previous century (ASI, Entwistle and Ramsden, 1983 and the SPQ, LASSI and ILP(-R) discussed above). After detailed analysis, Entwistle and McCune feel the major similarity between these inventories is the focus on study strategies and learning processes on the one hand and motives and intentions on the other hand. Most of these inventories are characterised by a threefold-structure, for study strategies/ learning processes and motives/intentions alike. The most commonly found strategies are deep/elaborative learning, surface/ rehearsal learning and well-organised/methodical learning. Each strategy is associated with its own set of motives and intentions: respectively intrinsic/personal interest motives, extrinsic/ fear of failure motives and finally achievement/effort motives. Biggs (1987) proposed that the logic of these relationships between strategy and motive is an example of 'psycho-logic': motive and intention define the strategy used in a particular learning situation. If passing a course is sufficient, then it is logical to focus on memorising only those facts (or pieces of knowledge) that one expects will be asked on the test. On the other hand, if a student has a personal interest and really wants to learn something, memorising is often not perceived as an appropriate strategy, and a strategy aimed at understanding and "building the big picture" will be more logical. While there is theoretical support for this 'psycho-logic', it has not always been supported by empirical results (Richardson, 2000).

The two other questionnaires discussed by Entwistle and McCune became available in the last decade of the previous century: the MSLQ (discussed above) and the ILS developed by Jan Vermunt (Vermunt, 1996, 1998). Jan Vermunt developed the ILS to extend the existing inventories with scales addressing "metacognitive aspects of student learning in higher education: regulation strategies and mental models of learning. [Vermunt attempts] to link these metacognitive aspects to students' cognitive processing strategies and to their study motivation, with the aim of enriching and broadening earlier conceptualisation of students' learning styles and strategies in higher education" (Vermunt, 1996, p. 26). In his view, metacognitive regulation strategies, and in particular self-regulation versus the external regulation of learning, play a central role in student learning in higher education (Vermunt, 1998, p. 153). In Vermunt's articles of 1996 and 1998 he describes the studies leading up to the development and final version of the multi-dimensional 120-item ILS.

The Inventory of Learning Styles (ILS)

The base of the ILS is a phenomenographic study where Vermunt interviewed 35 first-year students of the Dutch open university and a regular university. The semi-structured interviews covered five central topics – processing strategies, regulation strategies, mental learning models, learning orientations and affective processes[27] – and addressed all aspects of the students' experience of learning and studying. In the analysis, the five interview topics were used to organise the interview data per student by topic, facilitating the formation of emergent categories - each describing a qualitatively different experience of studying in the first year. Vermunt found four different categories and called them 'learning styles': "a coherent whole of learning activities that students usually employ, their learning orientation and their metal model of learning; a whole that is characteristic of them at a certain period [in time]", noting that they are "*not* conceived of as an unchangeable personality attribute, but as the result of the temporal interplay between personal and contextual influences" (Vermunt, 1996, p. 29). Careful examination of the four learning styles led us to conclude that each style is in fact a description of one of the learning-teaching conceptions we described in chapter 1.

Students who have an *undirected learning style* have difficulty with almost all processing strategies, often focusing on reading and rereading everything. They depend very strongly on external regulation of learning but "they experience insufficient hold on that" (Vermunt, 1996, p. 33). They experience anxiety about and little confidence in their study capabilities in higher education. All these aspects provide a picture of a student clearly in trouble and unable to meet the demands of higher education. The dependence on reading and rereading together with their extreme dependence on the teacher (and instruction) to provide structure, explanation and regulation reminds us strongly of learning-teaching conception 1.

The *reproduction directed learning style* is typified by memorising and rehearsing things one needs to know for examinations. Students put in a lot of effort and time into underlining and making summaries, moreover regulation is predominantly external and the goal of studying is passing exams (or obtaining a certificate). This description sounds fairly similar to the learning-teaching conception 2, where memorising, rehearsing and test orientation are typical and the role of the learner is mostly limited to asking questions for clarification.

Application directed students are preoccupied with the use of knowledge. They continuously look for the relationship between theory and practice, using their own experiences to make theory more practical or concrete. Regulation is partly internal (Can I use this? How would I use this?) and partly external, e.g. using knowledge in provided assignments (I have to apply this to ....). They always want to know how to apply everything they learn, anything without an obvious application is neither useful nor interesting. They try to apply what they know to their current life or save it for application in their future profession. "Learning for later" and "applying theory in practice" are characteristic phrases from the responses of learning-teaching conception 3 students. The need application-directed students express for discussion and asking a lot of questions etcetera is also common to teaching conception 3 students.

The *meaning directed learning style* is clearly different from the previous three. Students are capable of making connections, structuring, finding the main line or essence of the subject matter themselves. They have internalised regulation by asking their own questions, and are motivated by a need to understand, personal interest and personal goals (intrinsic motivation). In particular the description "becoming acquainted with the lines of thought in their subject area" (Vermunt, 1996, p. 41) is almost a copy of the emphasis in learning-teaching conception 4 on developing a "way of thinking". The internal regulation in this learning style echoes the goal of "learning to think for oneself" found in teaching conception 4.

Vermunt (1996) does not make the connection to the learning conception model of Säljö (1979a), or our own (e.g. van Rossum, Deijkers and Hamer, 1985), nor does he perceive these styles as stages in a developmental process towards self-regulation and complex meaning-making.[28] He does draw, we feel, the correct conclusion that two of the styles, undirected and reproduction directed learning are not appropriate ways of learning in higher education and therefore should be discouraged. He proposes to introduce process-oriented instruction to encourage application and meaning-directed learning styles (we discuss this in more detail in chapter 10). This type of instruction focuses not only on discipline specific knowledge but also on teaching discipline specific learning and thinking strategies necessary to apply or transform knowledge.

The 1996 study was a source of statements about learning, teaching, study strategies etcetera, Vermunt used to construct a large number of items for a questionnaire to apply and test Vermunt's "model of the regulation of constructive learning processes" (Vermunt, 1998, p. 153). This model consists of four major elements, where processing strategies are directly influenced by regulation strategies and both directly and indirectly by mental learning models and learning orientations.[29]

The first ILS was 241 items long, covering the four major elements mentioned above. In a series of three subsequent studies with open university students Vermunt revised and shortened the inventory to 120 items, still a questionnaire of considerable length. Each of the elements consisted of a number of subscales in the following manner:

1. processing strategies (27 items)
    a. deep
        i. relating and structuring
        ii. critical processing
    b. stepwise or surface
        i. memorising and rehearsing
        ii. analysing (stepwise)
    c. concrete processing
2. regulation strategies (28 items)
    a. self
        i. learning process and results[30]
        ii. learning content
    b. external
        i. learning process
        ii. learning results[30]
    c. lack
3. mental learning models (40 items) [30]
    a. construction of knowledge (meaning)
    b. intake of knowledge (reproduction)
    c. use of knowledge (application)
    d. stimulating education
    e. co-operative learning
4. learning orientations (25 items)
    a. personally interested
    b. certificate-oriented
    c. self-test-oriented
    d. vocation-oriented
    e. ambivalent

Factor analysis on the data of open university and regular university students resulted in mostly similar four-factor structures for both types of students.

Scales loading positively on the first factor were the deep processing scales, concrete processing, the self-regulation scales, the mental learning model scale of construction of knowledge and the learning orientation scale of personally interested. The learning orientation scale of certificate-orientation loaded negatively on this factor. All this is indicative of a meaning-directed learning style: a pattern that one would expect for learning-teaching conception 4. The scales loading positively on the second factor were the stepwise processing scales, the external regulation scales, the mental learning model of intake of knowledge and the scales certificate and self-test orientation. Vermunt identifies this factor as a reproduction-directed learning style and we feel it shows a pattern pretty similar to what one might expect for learning-teaching conception 2. The third factor, Vermunt named undirected learning style, has positive loadings for the scales of lack of regulation, intake of knowledge, stimulating education, co-operative learning, self-test-orientation and ambivalent. The final factor Vermunt interpreted as the application-directed learning style, with high loadings for the scales concrete processing, use of knowledge, personally interested, certificate-oriented and vocation-oriented. While for both groups of students the same scales load, it is notable that this factor seems to mean something different for each group. For the open university students this factor points towards a clear focus on application and future career/job and points less toward personal interest: a pattern we feel shows considerable resemblance to learning-teaching conception 3. For the regular university students however, this factor seems to mean the exact opposite. This mirror image interpretation could point towards a clear difference in motivation or a difference in epistemological development between the groups.

Overall, the regression of regulation strategies, mental learning models and learning orientations on processing strategies, as well as the regression of mental learning models and learning orientations on regulation strategies, confirmed the psycho-logic relations between scales of the four major learning elements (or components), leading Vermunt to conclude "no studies until now addressed mental models of learning, learning orientations and the use of processing and regulation strategies in their mutual coherence. This research showed strong interrelations between these learning components, so strong that one may indeed speak of learning styles" (Vermunt, 1998, p. 166). Other advantages of the introduction of this inventory are

- the use of concrete processing as a distinct strategy alongside the more familiar deep-surface dichotomy, which may prove valuable to measure differences in study strategies specific to higher professional education (Entwistle and McCune, 2004, p. 341),
- the explicit introduction of metacognition and regulation in the measurement of learning strategies or styles.

Whilst the ILS is considered to be an apparent improvement on earlier inventories, Entwistle and McCune (2004) observe that "[looking] through all the inventories there is a surprising lack of emphasis on emotion in learning. The positive forms are implicit in some of the scales describing academic interests and motivation, but only a negative form – anxiety or fear of failure – has been developed explicitly" (Entwistle and McCune, 2004, p. 340). We would like to add to this critique the fact that we also miss more explicit items referring to the interpersonal and identity dimensions of knowing and learning that are so clearly present in the work of Baxter Magolda (1992a, 2001) and our own (e.g. van Rossum, Deijkers and Hamer, 1985, and more strongly in van Rossum and Hamer, 2004). Perhaps interviews with more mature students – who have had time and experiences to develop further epistemologically – would suggest statements that could be used as items for these dimensions of learning.

Further use of the ILS

Vermunt and associates

Usually, this type of inventory is used to study consistency in ways of studying. The suggestion of Entwistle and McCune to use such inventories to measure the effects of different learning environments was adopted by Vermetten et al. in one part of their 1999 study (1999a), discussed below.[31] A third use is to test developments in, and changing relationships between components of, learning styles. An example of the latter use is reported in Vermetten et al. (1999b).

Vermetten et al. (1999a) used an adapted and shortened version of the ILS, focusing the items to address learning strategies used in a specific course (processing and regulation strategies[32], 50 items in total). In this study a within-subjects design was used to examine the effect of different courses on the learning strategies used. This approach is somewhat similar to the studies Schommer performed to examine domain (in)dependence of epistemological beliefs (Schommer & Walker, 1995; Schommer-Aikins et al., 2002). Two waves of first year students following four law courses (Introduction to Law, Private Law, Criminal Law and Administrative Law) during the second semester of their first year, were asked to fill in one 50-item ILS for each course followed. The two waves are referred to as Study 1 (n=85) and Study 2 (n=63). The differences between the four courses were established by interviewing lecturers about instruction and assessment and by inspecting study materials.

Of the four courses examined Private Law and Criminal Law appeared to differ from the other two in a number of ways. Where the Introduction to Law and Administrative Law courses were more general and abstract, Private and Criminal Law were more related to concrete issues and everyday experience, stated cases were used in teaching as well as assessment and both courses were well-organised and included various didactic resources (e.g. suggestions about task approaches). From the description given our interpretation of the difference between the two pairs of courses boils down to on the one hand traditional (learning-teaching conception 2) instruction for Introduction to Law and Administrative Law and on the other hand application-oriented (learning-teaching conception 3) instruction for Private and Criminal Law.

The effect of the learning environment on the students' learning strategies showed that in the courses of Private and Criminal Law students significantly more often used the processing strategies 'relating and structuring', 'analysing', 'concrete processing' as well as significantly more often reported the regulation strategies 'self- and external regulation'. Lack of regulation was significantly less often reported in Private and Criminal Law. The use of the processing strategy 'memorising' did not differ between the four courses. These results led Vermetten et al. to conclude that "learning strategies are susceptible to changes in the learning context" (Vermetten et al., 1999a, p. 16). In fact, the accumulative effect of good organisation and application orientation in the Private and Criminal Law courses resulted in "more frequent use of almost all processing and regulation strategies, [while reducing] lack of regulation" (Vermetten et al. 1999a, p. 18). Remarkable in this study is that strategies one might expect to be differentially influenced by the learning context (e.g. meaning directed vs. reproduction directed strategies), seem to be similarly affected by the learning environment. Considering the sample of relatively young first-year students, this result could be explained by the students' epistemological naivety.

Having four completed questionnaires per student, made it possible to examine the consistency in the use of learning strategies across courses. The analysis showed that for 55% of all correlation coefficients there was "a rather high consistency across courses, with 50% of the variance accounted for" (Vermetten et al., 1999a, p. 13). 'Concrete processing' and 'lack of regulation' were the least consistent, which is not unexpected as these two strategies were most seriously affected by the learning environment. The fact that Private and Criminal Law provided more opportunities for application and a lot of didactic suggestions (influencing regulation), may explain the found higher variability of 'concrete processing' and 'lack of regulation'. Vermetten et al. remark that their study does not provide an 'either-or' answer to the issue whether learning strategies are *consistent* across learning environments or that they *vary* by learning environment. We concur with them on this issue, while at the same time we would like to emphasise the importance of the students' level of epistemological sophistication as an influence on the extent of consistency and variability found (see p. 74–75 before).

Realising that within-subject longitudinal studies are scarce, Vermetten et al. (1999b) designed a further experiment to study developments in students' learning strategies, mental learning models and learning orientations from two perspectives. In the first uni-dimensional perspective possible development within each scale of the ILS (between first and third semester of university, one year apart) was examined separately. The multidimensional perspective focused on changes in intercorrelations between scales over the same period of one year – comparing factor structures of the ILS. This latter approach is identical to the approach described in Rodríguez and Cano (2007 in press) see above. Literature on the Model of Domain Learning led Vermetten et al. to expect that over time, interrelations between learning strategies, mental learning models and learning orientations would become stronger and the factor structure of the ILS more focused. This expectation is also true from the learning-teaching conception model perspective, because as students mature they become more aware of the complexity of learning and the structure of its components. A sample of 276 first-year students of Law, Economics, Social Sciences and Arts were asked to fill in a semester-specific 100-item ILS[33] version at the end of the first and third semester. In addition the students were asked to fill in the Inventory of Perceived Instructional Activities (IPIA). The IPIA was based on Vermunt's work and measures the "perceived adequacy of the amount to which the learning environment (teacher, book, study manual etcetera) performed the activity" (Vermetten et al., 1999b, p. 229). In this inventory students were asked to indicate on a 5-point Likert scale whether a particular instructional activity – e.g. providing guidelines, organising group discussions, raising interest, relating to students' own experience, etcetera – 'occurred much too little', 'occurred adequately' or 'occurred much too often'. The instructional activities were categorised into four main groups: directing, activating, motivating and concretising activities. The examples given above run parallel to these four main groups.

The uni-dimensional analysis was performed using a series of paired-samples T-tests. In the third semester students used significantly more often the cognitive processing strategies 'relating and structuring', 'critical processing' and 'concrete processing' and they reported significantly more use of 'self-regulation' strategies: these results indicating significant changes towards a more meaning-directed learning style. Regarding their mental learning models, only the scale 'intake of knowledge' changed significantly in such a way to indicate a decrease in the belief that learning is primarily reproduction of knowledge. Changes in their learning orientations showed a significant increase in 'personal interest' and 'vocational orientation' and a significant decrease in 'certificate orientation'. The IPIA results showed that students evaluated the amount of directing, activating and concretising activities as more adequate in the third semester (compared to the first semester). Motivating activities on the other hand were evaluated as occurring less often than deemed adequate in the third semester. Despite the changes found above in the uni-dimensional analysis, the correlations between students' scores on scales in the first and third semester were considerable: median correlation scores for learning strategies, mental learning models and learning orientations ranged from 0.58 to 0.64, indicating a large measure of consistency as well. Again these results confirm our position that the answer regarding development (variability) or consistency is not 'either-or', but 'both'.

Comparing the factor structure of the ILS over time, the first (meaning directed) and third (undirected) factors became more focused and more coherent, while the second factor (reproduction directed) remained mostly the same. The changes in the fourth factor were interesting because the factor loadings were quite different: the pattern for third semester students clearly pointing more towards an application directed style, while the pattern of the first year students Vermetten et al. qualified as "quite weakly defined" (Vermetten et al., 1999b, 232). We on the other hand, see a pattern where first semester students experience 'lack of regulation' and 'ambivalence' linked to their having little idea about the practical use of their knowledge (negative loadings on 'vocational orientation' and 'use of knowledge'). This interpretation is supported by the pattern in the third semester, where the students had a more clear idea about the practical use of their knowledge and ambivalence disappeared. From our learning-teaching conceptions model, these changes in the fourth factor are indicative of a development from learning-teaching conception 2 to 3 for third semester students.

The uni-dimensional analyses of the ILS and IPIA support our interpretation and Vermetten et al. draw a similar conclusion: "It would mean that, with the learning environment becoming more activating, directing and concretising (e.g., providing guidelines for studying, group assignments, and asking for possible applications), more deep-level and concrete learning strategies are employed" (Vermetten et al., 1999b, p. 235). Vermetten et al. reviewed several studies showing that factor structures often become temporarily less clear at the beginning of a new type of educational environment (the transfer e.g. from secondary to higher education) indicating a period of change, acclimatisation or friction, triggering students to change their perceptions of knowledge and learning. 'Friction' is a concept that over the years becomes more central to Vermunt's reflections on the practical implications of his work and we will return to this concept in the chapter Changing Teaching and Learning (chapter 10). If indeed, each transfer to a new learning environment is accompanied by a period of diffusion or friction Vermetten et al. conclude that this points "toward the importance of paying attention to learning processes in this [initial] period, which may be optimal to teach students how to learn, and to help them reflect on their learning conceptions and orientations" (1999b, p. 237).

In 2002, Vermetten et al. revisited the issue of the influence of context on the use of learning strategies, by studying the effects of a comprehensive, student-oriented educational reform (SOE) in the first two years of Law at Tilburg University. Among others, SOE was introduced to influence students' learning strategies towards more deep-level learning. In this study Vermetten et al. looked at the effects of instructional changes in four main courses in the Law department, Private Law, Introduction to Law, Criminal Law and Administrative/Constitutional Law, and two optional courses, Public Administration and Fiscal Law. In general all courses focused on the one hand on increasing more active learning: less lectures and more group work, more assignments and paper writing, more interaction, more cases and more application oriented treatment of subject matter. On the other hand teachers improved course structure and directions for studying. The level of changes implemented varied by course. To measure the effect of these 'powerful learning environments' on learning strategies, Vermettten et al. used 50 items of eight scales of the course-specific version of the ILS: the processing and regulation strategies. Two groups were compared, a control cohort following the courses in the year immediately before the introduction of SOE and an experimental group, the first group to follow the new Law programme. Only the changes in the Public Administration course turned out to be large enough to influence the students in the experimental group towards a more deep-level learning strategy. In interpreting these results it became clear that the changes in this course were more profound and that the Public Administration lecturers were considerably more positive about the reform than the lecturers of the other courses. The course was deemed particularly powerful due to "the extensive, actual case that students had to work on in small groups.

The case was supported by video materials and assignments and seemed to get students involved. Therefore, this course seemed to incorporate more constructivist elements compared with the others" (Vermetten et al., 2002, p. 273).

In an attempt to explain the lack of major effects of most of these changed learning environments on learning strategies, Vermetten et al. performed an additional study aimed at examining the importance of individual differences between students with regard to learning and thinking about learning. Second year Arts students filled in the learning strategies part of a semester-specific ILS as well as the part regarding mental learning models. Notable here is that Vermetten et al. now interpret the mental models scale as measuring learning conceptions. Cluster analysis of the responses to the ILS resulted in a three-cluster solution: 'inactive learners' characterised by low levels of learning activity, 'surface/undirected learners' who scored high on reproduction and external regulation, and 'deep learners' scoring high on deep processing and self-regulation. Consistent with our own research with beginning students (e.g. van Rossum and Schenk, 1984 or van Rossum and Taylor, 1987[34]) the group of 'surface/undirected learners' was the largest. In addition to the ILS, these Arts students had also indicated their appreciation and use of a number of instructional measures that were part of the SOE, using a questionnaire – the Responses to Instructional Measures Questionnaire, RIMQ. The six instructional measures included in the RIMQ were directions for studying, assignments, directions for exams, summaries, learning objectives and step-by-step manuals and students were first asked to indicate if a measure occurred 'too often', 'enough' or 'too infrequently' (appreciation) and secondly how they used each instructional measure (act upon it, use it as a check, use it afterwards, rarely use it). Deep learners and surface/undirected learners differed in their appreciation of instructional measures in a 'psycho'-logical way: e.g. "deep and highly self-regulated learners indicated that they do not need detailed manuals, whereas surface/ undirected learners would like to have them more often" (Vermetten et al., 2002, p. 281). Regarding the use of instructional measures the same 'psycho'-logical pattern was found, e.g. "deep learners with high self-regulation are inclined to apply their own methods, and find their own answers, and use instructional measures merely as a check" (Vermetten et al., 2002, p. 281) and at the same time surface-level learners "in general, more often indicate that they act upon instructional measures" (Vermetten et al., 2002, p. 278). In this sense, this second study clarifies that educational reform is not about objective entities perceived identically by all. Again, the view on learning (learning conception or learning strategy) proves to be a lens that distorts the objective image/innovation so that it fits the individual's level of epistemological sophistication. Students seem to seek congruence between their own learning preferences and the learning environment offered. However, to stimulate change (and development towards more deep learning strategies), Vermetten et al. propose to disturb this congruence, to introduce a constructive friction evoking critical reflection on the mismatch between students' current learning strategies (or conceptions) and the new demands, 'forcing' a change of viewpoint or strategy (see also Vermunt and Verloop, 1999 in the chapter Changing Teaching and Learning, 10).

In 2005 Vermunt changed his terminology, preferring 'learning patterns' to learning 'styles' because in his experience people too often "associate [style] with unchangeability, an invariant attribute of students, deeply rooted in personality" (Vermunt, 2005, p. 207). The study he reported in 2005 can be seen as comprehensive, relating the simultaneous influence of a number of personal (age, gender) and contextual (highest level of prior education, academic discipline) variables to the 20 scales of the 120-item ILS[35], now including the scales regarding regulation strategies and learning conceptions. Furthermore, Vermunt used the ILS scales to predict a number of academic performance indicators and – in contrast to other studies – included first-year students from seven disciplines who "had not yet passed the first year propaedeutic exam of their current academic discipline" (Vermunt, 2005, p. 211)[36] and who participated in a teaching-learning environment Vermunt characterised as "rather traditional in nature" (Vermunt, 2005, p. 231). The responses of 795 students were analysed using simultaneous regression analyses for the personal and contextual variables. The predictive value of the ILS for three performance indicators (mean exam score, percentage of exams passed and study pace) was also determined with regression analyses.

The results regarding the personal and contextual variables showed that

- Age was an important positive predictor for the scales associated with meaning-directed learning (e.g. 'construction of knowledge'). The positive relation between age and 'lack of regulation' was an unexpected outcome which Vermunt interpreted as perhaps indicative of students' confusion and lack of direction due to environment-induced reproductive learning conflicting with the older students' preference towards meaning-directed learning (Vermunt, 2005, p. 228) (see also our concept of disenchantment in the section When Worlds Collide);
- Gender had no consistent relationship with scales related to learning patterns. Men and women differed most on the scale 'co-operative learning', with women being more social and men more individualistic in their way of learning. This result reminds us of the gender-related reasoning patterns discussed by Baxter Magolda (1992a);
- The higher the level of prior education, the less students demonstrated signs of reproduction-directed learning. Reproduction-directed (and undirected) learning was strongly associated with students coming to university directly after completing secondary education, which made Vermunt conclude that "reproductive learning was adaptive in secondary education [in the Netherlands]" (Vermunt, 2005, p. 229); and
- Academic discipline proved to be the strongest predictor of students' scores on the scales of the ILS, indicating a measure of domain dependence of learning patterns. Meaning-directed learning was more strongly associated with Arts and Psychology, reproduction-directed learning was associated with Econometrics and Law, application-directed learning was also associated strongly with Law, and finally, undirected learning was strongly related to Economy and Econometrics. "In summary, the results show that academic discipline is an important predictor for all four learning patterns" (Vermunt, 2005, p. 223).

> Vermunt has an important caveat regarding this result. Although it may prove true that different disciplines make different demands on students' learning, it may also be possible that these differences have more to do with differences in teaching and assessment practices between disciplines than with differences between disciplines themselves.

Learning patterns – or learning conceptions for that matter – have proven to be notoriously difficult to change. Vermunt postulates that his study, where the learning patterns are closely related to a number of personal and contextual variables, might help to explain this stability of learning strategies: "The learning activities students employ are not only the result of instructional measures, but are apparently also embedded in a complex whole of personal and general contextual factors" (Vermunt, 2005, p. 229).

Because the pattern of results was identical for all three performance indicators, Vermunt (2005) only discussed the relationship between the ILS-scales/learning patterns and the mean exam score. In general, student learning patterns proved to be important predictors of academic performance in the predominantly traditional teaching-learning environment. Meaning-directed learning was positively associated with academic performance, reproduction-directed learning was mostly a negative predictor of academic performance[37] as was undirected learning. Lastly, application-directed learning was not a good predictor of academic performance, with inconsistent correlations. Closer examination of the separate disciplines revealed that of the processing strategies only 'relating and structuring' influenced exam performance for some disciplines, the other processing strategies did not seem to matter much in exam performance. Vermunt found this result striking: "in some disciplines relations between the use of processing strategies and indicators for academic performance were almost absent. In those disciplines it was apparently hardly relevant for exam results which thinking strategies students used to study subject matter" (Vermunt, 2005, p. 230). A second remarkable finding referred to 'lack of regulation' which proved to have a strong negative effect on exam performance. This led Vermunt to conclude "It seems that for exam achievements, it was less important whether learning processes were regulated internally or externally, as long as they were regulated in some way" (Vermunt, 2005, p. 230–231).

Other researchers using the ILS

In 1996 Lonka and Lindblom-Ylänne reported a study examining the relationships between a number of different theoretical constructs. This study is particularly interesting as an example of a study taking a complex approach to epistemology, treating the set of constructs as interdependent within a structure reminiscent of an epistemological ecology. The concepts linked in this study included students' conceptions of learning, epistemologies, learning approaches, criteria and study strategies used to monitor and assess comprehension and regulation strategies. In addition to the study of interrelations, this study also examines developments regarding the various concepts listed above using a cross-sectional design with first and fifth year students of medicine and psychology. Including two academic disciplines created the opportunity of also performing these analyses in the light of domain (in)dependence.

In total 175 students were asked to fill in a 'task booklet of learning' consisting of a number of open-ended, and a series of Likert-type questions. Of this sample the majority were medical students (n=116), 49 novice (first year) students and 67 advanced (fifth year) students. The 59 psychology students comprised 33 novice and 26 advanced students.[38] The two open-ended questions concerned the students' own subjective definitions of learning and a comprehension-monitoring probe examining how students determine that they had understood studied material (see also Ryan, 1984 in the section on Schommer). The responses to the learning question were analysed for 'active epistemology' (students taking an active or passive role), 'constructivity' (acquisition of existing knowledge vis-à-vis construction of knowledge) and 'representation' (the extent to which terms such as schemata and knowledge structures are used in responses). The responses to the comprehension-monitoring probe were scored for comprehension-monitoring criteria (use of knowledge versus use of comprehension/application criteria) and for suggested study strategies for assessing comprehension (e.g. rehearsal, elaboration). The 71 Likert-type questions were adopted from the ASI (Entwistle and Ramsden, 1983; 14 items on learning approaches), Vermunt's ILS (50 items referring to regulation strategy and conception of learning scales) and Ryan's dualism scale (Ryan, 1984a; 7 items).

Principal component analysis resulted in a four-component solution. The first component was called *externally regulated and reproduction-directed learning* (in the remainder referred to as reproductive learning) with the scales of 'surface approach', 'external and lack of regulation', 'intake of knowledge' and 'dualism' loading highly and positively. This component is recognisable as our learning-teaching conception 2. The second component was called *self-regulated, meaning-directed and goal-oriented learning* (in the remainder referred to as constructive learning) with positive loadings of the scales 'deep approach', 'self-regulation', 'construction of knowledge' and 'achievement motivation' and negative loading for 'surface approach' and 'lack of regulation'. This component is recognisable as our learning-teaching conception 4. The third component Lonka and Lindblom-Ylänne called *constructive epistemology* was characterised by high positive loadings of 'constructivity' and 'use of comprehension criteria' and by negative loadings of 'dualism' and 'use of knowledge criteria'. We disagree with the interpretation of Lonka and Lindblom-Ylänne that it represents epistemologies more than learning conceptions. We feel that this component in fact reflects the contrast between reproductive and constructive conceptions of learning and knowledge, the *contrast* between the first and second component in this analysis: in this it models the watershed we discussed in chapter two. The fourth and final component Lonka and Lindblom-Ylänne called *active use of knowledge* with 'use of knowledge' and 'active epistemology' loading high and this factor is reminiscent of learning-teaching conception 3 (aiming at the acquisition of knowledge to be used later in professional life). Three of the components (1, 2 and 4) are similar to three of the learning patterns Vermunt reported in 1998 (reproduction-directed, meaning-directed and application-directed).

Lonka and Lindblom-Ylänne proceeded to compare the component scores of psychology and medical students to examine domain differences and they compared the component scores of novice and advanced students (within each discipline) to examine development. The first component, reproductive learning, showed only domain differences: medical students scoring significantly higher on this component than psychology students. The analysis of the second component, constructive learning, resulted in no differences between domains or indications of development. The third component, constructivist epistemology, proved to be more interesting: psychology students scored significantly higher on this component than the medical students and students of both disciplines developed towards a more sophisticated epistemological level with psychology students developing further, but not statistically significantly so, than medical students. The final component, active use of knowledge, showed a domain effect and an interaction effect of domain and development: medical students being more application (and profession) oriented and scoring higher on this component than psychology students. In addition medical students tended to become even more application (and profession) oriented during their studies, while psychology students became increasingly less application oriented (but at the same time increasingly more constructivist). From our perspective, these results seem to indicate that the medical students grew towards learning-teaching conception 3 – coming to a halt just before the watershed – while psychology students seemed to cross the watershed in the course of their studies. While these results seem to indicate domain differences, Lonka and Lindblom-Ylänne are careful to describe the considerable differences in learning-teaching environments between the two disciplines: Finnish medical schools being very traditional, teacher centred and the psychology environment being more activating (Lindblom-Ylänne and Lonka, 2000). In later articles reporting on the same sample of students, the authors argue more and more towards the interpretation that these differences in learning/knowledge orientation and development reflect more differences in the teaching-learning environments, than in the disciplines themselves (Lindblom-Ylänne and Lonka, 1999, 2000, 2001).

From our epistemological perspective the third question addressed in Lonka and Lindblom-Ylänne (1996) was the more interesting one: the relationship between dualism and domain, and the development towards relativism. Consistent with the results above, psychology students scored lower on dualism than medical students, and furthermore both groups displayed an increase in relativist thinking during their studies. Regarding comprehension monitoring, dualists were considerably more fact oriented and relativists proved to be more comprehension oriented. The strategies used for assessing comprehension differed between relativists and dualists as well: relativists using more elaborative and affective[39] strategies while dualists used more rehearsal strategies.

By examining the interrelations between various concepts, as Lonka and Lindblom-Ylänne have performed here, they have provided us with quantitative support for our position on the relationship between epistemologies and conceptions of learning and they arrive at a similar conclusion as we do, that all these concepts (conceptions, epistemologies, approaches, criteria and strategies for monitoring and regulation strategies) seem to be in a dynamic process of interacting with each other in many complex ways. "In sum, interactions between conceptions of learning and conceptions of knowledge appear theoretically interesting. We can assume that these conceptions affect students' study habits by guiding their reading efforts … Conceptions of knowledge (epistemologies) may not only guide comprehension standards, but also, study strategies and orientations" (Lonka and Lindblom-Ylänne, 1996, p. 21). In short, we all (van Rossum and Hamer, 2004; Vermunt, 2005 and Lonka and Lindblom-Ylänne, 1996) have arrived at an 'epistemological ecology', where individuals exhibit a logically coherent system regarding these concepts at any moment in time, be it a reproductive pattern, an application-oriented pattern or a meaning-directed pattern. Because of the complexity, these systems (or patterns), while not unchangeable, will prove to be difficult to change in an educational context.

In a set of three subsequent articles, Lindblom-Ylänne and Lonka (1999, 2000 and 2001) further analysed the quantitative data of the advanced students above (medicine and psychology), using these data to examine individual study orchestrations (using a k-means cluster analysis) and linking these study orchestrations to measures of study success. An individual study orchestration "may be considered as [a] student's individual combination of different aspects of learning" (Lindblom-Ylänne and Lonka, 2001, p. 122): more concretely this means an individual's constellation of scores on the various scales included.[40] Lindblom-Ylänne and Lonka discerned consonant and dissonant orchestrations: consonant meaning that an orchestration contains 'psycho'-logical combinations for instance, an individual scoring high on 'deep approach' and 'self-regulation'. Dissonant orchestrations refer to individuals combining either e.g. 'deep approach' with the experience of 'external regulation' or combining 'surface approach' with the experience of 'self-regulation'.[41] In addition to this quantitative re-analysis of the data, the authors also performed a number of interviews with the advanced medical students (n=35) based on the responses given to the two open-ended questions in the 'task booklet of learning' (Lindblom-Ylänne and Lonka, 1999, 2001). A different qualitative approach was chosen for the advanced psychology students (n=24), who were asked to fill in an additional questionnaire with some open questions, and whose responses to these questions were examined through content analyses (Lindblom-Ylänne and Lonka, 2000). The interviews of the medical students were aimed at discovering the qualitative differences between students with consonant and dissonant study orchestrations (Lindblom-Ylänne and Lonka, 1999, only cluster 4) and examining the qualitative different ways in which students prepared for exams (Lindblom-Ylänne and Lonka, 2001, all four clusters). The content analyses of the responses of the psychology students were also performed to examine qualitative differences between consonant and dissonant study orchestrations (Lindblom-Ylänne and Lonka, 2000, both clusters).

The cluster analysis of the 67 medical students (Lindblom-Ylänne and Lonka, 1999) resulted in four clusters of study orchestrations, and so four groups of students:

- Cluster 1: meaning-oriented independent students (n=11 with 4 interviews), whose orchestration resembles our learning-teaching conception 4;

- Cluster 4: reproduction-oriented and externally regulated students (n=14 with 8 interviews) resembling our learning-teaching conception 2;

and two clusters resembling in our opinion two variants of our learning-teaching conception 3 (van Rossum, Hamer and Würffel, 2003): one variant linking reproduction to application (cluster 3), the other linking reproduction to selecting only main points expected to be necessary later in study or professional life (cluster 2):

- Cluster 2: meaning-oriented students with a novice-like conception of knowledge (n=25 with 12 interviews);
- Cluster 3: reproduction-oriented and application-directed students (n=17 with 11 interviews).

The effect of the traditional medical curriculum is reflected in the low number (n=11) of students that have reached a truly meaning-directed epistemological level of sophistication after almost 5 (!) years of university education, and that almost one "in every fifth advanced medical student" (Lindblom-Ylänne and Lonka, 1999, p. 15) seemed not to have developed epistemologically at all (remaining in cluster 4). In van Rossum et al. (2003) a similar distribution was found for students at the end of a traditional (tertiary level) hospitality-oriented curriculum in the Netherlands. The majority of students in this type of traditional curriculum may not develop beyond learning-teaching conception 3 and will not pass the watershed towards meaning-directed learning. The relationship between study orchestration and study success showed that meaning-oriented independent students (cluster 1) scored significantly higher than reproduction-oriented and externally regulated students (cluster 4) on preclinical grades. While the pattern for clinical grades was the same, the differences were not statistically significant.

Lindblom-Ylänne and Lonka reported only a qualitative analysis of the orchestrations of cluster-4 students and found two distinct groups within this cluster: students with consonant (4 interviews) and dissonant (4 interviews) orchestrations.[42] We will discuss only the students with consonant orchestrations, reserving the dissonant orchestrations for the section When Worlds Collide in chapter 8. In the interviews, the four purely reproduction-oriented students expressed a number of problems in their study strategies: while they were aware that their approach to studying was no longer appropriate, they seemed to be unable to change, to have problems to select the essentials, (still) to lean heavily on rehearsal of everything to be sure they at least 'know' it all, and they were puzzled about learning and applying knowledge.

> I study using an old, poor routine… I must admit that, even though I have tried to change [my study habits], I always start reading the same way: too late in a hurry, and I never have time to read the book through… I pay too much attention to detail, I can't choose the essentials of the text. It's very difficult for me to choose the essentials, because I don't know what is essential. I may have the bad habit of repeating what I have read all the time… Even when I was at comprehensive school I repeated things about ten times… (S3, Lindblom-Ylänne and Lonka, 1999, p. 12)

This type of extremely novice approaches to learning are usually found in the early years of higher education, and van Rossum et al. (2003) found a similar persistence of this naive epistemology in a traditional tertiary hospitality-oriented curriculum.

In 2000, Lindblom-Ylänne and Lonka examined the advanced psychology students in a similar way. For these 28 students a two-cluster solution was chosen: cluster 1, meaning orchestration (n=12, with 9 students for the qualitative analyses), and cluster 2, reproducing orchestration (n=16, with 15 students for the qualitative analyses). The first thing we notice here is that even in the activating psychology-curriculum, the majority of the advanced students still has a clear reproduction-orientation regarding learning. While meaning-directed students scored slightly higher grades and studied about 10% faster than the reproducing-directed students, these differences were not statistically significant. The content analyses showed that the meaning-directed psychology students all had a coherent study orchestration and expressed high motivation and personal interest, own initiative, and personal responsibility for their learning.

> I'm not expecting to really learning anything except through my own hard work. My own interest and initiative are the most important things... (S21, Lindblom-Ylänne and Lonka, 2000, p. 24)

As before in the reproducing cluster of the medical students, the second cluster of psychology students contained two types of orchestrations of which we will discuss the consonant, purely reproducing-orientation here, saving the dissonant orchestration for chapter 8 in the section When Worlds Collide. Reproducing students with a consonant orchestration were only moderately motivated and expected that their studies would give them good basic knowledge and skills, but "many believed that more profound knowledge and advanced skills as well as qualifications would develop through practice, that is, not during but *after* their studies" (Lindblom-Ylänne and Lonka, 2000, p. 24).

> I expect my advanced studies to provide me with concrete practice for working life. However, I don't believe good qualifications are everything – the real skill develops from experience. In working life I have to pray that I won't make serious mistakes. (S23, Lindblom-Ylänne and Lonka, 2000, p. 27)

While we will not go into detail here, we would like to remark that the forms of dissonance found for advanced medical and advanced psychology students were not identical or even similar. In fact they seem to express two types of friction (Vermunt and Verloop, 1999) or two types of incompatibility between students' and teachers' views on learning and teaching (Kember, 2001). We will discuss this further in chapter 8, the section on friction.

In 2001, Lindblom-Ylänne and Lonka do report a qualitative analysis of the *four* clusters of advanced medical students, focusing this analysis on the perception of assessment practices and on exam-preparation strategies, again using semi-structured interviews based on students' answers to the open-ended questions in the 'task booklet of learning'. The students in the four clusters did not in fact differ so much on the subject of the perception of assessment practices: "[students] in all four groups criticised quite similarly the examination practices of the Faculty of Medicine. According to the students, the examinations too often called for memorising instead of understanding and applying the knowledge. Furthermore, many of the students critically noted that the examination practices guide students towards superficial learning, which is not useful or functional for their future occupation" (Lindblom-Ylänne and Lonka, 2001, p. 136). The four groups of students did differ in their views on the best way to prepare for an exam.

The first group of meaning-oriented advanced medical students was not distracted from looking for meaning even though the exams were fact-oriented. These students were highly capable of thinking about how to prepare for different examinations and purposes, exhibiting metacognitive skills for planning and monitoring their learning and selecting study strategies. These students seemed to be 'immune' to the (detrimental) effects a traditional curriculum can have on students' study strategies and motivation. In a sense, we feel, that while these students have a consonant study orchestration, it is dissonant with the teaching-learning environment.

> ...I try to study the subject area from as many references as possible. I don't read the same text again, because I think it is important to learn how different authors write about the same issue... I never try to memorise. I'll construct the whole picture gradually from many references. (S14, Lindblom-Ylänne and Lonka, 2001, p. 126–127)

Where Lindblom-Ylänne and Lonka interpreted the orchestration of group 2, meaning-oriented students with a novice-like conception of knowledge, as conceptually close to the first cluster, we disagree (see above). In our opinion this group represents one variation of learning-teaching conception 3, which is basically reproduction-oriented but focuses strongly on an important new skill: selecting the essentials. In our model the fact that they interpret many meaning-oriented scales as descriptive of their behaviour, and thus are identified as meaning-oriented when measured by a questionnaire, is not unexpected. As we discussed in chapter 1, each learning-teaching conception uses and interprets significant educational concepts differently. The interpretation of meaning in the third level refers very often to being able to understand what is essential, important and useful in future. In this sense, these students see their skill of selecting meaningful parts of the subject matter as a meaning-oriented study strategy. This interpretation is supported by the scores of these students on scales such as 'deep approach' and 'construction of knowledge' where they often score themselves even higher than any other group (Lindblom-Ylänne and Lonka, 1999, table 3, p. 9). Typical of this learning-teaching conception (and the students in this second cluster) is the rejection of 'merely memorising' which led us – some years ago – to rename learning conception 3 "more than memorising". This emphatic rejection of memorising facts may deepen their overestimation of the meaning-directedness of their new study strategy. Three quotes below illustrate the type of comments these students have and their (relatively) flexible approach to exam preparation.

> I try to concentrate on the essentials of a text. Our knowledge consists of facts. Understanding makes learning easier. I formulate questions and problems through which I can evaluate how well I have learned ... (S1, Lindblom-Ylänne and Lonka, 2001, p. 127)

> What I don't like in studying medicine is that our knowledge remains fragmented. It is very difficult to form a coherent view of different subdomains of medicine... The examinations don't necessarily measure understanding but memorising instead... Learning by heart is silly... I have started to analyse my study habits more carefully and tried to develop them... Forming a coherent view of the material to be learned is the most important. (S3, Lindblom-Ylänne and Lonka, 2001, p. 128)

> We don't have to understand, only memorising is required ... I used to be a conscientious student. I have become more selective... I usually underline the main things, but if the examination material is difficult, I write notes... I try to apply knowledge to clinical situations. (S17, Lindblom-Ylänne and Lonka, 2001, p. 129)

The third cluster of students reflects we feel the more typical learning-teaching conception 3, they are much more focused on learning by reproductive application and less on understanding (what are the essentials). In a way, these students react in a similar way to the constraints of the learning-teaching environment as the students in cluster 1. While they are aware that exams are mostly fact-oriented, they focus on finding applications for their knowledge, hoping that at the same time this strategy will prove sufficient to pass their exams. In a way their strong focus on application "could be considered as their 'saviour'" (Lindblom-Ylänne and Lonka, 2001, p. 137) and it 'inoculates' them against the effects of the very traditional learning environment.

> I search for 'representative patients', that is, patients who represent to me different diseases. For example, I once met a patient who had all the typical symptoms of diabetes. This patients 'is diabetes' for me (...) Most of the examinations don't call for a broader picture, they only call for learning facts by heart. (S34, Lindblom-Ylänne and Lonka, 2001, p. 129)

> I study the subject matter from many references in order to read differently formulated explanations of the subject matter. I try to avoid pure repetition. When studying a disease, I relate what I have read to the symptoms of a patient I have met. It is like a puzzle - placing pieces from a book to the patient's symptoms. (S24, Lindblom-Ylänne and Lonka, 2001, p. 130)

> It is very important that you are able to apply theoretical knowledge in practice... Our examination books are very traditional. We usually have too little time to prepare ourselves for examinations. When studying for examinations, I try to concentrate on the essentials, to understand the main things and further try to carry out problem-based studying... (S5, Lindblom-Ylänne and Lonka, 2001, p. 130)

The fourth cluster of reproduction-oriented and externally regulated students with consonant orchestrations[43] we discussed earlier in this section (Lindblom-Ylänne and Lonka, 1999) and the problems they expressed there remain relevant also for exam preparation.

> I haven't any particular study habit, I've been frustrated from the beginning of my studies ... I feel that I can't read the way I should, and sometimes I feel that I don't understand what the examiners want ... I can't answer in the exams in the way they would like me to answer. Maybe I try too carefully to read every detail... At the beginning I felt lost, and I still feel lost ... I simply can't. (S27, Lindblom-Ylänne and Lonka, 2001, p. 131)

The quotes show, we feel, significant qualitative differences between the clusters of students, most clearly expressed in their flexibility towards exam demands and their level of metacognitive awareness. The first cluster displays the most flexibility and the larger sense of control of their own learning situation, including exams, while the fourth cluster contains students in 'despair'. These latter students clearly have no idea how to change what they *do* see as inappropriate learning strategies persisting after secondary education, perhaps because they do not understand what the teacher (examiner) in higher education expects from them. They seem to be unable to play the 'examination game'. In this sense we see in these results again a clear developmental process, where the higher developed group (cluster 1) has a larger repertoire of skills and strategies, and greater metacognitive awareness than the lower groups. Lindblom-Ylänne and Lonka close their article with suggestions for improving student development through a problem-oriented curriculum, metacognitive training (reflection on study skills and strategies) and appropriate assessment practices, aimed at application and competence. We will discuss these suggestions in the chapter Changing Teaching and Learning.

Broadening the base of disciplines to include the applied science of pharmacy, Nieminen et al. (2004) used a shortened version of the 'task booklet of learning' to examine relationships between study orientation (learning approaches, conceptions of learning, and regulation strategies), epistemology (dualism) and study success, and – in a longitudinal design – developments in orientation and epistemology. For us this study is interesting because the bachelor programme for pharmacy is in many regards higher professional education in the same sense as the bachelor of hospitality administration programme at the Hotelschool The Hague. On the other hand, the curriculum of the Hotelschool The Hague (see also chapter 6) central to our main study reported in later chapters (7 through 9), is much more problem-based and less traditional than the described pharmacy programme.

Nieminen et al. (2004) report on a final sample of 66 pharmacy students who had completed the shortened version of the task booklet twice, once at the beginning of their studies (September 1994) and once at the end (between May 1997 and March 1998)[44]. The shortened version of the task booklet included 8 scales for measuring approaches (deep and surface, Entwistle and Ramsden, 1983), conceptions of learning (2 ILS-scales, intake of knowledge and construction of knowledge), regulation strategies (3 ILS-scales, self-, external and lack of regulation) and epistemologies (dualism, Ryan, 1984a). Factor analysis of the scores on these 8 scales resulted in two second-order variables, meaning orientation and reproducing orientation. To measure study success three variables were constructed on the basis of course grades, the first-year GPA, a combined GPA for the last two years, and an overall 3-year GPA. The 3-year GPA was also used to form groups of above-average and below-average pharmacy students.

Intercorrelations between study orientation, epistemology and GPA were calculated for the first year and at the end of the students' studies. In the first year dualism was positively correlated with 'surface approach', 'intake of knowledge' and 'external regulation', and after three years dualism was positively correlated to 'surface approach', 'intake of knowledge' and 'lack of regulation' and negatively related to 'self-regulation'. These results pointed clearly to a strong relationship between epistemology and study orientation. The relationship with study success differed by wave, in the first year no relationship with first-year GPA was found, in the last year of study only 'lack of regulation' was negatively related to the combined GPA of the last two years. As mentioned above, factor analyses for the first and second wave separately resulted both times in two main factors, reproducing orientation and meaning orientation, with dualism loading highly on the reproducing orientation in both waves, and dualism loading negatively on meaning orientation only in the second wave. Together with a considerably more negative loading of 'lack of regulation' on meaning orientation, we feel that the factor structure after three years was slightly more 'psycho-logical' than the earlier factor structure, confirming the findings of Vermetten et al. (1999b). The relation between the second-order variables (meaning orientation and reproducing orientation) with the overall 3-year GPA was only (negatively) significant for the third-year reproducing orientation: the higher students scored on reproducing orientation after three years, the lower their study success as measured by the 3-year GPA. This result may be related to the finding that the combined last two years GPA was negatively affected by 'lack of regulation' and that the reproducing oriented students experienced increasing problems with regulation during their studies. As Nieminen et al. propose, "[s]tudents' regulatory problems became a component of the reproducing orientation. The results of the present study indicate that the reproducing orientation may be linked with problems of the regulation of learning" (Nieminen et al., 2004, p. 408). In this interpretation 'lack of regulation' no longer is part of a separate 'learning pattern' (e.g. 'undirected learning') as Vermunt proposed (e.g. Vermunt, 1998). The expected positive relationship between third-year meaning orientation and study success (3-year GPA) was only just not statistically significant ($p=0.075$).

In the traditional curriculum of the pharmacy programme, we would not expect much change in study orientation and epistemology over the years. Nieminen et al. found that for the group as a whole the meaning orientation did not change, but that the students with a reproducing orientation became moderately, but significantly less so. Comparing the development of above-average and below-average achievers, the pattern of development was slightly different. Both groups of students became less reproducing oriented over the years, with the above-average students changing significantly more than the below-average students. The changes in meaning orientation were also different for both groups, with above-average students retaining their original level of meaning orientation and below-average students decreasing their meaning orientation significantly. While neither group showed a significant increase in meaning orientation, as can be expected in a traditional curriculum, these developmental differences resulted in a significantly higher score on meaning orientation for above-average students at the end of their studies.

This study supports, as does the study by Lonka and Lindblom-Ylänne of 1996, our position that epistemologies and learning conceptions, or study orientations for that matter, are closely related theoretical constructs. Nieminen et al. (2004) do not answer the question about the possible causal relationships between these constructs. Concentrating on the question of causality, in our opinion (see also the section on epistemological ecology), all too often causality is assumed to be one-way, in the words of Nieminen et al.: "It is possible that dualistic conceptions of knowledge predispose students to perceiving learning as the passive intake of facts and to relying on the judgement of authorities instead of personal understanding" (Nieminen et al., 2004, p. 409). However, Nieminen et al. continue to describe an alternative approach to 'causality' which we feel fits more closely in our view regarding an epistemological ecology and Schommer's Embedded Systemic Model: "it is also possible that various factors, such as conceptions of learning and knowledge, study practices, and the nature of the subject matter itself, all shape each other in highly multidirectional and simultaneous fashion in the course of studying" (Nieminen et al., 2004, p. 409). Furthermore, the relationship between consonant/dissonant study orchestrations and study success is implicitly confirmed in this study, where the development towards more consonant study orchestrations of the above-average students (lower on reproducing with no loss –or small gains— on meaning orientation) was clearly different from the increasingly dissonant study orchestrations of the below-average students (lower on meaning ánd reproducing orientation). Nieminen et al. conclude on a positive note, "[since] the results of the present study indicate that in the same learning environment some students may be able to develop their study orientations in a more coherent fashion and others may fail to do so, it may be worthwhile to try to provide opportunities for low-achieving students to reflect on their views about learning and knowledge and to guide them to experiment with new ways to approach learning" (Nieminen et al., 2004, p. 413).

Richardson (2007, in press) used the mental models (or conceptions of learning) section of Vermunt's ILS to examine the learning conceptions of distance education students of the British Open University. The English version of this part of the ILS (25 items) was adapted to match the context of distance learning. While examining the results, Richardson addressed a number of methodological and theoretical issues regarding previous analyses performed by Vermunt and Lindblom-Ylänne and Lonka:

- the limits of the use of factor analysis,
- the choice of type of cluster analysis, and

– the need to perform further discriminant analysis to identify scales that best predict cluster membership.

Richardson argued that the use of factor analysis in e.g. the construction of the ILS, leads to support for "a theory of intellectual development that assumes a continuous progression along one or more cognitive dimensions rather than one that assumes a series of qualitatively distinct positions in some development sequence ... *In themselves*, the results will not provide evidence of qualitative variations in conceptions of learning, and *a fortiori* they will provide no support for a stage theory of intellectual development such as that espoused by Marton, Säljö and colleagues"[45] (Richardson, 2007 in press p6). Regarding cluster analysis, Richardson criticised the choice of k-means cluster analysis (see Lindblom-Ylänne and Lonka, 1999) as inferior to hierarchical cluster analysis. And furthermore Richardson argued that following cluster analysis, discriminant analysis is needed to be able to better interpret the characteristics of the clusters found. As the last step in his analysis, Richardson examined the clusters to see if they could be interpreted as forming an hierarchy typical for stage models.

Richardson used the complete answers to the 25-item mental models section of the ILS of 441 undergraduate open university students for his analyses. First a principal component analysis was performed on the five scale scores, resulting in a two-component solution. 'Intake of knowledge' (reproductive learning), 'use of knowledge' (application-oriented learning) and 'co-operative learning' loaded highly on the first component and 'construction of knowledge' (constructivist learning) and 'stimulating education' (learning stimulated by teachers and textbooks) loaded highly on the second component, lending in our opinion respectively a reproductive (surface) and constructive (deep) learning slant to the components. To formally evaluate the items of the adapted 25-item ILS, Richardson performed a principal component analysis on the answers to the 5 items within each scale. Each scale could be described by a single component, with all items loading highly. Then a second principal component analysis was performed over all 25-items, resulting in a four-component solution. Three components coincided with three original scales, 'co-operative learning', 'use of knowledge' and 'intake of knowledge', and the fourth component was a combination of the scales 'construction of knowledge' and 'stimulating education'. Only four of the 25 items loaded on a second component besides their own.

A hierarchical cluster analysis (complete linkage clustering using the city-block metric as measure of dissimilarity) on the students' scores on the five scales led to a four-cluster solution. The characteristics of these four clusters could better be interpreted after discriminant analysis – performed to predict cluster membership – which identified two significant discrimant functions. The first function combined 'co-operative learning' and 'intake of knowledge' demonstrating "an emphasis on learning with others for the purposes of memorizing and reproducing" (Richardson, 2007 in press, p. 14). The second function combined 'use of knowledge' and 'stimulating education' signifying "an emphasis on the application of knowledge in response to encouragement from tutors" (Richardson, 2007 in press, p. 14). The scale 'construction of knowledge' loaded on neither of these discriminant functions, implying that for *these students* this scale was not necessary to determine cluster membership.

Cluster 1 students scored low on both discriminant functions and Richardson interpreted this to mean that the students in this cluster were "meaning-oriented and independent" (Richardson, 2007 in press, p. 13, see also Lindblom-Ylänne and Lonka, 1999) and probably – according to Richardson – also more intrinsically motivated. Some 23% of the students belonged to this cluster, and if we interpret these students as representative for the 4th learning-teaching conception (or higher) this result is consistent with e.g. the share of epistemologically sophisticated people (about 20% evaluativists , see chapter 3, section on Kuhn) found by Kuhn when she measured the epistemological development of people of all ages and all walks of life (Kuhn, 1991). The largest second cluster (53%) contained students who scored moderately high on the first function, and Richardson interpreted this as reproduction-oriented students who, as Lindblom-Ylänne and Lonka found (1999, cluster 4), were externally regulated. Again the volume of this cluster is consistent with Kuhn's findings regarding the number of absolutists (Kuhn, 1991). Cluster 4 students, comprising only 5% of the sample, scored highly on reproduction as well as on application of knowledge and so can be seen as typical examples of learning-teaching conception 3 students. Cluster 3 students (19%) also scored (moderately) high on application, but scored considerably less reproduction-oriented (and so more meaning-oriented) than the cluster 4 students. Richardson interpreted this cluster as students who "were more likely to be studying to obtain qualifications, than for intrinsic personal reasons" (Richardson, 2007 in press, p. 14) and based on this characterisation we feel that cluster 3 students can be seen as a variant of learning-teaching conception 3 students. We have discussed similar variants of learning-teaching conception 3 before (see above in 'Other researchers using the ILS') in the discussion of Lindblom-Ylänne and Lonka (1999) who used more scales than the five Richardson used in this study. While Richardson had theoretical and methodological reasons to use different analyses (than Lindblom-Ylänne and Lonka 1999 and 2001), we conclude that the results are strikingly similar considering that the studies were performed with very different samples (medical students vs. a heterogeneous group of undergraduate distance learners) and using a different number of scales to measure learning orientations/conceptions.

Regarding the mental models (or conceptions of learning) section of the ILS, Richardson concluded that this part "is a relatively robust instrument when administered to students taking courses by distance learning in the UK" (Richardson, 2007 in press, p. 14). Unlike our interpretation above, Richardson does not see the four clusters as constituting "a simple developmental hierarchy" (2007 in press, p. 15) implying that "if course designers can be explicit about the particular learning patterns that they are trying to instil in their students, it should be possible to construct interventions to bring this about" (2007 in press, p. 15). Leaving the issue of whether change implies hierarchical development or not to the side, in principle one can agree with this, perhaps optimistic 'contextual' view on the effect that interventions might have on changing learning patterns (as Vermunt would call

Richardson's clusters). However, many studies who share our more 'developmental' view on learning have shown that interventions have to be carefully designed *and* tailored to the students' current epistemological level, creating what Kegan (1994) would call a holding environment and Vermunt a constructive friction (Vermunt and Verloop, 1999). And even then, changing learning patterns towards the desired level of epistemological sophistication in higher education, is found never to be quick nor easy.

Comments on Vermunt

Similarities between research using the EBQ and the ILS – discussing some theoretical and methodological issues

In Vermunt and Vermetten (2004) the authors discussed their contribution to the development of "a second generation of conceptualizations of student learning" (2004, p. 361) and they reviewed a number of studies using the ILS and its theoretical framework – linking processing strategies and learning orientations to regulation strategies and conceptions of learning.[46] Discussing this article, we will draw parallels between research with the ILS and research with the EBQ, and will examine the theory on students' development as learners that Vermunt and Vermetten constructed using the research with the ILS.

We have found ten parallels between the studies using the ILS and those using the EBQ, which we will discuss below. We use this summary as well to clarify a number of theoretical and methodological issues and place some annotations regarding particular findings.

1. The concept of friction between a student's learning activities and a teacher's teaching activities is discussed by both Vermunt and Schommer et al. (2002).

Friction can stimulate the way students learn or their epistemological development, but too much friction can be harmful for development. For instance when teachers expect too much self-regulation from their students. Without introducing the concept of friction, we presented an example of a similar destructive friction in van Rossum, Deijkers and Hamer (1985): "For teaching aimed at the students' development, this means that their interpretation of the context may in no way be discarded. … when one wants to give students more responsibility for their own learning, a slow process of growing familiar with it would, we feel, be necessary, because too much of 'a good thing' at once could possible be perceived as threatening (and therefore, no change will occur)" (p. 640).

2. The ILS and the EBQ both have become internationally well known and used inventories to measure we feel related concepts, epistemological beliefs and learning patterns.

Vermunt and Vermetten list the following countries: "From 1992 onward, the ILS was used by researchers in the Netherlands, Belgium, Finland, England, Cyprus,

USA, Brazil, Argentina, Indonesia, and Sri Lanka" (2004, p. 364). As we have discussed above the EBQ has been used in a number of countries outside the USA, including Norway, Belgium and China.

3. As in many studies in educational psychology, the most frequently used sample comprises of first-year higher education students.

From a developmental perspective this is unfortunate, as we expect that the relatively young first-year students will not often display the more sophisticated views on learning and knowledge that may prove to be more common among graduating or post-graduate students. Indeed Baxter Magolda's books (1992 and 2001) have shown clearly that epistemological development occurs during college, and especially after college in graduate studies and working life. This means that the factor structures (and the clusters) found in many of the ILS and EBQ studies are mostly characteristic of novice learners in (Western) higher education.

4. For both inventories, replications of the original factor structures (both by the way, four-factor structures) have been found, however there are also a number of studies that result in deviations of the original factor structures.

Vermunt and Vermetten (2004) mention that with other types of students (e.g. adult students in secondary education) and for students in other cultures (e.g. Indonesian university students) other factor structures, or even other factors can be found. In particular the Indonesian example is interesting because "Dutch students experience aspects of learning patterns as separate aspects that for Indonesian students can go well together. ... Marton et al. (1997) found that [Chinese] students do not experience memorizing and understanding as opposite poles, as is often found among Western students, but as phenomena that are closely interwoven" (Vermunt and Vermetten, 2004, p. 369–370).

We have our reservations regarding this particular evidence for cultural differences. As we have discussed in chapter 1, in van Rossum, Deijkers and Hamer (1985) and in van Rossum (1988), we have found for *Dutch* (first-year) students, that 'understanding' and 'memorising' (or dualism for that matter) *can* indeed and *do* go together, depending on the meaning students attach to 'understanding'. Säljö (1979c) described a similar phenomenon for (*Swedish*) students: while most students said they could use deep and surface strategies, only about half of them were able to describe clearly (and correctly) the difference in nature between a deep and a surface approach. This means that the other half – the ones unable to clarify the difference – obviously had a different interpretation of deep approach or understanding. The variation in interpreting 'meaning' is an issue also found in Lindblom-Ylänne and Lonka (1999, cluster 2 of *Finnish* students) and probably also in Richardson's analysis (2007 in press, cluster 3, *UK* students). In our experience (of over 25 years) 'memorising' and 'understanding' become opposites poles for students mostly when they are close to, or have recently passed the watershed and only just left multiplicity behind.

5. Both the ILS and the EBQ have been used to examine the development as a learner and in personal epistemology.

Vermunt and Vermetten carried this somewhat further than Schommer and proposed a theory for students' development as learners. Vermunt and Vermetten used studies with the ILS to show that as pupils (secondary) and students (higher) grow older and have more educational experience, the respondents are more capable of making differentiations within the four learning components of the ILS (processing strategies, regulating strategies, conceptions of learning and learning orientations), meaning e.g. for the component 'processing strategies' that students become more capable of recognising that there are different ways to approach a text. A second aspect of Vermunt and Vermetten's developmental theory concerns the increasing 'psycho'-logic or coherence of the factor structures found for somewhat older, and more educated students, meaning that students, as they become older and more experienced in education, recognise more clearly e.g. the coherence between a deep approach, self-regulation and personal interest. Vermunt and Vermetten interpreted the increase in coherence as symptomatic of the fact that "learning behavior is increasingly coming under the control of the views and motives of the learner" (2004, p. 370). They also discussed the influence of the educational context on the factor structures found, e.g. the seeming temporary disruption of factor structures at the transfer from one educational environment to the next indicating adaptation of students to new demands.

We feel both their development hypothesis (more differentiation and coherence or integration) and their context hypothesis are consistent with our view formulated in the eighties of the previous century: "We believe that we are neither dealing with stable individual characteristics, nor with qualities acquired by accident. Learning conceptions, in our opinion, show the *development* of the student from novice to expert in learning (see van Rossum and Hamer, 1985); a development that moreover is strongly contextually determined. When we read a [row of the table][47] of the prototypical answers, this development becomes more clear. To illustrate this line of reasoning we give the following example: the interpretation of 'active learning' develops itself from a reproductive notion to a more constructive view, during which five gradually more *differentiated* definitions of the concept are being used" (van Rossum, Deijkers and Hamer, 1985, p. 636–637).

6. The ILS as well as the EBQ have been used to examine consistency vis-à-vis variability of learning patterns over domains, or in Schommer's terms domain (in)dependence of epistemological beliefs.

Both ILS and EBQ studies demonstrate that the question of domain (in)dependence or (in)consistency cannot be answered with 'either/or' but that learning patterns (or epistemological beliefs) are both to a certain degree context specific (thus domain dependent), while there is also evidence for generality across contexts (or domain independent). We have referred to the former, context-specificity effect proposing that in some contexts some beliefs or patterns are more salient than in other contexts, and to the latter, generality-across-contexts effect as meaning that students do have similar learning patterns or epistemological beliefs in differing contexts. The conclusion that Vermunt and Vermetten draw regarding the learning patterns as measured by the ILS, is valid for the epistemological beliefs as measured by the EBQ as well: "the stability of these learning patterns is rather high, but not so high that they should be conceptualized as unchangeable phenomena" (Vermunt and Vermetten, 2004, p. 372).

7. The concept of dissonance in learning patterns can be related to Schommer's view that epistemological beliefs within a system need not develop in synchrony.

Dissonant learning patterns are becoming increasingly popular as objects of study in 'learning' studies and are interpreted as "unexpected, theoretically incompatible combinations of particular motives, intentions, strategies, regulatory mechanisms, contextual perceptions, learning conceptions, and so on" (Vermunt and Vermetten, 2004, p. 373). Vermunt and Vermetten list five types of dissonance that address in our opinion different issues. Some of the dissonances (those involving differentiation and integration), we feel if seen from a truly developmental perspective – such as our own or Vermunt and Vermetten's developmental theory (see also parallel 5 above) for that matter – should be interpreted *not* as unexpected combinations but as descriptions of lower levels of development. As an example Vermunt and Vermetten describe a group of low achieving university students with "several indications of dissonance in their learning patterns: they showed a lack of differentiation within learning strategies, conceptions, and orientations, and a lack of integration between these learning components" (2004, p. 373). They also list a dissonance – incompatibility – that seems to point towards a lack of 'psycho'-logic between learning strategies, conceptions and orientations within a student. It is this latter type of dissonance that could be an expression of asynchronical development proposed by Schommer.

The dissonances as discussed by Lindblom-Ylänne and Lonka (1999, 2000) seem to be of a different order altogether, with the dissonances referring to incompatibility between students' learning orientations and the demands of the learning environment and as such describing friction (Vermunt and Verloop, 1999). These latter forms of dissonance are more contextually defined, where the types of dissonance quoted above seem to refer to the students themselves, either to students' lower developmental levels or to asynchronical development. We feel that this discussion about dissonance would benefit if researchers made more clear whether they are discussing within-student dissonances or student-learning environment dissonances or friction.

8. Several studies with both the ILS and the EBQ have tried to establish relationships between learning patterns or epistemological beliefs on the one hand, and on the other hand personal (e.g. aspects of personality, gender) and contextual (e.g. level of (prior) education, discipline) variables.

Lonka and Lindblom-Ylänne (1996), Rozendaal et al. (2001) and Nieminen et al. (2004) in fact have linked the learning approach (of Vermunt) to the epistemological approach (of Schommer), showing that the reproduction-directed learning pattern was related to dualism (naive epistemological thinking) and the meaning-directed learning pattern to relativism (sophisticated epistemological thinking). Vermunt and Vermetten conclude "that it seems wise to see epistemologies and learning patterns as distinct but related phenomena" (2004, p. 380).

9. Relationships between learning patterns (or epistemological beliefs) and learning outcomes (or study success) have been established in studies with the ILS and the EBQ.

Where the studies with the ILS often had to focus on a rather narrow and quantitative measure of study success (exam results, GPA, study pace etcetera), we feel that Schommer was able to include a number of more qualitative measures of learning outcomes (e.g. writing a concluding paragraph to a dual position paper). We feel the measurement of the relationship between learning outcomes and learning patterns (or beliefs) would improve if studies were designed where

- learning outcomes are assessed in more open ways that facilitate differentiation between qualitatively higher and lower levels of thinking (also e.g. van Rossum and Schenk, 1984, making a summary; van Rossum, 1988, making a table of contents),
- and - as Phillips (1998, 2001 see comments on Schommer above) has shown - the assessment practice matches the types of epistemological beliefs measured.

10. The educational consequences of research with the ILS and the EBQ seem to overlap, leading Vermunt and Schommer to make similar suggestions for educational improvements.

Vermunt focuses on process-oriented instruction, "an educational concept especially aimed at promoting 'learning to learn', at discouraging undirected and reproduction-directed learning patterns and at promoting meaning- and application-directed learning patterns" (Vermunt and Vermetten, 2004, p. 377). On several occasions and often referring to Beers (1988), Schommer discusses the educational implications of her work which match the features of process-oriented instruction. Vermunt and Vermetten (2004) discussed a number of studies reporting positive effects of innovative 'learning to learn' courses (designed with process-oriented instruction in mind) on learning approaches, metacognition, study success and positive feelings towards education. We will discuss process-oriented instruction (Vermunt, 2003) in more detail in the chapter 'Changing Teaching and Learning'.

Besides the ten listed similarities, of course there are differences between the EBQ and the ILS research. For instance the EBQ has been used to examine epistemological beliefs in relationship to argumentation on controversial real-life issues such as abortion or gender-related conversation styles (Schommer-Aikins and Hutter, 2002). The ILS on the other hand has been used to measure the effects of particular learning environments on students' learning, examining whether the suggestions for better (more powerful) learning environments (see parallel 10 above) have the effects theoretically expected. Vermunt and Vermetten (2004, p. 375) reported on a study with the ILS where student-oriented learning environments emphasising relationships between topics (in Schommer's terminology a complex learning environment) led to meaning-directed learning, while learning environments emphasising memorisation and lacking incentives for students' active participation led to reproduction-directed learning (a simple learning environment). While at first glance, the study by Bråten and Strømsø (2005) could be interpreted as a study using the EBQ to compare different learning environments (an innovative teacher education programme versus a traditional business administration programme), the very limited format of the EBQ (only 24 of the 63 items) together with measuring first-year students only at the beginning of their study (without much experience of the two educational programmes) makes this study flawed in this respect.

The ILS as a Diagnostic Instrument

We would like to end this section on the current ILS with a study (Vermunt, 1995 reported in Vermunt and Vermetten, 2004, p. 378), where the ILS was used to diagnose a student's own way of learning. Based on this diagnosis, each student was provided with individually tailored instructional measures. The results of this study showed that because of this intervention students started to reflect on their way of learning. Furthermore, reproduction-directed and undirected students became more 'constructive' and the learning patterns of meaning and application-directed students became more integrated (more coherent). And very interesting for education is that the intervention had some transfer effects: the students received higher exams scores in another course.

'New Learning' and 'Old Learning' - How New is 'New'?

Vermunt and Vermetten (2004) place traditional education (reproduction and transmission-oriented) against innovative learning environments, stating that "[i]ncreasingly, people are becoming dissatisfied with these [traditional] types of teaching and learning environments, and the call for innovative teaching methods, stressing active, constructive and self-regulated learning, is increasing" (2004, p. 381). This controversy between traditional teaching and more innovative teaching is not new. In 'Experience and Education' John Dewey (1938/1997) distances himself from traditional education, saying "Learning here means acquisition of what already is incorporated in books and in the heads of the elders. Moreover, that which is taught is thought of as essentially static. It is taught as a finished product, with little regard either to the ways in which it was originally built up or to changes that will surely occur in the future. It is to a large extent the cultural product of societies that assumed the future would be much like the past, and yet it is used as educational food in a society where change is the rule, not the exception" (Dewey, 1938/1997, p. 19). And he continues to describe his vision and the common principles of progressive education: "To imposition from above is opposed expression and cultivation of individuality; to external discipline is opposed free activity; to learning from texts and teachers, learning through experience; to acquisition of isolated skills and techniques by drill, is opposed acquisition of them as means of attaining ends which make direct vital appeal; to preparation for a more or less remote future is opposed making the most of the opportunities of present life; to static aims and materials is opposed acquaintance with a changing world" (1938/1997, p. 19–20). Where Vermunt and Vermetten state that innovative active teaching is becoming more popular and mainstream, recent developments in the Netherlands show that there is a growing opposition[48] to what is called 'new learning' as a general label for innovative learning programmes. Actually this issue was already resolved to a certain extent in the Netherlands with the long-time existence of separate (primary and secondary) schools based on progressive education, e.g. Montessori or Dalton schools. The 'imposition from above' forcing *all* secondary school in the Netherlands to implement some form of new (or activating) learning (in 1999) may lie at the root of the current growing unrest about education in Dutch society.

Third Generation Inventories – What to Add

The ILS is considered a second generation inventory for assessing learning because it included metacognitive aspects of learning in addition to traditional aspects such as learning strategies and study motivation. Vermunt and Vermetten suggest that a third generation of conceptualisations of student learning and instrument development should "incorporate the affective and social/collaborative learning components more prominently" (2004, p. 381). With this recommendation, Vermunt creates a linkage to the interpersonal aspect of epistemological development which is such an important focus in the work of Baxter Magolda (1992, 2001). Based on her work (and Kegan, 1994) we would like to add a further recommendation: to include items or scales focusing on identity issues, either in a third or fourth generation instrument. An interesting dimension to examine would be identity development: from an externally defined identity to an internally defined identity (or self-authorship). Of course such statements would need to be derived from interviews with a variety of people of all ages and walks of life, perhaps even over sampling the more mature people, and not from a sample of first-year students.

Hofer

> *In our most mundane encounters with new information and in our most sophisticated pursuits of knowledge, we are influenced by the beliefs we hold about knowledge and knowing. What has been called personal epistemology, epistemological beliefs or theories, ways of knowing, or epistemic cognition, is activated as we engage in learning and knowing.*
>
> *(Hofer, 2002a, p. 3)*

We include the work of Barbara Hofer in this chapter as an example of an approach that, we feel, moves toward reconciling the more holistic traditional qualitative epistemological models (see chapter 3) with the more analytical and quantitative approach developed by Schommer.

Based on the review of epistemological models reported in 1997, Hofer and Pintrich analysed the epistemological dimensions most commonly found in the more holistic qualitative models. They proposed that epistemological thinking, as 'personal theories' (Hofer and Pintrich, 1997, p. 117–118, Hofer 2001, p. 361, Hofer 2002a), in general is characterised by two core dimensions[49]: beliefs about the Nature of Knowledge (what one believes knowledge is) and about the Nature [or Process] of Knowing (how one comes to know). Each of these core dimensions comprises of two more concrete aspects of (or beliefs within) an individual's epistemological theory: the Nature of Knowledge includes aspects about the certainty and simplicity of knowledge and the Nature [or Process] of Knowing includes aspects about the source and justification of knowledge. Hofer and Pintrich feel that limiting their model of epistemological theories to two core dimensions gives more direction to theorising on and research into personal epistemology.

To understand the model of epistemological theories (MET), we discuss the four main aspects here. Certainty of Knowledge refers to the degree to which one sees knowledge as fixed or changing and evolving over time. Simplicity of Knowledge ranges from knowledge seen as accumulation of discrete, concrete knowable facts to knowledge seen as highly interrelated relative concepts. At lower levels of the aspect Source of Knowledge, knowledge resides in some external authority (e.g. book, expert, teacher), while at higher levels the self as maker of meaning becomes central. Justification of Knowledge refers to how individuals support knowledge claims, ranging from simply accepting authority's claims through trusting "what feels right" to basing a knowledge claim on the evaluation of evidence from various sources (Hofer, 2004).

Hofer tested her MET of core dimensions in epistemological thinking in two studies. In 2000 she reported on a quantitative test, using a 27-item questionnaire specifically developed to represent the proposed dimensionality of personal epistemology (Hofer, 2000, p. 388). The questionnaire was administered to over 300 first-year college students and factor analysis resulted in a four-factor solution with the following factors:

- certain/simple knowledge (8 items)
- justification for knowing: personal (4 items)
- source of knowledge: authority (4 items)
- attainability of truth (2 items).

Hofer concluded that this result provided "some evidence for substantive validity of the suggested dimensions" (Hofer, 2000, p. 391). However, Simplicity and Certainty of Knowledge did not appear as separate factors, and the dimensions of Justification of Knowing and Source of Knowing appeared not to cover the full range to be expected within these aspects, the items loading on these factors representing only the lower end of the theoretically expected range of epistemological thinking. We feel the latter finding could be related to the relatively young sample, where higher epistemological thinking is more rare and as such the students may have problems to understand the meaning of items referring to higher levels of epistemological sophistication. An explanation that Hofer herself also acknowledged (Hofer, 2000, p. 399). Regarding this type of quantitative measurement of the MET, Hofer (2000, p. 402) concluded that "[m]ore work is needed to flesh out these dimensions in self-report measures".

In 2004, Hofer reported a qualitative study testing the MET and exploring the effects of two epistemologically different teaching environments within the lecture format. In this study, Hofer observed multiple lectures of three introductory courses, one psychology course and two chemistry courses. The chemistry courses differed considerably in the epistemological approach to teaching and learning: "[the organic chemistry] course offered the view that students are cognitive apprentices who can rise to the challenge of constructing knowledge much as scientists do, within a discipline in which knowledge continues to evolve. The [general chemistry course] presents a view that knowledge is chemistry consists of facts and formulas and that knowing chemistry means remembering and applying these formulas and recognizing contexts for their particular use" (Hofer, 2004, p. 143). In addition she interviewed 25 students twice during the semester in which they participated in these courses. The interview contained general questions taken from other epistemological studies (e.g. King and Kitchener, 1994) and questions specifically related to incidents and events occurring in the courses. Analysis of the interviews showed that the four dimensions of the MET could be found in the students' responses. To demonstrate how Hofer interpreted the answers as supporting the four dimensions we quote some of the more interesting answers below.

The dimension **Simplicity of Knowledge** was especially salient in the answers regarding the testing practices in the courses. Both chemistry courses were tested using mostly open-ended problems. When asked what students thought of this and why the test was constructed in this way, some students holding a more simplistic view of knowledge preferred the familiar high school multiple choice testing and using a note card with formulas necessary to answer the test questions.

> At my high school we had a note card and it had all the formulas…and she would give us questions but they were things we had seen before. So the stuff she went over in class was on the test, not the exact questions, but the same idea. And what was so different about *this* test was that these were things people had never seen before and that really threw us! (17a, Hofer, 2004, p. 144)

When these students were asked about how they studied, students mentioned memorisation as the main study strategy. Other students displayed a view on knowledge on the other end of the continuum of Simplicity of Knowledge and were more accepting of testing through open-ended problems.

> There are multiple things that can happen in each problem and they want you to think creatively…It separates people basically—those that can think creatively, because that's what an engineer does, or in chemistry or physics or whatever. They want people who can think creatively and problem solve. (7a, Hofer, 2004, p. 145)

Not only do these quotes illustrate the different ends of this dimension, the fact that they are both excerpts from a first interview[50] illustrates that at the beginning of college students already differ in their epistemological assumptions. We also found large differences between first year psychology students regarding their conceptions of learning in our early studies (e.g. van Rossum and Schenk, 1984). The question arises how such a diversity in students' epistemological (or learning) conceptions can be accommodated in the first year of higher education. This point is illustrated in Hofer's study by the difference in response of two students, the first with evidently more naive epistemological beliefs than the second, to the less conventional approach of the organic chemistry course.

> He was just trying to get us to look at stuff for what they are. I think when we get into more hardcore chemistry stuff he wants us not to forget what the basic things really are, not just what they stand for, but what they are and what they're made of, like seeing the tree instead of the forest. (id unknown, Hofer, 2004, p. 147)

> It's a totally different way of looking at chemistry. (And why do you think he does that?) To make people learn how to critically think. This seems to be a big thing in all our classes, the critical thinking. In the beginning of all our classes that's what's being discussed—that you're analyzing what you're learning and picking it apart (9a, Hofer, 2004, p. 147)

In particular the first response seems to indicate that presenting an introductory course on a fairly sophisticated epistemological level, even while explaining to the students the reasons for the approach, may prove to be counterproductive, with at least some students missing the point entirely.

Regarding **Certainty of Knowledge,** Hofer feels that in this study many students are likely to have evolved beyond the dualist phase. The examples provided in her article suggest that these students are already moving into the Perry stage of Multiplicity, where facts are substituted by opinions and every opinion is equally valid. However there was Dualism present in some answers regarding the definition of truth.

> Something that is known with absolute certainty. And something that is believed to be true, that is 100% true. Like mathematics concepts. (6b, Hofer, 2004, p. 148)

An example of a more multiplistic answer is

> Truth is different for everyone. You can believe something and it will be true to you but for the other person it's completely different. It's all about opinions…Truth to you is your particular view. (16b, Hofer, 2004, p. 148)

Within the analysis regarding this dimension, some responses contain evidence of epistemological development: where students described retrospectively how their thinking now differed from their thinking early in high school. To illustrate, below a response to the question "Do you think you always thought that?"

> No, I think before, more like early high school, I didn't think. More as I got into advanced placement classes in later high school years, and now that I came here, I think. I've developed more critical thinking and more openness to

> other perspectives and other findings, to be able to say 'I'm not as rigid, I can look at other people's argument and see what their side of the story is'. (2b, Hofer 2004, p. 149)

This finding is interesting with regard to the discussion about the value of retrospective questioning. However, retrospective questioning has a history in epistemological research, as Perry as well as Baxter Magolda base their models on some form of retrospective questioning. This approach is used also in studies regarding learning and teaching conceptions (e.g. Kember, 2001) and in our own work (van Rossum et al. 2003) to measure epistemological development. In the current study we have used it as well: a part of the data refers to retrospective accounts of epistemological development (see chapter 7).

With regard to the dimension **Source of Knowledge** Hofer found views on the source of knowledge ranging from "an external authority" to "the self as an active constructor of meaning". These opposite ends of the dimension are illustrated by the following two quotes in answer to the question "In learning something you really want to know, can you rely on experts?"

> Yes. I guess if I wanted to know something about chemistry, to give me the right answer, I guess I could rely on my professor to tell me the right answer and how to get it. (14a, Hofer, 2004, p. 151)

> To a point. I mean, you have to think about it yourself – people can only give you so much. There can only be so much input, then the information has to be assimilated and put together and made into what you know. (11a, Hofer, 2004, p. 151)

Some evidence for interrelationships between the dimensions studied by Hofer could be found in answers to the question "How do you know when someone is an expert?". On the one hand, experts were seen as people who have more knowledge, have studied for a long time, are certified and have found facts that have been proven to be "true": a simplistic and certain view on knowledge and expertise. In a more complex and tentative view of knowledge and expertise, experts were seen as people at the cutting edge of their field with original ideas and who tie things in with other things.

In discussing the differences between the views on the source of knowledge, Hofer was surprised at the persistence and strength of the students' belief in the primacy of textbooks as repositories of truth. The primacy of textbooks may even lead to incidents in assessment situations where students – confronted with contradictions between the views of the professor and what is said in the textbook – will give an answer consistent with what the professor said, while they actually believe that what is in the textbook is true (Hofer, 2004, p. 153). In this study only a few students had developed the ability to critically evaluate the source of knowledge (textbook or professor) which is elaborated with the following quote that also includes the suggestion of epistemological development.

> I guess I look at everything, ideas from everything, try to put them together, try to weigh what each person is saying, what each source is saying, and try to think what's the best – not truth, but the best sense you can make out of it.

> (...) When I was younger I just went with what the book said and what the teacher said, and they were usually the same because the teacher taught out of the book, and if the teacher said it, it must be true. I think that's how I was earlier. (When did that change, do you think?) Later high school. And now. I'm still changing, I think. (2b, Hofer, 2004, p. 155)

Hofer used this student's responses also to illustrate the more sophisticated end of the dimension Certainty of Knowledge (see the previous section) suggesting the interrelationship between the dimensions Certainty and Source of Knowledge.

In this study, Hofer found that the students' views on **Justification for Knowing** were the least sophisticated of the views on the dimensions studied. In the second interview this dimension was measured using a statement about verification and falsification of scientific theories. It proved that many students, even though they were familiar with this statement, were unable to interpret it in a way consistent with the common understanding of scientific practices and principles:

> Scientific theories cannot be verified? I would think they *can* be verified. I'm sure they can be falsified also. Well, by scientific study and experiment you can prove something is true, I would think. You can also prove that it's not. (20b, Hofer, 2004, p. 156)

In this response we feel there is also strong evidence for an interrelation between Simplicity of Knowledge and Justification for Knowing. It is a pity that in measuring this dimension, Hofer focused only on verification vs. falsification of scientific theories in the article. Kuhn's work would – in our opinion – offer more everyday questions referring to justification for knowing, and may have led to more rich and diverse responses (Kuhn, 1991). Hofer concluded from this study that the four proposed dimensions of the MET were present in the responses of the students, but she was less optimistic about the evidence regarding the dimensions forming a coherent way of meaning making. While she supposes it is probable that dimensions within one core dimension would be at similar positions (which she feels needs to be tested), she seems to ignore the evidence within her own study of the interrelationships between dimensions belonging to different cores.

Based on the interviews, Hofer introduced a fifth dimension possibly related to the four epistemological dimensions studied, **Sense of Self/Identity**, suggesting epistemological development and identity development are related: "[the] impact of college – and of the epistemological development that can occur in such an environment – is that it can challenge both beliefs and knowledge and thus a sense of identity and one's relationship to others" (Hofer, 2004, p. 160). With this observation, Hofer moves towards the work of Kegan (1994) and in particular Baxter Magolda's later work (Baxter Magolda, 2001, see also chapter 3) where Baxter Magolda discusses the interrelationships between three dimensions in the journey toward self-authorship:

1. epistemological (how do I know?)
2. intrapersonal (who am I?)
3. interpersonal (what relationships do I want with others?)

Furthermore, with relating identity and interpersonal relationships to epistemological theories Hofer places these theories back into a larger set of beliefs and conceptions, as we do, and at the same time seems to become less concerned with the issue of core and peripheral beliefs. We would end this discussion of Hofer's work with her own words, which we feel summarise also our own views on the role of students' views on learning and knowledge in their perception of educational practices, as well as the role of teaching in higher education in epistemological development. "Finally, it appears that students filter their perceptions of instructional practice through their own epistemological perspectives, a finding congruent with the existing body of research in this field. But such perceptions are malleable, and faculty members may be most effective when they take such filters into account, address epistemological assumptions, provide the rationale for particular instructional practices, and address not only *what* there is to know in a field, but *how* it is we know, and *how* what we know can be justified" (Hofer, 2004, p. 161–162, italics ours).

The usage of 'personal theory' as main concept within Hofer's (and Pintrich's) view on epistemological thinking (Hofer and Pintrich, 1997; Hofer, 2000, 2001, 2004) means that Hofer expects coherence and internal consistency with regard to epistemological dimensions within a person. Here, she retains the multidimensional character of personal epistemology proposed by Schommer, but rejects the independence of epistemological belief dimensions proposed in Schommer's model. Taking this position regarding personal theories, Hofer suggests a pragmatic approach where research "may be moving towards an integration of ideas from multiple models: *an identifiable set of dimensions of beliefs, organised as theories, progressing in reasonably predictable directions, activated in context, operating as epistemic cognition*" (Hofer, 2001, p. 377). Furthermore Hofer acknowledges that the two core dimensions (and the four dimensions therein) are related to the – in her eyes more peripheral – beliefs about learning and teaching: peripheral in the sense that beliefs about learning and teaching are outcomes of the core beliefs.

Conclusions

The epistemological belief system proposed by Schommer-Aikins contains a number of dimensions central to the six qualitative models discussed in the previous chapters: beliefs about

- the certainty of knowledge,
- the simplicity of knowledge (both captured in our learning conception),
- the locus of control of learning (covering in part the relationship to authority and our teaching conception), and
- beliefs about how learning takes place (covering the issue of effort vs. talent in learning and so recognisable in study strategies).

She found that the more students believed in simple or certain knowledge – i.e. the more naïve their belief system – the more conclusions were oversimplified and formulated in absolute terms, and that a naïve epistemological belief system had direct and indirect effects on study strategies, learning outcomes and study success. Various studies discussed above support Schommer-Aikins' finding that the more naïve the belief system, the less likely one is to take on multiple perspectives, acknowledge the complexity of issues and make decisions in a reflective way. The more people believe in certainty of knowledge, the more likely they are to incorrectly interpret, distort or even ignore tentative or contradictory information: in short to use a "make-sense epistemology" in which information inconsistent with one's personal opinion is disregarded and alternatives are not considered linking the results directly to argumentive thinking (Kuhn, chapter 3). Linking epistemic sophistication to performance, Kitchener proposed that solving of puzzles (well structured problems) is not hindered by relatively unsophisticated epistemic beliefs, but that the performance on ill-structured problems is seriously hampered by the inability of epistemologically naïve respondents to employ "a strategy to *construct* a solution" (Kitchener, 1983, p. 226, italics ours). Finally, the belief in quick all-or-none learning was related to less effort put into learning and to lower quality learning outcomes and results. A remarkable related finding was that girls were more convinced of the value of effort in learning – a quantified gender difference at last! [51] As many researchers before, Schommer-Aikins found that age, educational level of background and years of formal education all contributed to a more sophisticated belief system.

In 1993 Schommer moved towards a more holistic view on epistemological belief systems in formulating her Embedded Systemic Model (ESM), linking cultural and regulatory beliefs to learning and performance. Paulsen and Feldman (e.g. 1999a, 1999b, 2005) and Bråten and Strømsø (2004) added the link to motivation and test anxiety (both affect!), meta-cognition, management strategies and achievement goal-orientations, increasing complexity of the ESM. The link to learning strategies and the quality of learning outcomes was provided by e.g. Cantwell and Scevak (2004) and Rodríguez and Cano (2006, 2007 in press). We see many similarities to our own model here: the multidimensionality and multiple complex interactions within a person's individual belief system; the expectation that epistemological beliefs are domain independent to a degree (facilitating the inflexibility of naïve systems and the flexibility of more sophisticated ways of making meaning); the developmental nature by increasing sophistication and returning to familiar issues at increased levels of complexity; and finally the links to affect, study strategies and learning outcomes. Moving inevitably toward the complexity of the epistemological ecology, we increased the already impressive complexity of the ESM manifold by pointing out the interactions between belief systems of the various participants in education (e.g. teacher-student, student-student) and society (peer-peer, parent-child, etcetera). This only underpins Schommer's call for a concerted research effort to uncover the complexity. The main difference between her perspective and our own is that we perceive (and examine) these relationships as logically consistent, representing an underlying systemic development, where Schommer feels the relationships are not self-evident and need to be established by means of for instance path models and structural equation models. We suggest to address this in much the same way Hendrik

Lenstra approaches complex problems: cut them into one-study-sized problems and proceed gradually through all the separate smaller problems. A start has been made in the selection of studies that made use of the EBQ discussed in this chapter. We advocate more interaction between quantitative and qualitative research efforts, as both are necessary to define the range of and approach to the necessary studies. Further exploration will incur considerable effort, but then reaching true understanding always does.

Schommer (1993) comes to recognisable suggestions regarding the changes in teaching and learning necessary to lead to epistemological development (e.g. Baxter Magolda, 2004; Phillips 1998, 2001 above; Biggs, 1996 see chapter 11): modelling more explicitly the epistemological beliefs education aspires to instil in teaching and assessment. She also makes the link towards the effect of teachers' epistemological belief systems on teaching and learning referring to Beers, who states that "teachers who are aware of their own conceptions of knowledge and who monitor the articulation of those conceptions with the day-to-day activities of the classroom will stand the best chance of influencing students in a manner which is consonant with their primary educational objectives" (Beers, 1988, p. 92). However, Beers' comment about the finding that college teachers – as their students – display the full range of Perry's positions, we feel implicates that not all teachers have the epistemological sophistication to teach at the level necessary to promote epistemological development. We will return to this issue in chapter 5 on teacher thinking. A difference between our approach and Schommer's concerns her conclusion that – although she feels education should include the major controversies with a system of discipline – that congruence of teacher and student belief systems is optimal for learning, herewith ignoring the value of "constructive frictions" (Vermunt and Verloop, 1999) or "holding environments" (Kegan, 1994) necessary for epistemological development.

Acknowledging the complexity of learning, Jan Vermunt's Inventory of Learning Styles (ILS) linked cognitive processing strategies to metacognition (i.e. regulation and mental models of learning) and affective issues (i.e. motivation and study effort). The four learning styles found are recognisable as learning-teachings conceptions 1 through 4 of our own model, not surprising considering that the origin of the inventory lies with a phenomenographic study generating the items. Using different quantitative methods (Lonka and Lindblom-Ylänne, 1996) and combining different scales (Richardson, 2007) similar clusters of learning patterns were found in the now familiar expected volumes: approximately 20% is recognisable as learning-teaching conception 4, about half can be interpreted as learning-teaching conception 3 providing proof of the validity of the learning patterns/styles. In later work the learning styles (or more recently, learning patterns to counter the idea of permanence, Vermunt, 2005) were used much like we use our learning-teaching conceptions (e.g. Vermetten et al., 2002). While the ILS is already quite a large inventory and it can be seen as covering a section of the epistemological ecology, we feel it has not addressed two major non-cognitive domains affecting learning: both the interpersonal and identity dimensions of knowing and learning. On the other hand it was the first inventory to address the mutual coherence of various types of concepts and as such a first generation inventory towards unravelling the complexity of an epistemological ecology. Indeed we conclude that the studies performed by various researchers have been instrumental in providing us with quantitative support for our position on the relationship between epistemologies and conceptions of learning and that all these concepts or phenomena (conceptions, epistemologies, approaches, criteria and strategies for monitoring and regulation strategies of learning) seem to be in a dynamic process of interacting with each other in many complex ways.

The undirected and reproductive learning patterns/styles were interpreted to be inappropriate to higher education, leading Vermunt to suggest a process-oriented instruction with the now familiar characteristics: more explicit attention for learning and thinking strategies aimed at applying and transforming knowledge (see chapter 10). A suggestion that was later echoed by Vermetten et al. and Lindblom-Ylänne and Lonka who all proposed a more problem-oriented curriculum, meta-cognitive training (reflection on study skills and strategies) and assessment practices aimed at application and competence to foster appropriate learning patterns. Vermetten et al. used the ILS to study the effect of a more activating learning environment and found that "learning strategies are susceptible to changes in the learning context" (1999a, p. 16), but that an activating curriculum needed to be relatively comprehensive to make a difference. A number of studies pointed toward a measure of consistency of learning pattern/style across courses and the tendency of students to move towards more meaning-directed learning style and a clearer idea of the practical use of the knowledge over time (e.g. Vermetten et al. 1999a and b; Lonka and Lindblom-Ylänne, 1999, 2000, 2001; Nieminen, 2004). Most interesting for curriculum design, however, was the finding that the pattern of a learning pattern/style was less well defined at the transfer between educational environments, indicating a period of acclimatisation and perhaps an increased susceptibility to change (Vermetten et al., 1999b). On the other hand, Vermetten et al. (1999b, 2002) and Nieminen et al. (2004) also found that learning patterns/ styles had an internal logic: deep learners and surface/undirected learners differed in their appreciation of instructional measures in a 'psycho'-logical way, interpreting the learning environment in a way consistent with their own "way of knowing", underscoring the position that a learning conception (or way of knowing) is a lens that distorts the perception of reality to fit the logic of the ecology. Vermetten et al. proposed to disturb this congruence, to introduce a constructive friction evoking critical reflection on the mismatch between students' current learning strategies (or conceptions) and the new demands, 'forcing' a change of viewpoint or strategy (see also Vermunt and Verloop, 1999 in chapter 10, Changing Teaching and Learning). Additional evidence for the effect of the way of knowing on learning can be found in a set of studies by Lindblom-Ylänne and Lonka (1999, 2000, 2001) introducing consonant and dissonant study orchestrations. Considering the descriptions, dissonant study orchestrations can be seen as the first quantitative evidence of the destructive influence of (very) traditional education on the study approach of meaning-oriented students: disenchantment (see further chapter 8).

In a large multi-disciplinary study Vermunt showed that age and higher levels of prior education were positively related to a more meaning-directed learning pattern. However, he found almost no evidence for gender related differences outside a female preference for 'co-operative learning'. Interestingly enough Vermunt did find clear disciplinary differences, with Arts and Psychology being more strongly related to meaning-directed learning than Econometrics, Economy and Law. Not unexpectedly Law was slightly more application-directed than the former two. While this seems to indicate domain dependence, Vermunt was very explicit in his caveat that while it may prove true that different disciplines make different demands on students' learning, there is more than enough reason to believe that these differences have more to do with differences in teaching and assessment practices between disciplines than with differences between disciplines themselves. A conclusion Lindblom-Ylänne and Lonka increasingly agree with (e.g. 1999, 2000, 2001) quoting students' negative assessment of examination in a traditional study environment (2001). While a meaning- directed learning pattern was positively associated with academic performance, for some disciplines "it was apparently hardly relevant for exam results which thinking strategies students used to study subject matter." (Vermunt, 2005, p. 230), indicating the importance of assessment geared towards measuring ways of thinking and not only factual knowledge. Furthermore his study underpins our postulate that learning is embedded in "a complex whole of personal and general contextual factors" (Vermunt, 2005, p. 229) in short that learning is part of a complex ecology that is robust and often self-correcting.

A third family of studies discussed here make use of Hofer's model of epistemological theories (MET). Hofer started out making a distinction between core beliefs (simplicity and certainty of knowledge; source and justification of knowledge), and introducing 'personal theories' (Hofer and Pintrich, 1997; Hofer 2001, 2002) as more or less consistent constellations of beliefs that have far reaching effects on the perception of a learning-teaching environment, and so on learning strategies and learning outcomes. Simplistic views on knowledge were strongly related to a preference for reproduction-oriented testing and students' persistent belief in the primacy of textbooks as repositories of truth. Beliefs regarding the uncertainty of knowledge proved related to development beyond dualism, but the measurement of beliefs concerning source and justification of knowledge was problematic.

By using retrospective questions in her work, Hofer implied her position on epistemological development. By introducing a fifth dimension **Sense of Self/ Identity**, relating identity and interpersonal relationships to epistemological theories, Hofer suggested epistemological development and identity development are related. Not only that, Hofer rejected Schommer's assumption of dimension independence. Here we see her moving towards the work of Kegan (1994) and in particular Baxter Magolda's later work (Baxter Magolda, 2001, see also chapter 3), placing her personal theories back into a larger set of beliefs and conceptions, as we do and moving away from the idea of core and peripheral beliefs. In her later work, Hofer came to see personal epistemologies in much the same way as we do our learning conceptions: as filters through which students perceive the learning-teaching environment (Hofer, 2004). Such filters are not fixed and Hofer felt teachers need to be aware of these filters and need to take them into account when teaching. However, catering to large differences in epistemological sophistication in the same course would seem problematic: presenting an introductory course on a fairly sophisticated epistemological level, even while explaining to the students the reasons for the approach, may prove counterproductive, with at least some students missing the point entirely, resulting in this case in nostalgia (see chapter 8).

So what do these studies based on either the ILS, the EBQ or Hofer's MET have in common? Firstly, we feel evidence is clear that all three approaches result in similar set of configurations of epistemological beliefs, study approaches and related phenomena. The accumulated studies have done so in a wide sample of ages, cultures and educational environments, although strict reproducibility was not always achieved. We feel there is sufficient evidence to suspect that this may be less due to disciplinary or cultural differences than to differences in interpretation of the items due to varying shares of ways of knowing in quantitative approaches examined the development in personal epistemology, although the researchers involved were not of one mind whether the personal epistemologies or learning patterns formed a hierarchical set characterised by increasing complexity. Thirdly, all three approaches provided evidence of internal consistency, a "psycho-logic" within each personal constellation of beliefs, motivations, study approaches etcetera. Furthermore, they linked learning to a broad spectrum of personal characteristics (e.g. age, gender, prior education, chosen discipline, cultural background) and most importantly to study success and the quality of learning outcomes. A number of studies provided evidence for the complications (disenchantment and nostalgic despair, see chapter 8) resulting from a mismatch between students' and teachers' expectations and perceptions of the learning-teaching environment. Regarding less severe mismatches, Vermunt is more explicit in recognising both benefits and disadvantages of friction, while Schommer-Aikins focused mostly on the disadvantages. Hofer is alone in suggesting to add relational and intrapersonal aspects to the personal epistemology, a learning pattern and so her work forms a bridge to Kegan's, Baxter Magolda's work and our own. And finally, the formulated suggestions regarding creating a learning-teaching environment that will promote a more sophisticated epistemology are identical to our own.

It seems, even by following clearly different paths, we all have arrived at an 'epistemological ecology' (see below), where directionality of relationships is less and less the focus of study. We agree fully with Nieminen et al. who stated "it is also possible that various factors, such as conceptions of learning and knowledge, study practices, and the nature of the subject matter itself, all shape each other in highly multidirectional and simultaneous fashion in the course of studying" (Nieminen et al., 2004, p. 409). Because of this complexity of relationships and influences, these systems (or patterns), while not unchangeable, will prove to be difficult to change in an educational context.

In order to understand how to design the educational experience to successfully promote epistemological development towards a desired and necessary level of sophistication, in this study we have attempted to act on Hofer's suggestion of a pragmatic approach where research "may be moving towards an integration of ideas from multiple models" (Hofer, 2001, p. 377). Not only are we merging the outcomes of qualitative and quantitative models in this study, in the next chapter we will merge models of student and teacher thinking as well.

An Epistemological Ecology: A Temporary Psycho-logic

In chapter 3 we have quoted Perry's (1970) convincing case regarding the indivisibleness of (conceptions of) learning, teaching, knowledge and assessment.

> Where knowledge consisted of facts in a single frame of reference, the teacher's primary duties were to make the facts clear and to so correct his students in respect to the right or wrong of each fact as to allow of no error. The student, in turn, collected correct facts and procedures. Where knowledge is contextual and relative, the teacher's task is less atomistic as the student's is more integrational. The good teacher becomes one who supports in his students a more sustained groping, exploration and synthesis. His acts of evaluation must subtend more than discrete rights and wrongs, and extend through time to assist discrimination among complex patterns of interpretation. (Perry, 1970)

This argument is compelling and intuitively appealing, it is also remarkable in that it does not imply any directionality. In many studies causality and directionality of effects is implicit, and even sometimes explicitly formulated: e.g. where Hofer (2001) stated that a student who believes that knowledge is simple and certain will prefer a different learning environment than a student who believes knowledge is complex and evolving.

While this example seems logical, there is no indication that it describes the true causality. In reality of everyday teaching, students who are confronted with more constructivist teaching may experience – and indeed describe in the interviews (of Hofer, 2004) – the need to change their view on (good) teaching and learning. These changed views (on (good) teaching and learning) in turn make them realise that knowledge may be something else than they thought before, implying just the opposite causal direction and making views on knowledge the outcome of changed views on teaching and learning (e.g. Perry, 1970; Baxter Magolda, 1999a, 2001). Furthermore, if, in Hofer's example, you replace 'knowledge' by 'learning', 'simple and certain' by 'memorising' and 'complex and evolving' by 'understanding', the example becomes "a student who believes learning is memorising will prefer a different learning (or teaching) environment than a student who believes learning is understanding". This example then suddenly describes the relationship between learning conception and teaching conception as we have discussed in chapter 1. Again, we feel that the discussion about core and peripheral conceptions or beliefs does not contribute to the understanding of the determinants of student learning. Finally, epistemological beliefs are related to depth of processing and motivation in exactly the same way as learning conceptions are related to study strategies and motivation: the more sophisticated the epistemological belief (or the higher the learning conception) the deeper the level of processing and the more intrinsic the motivation (Hofer, 2001,1999; Hofer and Pintrich 1997; Paulsen and Feldman, 2005, 1999a, 1999b; van Rossum and Schenk, 1984; Entwistle and Ramsden, 1983).

In our opinion "conceptions of knowledge and knowing" (Hofer, 2001) and conceptions of learning and good teaching move in a coherent and logically consistent way, where we are not convinced that any one particular conception is always the weakest link leading to change and development. We feel that any conception – including for example self-concept, assessment or motivational beliefs – can be the origin of change. In this sense we would like to introduce the term *epistemological ecology*[52] in analogy of students' conceptual ecologies as proposed by Demastes et al. (1995). Change in any one of the dimensions (beliefs, conceptions etcetera) within an ecology, necessitates finding a new balance. David Kember takes a similar view on the interactions between conceptions and beliefs, where he remarks that in his study conceptions of learning, conceptions of teaching and epistemological beliefs "form a consistent and logically inter-related set. A belief in one of these areas influences the other two beliefs, and all act in concert to affect learning approaches and outcomes" (Kember, 2001, p. 206). The logic of the inter-related set of conceptions and beliefs is exemplified as follows: if knowledge is seen as defined by an authority (epistemology), it makes sense that the role of the teacher is viewed as transferring this knowledge (teaching conception) to the students, the students' role is seen as absorbing or memorising this knowledge (learning conception) and consequently assessment is expected to test the students' reproduction of this knowledge (assessment conception). Studies by Sheppard and Gilbert (1991), Rozendaal et al. (2001), Samuelowicz and Bain (2001, 2002), Buelens et al. (2002) and Cano and Cardelle-Elawar (2004, participants were secondary school students) support the notion of a logically consistent and inter-related set of conceptions or beliefs, and "confronting one or two elements of the set may perturb the whole set of beliefs" (Kember, 2001, p. 218).

Consequently, an epistemological ecology implicates that there may be many ways to stimulate epistemological development – e.g. changing the teaching practice or teachers' epistemological perspective, the culture of the educational institute, the image of a discipline, the assessment practice, the students' self-concept, motivation or study strategies, etcetera. This, in turn, may explain the divers nature of the many suggestions made by researchers and the divers effects of the various change strategies explored. Not only does this epistemological ecology approach imply that there are "many roads to Rome", it may also mean that choosing to change only one aspect may not be sufficient to dramatically change the balance within an ecology. Furthermore, because of the many inter-relations within a set, changing this set is difficult and traumatic for the student (e.g. Kember, 2001; King and Kitchener, 1994). Therefore, to stimulate epistemological change, it is probably necessary to confront students with a prolonged comprehensive and concerted learning environment[53] that provides students with time and support to change their initial naive epistemological perspectives and to cope with the more complex requirements of higher education (Kember, 2001). In our opinion, the epistemological ecology approach is theoretically consistent with the embedded systemic model proposed by Schommer (Schommer-Aikins, 2004). A epistemological ecology is also consistent with the findings and conclusions of Paulsen and Feldman (2005; 2007 in press) where they suggest that to develop students epistemologically, it is better to address more than one epistemological belief at any time (Paulsen and Feldman, 2005 p. 762).

NOTES

[1] Ryan found that of the 54 freshmen students, 61% were dualists. At sophomore, junior and senior level, taken together 37 students, only 38% were dualists.

[2] Naïve as opposed to sophisticated epistemological positions that e.g. require higher order thinking skills.

[3] The factor analysis was performed on mean subset scores and not on the individual items.

[4] The nutrition mastery test proved to be psychometrically invalid.

[5] It is not so much that there *is* metacognition, but more that there are *different qualities* of metacognition that is important to comprehension monitoring.

[6] An example of an Orderly Process item: It is difficult to learn from a text book unless you start at the beginning and master one section at a time.

[7] To a certain, extent the common practice of scoring Perry responses with a three-digit method (see Pavelich and Moore, 1996 in Comments on Perry, chapter 2) addresses this idea of frequency distributions.

[8] A major motive for our current study, was the new curriculum implemented at the Hotelschool The Hague in 1997. The curriculum was based on the didactic concept "Enterprising Learning" and aimed to increase the students' active participation in learning.

[9] If these researchers had adopted the developmental and inclusive view on epistemological development these results would not have been as puzzling to them.

[10] Such as work, parenting, partnering (Kegan, 1994) and juror reasoning (Kuhn and Weinstock, 2002).

[11] Correlations between thinking dispositions in most cases were very small.

[12] Following the convention introduced by Schommer to name the factors by the naive position.

[13] The students in this study were teacher candidates.

[14] The Chinese students were from a 'key' high school in Shanghai, and were a highly select sample of secondary school students. The sample of African, Hispanic and Asian Americans comprised honours students and as such also is a select sample of American secondary school students.

[15] Schraw et al. (1995) measured epistemic beliefs using the Epistemic Beliefs Inventory, which was constructed to measure – and indeed resulted in – a five-factor structure as proposed by Schommer in 1990, including Omniscient Authority as a separate factor.

[16] While Phillips confirms using a subset of Schommer's EBQ (personal communication), the examples given on page 117 cannot be exactly matched to the items of the EBQ (Schommer, 1998), still leaving some doubt about the exact phrasing of the items used.

[17] Here, Phillips' Committed Effort we renamed to Quick Learning, Uncertain Knowledge becomes Certain Knowledge and Abstract, Complex Knowledge is (Concrete) Simple Knowledge.

[18] Again we use the Schommer convention and for consistency sake have renamed Ability is Unlimited to Fixed Ability, Knowledge is Complex to Simple Knowledge, Learning is Gradual to Quick Learning and Knowledge is Uncertain to Certain Knowledge.

[19] The marginally significant relationship was found only for the self-testing scale of the LASSI. This scale measures 'deep-learning' strategies aimed at the consolidation and integration of knowledge across topics (Phillips, 2001, note 12, p. 29).

[20] The article by Hofer was first presented in 1994 and officially published in 1999. It will be included in the references under 1999.

21 Why the MSLQ scale of critical thinking was not included or analysed, either in Paulsen and Feldman 1999b or 2007, does not become clear from the articles.

22 The five scales were Rehearsal, Elaboration, Critical Thinking, Organisation and Metacognition, in total 31 items. In contrast to Paulsen and Feldman, Dahl et al. discuss the scale "critical thinking" explicitly.

23 The ILP-R is a 90 item, self-report, pencil-and-paper instrument.

24 From the perspective of learning conceptions, we would say that these students are typical of learning conception 3: while these students take more responsibility for their learning, their view on knowledge is reproductive and simple and applying is algorithmic, see chapter 1. We feel that this study reflects not only the issue regarding RPL students, but more generally the issues learning conception 3 students are confronted with when encountering complexity in learning. This interpretation is supported by the quotes indicating that some of the less successful RPL students have a clearly quantitative view on learning (Cantwell and Scevak, 2004, p. 141–143).

25 Although Rodríguez and Cano embrace the idea to use instruments such as the SPQ as a diagnostic (a 'barometer reading', Biggs, 2001) to measure how the educational system (curriculum) is functioning, they do not include such an analysis for the studied 'constructive curriculum'.

26 In Rodríguez and Cano the text on page 627 does not match the results given in Table 1on the same page. In personal communication, Cano confirmed the conclusions given above which are consistent with Table 1.

27 For clarity of reading we will use the terminology introduced by Vermunt in 1998, throughout the discussion of his model and questionnaire.
Examples of processing strategies are structuring (deep) and memorising (surface), regulation strategy examples are monitoring and reflecting, mental learning models are "conceptions and views that students have about learning and teaching" (Vermetten et al., 1999a, p. 3) or a combination of "conceptions of learning ... epistemological beliefs ... and beliefs about one's responsibilities or tasks in the learning process" (Vermetten et al., 1999b, p. 223), a learning orientation is the "whole domain of personal goals, intentions, attitudes, worries and doubts of students in relation to their studies" (Vermunt, 1996, p. 28) and affective process examples are motivating and effort.

28 While we see the application directed style as a stage between the reproduction and meaning directed styles, in 1998 Vermunt implies that the application directed style "develops later than the other styles" (Vermunt, 1998, p. 166).

29 The affective processes (Vermunt, 1996) seem to be no longer (an explicit) part of this model.

30 In Vermunt and Vermetten (2004) 'outcomes' has replaced 'results' and the term 'mental learning models' is replaced by 'conceptions of learning'.

31 At the time of these studies Yvonne Vermetten was a close colleague of Jan Vermunt.

32 The eight subscales used are relating and structuring, critical processing, memorising, analysing, concrete processing, self-regulation, external regulation, lack of regulation.

33 The 100-item variant used 25 items for mental learning models, 25 items for learning orientations and 50 items for learning strategies and students were asked to keep the previous semester in mind while answering the questions.

34 Some 15 years previous to Vermetten et al., Arts students from the same faculty of Tilburg University also participated in van Rossum and Taylor 1987.

35 For consistency with the changed terminology the ILS could be renamed to ILP (Inventory of Learning Patterns), but Vermunt continues to use the already well-known acronym.

36 The disciplines included were Psychology, Sociology, Arts, Economy, Econometry, Law and Management Information Science.

37 Only for Econometry 'analytical processing' was positively related to academic performance. We feel that this result supports the studies by Phillips (1998, 2001) where the logical connection between the strategy used (here organised, serial thinking) and the quality of the performance required was stressed.

38 In Lindblom-Ylänne and Lonka (2000) the same sample of advanced psychology students is used, but now in this study the number of students is 28.

[39] "Affective strategies aim at being alert and relaxed in order to help overcome test anxiety" (Lonka and Lindblom-Ylänne, 1996, p. 8).

[40] The scales included in these studies referred to four main theoretical concepts: conceptions of learning, learning approaches, regulation strategies and epistemologies.

[41] We choose these examples of dissonance with a specific reason: the former group will often experience – and express – a measure of disappointment in the learning-teaching environment, the latter group experiencing some confusion about what is expected from them. We will discuss these two types of frictions (Vermunt and Verloop, 1999) in the chapter When Worlds Collide.

[42] It remains unclear to us, why e.g. cluster 2, an inherently dissonant cluster combining a deep approach with dualism, was not examined qualitatively.

[43] The group with dissonant study orchestrations will be discussed in chapter 8, section When Worlds Collide.

[44] Nieminen et al. experienced a similar problem as we did with collecting the data from students at the end of their studies. One of the problems in our own study was that students differ considerably in the length of their study, some finishing after four years and some taking twice as long.

[45] In the theoretical discussion Richardson includes van Rossum and Schenk (1984), van Rossum, Deijkers and Hamer (1985) and van Rossum and Taylor (1987) as typical examples of studies describing stage models of intellectual development.

[46] Vermunt and Vermetten define learning conceptions broader than we do, including beliefs about "the task division between students, teachers and fellow students in learning processes" (2004, p. 362). These beliefs we do not include in conceptions of learning, but , in our model, are a part of the conceptions of good teaching.

[47] We refer to the table on pages 638–639 in van Rossum, Deijkers and Hamer (1985) summarising the development in *coherent* interpretations of concepts such as 'learning', 'good teaching', 'kind of exam question' (knowledge vs. insight), 'understanding and insight', 'application', 'active/passive learning'. The part on understanding and application is summarised in chapter 1.

[48] The members of the foundation 'Beter Onderwijs Nederland' [Better Education for the Netherlands] reject "new learning" and wish to return to traditional teaching. BON organised a kick-off conference in January 2007.

[49] Hofer and Pintrich suggest that cross-cultural studies of epistemological theories may provide evidence for other dimensions, e.g. the Purpose of Knowledge ranging from practical and utilitarian purposes to emphases on theory building (Hofer and Pintrich, 1997, p. 130). Such a dimension we would recognise as referring to the distinction between lower level learning conceptions and higher level conceptions.

[50] The first interview is indicated by the a following the student's id-number, the second interview is indicated with b.

[51] This finding may go a long way to explain the relative success of girls in the current Dutch educational system, they just put in more effort.

[52] Here we interpret epistemology to refer to a considerably wider set of beliefs than e.g. Hofer. In addition to beliefs about knowledge, we propose to include beliefs about learning, teaching and motivation, beliefs about self etcetera.

[53] The Enterprising Learning curriculum of the Hotelschool The Hague is currently being revised with this observation as main point of departure, see also chapter 6.

CHAPTER 5

TEACHERS' EPISTEMOLOGICAL BELIEFS AND CONCEPTIONS OF TEACHING

To a mind of flint, the teacher must be iron, and strike sparks. To the empty pitcher, the teacher becomes a well. To the fallow mind, a planter of seeds. To the cluttered mind, a gardener to weed, shape and clear a space for growing.

To the lens, the teacher is light, and to the mind of light, a lens.

Gerald Grow, 1977

In chapters 3 and 4, studies proved that educational reform aimed at promoting more sophisticated student epistemology was not universally successful. One issue that seemed crucial was the approach teachers took toward the implementation of educational innovations. This finding led us to take a closer look at teachers' epistemology and its expression in teaching practice and pedagogy. In particular we looked into the effects of compatible and less compatible teacher and student thinking.

In researching the question whether teacher thinking, and its effects on teaching, are compatible with student thinking there are two possible outcomes. On the one hand teacher thinking and student thinking may fit together in the sense that puzzle pieces fit together: both ways of viewing learning and teaching then are not identical, they mirror and complement each other. The other alternative is that teacher thinking in essence is identical to student thinking: teacher and student thinking fit in the sense that both are either in synchrony (teacher and student think alike) or teacher and student are out of phase. We discuss this issue using three sub-questions:

1. what are the epistemological beliefs or conceptions of teaching that teachers have,
2. is a teacher's teaching practice indeed consistent with his/her epistemological beliefs or teaching conceptions and what are possible obstacles preventing consistency; and,
3. do these beliefs or conceptions change and, if so, how

We will not discuss these issues consecutively, but will refer back to these three sub-questions as appropriate throughout the text of this chapter.

At the most fundamental level the central question of this chapter is formulated by Yero: "...what are teachers if not grownup versions of these children?"(Yero, 2002, p. 22). And isn't it then "reasonable to spend at least as much effort understanding teaching 'styles' as is spent studying learning styles? To admit teachers are *as different as* the students in their classes?"(Yero, 2002, p. 8, italics ours). In this chapter we review literature on teacher epistemology and conceptions of teaching and the effects of these on teachers' teaching practice and the quality of student learning.

Epistemology and Teaching

For discussing epistemological issues and clusters[1] Fitzgerald and Cunningham (2002) have – among others – two purposes that are relevant to this chapter:

- ".. to encourage educators to consider epistemological stances that are often implicit in educational organizational policies, journals, research methods, and popular educational practices.... Since education deals with knowledge, epistemology is really education's most fundamental concern. ...
- ... to help individual educators to clarify their own stances about knowledge and knowing [which] can ... enable informed change in personal outlooks on professional issues in education" (p. 209–210).

Elaborating on the usefulness of their epistemological framework for teachers, they say

- ".. many would argue that ideally, classroom instruction is driven by an underlying epistemological outlook. If you have a particular theory of knowledge, you are likely to teach and assess in ways that are consistent with that outlook. Different epistemological outlooks result in different forms of instruction and assessment" (p. 225, italics ours).

These three quotes refer to three fundamental issues regarding teacher thinking we wish to address in this chapter.

Answering the question regarding the relevance of epistemology to teaching, Lyons (1990) reported earlier work on the conflicts (or dilemma's) teachers face in their professional lives and how they dealt with them. Her first example described an experienced and popular history teacher's response to a student asking him when he was going to teach *them how to do it*?

> When I first started as a teacher, I was quite a showman .... I was a performer. I could hold ten balls in the air at once. The kids loved it. The parents loved it. I was considered a great teacher. .... But [the kids] weren't doing history, they were watching the show. It was only after ... six or seven years that I began to realize that I wanted to [change]. If memory serves me it was a student ... [who] said to me, "You know, you're really wonderful and it's exciting, but you have to show people how to do it. When are you going to *teach* us how to do it?" And that really forced me, it led me to try to do that. ... I had to make a decision. (Lyons, 1990, p. 160, italics ours)

What this teacher describes here is a development in teacher thinking[2], from a "teacher as an entertainer, who's the owner of the unseen (obscured) disciplinary method" to a "teacher who tries to teach kids (learners) to do what he can do" through unveiling the disciplinary way of thinking. In a sense, the first type of teacher is an illusionist, whose 'power' lies in keeping the disciplinary method hidden, while still entertaining the learners. This dilemma is moral and epistemological in nature: do I remain who I am – a teacher who entertains more than he teaches – or do I change? The development this teacher experienced, involved not only changing his teaching practice, but also his relationship to learners and to his own discipline: "Seeing that having students participate in class discussions made them foils to the achievement of his lesson, the teacher sets in motion different approaches to learning, changing his assumptions about his students as knowers and learners. In this reorganization, he comes to a new way to conceive of himself as a teacher" (Lyons, 1990, p. 161). Lyons proposed a Model of Teacher Change, which is of particular interest to the current study: it implies that teacher change "involves a changing logic, one that touches self, craft, relationships, values, and ways of knowing" (p. 175). The web-like complexity of teacher change speaking from this model – also recognised in Prawat (1992, p. 367) – is consistent with our ideas about student change from an epistemological ecology perspective (see final section, chapter 4). So we think teacher change – as we found student change to be earlier – is also not an automatism nor plain sailing.

That epistemology plays an important role in dilemma's and conflicts as described by Lyons, is found also in the interview with Ramon Parks, a secondary school philosophy teacher. Parks faced the dilemma whether or not to voice his own opinions on sensitive issues (e.g. abortion) within a classroom discussion: "They want to know my opinion and yet there is a danger in my mind of giving it too early because often the dialogue stops then. Now we know THE ANSWER, we can go on. Some kids don't do that, but a lot do.... [Do] I give my opinion ... running the risk that twenty-two kids will change their vote because this is what the teacher thinks, which is not what I want?" (Lyons, 1990, p. 166–167). Parks solved this dilemma by creating an atmosphere of willingness to question opinions, a holding environment (see Kegan, chapter 3), by playing a "sort of devil's advocate role ... to get them to do what the course, philosophy, is all about, to think, reason, construe arguments ... Not to change their mind, but to expose them to a methodology" (p. 170). Parks' dilemma is an example of a constructivist teacher having to deal with dualist (and perhaps a few multiplist) learners. The remark about exposing learners to a methodology of a discipline, together with the remarks below, lead us to see this conflict as again an epistemological one: Parks clearly has a different view on knowledge than the students have – Lyons sees him as a 'procedural knower'[3] (Belenky et al., 1997).

> ... I have never accepted the conclusion that is often drawn ... that everyone's opinion is equally valid, which kids tend to do. ... Well, some opinions are better than others and I believe that is an important value to me that kids realize that ... [Kids] maintain their opinion, and say, "Well, I'm entitled to my opinion." And my point at that point is that – and I guess this is a strong moral issue, I would say "No, you're not, you are no longer entitled to your opinion ... you can't hold an opinion in the face of contrary evidence." (p. 170–171)

Parks – to us – is a typical level-four-thinker in our model, with his reliance on disciplinary methods and using evidence to underpin opinions. These examples from Lyons (1990) show that at least some conflicts (or dilemma's) in teaching *indeed* involve (differences in) epistemological beliefs, and (changes in) teacher-student relationships[4]. Where Lyons feels that her article "suggests a way to *begin* to consider how to interpret the experiences of teachers. ... [while] the empirical mapping of these epistemological views is still underway" (p. 169, italics ours), we hope that the current study shows that much work has been done since then to trace epistemological beliefs in students and teachers, and to study their effects on learning and teaching.

Where Lyons' article treats examples of consistency between epistemological beliefs and teaching practice, Schraw and Olafson (2002) in their article on teachers' epistemological world views, describe obstacles leading to inconsistencies between beliefs and practice. As part of this study, they interviewed 24 elementary and secondary school teachers about their views on curriculum, pedagogy, and assessment, asking for specific examples from practice in their classrooms. The interviews also included a discussion about three vignettes summarising three epistemological world views (three sets of beliefs). Schraw and Olafson used these vignettes to measure – by ranking the preference for, or agreement with, each vignette – the teachers' beliefs about their own teaching:

- a realist world view seeming to emphasise transmission;
- a contextualist world view seeming to emphasise understanding and use; and
- a relativist world view seeming to emphasise independent thinking.[5]

One theme emerging from the interviews that is particularly relevant here, is the discrepancies found between teachers' epistemological world views and their classroom practice, leading Schraw and Olafson to conclude that "epistemological world views did not appear to be strongly related to teaching practices" (2002, p. 125). Where 95% of the teachers espoused the contextualist world view, their teaching practices differed remarkably in teacher versus student-centeredness. This was particularly evident in the way teachers used the Curriculum Essentials Framework (CEF, a guide provided by the school district). Teachers who followed the CEF closely used a teacher-centered approach: "You have to keep going over and over things at that age." Teachers who used the CEF as a set of general guidelines were clearly more student-centered: "The more students use the materials, make connections, and figure things out on their own, the more sense they will make of things" (both quotes from Schraw and Olafson, 2002, p. 125). More worrying even was that although most teachers believed (and claimed) to be highly student-centered, many of them talked about their own teacher-centered practices in transmissional terms, such as "I like direct teaching. My kids need direction. They need someone telling them every step of the way what to do" (p. 125). Teachers also gave reasons for their practice differing from their own world view: lack of experience, time constraints[6], administrative obstacles, lack of a professional culture (at their school), and assessment practices. Schraw and Olafson concluded that teachers do not always practice what they 'preach' because of (severe) limitations placed on their freedom to do as they believe best in their classroom.

However, they also found teachers who did seem to be able to follow their own beliefs about teaching: "These relatively few examples occurred when individual principals interpreted school district procedure and policy in less structured ways. For example, principals ... encouraged teacher autonomy in making curricular decisions. Three of our participants experienced the freedom to make classroom decisions regarding curriculum and instruction. These three participants also demonstrated the highest degree of consistency between world view and pedagogy..." (Schraw and Olafson, 2002, p. 129–130). This means that the question whether teachers' epistemological beliefs and their teaching practices are (in)consistent – this time – is not answerable with 'either-or' or 'both', but with 'it depends'.

Empirical Studies on Teachers' Epistemology

In this section we will discuss some empirical studies showing the nature of teachers' epistemological beliefs and teaching conceptions, and their impact on teaching and student learning.

The effect of teachers' epistemological beliefs – their beliefs about the nature of science or their philosophies of science – on the practice of their science teaching and the nature of their students' learning, was examined by Brickhouse (1989, 1990). Three secondary science teachers were selected for this study because of their widely differing conceptions of the nature of science. The three participants were then interviewed in-depth about their beliefs, and their classroom practice was observed for at least 35 hours each. The purpose of this design was to find out to what extent distinct (epistemological) philosophies were associated with distinct (teaching) practices and (learning) activities. Brickhouse discussed two teachers in particular, Cathcart and Lawson.[7] Cathcart's beliefs could be characterised by seeing

- scientific theories as 'truths' which are uncovered by rigorous experimentation. In his science teaching students were required to 'learn' these truths: assessment was aimed at reproduction of the 'right answers' and he "did not think that they were able to use the theories to solve new problems" (1990, p. 55);
- scientific processes as exact, predetermined procedures. By following these procedures precisely scientists will 'discover the truth'. In his classrooms typical science activities were aimed at following the directions and getting the correct answers. Similarly, laboratory instruction was so much focused on procedures that it practically obscured the theoretical concepts examined through the experiments. The focus on procedure also obscured the fact that scientists develop experiments based on a theory, they do not (usually) work by trial and error. For instance Cathcart's interpretation of the work of Edison – as being mostly driven by trial and error – is exemplary for this view "Scientists often, if not always, go back and check their answers. Remember Brother Edison? How many times did he try on a light bulb filament before he found the one that worked? Does anyone recall? Nine hundred and something" (1990, p. 56). More seriously was that his students did not learn to ask 'good' questions: they

learned to ask questions about procedures, showing little understanding of the theory: "[Interviewer:] Why do you do this … four times? [Student:] Because that's what he had on the board" (1990, p.56). Not only did Cathcart's students rarely ask philosophical questions about science, in fact "they rarely asked questions at all" (1989, p. 447);

– scientific progress as an accumulation of facts/knowledge. For Cathcart this led to the following view on the expansion of scientific knowledge: "We can read what's been done before and we don't have to go back and repeat that, once it's been repeated enough to be proven, obviously. Then we build upon that knowledge" (1989, p. 446). It is almost impossible to think that such a view on teaching could lead to anything other than the most profound form of 'teaching as banking' as described by Freire (2000, 1970) where the students can only receive, store and accumulate facts and knowledge and where learning is *not* seen as leading to qualitative changes in thinking: as seeing things in a new light, "a revisionary process rather than a cumulative process" (Brickhouse, 1990, p. 60).

Mr. Cathcart's beliefs and practice, while congruent, are examples of views on learning and teaching consistent with learning teaching conception 1, with an opening to the next level. In a Perry-like rating we would give Cathcart a 1, 1, 2 and, in Belenky et al.'s terminology, these students were – we feel – very close to being 'silenced' (Belenky et al., 1997).[8]

The more constructive teacher, Ms. Lawson, had totally opposed views on scientific theories, processes and progress, leading to an again congruent, and completely different teaching practice. Lawson saw scientific theories not as truths, but as temporary[9] tools for making predictions and generating new research, for solving problems and explaining observations. Brickhouse typified Lawson's classroom practice

– as aimed at using "scientific theories to solve qualitative and quantitative problems. [Epistemologically, Lawson] considered theories to be tools and believed that there is no value in knowing what they are without knowing how to use them" (1990, p. 55);
– toward scientific processes, as emphasising the importance of the interplay between theory and observation. In introducing a theory, Lawson would typically ask students to predict, based on the theory discussed, the outcome of a classroom demonstration that was to follow. In Lawson's classes students did raise philosophical questions about science, e.g. whether field lines really do exist. Her epistemological views are illustrated in her example of Einstein's reaction to the confirmation of one of his predictions: ".. one of [Einstein's] predictions was that the star would be displaced during the eclipse… When he got word that in fact it was displaced, he said, 'I knew it would! I knew it would be!' … That interplay between the theoretician and the experimentalist, that's science" (Brickhouse, 1990, p. 57);
– toward scientific progress, as portraying a view on learning *not* as mostly memorising (banking), *but* as 'building a pyramid': laying the foundations (the most fundamental concepts) first, building further by expanding (new concepts)

and connecting (to previous concepts), while the responsibility for making these connections was primarily the student's, making her students active participants within the learning environment and not 'silenced' at all. This approach to learning (with building as a major metaphor) is typical for learning-teaching conception 4. From an epistemological point of view Lawson saw scientific progress *not* as accumulated knowledge based on definitively proven observations, *but* as based on new observations as well as old observations re-interpreted in the light of new theories, showing the role of theory-based interpretation in scientific progress. As an example, Lawson explains the difference between Aristotelian mechanics – not recognising friction as a force – with Newtonian mechanics, leading to completely different interpretations of the same phenomenon. This replacement of Aristotle's world view with that of Newton is an example of the relative 'rightness' of theories, some theories being better (or more generally useful) than others in explaining phenomena within a particular context (here physics).

Brickhouse's studies show the consistency between teachers' epistemological beliefs and their teaching practices, and the effect of the teaching practices on students' learning behaviour and probably on students' epistemologies and understandings. The students in Cathcart's classes "rarely asked questions. When they did, the questions were nearly always procedural in nature. [While] Lawson's students were excellent problem solvers and tended to view physics as a problem solving activity" (1990, p. 61). The studies illustrate how important it is to address beliefs about learning, teaching, knowledge and knowing in teacher education and staff development. Brickhouse rightly remarks that "There is considerable rage among scientists and citizens in the USA when they hear of schools temporarily hiring uncertified teachers to instruct students in areas for which they have little formal content preparation. ... Yet we expect science teachers to teach philosophical and societal issues based on little, if any, formal preparation to help them understand what philosophers, sociologists, or historians believe about science" (1989, p. 447).[10]

Linder (1992) described some of the problems regarding students' learning, understanding and epistemological beliefs, that arise as a result of non-explicit epistemological assumptions underlying (traditional) teaching practices in (college) physics. His study expands on Brickhouse by linking the dominant epistemological position underlying teaching in *a discipline*, to students' learning behaviour and learning outcomes. Linder asserted that (college) physics teaching is a reflection of the epistemological belief *metaphysical realism*[11]: the belief that an objective reality is given and consists of mind-independent facts. Thus physics teaching in fact "reflects little appreciation for theory and model building, for the prediction of 'novel facts'..., that is, 'undreamt' of, or previously contradicted facts. Personal contributions are subjective and hence are not considered as physics" (Linder, 1992, p. 111).

To examine the influence of metaphysical realist teaching (MRT), Linder interviewed graduate physics students involved in a teacher-education programme about their understanding of sound. During these interviews it became clear that these teacher-education students had seriously deficient and incoherent understanding of the concept of sound, sometimes seeming to reflect on the concept for the first time. Linder stated that MRT makes students feel that learning is memorising, and memorising many facts and 'studying hard' is a necessary prerequisite for conceptual understanding. It also supports them in the epistemological unsophisticated perception that good teaching is the transfer of a lot of (proven) knowledge and methods – facts about reality and algorithmic procedures – from teacher to students. Learning is typically assessed with tests and quizzes that frequently can be passed *without* coherent conceptual understanding. MRT is characteristically free from discussion. So much subject matter (facts) needs to be covered, and discussion time eats into the time necessary for transfer. All this has a detrimental effect on students' conception of physics, it becomes "an extremely difficult subject [consisting] of laws, formulae and problem-solving algorithms, all to be *learnt* [memorised] in order to pass the final examination" (p. 112). Linder proceeded to give interview examples of the effect that this kind of teaching has on understanding, showing that MRT results in half-remembered, fragmented, inconsistent and poorly understood knowledge, and leads to a generation of future teachers (sic!) who believe in knowledge that is certain, proven and handed down by authorities (their current teachers). Considering that his subjects "obtained above average undergraduate grades from a reputable North American university" Linder finds their lack of conceptual understanding "disturbing" (p. 114).

In MRT, not only is memorising seen as a prerequisite for understanding, also success in solving sets of standard physics tutorial problems is seen as an indicator of conceptual understanding, without it ever actually testing the validity of this assumption. Solving multiple sets of this kind of problems cannot – Linder feels – lead to a coherent knowledge structure flexible enough to solve 'real' physics problems. MRT does little to bridge the divide between intuition and everyday experience, and the calculations students do in college physics classes. Physics thus becomes a *separate*, perhaps even paradoxical or unnatural, set of memorised procedures not connected to everyday life in any discernable way.[12] These students seem never to have been encouraged, or had the time, to connect what they learn in physics classes to what happens in everyday life. This lack of time may be aggravated by the rapid speed of instruction characteristic for physics teaching, which most teachers and students feel is unavoidable to cover the content and keep up the standards. This rapid instruction led Arons (quoted in Linder) to describe this approach with the 'length contraction metaphor',

> ...the premise of the vast majority of introductory physics courses [is] that if one takes a huge breadth of subject matter and passes it before the student at a sufficiently high velocity, the Lorentz contraction will shorten it to a point at which it drops into the hole which is the student's mind... The students have been 'told' but they have not made the concept part of their own. (Linder, 1992, p. 117)[13]

The result of MRT and the usual speed of physics instruction is that students usually have no time to play with and explore new concepts e.g. by using them in various contexts, nor to reflect on possible inconsistencies in their understanding of these concepts when applied in different situations. Linder concluded that this type of instruction leads more to 'student confusion' than to 'student understanding'. Especially troubling in this study is that the harmful philosophy of MRT is propagated to a future generation of physics teachers. Linder feels it is imperative that ".. we need to dissociate *covering* a range of topics and concepts in class, via speed-transmission of facts, from having *taught* those topics and concepts" (p. 120). In a sense this reminds us of the story of the 'showman' history teacher described by Lyons (1990) above. Reminiscent of the history teacher's student, Linder would want physics teachers "[to ask] students to *think about* and *question* what is being taught" (Linder, 1992, p. 120) and to show the students *how they do it*.

That students need some time to question and reflect on what is taught to reach true conceptual understanding in physics, becomes more clear if you consider that in particular the natural sciences require a totally new way of looking at things. A way of looking at things so at odds with intuition, that Wolpert refers to it as the 'unnatural nature of science' (Wolpert, 1994). Take gravity for instance. Wolpert gives a number of examples – of which we quote only too few – to illustrate the discrepancy between natural (common sense) thinking and the unnatural thinking required for understanding gravity.

> ...children suggest that the higher up an object is lifted, the more it weighs, since when it falls to the ground the impact is greater. (p. 15)
>
> ... when asked to indicate the forces on a ball thrown up, many students imagine an upward force to be present after the ball leaves the hand, whereas the truth is that at all stages after the ball leaves the hand it experiences only a downward force due to gravity. This is no simple problem and even Galileo got it wrong ... ... forces can either increase or decrease [an object's] speed. When a ball was thrown up, it would continue upwards forever if there were no forces like friction or gravity to slow it down. The force of gravity acts to accelerate the ball *towards* the earth ... so the ball is slowed down and eventually reverses its upwards motion (p. 4, this particular misconception returns in this chapter where we discuss Hashweh (1996)).

The unnaturalness of scientific thought lies in that it uses an unknown (and unseen), in this case the concept of gravity, to explain a familiar phenomenon. Considering the intuitively odd consequences and the fact that people are capable of performing everyday things without any need to understand the incredibly complex underlying physics – such as riding a bike (Wolpert, 1994, p. 11) or catching a ball – the concept of gravity actually takes some getting used to, requiring questioning and reflection, before it is a 'natural' part of one's thinking. As Wolpert says "[d]oing science ... requires one to remove oneself from one's personal experience and to try to understand phenomena not directly affecting one's day-to-day life, one's personal constructs." (1994, p. 17). In that sense, understanding science requires at least the fourth order of consciousness or learning-teaching conception 4.

Returning to Linder (1992), while he posed some interesting challenges for teachers (of physics), he might be overestimating the ease with which teachers are epistemologically able to fulfil his expectations. Martens illustrated, in a classic study, what might happen when willing, but epistemologically relatively unsophisticated, teachers are confronted with, and trained in, an educational innovation aimed at a higher level of epistemology and 'real' problem solving (Martens, 1992). Her study described the way a highly regarded, experienced teacher at an optional learning-center programme, Jean, tried to change her teaching from a content and teacher-oriented way to a hands-on problem-solving approach. Martens summarised Jean's epistemological beliefs regarding good teaching as liking "things to be very definite. Science, as strictly content, can be considered definite because then there are right answers to questions and facts to be known. Furthermore, ... problem solving is kept *separate* from content and the only discrepancies addressed are ones that have been planned for, results can be predicted quite accurately and success then almost guaranteed" (Martens, 1992, p. 152, italics ours). Jean, as teacher in change, had been trained in the new teaching philosophy by taking part in several workshops, in which she participated enthusiastically. In these workshops the primary aim was to engage participants in the process of problem solving and special attention was given to the "teachers' personally felt discrepancies regarding the availability of materials, time constraints, and classroom management issues as they related to teaching science in a hands-on, problem-solving manner" (p. 151). The data Martens used came from observations (during the workshops and later in Jean's class), interviews and analyses of documents.

From the data it became clear that a true problem solving approach to teaching elementary science proved to be beyond the reach of this teacher, a result that might have been expected considering her epistemological beliefs about teaching. Martens interpreted Jean's failure to change as "[having] only to do with some alteration of teaching strategies and the use of new materials. With no change in beliefs about her role as teacher when using these techniques, Jean is actually preventing her students from engaging in any problem solving" (p. 153). Two issues emerging from the data seemed to play an important role in the apparent failure of Jean to fundamentally change her teaching style:

– the need for ultimate teacher-control: organising students' success in finding the 'right answer' quickly, thereby preventing real problem solving.

  In a lesson in which students had to make their own telephone, Jean had prepared a model (the 'right answer'), and gave the students very clear directions how to replicate the model (how to 'find' the right answer). To ensure that her students would have every chance of success, she not only provided, but also prepared beforehand all the material to be used in class. As Martens described the situation, "Having a class make their own telephones is generally not something that can be accomplished in one 40-minute period. Jean, however, had cut all the wires to the specified lengths beforehand and also had stripped them so as to insure good contact points for the circuits. Furthermore, the presence of her model telephone could leave no doubt in anyone's mind about exactly what needed to be done in order to be successful" (p. 153).

– holding on to the dichotomy between the, in Jean's eyes, main purpose of science teaching, 'covering the entire book', and the diversion of 'solving problems' which she feared would eat up too much time if not heavily structured.

This separateness between teaching content or problem solving is finely illustrated by Jean's question to Martens as observer in her classroom, quoted on page 153: "Do you want to see a science lesson, or problem solving the next time?". As Martens concluded, Jean "does not know that content can be learned effectively *through* problem solving" (p. 154, italics ours) and so letting students work with material, allowing them to follow their own approach, to make their own mistakes and to 'really' solve problems, may seem to her "a tremendous waste of time" (p. 154).

From our perspective, Jean would be seen as a typical shaper, espousing to learning-teaching conception 3. Jean's focus on controlling all of the interactions in class makes her miss some opportunities to incorporate chance events in her teaching. Martens described such an event when, during a sudden violent thunderstorm, Jean did not actively respond to the students' spontaneous interest in thunder, the speed difference between sound and light etcetera. Martens felt – and so do we for that matter – that "[b]y attempting to foresee every possible obstacle and constantly alerting the students to what they must do in order to be successful, she does the problem solving for them. *The problems are hers and not theirs*" (Martens, 1992, p. 154, italics ours), and in teaching like this Jean does her students a disservice.

While this study usually is referenced to as a study about teacher epistemology, Martens seemed to interpret the obstacles to epistemological change to be – to a certain extent – contextual. Martens listed obstacles such as parents' expectations and pressures from school administrators, which may not lie in line with seeing teaching as 'real' problem solving – a phenomenon which Martens described as "discrepancies in [teachers'] daily lives" (p. 155). From a contextual point of view, Jean felt no reason "to change her belief about the role of a teacher or how to teach science ... There seems to be little or nothing in place which tells Jean or other teachers in her district that there may be more than one right way to accomplish a given task or that not knowing what to do is a prerequisite for problem defining..." (p. 155). This implies that, if a teacher's epistemological belief is fairly unsophisticated and the work environment remains traditional, not actively encouraging reflection on these beliefs, the probability of change and thus of real educational innovation – going beyond introducing a few new activities – is small indeed.

In an attempt to promote high-school students' scientific inquiry skills[14], Maor and Taylor (1995) –initially– studied the influence of a computerised learning environment. In the early nineteen-nineties the introduction of personal computers in school science classrooms was expected to provide a new, powerful learning context that would enable the development of inquiry-related higher order thinking skills (or HOTS). In this study the computerised learning environment included two main elements:

– a scientific database ('The Birds of Antarctica'), comprising real-life scientific data collected by research scientists during an expedition to Antarctica in 1982, namely "observational records of a range of behaviours of 26 species of sea birds (...) together with meteorologic information, times, dates, and the ship's positions and activities. This information created an artificial laboratory in which students could conduct investigations into inquiry-based learning" (Maor and Taylor, 1995, p. 841). The database aimed to encourage students to ask questions and formulate hypotheses and to use the data to look for evidence.

- an instructional student booklet designed to support students' (individual) use of the database. It provided "a series of worksheets designed to guide students toward attaining scientific inquiry skills ranging from the ability to conduct relatively simple investigations based on a single variable to designing and conducting complex investigations involving multiple variables" (Maor and Taylor, 1995, p. 841). Using the booklet provided a teacher with opportunities to better monitor students' progress and completed booklets provided evidence of students' work and their development in using scientific inquiry skills.

Initially, in preparation for this study, seven teachers of high-school computing were trained in using the database themselves and in using it in their teaching of an 11th grade applied computing course. In the research design these teachers were monitored and observed during the 20-week course while they were using the database to teach scientific inquiry skills. Very soon after starting the classroom observations, Maor and Taylor reported that "the nature of students' interactions with the computerized database varied among classes according to teachers' pedagogic styles. Teachers' pedagogies ranged from being very teacher-directed to very student-directed and provided markedly different opportunities for the students to interact with the database" (1995, p. 842). This led the authors to amend their study design and observe more closely two teachers, Ken and Sam, who differed remarkably in their epistemology and teaching approach in this computerised learning environment. Several methods of data collection were used, observations, interviews, monitoring students' thinking aloud and booklet-analysis.

Ken had a transmissionist epistemology, a belief linked by Maor and Taylor to "[p]edagogies that place a major emphasis on the learning of scientific facts and formulae and their confirmation by means of prescribed practical activities [and that] are the hallmarks of teachers who conceive of learning as the absorption and reproduction of the proven knowledge of the scientific community" (1995, p. 840). Ken's transmissionist teaching approach could be described focusing on three aspects, control, classroom discourse and the nature of the students' inquiries. In Ken's teacher-centered pedagogy, this meant that Ken's classes were characterised by

- teacher unilateral control.

  Ken proved to be an authoritarian lecturer, not supporting students' self-initiation and strongly controlling students' interactions with the database – up to talking them through all the details from the computer screen – and strongly controlling students' interactions with the instructions in the student booklet. Maor and Taylor concluded that Ken preferred "a structured, step-by-step teaching approach which enabled him to monitor closely each lesson, thereby giving students very little independence to investigate the database" (1995, p. 845).

- didactic classroom discourse.
  To illustrate this, Maor and Taylor described Ken's whole-class discussions – which already were limited regarding student-student interactions – as a teacher-controlled 'informative-type question/correct answer'-quiz, with Ken drawing almost all the conclusions himself, e.g.

  Ken: Where do you find the Snow Petrel?
  Student: 62°E. (Teacher writes on the board.)
  Ken: Where do you find the White-Chinned Petrel?
  Student: 82°E, 120°E. (Teacher writes on the board.)
  Ken: And the Antarctic Petrel?
  Student: 62°E. (Teacher writes on the board.)
  Ken: What is the preferred ice condition of the Snow Petrel?
  (Maor and Taylor, 1995, p. 846)

Maor and Taylor concluded that Ken "did not allow students to be engaged in discussions, to arrive at consensual understanding, and he restricted their verbal interactions" (1995, p. 846).

- students' narrow (factual) questions and simple (single variable) investigations.
  In this 'learning' environment, learning became "simple and certain" as Schommer would phrase it (see chapter three). Students formulated narrow, relatively superficial questions, usually following closely examples provided in the booklet, resulting in simple investigations and failure to explore the richness of the database.

  Tara's booklet ... concluded with investigations into the following questions: "How many South Polar Skua were seen when the air temperature was 5°C?" "When did [the voyage] start?" "What is the most preferred wind speed?" (p. 847)

  During the 20 weeks of the course, in Ken's class typically little change was found in the quality of the students' questions and investigations. Only a small number of Ken's students succeeded in performing more complex investigations, but even then the complexity was usually limited to increasing the number of variables used to pursue a still factual question. Maor and Taylor concluded that this showed that in such an environment, only a few students were able to "make a transition toward developing higher-level thinking skills" (p. 847). This minimal development reminds us of the transition from uni-structural to multi-structural learning outcomes as defined in the SOLO taxonomy (Collis and Biggs, 1979).

Sam, on the other hand, approached the use of the database in a totally different way. His constructivist epistemology was linked to a pedagogy that "places a major emphasis on engaging students individually and socially in problem-posing and problem-solving activities and in reflecting on the viability of the established and emergent understandings of themselves, their fellow students, and the scientific community" (Maor and Taylor, 1995, p. 840). Sam's teaching approach differed from Ken's approach on the same three aspects listed before, control, classroom discourse and the nature of the students' inquiries:

– teacher and students shared control.
  Sam stimulated students' independent interactions with the database and the instructions in the booklet, saying, "I will break the flow of work by posing questions, and promote class discussion and verbal interactions in the classroom as the need arises" (Maor and Taylor, 1995, p. 848).
– teacher-initiated, student-initiated and student-student negotiations.
  Sometimes Sam initiated whole-class discussion about e.g. problems with the database language (in the beginning of the course) or, later on, students' having different approaches to investigating the same question. Maor and Taylor reported that in the latter case, after much discussion, the students concluded "the method of investigation influenced the result and that therefore, there was more than one right answer to the problem" (p. 848), indicating that these students were developing towards a higher level of thinking.
  - In Sam's class student-initiated discussion and negotiation was encouraged and finally became an integral part of the teaching-learning process. Sometimes students would take on the teacher's role, discussing reasons for hypotheses or alternative investigations, while the teacher himself chose to adopt a more passive role, acting as "a facilitator for the negotiation of meaning in class discussions" (p. 850).
– students' creative questions and complex investigations.
  As the course progressed, in Sam's class, students formulated increasingly creative questions, requiring complex investigations even extending beyond the database and leading to additional research activities e.g. in the school library. One student, Edward, wondered about a particular species of bird (South Polar Skua) whose discrepant behaviour had attracted his attention.

> Basically, I set myself a task to explore the living conditions of the South Polar Skua, and I was sort of trying to work out things, like how did it interact with other bird life forms, and draw conclusions from that as to its general capacity for living in the Antarctic and how it actually lived there.

After investigating evidence relevant to this problem, Edward concluded,

> One thing I did find was that most of the other birds, when they were observed, were with other species. But with this bird, it was alone. I mean, it only appeared in ones or twos. Why does this happen when all the other birds interacted with each other? So the conclusion I drew from that was that possibly it was a bird of prey, a hunter. …

But Edward also offered alternative hypotheses that called for further research,

> … maybe they're smaller than other birds and they get preyed on when the other birds are around, or perhaps the conditions in which they hunt and the

> way they hunt are different from any other bird, and having any other birds around would lessen its chances of being able to find prey. ...

Such an inquiry-learning experience may facilitate students' epistemological development too, as Edward said,

> When I'm given information [from the database], I'm not just saying that's the information ... I'm sort of thinking, "But why is that so?" ... Now, I can actually draw my own conclusions from the information that I'm presented with. (Maor and Taylor, 1995, p. 850–851)

> Maor and Taylor described the effect of Sam's constructivist approach on his students as enabling "a *majority* of students in his class to generate creative questions and conduct complex investigations" (1995, p. 851, italics ours).

Where computerised learning is often seen as offering a powerful environment for enhancing inquiry-related higher order thinking skills, this study showed that such an assumption is *only* supported if the teachers involved have themselves a (constructivist) epistemology that supports the full use of the opportunities that computers offer. Maor and Taylor close with the suggestion that before engaging in computerised learning, teachers need to reflect seriously on the role and type of relationship with students they should adopt to make a success of inquiry-based learning: "it is important that the teacher not disempower students by exerting too much control over student-computer interactions. On the other hand, the teacher should avoid abandoning students to the isolation of individualized microworlds" (1995, p. 852). Here again, we find support for our earlier remarks that to encourage epistemological development, teachers must create a safe and secure holding environment (Kegan, 1994) and that the success of any educational innovation ultimately depends on the quality of the student-teacher learning partnership (Baxter Magolda, 2004, see also our remarks about 'mentored learning' before, in the section Comments on Perry).

We have now established that teachers differ in the way they implement educational innovations, and that these different ways are associated to their epistemological beliefs. Now the question remains, whether there is more evidence to support our assumption that constructivist teachers are better teachers than teachers with more naive views on learning and knowledge. Although we acknowledge that it is not possible to claim this to be true in all circumstances, Hashweh (e.g. 1996) has compared the effectiveness of teachers with different epistemologies in the context of conceptual change learning in science. In Hashweh's 1996 article a number of teaching strategies were ranked with regard to their effectiveness in inducing conceptual change:

1. repeated explaining (least effective): explaining a current scientific conception and repeating this explanation,
2. convincing: offering examples or demonstrations that "prove" the current scientific conception,
3. refuting: showing the discrepancy between the scientific conception and an alternative (or naive) conception a student might have[15],

4. restructuring: comparing the scientific and the alternative conception, demonstrating the relationship between them and attempting to resolve the conflict between them,
5. combining strategies (most effective): using multiple strategies simultaneously.

Hashweh developed a questionnaire to examine the types and frequency of teaching strategies used by science teachers. The questionnaire was returned by 35 Palestinian science teachers who, one year earlier, had been identified as either empiricist or constructivist teachers. Empiricist teachers view scientific knowledge as objective and permanent facts that are discovered rather than invented, while constructivist teachers see scientific knowledge as tentative and invented, accepting that absolute objectivity is impossible because observations are theory-laden. Empiricist teachers do not consciously acknowledge that students already have developed everyday ideas about scientific phenomena and so are not aware of students' alternative conceptions. Constructivist teachers see learning as an active process, and students as having their own alternative ideas about scientific phenomena which may be inconsistent with current scientific understanding. In the first section of Hashweh's questionnaire, teachers were asked to evaluate a set of two critical incidents – two vignettes – about their own subject and to describe how they would address such an incident in class. Each critical incident described a student expressing a common scientific misconception, e.g.

> *Physics Critical Incident*: The teacher asked students to identify the force or forces acting on a small object (a piece of chalk) if it is thrown vertically upwards after it has left the person's hand while moving upwards. The teacher asked the students to represent each force with an arrow whose length and direction correspond to the magnitude and direction of the force. A student drew the following diagram on the blackboard (see Figure 5.1).

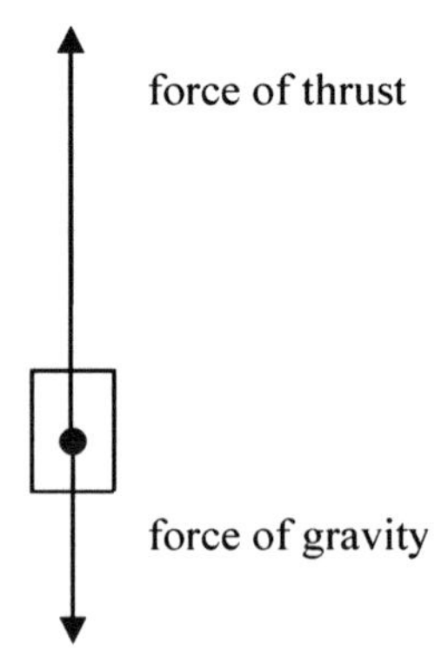

Figure 5.1. Forces on an object (based on Hashweh, 1996, p. 51, diagram ours).

In the second section of Hashweh's questionnaire the notion of students' alternative conceptions was explained, and teachers were asked whether they had a strategy (or strategies) to deal with this and to explain their strategy (or strategies). The third section described a number of strategies, similar to those listed above, and teachers were asked to rate them on frequency of use and importance.

The data from the first section, on the critical incidents, showed that empiricist teachers differed in a number of important ways from constructivist teachers. Qualitative analysis, using 4 prototypical teachers, demonstrated that an **empiricist teacher** may focus primarily on the incorrectness of the answer, without acknowledging or identifying the student's alternative conception, proceeding with a single-type strategy, *explaining* the correct answer.

The force in the upward direction is a momentary force that acts on the object only when it is in touch with the person's hand ... Therefore, when it is moving upward the only force acting on it is the force of gravity in the downward direction, and this force makes the object decelerate ... The representation given by the student is momentary at the instant the object is thrown, while the question asks about the phase after the object has been thrown. *The representation is wrong and the correct representation is this* (see Figure 5.2) (E2, Hashweh, 1996, p. 54, italics ours)

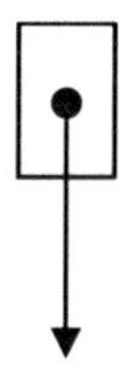

Figure 5.2. Gravitational force on an object (based on Hashweh, 1996, p. 54, diagram ours).

A **constructivist teacher**, on the other hand, may approach the incident differently, acknowledging the alternative conception in the student's answer and using the alternative conception to open a discussion. In the example below, according to Hashweh, this teacher used a multiple-type strategy, combining a *refuting* strategy, confronting the student with the consequences of the misconception, with a *convincing* strategy, giving more examples,

> This is a wrong answer of course, *but is very expected in the lesson about forces...* In such cases, I ask the student some questions about the concepts in the lesson. If I discover that he does not understand the concepts well I explain the concept and the definition of the force and its relation with acceleration and not velocity... This requires a long and detailed presentation that involves ...
>
> After that, I ask the student to rethink about his answer. If he does not reach the required answer I ask, "Which is bigger in your diagram, the force of

> thrust or the weight?" Therefore, in which direction is the object accelerating? Here, the student will discover that according to his diagram the object will accelerate in the upward direction because the net force is upward, which means that the object will never fall down... I finally shall ask further questions and give further examples to make sure that the student understood the concept of the lesson. (C2, Hashweh, 1996, p. 55)

We feel – in contrast to Hashweh – that this constructivist teacher combined three strategies, refuting, convincing *and* explaining. Either way, this analysis showed that constructivist teachers can and may use several qualitatively different strategies simultaneously in teaching science concepts.

The results of the quantitative analysis for all 35 teachers were also interesting regarding the frequency of use of single-type or multiple-type strategies by epistemologically different teachers. Constructivist teachers used more single-type strategies *and* more multiple-type strategies than empiricist teachers, who hardly used any multiple-type strategies at all. The majority of the empiricist teachers used the explaining strategy in addressing the critical incidents, with convincing as the second strategy of choice, while the strategies restructuring and refuting were hardly used or not at all. The constructivist teachers gave evidence of a much larger repertoire of strategies and of using the more effective strategies for affecting conceptual change more often. All four strategies were used, with a preference for using convincing followed by refuting and explaining, with restructuring being used least frequent of all strategies, but far more frequently than empiricist teachers used it.

The results of the 'critical incidents'-analysis was largely corroborated by the responses to the second section, where teachers described their strategy (or strategies) to deal with students' alternative conceptions. Empiricist teachers preferred convincing strategies - using this strategy far more frequently than the constructivist teachers. Constructivist teachers preferred convincing and refuting strategies almost equally. As illustrated by examples from the qualitative analysis.

> Teacher E2:
>
> 1. I emphasize the correct scientific concepts.
> 2. I give examples that demonstrate the truth of these concepts.
>
> Teacher C2:
>
> Changing students' concepts cannot be done by writing a group of laws on the blackboard but through the use of experiments that help the student deduce the required concept. Sometimes we use experiments that prove that the way the student thinks about a certain concept is wrong. Most importantly, the student should reach a stage of self conviction without causing him shame or embarrassment. (Hashweh, 1996, p. 58)

The self-reported preference of empiricist teachers for convincing strategies in this second section of the questionnaire, was in contrast to the responses given to the critical incidents (as a proxy for actual teaching behaviour). We expect that this may be explained in part by the social undesirability of *reporting* 'explaining' as primary strategy in dealing with alternative conceptions. It also supports Hashweh's conclusion that empiricist teachers may often fail to identify the existence of alternative conceptions, seeing only incomprehension in the critical-incident vignettes, and therefore feeling no need to convince a student of the 'right' conception.

The ratings of the teaching strategies, regarding their frequency of use and importance, as asked in the third section, showed that constructivist teachers judged the more effective teaching strategies more frequently as 'very important' and they also indicated more frequently that they used these effective strategies 'often', corroborating the earlier results.

From Hashweh's study one can conclude that – at least in the context of conceptual change learning – constructivist teachers are better teachers, having e.g. richer repertoires of teaching strategies and using more effective teaching strategies more frequently. Hashweh's research is interesting in particular because it is an example of relatively "large-scale studies that employ hypothesis-testing quantitative methodologies" (Hashweh, 1996, p. 48). He also concluded, based on this study and his own earlier research in the USA, that "the effects of science teachers' epistemological beliefs in teaching seem to be strong and stable across teachers' field of expertise in science, the educational level[16] at which they teach, or the culture[17] to which they belong. Finally, the fact that the period of 1 year separated the assessment of the teachers' beliefs and the investigation of the teaching practices of those teachers in the present study lends support to the claim that *teachers' epistemological beliefs are stable traits that strongly influence teaching*" (Hashweh, 1996, p. 61, italics ours). In addition, we find support for our 'epistemological ecology'-hypothesis (see chapter three) in the way Hashweh consequently linked the process of conceptual change to (teachers') views on the development of knowledge, on science learning and science teaching.

While Hashweh concluded that teachers with more sophisticated epistemological beliefs are better teachers, because they possess and use a larger repertoire of teaching strategies, it is not clear whether teachers always implement the teaching strategies that are consistent with their beliefs (see e.g. Schraw and Olafson, 2002). This issue is also the focus of the study by Lederman (1999). Lederman studied the classroom practices of five high-school biology teachers with epistemologically sophisticated views on the nature of science. These views included among others the beliefs that scientific knowledge is tentative, subjective (theory laden), partially based on human creativity, imagination and partially based on empirical evidence, and that scientific knowledge is socially and culturally embedded (Lederman, 1999, p. 917). The five teachers were followed over a one year period, using classroom observations, interviews (teachers and students, formal and informal), an open-ended questionnaire, lesson plans and instructional materials to study the relationship between teachers' epistemological beliefs and their classroom practice.

Two of the three more experienced teachers (John and Mary) exhibited a classroom practice consistent with their sophisticated views on the nature of science: "… these teachers included many inquiry-oriented activities (i.e., demonstrations and laboratories) that required students to collect data and infer explanations for the data that had been collected. These inferences were often subsequently tested and revised accordingly" (Lederman, p. 923). However, neither of these teachers indicated that they were "intentionally attempting to teach in a manner consistent with their perceptions of the nature of science. Indeed, neither teacher had students' understandings of the nature of science as an instructional objective or specified it as a goal" (Lederman, p. 923). The reasons behind their classroom practice were, in John's words,

> My main purpose for this demonstration is that the students really enjoy it, and it is a good way for me to get them to see that science is fun and that they can do it. How the students feel about themselves is a big thing for me. (John, p. 923)
>
> Students need to learn how to think. They also need to know that they can think and solve scientific problems. This is the first step in getting them to enjoy science. (John, p. 923)

We feel that, from a learning-teaching conception perspective these practices, and the reasons behind them – students learning to enjoy science, building self-confidence, and learning to think – are consistent with teachers' more sophisticated views on knowledge or science. While these teachers do not explicitly address the nature of science, they were constructing a holding environment towards a more explicit treatment of the nature of science. As John says,

> I know the nature of science is interesting … But first I need students to feel that they can do science. Then, I can hit them with the more abstract stuff. (p. 924)

In this example we see a first impediment for a fully consistent teaching practice at high school level, namely the 'logical' requirement to meet the students at their present level of thinking and understanding. In that sense these two teachers give prime examples of 'good mentoring' (Pavelich and Moore, 1996, see chapter two).

The classroom practices of the two less experienced teachers (Barry and Lisa) were far more at odds with their sophisticated views regarding the nature of science. Their inexperience with classroom management (the organisation and management of instruction) was a primary and constant impediment to developing more consistent teaching practices.

> I want students to have a global view of science as a way of knowing in addition to the factual stuff I need to teach. I just can't deal with that right now with all the management concerns I have. (Barry, p. 924)
>
> I want to teach more process and nature of science, but I need to feel that I have things under control first. (Lisa, p. 924)

These two examples illustrate what Schraw and Olafson (2002) concluded regarding inconsistencies between teachers' epistemological belief systems (or world views) and their teaching practices: "The most salient of these [inconsistencies] was that teachers are more teacher-centered in practice, and less student-centered, than they claim to be" (Schraw and Olafson, 2002, p. 134–135).

According to Lederman, the fifth, more experienced teacher, Alice, implemented teaching practices clearly and intentionally inconsistent with her views on the nature of science, because she felt that her (10th-grade) students needed foundational knowledge more than 'process skills', thereby separating content and process. In this sense, Alice reminds us of Jean (Martens, 1992 see before) who separated 'learning science' (covering the book) and 'problem solving' (practicing a skill).

> I have always felt that there has been much too much concern for process skills. It's not that process is not important, but you can't process in a vacuum. Students need to have some basic knowledge to use with their process skills. (Alice, p. 924)

From a learning-teaching conception perspective however, one might wonder if the sophisticated views on the nature of science Alice professed to when asked explicitly, are actually heartfelt. The view on knowledge expressed in this quote is more consistent with our learning-teaching conception 3, with its emphasis on building up a knowledge base that then can be applied. In that case, Alice's classroom practice would be *consistent* with her inner convictions regarding knowledge, learning and teaching.

From this study we can derive that Lederman identified at least two important impediments to implementing classroom practices consistent with teachers' epistemologically sophisticated views on the nature of science, namely teachers' inexperience (consistent with e.g. Schraw and Olafson, 2002) and teachers' perceptions of their students. What then – based on this study – can one say about the effects of these different classroom practices on the *students'* understandings of the nature of science? As Lederman says "the overwhelming majority of the students interviewed across all five teaches (46 of the 50) did not exhibit an understanding of the nature of science consistent with current wisdom and science education reforms" (1999, p. 926). Some examples of students' views illustrate this (p. 926).

> There really is no room for subjectivity in science. Otherwise, anyone could say whatever they want. (student of John)

> Scientists need to be creative in developing experiments, but the results should be seen the same way regardless of the scientist. This is why scientists do the same experiment many times. (student of Mary)

> Anyone can have a theory, but with evidence it eventually becomes a law because we now know it's the case. Things in the world happen in certain ways and we can eventually figure it out with science. (student of Barry)

> Scientists disagree all the time, but this is just because they don't have all the information or someone is interpreting the data wrong. (student of Lisa)

Despite the fact that these students had experienced clearly different teaching practices, this seemed to have very little effect on their views on the nature of science. Most students believed that "only certain types of scientific knowledge were tentative (i.e. theories) and that creativity, imagination, and subjectivity had a limited place, if any, in the development of scientific knowledge" (Lederman, 1999, 926). According to Lederman, this study showed that inquiry-oriented teaching alone – lacking explicit attention to the teachers' view of the nature of science – is insufficient to encourage students' conceptual change learning. Elementary to conceptual change is the realisation that one's current view is no longer sufficient. Therefore, to encourage change, teachers should explicitly confront students with a different view and discuss the advantages of this alternative view above the students' view. It is probable that none of the five teachers reached that point of confrontation in their teaching within the observed period. In Lederman's words, "Providing students with experiences in scientific inquiry is certainly a start, but students also need to have the nature of science made explicit through discussions and reflections about the nature of inquiry" (1999, p. 928).

Another study focusing on consistency between epistemological beliefs and teaching practice, now at academic level, is that of Quinlan (1999). Quinlan studied the beliefs academic teachers of one university department held about their discipline – history – and the effect these beliefs had on their teaching practice, educational goals and their evaluation of student work. A major argument for both this study and a later one (Quinlan, 2002) was the observation that "studies of beliefs about the subject or the disciplines are strikingly absent from the higher education literature on academics' beliefs about teaching and learning" (Quinlan, 1999, p. 448). Quinlan observed and interviewed eight history academics of various ages and both genders, at two different points in one academic year. In the first interview the respondents discussed e.g. their educational goals, their role as teacher, their perceptions of students' roles and students' work. In the second interview the academics were asked to respond to issues that emerged from the analysis of the first interview, these issues included teaching students how to construct historical knowledge, the difficulty students have with historical thinking, the role of texts and writing in history education. All these issues were discussed in the light of introductory and advanced history courses. Quinlan reported that the group of eight academics seemed to be (more or less) of one mind about,

- the goals of history teaching: e.g. illuminating the present, making students better citizens and improving intellectual skills, such as seeing connections and critical thinking;
- perception of students: students were mostly seen rather negatively as "lacking" in certain areas (foundational knowledge, reading and writing skills, time to study and motivation), "needing" structure and "expecting" spoon-feeding, with the academics partly blaming elementary and secondary education for this;
- the role of the teacher: besides inspiring students, academics saw their teaching approach primarily as didactic or traditional (conveying information or directive guidance);
- typical classroom practices: Quinlan observed predominantly classes in which academics did most of the talking making the connections for the students, with the main difference between introductory and upper-level courses lying in the

type of questions posed to students, respectively "fill in the blank" questions and more thought-provoking questions.

However, closer analysis of individual academics showed that the sample could be split into two groups with distinctly different conceptions of the nature of the discipline and/or historical knowledge. Using the two prototypical academics discussed by Quinlan (Colleen and Derek) we will attempt to illustrate these two epistemologically different groups and the consequences for their teaching (goals, practice and student evaluation).

Colleen, as an example of a group of five academics, saw history as "detective work" (Quinlan, p. 450), as a process of inquiry, using multiple primary sources, disciplinary methods and comparing historical arguments to construct a *reasoned* historical interpretation (as in Perry's position 4b, see chapter two), in contrast to students' preference for 'just any' interpretation (as in Perry's position 4a, multiplicity). Colleen was proud if "one of the things [her students] got out of [her class] was this sense that history was not just one story, but that it could be interpreted ... {and} the sense that there are right and wrong interpretations" (Quinlan, 1999, p. 454). The preference for revisionist accounts – looking to history from the perspective of disenfranchised groups (women, the poor, minorities, etcetera) – that characterised this group of 'detectives' derived from this belief that there are multiple stories in history. Colleen's views are an example of an academic teacher with our learning-teaching conception 4: the academics in this group themselves were active producers of historical knowledge following the ways of knowing (historical thinking and analysis) of their discipline.

Derek was prototypical of the remaining three academics, who saw history as "a story", which is about "people, their lives, their myths and their stories. He wants students to come out of his classes with a sense of the story and the flow of history" (Quinlan, 1999, p. 455). These academics used (personal) stories to bring history to life and make it more 'real'. Derek and his colleagues were less enthused about questioning the established, consensus interpretation of history - not wanting the "story to be too broken up with varying interpretations so that '[students] don't know which end is up when they finally get done.'" (p. 455). They also had a more consumer-oriented approach to historical scholarship: studying and sharing the results of others' inquiries. Quinlan summarised the difference between the two groups as "While Colleen basks in ambiguities ... Derek argues that in the end, 'you owe the students the right to know [the] consensus [version]'" (Quinlan, 1999, p. 457). Because Derek criticised views on history teaching emphasising memorising (facts) (learning-teaching conception 2), but simultaneously rejected 'ideological discourse' or too much 'subjective' constructive interpretations of history (learning-teaching conception 4), we place him at learning-teaching conception 3 level, where he applied people's stories to enliven the consensus version of history.

Colleen's view on history can be recognised in her views on learning and teaching history, her teaching practice and her evaluation of students' performance. Learning in her approach was more than memorising facts and dates, it was about getting the big picture, thinking more deeply and developing analytical skills.

"Ultimately, I don't think the facts they get from my class are as important as the analytical skills, the writing and the talking skills" (Quinlan, 1999, p. 457). Consistent with this view on learning, Colleen was not keen on using standard textbooks, "they are 'boring' and fail to support her interpretive goals: ... 'They are designed to give an overview of scholarship to this point, scholarship is tending in one direction and they will give that as the facts'" (Quinlan, 1999, p. 458–459). She preferred using selected sets of readings offering multiple perspectives on a particular historical issue. Students were required to write analytical essays based on these readings, which proved to be difficult for these students: the specific skill of being able to pull together a historical analysis of an issue based on various viewpoints seemed to be much more challenging than summarising the various readings: "The actual analytical skills tend to be the things they have the most trouble with – even figuring out what it is to write an analytical essay" (Quinlan, 1999, p. 459). For some of the academics in this 'detective' group the consistency between epistemological view on history and their teaching practice was less pronounced, in particular in the context of lower division or survey level courses. In these contexts these academics focused more on content and less on historical thinking: "...There is a certain kind of content that I think a student should have which is more important than that deeper methodological side, philosophical" (Quinlan, 1999, p. 458). It seems that for these academics, the perception of the students was an impediment for consistency between epistemology and practice (see also Lederman, above).

Derek, on the other hand, focused on students learning the story – the outcome of current historical scholarship, the consensus version of history – emphasising increasing (foundational) content knowledge above analytical or process skills. Academics like Derek, judge standard textbooks more favourably and often see their role as captivating their audience: "In the classroom [Derek] is a passionate and dramatic speaker and seems to enthral his classes with his rhetorical style and vivid stories" (Quinlan, 1999, 455). In particular, this description reminds us of the metaphor of 'the showman' as reported by Lyons (1990, see before). Yero (2002) remarks about such teachers – the 'performers' – that similar metaphors can mean different things: "Does that mean the teacher is a Jerry Seinfeld, constantly cracking one-liners for the sole purpose of keeping his kids amused? Or is she a Kiri TeKanawa, holding her audience spellbound as she reaches operatic notes seemingly out of the range of mere mortals? *Does the teacher's* performance *challenge, inform or merely entertain?*" (Yero, 2002, p. 44, italics ours). Derek also often required his students to read the original (classic) texts to give them a feel for the actual people who lived through history, making it all more real to the students. In Derek's experience too, students are not very good writers. However, in contrast to Colleen's evaluation that students lack a specific (analytical) skill, Derek felt students have difficulty with the general ability to organise their thoughts: "Students don't organize very well when they write. They put things here and there. It's a kind of a hodgepodge. It jumps into their head. They don't have a sense of the goals of their writing" (Quinlan, 1999, p. 459).

Quinlan remarked that the obvious differences between these two groups of academics within one department seemed "to fall along some of the same lines as the larger debates and changes that have marked the recent history of the historical profession" (p. 461), implying that these epistemological differences reflect the development of history as a discipline. The question is open what the effect of such epistemological differences is on students and their views on history. To prevent possible student confusion, Quinlan advised that academics should "articulate their points of difference to students so that the students, too, can learn to explicitly articulate their beliefs and perspectives on the nature of the field and their work within it" (1999, p. 461). Educational developers need to understand that there may be "subtleties and tensions within disciplinary cultures" (p. 461) that can have (severe and unexpected) consequences for their development work when not understood or acknowledged. Confirming these outcomes, Quinlan reported on a similar study about academics' epistemological beliefs regarding engineering education, finding similar groupings of academics within two divisions of a department of mechanical engineering (Quinlan, 2002).

Wineburg (2001) comes to the same conclusions regarding differences in teachers' epistemological views on history as a discipline, and the opportunities and challenges these differences lead to in teaching students. In Wrinkles in Time and Place[18] Wineburg and Wilson discussed the differences in performance of two secondary-school history teachers – Mr. Barnes and Ms. Kelsey – on a number of performance assessment exercises: evaluation of student papers, use of documentary materials and textbook analysis. As Quinlan concluded for academics, Wineburg came to the conclusion that also for teachers in secondary education "[i]ndeed, the differences we found between these two teachers represent major shifts in how we, as individuals and as members of academic communities, conceptualize teaching, learning and the discipline of history" (Wineburg, 2001, p. 200). Mr. Barnes's views on history and historical knowledge, learning, teaching and student motivation show great similarity with Derek's views discussed above: with history primarily seen as a shared "official story of the past" (p. 201) consisting of economic and political facts, teaching becomes correcting factual and spelling errors using the "old didactic approach" (p. 202), learning is perceived as the absorption of facts and getting enough practice, and student motivation is perceived as being primarily extrinsic, e.g. getting a good grade or the car for the weekend (p. 199). Mr. Barnes's views can be seen as an example of learning-teaching conception 2/3. Ms. Kelsey on the other hand, displays more similarities with Colleen (above). Ms. Kelsey saw history as "interpreting the past" (p. 193) and historical knowledge primarily as the result of reasoned argumentation and use of evidence. She felt that in teaching students need to be supported in constructing their own historical understandings by teachers "building bridges" (p. 190), learning is "learning to think historically" (p.189) and "getting the big picture" (p. 187), and that student motivation is the result of challenging tasks – e.g. working with primary historical sources – so that students "really get in and re-experience" history (p. 191). In this description we recognise many characteristics of learning-teaching conception 4.

Our comparison of Derek and Colleen with respectively Barnes and Kelsey is further supported by Wineburg's description of the different approaches Barnes and Kelsey had to evaluating students' papers : "[r]ather than addressing the historical content of the essays, Barnes's comments focused on *generic* [italics ours] issues of writing and expression. While she did not ignore problems of composition, Kelsey focused primarily on making these better *history* essays" (Wineburg, 2001, p. 183–186). In comparing Barnes and Kelsey, we feel Wineburg (2001) also showed that Kelsey was the teacher with the richer repertoire of teaching strategies. For instance regarding the use of historical documents in teaching, Barnes and Kelsey differed remarkably in the number of potential uses they saw for primary/secondary historical documents in teaching. In Table 8.4 (p. 191) Wineburg contrasted the three possible uses Barnes mentioned while also limiting them to only his better students, with the eleven uses that Kelsey could imagine for students at various levels. A similar picture emerges when we look at the task of evaluating student papers: Kelsey's comments accompanying her evaluations were more elaborate, and her plans for remediation more specifically aimed at improving their essays. And again, in the task of analysing a textbook, Barnes showed his smaller – binary – repertoire in evaluating a textbook as either appropriate or not. While in Kelsey's more adaptive repertoire even less appropriate textbooks offer enormous teaching opportunities, for instance by cueing students to the various viewpoints possible in history. These results indicate (again) that less epistemologically sophisticated academics/teachers such as Derek and Barnes have a smaller repertoire of teaching strategies (and thus are less versatile teachers) and they are consistent with e.g. Maor and Taylor (1995) and Hashweh (1996). Our repertoire interpretation is – in a sense – supported by Wineburg when he discussed – in the context of the use of historical documents in teaching – the different types of 'historical detectives' Barnes and Kelsey seemed to be: "Indeed, whereas Kelsey corroborated evidence, speculated about the origins of documents, raised multiple competing hypotheses, and generated themes that captured patterns in the evidence, Mr. Barnes talked only of a single dimension in the documents: the dispute over who fired the first shot [at Lexington]. Although Barnes and Kelsey may both view history as 'detective work', Kelsey appears – at least in this exercise – to be the *shrewder detective*" (2001, p. 194, italics ours).

Finally, Wineburg seems to share our epistemological ecology hypothesis where he speculated about the sources of the differences between Barnes and Kelsey, namely differences in conceptions of learning, in conceptions of teaching or differences in conceptions of historical knowledge or history itself. "Yet it is difficult to say whether these differences [in teachers' views] stem from teachers' beliefs about *learning* or conceptualizations of *historical knowledge* ..., for the two go hand-in-hand. If knowledge comes prepackaged, teaching is straightforward: Just deliver the packages. But if knowledge is dynamic, teachers cannot simply hand over prepackaged facts, for understanding these 'facts' rests in no small measure on understanding the ever-shifting interpretative frameworks in which they are embedded" (2001, p. 193, italics ours).

In the previous paragraphs we have described studies based on active – in-service – teachers and academics. There are studies that focus on the beliefs of pre-service student teachers, for example Joanne Brownlee's work with Australian students (e.g. Bownlee et al., 2001). To illustrate that pre-service teachers already have certain epistemological beliefs that will influence their practice when they actually become teachers, we will discuss a study with pre-service (or student) teachers who were asked to contemplate their reaction to a problematic classroom situation (White, 2000). In designing this study, White made use of the four epistemological dimensions as defined by Hofer and Pintrich (1997, i.e. certainty and simplicity of knowledge, source and justification of knowing). White used a small set of questions to categorise the student teachers' epistemological beliefs and their approach (e.g. chosen alternative for action or solution) to a problematic classroom situation.[19] In White's study 20 pre-service teachers were interviewed using a scenario, where the interviewee "was to assume the role of a first-year teacher who had become aware of some problematic situation in his/her classroom"(White, 2000, p. 282), e.g. a discipline or pedagogical problem. In this scenario, the interviewees were to think of themselves as a member of a team discussing this problem. This team would generate five (imaginary) alternatives that the interviewee would consider on returning to the classroom: "[the] interview questions explored the students' thinking as they considered the five imaginary alternatives" (White, 2000, p. 282) and their responses were used to construct five categories of epistemological thinking (summarised in Table III, p. 290):

- Departing Absolutist (n=2)
  These student teachers indicated that all problems have one best solution, something that works, and that experts (i.e. experienced teachers), because of their larger experience, probably know for sure what this correct answer/ solution is and that *their* advice should be followed.
  Their view on problematic classroom situations was simple: "[n]ot bothered by considerations such as whether what will work for some students may have negative effects on others or whether what works in the short run may cause more problems in the long run, they use one criterion to choose an alternative … finding an alternative that will work" (White, 2000, p. 289).
- Intuitive Relative (n=3)
  These students believed that every student, teacher and situation is unique, different from any other, and that everything is in a constant state of flux: "I don't think you could say that the old stuff is right because it worked before" (White, 2000, p. 291). This means that no knowledge is certain, no solutions lead to predictable outcomes. These student teachers were suspicious of experts and textbooks as reliable sources of knowledge. As one student teacher said: "An expert isn't any better than a person without the knowledge" (White, 2000, p. 292). A quote that reminds us very much of the multiplicity examples of Kuhn (1991, see chapter 3). They emphasised that the determining factor for success is not necessarily the alternative chosen, but more the person carrying it out: "[w]hatever alternative doesn't matter; it's how you do it. It pretty much

depends on the person and what they're capable of doing—how they can best take the alternative and make it work for them." (White, 2000, p. 293).
Although situations are in constant flux, and therefore uncertain, approaching problematic classroom situations is seen as simple: following the teacher's instinct or gut feeling. In a respondent's words: "You look at the situation, thinking what the situation is. You pick an alternative. You're going to have to do it [select and alternative] from your instincts—what you think would be best… [but] not saying which is better because you never can say what's better" (White, 2000, p. 291).

– Selective Relative (n=10)
This group was by far the largest of the five. While these students still relied mostly on their own feeling when deciding on a course of action, they were less cynical about expert information: there might just be something you would be able to use. They selected (expert) information based on their expectation of future use – a course of action that is typical for learning conception 3 (van Rossum, Hamer and Würffel, 2003, and chapter 1) and as such it does not surprise us that this is the largest group, see also the discussion on Transitional Knowing of Baxter Magolda (1992 and chapter 3). In the words of one student "… a lot of the things in textbooks—some are recent, but they are really based on studies that were done a long, long time ago. … It's hard for me. You know, some of the things in textbooks are good. I read it, and I'm like, that makes sense to me … It makes sense, but applying it to a case-study straight out of the book might be kind of hard because [student changes in mid-sentence] I'm an advocate of you have to try something new to see if it will work or not … I would do my way and in a sense I would try my way but still have in mind what the textbook was saying" (White, 2000, p. 294).
These student teachers viewed a problematic classroom situation still as simple, but took a broader view – including the viewpoints of both teacher (or expert) and students. In looking for a solution that would work for themselves, all also considered the benefit for the students in deciding on a course of action. In this sense these student teachers viewed teaching as an interaction, again typical for the third teaching conception. In addition, where in the previous two categories student teachers had a uni-structural view on problematic classroom situations, these students were characterised by a multi-structural approach (Collis and Biggs, 1979).

– Informed Relative (n=2)
The major difference between the Intuitive and Selective Relatives and this small group of student teachers, was their budding notion that some solutions *are* better than others. These student teachers began to understand that using and prioritising criteria helps to evaluate solutions and choose the better one above any other. For example, one possible criterion that limits the range of solutions the pre-service teacher would consider, is his/her view on teaching: a preference for student-oriented teaching results in a different choice of action in a particular problematic situation than a preference for teacher-oriented teaching. One student

elaborated: "From what I understand there are different bases of teaching and some people are more teacher-oriented. I will tend to focus on the students' role, and so I will lean toward alternatives that benefit the students most, rather than benefit the system or the curriculum."(White, 2000, p. 295).

While these students acknowledged the worth of expert knowledge, they were more like the previous category in that they valued their own (concrete and immediate) experience and knowledge of their pupils above the abstracted or generalised knowledge from textbooks and experts: "[t]here's been so much research done in those [textbooks], but I still think they're just guidelines. Once again, they are generalised and so in order for them to be situation-specific is just impossible. I would take those, but then also, if I can refute the evidence with my own situation, I would say, 'Well, that might be true for most situations, but I have a unique group of people here'."(White, 2000, p. 296). The last quote reflects that for these students, ultimately their own experience prevails above evidence, however, at the same time they at least strongly feel the need to be familiar with the body of expert knowledge. We would interpret this to mean that these student teachers are in-between stages, in this case moving from learning conception 3 to learning conception 4.

White categorised this group as the first to view a problematic classroom situation as inherently complex, and solutions are selected based on a set of criteria. In discussing the criteria to apply, one student teacher said: "First would be if it was in my realm of philosophy. What is my particular situation? How well do I know my students, and how are they going to react to these different situations [alternatives]? Also, is it similar to something I've already tried? So, it's somewhat of a process of elimination by the basis of what are my students like, and how do I know that they'll respond to this. What is the particular need that I'm trying to solve, and have I tried something similar to this before (is this a possible solution)? Some of it may be a budget problem, and I couldn't possibly do that, or maybe just a logistics problem that I'm not able to do it."(White, 2000, p. 295). Their status of 'in-betweenness' is illustrated by the fact that choices are still dominated by personal feelings and experience (learning conception 3), while simultaneously these students are aware of the existence of a system of rules one can apply (learning conception 4) to arrive at a solution that feels right.

– Reflective Relative (n=3)[20]

These students trusted expert knowledge highly, they used multiple sources of knowledge which made them feel that they could indeed identify the better solution. White interpreted the responses of this group of student teachers as a revisiting of the belief in certainty of knowledge so characteristic of her first category. In a sense, these students do revisit a notion of certainty, because they have considered the evidence and have reached a conclusion, using a set of rules and the available evidence. So while they are certain, it is 'considered certainty', which is very different from the 'simple certainty' that the Departing Absolutists adhere to. In their considered certainty they are typical of the judgemental learning-teaching conception 4. As one student indicated, there is no absolute certainty about the outcome of a course of action, but based on expert knowledge, educated reasoning and taking into account that experts may not have the details of each classroom, one can make a prediction with a fair amount of probability: "[t]here's always the possibility that the alternative won't work turn out like you think it will because outside factors are possible to come in, but you can make an *educated guess*" (White, 2000, p. 297, italics ours).

White felt these students had the greatest understanding of the complexity of problematic classroom situations, being fully aware of, and using, many more types of criteria and multiple sources of evidence in constructing and evaluating possible solutions than any previous group. Typically all student teachers in this group considered best solutions those that solve the problem without causing more (or other) problems: "... adverse effects of alleviating the problem like if I ... like a lot more problems I could have created by solving this one. I need to have a clear understanding of the problem so I can know if it [the alternative] worked." (White, 2000, 298).

Looking at these categories while concentrating on the approach to the solution to the problematic classroom situation, we recognise the levels of application as they are characteristic for the various learning-teaching conceptions (see chapter 1, the section on 'conceptions of applying') and the various epistemological levels of thinking. From this perspective, Departing Absolutists view applying as doing as you are told by authority, which places these student teachers in the lowest epistemological levels of all the models discussed previously, e.g. learning-teaching conception 2.

Intuitive Relatives take their own feelings into account and applying is seen as following your instincts, your gut feeling, connecting this category to learning conception 3, multiplicity or 'subjective knowing'. This interpretation is supported by the student teachers' view that the success of any solution depends on the person carrying it out, so that the person is (part of) the solution. As such the teacher is had by the solution, and does not have a solution, which is typical of the third order of consciousness (Kegan, 1994 and chapter 3). Selective Relatives have a reproductive but selective view on application, which we feel places them in the same category as the Intuitive Relatives, learning-teaching conception 3. These two categories do differ in some sense, which brings us to propose again that the categorisation of White may reflect development within a stage or between adjacent stages. In this sense Intuitive Relative would be an earlier stage of learning conception 3, with Selective Relative coming into the full bloom of learning-teaching conception 3. Such a gradual growing into a next stage would not seem illogical, as you might not just wake up a level-three-thinker one morning, after being a level-two-thinker for some time. We have encountered such subgroups in our own work (e.g. van Rossum and Taylor, 1987), but we have chosen to focus on the main categories in an effort to simplify and clarify our learning-teaching conception model. Of course, studying the details of the development between adjacent conceptions or beliefs is very interesting and useful. We discuss such developments in chapter 7.

In the case of Informed Relatives, application becomes a complex problem in itself, placing these student teachers beyond the third learning conception or

Transitional Knowing. The complexity lies in using some form of reasoning by applying criteria, but the use of evidence is still limited, which makes us doubt their full-fledged membership of learning conception 4 or Independent Knowing. The final category identified by White, Reflective Relatives, is a fair description of application at the level of learning-teaching conception 4: using (expert) knowledge and applying a set of reasoned rules to construct a (logical) solution they have confidence in.

White (2000) is often cited to support a non-developmental stance with regard to epistemology, quoting her statement (p. 279) that "Pre-service teachers do not move from category to category of epistemology in [a] stage-like fashion" (e.g. Schraw and Olafson, 2002). We clearly disagree, and perhaps White does as well where she says "The arrangement of the sequence of the five categories is that which would be predicted by King and Kitchener (1994) and by Dewey (1933)" (White, 2000, p. 286). Her paper is much more interesting than that: White's results may be exploring the gradual development within and between stages. As such this study is an important one and one of the few we know that addresses the issue of how development between adjacent stages takes place.

Even more important to the current study, is White's proposition that each of the five epistemological categories found for pre-service teachers, represents a web of interconnected, logically consistent and coherent beliefs for which she gives the following example.

> It is logically consistent, for example, for an Intuitive Relative pre-service teacher to believe that her choice of an alternative to follow in a problematic classroom situation would be better than even an expert's choice since experts, all having different answers, are obviously touting their own opinions. Because all ideas about which alternative to follow are somebody's opinion, why should these pre-service teachers choose to follow the dictates of another when it would be they trying to implement the alternative? *One opinion is, after all, as good as another.* It is also consistent that choosing one alternative to pursue is not a major concern for these pre-service teachers since the problematic classroom situation, no matter what its nature, is changing so rapidly that any alternative chosen before the fact will be a mismatch with the situation by the time it is actually implemented. As would be expected, these pre-service teachers voice the importance of the teacher being able to 'go with the flow' of the classroom, adapting as needed to deal with the changing situation. The world view of the pre-service teachers in *each* category is likewise coherent…." (White, 2000, p. 299–300, italics ours)

'One opinion is as good as another' is the epitome of Perry's multiplicity, and the example again presents strong evidence for the existence of a psycho-logic within each epistemological way of knowing and also for our epistemological ecology hypothesis (see chapter 4).

Thirdly, White seems to have a keen perception of the many obstacles to overcome when crossing the watershed between Intuitive/Selective Relative and Informed/Reflective Relative – between learning-teaching conception 3 and 4.

> The vast majority of the pre-service teachers in this study believe views about problematic situations and the knowledge that might inform them to be a matter of opinion. ... ... most lack the understanding of the nature of knowledge or the ways of reasoning that would enable them to make judgements that are defensible. Bereft of such understanding and reasoning ability, they fall back on their natural basis of verifying credibility for the purpose of judgement making on the beliefs they have acquired through lived experience. ... [What they need is] the disposition to seek and assess critically and honestly all available information and to reason dialogically with that information, all the while refraining from rushing to conclusions."(White, 2000, p. 302)

Finally, White concludes that encouraging epistemological growth is a "starkly daunting task" (p. 302). Using her categories she suggests a number of educational activities addressing and stretching each category's typical aspects, constructing a type of holding environment to aid epistemological growth (Kegan, 1994). We will discuss these suggestions (seen as good practices) – as well as her position that changing epistemology "can be accomplished only through a programmatic emphasis that is concerted and sustained" (White, 2000, p. 304) in our chapter Changing Teaching and Learning.

In the context of mathematics instruction, Stipek et al. (2001) measured and interrelated several teachers' beliefs and practices. A major subtheme in this study was the controversy – in the literature, the minds of teachers and the general public – between inquiry-oriented instruction and more traditional instruction. The NCTM standards for mathematics instruction in the United States (1991) emphasised that "mathematics need to be taught as a dynamic tool for thought, not just as a set of operation to be learned."(Stipek et al., 2001, p. 214).[21] The role of the teacher in this type of instruction is "to support and guide this constructive process rather than to transmit discrete knowledge" (p. 214). Stipek et al. viewed this approach to mathematics as being in stark contrast with the conception of mathematics and its instruction that most (American) teachers hold, namely "as a static body of knowledge, involving a set of rules and procedures that are applied to yield one right answer. 'Knowing' mathematics means being skilful and efficient in performing procedures and manipulating symbols without necessarily understanding what they represent..." (Stipek et al. 2001, p. 214). In this more traditional instruction, the teacher is in control, and "in a typical American lesson the teacher reviews or introduces a new procedure, provides students with step-by-step instructions, then assigns students problems on which to practice the procedure..." (p. 214). These practice problems are in our experience usually identical or very similar to the examples introduced in the lesson. We recognise in these two stances on the one hand learning-teaching conception 4 (i.e. inquiry-oriented instruction) and learning-teaching conception 2 (i.e. traditional instruction). The controversy discussed by Stipek et al. is not unique to the United States, also in the Netherlands we have an ongoing, public discussion on the controversy between so-called "new learning" and "old learning", not only with regard to mathematics, or any other specific subject. In the Netherlands the discussion covers the whole range of education, with a focus on secondary schooling.

Stipek et al. is noteworthy in our review for a number of reasons. It is the first study in this chapter which is completely quantitative in nature, and as such has similarities with the studies of e.g. Paulsen and Feldman and also Cano on students' learning strategies (see chapter 4). In the instrument used to measure teachers' beliefs we see also some similarities with Schommer's EBQ and Vermunt's ILS. Secondly, it focuses on (twenty-one) primary school teachers, measuring divers teacher beliefs and teacher practices, as well as pupils' feelings of competence and enjoyment. Thirdly, the pupils themselves (n=437) were not typical of much educational research on teacher beliefs, coming from low-income families and from divers ethnic backgrounds.

The questionnaire Stipek et al. used to measure the teachers' beliefs consisted of 43 relevant statements. The following five aspects of teacher beliefs about mathematics and mathematics instruction were measured at the beginning and the end of the school year:

- The nature of mathematics (5 items, a set of operations vs. a tool for thought)
- Mathematics learning (7 items, getting the right answer vs. understanding)
- Teacher control (6 items, teacher control vs. pupil autonomy)
- Mathematical ability (11 items, fixed entity vs. incremental)
- Motivational strategy (5 items, extrinsic vs. intrinsic)

In addition the questionnaire included 9 items about confidence in teaching math and enjoyment of math. Teaching practice was measured by scoring videotaped instructional periods (lessons) on seven dimensions, and by a questionnaire about teachers' criteria for formal evaluation of pupils' work. The lessons were scored on the following seven dimensions:

- Emphasis on performance outcomes (e.g. praising or criticising performance)
- Emphasis on speed (e.g. "you should be done by now")
- Psychological high-risk environment in the classroom (e.g. conveying low expectations of certain pupils)
- Encouragement of pupil autonomy (e.g. giving students choices in how to solve problems)
- Emphasis on student effort (e.g. encouraging students to keep on trying)
- Focus on understanding and mastery (e.g. asking pupils to apply concepts in new contexts)
- Teacher's enthusiasm and interest (e.g. low score for comments as "I know math isn't fun, but I had to learn it and so do you")

The questionnaire about teachers' evaluation criteria focused on four aspects – a pupil's effort, relative score, creativity and independence – of their grading (term grades) or written reports to parents.

Finally, the pupils were asked to fill in a questionnaire about their own math competence/confidence and their enjoyment of math at the start and finish of the school year.

Over the year, teachers' beliefs proved to be fairly stable, in particular the beliefs about mathematics learning, teacher control, motivational strategy and their confidence in (teaching) math. This result is not exceptional, as much of the literature reviewed here shows that beliefs of teachers (and of students for that matter) are notoriously difficult to change. A factor analysis of the teachers' beliefs revealed a two-factor solution. High scores on the beliefs loading on the first factor represented aspects of traditional thinking about mathematics, mathematics learning and mathematics teaching. Stipek et al. summarised this coherent set of beliefs as follows: "[f]ive dimensions of beliefs were strongly associated with each other: (1) mathematics is a set of operations to be learned; (2) students' goal is to get correct solutions; (3) the teacher needs to exercise complete control over mathematics activities; (4) mathematics ability is fixed and stable; and (5) extrinsic rewards and grades are effective strategies for motivating students to engage in mathematics". (2001, p. 222). The association of a belief in a fixed and stable ability and the belief in firm teacher control is consistent with the link between learning-teaching conceptions and conceptions of intelligence (see chapter 1).

Remarkable for this first factor are the negative loadings for confidence in teaching and enjoyment of math indicating that teachers scoring high on traditional beliefs were "less self-confident about teaching mathematics and enjoyed it less" (2001, p. 221). Confidence and enjoyment seemed to form the second coherent set, both loaded with the first. Stipek et al. concluded that these results may indicate that "less confident teachers are drawn to a set of beliefs and practices that require relatively less teacher judgment and decision making ...following the procedures described in the textbook and even using the answer sheets in the teacher's manual to correct student work" (2001, p. 223). This would mean that to encourage the adoption of inquiry-oriented instruction, it may prove necessary to build up teachers' self-confidence in math, by building up their mathematical understanding. In short, contrary to popular belief, the coaching role of teachers within inquiry-oriented instruction would seem to require a deeper understanding of the subject matter than may be necessary for traditional teaching.

The relation between the first five teachers' beliefs and their observed teaching practice was strong. In particular, the beliefs that math is a set of operations and procedures to be learned, that the teacher is in firm control and that extrinsic motivation is more effective, were positively associated with an emphasis on performance outcomes (good grades, correct answers) – and to a lesser degree with an emphasis on speed – as opposed to an emphasis on understanding and learning. Not surprisingly, these traditional beliefs were negatively associated with creating a low-risk environment, pupil autonomy, an emphasis on understanding/mastery and teacher enthusiasm. This means that more traditional beliefs were (strongly) associated with more traditional practices, making the influence of traditional beliefs on practice evident. The final statistically significant relationship found was between belief in an entity theory (ability is fixed) and an emphasis on performance outcomes. Stipek et al. felt this meant that these teachers were more likely to group pupils of the same perceived ability level together, adjusting their teaching to the expected performance level instead of focusing on individual understandings of a particular problem in a particular context.

The relationship between teachers' beliefs and their evaluation practice showed that teachers who believe in firm control and finding correct answers (the more traditional teachers) focus less on effort and creativity as criteria in their evaluation of student work. The unexpected result that pupil independence was positively associated with four of the five traditional beliefs, might be an artefact of the design. The concept of pupil independence was not elaborated upon and was, Stipek et al. think, probably interpreted by the teachers as the pupils' tendency *not* to ask questions and *not* to ask for help. If so, it is consistent that for teachers with inquiry-oriented beliefs this would be a negative sign, a sign of lack of interaction between pupils and teacher, explaining the low value given to this aspect by inquiry-oriented teachers. It is interesting to note that here again we find a popular misconception about inquiry (or new) learning. Within inquiry learning, independent learning – seen as not asking for help or lack of interaction – is not a desirable phenomenon. Inquiry learning supposes a good (and intensive) relationship between pupil and teacher and would indeed require '*dependent learners*', namely pupils not afraid of asking questions about something they are working on, and not 'independent learners'. We have introduced before the term 'mentored learning' (see chapter 3) to replace the commonly used term of 'independent learning' in order to eliminate this particular misconception about inquiry-oriented instruction (or new learning).

Combining this latter conclusion with the conclusion formulated before with regard to the level of subject-matter understanding required for inquiry-oriented teaching, one may conclude that inquiry-oriented instruction (or new learning) needs teachers with a deeper subject-matter understanding, and students ánd teachers who are willing to interact frequently and openly, learning together. In short inquiry-oriented instruction and learning aim for learning partnerships (Baxter Magolda, 2004), in order to be successful, *closeness* - and *not* distance – is required.

Considering all this, one might ask what this means for students. Stipek et al. addressed this issue when they asked students to report on their enjoyment of math and confidence in learning math. They found that the teachers' self-confidence as math teachers was significantly positively related to the students' perceived confidence as math learners. This supports the earlier conclusion about the importance of teachers' mathematical understanding: "[i]ncreased understanding of mathematics should enhance the quality of their teaching and give them self-confidence, that may, directly or indirectly, contribute to their students' self-confidence as math learners" (Stipek et al., 2001, p. 224).

Stipek et al. (2001) closed with a discussion about the consequences of their findings for changing teaching practices and staff development. We will return to this study in the chapter on Changing teaching and learning. For now we close our discussion of Stipek et al. by quoting their final sentence: "Whatever approach [to staff development] is used, *it is clear that* [at least for traditional beliefs] *beliefs and practices are linked*, and emphasis in teacher professional development on either one without considering the other is likely to fail" (2001, p. 225, italics and caveat ours).

Martinez et al. (2001) examined and compared the metaphors evident in the tacit theories of experienced and pre-service elementary school teachers about learning and teaching. While Martinez et al. did not explicitly define their use of the concept metaphor, we feel that the definition of Yero (2002) covers the meaning of metaphors well: "For the sake of simplicity, I plan to use the word *metaphor* to mean any circumstance where a person uses one conceptual category, experience, or 'thing' to describe or define another conceptual category. It may be simple or extended, and with or without the words *like* or *as*. 'The essence of metaphor is understanding and experiencing one thing in terms of another.'" (Yero, 2002, p. 40 and below). Three assumptions lay at the root of this study on metaphors, namely

- Relevance of teachers' metaphors: "In education as well as in other sciences, researchers and practitioners are unconsciously guided by images and metaphorical patterns of thought recurring in their field, which can be seen as 'archetypes' of professional knowledge or from a merely functional point of view as *blueprints of professional thinking*" (Martinez et al., 2001, p. 966, italics ours).
- Effects of metaphors on teachers' conceptions of learning and their teaching practice: "As blueprints of thinking, metaphors of learning will guide and facilitate teachers' understanding of *what it means to learn*, but these same tools of thinking may also limit the thoughts, attitudes and *actions* of prospective educators" (Martinez et al., 2001, p. 966, italics ours). Martinez et al. give an example.

  > ... if a teacher prefers the captain metaphor, he or she will probably tend to practice strict control over the students, while a teacher preferring the entertainer metaphor will be first of all friendly and humorous in the classroom ... The inherent potential of metaphors to influence teachers' educational practice makes them important tools for the education of teachers. (Martinez et al., 2001, p. 974)

- Professional development: change is easier in collaborative groups (i.e. in communities of teachers as learners, Beishuizen, 2004): "... we prefer to promote educators' professional development by—among other strategies—sharing their metaphors of education in collaborative groups of colleagues ... In this process, metaphors may function as stepping stones to a new vantage point from which a teacher can look at his or her own practice as educator from a new perspective" (Martinez et al., 2001, p. 974). In a community of teachers as learners, in-depth analysis of the subjective experiences and the collaborative reflections on the metaphors within the group often requires additional guidance. Questions and probes from trainers may help in the discovery of unexamined or controversial aspects of the metaphors and thus may lead to heightened awareness of the teachers' implicit theories. This awareness can in turn lead to refinement or even change of teachers' metaphors and consequently

> in teachers' educational practice. This is true in particular, when exercises in collaborative reflection are not incidental, but continued over longer periods of time (p. 974).

It is interesting to note that Martinez et al. used an a priori grouping of metaphors to analyse the metaphors of their subjects. The first group of metaphors was labelled 'behaviourist/empiricist' and these metaphors portrayed the mind of the learner as a "wax plate onto which our experiences in the physical world are engraved" (Martinez et al., 2001, p. 967). The learner is seen as a more or less passive member of the student-teacher relationship. This group of metaphors fits nicely with our lower learning-teaching conceptions. The second group of metaphors was labelled 'cognitive' and these metaphors portrayed the mind of the learner as "pro-active, problem-orientated, and interpretative" (Martinez et al., 2001, p. 967). Learning is seen as the active process of schema (re)construction. This group of metaphors has the flavour of learning-teaching conception 4. The third and final group of metaphors was called 'situative or socio-historic' and in this group the mind of the learner depends on dialogic exchanges and learning is a "consequence of authentic participation in the activities of a community of practitioners, and during the process of learning, the individuals as well as their community acquire knowledge and skills..." (Martinez et al., 2001, p. 967–968). Formulating learning like this is typical for learning-teaching conception 5.

The metaphors found in a group of 50 experienced teachers, who were in an in-service training to become school counsellor, were compared to the metaphors found in a group of 38 pre-service teachers. For both groups of teachers the metaphors were gathered and exchanged in small groups (4 to 6 members each). The experienced teachers discussed their metaphors of learning in their own group and recorded the metaphors that best represented the group's view on learning. The metaphors of the pre-service teachers were gathered when they were asked to give a personal answer to the question "How do you understand 'learning'?"[22] in the framework of an analysis of curriculum design approaches. Before discussing the results, Martinez et al. (2001) made two interesting remarks about these metaphors:

1) Some of the metaphors found seemed to be 'hybrids' revealing a combination of types of metaphors. Where this may have surprised Martinez et al., Yero (treated below) has a viable explanation for this phenomenon. In Yero's experience it is not the metaphor itself that gives insight into teacher thinking, it is how the teacher gives substance (and meaning) to the metaphor. We will discuss this in detail below.
2) Only in one case, Martinez et al. were unable to categorise a metaphor into one of their three a priori groups of metaphors, indicating the fairly comprehensive nature of their three analytical categories for this group of teachers.

Considering the fit with our model of learning-teaching conceptions, we would tend to agree that these three categories would cover by far the most frequent implicit teacher theories about learning and teaching. In stating this, we anticipate on our conclusion of this chapter, that student and teacher thinking are really not that much different. For, as Yero states, "...what are teachers if not grownup versions of those [students]?" (Yero, 2002, p. 22). And isn't "it reasonable to spend at least as much effort understanding teaching 'styles' as is spent studying learning styles? To admit teachers are *as different as* the students in their classes?" (Yero, 2002, p. 8, italics ours).

The majority of metaphors (57%) formulated by the experienced teachers could be classified as belonging to the behaviourist/empiricist category, describing the teacher's role as transmitting (externally determined) knowledge or training skills, and the student is seen as an empty container or slate, ready to receive the knowledge. Yero (2002), in reviewing various studies on metaphors, found a similar percentage (55%) of teacher metaphors implying authoritative control by the teacher over the students (p. 67). This large group of metaphors Martinez et al. found displayed consistent (traditional and epistemologically fairly unsophisticated) views on student learning, teaching and knowledge/knowing, supporting our epistemological ecology hypothesis. Within these metaphors some subgroups could be discerned, metaphors dealing with visual perception, the absorption of knowledge, training, food or eating, and directive teaching. We will give examples of this group (and the following groups) in Table 5.1. Metaphors referring to the military, sports, economy or technology were rare, and, surprisingly to Martinez et al., no metaphors for the mind "as a computer" were found at all in this group.

The second largest group of metaphors (38%) could be categorised as constructivist/cognitive, which again surprised Martinez et al. because "... the official curriculum of the Autonomous Community of Valencia (...) where our subjects are teaching, is focused on the constructivist approach" (Martinez et al., 2001, p. 970).[23] The teachers' epistemological ecology for this group of metaphors is characterised by a (re)constructive view on student learning, the teacher's role is likened to facilitator and coach and, in most respects, knowledge is not seen as fixed nor stable, but as flexible and malleable. Metaphors refer to students actively dealing with the environment, empirical research activities, architecture and building, and independent learning (although teachers acknowledge the supportive role of others).

The remaining 5% of the metaphors were categorised as referring to "socio-historically based notions of situative learning" (p. 971). These metaphors were fundamentally constructivist, describing learning, teaching and knowledge/knowing as joint practices between equal partners, and based on mutual care. We are not surprised by the relatively small size of this category, it is consistent with our finding that learning-teaching conceptions 5 and higher are rare in the total population, and even relatively rare in the population of highly educated people (see also Kuhn, 1991 and chapter 3). However, Martinez et al. seemed to be rather disappointed about the size of this group of metaphors, especially as they referred to the quality of teacher education in Spain and its emphasis on situated learning: "The perspective of situated learning is by no means absent in teacher education. Throughout their teacher studies, our subjects had 'received' much information on socio-historic points of view. For example, Habermas' (...) construct of an ideal community of dialogue and its contribution to overcome highly subjectivist and individualist ways of life was part of their studies" (Martinez et al., 2001, p. 971).

The reference to Habermas seems to refer to the often confusing difference between multiplicity (learning-teaching conception 3) and relativism/dialogue teaching (learning-teaching conception 5, see chapters 1, 3 and 4). In their disappointment about the unexpected low level of teacher thinking Martinez et al. came to an important conclusion about the effort needed to bring about change in teacher metaphors/beliefs: "… development towards considering the social nature of learning [depends on] a process of restructuring the teachers' epistemological, ontological, emotional and social assumptions. Metaphorical and conceptual reconstructions depend on a *collage* of metaphors and 'literal' conceptions which interact and support each other" (p. 972). In this conclusion they summarise our view on the role of the epistemological ecology in staff development, it is not sufficient to focus on one or two aspects of teacher thinking – such as introducing only one foreign life form in a robust ecology. It is potentially much more successful to 'disrupt' the robust epistemological ecology by weakening it in many and fundamental ways simultaneously, including "The Heart of [the] Teacher" (Palmer, 1998).

The somewhat disappointing results from the experienced teachers were compared to the distribution of metaphors formulated by the prospective teachers,

Table 5.1. Examples of teachers' metaphors

Metaphor group	*Example*
Behaviourist	
visual perception	Learning is like a video camera which records the world.
absorption	Learning is like a sponge, which soaks in the water.
training	Teaching is like taming a horse.
eating	Teaching is like eating, it satisfies a necessity.
directive teaching	Teaching is a game of billiards … you have to know how to aim, to push […] at he right place in order to send it into the right direction.
Constructivist	
active approach	The student is like a silkworm that does not know … that it is going to be converted in a long process step by step into something beautiful, where the beauty is like the fruit of something it has constructed from what it has eaten.
research activity	Learning is a detective who looks for things and into things…
architecture	Learning is like setting the bricks of a house. The student is the mason… the house… the owner... The teacher is the site foreman.
independence	It is like learning to walk … Various forms of assistance, given by parents, relatives, etcetera are necessary … until we are able to 'walk' by ourselves.
Situative	
joint practice	Teaching is like a tourist guide who negotiates a route *with* the tourists.

Source: Martinez et al. (2001), tables 1, 2 and 3, italics ours.

who by the way had no practical experience in teaching. The difference was striking. The relative size of the categories behaviourist and constructivist was nearly inverse: 22% behaviourist and 56% constructivist, with another 22% of the metaphors being categorised as situative. The difference was attributed to the fact that the pre-service teachers had been exposed to constructivist theories throughout their four years at university, while the experienced teachers had no recent contact with these theories and, according to Martinez et al., constructivist ideas were extremely rare in their daily practice in nursery and elementary schools in Spain. The implication of this argument is that beliefs or metaphors are social constructs, they are fed – and can be changed – by (in)formal everyday experience. Yero (2002) proposed a similar explanation: "[t]he point is a teacher's behaviors frequently spring, not from higher-level thinking processes, but from habit" (p. 6).

Judith Yero, a Canadian science teacher with many years experience wrote a humorous and informative book about metaphors and teaching—Teaching in Mind—and she clarifies with many examples what metaphors can mean in teaching. As Yero (2002) remarks, we all (teachers, students, in fact everyone) use metaphors regularly. It is a convenient way to describe a complex situation in a few words. In a way a metaphor is like a caricature, it emphasises some aspects, e.g. a big nose, a heavy five o'clock shadow, a pair of spectacles, so that with very few clues one can identify the person intended. Metaphors are much the same in the sense that, when you describe a particularly difficult class with the words "Class was a zoo today", almost everybody will understand you immediately. Of course it definitely does not mean that the students have suddenly changed into sloths, parrots, and monkeys, it's only a figure of speech. So what does this have to do with teaching, how could such mental images influence a teacher and his/her practice? The same way a caricature reduces the person depicted to a few body or facial aspects, a metaphor has in it the danger that it obscures the full detail of each situation, while its interpretation may reflect some deep – perhaps unexamined – beliefs about teaching and learning.

Yero stresses that it is important to realise that as there are no absolutely 'wrong' metaphors, there are also no immaculately 'right' metaphors. It's all about what the metaphor means to the teacher who uses it. Here may be the underlying explanation for the hybrid-type metaphors that Martinez et al. (2001) reported above. The hybrid-ness may lie in the different meanings given by teachers to the same words, i.e. what each metaphor entails for an individual. For instance, if a student is seen as a sponge (an a priori behaviourist metaphor, Martinez et al. 2001), does that mean he/she is passively soaking up all knowledge (as a dead – behaviourist – sponge may do in your bathroom) or does a student, as a living – learning-teaching conception 3 – sponge, select specific, nutritious, parts of what knowledge is floating by? In Yero's words: "People assume that when they use the same words they've reached agreement. (...) Educators constantly toss around words such as *successful, effective, appropriate, respect, learn, understand* and *teach*. What, specifically, does each of those words mean to you? What is *your* measure of *success*? Is it the same as that of a student? The student's parents? The experts writing educational standards? The people urging more individualized learning environments? When teachers try to motivate students to *succeed*, whose definition are they using?"(Yero, 2002, p. 53). Here, in the final question we recognise the fundament underlying our own body of research.

As Martinez et al., Yero noted various categories of metaphors. For instance, ideas are seen as things, sometimes food, or plants or commodities. A few examples of ideas
as food:

> "All this paper has in it are *raw* facts, *half-baked* ideas, and *warmed-over* theories ... That argument *smells fishy* ... That's *food* for thought! ... We don't need to *spoon-feed* our students";

or as plants:

> "That idea *died on the vine* .... Mathematics has many *branches* .... She has a *fertile* imagination";

or as commodities:

> "It's important how you *package* your ideas ..... That idea just won't *sell* ... There is always a *market* for good ideas" (all examples Yero, 2002, p. 41).

And teaching is sometimes seen as cooking, with lessons seen as "*mental meals* ... meals intended to *nourish* the mind" (Yero, 2002, p. 82).

As we have seen above (Martinez et al.), metaphors teachers use influence their teaching practice and their teacher-student interactions. This means that metaphors are *not* merely ornamentation of speech. Metaphors seem to work somewhat like an eye (or a lens) with which you perceive reality, in this they are very like conceptions or beliefs etcetera. Yero uses the terms metaphor, beliefs, meaning etcetera almost interchangeably and doesn't seem to see the need to use so many different terms to describe teacher thinking. She is not alone in her position, e.g. Tsai (2002) and Pajares,

> Educational psychology does not always accord its constructs such precision, and so defining *beliefs* is at best a game of player's choice. They travel in disguise and often under alias—attitudes, values, judgments, axioms, opinions, ideology, perceptions, *conceptions,* conceptual systems, preconceptions, dispositions, implicit theories, explicit theories, personal theories, internal mental processes, action strategies, rules of practice, practical principles, perspectives, repertories of understanding, and social strategy, to name but a few that can be found in the literature. (Pajares 1992, p. 309, italics ours)

In the spirit of this study, we would like to add e.g. 'ways of knowing', 'positions', 'epistemological theories' and 'orders of consciousness' to this list.

If metaphors function as a lens, each person will interpret their own metaphors to fit their own beliefs about teaching and learning. Yero feels that this means that while metaphors are a window onto teachers' implicit theories about learning or teaching, they should not be taken at face value: not all sponges are alike. They need to be examined more closely to uncover the deeper structure or their real meaning to the teacher. To illustrate Yero's claim, let's examine another very common metaphor in teaching—learning seen as a journey—and its underlying meanings, the *metaphor-as-meant*: "[e]xamining the subtext—the entailments of a metaphor—yields fascinating insights into the role of the teacher, the student, the curriculum, discipline, and many other aspect of the education environment" (Yero, 2002, p. 44). In the current study, we primarily discuss the *epistemological* aspects of the metaphors' meaning, the metaphor-as-meant. These epistemological aspects are e.g. the views on learning, teaching, knowledge/ knowing and sometimes assessment, that speak from the underlying meaning (the story) of the metaphor. In a sense Yero does the same, however, she also acknowledges that there are other dimensions of meaning that shape the metaphor-as-meant.

In the *coverage-oriented* interpretation of the journey metaphor, such a journey is one where concepts and facts are objects that can be collected and possessed, content needs to be covered much like a landscape, and students need to be kept on track like a train. If so, what then is the destination of this journey? Is it a visit to Hotel Application, to Understand City or Testland? Not only the destination can vary, what kind of journey are we talking about? Is it a whirlwind tour of the world, with the students – much like Japanese tourists – snapping uncountable numbers of pictures to make sure that once they are back they can show you where they have 'been'? Or, does the teacher (as an intrepid explorer) invite the students to "boldly go where no-one has gone before", to seek out and *construct* new knowledge? Or is it a leisurely trek across the land, with frequent stops to examine the local flora and fauna together, to get the feel of each locale? The latter would be an example of a *discovery-oriented* interpretation of the journey metaphor. As Yero puts it,

> In the [coverage-oriented interpretation of the journey] metaphor, one can visualize the *journey* as a busload full of students with the teacher driving at full speed along a predefined road to reach the destination before nightfall—the test. In a discovery-oriented interpretation of the metaphor, the teacher and students travel more or less together, along a somewhat defined route, but they make frequent stops along the way as students notice something of interest that they wish to explore. There are occasional interesting side trips to unexpected places. At times, groups pursue different paths and, after returning to the main road, report to the class about what they have found. (Yero, 2002, p. 47)

A third example from the more behaviourist category to illustrate the concept of metaphor-as-meant: if teachers see students as receptacles – things they can pour facts and knowledge into – what does that say about each separate student? Are their heads all equally large and can all contain the same amount of knowledge? If the teacher pours harder (teaches faster) will the students' heads fill up more quickly? Are all the holes in their heads of equal diameter, so that they can take in knowledge at an equal rate? (Yero, 2002, remember the Lorentz contraction metaphor explained before, Linder, 1992).

While Yero takes a strong position about the relationship between teachers' metaphors and their entailments for teachers' beliefs about learning, teaching, knowledge and knowing, and assessment, she remains unclear about the nature of the relationship between beliefs and metaphors. On the one hand, metaphors seem to reflect underlying beliefs (i.e. the interpretation or story of the metaphor, Yero, 2002, p. 63), so that the same metaphor can mean different things to different people. On the other hand, Yero feels that changing the metaphors could change the teachers' beliefs so that "metaphors act like a 'master switch' for beliefs" and the changing of the metaphor's story (the beliefs) is implicit. (Yero, 2002, 51). We feel it might prove more complicated than that: what stops teachers from interpreting their new metaphor within their existing belief system? For example, what happens if we change the journey metaphor to a garden metaphor - from covering the material to nurturing the students - without addressing the story/ beliefs explicitly? Yero has an appropriate paragraph on this as well.

> The image of *teacher as gardener,* nurturing her students, sounds benign and helpful, but all gardens are not created equal. The general metaphor turns out to be less important than the subtext—the entailments that go along with the story as a result of the particular *meaning* assigned by the individual. Here are a couple of examples.

1. Gardener number one first plows the land to remove all the weeds. The ground is then laid out in neat plots and the same type of seed is planted in each plot. The gardener regularly waters the seeds and gives hem doses of fertilizer. What the gardener expects from those efforts is a field of healthy plants that will yield a productive harvest. They are, of course, all the same plants. Failure to grow and produce is seen as the fault of weak and stunted plants—the bad seeds. The gardener is judged by the yield of his fields (test scores).
2. Gardener number two creates unique and beautiful bonsai trees. Working with what is already there, the gardeners judiciously snips and prunes, feeding each tree with just the nutrients it needs to become a one-of-a-kind specimen. The gardener seeks to bring out the innate beauty of each tree.
3. Gardener number three tends a large botanical garden. Different plants occupy each area of the garden. Some require more or less water, more or less fertilizer, more or less sunlight. The gardener recognizes the unique requirements of each type of plant and provides the environment most conducive to growth and development. The gardener's reward is in helping each plant produce the healthiest flowers and fruits that are within its nature. (Yero, 2002, p. 70–71)

Even if a teacher changes his/her metaphor from the coverage-oriented interpretation of the journey metaphor to the gardening metaphor, if his/her underlying beliefs are not addressed what kind of gardener can we expect? So, changing teachers and their practice is more complicated than simply switching metaphors. It is not the metaphor that needs changing, but the 'metaphor-as-meant'. If anything, the metaphor-as-meant is the 'master switch'. Therefore, looking back at Pajares' list of definitions for beliefs, we feel that yet another alias needs adding: metaphors-as-meant.

While this is all very interesting (and entertaining), one might still wonder what is the purpose of changing metaphors-as-meant? The importance for Yero lies in the direct relationship between the metaphor-as-meant and teaching practice: "[t]eachers' beliefs and values [hidden in metaphors] shape the *atmosphere* of the classroom itself. Within that atmosphere, from the interactions among teachers and students, students learn their most pervasive lessons. These are lessons about respect, values, the nature of knowledge, thought processes, self-worth, and expectations" (Yero, 2002, p. 2). Applying this to the use of a tool-metaphor in relation with teaching practice, Yero discusses – as an example – the effects of different metaphors-as-meant for concepts or principles to be learned: "tools to be used" versus "tools, as objects one can possess". Yero describes the practices of two teachers using these different metaphors-as-meant.

> The behavior of a teacher who thinks about concepts and principles as *tools to be used* is quite different from one who thinks about them as *objects to be collected or possessed.* The first teacher is more likely to spend time having students learn to use the tools once they have collected them, She might, in fact, give students a problem requiring a specific tool that they didn't already have. When students recognize that they need the tool, the motivation is in place to acquire that tool.
>
> Once they possess sufficient tools, the teacher often has students confront real issues, real situations, to see how their tools can be used to operate on those issues. Students explore the range of situations in which they can use each tool and begin to recognize places where the tool's usefulness ends and what other kind of tools they might need. (Yero, 2002, p. 49)

In this description we recognise a transition from learning-teaching conception 3 (simple application) to learning-teaching conception 4 (complex, real-life application). In a sense we also recognise a transition from mindless application to mindful application (Langer, 1997).

> On the other hand, a teacher who believes every educated person must possess the same "body of knowledge" will employ the tool metaphor in an entirely different way. If concepts and practices are tools, that teacher will perceive his job as *giving* those tools to the students. He will feel he has done his job well when each student *possess* the deluxe set of tools (the 512-piece set complete with metal boxes and compartments into which each tool fits). Even though concepts have been described as tools, these teacher's goal reverts to *possessing* those tools—the concepts and principles—rather than *using* them. Therefore, examining the beliefs behind the interpretation of the metaphor is essential. (Yero, 2002, p. 50)

This example clearly shows the direct – epistemological – relationship Yero assumes between teachers' metaphors-as-meant and their practice. In yet another example that Yero elaborates, she discusses the differences in practice that may result from different metaphors for the classroom: it surely makes a difference if one sees the classroom as a workplace, a learning place or a learning community (p. 79). However, the direct relationship is sometimes obscured by other (non-epistemological) considerations. For instance, Yero describes a teacher, Ed, who "says he values higher-level thinking skills. Yet his tests rarely require students to do anything more than simple recall or recognition (...) This doesn't mean Ed is lying. He simply has another value of which he is unaware—perhaps time to spend with his family" (Yero, 2002, p. 27). This finding is consistent with the results of e.g. Lederman (1999) and shows once again that any number of (practical, emotional, organisational, etcetera) obstacles can blur the relationship between beliefs (metaphors-as-meant, conceptions, etcetera) and teaching practice—especially for the higher levels of epistemological thinking.

Yero feels that changing teachers' beliefs, metaphors-as-meant and through this their practice is difficult, and that this may lie at the heart of most failures of educational reform (see also Marchese,1998; and chapter 1). The fact that many teachers are unaware of their beliefs, metaphors-as-meant etcetera means that the subsequent failure of an innovation need not be intentional or even a conscious decision. Furthermore, even introducing new ways of teaching while consciously and purposefully addressing the belief structure underlying this innovation on a cognitive level, may prove to be insufficient to result in success. Using the example of the failure of an innovation based on ideas of Piaget (i.e. the student as the constructor of knowledge), Yero comes to the conclusion that "[w]hen teachers hold a fundamental belief that learning *means* accumulating knowledge objects, they may *cognitively* accept the wealth of research supporting internally generated knowledge, *but it will not significantly affect their practice.*" Using a metaphor of her own she states: "It's difficult to build an effective rocket ship on the framework of a Model T Ford!" (both quotes Yero, 2002, p. 55). In Kegan's terms (1994), teachers driving a Model T Ford are almost surely unable to create the holding environment that leads to students constructing an effective inter-planetary vessel.

So, while this excursion into metaphors is interesting because it provides an intuitively attractive – and perhaps less threatening – approach to (the development of) teacher and student thinking, one must be aware that what goes for ubiquitous concepts such as understanding, applying, intelligence, learning, good teaching, good assessment, good leadership etcetera goes for metaphors as well. Metaphors may seem deceptively 'simple', but they are in fact truly complex. From our perspective, each metaphor needs to be interpreted within the frame of the user's epistemological level of thinking. When a level-three-thinker and a level-five-thinker are speaking of learning as a journey, can one really expect that they are talking about the same type of journey? Hence, Martinez et al. are right, you – the teacher or academic – need someone else (e.g. a trainer, a teacher educator) to look beyond the words, to draw the attention towards the underlying meanings – the metaphors-as-meant – and to help you discover the implications of the various possible interpretations. In addition, Martinez et al. suggest that teacher educators use more sophisticated (e.g. situative) metaphors to create an epistemological stretch. We feel that teachers could use a similar tactic to help students to develop epistemologically. For this the trainers and teachers need to be able to anchor both sides of the bridge that is the holding environment necessary for epistemological growth (Kegan, 1994).

A final point made by Yero explores the issue of 'the better teacher' through the concept of *the reflective teacher* (p. 9–18). Assuming that teachers' metaphors-as-meant are often unexamined and limiting the holders in their choices, there is reason to believe that exploring multiple metaphors, and thus the multitude of stories underlying these metaphors, may open up new choices from a range of unknown options and possibilities. Connecting with Hashweh's point (1996) that better teachers are more flexible and possess a larger repertoire of strategies, Yero states that "Everyone has choices. (…) The more you know and the more alternatives you explore, the more choices you will have. The more choices you have, the greater your flexibility." (Yero, 2002, p. 55). Interpreting alternative metaphors-as-meant as providing maps of various aspects of learning and teaching – much like an atlas contains different maps that fulfil different purposes (Yero, 2002, p. 76) – the reflective teacher explores multiple maps.

> Perhaps the most compelling reason for teachers to explore the beliefs that shape the topography of their inner landscape is contained in these words by Parker Palmer:
>
> "When I do not know myself, I cannot know who my students are. I will see them through a glass darkly, in the shadows of my unexamined life –and when I cannot see them clearly, I cannot teach them well." (Yero, 2002, p. 25)

The importance of being aware, or *mindful* of one's views on learning, teaching, knowledge and values, and of the impact of seemingly inconsequential issues has been studied by Ellen Langer (1997). To teach in a mindful way, it is necessary to examine "your own beliefs about teaching and learning; and about what you really value for yourself and your students, and how your actions support those values. Being a reflective teacher means deliberately switching from *mindless* teaching to a *mindful* practice" (Yero, 2002, p. 13–14). We will discuss Langer in detail in the chapter on Changing teaching and learning.

Tsai (2002, 2007)[24] researched a number of questions raised above and important to our own work and our epistemological ecology hypothesis. He used a combination of qualitative and quantitative methods to find answers to the following questions:

Are secondary school science teachers' scientific epistemological beliefs closely aligned[25] with their

- own beliefs about teaching and learning science? (in both studies)
- own teaching practice? (2007)
- students' scientific epistemological beliefs? (2007)
- students' perceptions of the science learning environment in class? (2007)

In earlier studies, Tsai (1998, 1999) found that students' scientific epistemological beliefs were related to students' approaches to learning science and the quality of their resulting knowledge structures, in much the same way that we (van Rossum and Schenk, 1984) established relationships between learning conceptions, study strategies and learning outcomes, strengthening the similarity between the two research approaches: the study of learning conceptions and the study of epistemological beliefs. A further similarity with our learning-teaching conception approach is, that Tsai refers to both epistemological beliefs ánd teaching approaches where he speaks of categories of scientific epistemological views, such as constructivism (Tsai, 2007, note 1 on p. 223).

Tsai switched focus from these earlier studies with students to teachers, because "little research literature is found to [explicitly] explore the relationships among science teachers' beliefs about teaching, learning and the nature of science." (Tsai, 2002, p. 771–772). Furthermore, the studies discussed below are interesting because the "research about how teachers' [scientific epistemological beliefs] translate into actual classroom practice remains a crucial issue. ... Also, most of the studies regarding [this] relationship ...were conducted in western countries, while little research about this has been undertaken in eastern countries. This study would explore this relationship on some Taiwanese science teachers" (Tsai, 2007, p. 224).

In 2002, Tsai interviewed 37 secondary school science teachers of differing experience levels and from different geographical regions in Taiwan. To obscure the purpose of the study, Tsai focused, in three consecutive interviews, on three dimensions of teachers' beliefs respectively:

1. beliefs about teaching science: e.g. Could you describe what an ideal science teaching environment would look like? Why?
2. beliefs about learning science: e.g. In your view, science is best learned in which ways?
3. beliefs about the nature of science: e.g. What are the differences between scientific knowledge and other knowledge? (all example questions Tsai, 2002, p. 772–773).

In scoring these interviews, Tsai used an a priori framework to categorise the teachers' beliefs into 'traditional', 'process' or 'constructivist'. The traditional category was exemplified by descriptors such as e.g. "transferring of knowledge" or "practicing tutorial problems", the process category used descriptors as e.g. "teaching the scientific method" or "working on the processes of verification", and finally, the constructivist category was exemplified by such descriptors as "paying attention to students' prior knowledge or misconceptions" and "helping students make interpretations" (Tsai, 2002, Table 1, beliefs about teaching science). Based on the interview transcripts included throughout the article, we would have labelled these categories learning-teaching conception 2, 3 and 4.

More than half of the teachers (n=21, 57%) had closely aligned beliefs about learning, teaching and the nature of science. The largest subgroup within this group (n=15) had traditional views on all three: "The 'traditional' category perceives teaching science as transferring knowledge from teacher to students, learning science as acquiring or 'reproducing' knowledge from credible sources, and scientific knowledge as correct answers or established truths." (Tsai, p. 773). The consistent 'process group' of four teachers all perceived "teaching science and learning science as an activity focusing on the processes of science or problem-solving procedures, and scientific knowledge is viewed as facts being discovered through 'the' scientific method or by following codified procedures" (Tsai, 2002, p. 773). The final consistent subgroup, the 'constructivist group', was very small, n=2, and furthermore consisted solely of relatively less experienced teachers (8 years or less). These teachers viewed "teaching science as helping students construct knowledge, learning science as constructing personal understanding and science as a way of knowing" (Tsai, 2002, p. 773). When examining the results from a developmental learning-teaching conception model[26], they become even a little more convincing regarding alignment. In our view any combination of traditional and process views is consistent, as both these ecologies are fundamentally fact-oriented and reproductive. This means that the number of teachers with consistent or aligned beliefs increases to 31 (21+5+3+1+1= 84%, see Table 5, Tsai, 2002, p. 777). In the table, six teachers combined constructivist beliefs with reproductivist beliefs, showing misaligned beliefs about learning, teaching and the nature of science. It is possible that a basically epistemologically constructivist-oriented teacher may have experienced sufficient external constraints that have resulted in a traditional or process view on teaching and/or learning science (n=2, 5%). We feel the final four teachers (11%) reflected truly divergent belief structures. These results then represent strong support for our epistemological ecology hypothesis.

Tsai further examined the congruence between teachers' beliefs about learning and teaching, which is relevant to us as we advocate a congruent learning-teaching conception model in chapter 1. Using a strict congruence criterion (same categories only), Tsai found 30 congruent teachers (81%). We find 32 (87%) teachers with congruence between views on learning and teaching science, as we accept the combination traditional-process as epistemologically congruent. Either way, we feel that this study again underpins our position on the strong coherence between views on learning and teaching. In comparing his study with an Australian study, Tsai concluded that "many teachers' beliefs about teaching and learning show a good consistency, despite the fact that a huge cultural difference exists between Taiwan and Australia" (Tsai, 2002, p. 778). And we see, what holds for student thinking, indeed seems to hold for teacher thinking as well.

Giving up numbers for depth, and in an attempt to clarify the "relationships between teachers' beliefs and teaching practice" (Tsai, 2002, p. 781), Tsai's 2007 study focuses on four secondary school science teachers and their students. The four teachers included in this study were purposefully selected using a five-dimensional epistemological belief questionnaire, measuring:

1. the theory-laden quality of scientific exploration (vs. objective observation)
2. the creative nature of science (vs. discovery)
3. the tentativeness of scientific knowledge (vs. certainty)
4. the role of social negotiation in the scientific community (vs. individual exploration)
5. the cultural impact on science (vs. culture-free scientific knowledge)

Two teachers scored extreme on these five epistemological dimensions, with Andy typical of the positivist pole, and David typical of the constructivist pole. Teachers Betty and Cindy were chosen to reflect more intermediate (or 'mixed') positions. The selected teachers were interviewed about the nature of science and their "responses were classified as a position ranging from positivist to constructivist perspective [on the five above mentioned epistemological dimensions]. By doing this, this study did not make the simplistic positivist/constructivist dichotomy; rather, this study believed that a teacher might display different [scientific epistemological belief] positions across various … dimensions" (Tsai, 2007, p. 226). In addition, the teachers were interviewed about their beliefs regarding science teaching and learning.

The teachers' instructional practice was determined by quantifying the time spent, minute by minute, on six types of instructional activities during eight classroom periods, resulting in time-allocation percentages per activity type. The six instructional activities were 1) one-way lecture, 2) tutorial problem practice, 3) in-class examinations, 4) laboratory or small-group inquiry activity, 5) interactive discussion and questioning, and 6) other, e.g. making jokes. The first three of these practices can be seen as reflecting more traditional instructional practices, while types 4 and 5 are more common in more constructivist instructional environments.

Students' scientific epistemological beliefs were measured using a questionnaire Tsai had developed earlier together with Liu. This questionnaire focused on the same five epistemological dimensions listed above. Finally, the students' perceptions toward the learning environment in their science classes were measured using the CLES (Constructivist Learning Environment Survey) containing four subscales:

1. student negotiation: e.g. the opportunity to interact with others in class,
2. prior knowledge: e.g. the opportunity to integrate prior knowledge with newly acquired knowledge,
3. autonomy: e.g. the opportunity to think independently,
4. student-centeredness: e.g. the extent to which students experienced support from the teacher in resolving problematic experiences in class.

The analysis of the teacher interviews supported the selection criteria for the teachers, with Andy and David representing opposite – positivist and constructivist – poles on the epistemological dimensions. While Betty and Cindy both had 'mixed' profiles, in general Betty was more like Andy and Cindy was more like David. The relationship between the teachers' scientific epistemological beliefs and their views on teaching and learning science were summarised in Tsai's Table 2 (2007, p. 232). According to our learning-teaching conception approach, Andy and Betty were clear proponents of the traditional, fundamentally reproductive learning-teaching conception 2. Both focused on providing students with information, using primarily one-way lectures, in-class examinations and tutorial problem exercises, and students were expected to work hard, to acquire knowledge and facts and to get good grades. In Andy's words

> In science, there are a lot of formulae and definitions. If students cannot memorize them carefully, they will experience great difficulties in solving science problems … Then, they cannot attain high scores. (Tsai, 2007, p. 233)

Cindy on the other hand, had a more pragmatic view on learning and teaching science, stressing the application of scientific knowledge. Interestingly, Cindy "claimed that a science teacher should be an information provider, [but] she also thought the teacher should ... model ... using scientific knowledge, concurring with her belief about the purpose of learning, that is applying scientific knowledge" (Tsai, 2007, p. 231). With her focus on memorisation followed by using what is learned, together with an emphasis on small-group activity, Cindy is an almost perfect example of learning-teaching conception 3. In our view she does not have a 'mixed' view on learning and teaching, but a separate, coherent and identifiable belief system.

> I think, in addition to regular lecture class, the use of laboratory work or small-group learning activity is important for science students. By laboratory work, they can know how to apply scientific knowledge. By small-group learning activity, they can learn how to solve a problem and how to communicate with others. These will help a lot when they are in the job market, no matter [whether] they are in a science-related career or not. (Tsai, 2007, p. 233)

Finally, David, the constructivist teacher, focused on developing students' scientific understanding, addressing students' prior knowledge and misconceptions, and the application of scientific knowledge to real-life situations by means of open-ended inquiry activities. He saw his role as facilitator and engaged in interactive discussions with students, giving a fair example of learning-teaching conception 4: student-centred teaching.

> Students often have some "misconceptions" in science. The use of some instructional approaches to challenging their prior knowledge is very important. Some interactive discussion or questioning activities may be helpful for this. Also, it is important for students to develop a better understanding of scientific knowledge in classrooms. I think some inquiry activities are helpful for this. By open-ended inquiry, they will think and apply the scientific knowledge thoroughly, thus constructing a better understanding. (Tsai, 2007, p. 233)

These results again point toward very high coherence between teachers' epistemological beliefs and their beliefs about learning and teaching science.

Tsai's analysis of the coherence between teachers' scientific epistemological beliefs and their instructional practice was summarised in Table 3 (p. 234, reproduced slightly modified in Table 5.2 below).

Table 5.2 shows a strong coherence between teachers' epistemological beliefs and their instructional practice, with the reproduction-oriented teachers (Andy and Betty) emphasising the more traditional practices. David, as the most constructivist teacher, used predominantly constructivist type activities, allocating the most time of all teachers to interactive discussion and questioning and considerably less time to one-way instruction than any of the other three teachers. Cindy's time allocation is almost a mirror image of David's, spending about half her time on traditional activities, but she also spends quite a proportion of her time in lab or small-group activity,

Table 5.2. Teachers' time allocation per type of instructional activity

Instructional activity	*Teacher*			
	Andy (%)	*Betty (%)*	*Cindy (%)*	*David (%)*
One-Way (teacher-directed) lecture	38	35	31	15
Tutorial problem practice	25	22	14	10
In-class exams	24	5	8	9
Subtotal 'traditional' practices	*87*	*62*	*53*	*34*
Lab or small-group inquiry activity	0	17	30	26
Interactive discussion and questioning	2	5	6	26
Subtotal 'constructivist' practices	*2*	*22*	*36*	*52*
Other	11	16	11	14

Source: Tsai, 2007, Table 3

which matches the learning-teaching conception 3 need for 'interaction' (see chapter 1). Tsai remarked that these "results were quite consistent with their interview responses. That is, the teacher with positivist-oriented [scientific epistemological beliefs] (e.g. Andy) tended to use one-way lecture, tutorial problem practices, or in-class examinations in real teaching practice, whereas the teacher with constructivist –aligned [scientific epistemological beliefs] (e.g. David) tended to allocate more time on inquiry activity and interactive discussion [as established] by actual classroom observations" (Tsai, 2007, p. 234).

Tsai found that while there was some evidence that teachers' scientific epistemological beliefs and those of their students were aligned, the relationship was less strong than expected. The students in David's class, compared to Andy's students, displayed more constructivist views on three of the five epistemological belief dimensions, the theory-laden quality of scientific exploration, the tentativeness of scientific knowledge, and the cultural impact on science. The finding that David's students were more constructivist with regard to the theory-laden quality of scientific exploration than Andy's students is consistent with the difference between learning-teaching conceptions 2 and 4. In addition, Cindy's students displayed more constructivist beliefs than Andy's students on the dimension tentativeness of scientific knowledge, a finding consistent with the difference between learning-teaching conceptions 2 and 3. While we agree with Tsai, that ideally the alignments between teacher and student thinking could have been stronger, considering that these students had been exposed to each teacher for at least 8 months (Tsai, 2007, p. 225) but presumably for only a few hours a week, and considering the general finding (by many, see above) that changing epistemological beliefs is notoriously difficult, we feel that these findings are significant.

Students' perceptions of the learning environment in their science classes displayed more variation (see Table 5, Tsai, 2007, p. 237). Students in David's class experienced their learning environment as providing more opportunities for student negotiation, exploring their prior knowledge and student autonomy than Andy's or Betty's students. David's students also felt, more than Andy's students, that their classes were student-centred, and compared to Cindy's students that their classes provided more opportunities for student autonomy. Compared to Andy's students, Cindy's students felt their classroom environment was more open to student negotiation and their prior knowledge. Compared to Betty's students, Cindy's students felt their prior knowledge was taken more into account. These results clearly show that students are able to perceive different learning environments differently, indicating that students seem to be less limited by their own lenses (or beliefs) than is often assumed. The fact that they can and do perceive different learning environments differently, provides a window on a possible approach to changing their beliefs, namely consistently exposing students to coherent constructivist learning environments (see e.g. Biggs, 1996, Enhancing teaching through constructive alignment). Based on Tsai's findings one would expect that creating a coherent constructivist learning environment requires constructivist teachers. To help the positivist science teachers, the majority of secondary school science teachers (Tsai, 2002), to develop more constructivist beliefs and approaches to teaching, Tsai recommended that these teachers are explicitly trained in the epistemological fundaments of their discipline and in the use of inquiry-oriented instructional practices, while simultaneously they are supported over a considerable period of time by trainers to help them uncover and reflect on their own tacit scientific epistemological beliefs, see also e.g. Martinez et al. (2001).

Overall, all the discussed studies here show that teachers' thinking about learning and teaching and their epistemological beliefs about science are fairly coherent, and that teachers' views and their practice are also closely and psychologically related. We are happy to agree, but feel the need to stress that inconsistencies between epistemological beliefs and teaching practices remain possible without disproving immediately the epistemological ecology hypothesis. Such inconsistencies are far more likely to occur when epistemologically sophisticated teachers are confronted with major impediments, e.g. state (compulsory) curricula, time constraints, institutional cultures, standard testing practices, students who are not (epistemologically) ready yet, their own lack of (teaching) experience, etcetera. A point nicely made by Lotter et al..

> The *teachers' conceptions* of science, their students, effective teaching practices, and the purpose of education were found to influence *the type and amount of inquiry instruction performed* in their high school classrooms. The four core conceptions indicated in our model can provide positive and negative influences on the teachers' decisions regarding the use of inquiry-based practices. Inquiry teaching was limited, for example, when a teacher believed that his or her students were incapable of solving problems on their own or when they viewed science as a body of knowledge that hey needed to transmit to students in a limited amount of time. Inquiry teaching was enhanced, however, when teachers viewed science as a process of solving

> problems using various methodologies or when students were given the freedom to explore their own questions and discover content for themselves with teacher guidance. …
>
> Future research studies should investigate whether changes in teachers' core conceptions toward more reform-based instructional strategies actually result in increased use of these strategies in their classrooms given *the many external constraints* (testing, content standards, school culture) influencing teachers' instructional choices. (Lotter et al., 2007 in press, p. 24–25, italics ours)

In all these studies above, we observe that teachers (at all levels, from nursery school to academia) can be divided almost always into a group consistent with learning-teaching conceptions 2 and mostly 3 (fundamentally reproduction-oriented), and a group with learning-teaching conception 4 and sometimes higher (with constructivist beliefs). We feel this finding supports our proposition that the epistemological watershed must lie between levels 3 and 4, and that – even for teachers themselves – the shift from 3 to 4 may be the most disturbing one to make in any educational setting. Furthermore, we feel we have reaffirmed the constructivist truth regarding the importance of using a sound, sufficiently detailed theoretical framework to design research and to analyse empirical findings. The lack of such a framework – using e.g. only two opposite categories and one mixed category - has, we feel, led to interpretation problems, which in turn may have led to muddling the picture, instead of clarifying it (e.g.Tsai, 2007; Brickhouse, 1989, 1990).

To illustrate this last point we discuss shortly the categorisation of the teacher Jerry in Kang and Wallace (2004). Where Kang and Wallace found clear coherences between epistemological beliefs and teaching practice for two of the three teachers studied, they had difficulty interpreting Jerry's approach to lab work. In particular, they were confused by the juxtaposition of Jerry's sophisticated epistemological beliefs about science and his rather teacher-dominated, procedural approach to his students' lab activities, which they found contradictory. However, looking at Jerry's approach as summarised in Table 3 (Kang and Wallace, 2004, p. 148), it becomes clear that Jerry is not structuring the *content* of science (the information or facts), as you would expect for an unsophisticated learning-teaching conception 2 or 3 teacher. He is structuring the *procedure* – the scientific way of knowing - that students must learn to understand the process of scientific thought. In this we recognise the Procedural Knower (Belenky et al., 1997) who is training his students quite rigorously in a particular way of thinking, or a teacher at Perry's position 4b: "The way they want us to think". Indeed, students can feel pressured (Belenky et al., 1997, see chapter 3) into following this external formula of a disciplinary way of thinking (Baxter Magolda, 2001). Jerry is indeed relatively sophisticated in his beliefs, but he also feels his students are not capable yet of doing "real science", he is teaching them the way to think they will need for doing "real science".

It is not that there is a lack of more detailed models, it is only that these models use a different set of aliases for the same conceptual framework. Furthermore, many of these models are of European or Australian 'descent' and not very familiar to the teachers' epistemological beliefs research community in North America. We will discuss but a few in the next section.

Empirical Studies on Teachers' Conceptions of Teaching

One of the first studies – that we know of – that focused on teachers' conceptions of teaching was reported by Staffan Larsson (1983), in which he described a number of paradoxes teachers experience in their teaching practice. For this study Larsson interviewed 29 adult education teachers (secondary school level). The analysis of the interviews followed the phenomenographical method (Marton, 1981), which is a common method used in educational research to study people's conceptions of phenomena, such as learning or teaching, from a second-order perspective.

Larsson found two fundamentally different views on teaching:

- "*Conception A*: The essence of teaching is that a content should be presented and structured for the students. This means that the content should be prepared so that the students can learn without too much interpretation.

  This conception is built on the view, taken-for-granted or not, that the teacher must do some of the interpretational and/or structuring work for the students. In some cases those teachers holding this conception do think that the students could themselves do this interpretation and structuring, but only as a complementary task to the fulfillment of conception A." (Larsson, 1983, p. 357)

  In hindsight, with our model in mind, we recognise in this description two strongly related conceptions, namely learning-teaching conception 2 – where the teacher structures all the content – and learning-teaching conception 3 – where students are allowed to 'mess about with the content a bit' in order to do a little bit of structuring themselves.

- "*Conception B*: The teaching ought to involve the students in interpretational and structuring work. If they are not involved, real changes will not occur or they will not develop real knowledge.

  This conception has two parts, one concerning the essence of teaching and one that is a criticism of conception A, explicit or implicit. The criticism is in all cases built on the idea that the learning effect of such [conception A] teaching is weak. In some cases the teachers referred to their own experiences as students. Mathematics was sometimes excluded as a subject impossible to teach from a conception B basis." (Larsson, 1983, p. 357–358)

  In this description the phrase that students need to be involved in interpretation and structuring points to learning-teaching conceptions 4 or 5. Which of these two the teacher is referring to depends on the nature of the students' involvement and the nature of the student-teacher relationship.

In examining the practices of these two types of teachers, Larsson used 'the level of teacher control over communication in the classroom' as the central criterion. Strong teacher control was present in activities such as one-way lecturing, going through the content of the lesson and teacher-led discussion. Weak teacher control activities were listed as e.g. problem-oriented teaching, group work or explorative classes. Larsson immediately found a pattern: conception-A teachers preferred only strong teacher control activities, and of the conception-B teachers some preferred strong teacher control and the others preferred weak teacher control activities. This finding could be interpreted as inferring only a weak relationship between conceptions of teaching and teaching practice. However, again in hindsight, we see here a first affirmation that teachers with more sophisticated levels of thinking (conceptions) have a broader choice (see e.g. Hashweh, 1996), they can choose between strong and weak teacher-controlled activities, whereas conception-A teachers lack that flexibility.

Larsson proceeded to examine possible explanations for the fact that most of the conception-B teachers actually used strong control over communication in their classrooms. The teachers reported as most important constraint defining their chosen approach, the students' conception of teaching. "Not every teacher [reported] the students' view on teaching, but everyone expressing a view on the matter reached the same conclusion. Fifteen out of sixteen teachers with conception B and two of the eight with conception A reported the students' conception as one that could be described as conception A" (Larsson, 1983, p. 359).[27] This quote shows that conception-B teachers are more aware of their students' ways of thinking than conception-A teachers, emphasising the essential student-centeredness of conception B. Larsson on the other hand, felt that the beliefs of conception-A teachers and conception-A students were in harmony, resulting in these teachers simply not seeing student thinking as a restriction.

The two groups of conception-B teachers, represented different ways of dealing with this restriction of the students' conception of teaching. In Larsson's interpretation it is a matter of power: is the teacher powerful enough to pressure the conception-A students to accept his conception-B teaching, or is he pressured by the students to accept their preferred way of teaching? In Kegan's (1994) words, is the teacher able to create an epistemological stretch or not? The first quote below is from a teacher who has had to give in to the students.

> … I think that I can control my working situation rather a lot, at least in theory I can do that … … I can obviously choose the form of teaching just as I like… … In practice I do *not* think that the freedom is that wide since the students, as I see it, want a textbook and become very disturbed when you read things that cannot be found therein and want to know where it can be read and what they should prepare. We have talked about grades now. It is said in certain quarters that most students do not want grades in school; I have never believed that. …… [The students] want to see a result, they want to be rewarded at once. And that means that one *must* then work in a certain way, so that it is possible to have a test, so to speak… (Larsson, 1983, p. 359–360, italics ours)

The paradox here is that "the students use their control to *press* the teacher to exert *control over them*" (Larsson, 1983, p. 360, italics ours). Another conception-B teacher who seems to have won – at least partly – the conflict with the students, said,

> There *can* be problems in certain classes to *enforce* such a form of teaching. I think in fact that I have succeeded in most cases. I do not think that I have been confronted with such resistance that I have had to leave the idea and go back to one hundred percent lecturing. But neither is it so that I only have problem-oriented teaching, nor have [I had] to make a summary of certain central points in social science. (Larsson, 1983, p. 360, italics ours)

A third conception-B teacher looked with some trepidation to the next term, where he/she would have to engage students in the struggle for control and lure them into conception-B teaching:

> And I shall probably start a new course in physics in the spring and then I want to build further on what I have worked with during this period. And this will be a very difficult start, difficult to start and difficult to know how to structure it and how you should make them accept a different way, because there is a restriction there too… one could call it *a conservative perspective on what teaching in physics means*. (Larsson, 1983, p. 360, italics ours)

The paradox confronting these conception-B teachers is that here "the teachers with conception B *force* the students to accept their *weak* control of the communication process" (Larsson, 1983, p. 361, italics ours). These reports show clearly that "good education may leave students deeply dissatisfied, at least for a while …students who have been well served by good teachers may walk away angry—angry that their prejudices have been challenged and their sense of self shaken. That sort of dissatisfaction may be a sign that real education has happened" (Palmer, 1998, p. 94). However, the conception-A preference of students may have a rational – perhaps to epistemologically more sophisticated knowers objectionable – origin: "To master their own achievement, it is then logical that students need a situation where the teacher who is also the examiner shows the criteria as clearly as possible. Teaching according to conception B is weak since it is difficult to gain insight into the rules and, in fact, even the teachers find it difficult to assess the students in such a teaching system. So, from the students' viewpoint it is a rational maneuver in the given context to force the teacher to control the situation" (Larsson, 1983, p. 364). In short, teachers and students may have opposite goals and conflicting agendas, leading to various types of friction in classrooms (e.g. Vermunt and Verloop, 1999; van Rossum, Würffel and Hamer, 2003; see also the chapter Changing Teaching and Learning).

Kember (1997) compiled a convenient review of 13 – predominantly qualitative – studies regarding academics' conceptions of teaching, mostly reported in the early nineteen-nineties. Most of these studies referred to Australian academics, with a sprinkling of Asian, North American and UK respondents. Kember found a high degree of communality in the categories of description (conceptions of teaching) reported in these studies, which made it possible to distil a set of five conceptions of teaching that best reflected the various conceptions of teaching described in these 13 studies. This review significantly expanded the epistemological framework to study teacher thinking. Furthermore he made the distinction between 'orientations' and 'conceptions', where an orientation "is taken as a broader level of categorisation encompassing two or more conceptions" (Kember, 1997, p. 257). Consequently, the set of five conceptions could be regrouped into two major orientations, and one intermediate category/conception, as reproduced in Figure 5.3.

In this model, the shaded areas between the two conceptions within each orientation reflect a relatively 'easy' development across each pair. Following this model, Kember expected the transition between the two orientations "requiring a more significant change" (Kember, 1997, p. 264), evoking a suggestion of the watershed we have discussed in detail in chapters 1, 3 and 4. However, Kember was not sure about the exact placement of this shift between orientations (the watershed), and placed it more or less around the so-called "intermediate conception". In our model this intermediate conception is part of the (reproduction) orientation to the left of the watershed. This placement of the watershed between the reproduction and construction-oriented conceptions/orientations was supported, more recently, by Samuelowicz and Bain (2001). The – by modellers – often felt wish for symmetry can be satisfied by adding our sixth learning-teaching conception to the far right of Kember's model.

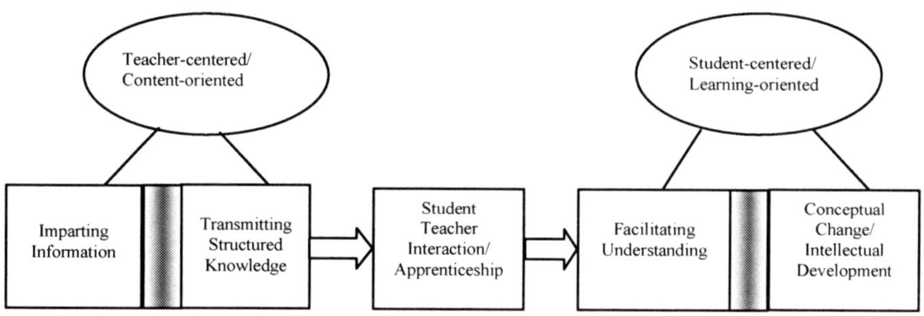

Figure 5.3. A multiple-level categorisation model of conceptions of teaching.

(*Source*: Kember, 1997, p. 264)

The five categories of teachers' views on teaching given below, Kember interpreted as five positions on a continuum running from teacher/subject-oriented views on teaching to student/learning-oriented views.

> ...the alternative conceptions of teaching are better regarded as an ordered set of qualitatively differing conceptions. When change does occur, lecturers seem to move from one belief to another, and do not retain all elements of previous beliefs. Further, that development or progression through ordered categories does happen but it is unlikely to be a rapid or easy process ... The categories of conceptions of teaching are perhaps, then, better portrayed as *well-established positions within a continuum.* (Kember, 1997, p. 263, italics ours)

Imparting Information/Broadcasting: Teaching is seen as purely presenting information and the student is a passive recipient without a clear role in the teaching-learning process, if the student is considered at all. This disregard for the other, the student, taking part in this 'meeting' that is education, is eloquently put by Fox and Samuelowicz and Bain below.

> ... the broadcast theory which views teaching as scattering seeds to the wind rather than transferring them to specific containers. All that is required of a teacher is that he deliver himself of his nuggets of wisdom. Whether or not these are relevant or applicable in particular contexts or whether they make any sort of sense to anybody but himself is not his concern. His responsibility is solely concerned with ensuring the purity of the seed. (Fox, 1983, p. 153)

> [teaching] means that you're imparting information ... that they [students] are expected to get because they are enrolled in that course. (8/T/S, Samuelowicz and Bain, 1992, p. 101)

Transmitting Structured Knowledge: Teaching is still seen primarily as content-related, but now at least the recipient is acknowledged. However, teachers do not expect much from the students: in order to ensure correct receipt, the teacher is responsible for the highly organised or structured transmission.

> Teaching is transmission of concepts and skills *in such a way that the students can acquire them*, ... that sounds [like a] very rudimentary sort of approach, but I think there is a body of knowledge and skills that students need to start off with (10/T/S, Samuelowicz and Bain, 1992, p. 101, italics ours)

Kember described this conception with a sports metaphor: "The student enters the picture more but is still a passive receiver. The lecturer does a least recognise that there is a receiver out there and does need to catch what is thrown. The ball, then, needs to be thrown carefully and accurately so that it can be caught" (Kember, 1997, p. 266). As parents ourselves, we also recognise the well-meaning care that some teachers seem to take to remove all difficulties and effort associated with learning for the students by reducing the whole lesson (meal) into a bland puree and spoon feeding it to the young minds in their classroom, in short the baby food manufacturing conception (Fox, 1983),

> ... the teacher sees his job as one of processing very tough material into more easily digestible nutrient for rather simple minds. This seems to be quite an important defence position to be taken against the charge that the subject-matter is being distorted during the process of transfer ... ...

> [This] distortion ... is justifiable on one of two grounds. Either it is the only possible way of getting any material at all into such puny containers or it is only a first stage in the development of a digestive system that later will be able to cope readily with the toughest of conceptual steaks." (Fox, 1983, p. 153)

Student-Teacher Interaction/Shaping: Teaching is still teacher-dominated and content-oriented, but the importance of interaction between teacher and student becomes more pronounced, resulting in a larger role for the student. The students' 'understanding' and discovery are taken seriously within a clearly defined area of knowledge (the discipline). As Trigwell et al. (1994) put it "the teacher believes the students need to be active in their learning, and so engages in an interaction with the students. But the teacher maintains responsibility for the teaching situation" (p. 80).

> But I don't want students to take everything I say at face value. I like them to think for themselves so I try to get them to interpret before I tell them, if possible. So if I do a demonstration, I won't tell them what the result will be.... I often ask them to predict the result, having given them the principles. (Trigwell et al., 1994, p. 80)

According to Kember, a number of the studies reviewed reported the teachers wanting to mould or shape students' behaviour toward a predetermined model. A shaping theory is a second major aspect of this conception of teaching.

> There are many varieties of shaping theories. One subset of these theories views students, or at least student brains, as raw material (metal, wood or clay) to be shaped, or moulded, or turned to a predetermined and often detailed specification. ... ... The typical teaching environments of shaping theorists are not only lecture theatres but also science laboratories, engineering workshops, problems classes, gymnasia and studios of various kinds. In workshops and laboratories students will be set specific exercises and they will be given copious instructions on detailed workshop or laboratory schedules. They will be closely supervised by assistants called 'demonstrators'. The exercises all have quite specific predetermined outcomes and they success of the students in their practical work is judged according to how closely they approach these specified models. (Fox, 1983, p. 153–154)

Maybe the different emphases within this conception on, on the one hand, 'interaction' and, on the other hand, 'shaping' can be seen as reflecting a teacher's preference for either 'connected knowing' or 'separate knowing' (Belenky et al., 1997) or they may reflect merely a difference in focus (teaching versus learning).

Facilitating Understanding: The teacher, as facilitator, focuses on the students' learning and understanding[28] of the subject matter (e.g. by assessing their application in more complex, realistic situations) and thus the teacher in this conception is fundamentally student-centered. The teacher designs a variety of learning environments that facilitate 'real' learning, advising students during the learning process and ultimately ascertaining to what extent the student has understood the subject matter.

> You've got to be able to make an environment where students really want to learn. If you do that, they are much more likely to understand why they learn. And then I think after that, the teacher should be a resource person, ... Generally to guide the students, I don't see it as spoon-feeding. (L8: Rehabilitation Sciences, Gow and Kember, 1993, p. 23)

> ...they [students] have learned because they could apply it in some real situation and make sense of it. (2/D/S) Samuelowicz and Bain, 1992, p. 100)

> [teaching is] ... any form of presenting information or allowing students to find their own information that helps them ... it can be on occasions didactic, can be a student activity, it can be solving problems, it could be anything as long as it promotes the student having a clear understanding of what they are learning. (7/D/S) Samuelowicz and Bain, 1992, p. 100)

The latter quote shows clearly that teachers with more sophisticated views on teaching are more flexible in the choice of teaching practices (see e.g. Hashweh, 1996). From this description we can construe as well, that it is not lecturing per se that defines the reproductive or constructive level of teaching, it is the way the lecture is used or performed in the total of the learning experience.

Kember presented a possible mixed conception – **Conceptual Change/ Intellectual Development** - as the fifth one in his model, perceiving these two aspects as alternative descriptions within one conception. We would like to treat them as Samuelowicz and Bain have (1992, 2001), namely as separate conceptions, bringing Kember's model more in line with our own learning-teaching conception model.

Conceptual Change: Good teaching leads to development/change in students' views on reality by helping students to become aware of their own views and to expand these views. This means teachers need to focus even more than before on the students' thinking: "Changing student conceptions is not an easy process..." (Kember, 1997, p. 268).

> ... I [student] have theoretical models that help me like [a] pair of glasses that I put on and it can order the world for me and I have, you know, the theories and the magnifying glass that I can discern more definite patterns out there instead of the chaos ... (9/T/SS, Samuelowicz and Bain, 1992, p. 99)

> ... [Conceptual understanding is developed] by arguing about things, and trying to apply ideas, and being again confronted by differences between what you think and what actually happens... to get people to make predictions about what's going to happen, and then when it doesn't happen, maybe they might backtrack and revise their ideas about things...what's going on their heads...What we're trying to achieve in learning physics, is for people to shift their view from the layperson's view, to what we would call a scientific/physicist's view...view of the world. I think that's what I'm, on about. (P2, Prosser et al., 1994, p. 225)

A common metaphor used to describe teaching in this conception is travelling (together) – we have used it ourselves, see chapter 1 – and Fox describes it as,

> Education is seen as a journey and the subject being studied represents one of many interesting and challenging areas of countryside to explored. ... ... The teacher in this analogy, is a local guide. He has climbed all the hills and

> mountains; he knows most of the views. He walks along the tracks and by-ways with the assurance of one who has seen in all in context—but he is still exploring. ... He enjoys sharing his experience with newcomers; he can provide maps and compass and other travelling equipment and he will accompany novice explorers as a travelling companion with lots of helpful suggestions about the best routes and about what to look for on the way. He can help others to make sense of the views from the tops and he often finds himself learning something new himself ... he recognises that he will never know everything and he shares the excitement of being a fellow explorer—albeit an extremely knowledgeable and experienced one. ... ... No guide though, no matter how competent or experienced can do your exploring for you. Exploration is a personal activity. ...
>
> ... education is a journey. But it is a journey of exploration, not a direct trip from A to B. The teacher is a local guide and equipment supplier, not a coach driver on a packaged tour. (Fox, 1983, p. 156–157)

The effort that Fox takes to explain the exact nature of the journey-as-meant in this conception of teaching, shows that he is well aware of the fact that it isn't the metaphor as such that matters, but the metaphor-as-meant (see also Yero, 2002 and before).

Intellectual Development: Here, teaching focuses not so much on content, or procedures or ways of thinking, but more so on authentic interpersonal relationships, in particular between student and teacher. Where in previous conceptions the emphasis was on cognitive aspects of teaching and student learning, here we see a clear extension in emphasis: while retaining cognition, feeling and emotion become acknowledged aspects of the teaching-learning process. Student learning is a holistic developmental process facilitated by a teacher-student relationship based on mutual respect and understanding. Students are provided with the necessary space to grow as a learner/person, being nurtured by the teacher, and as such this orientation is very similar to Fox's growing theory, described by Northedge (cited in Kember, 1997; Fox, 1983). In this teaching conception the teacher is seen as

> ... a gardener with the student's mind ... an area of ground ... already covered with vegetation (concept systems), some of which is clearly worth retaining and cultivating. ... ... In the garden plants will tend to grow quite readily regardless of intervention from the gardener, and it is his aim to encourage certain plants at the expense of others; finding ways of acting as a catalyst in bringing out the best he can from the available ground. The gardener does not work towards a precisely defined end, since the garden is continually changing as different plants come to their prime. He has broad plans as to how he want he garden to develop (probably rather flexible ones, which change as possibilities within the garden reveal themselves), but he does not attempt to specify the exact dimensions that each plant (or concept structure) is to achieve. (Fox, 1983, p. 157)

Samuelowicz and Bain (1992, see also below) found this conception only in postgraduate teaching, where "students are not only responsible for their own learning process but also are in control of the content of their learning." (p. 98).

> ... postgraduate teaching is ... different ... personal interactions with the student are very important in terms of being able to get their confidence and also attempting to be able to guide them in terms of organization of their work. (10/T/S, Samuelowicz and Bain, 1992, p. 98)

From a student's point of view this approach to teaching and learning could indicate that students can only then become fully responsible for their own learning process, once they have become expert (autonomous) learners themselves (van Rossum and Hamer, 1985), and as such it mirrors the development for teachers, from novice, textbook-bound teachers, to expert, flexible ones (see Entwistle and Walker, 2000, discussed below).

In his review, Kember emphasised the communality in the categories of description found in the studies discussed. With his summary he did indeed cover most of the categories of description, only for one conception, found by Pratt (1992), Kember could find no further evidence and he did not include this conception in his five conception model. Pratt interviewed 253 people from various countries (including Western and Asian respondents) and found five conceptions of teaching:

- engineering conception (combining imparting information and transmitting structured knowledge);
- apprenticeship conception (shaping);
- developmental conception (combining facilitating understanding and conceptual change);
- nurturing conception (intellectual development); and
- social reform conception (no match).

The social reform conception was remarkable in that an explicitly stated ideal dominated all elements within this conception. Teaching then "was framed from within a conviction that this ideal was appropriate for all people and necessary for a better society" (Pratt, 1992, p. 216). There was no single ideology that dominated this conception, ideologies could be taken from religion, politics, social reform (e.g. feminism), etcetera. The paramount emphasis on teaching for the 'greater good' resulted in a focus shift from micro (e.g. student thinking) to macro (e.g. societal) concerns: "Actors and content were secondary to a broader agenda and there was a shift in emphasis from the individual to the collective." (Pratt, 1992, p. 217). Freire's work, Pedagogy of the Oppressed (2000), can be seen in this light, as an attempt to change (the view on) pedagogy based on a societal ideology. We may have encountered a possible (weak) variant of this conception in our early work, where we defined learning- teaching conception six as "a conscious process, fuelled by personal interests and directed at obtaining harmony and happiness *or changing society*." (van Rossum and Taylor, 1987, p. 19, italics ours).

Kember conceived a model to link his five teaching conceptions to teaching approaches, student learning approaches and learning outcomes, attempting to show the educational relevance of teachers' conceptions of teaching. In this model teaching approaches are directly influenced by teachers' conceptions of teaching but discrepancies between conceptions and approaches are possible due to external constraints such as e.g. departmental or institutional pressures. These external constraints work both ways, pressuring epistemologically unsophisticated as well as sophisticated teachers, but with different outcomes. On the one hand, those teachers "holding student-centred conceptions of teaching may at times still have to employ approaches which appear inconsistent with that belief" (p. 270) and the work of Larsson (1983) is a clear example of this. On the other hand, teachers holding traditional beliefs may be forced by their institute to "make teaching less didactic and more interactive" (Kember, 1997, p. 271) and to modify their course to include e.g. tutorial sessions. As Kember described "... observation of [these] tutorial classrooms ... revealed ... very low levels of student participation. They were dominated by exposition from the tutors, who turned the tutorials into mini-lectures. ... Those who held conceptions in the teacher-centred/content-oriented domain ... would be worried about covering content, so viewed the tutorial as an extra session for transmitting knowledge" (Kember, 1997, p. 271). Here we see that changing teaching is not really realistic without changing the teachers' underlying beliefs (conceptions) of teaching. And Kember further concluded that "short workshops which focus upon teaching skills or approaches may have limited outcomes if the underlying beliefs of the participants are inconsistent with the conceptual framework of the initiative" (Kember, 1997, p. 272).

Kember concluded, based on his review, that there "... seems to be little value ... in further exploratory studies to classify academics' conceptions of teaching" (1997, p. 273). However, we feel this is a little 'too early to call', dismissing this area of research all too quickly. We will proceed to discuss a later study by Samuelowicz and Bain (2001) who derived a model with seven conceptions of teaching that is largely similar to our own learning-teaching conception model. This model solves the somewhat unsatisfying artificial position of the 'intermediate conception' and provides more evidence for the placing of the epistemological watershed as we describe it.

To study conceptions of teaching in more detail, Samuelowicz and Bain (2001) interviewed 39 academics representing a large variety of disciplines. Their main motive to revisit their earlier 1992 study, was to establish the robustness of their findings: five conceptions of teaching, 1) Imparting information, 2) Transmitting knowledge, 3) Facilitating understanding, 4) Changing students' conceptions and 5) Supporting student learning. A second reason was to examine the plausibility of the existence of an intermediate position (Facilitating understanding in 1992). The method of validation was increasing sample size and discipline mix. Samuelowicz and Bain now found seven orientations (conceptions of teaching) towards the teaching-learning process, each of which could be characterised by a unique pattern on nine belief dimensions. The nine belief dimensions found "were required to characterise the major differences between the orientations in [the] sample. These dimensions varied in the number of beliefs constituting them, but in all cases it was possible to order the beliefs to reflect variation ranging from teaching-centred (transmissive [indicated with A or A/b]) to learning-centred (facilitative [indicated with B or B/a])" (Samuelowicz and Bain, 2001, p. 304). The nine belief dimensions were 1) desired learning outcomes, 2) expected use of knowledge, 3) locus of responsibility for organising/transforming knowledge, 4) nature of knowledge, 5) taking into account students' existing conceptions, 6) nature of teacher-students interaction, 7) control of content, 8) professional development and 9) locus of interest/motivation. These nine dimensions were used as a set of nine criteria to score the interviews. Each interview received nine scores, one for each dimension: scores ranging between A, A/b, B/a and B. Numbering these scores made it possible to do a quantitative (hierarchical cluster) analysis of the interviews. The seven orientations (conceptions of teaching) found are given in Table 5.3 which is based on Table 2 of Samuelowicz and Bain (2001, p. 306–307).

Examining the score pattern of each conception of teaching in Table 5.3 one can deduce that the first three conceptions are very similar and dominated by A-scores. The latter four are dominated by B-scores and also pretty similar to each other. Consequently the smallest overlap between these seven conceptions is between the third and the fourth conception. An hierarchical cluster analysis confirmed this finding and also provided evidence that conceptions 5 and 6 are relatively most similar to each other (Euclidean cluster distance 0.50), while the largest distance between clusters was found between conceptions 1–3 and conceptions 4–7 (Euclidean distance 16.11). Both these findings confirm to us that

- firstly, the epistemological watershed, the most disturbing transition between conceptions, lies between Providing and facilitating understanding (3) and Helping students develop expertise (4).

  Samuelowicz and Bain drew the same conclusion where they said that this transition – in addition to the shift in interpretation of the nature of the student-teacher interaction – "appears to require a profound shift in what the venture [teaching] is about, so much so that six other beliefs would also have to change .... Thus the boundary between teaching-centred and learning-centred orientations appears to be relatively 'hard' and may require the equivalent of conceptual change (i.e. an accommodative process) to cross it. Boundaries *within* the two broad groupings on the other hand, may be relatively 'soft', as Kember [1997] has proposed, because the differences between adjacent orientations are small in number and often subtle in character." (Samuelowicz and Bain, 2001, p. 322); and
- secondly, that conceptions five and six in our opinion may reflect two alternative descriptions of the same fundamental conception of teaching.

Samuelowicz and Bain also included two illustrative stories, portraying two academics with teaching conceptions at either side of the watershed (academic A: Providing and facilitating understanding vs. academic B: Helping students develop expertise). Their purpose was "to demonstrate how dissimilar these two orientations are, notwithstanding their proximity ..... The stories also illustrate how closely coupled an academic's beliefs and practices tend to be..." (Samuelowicz and Bain, 2001, p. 312).

Table 5.3. Conceptions of teaching, quantified and compared

Conceptions of teaching	*Score pattern*	*Identical scores with previous conception (total overlap)*
1. Imparting information	9 A-scores	-
2. Transmitting structured knowledge	6 A-scores and 3 A/b-scores	6 A-scores (6)
3. Providing and facilitating understanding	5 A-scores, 3 A/b-scores and 1 B/a-score new conception*)	5 A-scores, 2 A/b-scores (7)
4. Helping students develop expertise	2 A-scores, 1 B/a-score and 6 B-scores new conception	**2 A-scores (2)**
5. Preventing misunderstandings	1 A-score, 1 B/a-score and 7 B-scores new conception	1 A-score, 6 B-scores (7)
6. Negotiating understanding	1 A-score, and 8 B-scores new conception	1 A-score, 7 B-scores (8)
7. Encouraging knowledge creation	9 B-scores previously (1992) called Supporting student learning	8 B-scores (8)

*) new conception means this conception was not found as a separate category in Samuelowicz and Bain, 1992.

Academic A's views on learning, teaching and knowledge are summarised in the first three lines of the story and form in our opinion a quintessential example of learning-teaching conception 3:

> What underpins Academics A's views about teaching is his desire to provide an established understanding of his subject matter to his students so they will be able to use the knowledge and understanding in the future. (p. 312)

In his beliefs about learning Academic A makes a distinction between what he wants his students to be able to do now and in the future.

> … he expects them to remember techniques and methods needed to solve problems, to be able to remember 'how it works' and reproduce it, to be able to recall his reasoning in similar situations in the future: "…You end up being in Siberian oil fields and the boss says 'Analyse this oil and tell us if it's worth drilling for more'. What do you do? Phone me? No, you think about it and say 'how would Peter do it' and you do it". For now, he expects his students to be able to solve problems that illustrate theoretical concepts taught in the course: "… so they can say, 'oh, I remember the way to do this', and then apply the knowledge", but at he same time [Academic A] chooses problems that are likely to arise in practice. (p. 313)

Knowledge to Academic A is

> ...a corpus of knowledge as defined by the discipline and developed by great thinkers, ... he sees the knowledge and understanding to be gained by students as externally constructed, he tries to involve students in the process of teaching by "...giving them some facts and drawing out some from them". (p. 313)

And his conception of teaching - the roles of teacher and student, and the nature of their interaction – is characterised by the belief that

> ... the interaction between himself and students improves their understanding of the subject. Consequently he encourages students to interrupt him during lectures to *ask questions* to clarify their understanding: "... a student might say 'excuse me, but why does this nitrogen attack that H over there?' so I stop and explain". ... he gives them an opportunity to be active, albeit in a limited way: "I give them some facts and then I *play with the facts* and try to drag answers out of them and try to connect it to many things in the world around them". ......
>
> Academic A stresses *his* enthusiasm and interest ... as factors that should motivate students ... He tries to make things less boring by using humour, by trying to make the content relevant to students, by giving examples of substances known in everyday life, familiar to students. (p. 313–314, italics ours)

From these quotes one can conclude that Academic A's beliefs or conceptions of learning, teaching and knowledge are closely aligned and represent a 'psycho'-logically sound ecology of related beliefs.

Academic B's views on learning, teaching and knowledge also form a coherent whole, emphasising students becoming independently thinking professionals within a particular – in this case applied – discipline (architecture). For her, students "take the centre stage" and teaching is "a challenging two-way process" (p. 315).

Academic B's beliefs about learning stress students

> ... to develop professional knowledge, attitudes and skills and to use them appropriately for the tasks and the contexts encountered in real life.
> ... to learn to think and act as architects. ......
> ... to reflect on their approaches, to be able to judge what works and what does not, and to identify the reasons for successes and failures [as part of developing their professional expertise]
> ... to be involved in assessing their work as well as the work of their fellow students. (p. 315)

Her view on knowledge is clearly discipline-related, seeing her own discipline (architecture) more as a system than as a body of knowledge (facts and procedures):

> ... architecture synthesises information from various sources, jumbles it up somehow, proposes it as a scheme, evaluates that as a scheme, tests it, builds

> it, learns from it, criticises it, all that. .... students [are] the ones who develop their knowledge, the ones who unpack and repack it, the ones who analyse and synthesise it, the ones who transform it, the ones who make it their own. (p. 316)

Teaching, as seen by Academic B – her view on the roles of teacher and students, and their interaction –is very different from Academic A's view.

> [Teaching] means working with students, not doing learning for students. It means defining the content, setting up a learning environment where learning is possible, making expectations clear, expecting students to produce high quality work, treating students as adults, being fair but demanding. She calls it "a tough love". ...
>
> Academic B regards the interaction between herself and students as vital to the process of learning. It is through this interaction that students become involved in their learning and this is how they develop the understanding, knowledge, attitudes and skills needed in their future profession.
>
> ... she uses, for example, role-play simulating real life situations where not everything is predictable, where the unexpected happens: "... it brings reality into their lives, and they enjoy it; it's fun". (p. 316–317)

We agree with Samuelowicz and Bain that, although these two academics may seem to be close together (in their thinking) as their conceptions of teaching are adjacent on the continuum teacher-centeredness to student-centeredness, one would be indeed hard pressed to imagine two people thinking less alike about most aspects of teaching and learning than these two, illustrating the vastness of the 'divide' (Samuelowicz and Bain, 2001, p. 312). These two stories also illustrate that using only two belief categories (teacher vs. student centeredness) cannot be anything but insufficient to understand the epistemological strengths and weaknesses of the various conceptions and thus they underpin our position on the need for, and the benefit of, using a sufficiently elaborate theoretical model.

In their discussion, Samuelowicz and Bain examine the relatively small difference found between Preventing misunderstandings and Negotiating understanding, both categories in their 1992 study seen as belonging to one category of description: Changing students' conceptions: "Both are learning-centred, in part because they place importance upon students' understandings but they make different use of this knowledge, one by seeking to *prevent* common mistakes from happening, the other by assisting students to *move away from* inadequate interpretations." (2001, p. 320, italics ours). In our opinion, these two categories may reflect two stylistic variants of one underlying conception: our learning-teaching conception 5, where *awareness* of alternative interpretations of issues and *dialogue* about these differences are important. Fox's local guide in Preventing misunderstandings, seems to be a little bit more directive than the local guide in Negotiating understanding, but in both situations both guides are 'good travelling companions'. On the other hand, it may just be a difference in "tone of voice", with the latter aiming more for connectedness and the former aiming more for mastery and separateness. (Belenky et al., 1997).

It is somewhat disappointing (to us) that Samuelowicz and Bain (2001) paid relatively little attention to discussing the seventh (perhaps sixth) teaching conception that they found and renamed from Supporting student learning (focusing on what is expected from the teacher) to Encouraging knowledge creation (focusing in turn more on what the student is expected to do). This conception is only found by Samuelowicz and Bain at postgraduate level, and from the student's point of view it stresses the "creation of original knowledge" (p. 321) or the "constructing and defending a potentially new interpretation" (p. 321). We feel that both these interpretations fall short of our sixth learning conception, or Baxter Magolda's Internal Foundation, in the sense that Samuelowicz and Bain's conception seems to be more knowledge oriented and we see no indications of identity issues emerging here. The emphasis on "*personal* interactions" that was present in the description of Supporting student learning in the 1992 study (p. 98, italics ours) is more in line with what we (and perhaps Baxter Magolda) would expect at this level of teacher thinking. Therefore, we would like to champion the earlier label and its interpretation as, we feel, this earlier category of description is more in line with the issue of teaching. Furthermore, we propose to reserve the latter label for a conception of student learning that may or may not be linked to the sixth learning conception.

Finally, Samuelowicz and Bain strongly believe that their research is not only about views on teaching and learning, but also – while perhaps not explicitly addressed in their studies – about the relationship between conceptions of teaching and teaching practice: "… we nevertheless claim that the belief orientations we have reported here reflect our participants' characteristic perspectives and dispositions *to teach* in particular ways. These claims derive from the method which …. sought the characteristic perspectives of the participants exemplified with descriptions of their usual educational practices. … [However,] the coupling between belief and practice should be examined more closely … [and] because efforts to improve teaching are predicated on the assumed link between teaching and learning, this relationship [too] has to be investigated further…" (2001, p. 322–323). Below, we discuss – with a few examples – research efforts to address precisely these two final issues.

Before this, we will point out that Samuelowicz and Bain (2002) touched on the relationship between orientations to/conceptions of teaching and assessment orientations. They found that both types of orientations were highly correlated indicating "that academics who view teaching as exposition, and learning as reproduction, tend to believe that assessments should determine how well students can reproduce the knowledge they have been given and how well they can use that knowledge in much-practised tasks. On the other hand, those who view teaching as facilitating learning, and learning as constructing a personal understanding based upon established knowledge and procedure, tend to believe that assessments should require purposeful transformation of knowledge to address open-ended issues or problems not previously encountered" (Samuelowicz and Bain, 2002, p. 196). It seems to us that these orientations are also logically congruent, forming yet another support for the idea of a temporarily balanced epistemological ecology of beliefs.[29]

What does this mean for Teachers' Teaching Approaches?

While summarising their work from the nineteen-nineties Prosser and Trigwell (1999) compared the teaching approaches of two first-year university science teachers. Again in the quotes below, comparing a teacher from their least sophisticated category (A) with one from the most sophisticated category (E), we recognise now very familiar differences.

Lecturer A's approach:

> ... in preparing for an hour lecture I decide what I want he students to get out of this lecture, specifically what I want them to be able to do as a result of this lecture. So that is one of the first parts of planning my list if you like, planning my lecture. I also plan them in a way so that I know the notes that I want the students to get. I'll write my notes in such a way so that the students don't have to decide when to take notes, I tell them to. I'll dictate to them, I have handouts prepared, I have gaps in them that they fill in and I take that decision away from the students about when and how to take notes... ... ... I think it's important they come away with a good set of notes. After all there are exams we expect these students to pass, and you know, we could debate the merits and demerits of examinations but the point is they have to pass formal examinations. (Prosser and Trigwell, 1999, p. 139–140)

Lecturer E's approach:

> ...[I] use a reasonable number of what we call buzz sessions. ... getting the students to eh, to think, to be actively involved in what's going on, to think about it themselves ...... what I want to achieve with, eh, buzz sessions and the questions, and stuff is confronting students with their pre-conceived ideas about he subject which quite often conflict with what we're talking about, the official dogmas as it were. Um, so you've got to bring out that conflict and make the people aware that what they already know may not be what is the official line, as it were. (p. 140–141)

Prosser and Trigwell, confronted with these obvious differences, then asked themselves "If these different approaches represent fundamentally different ways of approaching teaching .... do such fundamentally different ways relate to different ways in which these lecturers conceive of learning and teaching?" (1999, p. 142). Based on interviews with 24 first-year university science teachers, Prosser and Trigwell reported six categories of teaching conceptions and five categories of teaching approaches.[30] The six conceptions of teaching could be re-categorised into three groups: A and B were characterised by transmission of information (n=10), C and D focused on the acquisition of information (n=6), and E and F, the smallest group (n=2), emphasised developing and changing students' conceptions. For six teachers only mixed conceptions could be reported (A&B, A&C, B&C, B&D, Prosser et al. 1994, p. 225). On closer examination of the quotes used to illustrate teaching conceptions C and D, it would appear necessary to move conception C into the group focusing on transmission: A and B

> I'm committed to the syllabus – the reason we have the syllabus is to give that student the foundation he or she needs, to go on to the rest of the course. I am committed to that syllabus. I believe that's very important for the student. What I've got to do is to conduct classes in such a way that the students understand the basic physics concept of what's going on in the topic that I'm teaching ... I'm viewing it (knowledge) as hierarchical. I put the topics in a logical way, and then it's students actually building up the concepts. (M3) (Prosser and Trigwell, 1999, p. 145–146)

In this quote we see an atomistic view on teaching, one concept followed by another, and another, without any reference to relationships between them. This conception of teaching looks very much like Kember and Kwan's *second transmission conception* of teaching (2000, p. 484). In addition we feel teaching conception D deserves a separate position, as it is the first conception that mentions interaction, although one could reason that the teacher-student interaction is of a somewhat virtual kind: the teacher imagining what students would think or know or want to know, and not asking them in any direct way.

> When I sat down to write the course *I* thought two things: what do they need to know, and what are they likely to want to know. And the two things are quite different ... in terms of how I develop my course is I try to relate the need to know to the wants to know. If I can do that then there's a chance that as a teacher I can get the interest of the students. ... So I guess that's really where I see teaching, as *relating* what I think they need to know with what they already know... (P6) (Prosser and Trigwell, 1999, p. 146, italics ours)

Furthermore, it seems to us that teaching conception D matches seamlessly with the *first learning-facilitation conception* of Kember and Kwan (2000):

> I will say that good teaching is ... if the students learn what they want to learn, then I have done my job, irrespective of the teaching media, or the teaching support. The most important thing is that we recognise the needs of our students, and base our teaching upon their needs. (ENG-5, p. 484)

In the same group of teachers, Prosser and Trigwell found five teaching approaches, two teacher-focused strategies (A and B, n =19), two student-focused strategies (D and E, n = 2) and one strategy focusing on teacher-student interaction (C, n=3). Reorganising Table 7.3 from Prosser and Trigwell (1999, p. 155) using these combined categories of description, we arrive at a clear pattern (see Table 5.4).

Table 5.4. The relationship between teaching conceptions and teaching approaches

Teaching conception	*Teaching approach* *A,B*	*C*	*D,E*	*Total*
A, B, C and their combinations	15	0	0	15
D, D&B, D&C	4	3	0	7
E, F	0	0	2	2
Total	19	3	2	24

Source: Prosser and Trigwell, 1999, Table 7.3

In this table the pattern becomes remarkably clear: the – less complete (Prosser and Trigwell, 1999, p. 147) – teaching conceptions A, B and C are not related to teaching more sophisticated than transmission of content. On the other hand, for the more epistemologically sophisticated – and more aware – teachers with more complete conceptions (E and F), the teaching approach is always aimed at developing/ changing conceptions. These results then are almost identical to the pattern found for student learning conceptions and the related study approaches (van Rossum and Schenk, 1984), linking again student and teacher thinking. The results as presented here are to be expected when one assumes the validity of the developmental models presented in chapters 1 and 3 and applies these models to teacher thinking (as we have done). Prosser and Trigwell on the other hand do not make this assumption, they feel that coherence between conceptions, beliefs, approaches etcetera, is context specific. In this case, they would expect to find different patterns in different teaching-learning situations: "There is substantial coherence between [the teachers'] conceptions, perceptions and approaches. Remember, we are not talking here of general orientations, but specific responses to perceived specific situations. The same teachers may well have different conceptions, perceive their teaching situation in different ways and adopt different approaches to teaching in different teaching contexts. *But if we get teachers to focus on their teaching for a specific teaching situation, they exhibit substantial coherence in their experience of that situation*" (Prosser and Trigwell, 1999, p. 156–157, italics ours). We agree that this could be the case for the more aware teachers, who may adapt their teaching to e.g. the epistemological level of the students, but can one honestly expect Lecturer A to teach like Lecturer E in a different situation? In fact, Lecturer A even tells us himself that he teaches the same way in all situations (years): "And indeed in the very first lecture *of any class* I have, not just first year students, I explain to the students about my lecturing style, so they know where they stand. I explain to them the sort of things I'm just telling you, that is, they don't have to worry about when to take down lecture notes. I'll tell them .." (Prosser and Trigwell, 1999, p. 139, italics ours).

In Table 5.4 there were four teachers (with teaching conception D) who seem to perform at a lower – more transmissive – level than one would expect, in our opinion showing the role of constraints (perhaps external) on their chosen approach. In closing, Trigwell and Prosser (1996) discuss these results in the light of staff development: "... in academic development, the focus should be more on the way academic staff conceive of teaching and learning, and less on teaching strategies ... [p. 282] ... in designing programmes for teachers in higher education, a major focus needs to be on helping staff examine and change their conceptions of teaching and learning" (p. 283). If indeed the coherency between conceptions of teaching and teaching approaches is context specific, following Trigwell and Prosser's reasoning, this would mean that staff-development programmes would need to take into account all the possible contexts or situations such teachers would be confronted with within higher education. We surely hope this is not the case! Changing coherent beliefs has been proven to be already difficult enough within the developmental models described in the first two chapters of this book, without needing further complications.

Kember and Kwan (2000) strongly criticised the way in which Trigwell and Prosser (1996) established the relationship between conceptions of teaching and teaching approaches. Their main points of critique were that Trigwell and Prosser did not define the constructs used (conceptions of teaching and approaches to teaching), and secondly, that occasionally they seemed to use nearly identical labels for conceptions and approaches. Furthermore, Kember and Kwan observed that Trigwell and Prosser did not make clear whether the data defining the teaching conception and the teaching approach came from different parts of the interview. In an attempt to answer the same question Trigwell and Prosser had studied – the relationship between conceptions of (good) teaching and approaches to teaching – Kember and Kwan interviewed a selected but representative sample of 17 university lecturers, who were assumed to be typical of their university and all taught both "adult part-time and adolescent full-time students" (Kember and Kwan, 2000, p. 473). The respondents were interviewed regarding five themes: their 1) views on what constituted 'good' teaching, 2) use of motivational strategies, 3) expectations of students' learning activities, 4) views on the most effective teaching strategies, and 5) perceptions of adult (part-time) and adolescent (full-time) students (e.g. whether these groups required different teaching approaches).

In an initial analysis of the interviews a remarkable result was that it proved to be difficult to find differences between teachers when focusing on teachers' descriptions of their use of teaching methods or techniques: lectures, class discussions, case studies etcetera. Kember and Kwan posed that "[the] teaching methods utilised did not seem to be determined by any fundamental beliefs about teaching" (2000, p. 475). This counter-intuitive result – considering the previous studies on teachers' epistemological beliefs – may be the consequence of two design choices: collecting data on the use of teaching methods and techniques only by interviewing lecturers about their own teaching (i.e. no observations) and secondly focusing on the techniques or methods as such, and not focusing on the nature of the use of each technique or method (that is, not on techniques-as-meant or methods-as-meant).

Kember and Kwan proceeded to examine the transcripts more closely for broad categories of approaches and their underlying dimensions. This approach resulted in two broad teaching approaches, *content-centred* and *learning-centred*. The final allocation of each lecturer to one of either categories depended on their profile, their approximate positions, on six teaching-related dimensions (2000, p. 482): 1) using external motivators vs. intrinsically motivating students, 2) providing knowledge vs. encouraging discovery and construction, 3) whole-class orientation vs. individual orientation, 4) assessment by tests and quizzes vs. flexible assessment, 5) catering to students' weaknesses vs. remediating their weaknesses, and 6) using teachers' experience vs. using students' experiences. In allocating "lecturers to categories, [Kember and Kwan] decided that each dimension did *not* have to be present for classification, simply because not every dimension had been mentioned in all of the transcripts. [They] further agreed that allocation would be based upon a *holistic judgement* of all evidence that could be found in the transcripts rather than focusing on individual dimensions. [They] also took great care to ensure that evidence supporting the categorisation was *not* taken from the part of the transcript used to identify conceptions of teaching, ... unless there was corroborating evidence from another part of transcript not used to identify conceptions." (Kember and Kwan, 2000, p. 482, italics ours). This allocation method led to two equal-sized groups of teachers/teaching approaches (nine content-centred teachers, and eight learning-centred teachers).

The lecturers' conceptions of 'good' teaching were based on the responses to the question , 'What is good teaching?'. Analysis of the responses led to four teaching conceptions, the first two seeing teaching as transmitting knowledge, and the last two seeing teaching as facilitating student learning:

1. Teaching as passing information (T1): emphasis on covering the syllabus and meeting examination requirements. ".... I will cover the syllabus fully. Although I am the one who sets the examination paper, I will not skip any part of it, and I will not teach only the materials that will be examined....(ENG-1)" (Kember and Kwan, 2000, p. 483).
2. Teaching as making it easier for students to understand (T2): recognition of the teacher's responsibility to structure and organise the material, to help students understand and remember. "... For my course, I expect to deliver the lecture, present the ideas and theories, conceptualise as precisely as possible, and use concrete ... and updated examples...(SS-3) " (p. 484)
3. Teaching as meeting students' learning needs (F3): recognition that students' needs differ and the teacher should take this into account. "... The most important thing is that we recognise the needs of our students, and base our teaching upon their needs. (ENG-5)" (p. 484, quoted before in discussing Prosser and Trigwell, 1999).
4. Teaching as facilitating students to become independent learners (F4): emphasis on a student's individual growth rather than on specific knowledge and skills. "I think .... 'good teaching' means that you can stimulate the students' interest in the subject matter. You can help them to learn the method for studying the subject matter, because different subjects may require different learning

methods. The third thing is to help them to become responsible for their own learning. (SS-6)" (p. 484–485).

Contrary to Kember and Kwan's conclusion, we do not feel that conception F3 is similar to the facilitating learning/understanding category Kember defined in 1997 (see also above), and we feel that only F4 has definite similarities with facilitating learning/understanding. As we discussed before, in the section on Prosser and Trigwell, F3 is much more like the interactive category Kember described as the 'intermediate category'. Either way, Kember and Kwan found considerable coherence between conceptions of teaching and approaches to teaching: all knowledge-transmission oriented teachers but one, used a content-centred teaching approach, while all learning-facilitation oriented teachers but one, used a learning-centred approach.

> ... lecturers who perceive teaching primarily as a process of transmitting bodies of knowledge tended to adopt a content-centred approach to teaching: they were more likely to rely on extrinsic motivators, supply a lot of notes and references, focus on the whole class, employ frequent tests and quizzes, teach to their students' strengths or cater for their weaknesses, and give examples and illustrations from their own experiences. Lecturers placed in the two facilitative categories, on the other hand, tended to adopt a learning-centred approach to teaching. They were more inclined to recognise the need to motivate students as an intrinsic part of their role as a teacher, encourage students to discover knowledge on their own, deal with the needs of individual students, employ a more flexible system of assessment, make conscious attempt to remediate the weaknesses of their students, and respect and make good use of the students' experience in their teaching. (Kember and Kwan, 2000, p. 486)

This result made Kember and Kwan conclude that, contrary to the conclusion of Prosser and Trigwell, teaching approaches are relatively stable across situations and contexts, because they are heavily determined by the teacher's conception of teaching. Although they recognised that teachers may be influenced by external influences (e.g. large classes, heavy teaching loads, different types of student, etcetera) their data led them to suggest that "... the context dependent aspect was weaker than the predominant effect [of the teaching conception] .... Radical shifts from one pole to another do not seem likely, and our data showed no evidence of ... lecturers shifting from one pole to another and back again, depending upon the class they were teaching at the time" (Kember and Kwan, 2000, p. 488). This conclusion in turn, leads us to reiterate the now familiar stanza: "Fundamental changes to the quality of teaching and learning may only result from changes to conceptions of teaching." (Kember and Kwan, 2000, p. 489).

What does this mean for student learning?

In the above section we have established that teachers' conceptions of teaching are strongly related to their teaching approach. The question that can be asked now was asked about a decade ago by Marton and Booth: "What can we identify in the teacher's teaching that might lead to a variation in how students learn what they are intended to learn?" (1997, p. 175). Prosser and Trigwell also put this issue on the agenda, formulating it more dramatically, "Everything … would be for naught if we were not able to find a link between the way …. teachers teach and the way their students learn" (1999, p. 157), where 'everything' refers to the existing research into teachers' teaching conceptions, teaching approaches and their relationship in particular. In short, if different teaching approaches do not lead to different learning approaches, then all is theoretically perhaps interesting, but not very relevant in everyday teaching.

Trigwell, Prosser and Waterhouse (1999) tried to establish this "missing link", using a more quantitative approach to study teaching approaches and students' learning approaches. The university science class was the unit of analysis in this study, where Trigwell et al. administered a context-specific version of a study approach questionnaire (SPQ, Biggs, 1987) to 3956 students of 48 science classes taught by 46 university science teachers. The teachers filled in a questionnaire (Approaches to Teaching Inventory, ATI), measuring their approach to teaching in the context of their first-year science class, developed by Prosser and Trigwell some years earlier. The ATI consists of two main scales, measuring an information transmission/teacher-focused approach (ITTF) and a conceptual change/student-focused approach (CCSF), and the SPQ measures three learning approaches, of which we will discuss only the two for this study relevant ones: the surface approach and the deep approach to learning. Factor analysis of these combined approach variables (the teachers' approach to teaching and the students' approach to learning) resulted in a two-factor solution.[31] The first factor linked a teacher's ITTF teaching approach to students using a surface approach (and a non-deep approach) to learning. The second factor on the other hand linked a teacher's CCSF teaching approach to students using a non-surface approach to learning, while not linking CCSF to a deep approach as one might expect. This result shows, we feel, that encouraging students towards deep learning may be much more complicated than getting students to use a surface approach to learning. A second analysis involved cluster analysis of the classes, identifying subgroups of classes "with similar approaches to teaching and approaches to learning" (Trigwell et al., 1999, p. 65). The first cluster (19 classes) was characterised by teachers using the ITTF approach and students who reported surface or non-deep approaches to learning. In the second cluster (29 classes) teachers reported a non-ITTF approach to teaching, and students used deep and non-surface approaches to learning. These two clusters more or less confirmed the factor analysis and linked the ITTF approach to teaching with surface or non-deep student learning, a result having obvious consequences for students' learning outcomes (van Rossum and Schenk, 1984). The CCSF teaching approach did not discriminate well between clusters: classes with teachers using a CCSF teaching approach were less unambiguously linked to any particular approach to student learning. However, a non-ITTF approach was associated to a deep approach (and non-surface approach) to learning. This result might be an indication that the dichotomy ITTF and CCSF, or surface vs. deep approach for that matter, is not sufficient to describe the complex reality in these 48 (or any other) classes, supporting our position that a more elaborate epistemological framework is necessary for this kind of research. Pulling their body of research together, Prosser and Trigwell concluded that

> ... university teachers who focus on their students and their students' learning tend to have students who focus on meaning and understanding in their studies, while university teachers who focus on themselves and what they are doing tend to have students who focus on reproduction." (1999, p. 142)

This conclusion has vast implications for university staff and staff development: it points out the vital importance of promoting the adoption of higher quality – i.e. more epistemologically sophisticated – approaches to teaching, while simultaneously, through reflective 'learning by doing', changing the teachers' underlying conceptions of teaching and (student) learning. Otherwise, especially university teaching will not fulfil its purpose: educating students towards an expanded awareness of learning and knowledge (e.g. Entwistle and Walker, 2000; Åkerlind, 2003, and below).

Taking the unit of analysis another step up, from teacher to class level and now to academic department level, Gow and Kember (1993) studied the relationships between teachers' (general) orientations to/conceptions of teaching and students' approaches to learning. In the initial phase of their study, Gow and Kember interviewed 39 university lecturers, in order to establish categories and items related to teachers' beliefs about, and approaches to, teaching and learning. The outcomes of this phase were used to develop a pilot version of their Teaching Orientation Questionnaire, which in turn was tested and revised resulting in a final version. The revised version with 14 scales was administered to lecturers of in total 15 departments of two polytechnics in Hong Kong. Analysis of the revised version led to the final version consisting of nine scales (or categories) of teacher beliefs, teaching approaches, and pursued (student) learning approaches and outcomes, reflecting two main orientations to teaching:

A. Learning facilitation
   - Problem solving
     (sample item: After completing a course, students should be able to analyse a situation and display logical and rational thinking)
   - More interactive teaching
     (sample item: In my teaching I have tried to develop participation from the students to make it more lively)
   - Facilitative teaching
     (sample item: I guide students in learning rather than force things down their throats)
   - Pastoral interest
     (sample item: A good tertiary lecturer is someone who cares for the students and is in-tune with their problems)
   - Motivator of students
     (sample item: A successful lecturers is able to enthuse students)

B. Knowledge transmission
- Training for specific jobs
  (sample item: A most important function of higher education is to produce graduates for certain professions within the community)
- Greater use of media
  (sample item: Information can only be properly presented if audio-visual materials are used)
- Imparting information
  (sample item: A lecturer imparts information to the student)
- Knowledge of subject
  (sample item: A sound knowledge of their discipline is vital for all academics)

(Gow and Kember, 1993, Table 5, p. 27)

In our opinion, the first orientation includes items that are consistent with learning-teaching conceptions 3 and 4, whereas the second orientation includes items that could be examples of learning-teaching conceptions 1 through 3. A second observation that we can make here is that these teachers teaching in Hong Kong, display the same types of conceptions of learning and teaching as found in the more West European and Australian studies. In comparing these two teaching orientations to models of teaching, Gow and Kember came to the surprising observation that "... the learning facilitation orientation seems consistent with a wide range of teaching models in different families. It is difficult, though to find any teaching models consistent with the knowledge transmission orientation because of its *neglect* of the student in the information transmission process. This orientation appears to assume that what is transmitted is received as sent: as assumption which teaching models do *not* seem to accept" (Gow and Kember, 1993, p. 28, italics ours). It is interesting (to say the least) that such a commonly held orientation to teaching (i.e. knowledge transmission) seems to have been absent in literature about teaching models.

The students' learning approaches were gathered using the SPQ (Biggs, 1987; again we will focus only on the surface and deep approach scales in this discussion) administrating the SPQ at the beginning and at the end of the academic year. In the analysis Gow and Kember focused on a student's final score (on deep or surface approach) and a change-in-approach-score, as the basis for calculating a "departmental mean score" (1993, p. 29). The students' departmental-mean-scores were "Mean scores by department ... calculated for deep [and] surface ... approaches. For each approach, one departmental mean score was taken from the application of the questionnaire just after the cohort started the course and 'final' scores from the application prior to the final examination" (Gow and Kember, 1993, p. 29). The change-in-approach-score was calculated by subtracting the initial departmental-mean-score from the final departmental-mean-score. A similar procedure was performed to arrive at teachers' departmental-mean-scores for each of the nine teaching scales as well as for the two orientations to teaching.

Analysis of the 44 correlations relevant to this discussion (Gow and Kember, 1993, Table 6, p. 30) and only reporting the significant relationships, showed that

- The knowledge transmission orientation was negatively related to the final deep approach score and to the change in deep approach score: "... in departments where the predominant orientation is towards knowledge transmission, the students' use of [a] deep approach is likely to *decline* through the period of the course of study" (p. 30, italics ours). This effect seemed to originate from two scales in particular, Imparting information and Knowledge of subject.
- The learning facilitation orientation was negatively related to the final surface approach score: "...departments with a propensity towards learning facilitation tend to *discourage* the use of surface approaches. The effect of an orientation towards learning facilitation is perhaps more likely to manifest itself in this way, rather than as a positive advance in the use of a deep approach, because of the difficulty of inducing students with a propensity towards a surface approach consistently to adopt a deep approach..." (p. 30–31, italics ours).This effect of the learning facilitation orientation is consistent with what Trigwell et al. (1999) found for the CCSF approach in their two-factor solution (discussed above). This effect seemed to originate from two scales in particular, Problem solving and Motivator of students.
- The scale More interactive teaching - part of the learning facilitation orientation - had a positive effect on both the final surface and deep approach score, and a positive effect on the change in deep approach score, a pattern which Gow and Kember found difficult to interpret. However, from our perspective, this effect is probably related to the discussion above. There, we elaborated the different meanings of student-teacher interaction as illustrating one of the dimensions that define the distinction between learning-teaching conceptions 3 and 4: from which side of the divide or watershed (Samuelowicz and Bain, 2001; chapters 1 and 2) are we looking at the nature of the interaction?

These quantitative results[32] led Gow and Kember to conclude that

> The combination of the significant correlations and the consistent directions of the remaining correlations establishes a clear relationship between knowledge transmission and less desirable study approaches on the one hand and learning facilitation and more meaningful student learning approaches on the other hand. (Gow and Kember, 1993, p. 31)

Of course, inconsistencies between teachers' teaching conceptions and their teaching approaches –with the now well known effects on students' learning approaches and outcomes– remain possible, even from a developmental stance and Richardson (2005) discussed a number of these in his review of the state of the art in teachers' approaches to teaching in higher education.

> ... in Trigwell and Prosser's study [1996], more than half of the teachers described approaches to teaching that were less learner-focused and more teacher-focused than would have been expected from their reported conceptions of teaching. This drift towards teacher-focused approaches to

> teaching and away from learner-focused approaches to teaching was confirmed in the study by Norton et al. (2005). It suggests that contextual factors tend to frustrate teachers' intended approaches to teaching (....). Senior staff who hold traditional, teacher-focused conceptions of teaching may raise issues about standards and coverage of the curriculum (...), or else the students themselves may conspire to induce the teachers to adopt a more didactic approach (....)" (Richardson, 2005, p. 678)

Richardson also stated that there

> ... is, in fact, little evidence that teachers' conceptions of teaching really do develop with increasing teaching experience (...). There is also little evidence that conceptions of teaching change as a result of formal training..." (p. 677–678) ...
>
> So, if institutions of higher education want their teachers to adopt a more student-focused approach to teaching, they need to ensure that their teachers hold a commensurate conception of teaching – *and a brief training course will not be sufficient to achieve this.* (p. 678, italics ours)

To eleviate the possible gloom that might have settled in the readers' minds regarding the possibility to change teaching and learning, we will now discuss some studies showing positive developments in teacher thinking and a successful intervention to influence teacher thinking.

The Development of Teacher Thinking

In 2000, Noel Entwistle and Paul Walker embarked on a journey to explore the nature of 'good' teaching, which they interpreted as an (epistemologically) sophisticated conception of teaching. Their starting point – perhaps an odd choice to some – was based on studies on students' intellectual development, which showed that "... higher level conceptions emerge out of the lower ones through reflection and integration, resulting in *an expanded awareness*[33] of the nature of learning and academic study." (Entwistle and Walker, 2000, p. 335, italics ours). More specifically, they based their assumption on e.g. Perry's model (1970) which suggested that "intellectual development in higher education involves the gradual integration of previously separate personal characteristics and ways of thinking, leading to an expanded awareness of the complexities of academic knowledge." (Entwistle and Walker, 2000, p. 338), and on Marton's and Säljö's work (Säljö, 1979a; Marton et al., 1993) which suggested that "[i]ndividuals who recognised the importance of understanding for themselves [learning conception 4 or 5] were still ready to use rote learning when necessary, but were conscious of the variety of forms of learning available, and how they could be used. I.... Overall, these six categories ... seem to form a nested hierarchy..." (Entwistle and Walker, 2000, p. 338). Their main question was if the notions of 'expanding awareness' and 'nested hierarchy' were viable explanations for teachers' intellectual development, with a focus on the development in their conceptions of teaching. If this proved to be the case, this would mean that student thinking and teacher thinking indeed are parallel phenomena, as is one of the main themes of our current study.

For their exploration they used Paul Walker's recollections of his own development as a physics teacher, using an elaborate retrospective narrative of this development. We will be quoting from this narrative freely to illustrate what we feel are the most clear examples of Walker's expanding awareness of the nature of knowledge, learning and teaching, and we will be linking these quotes directly to our model of student thinking. All quotes come from Entwistle and Walker (2000, p. 345–351), and to improve readability we will refrain from page numbers in the quotes from the narrative. This narrative cumulates in a description of a teaching approach that Entwistle and Walker feel is appropriate to a sophisticated conception of teaching.

In the beginning of his teaching career, Paul Walker seemed to have been a typical novice teacher

> The focus of my own learning up to this point, and of my early teaching, was very much on course content and on learning as the intake, retention and reproduction of this course content …

> … my early teaching experiences were something of an act, in being the authoritative source of knowledge as well as being in control of the process, …

Here we see the focus on (covering the) content and control of the communication typical of learning-teaching conception 2. However, Walker was already aware of the incongruence between the course content and physics in everyday life, but he separated school physics from 'real physics'. The outcome for Walker himself of this approach to teaching was somewhat unexpected

> … I found that my own understanding of the concepts increased markedly. In some instances, there were flashes of insight which allowed me to make sense of things I had only partly understood as a student.

A similar outcome for teachers at this level of thinking is reported in Åkerlind (2004) discussed in the next section. Walker's improved understanding of physics concepts, and his seeing this understanding as the outcome of learning, led him to start altering his teaching approach to encourage a similar understanding in his students.

> The focus on course content remained, with understanding being really still a means to an end (success in examination-based assessment), but with a gradually emerging intrinsic worth (understanding of, and practical application to, the real everyday world).

The lingering focus on content and examination-based assessment, coupled with the aim for practical application, and perhaps using everyday examples, is typical of learning-teaching conception 3. While working as a doctoral student and a physics teacher at a technical college, Walker realised that the 'practical understanding' that had characterised his teaching did not match his own growing understanding of the "deep structure of knowledge" in his own discipline (physics). In an attempt to counter students' tendency to make lists of formulae and equations to remember, he started to stress the connections between them.

> I began advising students in class explicitly to the effect that understanding was a key objective, ... I told them that if they appreciated the connections between the various facts and formulae, there was less need to blindly remember these in isolation.

Walker became more aware that understanding as a concept had more aspects than he had realised before.

> As well understanding course content, there were opportunities to understand aspects of the real world in terms of the course content, and also the course content in terms of the real world.

This seeing of connections and tackling real world problems are two aspects that dominate learning-teaching conception 4. Over time, Walker began to explore the epistemological aspects of physics as a discipline. Re-confronted – in this new light of understanding – with a number of well-known paradoxical issues in modern physics[34], he became aware that,

> ... the world is not as it ordinarily appears – indeed, this ordinary appearance could be largely a matter of consensus. ... ...
>
> ... the edifice of human knowledge, including the solidity of physics, has been fabricated by human beings no better or worse than oneself ...
>
> Ideas about the nature of knowledge and learning thus became a matter vital personal concern for me ...

Walker had now become aware that there are more ways to see (anything) and that each way of seeing has its own merits and limits. This is the crux of Relativism (Perry's position 5, see chapter 3), and Walker had now himself arrived at learning-teaching conception 5. He found this expansion of his awareness

> not easy to reconcile with the requirements of day-to-day teaching.

So how did he resolve this? It was a gradual process starting with changing the nature of communication in the classroom.

> My lectures thus began to be less a matter of delivering students the facts handed down from higher authority, and more a conversation designed to stimulate their engagement, not only in the content and concepts of the discipline but also in learning as an intrinsically rewarding endeavour.

And how did the students react to this conversational approach to teaching? Not so well initially it seems.

> I experienced indifference, even hostility, ...[because] this shift of focus was at the expense of duly delivered information. It created apparent unease and concern about how this might relate to what was on the examination papers.

It took Walker some time and effort to find a solution to this power struggle (Larsson, 1983). Over time, he developed what he called a 'multiply inclusive approach' to teaching:

> ...information is provided in logical order for those who want it, but with the oft-repeated rider that relying on my lectures for complete and accurate information is fraught with danger – I might be mistaken (as I have been many times and not realised it until later) or even deliberately misleading (temporarily, to make a point). For students who need to relate to other course content or to the world, there is a thread of conversation making such links, often unexpected ones. This approach is not unusual; physics teachers often highlight examples and provide practical illustrations of the abstract concepts in physics courses. For students who seek to apply the knowledge, there is at least conversational reference to that, which again is not unusual. *But an explicit awareness of inclusively serving the interests and learning approaches of a diversity of students seems to be much less common.* (italics ours)

In this approach we recognise a layered structure, various types of students are catered for, while only "partially fulfilling" the students' expectations – maybe in this partial fulfilment providing an epistemological stretch (Kegan, 1994). While this description seems to confirm Hashweh's (1996) conclusion that epistemologically more sophisticated teachers have a wider range of effective teaching strategies, this application of multiple strategies simultaneously seems – at least to us – a devilishly difficult juggling act to manage. Even so, Walker came to realise that "Still this was not enough",

> ... the learning outcome that I came to value most was an awareness of learning itself as a transformative agent, a means of redefining an individual's relationship with the world and thus fundamentally altering both that individual and his or her world... It was *being* a *learner* that was important, and for intrinsic rather than merely instrumental reasons. ...
>
> It did not imply the need for radical changes in the curriculum, but simply sought to engender *a spirit of inquiry* in the broad majority of students ... (italics ours)

In introducing this new view on teaching, Walker made some consequences for the students explicit and an object of discussion and reflection in the classroom,

> ... [it] might sound attractive, but it ... demands of the students a new level of personal commitment to learning, a deep intentionality and willingness to experience discomfort. This is a challenge which rather few students are, initially, ready to embrace. ... ... I have come to see a quest for personal meaning as an important catalyst for high quality learning and I have attempted to develop ways of fostering this kind of commitment by making my teaching more *an authentic conversation with students* than a delivery, based on the stereotypical roles of lecturer and student. (italics ours)

In this quote we recognise the conception of good teaching advocated by Palmer (1998), teaching as an authentic conversation between people who 'know as they are known'. In the teaching approach we also recognise the learning partnerships of Baxter Magolda (2004) and the teaching conception that is linked to learning conception 6, see chapter 1. Walker's current teaching approach is complex to perform indeed:

> The process requires skilful management – to keep directing attention to issues that are just beyond the current horizon of students' awareness and thus stimulate the expansion of that awareness.

Clearly, expanding students' awareness had now become the object of teaching, making awareness the object of reflection as Kegan would say (1994). While from the inside, actions are taken with a specific epistemological goal in mind, from an outside (and perhaps less informed) standpoint, Walker's practice would seem to be fairly standard

> But from my point of view, as the one teaching, it looks very different, and my awareness of what happens is class contrasts markedly with how it used to be. In the early days it was a matter of being prepared, presenting content confidently and accurately, and being in control. Some days it worked well and others it was a struggle, and I never knew quite why – it must have been the students or perhaps the weather that day. Later, as I developed more mastery, I could teach in a more conversational style, maintaining the sense of theatre, creating and taking opportunities to engage students' interest and thinking. Examples, demonstrations and questions can be chosen to maximise such engagement and wherever possible to elucidate and challenge students' preconceptions. The experience of teaching now, from my point of view, is more akin to a masterful jazz musician improvising and interacting with partners, allowing the instrument itself to speak, to express and inspire – rather than having to clumsily pluck or blow to force a predictable outcome.

By likening his practice to jazz improvisation with partners, Walker emphasised that the students have an active, equal and authentic role in the teaching-learning process. However, one might wonder how an observer (e.g. an educational researcher in the study by Tsai, 2007, see above) would score Walker's teaching practice? Although the intent of many activities is clearly different, would Walker's time allocation to activities differ that much from David's?

The use of Walker's retrospective narrative showed how more advanced conceptions of teaching emerge out of less advanced conceptions. Secondly, it showed that each more advanced level is *inclusive* of the skills, knowledge, etcetera characteristic of the previous level, although, as Entwistle and Walker say, "earlier techniques [can be brought] back into play, but in a qualitatively different way" (2000, p. 353). Each new level is shown to be a *more complete* experience of the phenomenon of teaching (Åkerlind, 2004). Furthermore, Walker's narrative showed explicitly that changes in awareness and changes in conceptions of teaching seem to precede changes in teaching approach and practice, underpinning the conclusions drawn repeatedly above, but now seen from the viewpoint of a developing teacher: to change teaching one needs to change the underlying conceptions, either first or at least as well. Finally, a fully sophisticated conception of teaching – in Walker's narrative – should lead to a teaching approach that is characterised by "strategic alertness"

> ... capitalising on chance events in the classroom to create springboards to significant learning. (p. 357)

We feel that, to enable this kind of teaching to take place, one needs teachers with a profound and passionate understanding of their discipline itself and its place in everyday reality. Entwistle and Walker concluded

> [Our] view of good teaching ... goes well beyond the listing of individual competencies. It represents a sophisticated conception of the relationship between learning and teaching, and a commitment to encouraging students to reach higher epistemological levels and a deeper understanding of the discipline or professional area. Expanded awareness of the nature of both disciplinary knowledge and student learning allows staff to become strategically alert to events in the classroom which can be transformed into 'teaching moments' ... ... Staff who follow a developmental path towards such an expanded awareness of teaching are likely to find classroom activities *much more rewarding*, not just through the higher levels of understanding acquired by students, but through being able to reflect knowledgeably on the complex experiences involved in bringing such achievement about. (p. 359, italics ours)

In the final sentence of this quote, Entwistle and Walker touch on the outcomes of epistemological development for teachers. They are referring to a possible intrinsic motivator for teacher development hitherto neglected: the continued enjoyment in teaching. Åkerlind (2004) has studied teachers' outcomes more fully and we will return to this issue in the next section.

Moving now from the narrative of an experienced and fully epistemologically developed teacher, to the development of views on teaching of student teachers, we discuss Wood's (2000) study. Wood described an explicit intervention aimed at changing student teachers' understanding of teaching (economics). The intervention in this case was a one-year programme of postgraduate initial teacher education, with the purpose "that student teachers should teach with the intention of making [secondary school] students' economic understanding the object of their reflection. This process of exploration of [secondary school] students' understanding should make possible conceptual-change learning on the part of the student teachers. Consistent with this view of learning, the programme set out to make teaching economics the object of the student teachers' reflection in order to explore their understanding with other student teachers and the tutors on the programme" (Wood, 2000, p. 89). In this programme we can recognise three main elements: a focus on

- secondary school students' understandings of (economic) concepts,
- student teachers' understandings of learning and teaching, and

- collaborative reflection on the student teachers' given lessons (in practicum schools).

These three elements were bound together by the phenomenographic approach, and the course was 'taught' from this approach to teaching which the student teachers were expected to learn, understand and apply themselves. A further aim of the programme was to provide the student teachers with a notion of competence about their own way of seeing and approaching teaching.

Throughout the programme student teachers were interviewed four times, at the start of the programme (October 1991), after five weeks and just prior to the first stint of teaching at a practicum school (November 1991), before the second period of teaching at a practicum school (February 1992) and at the end of the course (June 1992). In his discussion of the results, Wood did not include the final interview in establishing the conceptual change of the student teachers. The analysis of the interviews focused on student teachers' "understandings or experiences of teaching present in the data" (p. 80). Wood found three student teachers' conceptions of teaching that formed a "hierarchy of levels of understanding of, or ways of experiencing, teaching" (p. 83)

- A: Focus on the agent of teaching (the teacher)
  Good teaching is seen as teachers imparting knowledge to students (transmission): "... the hardest thing, ... to get respect from the pupils you're working with when you've got to transmit information in a clear and logical way..." (Rehana, October, p. 83).
- B: Focus on the act of teaching (the interaction)
  Good teaching is preparing students to use knowledge, is characterised by two-way interaction between teacher and students, and students are shaped in the interaction in the right direction (interaction and shaping): "Managing the learning process so that it goes in the direction you want without veering off in directions you don't want..." (Katerina, October, p. 84).
- C: Focus on the object of teaching (the learner)
  Good teaching is seen as diagnosing (secondary school) students' initial conceptions of the content and where necessary changing their conceptions or understandings (facilitating understanding): "... All issues which we did raise with the role play but they tried to avoid...We thought raising the issue would be enough and it wasn't ... it's what *they* make of it ... We then have to look at what they are making of it—and look for something that will challenge what they're doing with it, rather than what we see that they should be doing with it..." (Salif, February, p. 84)

In these quotes we recognise respectively learning-teaching conception 2 (A), 3 (B) and 4 (C). In Table 5.5 we have summarised Wood's Table 1 (2000, p. 86), focusing on the largest period between measurements. For most student teachers this was about 5 months (October – February). For 4 student teachers one of these measurements was missing, and we used the next nearest measurement. For two of these four student teachers, this procedure might have led to an underestimation of the effect of the programme.

Table 5.5. Changes in conceptions of teaching over 5 months

Teaching conception (October '91)	*Teaching conception (February '92)* A	B	C	*Total*
A	2	7	4	13
B	0	4	6	10
C	1	1	2	4
Total	3	12	12	27

Source: Wood, 2000

From a developmental perspective, the cells below the diagonal (in Table 5.5) should have been empty. The fact that they are not indicates that only two student teachers showed a odd score pattern. The number of student teachers with an A-conception dropped from 13 to 3, while the number of student teachers with a C-conception increased inversely from 4 to 12. The number of student teachers with a B-conception remained about the same. Closer examination reveals that 8 student teachers did not seem to react to the programme. This shows we feel that there are three types of reaction here: 1) no development, 2) some development and 3) larger development. These three types of development become more clear looking at Table 5.5, showing that 63 percent (17 of 27) of the student teachers developed one or even two levels upwards within a period of only five months. In particular the fact that 15% of the student teachers developed from A to C is pretty remarkable, as a development of about one level in four years (e.g. Baxter Magolda, 1992) is far more common. The stability of the size of category B is the result of A's moving into the B category, while B's are moving out at approximately the same rate.

From the additional qualitative case studies, it became clear that development in this programme meant that student teachers' awareness of various aspects related to teaching and learning was significantly expanded, e.g. the growing awareness of other student teachers' conceptions and becoming aware that not all colleague student teachers were on the same level of sophistication.

> … you're continuously learning, but you're never going to reach a point whereby you think, I've done this, I've reached the zenith, I'm a teacher. You're a teacher but you're never going to be the ultimate teacher. I think it's important for student [teachers] to realize that. I think there're still people on the course who want something prescriptive and want some kind of path, a bulldozed path, through to being a teacher at the end of it. *And it just doesn't work like that.* (Matthew, June, p. 86, italics ours)

In addition, the case studies proved that the impact of the programme could have been (even) larger, if all the school-based tutors (and other teachers) at the practicum schools had been more aware of the goals and approach of the progra-mme themselves: "In some cases, the classroom experiences provided by the practicum differed so markedly … from those intended by the programme that student teachers felt able to distinguish between 'real' teaching in school and teaching as it is seen to be perceived by the university-based tutors" (Wood, 2000, p. 90).

Åkerlind (2003) studied academics' conceptions of their own growth and development as a university teacher, linking these conceptions to academics' conceptions of "being a university teacher" (Åkerlind, 2004, p. 364, called 'conceptions of teaching *per se*' in Åkerlind, 2003, p. 383). Åkerlind interprets conceptions as forming a hierarchy of inclusiveness, meaning each higher level conception is a more complete experience of the studied phenomenon: "Empirically, quantitative understandings of learning have been shown to occur without an awareness of the possibility of qualitative forms of learning, but *not* vice versa ... Consequently, from a phenomenographic perspective, qualitative understandings of learning are seen as inclusive of quantitative understandings" (Åkerlind, 2003, p. 377). The standpoint of hierarchical inclusiveness is central to phenomenographic analysis: "...the hierarchy of inclusiveness that phenomenographic analysis searches for is one of increasing breadth of *awareness* of different aspects of the phenomenon being investigated" (Åkerlind, 2003, p. 378, see also Marton and Booth, 1997). Furthermore, it is consistent with our own (see chapter 1) and Entwistle and Walker's (2000) view that development in conceptions of learning and teaching – whether it be students' or teachers' development – reflects expanding awareness of aspects related to learning and teaching. To establish conceptions of growth and development, Åkerlind interviewed a diverse group of 28 academic teachers of an Australian university, a process leading to three conceptions representing different ways of experiencing growth and development as a university teacher.

1. *Teacher comfort* focused understanding of teaching development

   This conception was entirely teacher focused, and contained two sub-understandings, 1A) teaching becoming *easier* and 1B) growing *confidence* in one's abilities as a teacher.

   1A: "As far as teaching goes I look forward to the day when teaching a course isn't hard and does not occupy such a large fraction of my time. I see that as coming especially when I'm teaching a course a second or third time" (p. 381)

   1B: "There's still a lot of growth in teaching that I can make. I want to be so comfortable with teaching that I can walk out there with hardly any preparation and deliver a wonderful lecture" (p. 381).

2. *Teaching practice* focused understanding of teaching development

   This conception as well was teacher focused, but "the experiential focus has *expanded* to include teaching practices as well as feelings. The intention is to become more effective as a teacher" (p. 381, italics ours). Teacher effectiveness was seen in terms of student satisfaction: "It's just like the student is here as a customer to get some services and I have to provide these services to the best quality I can" (p. 382).

   2: "I've always asked colleagues if I can attend their classes, and actually I've done that a lot. They've been like models to me. I want o be as good as they—the way they speak, the way they articulate ideas, the way they organise lectures, the way they deliver them, the techniques they use..." (p. 382)

3. *Student learning* focused understanding of teaching development
   This third conception indicated "a critical expansion in the experience to include awareness of developmental changes for students, in terms of student learning outcomes and their development as learners in the subject. I call this an expansion because, while students' experiences of teaching and learning become the primary focus of awareness (rather than the teacher's experience), there is also awareness of the potential for changes in the teacher's feelings and skills, as in the previous categories." (p. 382–383).
   3: In talking about the usefulness of observing other people's teaching, an academic remarked "because you see, well you're observing, you're seeing the effect it has on you, as somebody who is a potential learner and you also are, having taught for a while, you see what they are attempting to do from the technique that they are adopting. So you see it from both ends, and you then see the reaction it has on you as a potential learner and you try to discern whether that's a technique that will adapt itself." (p. 383).

In line with the standpoint of viewing the categories as forming a hierarchy of inclusiveness, Åkerlind (2003) stated that "the experience of growth and development represented by categories higher in the hierarchy includes awareness of the aspects of growth and development represented by categories lower in the hierarchy, though these aspects need not be the primary focus of the experience, tending to be in the background rather than in the foreground of awareness" (p. 383). These three understandings (conceptions) of growth and development were related to the four conceptions of teaching *per se* found for the studied academics: 1) Teacher transmission focus—teachers imparting information and students absorbing it, 2) Teacher-student relations focus—teachers developing good relations with students leading to satisfaction about teaching, 3) Student engagement focus—involving students in active learning activities, and 4) Student learning focus—encouraging students to think critically and originally. Broadly these four conceptions of teaching match our own learning-teaching conceptions 2 to 4. As with the conceptions of growth and development, Åkerlind saw these categories forming a hierarchy of inclusiveness, with the focus expanding from 1 through 4 from content transmission towards student learning.

The relationships between conceptions of growth and development and conceptions of teaching were summarised in Figure 4 of Åkerlind (p. 386), which showed that

- the 'teacher transmission' conception of teaching was aligned with a growth conception of teacher comfort,
- the two teaching conceptions 'teacher-student relations' and 'student engagement' were both aligned with two conceptions of growth, 'teacher comfort' *and* 'teaching practice', and finally, that
- the 'student learning' conception of teaching was related to both 'teaching practice' *and* 'student learning' growth conceptions.

The fact that the first three – teacher focused – teaching conceptions were related to teacher focused growth conceptions, and the student focused growth conception only emerged in relation with the fourth – student learning focused – teaching conception, led Åkerlind to conclude that "increasingly sophisticated understandings of teaching tend to be associated with increasingly sophisticated understandings of teaching development." (2003, p. 386). Åkerlind noted that the student learning conception of teaching was also related to a teacher focused conception of growth, but within the concept of hierarchy of inclusiveness this phenomenon is not problematic: "the 'either/or' relationship between conceptions of teaching .... is reconceived as an 'and' relationship, and it ceases to be a surprise that student-focused conceptions of teaching may be combined with teacher-focused conceptions of teaching development" (2003, p. 387–388). We have come to a similar conclusion in chapter 4. On the other hand, and to circumvent the danger of using only a potentially circular argument, the issue of why these apparent inconsistencies between conceptions of related phenomena appear, might also lie in (internal or external) constraints, for instance a training programme for epistemologically sophisticated teachers focusing on 'tips and tricks'. Or it may even refer to re-interpreting an already familiar conception (e.g. the teaching practice focused growth conception) in a qualitatively different (more sophisticated) way. In the latter case it is not the teaching-practice-as-performed (tips and tricks) that is important, but the teaching-practice-as-meant (e.g. Walker's multiply inclusive teaching). Either way, Åkerlind concluded that "in the area of teaching-related phenomena ... an expanding awareness of phenomena related to teaching and learning may follow a predictable direction, with a broader awareness of aspects of teaching preceding a broader awareness of aspects of student learning, approaches to teaching and growth and development as a teacher" (2003, p. 388).

What's in it for the teacher?

In Trigwell et al. (1999) the authors developed a model linking teacher thinking to student thinking (Figure 1, p. 60) and so found an omission in the research on teacher thinking. In the student learning literature evidence has been found regarding relationships between students' conceptions of learning, their approaches to learning and their learning outcomes. For teachers, the latter matching concept – the teachers' teaching outcomes – had not been studied to their knowledge: ".... we have found no research reporting on the outcomes for teachers from their approaches to teaching" (p. 68). This challenge has been taken on by Åkerlind.

In 2004, Åkerlind published a study describing in more detail the perceived teaching outcomes for teachers with various conceptions of being a university teacher. The study is closely related to Åkerlind's 2003 study: it is based on the same 28 university teachers, elaborating on the four teaching conceptions *per se* found and relating these to the perceived benefits for teachers and students. Referring back to the four teaching conceptions *per se* described above, Åkerlind found that teachers with

- a 'teacher transmission' conception of teaching gained either nothing (when they were familiar with the material) or new content knowledge (if they encountered content that they were less familiar with):

  "... But the reason I like to teach is because I found that in some students' case it is fun. In other words, I can think about things from one point of view and probably I know 90% of it, but the students do teach me the rest, 10% to reach 100%, and that makes me improve in knowledge and teaching. ...

... but I have to say, nowadays .... I don't get as much feedback as I had before and that disappointed me, a little bit ... More like a one way transfer now. You teach them everything you know, but really you can't get any feedback from them so you can improve yourself."(Åkerlind, 2004, p. 367)

- either of the two teaching conceptions 'teacher-student relations' and 'student engagement' gained new content knowledge *and* a sense of satisfaction or enjoyment from the teaching experience:

  "... I'm more interested in what I can give them as a teacher than as a lecturer... Enthusiasm for pursuing something. Encouraging engagement, I suppose. ...

  Why is that important for me? Because it certainly makes the teaching process more enjoyable and interesting ... The hour just goes quickly and you have enjoyed it and they have got pleasure out of it. They will say that. And there is group dynamics and I think that's really nice." (2004, p. 368, example from the 'student engagement' conception),

- a 'student learning' conception of teaching gained new content knowledge (occasionally), enjoyment *and* "an opportunity to extend his/her own understanding of the area" (2004, p. 369):

  "... So, this area of knowledge you've been wrestling with and cultivating, and you too are being cultivated by it, and you become entangled in it. The classroom becomes the area where you disentangle it, where you share whatever you've been learning with others. And I think the greatest thing about that is, once you tell or disseminate it in the classroom, suddenly it becomes something else that everyone owns or appropriates it with you, and I think that is fairly dynamic..." (2004, p. 369).

In this hierarchy of inclusiveness of the teacher's perceived outcome one can see that epistemological development has a definite benefit for the teacher, namely enduring enjoyment in teaching and changing understanding of one's own area of expertise. So this may prove that teachers' epistemological development does not only affect students, but it has an intrinsic worth for teachers themselves as well, it can keep them fresh and enthused about the career they chose: "It seems likely that the sense of satisfaction, enjoyment and development in content understanding that forms part of some academics experiences of being a teacher would encourage a commitment to teaching that would not be felt by academics who experience little personal benefit from teaching" (Åkerlind, 2004, p. 374).

Linking Teacher Thinking and Student Thinking

In the above sections we have first discussed studies regarding teachers' epistemological beliefs about teaching. Here we found a lack of detail, which we feel is unfortunate and has hampered understanding of teacher thinking. In the second section we discussed studies viewing teaching from a different school of thought, teachers' conceptions of (good) teaching, which gave us ideas and models to form a more elaborate model of teachers' epistemological development. This attempt was supported by earlier work by Entwistle and Walker in particular. Below we propose a model linking teacher thinking to our own model of student thinking regarding teaching and learning. Our proposition here is that teacher thinking matches student thinking, for - as we quoted Yero before - "...what are teachers if not grownup versions of those [students]?" (2002, p. 22).

Table 5.6. The parallel views of students and teachers on learning, teaching and knowing

	Student thinking on learning and teaching		*Teacher thinking on teaching and knowing*	
	Learning conception	*Teaching conception*	*Epistemological belief*	*Teaching conception*)*
1	Increasing knowledge	Imparting clear/well structured knowledge		Broadcasting[†]
2	Memorising	Transmitting structured knowledge (acknowledging receiver)	Positivist	Transmitting structured knowledge (acknowledging receiver)
3	Reproductive understanding/ application or Application foreseen	Interacting and Shaping		Interaction and Shaping
4	Understanding subject matter	Challenging to think for yourself / developing a way of thinking		Facilitating understanding and building expertise
5	Widening horizons	Dialogue teaching	Constructivist	Travelling with equals
6	Growing self awareness	Mutual trust and authentic relationships: Caring		Nurturing the mind garden

*) *source*: Van Rossum and Hamer, 2004
†) *source*: Fox (1983).

The first two columns of Table 5.6 summarise our model as presented in chapter 1, the third column reflects the literature discussed in the first section of this chapter about teacher beliefs. The most right column is the summary of the studies regarding conceptions of teaching as we interpreted the communalities between them and the relationship of these communalities with our own learning-teaching conception model based on student thinking.

Consequently, this proposed developmental model of teacher/student thinking proves that for any educational innovation to succeed it is necessary to consider the teachers' beliefs as closely as – and in relationship to – those beliefs the innovation wants to foster in the students. To close this chapter, we would like to repeat our answer to Yero's earlier question whether it is reasonable and necessary "to spend at least as much effort understanding teaching 'styles' as is spent studying learning 'styles'? To admit teachers are *as different as the students* in their classes?" (Yero, 2002, p. 8, italics ours). We feel that the answer is, 'Yes, it is both reasonable and definitely necessary'. So we disagree deeply with Kember (1997), and agree with Åkerlind that "...we may still have much to learn about the various facets of .... teaching" (2004, p. 373).

Conclusions

In the studies reviewed in this chapter it is obvious that teachers differ, sometimes dramatically, in their views on knowledge and knowing, the best way for students to benefit from education, how to motivate and influence their students to enjoy their studies and to perform well academically. In epistemological belief literature, teachers are often split between traditional (or empiricist) and more constructivist views on knowledge, knowing, learning and teaching (Brickhouse, 1989, 1990; Linder, 1992; Lederman, 1999; Quinlan, 1999, 2000; Wineburg, 2001; Hashweh, 1996, to name a few), a split that is also usually characterised as opposing each other in teacher versus student centeredness. Some studies recognise intermediate ways of knowing (e.g. Brickhouse, 1989), some but not all describe these mixed or intermediate ways of knowing in detail, linking them to teaching practices (e.g. White, 2000; Martinez et al., 2001; Tsai, 2002, 2007).

The most common view on teaching can be characterised as **traditional and positivist**. Using metaphors as an indicator for personal views on teaching and learning, Yero (2002), Martinez et al. (2001) and Tsai (2002) found that between 40 to 55 percent of experienced teachers expressed beliefs consistent with a traditional positivist view on learning and teaching. A traditional positivist teacher believes in truth and certainty of (scientific) knowledge, interpreting scientific theories as representing truths about reality. Fundamentally, they interpret the body of scientific knowledge as an accumulation of predetermined procedures and facts constituting reality, not describing it. The goal of education for such teachers is to transmit this body of knowledge (which *is* reality), and learning then is accumulating and reproducing established truths passed down from credible sources. Occasionally such teachers attempt to invite students to expand on scientific knowledge, without really questioning the basic assumption that knowledge equals reality, but mostly the students are seen as passive members in the student-teacher relationship (Martinez et al., 2001). Very often teaching is very teacher-centred and it is characterised by high speed teaching or pressures to cover the (prescribed) content (e.g. Linder, 1992). Such teachers focus on providing information – most often by one-way lectures – and reproduction oriented testing, students are expected to work hard and get good grades (Tsai, 2002, 2007), and grades are an effective way to motivate students (Stipek et al., 2001). At the most extreme the teacher is a showman, an illusionist who entertains the audience (students) without letting them see *how it is done* (e.g. Lyons, 1990), in other instances the teacher obstructs anything but reproductive learning by making student mistakes almost impossible (e.g. Jean in Martens, 1992) or reducing questions to a 'fill in the blanks' exercise (e.g. Ken in Maor and Taylor, 1995). Very often these teachers are highly regarded by management, parents and students (e.g. Martens, 1992; Lyons, 1990) because they have the teaching-learning situation totally under control.

The second most common type of views on teaching and learning recognised in studies on teacher epistemology are the constructivist views (about 40% of experienced teachers profess to this type of thinking, Martinez et al., 2001). For **constructivist teachers**, knowledge is constantly being re-invented, the goal of education is not to transmit a body of knowledge constituting reality, but to engage students in a process designed to make them think about how 'facts' come about, how theories are made, how observation is unavoidably coloured by theory or expectations: in short to teach them *how to think* and perhaps even to *think about thinking*. Scientific theory to them then is a tool, a tentative model designed to provide adequate (or better) solutions to old questions, to solve new problems, to predict new avenues of study and to provide insight into new ways of understanding (e.g. Ms. Lawson in Brickhouse 1989, 1990; David in Tsai, 2002; Stipek et al., 2001). Such teachers do not eliminate lecturing from their repertoire, but alternate between more traditional instruction activities such as lecturing, tutorial practice exercises and in-class exams, and constructivist instruction activities such as small group inquiry activities, discussions aimed at addressing students' prior knowledge and their misconceptions, and the application of scientific knowledge in everyday situations (e.g. Tsai, 2007). When teaching from a constructivist epistemology, the teacher is much more aware of students as individuals with their own interpretation of reality who come into the classroom with preconceptions about what and how they are going to learn: students' understanding is the focus, not the teacher's control of the teaching-learning situation. In the latter we may have captured the aspect of constructivist teaching and learning most difficult to understand and implement: letting students develop their own thinking and independence in learning without leaving them out in the cold: in short, implementing **mentored learning**.

In-between these two most common beliefs about teaching, some studies recognise a more **process oriented approach** to teaching (e.g. Tsai, 2002). For these teachers teaching science is an activity focusing on the process of problem solving and scientific knowledge is seen as facts discovered through following the scientific system. Such teachers stress the application of scientific knowledge they provide, and usually include a measure of group work to facilitate students learning how to apply the knowledge.

A fourth set of teacher beliefs more sophisticated than those of constructivist teachers in epistemological literature is described in Martinez et al. (2001). These beliefs may prove to be fairly rare in the current teaching body (Martinez et al. found only 5% of experienced teachers viewing teaching in this way), but they may become more frequent as more student-teachers are brought up in the constructivist pedagogy (22% in prospective teachers, Martinez et al., 2001). In this **socio-historic approach** the mind of the learner depends on dialogic exchanges and learning is a result of a community of learners (Beishuizen, 2004).

Comparing these descriptions to our own model of student thinking we see that empiricist teachers often express a view on learning, scientific knowledge and teaching that is consistent with learning-teaching conception 2. The less commonly described process oriented teacher seems to view learning and teaching in a way that completes the picture of good teaching to match the way students view it from learning-teaching conception 3. Constructivist teachers have much in common with learning-teaching conception 4, with the focus on learning a way of thinking, the scientific procedure. The least often described epistemological category can be recognised as teachers teaching from learning-teaching conception 5, with dialogue in teaching and learning. There is some evidence that teachers' teaching beliefs also reflect changes in current views on the nature of the discipline (Quinlan, 1999), with younger teachers on average more often viewing teaching from a more constructivist viewpoint (e.g. Martinez et al., 2001; Quinlan, 1999), but other studies seem to point in a completely opposite direction, with pre-service teachers functioning overwhelmingly within the reproductive range of teaching beliefs (White, 2000).

Initially in phenomenography, teacher thinking was perceived as basically dichotomous (Larsson, 1983), with teachers differing most in the control they exerted in the classroom and the role of students in knowing. In about a decade and a half, the different ways teachers were found to view teaching and learning had grown to five or six (as reviewed by Kember, 1997). These conceptions of teaching could be grouped into two main orientations: a set of two mostly reproductive conceptions characterised by a teacher centeredness and content orientation, and a set of two (or three) more student centred and learning oriented teaching conceptions. The place of an intermediate teaching conception, aimed at teacher-student interaction and apprenticeship, was not clear at that time.

The two reproduction oriented teaching conceptions were Imparting information or **Broadcasting** – without paying too much attention to the recipient by the way – and **Transmitting structured information** – with a recognition of the recipient as a player expected to catch the ball, and the teacher responsible to make the ball catchable. Here we see exactly the characteristics present in learning-teaching conceptions 1 and 2. The intermediate teaching conception (Kember, 1997) is characterised by significant **teacher-student interaction**, with the teacher believing that students must become more active in learning. Students are put to work on many exercises while provided with clear instructions and guidelines how to proceed in order to reach specific, well defined outcomes in a specific and well defined way. Students are moulded, and shaping is a preferred teaching strategy in learning-teaching conception 3. So where Kember was unsure where to put this category, we would situate it on the teacher centred, content and reproduction oriented side of the watershed.

The more constructivist teaching conceptions focus on **Facilitating student understanding** and the application of knowledge to new, more complex problems requiring flexible, non-algorithmic use of knowledge – learning-teaching conception 4 – and on **Conceptual change**, helping students become aware of their own views and to expand these views – widening horizons, or learning-teaching conception 5. Kember clustered a sixth teaching conception found by Samuelowicz and Bain

(1992) with Conceptual change. But on closer reflection it would seem that, as this teaching conception, **Intellectual development**, emphasised an authentic student-teacher relationship and a disregard for teaching procedures, Samuelowicz and Bain found the rare sixth teaching conception using qualitative as well as quantitative approaches. Not only they found this sixth conception, Pratt (1992) described the social ideological variant of the sixth learning-teaching conception as well. Kember found both these categories difficult to place, but we recognise both descriptions as part of the sixth learning-teaching conception and would place them together on the far side of the watershed.

Not only are all the categories recognisable using a model of student thinking, teachers do not mirror the views of students in the sense that they complement student thinking. No indeed, teachers describe their views on learning and teaching from the same standpoint students do, only differing in the role each player fulfils in the teaching-learning situation. For instance, in the reproductive teaching conceptions, teachers act exactly the same towards experts and teaching material as they expect students to act towards them: acceptance of established truths passed on to them. It seems **teachers are indeed students grown up** (Yero, 2002), and functioning somewhat further along the track of intellectual development. But we must add, in many cases a lot less further than we might have expected, and sometimes teachers are even overtaken by students on the intellectual highway with detrimental effects on student learning (see chapter 8).

An interesting finding underpinning our positioning of the watershed is provided by Samuelowicz and Bain (2001), where they find that although "providing and facilitating understanding" (learning-teaching conception 3) and "helping students develop expertise" (learning-teaching conception 4) are adjacent, it would be difficult to construct two consecutive conceptions that are more different from each other on the dimensions they used to categorise teacher interviews (Samuelowicz and Bain, 1992, 2001). A finding that was confirmed again in cluster analysis.

A final remark on the transmission oriented views on teaching where students are mostly not included as an actor in the learning-teaching process: Gow and Kember (1993) remark that this most common view on teaching in formal education (and perhaps in society at large) seems to be *absent* from the literature about teaching models. It seems that theory formation about teaching has long failed to consider this most common and epistemologically naïve approach, in-depth knowledge of which might have added significantly to understanding less than successful implementations of educational innovations.

In all the studies reviewed here, we find that the majority of teachers at all levels, including academic and other higher education, view teaching and learning in a fundamentally reproductive way. They describe good teaching in a way that is consistent with the expectations of students at the same level of epistemological sophistication. A minority has been able to cross the watershed, into reasoned thinking and learning-teaching conception 4, which only confirms our hypothesis that it is this particular move that is the most disturbing, and most difficult one to make. However, it would seem that for (higher) education to attain its goals, it is a necessary move for *all* teachers to make (see chapter 10).

Quite a large body of research suggests that teaching practice is highly influenced by the epistemological beliefs or conceptions of the teacher. In particular the effects on teaching practice with regard to the measure of teacher versus student-centeredness are clear. Epistemologically less sophisticated teachers being most often teacher-centred, and thinking, speaking en teaching in transmission terms influencing all aspects of the teaching-learning practice including the use of teaching materials such as books, educational software or multimedia materials, and the position of demonstrations and practice in the curriculum, etcetera (e.g. Schraw and Olafson, 2002; Martens, 1995; Maor and Taylor, 1995; Tsai, 2007).

However, the **relationship** between epistemological beliefs or teaching concept-tions and **teaching practice** is not symmetrical. In keeping with Hashweh's (1996) finding that more sophisticated teachers have access to a greater range of teaching strategies, it seems that more constructivist teachers can use both traditional trans-missive strategies as well as teaching practices more aimed at constructing meaning (Maor and Taylor, 1995; Wineburg 2001). In addition, epistemological sophisticated teachers may run into any number of obstacles preventing them to teach in a way consistent with their views (see below). On the other hand traditional, positivist teachers almost invariably and exclusively use traditional teaching strategies aimed at knowledge transference and reproduction of knowledge. This means that the answer to the question of the alignment of teacher beliefs/conceptions and teacher practices is not a simple yes or no, but it depends. The result is that, as with student learning, it is easier to move teachers towards content and transmission oriented ways of teaching – for both epistemologically sophisticated as unsophisticated teachers have access to these skills – than it is to foster constructivist teaching for the simple reason that less epistemologically sophisticated teachers do not possess the skills or the understanding to implement such teaching.

So what is the effect of these clearly very different ways of teaching on **student learning**? For as Prosser and Trigwell stated, all this interest in teacher thinking "would be for naught" if we are unable to find a link between the way teachers teach and the way students learn. Well, we can rest assured, there is a clear link, although the relationship – as with teacher beliefs/conceptions and teaching practice – again is not symmetrical. Not only that, there is ample evidence that the measure of constructivist beliefs expressed in teaching practice has a differential effect on student learning (Tsai, 2007): the more explicitly constructivist the teaching, the larger the expression of constructivist student beliefs as well. However, education is not only about cognition and epistemology, it is the whole of the classroom atmosphere that creates and sends explicit as well as hidden messages that define the students' "most pervasive lessons. These lessons are about respect, values, the nature of knowledge, thought processes, self-worth and expectations" (Yero, 2002).

Traditional, positivist, content and teacher oriented teaching almost always leads to low quality (surface oriented) learning outcomes - factual and sometimes incomplete knowledge, inconsistent and poor understanding of concepts, student beliefs in certain and proven knowledge handed down by experts (e.g. Linder, 1992), poor inquiry skills (Maor and Taylor, 1995), passive students who limit their questions to procedural ones or requests for additional clarification (e.g.

Brickhouse, 1990; Stipek et al., 2001). Teachers expect students to be able to recall facts, procedures and techniques and to perform much practiced tasks faultlessly (e.g. Prosser and Trigwell, 1999).

The learning outcomes associated with constructivist teaching are more often meaning directed and therefore of a higher epistemological quality. Such learning outcomes include complex and creative investigations (e.g. Maor and Taylor, 1995), active student participation in inquiry, discussions and the formulation of questions regarding the nature of concepts (e.g. Brickhouse, 1989, 1990) and a questioning attitude towards teaching materials provided and looking for other sources (e.g. Maor and Taylor, 1995; Quinlan, 1999). These teachers convey clearly different demands to students, namely the expectation that they can perform well and produce high quality work, that interaction is a large part of learning, and that understanding is best measured by "purposeful transformation of knowledge to address open-ended issues or problems not previously encountered" (Samuelowicz and Bain, 2002).

Students exposed to constructivist teaching often view science as a problem solving activity (e.g. Brickhouse, 1989, 1990), however, Lederman (1999) expects that this latter aspect requires that teachers address issues regarding the nature of science and scientific inquiry explicitly, and that inquiry activities alone are insufficient to cause conceptual change learning. The fact that students are capable to respond to a teaching-learning environment geared towards more sophisticated epistemological views on knowledge, knowing and learning (Tsai, 2007) would seem to indicate that all is not "for naught", and students can indeed change when exposed to an epistemologically more sophisticated environment.

However, encouraging students towards deep-level and meaning-directed learning will prove to be much more challenging than getting students to use surface approaches to learning, for it is not only the atmosphere created in the classroom by each individual teacher that forms students' perception of knowing, learning and shapes their values. Messages regarding the desired views on knowing and learning are transmitted by departments, institutes, governments (e.g. Gow and Kember, 1993; Martens, 1992), and even society. Not only can these messages form an obstacle to higher quality student learning, when confronted with exceedingly transmission-oriented teaching, students can indeed rebel or become despondent (see chapter 8). In these cases students' deployment of meaning directed learning might even decline during the period of education, with students possibly persisting in surface learning strategies for some time in their professional life.

Variables that increase the likelihood of traditional, positivist teaching practices are first and foremost the epistemological beliefs or teaching conceptions of the teachers. If these are traditional and positivist, then teaching practice will be so too. There is another, often neglected obstacle to the development of traditional teacher beliefs towards more sophisticated beliefs, namely the fact that these teachers lack the incentive to change: managers, colleagues, students, pupils and parents as well as society as a whole perceive them to be excellent teachers in complete control of the teaching-learning situation (e.g. Martens, 1992). However, when a teacher professes to more sophisticated views on knowledge, learning and teaching, in quite a number of cases they do not teach in a way consistent with their own beliefs (e.g. Schraw and Olafson, 2002). Here we see a similar, asymmetrical relationship we encountered before when considering the relationship between students' epistemological sophistication and their study strategies that bewildered Marton and others (see the introduction of chapter 3), but which is quite consistent with the hierarchical nature of epistemological belief systems.

What then are these other **obstacles** that especially prevent teachers with a more sophisticated view on knowledge, learning and teaching from teaching in a way consistent with their beliefs, usually meaning that these teachers will teach in a more traditional and more teacher-centred way. Obstacles often found are lack of experience with classroom management issues, time constraints and pressures to "cover the syllabus" (e.g. Schraw and Olafson, 2002), lack of professional culture and traditional assessment and evaluation practices (e.g. teaching to the test issues), lack of confidence in a teacher's own subject expertise and self-efficacy, a power struggle with students with regard to the measure of control in the classroom (Larsson, 1983), parents' expectations and pressures from school management to conform to a more traditional teaching practice (e.g. Martens, 1992; Lotter, 2007), the need to meet students at their current (perceived) epistemological level (e.g. Quinlan, 1999), and lastly perhaps unexamined personal values that interfere with the aim of consistent constructivist teaching (Yero, 2002).

To answer the question whether constructivist teachers not only teach in a different way, with different results, but really are **better teachers** requires some consensus on the meaning of better. In the current study we would propose to take *better teacher* to mean a teacher who is *at the very least* capable to address and remedy incorrect and incomplete prior student knowledge, who encourages a body of knowledge in students while training students' minds to reason well: to observe and evaluate new information critically in the light of evidence and arguments. Ideally, such teachers would also be able to inspire and motivate students to seek out the limits of their capabilities whether in the teacher's own area of study or more in general. Such an interpretation is in keeping with the meaning of the latin verb educere: to lead out, upwards or onwards to new things.

When confronted with students' incorrect interpretations, empiricist teachers will most often focus primarily on the incorrectness of the interpretation, without delving deeply into the roots of the misconception. Indeed, because these teachers are far more teacher-focused, e.g. Hashweh (1996) doubts if such teachers are really aware of the roots or the nature of the student's misconception and so they cannot use this in their strategy to redress the misconception in the classroom. Empiricist teachers often choose a strategy of repeated explanations to convince the student of the correct interpretation, a strategy not particularly aimed at conceptual change. The result most probably will be a student who accepts the interpretation of the teacher for "school science" and "book knowledge", interpreting school science and knowledge to mean a lot of memorising of sometimes incomprehensible facts and findings in order to pass. Such students need not do bad in current (higher) education, they may even attain master degrees from respected academic institutes. But students nonetheless whose initial misconceptions will probably persist in everyday life. Indeed this is often the result of what Linder calls metaphysical realist teaching (1992) which is not at all uncommon even in academic circles. Empiricist teachers further often emphasise (and thus also assess) content knowledge above analytical competence, have low expectations of students and what they are capable of (e.g. Quinlan, 1999), see only limited uses for additional sources than the textbook (e.g. Wineburg, 2001) and then only for honours or advanced students reaffirming their low expectations of students in general. Looking back at the definition of a better teacher above, we feel we cannot conclude otherwise than that such teachers, even when highly respected, do not encourage learning of sufficient quality for higher education.

Well, how well are constructivist teachers doing then? Firstly, constructivist teachers are more consciously aware that students have prior knowledge. When confronted with incorrect prior knowledge, they more often use it in a discussion to point out inconsistencies, using not only repeated explanation of the correct interpretation, but using other student knowledge and their own knowledge about the nature of the misconception to refute it and to convince the student of the need of conceptual change (e.g. Hashweh, 1999; Wineburg, 2001), leading a student through an argumentation ending in the more correct conception. Not only do they use more effective strategies, often simultaneously, in addressing student misconceptions, they use more different and more effective teaching strategies at all times in the teaching-learning process while they are able to vary teacher control of the learning process as well (e.g. Brickhouse, 1989, 1990; Maor and Taylor, 1995; Hashweh, 1999; Wineburg, 2001). Constructivist teachers are not only more versatile themselves, they see more uses for additional source materials and more different options regarding teaching materials than empiricist teachers (e.g. Wineburg, 2001). Constructivist teachers value analytical process *as much as* content knowledge, for without content knowledge, there is nothing to build an analysis on. Constructivist teachers expect students to be able – or at least willing – to perform well and sometimes admit that theirs is a "tough kind of love" but one necessary to true education (Samuelowicz and Bain, 2001). Initially such teachers may experience resistance to their teaching, because students are unsure of the new demands and criteria for passing (e.g. Larsson, 1983). But very soon constructivist teachers see students responding well, with students admitting to feeling forced to learn to think according to particular rules, but obliging none the less and learning more about themselves on the way. On average, students in secondary and higher education have already proved sufficiently that they are able to find out what a teacher wants and to deliver it (e.g. Belenky et al., 1997; the current study). Here we come to the crux of the matter: if a teacher expects little independent thought from students and does not include thinking as a criterion for graduation, students see no incentive to include serious thinking in their curriculum or perhaps even in their life. Then even higher education will not lead them out, onwards or upwards to new things. It will not change their way of knowing nor encourage knowing themselves in significant ways. Thinking well, examining one's own prejudices and misconceptions are skills that need to be practiced, these are things that can be learned and improved. Where else to practice and improve these skills better than in interaction with real educators and mentors who encourage learning to think. So, constructivist teachers are, to all intent and purposes, the better teachers.

Consequently, if constructivist teachers are better teachers, and most teachers currently profess to empiricist beliefs or reproduction-oriented teaching conceptions, it is important to know **if teachers can change**. Well, as teachers are students grown up, and students have proved more than capable to change, then logically teachers can too. Of course, as teachers are students grown-up, we might find that changing teachers' beliefs and teaching conceptions is a challenging task as well. And indeed the literature (in this chapter and in chapter 11) would support this conclusion. What would teacher development look like? Our six-stage developmental model – which we feel describes student and teacher thinking alike – together with the models discussed in the chapters 3, 4 and the current chapter, would seem to give sufficient clues to answering that question, but there is other evidence too. On occasion, teachers have an introspective bent, and move through various stages of development without much encouragement from outside (e.g. Entwistle and Walker, 2000 Akin, 2002). Walker's discovery that in teaching he reached a deeper understanding of physics himself is not unique. This deeper understanding then leading to a more profound wonderment about the world as we perceive it and the world according to science is one very familiar to many natural scientists including the second author of the current study. But we need not rely on individuals' own impetus alone to improve the quality of teaching. A logical outcome of this review would be for educational innovators to focus not only on improving the education of students, but to focus on educating the educators as well.

Our suggestions regarding improving student education towards a more consistent constructivist nature, *without* necessarily implying large and costly restructuring of current educational systems, are the subject of chapter 10. As Judith Yero, Paul Walker and many others have discussed (see above), it is not the observed methods of education that matter, but the methods-as-meant. To uncover how teachers can change their perception of education towards more meaning directed methods-as-meant, current and future educators need to examine more closely their own views, beliefs and prejudices towards teaching and learning.

Furthermore, policy makers, educational innovators and empiricist teachers need to realise that constructivist teaching is *not* in fact teaching less, requiring *less* subject knowledge and *less* interaction. It is in reality *teaching more,* requiring deeper understanding and a different type of interaction: constructivist teaching is indeed a "tough kind of love." A love, perhaps, that teachers themselves need to experience first, before they can bestow it on their students. How and to what level to educate our educators in order to improve student learning is the subject of chapter 11.

NOTES

1 Fitzgerald and Cunningham proposed five epistemological clusters that differ in their combined stance on seven epistemological issues (2002).

2 After much work on student thinking, 'teacher thinking' became popular as a specific field of research in the early nineteen-eighties, formalised in the foundation of the International Study

Association on Teachers and Teaching (ISATT), with a first conference in 1983 at Tilburg University, Netherlands, which one of the current authors attended.

3 But his challenging attitude – playing the devil's advocate – would seem to imply that his teaching approach may not be an example of 'connected teaching' (Belenky et al., 1986).

4 This aspect is covered in our model within the teaching conception.

5 In our opinion much can be said about these vignettes, as e.g. Hofer (2002b) did before us. We have considerable difficulty with the internal consistency and coherence of these vignettes. For example, the relativist vignette contains contradictory elements, such as "one opinion is as good as another" – without mention of the role of evidence in forming an opinion, which probably led Hofer to interpret this vignette as multiplist or third level thinking – and the contention that "students can learn to think independently" which is typical of level four thinking. And the sentence "I don't believe that I can really teach my students what is important, since they all need to know different things" might even be interpreted as an expression of the rather cynical approach taken in deconstructive postmodernism (level five thinking, see section on Kegan, chapter 2).

6 A common rationale used by schools and teachers alike to *not* engage in educational reforms. See also Nelson (1999), who refers to this phenomenon as the persistence of the mythical unicorn: that there is a trade-off between covering content and teaching (important) skills.

7 The third teacher, Mr. McGee, provided Brickhouse with problems of interpretation, and she placed him somewhere between Cathcart and Lawson. We feel that Brickhouse, perhaps unintentionally and unknowingly, made the right decision here, as we see McGee as an exponent of multiplicity. McGee is characterized by the juxtaposition of a strong believe in 'the [objective] scientific method' and the 'infusion' of subjectivity in 'true science': "I would say that *true* science is subjective ... you taking something they've done and then adding yourself to it." (1989, p. 444). In addition, McGee professed to the belief that "scientific theories were not the absolute truth, but that they were close to it" (p. 447) exemplifying the temporary uncertainty acceptable to multiplists.

8 In Belenky et al. 1986 they use the term silence, but later renamed this to silenced.

9 Although some theories prove to be incorrect (or incomplete), they are not always discarded completely. Usually because these theories are a good approximation of, and thus very useful in, everyday situations. See Nelson, 1999, quoted in chapter 1.

10 In light of the remark about uncertified teachers, it is interesting to note that in recent years it has become necessary to hire under-qualified teachers to teach science in secondary education in the Netherlands, because there is a significant (and growing) shortage of qualified science teachers!

11 Metaphysical realism belongs to one of the five epistemological clusters mentioned in Fitzgerald and Cunningham (2002).

12 While often the 'unnatural' and 'paradoxical' are reserved for science and mathematics, the experience of scientific 'unnaturalness' can also be found in the humanities, consider for instance "Historical Thinking and Other Unnatural Acts" by Sam Wineburg (2001).

13 For the non-physicists among our readers: the Lorentz contraction refers to the length of an object that is observed by a moving observer. The contraction only becomes noticeable at speeds approaching fractions of the speed of light, which is about 300,000,000 metres per second: e.g. a 5% shortening of an object's perceived length is obtained at speeds 0.3 times that of light, that is at a velocity of 324,000,000 kilometres per hour.

14 Practicing these skills, students learn to work like 'real' scientists through asking questions or formulating hypotheses, designing investigations, collecting evidence and using it for drawing conclusions.

15 Science requires a particular, often less 'natural' way of seeing things (Wolpert, 1994). When students enter science classes, they already can have alternative, 'everyday' views on scientific concepts. When not acknowledged, these views may make (real) understanding of scientific concepts difficult.

16 Hashweh studied school and college level teachers (Hashweh, 1996).

17 According to Wolpert (1994) practicing science is only possible after adopting the (peculiar) Western scientific way of thinking. So within science teaching, Wolpert would not expect culture to make a difference.

[18] This chapter was published earlier in 1993 by Wineburg and Wilson (*American Educational Research Journal*, vol. 30, pp. 729–770).

[19] While the view on the problematic classroom situation was measured as one of the epistemological dimensions (namely simple vs. complex) we discuss this study as if it is a design with independent and dependent variables, respectively the students' epistemological beliefs and their views of a problematic classroom situation.

[20] While the category is listed as Reflected Relative in Table III (p. 290) the correct and consistent label, Reflective Relative, can be found many times in the text, e.g. on page 287, 298, 299, 300 etcetera.

[21] This approach to mathematics as a learner-focused, creative, constructive process and a conceptual structure enabling students to personally construct mathematical knowledge, reminds us of the 'reinvention principle' of Freudenthal and the vision on mathematical instruction advocated by the Freudenthal Institute in Utrecht (the Netherlands).

[22] In the past decades we have asked a very similar question, "What do you mean by 'learning'?". However, we always added the same elaboration, asking students to describe when they felt they had "really learnt something", emphasising our focus on their own *best and personal* experience of learning.

[23] Yero (2002) puts the importance of 'official curricula' in perspective where she remarks that a "school may publish its goals, objectives, and standards to represent its *intended* purposes and subject matter coverage. However, any uniformity outside of those published lists is largely mythical." (p. 1).

[24] Contrary to our practice, occasionally we have not been able to quote Tsai verbatim. We felt the need to change or insert words here and there to improve the readability of the English language text.

[25] Tsai uses the term 'nested epistemologies' to indicate a large measure of congruence or coherence between beliefs, we prefer the term alignment, see also Biggs (1996).

[26] We prefer the developmental stance of our own epistemological model (and those of others, see chapter 2) to interpret Tsai's data and so reach a somewhat different conclusion than Tsai.

[27] Larsson reported that for 5 teachers it was not possible to identify their conception of teaching.

[28] There may be more interpretations of (real) understanding than become apparent from the quotes used for this conception of teaching (see also chapter 1). Indeed, Samuelowicz and Bain (1992) discuss alternative interpretations of understanding: e.g. understanding concepts and their inter-relationships, or understanding as a way of thinking within a particular perspective (or discipline). The deep approach to reading texts (van Rossum and Schenk, 1984) includes a definition of understanding as connecting with the intention of the author.

[29] We have collected students' views on their 'ideal assessment' format or questions together with their views on learning and 'good' teaching, to make this link for student thinking. We will report on these data separately from the current study.

[30] The data used here come from studies which were co-authored by Philip Taylor (Trigwell et al., 1994; Prosser et al., 1994).

[31] This study was discussed in Prosser and Trigwell (1999), where only a single-factor solution was presented. The interpretation of the single-factor solution may differ from the interpretation of the two-factor solution.

[32] Marton and Booth (1997) refer to a qualitative study that comes to the same conclusion (Patrick, 1992). Patrick's study expands on the work of e.g. Quinlan (1999) and Wineburg (2001) by showing the effect of teacher thinking on students' learning.

[33] We introduced the notion of expanded awareness in Chapter 1.

[34] Such paradoxical issues as the relativeness of time or the fact that "the underlying nature of seemingly solid objects involves strange waves of probability" (Entwistle and Walker, 2000, p. 347).

CHAPTER 6

THE CONTEXT OF THE EMPIRICAL STUDIES

The current students would probably pity us if they could see scenes from the 1947-1948 course. Filleting a wooden chicken or sole in evening dress. Knowing the origin and preparation qualities of 10 or 12 types of rice. Recognising 8 types of coffee beans and their characteristics. Picking strings of wool, cotton, linen or (very new) suran and velon from a piece of cloth and determining the utility. Silly stuff? Not in those years. ... Of course our training was not very broad and pretty craft oriented, but I really feel that the school should not become too narrowly managerial. When staying in major hotels, it has happened to me a number of times that 5 or 6 neat youngsters with badges and impressive looking stacks of paper walked by my table before someone would ask me if he/she could be of service.

(John Fagel, student during 1947–1948, Hotelschool The Hague, 2004, p. 55, translation ours)

In this chapter we will first give some background information about the Hotelschool The Hague and her students, painting the context of our study and a background for the results described in the next chapters. The Hotelschool is located in Scheveningen, a small seaside resort bordering The Hague, the governmental centre of the Netherlands and its third largest city. The Hague is also home to all Embassies to the Netherlands, and many international organisations. It is well known as the residence of the International Court of Justice, the International Criminal Court, and it is the fourth United Nations city of the world. In 1995, Boutros Boutros Ghali, the then Secretary-General of the UN, referred to The Hague as the city of peace and justice, reaffirming an ambition that the city has aspired to since the opening of the Peace Palace in 1913. Here we see the international outlook that figured prominently in the Hotelschool The Hague educational process of the last 25 years.

Below we will describe, in short, the history of the school, including its mission, some facts and figures and interweaving portraits of students. In the second section we describe the inception and development of Enterprising Learning[1] as appropriate to the current study. We finish this section with a description of Enterprising Learning as a truly developmental concept, a version of Enterprising Learning that is less relevant to the results described here, as most students in this study finished their studies before version 3.0 (see below) was conceived. In the final section we detail the data analysis procedure followed leading to the results described in chapters 7, 8 and 9.

The Hotelschool The Hague

The Hotelschool The Hague is a small scale, independent institute of higher professional education in the Netherlands, aimed at providing students with a background necessary for management positions in the international hospitality industry. One of its courses, the four-year (inter)national course, leads to an accredited Bachelor's degree in Hotel Administration (BHA). It is this course that the students that participated in the current study were following. The vast majority of these students entered the school immediately following secondary education.

Dutch higher education is divided in institutes for university or academic education and institutes of higher professional education, in Dutch "Hogescholen". Internationally, the Hogescholen are referred to as Universities of Applied Sciences and their bachelor's degrees comprise of four years. In general Hogeschool graduates are assumed to have a somewhat less academic, and more practical outlook on their profession than university graduates. As one university teacher said about graduates from higher professional education entering university, "At the Hogeschool it's all very different, that's what students tell me. At the Hogeschool theories are presented and that's about it. Here [at university] they are also introduced to the critique on these theories and to the fact that some of a theory's assumptions may be not very well researched yet. I see them get into trouble. They are not used to taking different viewpoints. They get a case about an issue in a company and they tend to apply one theory. They assume that this theory will be the *right one* to use, because it was thought out by smart people" (Zuidweg, 2003, p. 29–30, translation and italics ours). And students concur, "I experienced the transition from higher professional education to university very consciously. Only after having worked on three cases, did I suddenly realise that there might be more than one answer. The one-and-only right theory does not exist. You can look at organisations wearing different theoretical glasses. *Then I realised very consciously, 'Oh, so this is university.'* " (Zuidweg, 2003, p. 30, translation and italics ours). Although we would not want to deny this university teacher's nor the student's experience, our own research over the years gives us reason to suspect that the epistemological differences between the two types of students are smaller than pictured here. Also Baxter Magolda's 1992 study seemed to indicate a less extreme difference between higher professional and university graduates, as in her study college graduates rarely developed beyond Transitional Knowing (learning-teaching conception 3), which is characterised by (reproductive) application and not by critical thinking.

At the time of the study, there were two other similar schools in the Netherlands, in the North (Leeuwarden) and South (Maastricht). However, the Hotelschool The Hague is the oldest of the three and already for many years it is considered a member of the elite top-three hotel schools of the world, "The Hotelschool, along with the Ecole Hôtelière de Lausanne (EHL) in Switzerland and the School of Hotel Administration at Cornell University in the USA, make up the big three international centres of hotel education. All three are recognised around the world as beacons of excellence and have turned out many of the world's top-level hotel managers " (Bignold, 2006, p. 23). The latter statement was supported by an article in the leading Dutch trade magazine Misset Horeca of 2005 claiming that in about 30 percent of the top-100 of hospitality companies in the Netherlands, graduates of the Hotelschool The Hague fill management positions (Hotelschool The Hague, 2005).

History

The school was founded in 1929 as a one-year course for personnel in hotels, restaurants and cafés, founded by Horecaf, the employers' organisation for the hospitality industry (Hotelschool The Hague, 2000, p. 27). In 1938 women first entered the course, and while they were successful students, until the 1970's their number remained fairly small in part due to difficulties for women in attaining jobs at the appropriate level at that time. In 1953, the first two-year course started, and by 1959 the course was expanded to cover three years. During these years, the school became officially recognised by the government, making it eligible for government funding. From the start, the location of the school moved several times, ending finally in 1966 at the location Brusselselaan in Scheveningen, which is also the location where the students in the current study spent their study time. From 1971 onwards female enrolment increased markedly, nearing equal participation in the nineteen-eighties.

In the early eighties, the first four-year curriculum was introduced. Throughout this study this four-year curriculum is referred to as the *old* or *traditional curriculum*. In six of the eight semesters, students participated in practicals and in various courses aimed at business management subjects (e.g. finance, marketing, personnel and organisation) and support subjects (e.g. languages, statistics). The courses were given in a mainly traditional way and increased in level of complexity in the higher semesters, from introductory to advanced (management) level. Two semesters, the fourth and eighth, were reserved for (external) internships. By 1989, about 90% of these internships were completed outside the Netherlands: "From the USA to Hong Kong, from Australia to Great Britain. Many large internationally operating hotel chains visit the school to present themselves and to recruit students" (Hotelschool The Hague, 2004, p. 26, translation ours). By 1989, the school had about 900 students.

In 1997 the old curriculum was replaced by a new curriculum, referred to as Enterprising Learning. It is this new curriculum, in particular students' perceptions of it, that was the object of the current study.

The Hotelschool by the End of the 1990's

In the last decennium of the previous century, the educational landscape for schools for professional and vocational education changed dramatically in the Netherlands. A policy promoting mergers based on expected economy of scale advantages led to major concentrations of institutes, sometimes leading to higher education institutes of 30,000 students or more, forming Universities of Applied Sciences (in Dutch,

Hogescholen). The three Hotelschools, together with a small number of other specialized schools, put their heads together and lobbied successfully to remain independent. However, the pressure to expand and innovate was great as the Hotelschool The Hague aspired to become an internationally acclaimed "top school" aimed at business management for the hospitality industry (Hotelschool The Hague, 2004, p. 29). An example of the results of this aspiration was the introduction of the bachelor programme European Hospitality Management (EHM), an English language version of the Dutch bachelor programme. By the end of the century, the international programme comprised about 20% of the students. In the same period the school grew to about 1300 students, and the EHM programme contributed greatly to the diversification of the student population to include many different nationalities. As the school grew, the staff grew as well to more than 100 employees, about two-thirds of which were teachers. At the same time information technology made its entrance as a means to improve student-teacher and school-student communication, as well as it becoming a new resource for instruction (e.g. through internet connections and personal email for all students and teachers). Finally, to illustrate the increased international focus of the school, the Hotelschool set up (or helped set up) courses and eventually similar schools in many parts of the world: "Training courses were provided all across the globe and Hotelschool The Hague participated in the development of hotel schools. From Mongolia to Chile, from Tanzania to Macao, the Hotelschool The Hague was active everywhere" (Hotelschool The Hague, 2004, p. 32, translation ours).

Unique Features of the Hotelschool The Hague during the Study[2]

Student hostel. From the start, all students of the Hotelschool were expected to live in a school residence (student hostel), for at least part of the study time. This is very unusual for the Dutch higher education system, where university campus life with dormitories is virtually unknown. In 1992 the most recent student hostel, the Skotel, was opened. Students not only live and study there, but by running the school hotel, which is also located in the Skotel, they perform part of their practicals as well (Chênevert et al., 1993).

> [Semester] 1987–1 was characterised by [the three student hostels] Bella Vista, Paviljoen and Schakel. ... The inhabitants of Schakel lived in a wonderful building, perfectly equipped and with ballroom sized rooms! A rec room with French doors, one kitchen and shower per four students. Schakel dwellers turned out to be the more laid back types, hanging their feet over the balcony on Friday afternoon while reading the newspaper or boning up on 'nutrition'. They got better grades than the rest of us. The Paviljoen was inhabited by all sorts! In some parts of the house it was calm, in others it was never a dull moment. ... Bella Vista left a life long impression on her inhabitants. And on their parents who formed an action committee on the first day of the first semester. Alas very little actually came of all the plans for improvements, promises and commitments. Bella Vista became "Vile Bella" and remained so. Her inhabitants were

> characterised by a passionate drive to survive! All possibilities of Bella were explored to the fullest, and the building became less inhabitable by the day (but also a lot more fun). ... (Gwen van der Meer, student during 1987–1991, Hotelschool The Hague, 2004, p. 103–104, translation ours)

Student selection. In principle Dutch higher education is open to all students who have successfully completed secondary education at an appropriate level. In most cases entry to various studies is based on the subjects completed and the diploma level. Secondary education is divided into three major streams, pre-university (vwo), pre-professional (havo) and vocational (in two levels, lower = vmbo and secondary = mbo), three diplomas of which (pre-university, pre-professional and secondary vocational) give entrance to the Hotelschool (see also Appendix). A further requirement is good command of at least two (foreign) languages (English and one other European language). However, as the Hotelschool traditionally received more applicants than could possibly be taken on, it proved necessary to employ a strict and elaborate selection procedure based on information from three face-to-face interviews (with a lecturer, a senior student and a representative of the hospitality industry), the observation of a management group assignment, and a number of externally performed personality tests. Selection criteria included e.g. independence and initiative, communication and organisational skills, team spirit, a businesslike attitude, motivation towards the industry and appearance (Chênevert et al., 1993, 2000).

> Anybody who has anything to do with the hotel schools in the Netherlands, knows that there was an ongoing "vendetta" between the Hague and Maastricht. ... I personally witnessed a number of get-togethers, and what struck me was that the "Hagenezen" [students from The Hague] were much more self-confident than the "Limbo's" [students from Maastricht]. All too often it happed that those "from the south" initially registered for both schools, but had been turned away in The Hague. And of course we, the Hagenezen reminded our southern friends of that with glee. (Lutze van der Ploeg, student during 1989–1993, Hotelschool The Hague, 2004, p. 108–109, translation ours)

International internships. Within the curriculum at the Hotelschool The Hague two semesters are reserved for hands-on experience in leading hospitality and leisure industry companies. The first – practical – internship focuses on improving and expanding students' operational skills in departments such as kitchen, reception, housekeeping, etcetera. The policy for these internships was to provide placements mostly within Europe (approx. 66%, with only 5% in the Netherlands), including the Dutch Antilles (approx. 16%), with an additional advantage of practicing modern language skills (English, French, German and Spanish). A minority of students preferred and received a placement in other countries located across the world, most often in the America's and in the Far and Middle East.

> To improve my French I chose to do my [practical] internship in France. Together with a fellow semester student, I travelled to Nice! We were very

> lucky with our internship mentor, who did everything to make this not only a meaningful, but also a fun time. We worked in all departments of the Holiday Inn and spent the rest of our internship on the beach. By the end of our time there we had a house full with 10 fellow students, who had come to spend their summer break with us. (Cleo Vehmijer, student during 1988–1992, Hotelschool The Hague, 2004, p. 113–114, translation ours)

In the second – management – internship, aimed to develop students' managerial skills, students worked as assistant manager on a departmental level, for instance as assistant of the marketing and sales director, the food & beverage manager or the accommodation manager. Students were also expected to be able to analyse issues at departmental level, to provide solutions and to make suggestions on how to improve efficiency and effectiveness.

> I was offered a management internship on Bonaire. It was supposed to focus on yield management. The placement office asked me if this would be a problem, and I answered quite convincingly that this would not be the case. As finance major I should know all about this, but I felt a little bit unsure and I spent an intense week in the library to dive deeper into the subject. I travelled to Bonaire and in my intake interview the concept of yield management came up. It became clear that my internship mentor knew very little about it. I was quite relieved and I had a wonderful time. (Cleo Vehmijer, student during 1988–1992, Hotelschool The Hague, 2004, p. 115, translation ours)

Placement for the management internships was less internationally oriented, with the share of Dutch placements increasing from 25% to about half by the end of the decade. This shift was probably partly the result of students' changing perceptions of immediate job opportunities. The other management placements were distributed across the world in a way comparable to that of the practical placements.

Studying at the Hotelschool The Hague

As indicated in the previous section (see e.g. the paragraph on student selection) the students of Hotelschool The Hague are often rather unique young people, characterised by a go-getting attitude and a specific blend of flair, daring and perseverance that often proved to support them well in difficult times and in very different cultures. Below we include two more full portraits of students, one of the old curriculum, and one who participated in our current study. These portraits further illustrate the typical Hotelschool student and the experience of studying at the Hotelschool The Hague. Two portraits that include tales of culture shock, (near) disasters, daunting challenges and pushing past one's own limits to discover self-confidence.

> Coming directly from the rural area of Brabant to the Hotelschool in the Hague, a step in my life that would change my view of myself and the world forever. … Two periods during my studies that stand out in particular are my internship in Florida and my position as student-assistant in the marketing

and communication department. Let me start with my internship in Disney World in Florida. After an 8 hour flight I arrived in New York to miss my connecting flight to Orlando and I had to wait 4 hours for the next one. Arriving in Florida at last, I was surprised by Mickey Mouse himself!! That the Mouse had time to stay and wait to collect us from the airport made us feel like VIPs. This feeling of self-importance would only increase during that first week. In the introduction courses you are informed that you are one of the chosen who may – together with about fifty thousand other Cast Members (Disney does not have wage slaves) – work for the Main Mouse (Mickey). My position at Disney was that of "seater" in Citrico's, a restaurant in Disney's Grand Floridean Resort and Spa, Disney's flag ship resort. And you may have guessed, with a general manager ... from the Hotelschool The Hague. So obviously you feel you have an advantage coming from The Hague. The living experience at Disney means you share a bungalow park setting with about 4500 fellow young people, sharing your room with a total stranger, much like the first year at the Hotelschool. My roommate was from Kenya, a nice guy but with very different customs than I was used to. That is when you appreciate fully the learning experience of the Skotel, a lot of potential problems were avoided because I was accustomed to sharing with a relative stranger. In truth the seven months at Disney flew by and I learned a lot, not as much about being a "seater" but a lot about cultural diversity and how to cope with it. That was something that came in handy many a time later in my studies.

I learned a lot of useful facts during my studies, but as student-assistant I was able to apply a lot of theory I had learned and occasionally I was able to make innovations. ... The fun thing was that when I started in the department, it was in its infancy itself. I had interesting projects, such as writing a marketing plan for the Scandinavian market, focusing on Norway. This was my first plan ever that could result in someone making real investments. Although I was supervised .... and everything was checked ... this was a totally different kettle of fish than doing a project for the marketing course. I invested a lot of research time before writing and presenting a first plan. Parts of the plan were approved for implementation. I had made a selection of attractive student recruitment fairs where the Hotelschool could present itself. One of these fairs was in Oslo. Together with [the school's director, a teacher and a member of the marketing and communication department] we travelled to Oslo to promote the Hotelschool. Once in Oslo, we were unpleasantly surprised by the disappearance of our bags! They had been shipped to a warmer climate while we were standing in Oslo at -40 degrees centigrade. No hat, gloves, or winter coat, nor *Tenue de Ville*. A slight panic ensued. Luckily three days later, just before the fair started, our luggage arrived at our hotel. Despite this mixed-up start we had a really successful fair and following it the Scandinavian enrolment rose considerably. Actually, if I look back on my five years at he Hotelschool, it was a period which I thought could not just end some day. In hindsight it flew by like a shot and I still remember it fondly. A time I would not have liked to miss

> and if I had to do it again, I would not change a thing. (Antoine van den Oever, student of semester 97–2, Hotelschool The Hague, 2004, p. 117–118, translation ours)

To show that the Dutch students were not the only ones to feel challenged by the school's expectations, and to feel reassured by the trust given to them that they would perform well, we include the story of one of the first international students, Tracy Ricard, a student of the EHM course enrolling in 1994.

> We are tempted to remember our college experiences as sleeping late, getting drunk, and hunting the opposite sex as much as possible, but in truth I only remember how hard I worked and how much I studied at the Hotelschool The Hague. Don't get me wrong; I participated in my share of the fun stuff. But I was made quickly aware of how different this education was going to be as opposed to an American college, namely failing out of the Hotelschool could be fast and swift. You see, the system of taking 8–10 courses in a semester, having to pass them all in one week, and having to go into a ("intermediate") semester if you didn't [as was the case in the old curriculum], was completely unfamiliar to me as an American. I was going to have a hard enough time paying for four years of this school in a foreign country where I could only get (illegal) under the table work, let alone repeat a semester or two and pay for those extra years. But this convinced me that I was in the right school. I wanted to go to an elite institution that would make me competitive in the working world. And the Hotelschool curricular format didn't appear to be (f***ing) around. I remember in the first semester we had English that was compulsory. Although I had been out of high school a year before entering The Hotelschool, I figured I had a unique advantage. I was the only foreign national that had English as … native language. Naturally this was going to be a breeze for me, until what seemed as if every lecturer and every Dutch student came up to me and squealed, "You didn't pass English? An AMERICAN!?". Or what they probably were thinking "a stupid American". But I appreciated that about the school and its intimacy as well as the Dutch people's directness. It definitely humbled me and quickly got through to me that I was going to have to give it my all just to "pass" at this school. I think what was most exceptional about my education at the Hotelschool was the small intimate class rooms with eccentric lecturers who were teaching from recent practice, not 20 year old theory. Lecturers … were especially kind to me. I always had the feeling with every lecturer that they wanted to be there and that they wanted to teach things that were fresh and relevant. The expression "those that can't, teach" did not apply with these lecturers. I also can not forget a few of my fellow class mates …. that made up some of the few first four-year international English stream. They too were determined and flexible with the adjustment pains of a pilot program. They all had such amazing backgrounds and wonderful personalities. We spent many memorable moments on group projects discussing, arguing , and getting on each other's nerves, but ultimately we pushed each other to think harder and more creatively, and never did it seem that we settled for the easy completion. ….

> Being an American, I feel blessed that I even found The Hotelschool The Hague let alone graduate from it. Its entrepreneurial like education I give credit to endowing me with the confidence I needed to start and build my own successful company of four years. Moreover, I give it credit for providing me with such a rich cultural education that has made me very competitive in the working world and has profited me greatly. … (Tracy Ricard, international student of the old curriculum 1994–1998, Hotelschool The Hague, 2004, p. 115–116)

Designing a New Curriculum: Enterprising Learning

The Dutch 1998 national student monitor (Chênevert et al., 2000, p. 34) revealed that 86% of the students graduating in the final year of the traditional curriculum found work within three months after graduation (and 96% within six months). Research by the Hotelschool also showed that the industry rated the performance of the Hotelschool students as "good to very good" (Chênevert et al., 2000, p. 33), rewarding an average 85 grade (out of 100) for management trainee performance, and that in "75% of all cases the first jobs [were] a continuation of the management placement". Considering further these students' satisfaction (see above) with their school experience as well as the Hotelschool's existing reputation of an elite institute, one could ask, "Why consider to change the curriculum?"

The aim of the school in the nineteen nineties was to provide

> higher education courses in hotel management, to train people to become managers of, and entrepreneurs in, the hospitality business both at home and abroad. (Chênevert et al., 2000, p. 9)

With a general mission statement (formulated around the turn of the century) that positioned the Hotelschool The Hague as

> .. an institute that to (potential) students, its employees and the international business community, is one of the foremost and leading innovative international business schools focusing on the hospitality industry (in the broadest sense) (Hotelschool The Hague, no date, translation ours).

It seemed that the school was already succeeding to meet these aims. However, in the last decade of the twentieth century the general feeling in society evolved that (at least) in higher education a traditional didactic approach was insufficient to ensure graduates who could meet the modern challenges of the information age and be as successful in the twenty-first century.

The Immediate Cause for Change

In the early nineteen nineties, an international accreditation and visitation committee evaluated the three Dutch hotel schools. This evaluation was based on a self-evaluation report provided by each of the hotel schools (for the Hotelschool The Hague see Chênevert et al., 1993) and a two-day on-site visit. The impression the three schools left was very positive, bringing the committee to conclude that the

> three schools are clear in their mission: to prepare students for management level jobs in the international hospitality industry. The schools are well-equipped to achieve these objectives. The Dutch hotel management schools have definitely put themselves on the international map. Their graduates are praised for their flexibility, practical approach, knowledge of foreign languages and 'an eye for people'. (HBO-raad, 1994, p. 13)

However, the committee also made a number of recommendations for each school. For the Hotelschool The Hague the first recommendation regarding the pedagogical approach was the turning point that led to the development of a new, more problem-based curriculum (Enterprising Learning) and ultimately to the current study. The committee recommended that

> the school should review its pedagogical approach to teaching. A more progressive approach is recommended, where students take greater responsibility for their own study and learning, where there is less reliance on the lecture as a means of imparting knowledge and information, and where there is a more integrated approach to the curriculum. (HBO-raad, 1994, p. 32)

Following the recommendation the Hotelschool formed a number of internal committees to discuss the options and formulate an appropriate, well considered response. Important issues that framed the development of the new curriculum were,

- designing learning environments that would activate and challenge students more and using information technology to its potential;
- increasing integration of subject areas;
- increasing variety in assessment format and content, assessing more than factual knowledge alone;
- encouraging students to use higher order thinking skills, in particular critical thinking and reflection skills;
- requiring new roles for teachers and students: teachers should develop toward learning facilitators and students to less reactive learners (van Rossum and Würffel, 1995).

By the end of 1995, the Hotelschool decided to follow a two-pronged strategy towards a new pedagogical approach. Firstly, the former two-stage curriculum was restructured to form a three-stage process, each stage or phase with its own focus. Secondly, a more activating and problem-based didactic approach was adopted. This strategy led to a first version of Enterprising Learning, version 1.0, which was implemented for a short period only (January 1997 – August 1998), and was replaced by version 2.0, the version that was leading during the current study.

Enterprising Learning, Version 1.0[3]

A prominent difference between the traditional and the Enterprising Learning curriculum was the introduction of a modular structure in teaching. All modules were the responsibility of the teachers developing and implementing them as the first year proceeded. Assignments and tasks to be performed formed an integral part of the problem-based approach of the new curriculum. In version 1.0 the educational modules were six weeks long, this proved to be rather short, often resulting in setting a more or less desperate pace to finish within the allotted time. This experience of 'inappropriate hastiness' was aggravated by the subsequent lack of reflection on what was learned during each module. In addition, contrary to the initial objective of subject integration, many of these early modules were in essence mono-disciplinary.

The three phase structure was built around the notion of increasing scale of complexity of a (hospitality oriented) business. The first phase therefore focused on the issues of a small business. The plan was to proceed in the second phase to issues linked to departments of larger hospitality businesses. In the final third phase students then would have been expected to address those issues belonging to general management. This approach was coupled to the notion of "concentric learning", referring to the revisiting of concepts at increasing levels of business complexity. In the experience of the Hotelschool teachers, this principle of increasing scale of business complexity proved a difficult one to apply to concentric learning.

The new curriculum required new roles for teachers and students, each of which had many characteristics consistent with constructivist learning and teaching. Teachers were expected to move away from their traditional role of transferring knowledge and toward "new forms of instruction, coaching students and giving feedback on students' work. The lecturer gradually lets go of the control he has over the student's learning process" (Chênevert et al., 2000, p. 38). Students in turn, were expected to adopt (all at once) a new, more active role in the teaching-learning process. This new role was characterised by

- autonomy: the student is less dependent on the teacher and is more proactive (for instance by seeking out information himself, or by independently applying theories in practice);
- task-orientation: the student is result oriented, a team worker and self-disciplined while working on assignments;
- information-processing: the student aims to seek out multiple sources and use multiple media in collecting appropriate information to tackle issues and assignments;
- innovation: the student realises that nothing is self-evident nor necessarily true or certain, this enables the student to depart from well-worn paths and come up with innovative ideas and solutions; and
- reflection: the student is able to plan, monitor and (if necessary) adjust his/her learning process, e.g. to increase its efficacy.

(Reuland et al., 1997)

While occasionally, in the literature on Enterprising Learning 1.0, the gradual development of the new roles is implied, in reality both teachers and students at that time felt that the new roles were expected to come to life in full bloom almost immediately (see also chapters 6 and 7). In a sense the developers (Reuland et al., 1997) explained the new roles for teacher and student as more or less static and unchanging. The roles described were more or less consistent with the aims of higher education (see also chapter 10), and implicitly these roles referred to learning-teaching conception 4. It is important to note that at that time the developers definitely did not present the new student role as a desired endpoint to a developmental process covering several years. With regard to the new teacher role, the developers further failed to provide the teachers with a timely and clear toolkit to help them visualise their own gradual retreat from the dominant position in teaching. Although the Hotelschool provided all teachers with an initial teacher training based on the new (fixed!) role for the teacher, the teachers themselves reported that developing the new modules took up all their time and energy. This left them with too little time to invest in developing their new didactic role.

There is some anecdotal evidence that even this imperfect, first version of Enterprising Learning "shocked" some students into epistemological development

> Just after I came to the Hotelschool I tended to learn everything by heart. Sometimes I really didn't even understand what I had learned and I forgot it again quickly. I used to focus on detail too much, and lose sight of the main point of the material. Now I learn in an 'understanding way' ... I try to link things together. The knowledge I have I now use to solve new problems, even if I have to dig deep now and then. This way I make myself use my brains. (Rosanne, student 97–1)

However, several issues mentioned above quickly led to the realisation that perhaps the current choices could be improved upon. So, while the students of 97–2 were still proceeding through this original version, a working group came up with an adjusted version, Enterprising Learning 2.0 (van Hest et al., 1998). The students of 97–2 enrolled into this improved curriculum in their fourth semester, on return from their practical internship.

Enterprising Learning, Version 2.0

Enterprising Learning version 2.0 was implemented in August 1998, for both the freshmen of semester 98–2 and for the returning semester 97–2 students in their second year. New modules were developed simultaneously for the first and second phase. It is this "new and improved" version (in memo's often referred to as the new-new curriculum) that was the curriculum experienced and evaluated by students in the current study.

The issue of too short modules was addressed by increasing the module length to eight weeks, resulting in 5 teaching periods (blocks) a year during which various modules were offered. In addition to regular holidays, a short break was introduced between block periods. At the same time teachers were encouraged to develop more multi-disciplinary modules. For example in phase 1, new modules included "Money & Markets" and "People and Technology".

In response to the teachers' comments on the use of increasing scale complexity as a guiding principle for concentric learning, in the new version the phases were structured around what can be interpreted as a focus on increasing complexity of thinking. This notion was loosely based on the developing epistemological model of learning-teaching conceptions introduced in chapter 1. The new three-phase curriculum was introduced as aiming at

- Hospitality performance: "doing the existing well"
  "The student is ... taught the basic skills for positions on the work floor ... He is also introduced to basic hotel management theories and learns to apply these when solving practical problems";
- Tactical hospitality management: "improving the existing";
  "The student learns to use the knowledge from [the various management] domains when resolving management issues...";
- Strategic hospitality management: "searching for new combinations".
  ".. the student is taught to think strategically, to find solutions for difficult, potential problems in a creative way."

(Hotelschool The Hague, 2000, p. 33).

This reinterpretation of complexity within the guiding principle implied an adjustment in the type of assignments used in the three phases, with problems becoming increasingly ill-structured and realistic as the student moved through the curriculum. Again we see here aspects in the teaching environment as designed for the Hotelschool which are consistent with a constructivist view on knowledge and learning.

In this new version, the view on the new roles of students and teachers did not change: still these roles were introduced as fairly static and expected to develop more or less overnight. The issue of having too little time to invest in changing their own role remained a problem for teachers. In 2000, they still said "that the new concept is not always consistently followed in everyday practice" (Chênevert et al., 2000, p. 40). Apparently, even after several years of implementing Enterprising Learning, teachers continued to feel a need for more face-to-face instruction, a return to the traditional education system, but by then they indicated that that was largely the result of lack of adequate training and support (Chênevert et al., 2000, p. 40).

An internal audit of the developed modules (Chênevert and van Muyden, 2001) concluded that the modules differed greatly with regard to the measure in which they embodied Enterprising Learning. Obvious shortcomings were

- a too dominant role of the teacher in the teaching-learning process (focusing on transfer of knowledge) often partnered with a strong emphasis on mono-disciplinary content,
- too little attention given to clarification of the expected role of the student, and
- ambiguity with regard to the role of assignments for the processing of subject matter.

In short, the audit committee recommended that the "desired roles of students and teachers in Enterprising Learning needed to be described more explicitly" (Chênevert and van Muyden, 2001, p. 2, translation ours) and added that management should be more clear in their commitment to and appreciation of the desired teacher role in Enterprising Learning (Chênevert and van Muyden, 2001, p. 3). On the other hand, in 2000, the then accreditation committee was far more positive about the Enterprising Learning curriculum at the Hotelschool (HBO-raad, 2000). The committee acknowledged that the new curriculum was a direct outcome of the main recommendation of the 1993 accreditation committee (HBO-raad, 1994, p. 32). More importantly, it felt that the quality of the Hotelschool The Hague programme had improved considerably because of its implementation (HBO-raad, 2000, p. 57).

Beyond Enterprising Learning 2.0: A True Developmental Approach

During the first years of the implementation of Enterprising Learning 2.0, it became increasingly obvious that the predominantly static interpretation of the concept Enterprising Learning – and of the teacher and student roles therein – was unsatisfactory. This realisation resulted from the current authors' ongoing work in developing a linked learning conception-teaching conception model. This model emphasised more strongly the *developmental* nature of the set of views on learning and teaching (van Rossum and Hamer, 2004). Furthermore, in this more elaborate model, the students' views on learning and teaching were linked to matching teachers' views. The model's developmental stance translated into a recommendation for major adjustments with regard to the nature of teaching and learning in each phase (van Rossum et al., 2004a). It was felt that the stages needed to consider the finding that the majority of students enter the Hotelschool (or any other formal higher education for that matter) with a learning conception 2, and that higher education aims to have students graduate with at least learning conception 4 (see chapter 10). Enterprising Learning 2.0 completely ignored the effort needed to make this journey, and more or less assumed that this new way of learning (and teaching for that matter) was a question of simple adjustments and sufficient practice for both parties involved.

From this new, developmental perspective, perhaps phases could be better organised as an epistemological staircase instead of one single high-jump effort at the start. The existing three phases in the curriculum provided a relatively straight forward way to model them to the learning conception levels that would need to be traversed. In this new design of Enterprising Learning 3.0, in each phase teachers would create a holding environment (Kegan, 1994) challenging the majority learning conception at entry, and supporting students in their development to the next level of thinking. In van Rossum and Hamer (2004) we described how such a developmental curriculum (Enterprising Learning 3.0) could be fitted into the ongoing innovation at the Hotelschool The Hague.

> Stage 1 focuses on the operational side of the hospitality industry, and strives for an end level learning conception 3. To stimulate the development from (mainly) learning conception 2 to 3, teaching needs to be organised around interactive lectures, in which the students are challenged to think themselves (and ask questions), while assignments lie close to the subject matter treated. The teaching method of 'shapers' [Fox, 1983] fits well in this stage and as this is very similar to traditional methods in higher [professional] education no significant problems are expected.

> Stage 2 focuses on acquiring insight on a management level and applying this on – preferably hospitality related – realistic problems. As this stage should encourage the development towards learning conception 4, assignments should be more complex, while assessment needs to focus on constructive application. The teacher assumes a more coaching role to facilitate understanding, and teachers using the teaching method of 'builders' [Fox, 1983] are effective in this stage. …
>
> In Stage 3 personal development is the central theme. This stage focuses on a development to learning conception 5 and elaborates this in the three main sections within this stage; a strategic case, the graduation project and the management internship. The teaching environment emphasises counselling and guidance, giving the student ample space to make choices and to determine his own development. Assignments are ultimately formulated and elaborated by the students themselves, while assessment increasingly focuses on the personal view of the student. Ideally teachers see themselves as 'local guides' [Fox, 1983] travelling together with the students through a landscape of real life assignments.
>
> (van Rossum and Hamer, 2004, p. 131–132)

Later in 2004, van Rossum et al. further filled in the requirements of each phase of Enterprising Learning 3.0 using four criteria: teacher role and feedback, student role, complexity of assignments, and assessment method (van Rossum et al., 2004b).

A major hurdle of this approach is that the teacher's role differs per phase and that in turn implies that teachers should be capable of switching between roles as they teach various groups of students from different phases. This seems to be a major weakness of the concept of a developmental curriculum, namely that perhaps teachers are less able to switch between roles, than management and developers seem to think. From the body of literature on teacher thinking (see e.g. chapter 5) it would seem that only teachers who themselves are fairly well developed epistemologically are able to perform this quick switching. In chapter 9 we will describe the epistemological thinking of teachers at the Hotelschool The Hague during the current study. This analysis will show that the majority of teachers would probably be unable to perform the different roles as described above. This may mean that if an institute is serious about implementing a developmental curriculum, knowledge of teachers' views on learning and good teaching (their epistemology) would necessarily be an important part of the implementation of the curriculum. With regard to the existing staff, this might mean that considerable investments would need to be made to help teachers develop epistemologically so that they can function within the new curriculum. Secondly, with regard to hiring new staff, teachers' epistemology would also necessarily be part of the selection procedure of new teachers. Either way, an institute would further need to decide either to assign teachers – based on their epistemological sophistication – specifically to particular phases, or to train new and existing teachers until they are capable to teach in all phases. Of course a mix of these strategies is also an option.

Baxter Magolda identified Enterprising Learning 3.0 (as described above) as an example of a Learning Partnerships curriculum (Baxter Magolda and King, 2004) and based on her experience, in such a curriculum "developmental growth occurs when the context demands it and sufficient support is available to meet that challenge" (Baxter Magolda, 2008, p. 61). Even given the drawback mentioned above concerning the less than perfect ability of teachers to switch their teaching roles, she felt that "higher education can be organized to intentionally promote personal epistemology."(2008, p. 61–62) and that Enterprising Learning 3.0 was a curriculum aimed to do precisely this.

Analysis of the Empirical Data

In the current study data of 244 students of two separate semesters of the Hotelschool were included as well as 43 essays of teachers of the Hotelschool. The data consisted partly of handwritten (or typed) responses to essay questions, and of prints of emails. All data included name or student identification number, so that it was possible to establish which responses were provided by the same student or teacher. In addition date of response, semester identifier and gender were easily established. The student data were sorted, with all materials pertaining to each individual student organised in chronological order and inserted in a separate sleeve. The data were organised into separate semesters. The teacher data were sorted by name.

It is important to stress here, that during the data collection and prior to analysis the two judges, co-authors of the current study, deliberately refrained from discussing any impressions they had gained of individual responses. Prior to the analysis the judges prepared a list of characteristic expressions and defining aspects per category/conception of learning. This identification scheme was based on the outcome of the chapters 1, 3 and 4 and is given in table 6.1. In addition each judge prepared a log with the purpose of logging impressions, arguments and category allocation of each student or teacher by name.

Analysis sessions covered between 2 hours to at maximum 4 hours. On average, in each session the epistemological level of between 10 to 20 students was established, with all measurements (entry, intermediate if available, exit as well as retrospective) categorised at the same time. Categorisation involved reading through one measurement at a time, noticing (and often logging) distinctive features of the responses to the learning and teaching conception questions. Logged features included "signature utterances" of a category of description, such as included in Table 6.1, but also segments or comments that seemed to put these utterances in perspective or a different light. While reading judges consciously attempted to suspend their own interpretation, remaining open to familiar as well as new aspects included in each essay, refraining from allocation until a picture of the whole essay was clear in their mind. By incorporating new information the analysis was not an exercise in allocation of categories only, but included an element of refinement of categories of description as well, putting it well within the phenomenographic tradition (see chapter 2). Many of the issues noticed through

Table 6.1. Category identification scheme

Category	*Characteristic usage*
1	Listing activities, synonyms Listing means of learning Relying on luck, improvisation No strategy, simply cramming everything Lacking signs of understanding the question; lack of reflection
2	Learning to pass exams, tests Learning for parents, teachers Testing yourself, rehearsing Knowing is reproducing Understanding is knowing each separate word, each sentence Being able/allowed to ask questions Explanation by examples Working hard in class, cramming but with selection (main and sub points) Enthusiast/impassioned teacher
3	Learning is not only theory, it is also doing/experiencing Learning only what is expected to turn out to be useful (later): becoming more selective in learning Learning for the future, to use in your career (after school) Learning for yourself More than memorising (for tests)! Making realistic assignments, doing cases; reproducing reality in assignments Advocating discussions/exchanging different viewpoints/opinions in class Being able to apply theory/what is learned in similar situations Developing personal opinions, all opinions are equally valid because personal Recognising theory in everyday situations
4	Learning is a new way of thinking; technical flavour to descriptions Thinking for yourself, critical thinking, thinking things through Challenging what you see and hear Some opinions/conclusions are better than others, because they are based on evidence Discussions based on arguments not opinions Identifying structure in texts, making connections between texts and what you already know Applying theory when possible, but recognising when theory needs adapting Thinking about new applications, combining theories (within one way of thinking) Teachers are flexible and are responsive to student thinking Being proud of what you do and make, striving to do your best, to deliver quality
5	Learning is dialogue Learning to see things from different perspectives; widening horizons Learning is finding/knowing your limits What you see depends on which way you look, what perspective you take There are no simple problems with one correct answer Everything is complex, multi-facetted Good solutions depend on the context/ way of looking/ the glasses you use

Table 6.1. (Continued)

6	Learning is becoming a better, wiser person Harmony with reality, others Getting to know who you are, what is important to you and what is not Language of growth, organic metaphors Teaching is caring, authenticity and passion are more important than technique I decide what to accept/learn and what to ignore (sense of agency) I learn from you, you learn from me; learning is two-way

this open attitude are reported in chapter 8, Issues in Enterprising Learning, following the thematic approach to the outcome description recommended by Ashworth and Lucas (2000, see also chapter 2). After reading through the data for one measurement one or more times, a category was assigned. In assigning a category judges weighed the utterances by relevance and coherence, with single or more or less "unanchored" utterances receiving less importance than longer, logically connected fragments. In most cases the judges used single digit categorisations. On occasion a three digit Perry-like categorisation was used to indicate room for discussion and the need for explicit argumentation (see chapter 3 on Perry). This procedure was then repeated for the remaining measurements of this student. During categorisation judges did not discuss any of the students.

Each session was concluded with data entry of the categorisation of the two judges separately, after which the interrater reliability was updated. Interrater reliability was based on the agreement on all measurements included in the current study, meaning that if the raters initially disagreed upon two of the three measurements available for a student, this was counted as two disagreements out of three. Subsequently students whose categorisations did not match for one or more measurements, were discussed, using the raw data, the log entries and the categorisation scheme. In all cases judges came to an agreement. Initial disagreements almost always concerned a difference of only one category. Many of the initial disagreements could later be attributed to small developments within a category (see chapter 7, section No change at all?) or such a simple thing as analysis fatigue.

Categorisation of the teachers learning-teaching conception was performed following the same analysis procedure as described above. The data of the teachers, only 43 in total, were read separately from the screen by both judges who again made log entries and allocated teachers to a learning-teaching conception using more or less the same scheme as given in Table 6.1. After categorising all teachers, interrater reliability was established. Finally the judges discussed those teachers they disagreed upon until agreement was reached.

NOTES

[1] The curriculum was introduced as "Ondernemend Leren" and continued through 2008 under the [incorrectly translated] name of Entrepreneurial Learning at the Hotelschool. However, as one of the major designers, we feel "Ondernemend Leren" never aimed at training entrepreneurs. It aimed at making learning an enterprise, a student's exploration of learning and self. Therefore we consistently

used (and will continue to use) the more precise term Enterprising Learning as suggested by Noel Entwistle during our visit in 2001.

[2] The facts and figures included in this section are taken from two self-evaluation reports (Chênevert et al., 1993 and 2000) and cover the period 1990–1999.

[3] The information on version 1.0 is mainly based on an internal email correspondence with Ruud Reuland, former member of the Board of Directors responsible for education matters, and on Reuland et al. (1997).

CHAPTER 7

STUDENT DEVELOPMENT IN ENTERPRISING LEARNING

My management internship in Tianjin, China was a bizarre experience. Because the hotel had just opened, and without any specific training, they gave me the responsibilities of Guest Service Manager, Restaurant Manager, and Executive Lounge Manager.

So here I was constantly learning. I had no social life whatsoever and still it was the most exciting time. Each morning I got up with a fear of the unknown, for everything I would be doing that day, for everything I had never done before. At times I felt like I had never even been to the Hotelschool – and I'm not talking about the quality of my education there. And every evening I went to bed with the same satisfied feeling that I could *cope and I had learned so many new things.*

(Willem, level-three-thinker, 98–2)

The question addressed in this chapter concerns the epistemological development that occurred in the respondents of this study who were exposed to an activating curriculum, Enterprising Learning. Underlying this main question are issues regarding a stage like development, the espoused goals of the Enterprising Learning curriculum, and new insights gained from this relatively large scale phenomenographic study into student learning. The data from 244 respondents are described in terms of epistemological development, paying attention to methodological issues. The current results are compared to data from earlier studies and in the final empirical section of this chapter new insights are shared regarding smaller developments within larger epistemological structures.

In this chapter (again) we consistently use the convention to refer to students functioning at a particular epistemological level by level-x-thinkers. Level-three-thinkers therefore refer to students viewing learning and teaching from the perspective of the third learning-teaching conception. This convention in no way should give the impression that the epistemological position refers to a fixed and unchangeable personal trait. On the contrary, we agree with Csikszentmihalyi that "every human brain is able to generate self-reflective consciousness, [although] not everyone seems to use it equally" (1993, p. 23). Furthermore, we believe that education can foster the development of such "self-reflective consciousness".

A Stage-Like Development in Conceptions of Learning and "Good" Teaching?

There may be those among our readers who still feel the evidence regarding epistemological development through a stage-like and hierarchically inclusive sequence of 'ways of knowing' is not all together convincing. However, occasionally, as one reads students' essays, one may come across examples almost irrefutably supporting our assumption underlying the current study, namely that students, when sufficiently encouraged, do indeed develop in an orderly and stage-like fashion. One such an example is the story of Noor, a level-four-thinker in 2002 at the end of her studies. Noor described in two retrospections the whole development from a level-one-thinker through to a level-four-thinker. Furthermore, she clearly indicated that, as a level-four-thinker, all previous ways of knowing and learning remained open to her to be used when appropriate. Before presenting the results of our study of students who experienced Enterprising Learning, we quote her story below to underpin not only our assumption of stage-like progression, but also as support for the hierarchically inclusive nature of these developmental stages.

In her first semester at the Hotelschool, when asked to think back on her learning in the final year of secondary school, she clearly indicated that while entering the Hotelschool as a level-two-thinker, she remembered a different approach to learning when she was younger

> My favourite way of learning was mainly making lots of summaries. Rereading these regularly. Learning words, I reread repeatedly, but only for short periods at a time. For math and biology I did a lot of questions and sample exams or I thought up questions to check myself.
>
> Before that learning to me was "*as long as I've done it*". In my final year [of secondary school it was] "as long as I know it!" (Noor, level-four-thinker, 98–2, italics ours)

To us, the first lines indicate that she entered the Hotelschool as a level-two-thinker. The italicised line following these, sounds to us a lot like the position of Silence (Belenky et al., 1997) which we link to learning conception 1. In Silence, learning is not reflected upon, it is something one "does". According to Belenky et al. there is *no knowing* possible at this level, and people describe themselves/their knowing in terms of movements or activities, much as Noor did above. And some four years later, Noor, in her final year of the Hotelschool – while analysing the types of learning she has to her disposal – sketched the subsequent development in her views on learning from level two to four

> Learning means to me, making something my own! I can learn in different ways and in different circumstances.
>
> – Learning by heart: You can learn words by heart, for instance in learning a foreign language, remember definitions and this usually boils down to pure rote learning.
> – Learning by example: looking at an example and copying this (especially in our practical), for instance learning to cut onions correctly in the kitchen. The teacher shows you how to cut and I imitate.
> – Trial and error learning: Learning by practicing and making mistakes. 'Learning to walk' with falling down and getting up again, doing math sums by practicing, *practice makes perfect.*

> – Problem-based learning: by encountering a problem. To experience what this means and how to handle it. To solve it or not, but through evaluating the experience it can be very educational. What went well, what went less well, and how can I improve the way I handled this type of problem should I encounter a similar one?
> – Analytical learning: I mean making the combination of facts you learn and what you already know. You need to rise above the subject matter and look down with a helicopter view so that you can make connections and relationships.
>
> ... At the Hotelschool I encountered for the first time problem-based learning. Most of the projects and cases we had to work on at the Hotelschool were constructed around a problem [from professional practice]. ... In that way learning to me now means something very different than in 1998. In [secondary school] I was mainly preoccupied with learning facts, definitions by heart... (Noor, level-four-thinker, 98–2)

Finally, Noor also indicated that Enterprising Learning, with its focus on solving cases from practice and group work, played an instrumental role in her development to level-three-thinker – by applying knowledge in problem-based learning – and subsequently level-four-thinker – when she learned to think critically and look for connections between new and existing knowledge.

Another example is Katja's story (level-four-thinker, 98–2). She described almost the same development (from level-two-thinker through level-four-thinker), indicating that her epistemological development was fuelled by her experiences at the Hotelschool.

> When I started at the Hotelschoool in August 1998 I proceeded in much the same way as I had done at secondary school. This meant I went through all the required literature and learned it all by heart. Rote learning, rote learning and more rote learning. I thought I would learn a lot this way.
>
> Pretty soon I found out that rote learning actually doesn't get you very far. It was all about *applying* what you learnt/know, using it in practice.
>
> [Then] the *why* became more important. I mean the reasons you have for doing something in a particular way. In addition I learned that it very often was not a question of right or wrong, but that it was your arguments that counted.
>
> Through the cases at the Hotelschool I encountered a completely different way of learning. Here we were dropped in at the deep end with little information to go by, and we just had to see how to arrive at an acceptable end product. In this way we learnt how to find the information needed and (how) to select from the abundance of information we found. In addition, we had the opportunity to deepen our knowledge of subjects that caught our interest ... reading different sources in gathering our knowledge followed by comparing different viewpoints on issues.

> Especially during the final project I experienced that knowledge and theory alone is never enough. A structured approach and a logical way of thinking together with insight into the situation are crucial. (Katja, level-four-thinker, 98–2, italics ours)

Her epistemologically fairly sophisticated views on learning and good teaching had consequences for the kind of feedback she felt students needed to learn and improve.

> When [students'] independence is the focus, the teacher must focus on advising and coaching. Good feedback becomes important .. not only in the form of a mark indicating *only* the quality of the finished product. A mark says nothing about what mistakes were made, existing gaps, nor about points for improvement, etcetera. Such feedback would contribute greatly to good teaching. (Katja, level-four-thinker, 98–2, italics ours)

Where most students would probably be more than happy with a mark indicating good quality, Katja prefers to know much more about her end product in order to improve her performance. As we will see in the next chapter, feedback in all its types is an area of particular interest for students.

Considering these stories, we feel more than confident to present the tables with the entry and exit learning-teaching conceptions of the students of two semesters as proof of epistemological, stage-like, and hierarchically inclusive *development*, and not as "mere" changes in students' learning approach within a particular context. We also feel confident to present this development as being – at least in part – due to the Enterprising Learning curriculum at the Hotelschool.

First Student Cohort of Enterprising Learning (semester 97-2)

Enterprising Learning (version 1) was implemented at the Hotelschool in January 1997. The first cohort we followed over the years was not the first semester in this new curriculum[1] but the second. Of this second semester to fully experience Enterprising Learning, starting in August 1997, some three years later 135 students were still registered as studying at the Hotelschool. Each student of this semester was included in the study if and when he/she started the final project. This procedure led to 126 students receiving an open-ended exit-questionnaire. After a thorough follow-up procedure, 120 exit-questionnaires were returned (95%), 46% of these respondents were male. During the study of our first cohort student-email was introduced at the Hotelschool. This meant that initially students filled in hard-copy questionnaires, and later on students received the questionnaire by email. For many of the latter group the questionnaire grew into what we call an *email conversation* (or *email-interview*) consisting of requests to elaborate on specific phrases or issues. Some of these conversations were concluded within a day, some took a few months or more to reach their conclusion. While the research procedure was keyed to receive a measurement of students' views on learning and good teaching while they were participating in their final project, a number of responses were received considerably later during students' final management internship, with students apologising because of heavy workloads. One or two students only responded after graduation. Only the 120 students with both an entry and an exit-questionnaire were included in the analysis.

Now and then the persistence of the follow-up procedure was commented upon, occasionally favourably (see Rico below), usually with good-natured acceptance,

> Dear Mr. van Rossum,
>
> Thank you for your patience. I do admire your follow-up procedure, many a business loses contracts because of a lack of it.
>
> (Rico, level-three-thinker, 97-2)

The entry-questionnaire, administered in August 1997, consisted of an introduction and two essay questions, each on a separate page:

1. Firstly we would like to know what was **your favourite way of learning** in the last school year before you came to the Hotelschool. How did you study for certain subjects, how did you know that you had learnt the subject matter, what was the goal of your learning, etcetera …?
   Please describe as fully as you can how you felt then.
2. Lastly, we would like to know what was **your favourite way of teaching** in the last school year before you started at the Hotelschool. In which type of lessons did you feel you learned the most, what are in your opinion the most important characteristics of a good teacher, how does a good teacher introduce and present the subject matter, etcetera …?
   Please describe as fully as you can how you felt then.

Both the learning and teaching conception were used to allocate each student to a entry-category learning-teaching conception.

The exit-questionnaire used consisted of three main questions:

1. Could you please describe how you see learning and studying today?
   a. What is **currently your way of learning**? How do you learn for instance for different subjects?
   b. When do you feel you have really learned something?
   c. Has your way of learning changed during your period at the Hotelschool?
   d. What does learning mean to you (here or elsewhere)? What do you hope to achieve with learning?
2. Could you describe how you see (good) teaching today?
   a. What is your ideal way of (good) teaching? From what kind of teaching do you feel you learn the most?
   b. What characterises the ideal teacher?
3. Assignments are an important feature of Enterprising Learning. What do you think is a good assignment, that means to say an assignment that really meant something to you?

Questions 1 and 2 were used to allocate the students to an exit learning-teaching conception. The responses to question 3 were not included separately in this study, but were used to corroborate the allocation of the exit-level. Question 1c was used to ascertain how well the students could establish their epistemological development since entering the Hotelschool. The responses were used to analyse the reliability of a retrospective question spanning multiple years. The question as administered here was less than satisfactory, because e.g. with some regularity answers consisted of a yes or no answer, followed by an elaboration on the current learning conception without sufficient information about the learning conception at entry of the Hotelschool. For this cohort this was not a problem as we had entry-questionnaires for all participants. This question was amended in the questionnaire for the next cohort (98-2, see below) in order to increase the quality of the retrospective process.

In this and in the follow-up procedure, occasionally the email-reminders included slightly differently worded versions of the questions given above. The main themes were retained throughout the study of this group.

Entry and Exit Levels of Cohort 97-2

In Table 7.1 below, the entry and exit levels of the 120 students included are presented. Students were allocated to an entry and an exit-level by the two authors separately. Interrater reliability for this first semester analysed was 80% (Cohen's Kappa was 0.69). All remaining students were allocated to a developmental position after discussion and subsequent agreement.

By far the most students entered the Hotelschool directly from (primarily traditional) secondary schools and so it is hardly surprising that 93% of these freshmen higher professional students had learning-teaching conception 2. This result is even more extreme than found by van Rossum and Schenk (1984) where the respondents were freshmen psychology university students. Sixteen of the 120 students (13%) did not change their views on learning and teaching in the period at the

Table 7.1 Epistemological development of semester 97-2 students

	1997 entry level							
exit	*1*	*2*	*3*	*4*	*5*	*6*	*exit*	*%*
1							0	0%
2		12					12	10%
3	1	85	3				89	74%
4		12	4	1			17	14%
5		1					1	1%
6		1					1	1%
entry	1	111	7	1	0	0	120	
%	1%	93%	6%	1%	0%	0%	100%	

Hotelschool. The overwhelming majority of the students (71%, 85 of the 120) developed one stage up, from learning-teaching conception 2 to learning-teaching conception 3, moving from pure reproduction to application (foreseen). Some 16 students (13%) moved across the watershed upward to learning-teaching conception 4. Two students displayed a considerably larger development, moving way beyond the watershed (2%). Both these students are included in the qualitative analysis below. As we would expect, given our interpretation of the developmental sequence, we did not find any students "moving backwards" towards less sophisticated levels of thinking.

By the end of the Hotelschool three-quarters of the students of 97-2 saw learning as something that should lead to application or at least to something that would prove to be useful in future (learning-teaching conception 3), some 16% had crossed the watershed and had moved into constructive learning.

Second Student Cohort of Enterprising Learning (semester 98-2)

The student cohort starting in August 1998 (98-2) was the first to experience Enterprising Learning version 2. Of this semester 126 students who started their final project were sent an open-ended questionnaire by email from August 2001 onwards, in the months before they started their final management internship. This exit-questionnaire was sent to their student-email address. The same, rather persistent follow-up strategy resulted in 125 returned questionnaires (99%), with one remaining student refusing to respond by email. His interview and the questionnaire of one other student proved to contain insufficient information and these two students were removed from the final analysis. So, the final response rate was 98%, where 47% of the students were male.

As before for parts of semester 97-2, the exit-questionnaire often grew into an email conversation. These conversations were again sometimes concluded within a day, some took considerably longer to reach their conclusion, with students apologising again for the delay due to a heavy work schedule. The overwhelming majority of the students was amendable to these conversations, occasionally providing additional contact information of fellow students who had not yet responded. A small number of students commented – more or less jokingly – on the persistence of the follow-up, having been warned about it by fellow students.

> Dear Mr. van Rossum,
>
> In the future, the word "persistent" and your name will be closely connected for me… Good thing though, because I must admit that I had forgotten about your survey. (Davy, level-three-thinker, 98-2)

Davy, while having been "bothered" by Mr. van Rossum two times already, was interested enough to inquire about his responses in 1998, and wanted to know when the results of the whole study would become available.

Other students also commented as well that they enjoyed the insight they gained in their own learning and themselves by having to explain something they usually did not think much about to someone so interested.

> Good morning Mr. van Rossum,
>
> Because of your questions I've started to think about it more and more and I realise that it isn't really that simple to explain it to someone. Funny really.
>
> ... I hope I've been more clear now, if not please let me know.
> (Iris, level-three-thinker, 98-2)

The exit-questionnaire underlying the analysis of epistemological development in this cohort consisted of five essay questions, which were slightly adjusted in phrasing in response to problems encountered with semester 97-2, while covering the same themes:

1. Learning has many meanings. I would like to know
   - What learning means to you **now,** at this moment?
   - When do you feel that you have **really learnt** something?
2. The same question as above, but then about **learning in 1998**. You can think back to what you did/thought in 1998 when you learned something at the very start of your Hotelschool period, or at the end of your previous education/ school. In short, what did learning mean to you in 1998?
3. If you compare the answers to both questions above, do you feel your **ideas about learning have changed** over the years? Have you come to think differently about learning?
4. What is **good teaching** to you now? And what may you expect in good teaching from a) you the student, and b) the teacher? What roles should student and teacher play in good teaching?
5. What is a **good assignment**? An assignment you really felt you learned something from?

Questions 1 and 4 were used to allocate students to their exit learning-teaching conception category. Questions 2 and 3 were used to establish firstly a student's own perception of his/her views on learning at the start of the Hotelschool and secondly the measure to which they felt sure about a possible change in their thinking. In the instances that there was an entry-questionnaire (60, see below) the allocation of this initial questionnaire was used to establish the entry learning-teaching conception. Where no initial questionnaire was available, the retrospective estimation was used as indication for the entry-level. As before, question 5 was not included separately in the current study, but was used to corroborate the allocation of the exit learning-teaching conception level.

Of the 124 students who had filled in the exit-questionnaire, 60 had previously, at the start of their first year, filled in an entry-questionnaire. This first questionnaire was identical to the entry-questionnaire of 97-2 and asked about the way they saw learning and teaching in the year before they started at the Hotelschool (see above). In many cases the responses referred to their experiences in (traditional) secondary school, which in part explains again the overwhelming majority of students entering the Hotelschool with learning-teaching conception 2 (see Table 7.2 below). This group of 60, having both an entry response and a retrospective response regarding their entry level, facilitated analysis regarding the validity of using a retrospective question across multiple years to ascertain the entry-level learning-teaching conception. The results of this latter analysis regarding the retrospective question, together with the corresponding analysis for all 120 students of the earlier semester (97-2) are discussed below in the section on methodological issues.

Entry and Exit Levels of Cohort 98-2

In Table 7.2 the entry and exit levels of the 124 students included are presented.

Students were allocated to an entry and an exit-level in the same way as for semester 97-2. Interrater reliability for this second semester analysed was 84% (Cohen's Kappa was 0.65). All remaining students were allocated to an entry-exit position after careful rereading, discussion and subsequent agreement.

As already mentioned above, the large majority of these freshmen higher professional students (86%) had learning-teaching conception 2, which is slightly less than found for semester 97-2. Twenty of the 124 students (16%) did not change their views on learning and teaching in the period at the Hotelschool. Oddly enough in this group again 71% (88 of 124) developed one stage up, from learning-teaching conception 2 to learning-teaching conception 3, moving from pure reproduction to application (foreseen). Sixteen students (12%), the same number as in semester 97-2, moved across the watershed upward to learning-teaching conception 4. Unlike semester 97-2, no students of 98-2 developed beyond learning-teaching conception 4, probable reasons for this we will discuss in the qualitative analysis below. Again we did not find any students "moving backwards" towards less sophisticated levels of thinking.

On leaving the Hotelschool, somewhat more students than in semester 97-2 had reached learning-teaching conception 3 (83%), and 14% had crossed the watershed and had moved into constructive learning.

Table 7.2. Epistemological development of semester 98-2 students

	1998 entry level							
exit	*1*	*2*	*3*	*4*	*5*	*6*	*exit*	*%*
1							0	0%
2		4					4	3%
3		88	15				103	83%
4		15	1	1			17	14%
5							0	0%
6							0	0%
entry	0	107	16	1	0	0	124	100%
%	0%	86%	13%	1%	0%	0%	100%	

Comparing Developments within Enterprising Learning and Before

Examining the two semesters (97-2 and 98-2) we see large similarities in the pattern of development over the years. Furthermore, we note that no students described a negative development in their conceptions of learning and teaching. We interpret this latter finding as a positive outcome of Enterprising Learning, as in some research students have been found to regress to more surface level approaches to learning during higher education (see chapter 10). Finally, the semesters of Enterprising Learning differ in three respects:

- In semester 98-2 almost no students (3%) leave the Hotelschool at learning-teaching conception 2, whereas in semester 97-2 about 10% left higher education with this unsatisfactory level of thinking.
- In semester 98-2 the proportion of students remaining at level 3 thinking is much larger than in semester 97-2. We will discuss this issue in more detail in the methodological section below.
- In semester 98-2 no students developed further than level 4 thinking.

In Table 7.3 we have reproduced the results of an earlier study, with 70 students of the traditional curriculum before Enterprising Learning (van Rossum, Hamer and Würffel, 2003). These students came from various semesters, and all participated in a final project coached by the first author.

In the old curriculum almost two-thirds (63%) of the students entered the Hotelschool with learning-teaching conception 2. This is considerably less than was found for the later semesters, but simultaneously this sample contained quite a few students with more sophisticated entry-levels of thinking. [2] It is important to note that this set of students was perhaps not a random selection of the general student population. While this may be unfortunate, at this moment we are more interested in the pattern of developments that these students revealed. In this regard, there are large differences between thc old and the Enterprising Learning curriculum. In the old curriculum 42 of the 70 students (60%) failed to develop

Table 7.3. Epistemological development in the old curriculum

	old curriculum, entry level							
exit	*1*	*2*	*3*	*4*	*5*	*6*	*exit*	*%*
1							0	0%
2	2	18					20	29%
3		15	8				23	33%
4		9		12			21	30%
5		2			4		6	9%
6							0	0%
entry	2	44	8	12	4	0	70	100%
%	3%	63%	11%	17%	6%	0%	100%	

Source: van Rossum, Hamer and Würffel (2003)

even one stage upward, with the largest set of non-developers (18 of 70, just over a quarter of all students!) remaining at level 2. Looking at the distribution of students across exit-level learning-teaching conceptions 2, 3 and 4 we see a more or less equal split, which might lead one to say that the traditional curriculum led to higher exit-levels. However, in fact it is the result of a larger proportion of students entering with a sophisticated level of thinking and who remain at this level, failing to develop further.

Looking in particular at the spectacular decrease in the unsatisfactory exit-level learning-teaching conception 2, from 29% in the old curriculum to 10% for 97-2 and only 3% for 98-2, it is clear that Enterprising Learning *at the very least* is considerably more successful in promoting epistemological development than the traditional curriculum.

From a less positive perspective it is unfortunate that Enterprising Learning has failed to encourage development for the majority of students across the watershed and so into the espoused level of thinking aimed for by higher education. In the next two chapters we will discuss some possible causes for this less than optimal result.

On the other hand, the finding that the largest proportion of higher students leave their studies with a level of thinking consistent with the third order of consciousness (learning-teaching conception 3 or Transitional Knowing) is not uncommon, see chapter 3. Baxter Magolda's 1992a longitudinal study found *almost identical* outcomes, with about 80% of the seniors functioning at a level of Transitional Knowing and 16% at the level of Independent Knowing (learning-teaching conception 4).

Radloff (2002) is another example with similar results. Radloff's longitudinal study is perhaps even more relevant to our own than Baxter Magolda's 1992a study as it focused on student development in a degree-level higher professional education programme. Although the respondents in Radloff's study were Technical and Further Education lecturers and somewhat older than the students of the Hotelschool, their initial attitude towards learning in this two year programme was very similar to that of our own respondents: focused on obtaining qualifications, passing exams with minimum effort, using predominantly rehearsal strategies to learn (e.g. rereading, copying, highlighting), and seeing learning in quantitative terms. At the end of the programme the main changes in these students/lecturers were shifts

- in focus from qualification (17%) to job training (70%), i.e. "improving job prospects and future study opportunities" (Radloff, 2002, p. 276),
- in conceptions of learning focusing predominantly on applying knowledge,
- in learning strategies from primarily rehearsal strategies to organisation strategies (i.e. grouping, outlining, selecting relevant material)

An example of the epistemological change is given by T06 in the third wave

> I'm able to look very quickly at things and say that's relevant, that's relevant. I'm a quicker learner, I don't waste time in what I was doing. I think in the beginning the time was spent wasting around. Well, I don't do that anymore. You get one book or two books and get a hell of a lot out of that. I'm more

> efficient. I think also what it's taught me is that I might get very heated in discussions or whatever, whereas now I can sort of sit back as well and listen to what other people are saying without sort of butting in and saying, no that's not right or whatever. I am able to say, well that's your point of view and communicate better in a group situation. (T06 3, Radloff, 2002, p. 280)

In the qualitative analysis presented below, we shall see the same themes – efficiency and selectivity in learning, and preference for discussion in teaching – emerging in the responses of the largest group of our students, those moving from learning-teaching conception 2 to level 3. The epistemological development was reflected in the way Radloff's respondents changed their ideas about teaching

> My ideas have changed. The idea of the way I would like to teach has changed ... As far as I'm concerned, if you are not doing something, you can't learn ... The way to learn is to do something ... to be active all of the time... there has to be more application, being able to solve problems in their work environment. ... (T05 3, Radloff, 2002, p. 282)

And in their actual teaching practice as well

> I used to stand up and deliver ... Now I let them talk a bit more, let them talk and find out for themselves and discuss it more with them. (T21 3, 2002, p. 283)

From this study we can conclude two things. Firstly, that student-teachers/lecturers who develop towards a coherent learning-teaching conception 3 level of thinking, once aware of their own preferences in learning and teaching, will *indeed* change their teaching practice towards one consistent with this level of thinking. Secondly, as all respondents graduated and many with high grades, we see here as well that it is entirely possible to "gain a professional qualification in teaching *without* necessarily holding or developing sophisticated views of learning and teaching" (2002, p. 285, italics ours). We will come back to these two conclusions in later chapters.

Finally we see in this study a further argument to suggest the abolishment of the artificial divide between student thinking and teacher thinking (see also Vermunt and Verloop, 1999).

Contamination: Old-Curriculum Students in Enterprising Learning

The data used to establish students' epistemological development during the old curriculum were gathered at more or less the same time that the new curriculum based on Enterprising Learning was implemented. This meant that some respondents of the old curriculum had heard about the new curriculum and had formed an opinion about it. As it happened a small number of students following the old curriculum still needed to complete a few study requirements and were confronted with the fact that a particular course was no longer available in the traditional format. This meant that they had to do the missing course as an

Enterprising Learning course, and so actually had some limited experience with the new curriculum. In research such mixing of cohorts is considered contamination, which could have influenced the results with regard to the old curriculum students. However, this happenstance also meant an unexpected but interesting insight into how students with different learning conceptions and accustomed to a more traditional curriculum viewed the new activating curriculum. This is particularly interesting because the group of old curriculum students included more students with relatively sophisticated views on learning (learning-teaching conception 4 and upwards).

The analysis of the contamination showed that in particular students with a less sophisticated view on learning had a very different opinion of the new curriculum than those with more sophisticated views. As one might have expected, the students with an exit learning-teaching conception 4 or 5 were quite pleasantly surprised about enterprising learning. We quote two students to illustrate this,

> [In the old curriculum] the strange thing is that I do know what the subject matter is about: I've explained it often enough to my fellow students (...), but this doesn't show in the exams because of the amount of details asked.
>
> (...) I was lucky enough to be able to do some courses of the new curriculum and I must say this approach fits me better (for some subjects!). (...) you use only those parts of the books you need (keeping to the main line, instead of details) and in the end you have mastered the subject anyway.(Jan, old curriculum, level-four-thinker, van Rossum et al., 2002)
>
> I feel I'm just biding my time at the Hotelschool. I feel my time here is just holding me up in my development. (…) I'm only studying to get my diploma. (...) Enterprising Learning is a relief. (Chris, old curriculum, level-five-thinker, van Rossum et al., 2002)

At the same time, the first version of Enterprising Learning seemed to present a large, perhaps too large, challenge for students with a relatively less sophisticated learning-teaching conception (exit levels 2 or 3). For these students it seemed Enterprising Learning would require a proper introduction.

> That concept of enterprising learning may be the future, but I think you should also be given a chance to follow lessons. (…) Self study sounds fine, but I don't think it fits the image of the Hotelschool. You can only learn from guidance, help and explanation in class. (Bo, old curriculum, level-two-thinker, van Rossum et al., 2002)
>
> I am a passionate advocate of traditional teaching. I like to attend a lecture where the teacher just teaches. Every student can then find important elements in the subject matter in his/her own way. (…) This system has worked fine since the ancient Greeks, and therefore I seriously doubt the effectiveness of Enterprising Learning. (…) In my opinion, the new system has no advantages whatsoever. (…) I think Enterprising Learning is very patronising, it damages higher professional education in the sense that

> students' independence is lessened. Furthermore, I believe that the craft of teaching is endangered because the teacher becomes more of a counsellor or coach. (Sam, old curriculum, level-three-thinker, van Rossum et al., 2002)

It is probable that these latter negative perceptions were partly the result of the unexpected and unprepared confrontation with a more activating curriculum. In our current study we found that many of the students who experienced Enterprising Learning entered the Hotelschool with a similar level of thinking (see Table 7.1 and 7.2) and found it to be a move upward from their traditional secondary education. On the other hand the negative perception of Enterprising Learning was also an indication that some students, in particular those entering the Hotelschool with less sophisticated views on teaching and learning, might experience disappointment and express disengagement with the Hotelschool.

The current study, evaluating the epistemological development of the students who followed the complete version of Enterprising Learning showed that this particular potential problem mostly sorted itself out in practice. In addition, the few cases of contamination also showed that even a very short exposure to Enterprising Learning could lead to significant epistemological development. Annika, a student of the old curriculum, was very explicit in attributing part of her development from level-two-thinker to level-three-thinker to having followed a course in the new curriculum,

> ... I **have** seen that you learn more from 'practice' (through projects) than from only memorising old exams. I saw this clearly following Finance. In the old curriculum you went to lectures, did your homework and took exams. If the subject matter wasn't your cup of tea you failed, which I feel is clear from the grades. In Managerial Finance of the new curriculum you first learn that what you are doing is related to something, while at the same time it is not all spelled out. (Annika, old curriculum, level-two to level-three-thinker, van Rossum et al., 2002)

Qualitative Analysis of the Developments

Below we will illustrate qualitatively the major developmental moves, which we have divided into three sections:

- development within reproductive learning (moving to three), by far the largest group in our study,
- development across the watershed, and
- development beyond level 4.

In each section we have composed a storyline around a few typical students, sometimes adding short quotes from other students as well to illustrate other important aspects of the development concerned.

Moving to 3

The development to level three was the dominant development found in this study. First, we will introduce three students who developed from level-two-thinker to level-three-thinker and use their stories to illustrate the main issues in this development. Our first student, Hugo, started his study at the Hotelschool with the following views on learning which were based on his experiences in secondary education.

> For "do" subjects: I started to learn about 3 to 4 days before a test. For exams I started about a week beforehand. That worked fine. As I learned I also did exercises. If I could do these I felt I had mastered the subject matter.
>
> For "theory" subjects it is important to keep pace with them. That is what I did as much as I could. That makes a big difference for your learning work. It is also important to repeat it (also important for the "do" subjects). And for these subjects after learning I also did exercises which we discussed in class. If I could do the exercises then I knew I mastered the subject matter. (Hugo, level-two-thinker in 1997)

As a level-two-thinker, Hugo preferred "fun" classes, with a teacher who made jokes, kept the students interested and involved in what was going on, but most importantly who explained everything well. At the end of his studies – in becoming a level-three-thinker – Hugo realised that his views on learning had changed, and that the new way of learning which he developed at the Hotelschool as a result of (his perception of) Enterprising Learning was more to his taste.

> My view on learning has changed considerably over the years. At secondary school it was primarily cramming, cramming and more cramming followed by an exam. Here, I really needed to get used to the new learning style (mastering the subject matter through applying it in assignments).
>
> I must say, my current way of learning is more to my taste than the one I had to use in secondary school. I never was very good at cramming. By applying the subject matter immediately, you understand it and remember it for a longer period of time. …
>
> You only really learn something when you have to apply it in practice. So, doing cases. That is my experience over the years. ... Cases at school then need to be as close to reality as possible to create a good learning situation. And if we get a case that is not based on reality or even nowhere near reality, I wonder about the use of doing this case. … That is why I say, "the more realistic a case, the better a student understands the possible applications of the subject matter". (Hugo, level-three-thinker)

Hugo also realised very well that the approach to teaching at the Hotelschool – in his view the teacher as consultant and the student as independent operator capable of timely asking for teacher guidance/advice – could spell trouble for freshmen because they had not learned to learn/work in this way at secondary school. He felt that a bit more 'mentored learning' in this respect in the first year would help students adapt to this new learning style expected at the Hotelschool. The issue of a more gradual introduction to Enterprising Learning is something we will see mentioned by other students as well (see e.g. Georgina in "across the watershed" below).

The second student we quote as a level-three-thinker at the end of her studies is Nicole (97-2), who started as a typical level-two-thinker, coming straight from pre-professional secondary education. She had a good idea about her view on learning at the start of the Hotelschool and referred to it as well in her exit questionnaire.

> Now I learn mostly by doing instead of the way I learned at secondary school. For instance the elective Training, I learned a lot from that (in this course you need to give two training sessions to fellow students). For my first training I only looked at the theory. I did not do a dry run of my session. Consequently it was really lousy. I learned so much from that training just by doing it. In other words, I changed from "learning and cramming" to "learning by applying". ...
>
> [I really learned something] in the third phase, in the Restaurant case and Hotel case. Everything/all the tools you learned come together there. (Nicole, level-three-thinker)

Nicole seemed to be aware that "applying" knowledge is not the end of her development. She wanted to know and learn more before she felt sufficiently prepared to take the professional position she saw in her future.

> I'm really a curious person. I want to know everything ... And I want to develop myself personally by participating in many [extra curricular] activities (currently I am vice-president of the Student Council). After this school I want to go to university, probably Personnel Science, to hone my analytical and research skills. (Nicole, level-three-thinker)

Nicole's interest in personal development is distinctly different in character from views on personal development we encounter in levels 5 and 6, here at level three it is linked to experiencing activities and acquiring skills. On the other hand, the skills she wanted to acquire would seem to indicate a sense of what is needed in level four. In this sense, Nicole could also have been categorised as developing from level-two-thinker to level-four-thinking-foreseen (see below in the section No change at all?). Nicole's views on the skills that teachers need to teach well illustrate well a prototypical level-three-thinker's views on good teaching.

> [An ideal teacher] needs to possess up-to-date knowledge of the subject he/she teaches. [He/She] needs good social skills, to be open to feedback and discussion. Someone who encourages interaction, is interested in students, in other words someone whose door is open when you run into trouble with your group etcetera. ... I like to hear teachers' examples from practice when relevant to the subject matter. (Nicole, level-three-thinker)

Where Hugo and Nicole both illustrated the dominant aspect of level-three-thinking, reproductive application and understanding, Nicole added the preference for interaction and discussion in the classroom. Nick, our third student here, added a third very common aspect of thinking about learning at this third level, namely an increased selectivity with regard to what to learn. Main criterion here is what students expect that will prove useful, either immediately in doing assignments or later in their professional lives.

> Learning to me is taking in the knowledge that can be useful in everything I do or will do. For me it is very important that the subject matter I learn can be applied in practice. I have to know what I can do with the information and have to understand it before I can take it in. Learning is best by filtering the information for the important points as I see them. (Nick, level-three-thinker)

When asked to elaborate on the "filtering for important points", Nick explained what he meant.

> If you remember those points that you need to be able to apply the subject matter or to use it, then I think you have 'filtered' the information correctly. (Nick, level-three-thinker)

Oddly enough students interpreted this new (or improved) ability to filter (or select) information, resulting in learning less facts, as a loss for learning. They felt they now were learning less thoroughly. Some even mentioned that it felt a bit like cheating because now that they "knew less" they got better grades. Nick also included in his responses a motivational aspect of level three thinking. Whereas intrinsic motivation is usually placed at level four, at this third level students already start to mention that learning is something you do for yourself – and your career in the future. This view on learning is often contrasted to the view of the previous level where learning was seen as something done for parents or to pass exams.

> In 1998 I saw learning primarily as a necessary evil. I did not learn to take in the information but just to get a pass. In the beginning it is al new at the Hotelschool, but after a while you get used to it and you fall back into the attitude of secondary education, school is something you have to get through to move on. (Nick, level-three-thinker)

When responding to the question about his own perception of change since the start of his studies in 1998, Nick was emphatic.

> Absolutely, I know better now. *Learning you do for yourself.* That's why I think it is so important to filter the right information. ... I really don't mind narrowly passing an exam, as long as I know the information I need later in practice or that I know where to find it. (Nick, level-three-thinker, italics ours)

Hugo, Nicole and Nick together give a good overview of what is important for a standard or prototypical level-three student: reproductive application and understanding, selection of information to learn, interaction in class, and learning for yourself/your career. Since in this study the large majority of students graduated from the Hotelschool as level-three-thinkers (see Tables 7.1 and 7.2), we would like to add touches of colour to this standard likeness, deepening our understanding of various themes that play a role at this level of thinking, and the influence of Enterprising Learning on the development of it.

Interaction, both between students and between students and teacher, is an important aspect of the learning environment for students at this level of thinking. In class the interaction often takes the form of a discussion, in which students exchange opinions about the subject matter. Students often mentioned that it helped them 'understand' the subject matter (and thus remember it) better. Something similar was expected from discussion in teams, while doing e.g. cases. Katinka and Maud (both 98-2) both commented on the positive effect of discussing various points of view in a team.

> I must say, now that I'm really used to working in teams I see it in a very positive light. You see, I feel that with a team you get better results. Each member has a certain view and a certain opinion, and when you work in a team you have the opportunity to for instance look at a problem from different viewpoints. (Katinka, level-three-thinker)

> It is good to do an assignment with a team, everybody has different ideas and different views on things and so you can learn from each other. (Maud, level-three-thinker)

At this level many students used the words viewpoint or view when they were actually talking about opinions in a more multiplist sense. Dirk (98-2) made the multiplist nature of views and viewpoints very clear when he discussed the interaction between student and teacher.

> I feel that there should be more mutual respect. I understand that the life experience of a teacher cannot not easily be matched by students, but that doesn't mean that we students have wrong ideas, views or interpretations of theories/situations. More strongly: there is no wrong in interpretations, views or ideas. There may be differences, but wrong does not exist. (Dirk, level-three-thinker)

Here Dirk rephrased almost perfectly the typical multiplist standpoint that any opinion is as good as another. In this multiplist way of thinking 'creativity' is seen as an outcome of the exchange of opinions. It can be interpreted as a synonym for 'following your own ideas' and 'using your common sense' and it has its own place beside (reproductive) application of knowledge. So, creativity here is not theory driven and can be seen as an aspect of subjective knowing (Belenky el al., 1997). Creativity was often mentioned in relation to good assignments.

> A good assignment should
> - give students space to use their creativity,
> - give students the opportunity to use their knowledge,
> - match the subject matter, and
> - be feasible (Katinka, level-three-thinker)

> Case studies are the future. ... students' ideas should be taken seriously. At the Hotelschool they look to some guru's theory too much and the ideas and creativity of students are suppressed. ... Case studies are I feel "good assignments". These assignments are characterised by the creativity or freedom they give to students or student teams. ...
>
> ... it is important that these assignments are evaluated in the right way, I mean that not all problems can be solved using the theory as prescribed by an authority. Theories can be interpreted and can be used in very different ways. Some situations are also solvable by "common sense", use your own mind! That is often forgotten. (Dirk, level-three-thinker)

Dirk's rejection of pure reproductive application, using the theory exactly as the authority (or teacher) prescribed, is echoed by Willem, who, confronted with cultural differences, also had to improvise to make the theories he had learned applicable,

> For instance, now I manage the Executive Lounge and I have to make sure everything runs smoothly. And to make that happen I use a lot of the things I learned at [the Hotel]school. But that does not mean that it does run smoothly. In the first weeks I ran into problems I never learned anything about at school. Logical of course, you cannot be prepared for everything. But what school did teach me is ways to solve the problems.
>
> To give another example. At school we had the subject Marketing Management. A wonderful subject by the way. And as this is a newly opened hotel I had a number of projects going on, e.g. increasing "the brand name" of the hotel. In setting up these projects I used a lot of the theories that I learned [at school]. Only, in China it doesn't really work the usual way. And so I had to bend the theories to make them applicable to [China]. (Willem, level-three-thinker)

Perhaps here Dirk and Willem also illustrated an aspect of a more gradual or continuous development from one stage to another than is captured in the current developmental model. Both could perhaps have been categorised as level-four-thinking-foreseen, as Nicole above. In the so-called Perry ratings Dirk, Willem and Nicole might have been categorised as 3,3,4 (see chapter 3). Although sometimes we saw movement within this level 3 thinking, one common characteristic of many of these stories placed them firmly in the reproductive part of the model, namely the students' quantitative view on knowledge. Very often, when asked about what learning and knowledge meant to them, these students used metaphors that indicated having or collecting 'things', items that may prove useful later on (see also chapter 1). Dirk did not only see knowledge as a collection of things, he saw his future mainly as collecting even more things

> I think I will keep on learning all my life. What I want to achieve is possessing a lot of information about many different issues ... to learn more about cultures, people, etcetera ... The shop-trolley that is my life should be well filled before I leave this existence. (Dirk, level-three-thinker)

Eline (98-2) used a somewhat more common metaphor for knowledge as a collection of items, in this case luggage with essential items you may need at your next destination, your (working) life

> Good teaching … is getting the feeling that you have collected knowledge that really is useful. It has to be tangible. … Knowledge should be a whole, [it's] the luggage you are given to take along as you enter the labour market. (Eline, level-three-thinker)

When asked to explain what she meant when she described knowledge as "tangible" Eline responded

> … tangible: the idea that it is useful to learn because you will be able to apply it later and you can change what you know into meaningful work. You need to feel that what you learn is leading you somewhere and that it has a use. (Eline, level-three-thinker)

This preoccupation with the use of knowledge, that students themselves often recognised as a major development in their learning, some students attributed to the new way of learning they encountered at the Hotelschool, see for instance Christine, Katinka and Maud below.

> When I came to the Hotelschool in 1998, what really surprised me was that we were forced to learn in a different way. I mean we were "cut loose" and had to look for information ourselves. It wasn't presented to you on a platter anymore. (Christine, level-three-thinker)

> I think [my ideas about learning changed] because of school. The system at the Hotelschool is based on enterprising learning, I think I just got used to it. It could be that if a different "system" had been in place, I would have changed in a different way and my idea of learning would be based on that [system]. If I had gone to university I probably would have gotten a different view on learning. (Katinka, level-three-thinker)

> … I know I used to cram a lot in secondary school (pretty unavoidable when you are doing four foreign languages) and I think I thought that was normal. We hadn't done anything that looked like "enterprising learning". At the Hotelschool you start out with theory and then gradually you start to apply more and more, with the underlying theory in you memory. Secondly, the information you need is not just lying around, you have to go out and look for it on internet/in the library. That's what I think is normal now, so perhaps you can say my view on learning changed from "cramming" to enterprising learning and applying theory in practice. (Maud, level-three-thinker)

It is interesting to note that for many of the graduates of the Hotelschool, level three thinking is the meaning they gave to Enterprising Learning. Zoë, a level-three-thinker from 98-2, was even more clear than Maud in her interpretation of Enterprising Learning

> Currently learning to me is the so-called "enterprising learning"... meaning to me that in phase 3 you are fairly broadly "developed", you know about a lot of things. The assignments in phase 3 are also broad, so that you know you need to look for information, what do you need to know exactly, what way you need to go about finding this information and how you need to analyse it to make it useful. In the modules of phase 2, the nature or aim of a lot of assignments remained the same over the years, so that you could always find an example to look at and see what the purpose or aim of an assignment was. Because the Hotel case and the Restaurant case are fairly specific, [in phase 3] this is not an option and a student is forced to go out and actively look for relevant information (what do you need, what are you going to use it for, where do you think you will find it within the timeframe given). ... You ask the teachers of phase 2 questions. ... [You] go to the library more, read more about issues that you are not familiar enough with. Before this you could get pretty far with only [a few basic] books. In phase 3 that all changes. (Zoë, level-three-thinker)

Zoë saw a progression in required 'depth' of learning in the curriculum. Not all students saw this and some became disillusioned. We will discuss responses of these latter students in the next chapter in the section on frictions, disenchantment and nostalgia.

As we have said before – and it will be argued again in the final chapters of this study – level three thinking, while very common among graduates of higher education, is not actually seen as satisfying the espoused goals of higher education. That assertion, and the constant reminder that this development is within the reproductive range of views on learning, might make readers underestimate the students' achievement in developing so far. For many students it was a major effort and definitely "nothing to be sneezed at". As Ian wrote in discussing the move from memorising to applying, and explaining how he himself found out that learning through applying knowledge proved more useful than memorising and reproducing it on tests

> In my opinion memorisation (...) of facts is useless, unless you understand how to apply the knowledge. ... I think a few examples might help [to] explain ... ... [Reading] a book on wine or several books for that matter ... doesn't mean that you are a sommelier. ... you need to be shown how, what you read in books translates into the real world and how to identify it. ... This is not so much a new element [in learning] but something that I think is overlooked by a lot of educational institutions as they feel that the translation of their theory into the big wide world is merely the next obvious step. *But it's always easy once you know how*. (Ian, level-three-thinker, 98-2, italics ours)[3]

That Enterprising Learning was a pretty unique approach at the Hotelschool, a way of working and learning that was so embedded in the 'culture' of the school that hardly any student paused to question it, only emphasises that Enterprising Learning was an external formula that students were taught to follow, sometimes willy-nilly. This formula not only "constrained" students to work in a certain way but – by its repetition and thoroughness – it built up students' confidence that they were ready for the next step, the real world. As Eline said, she realised that now at the end of her studies it was time to stop following what other people said she should do. It was time to start making her own decisions and Enterprising Learning had given her the confidence to feel she would be able to

> I think in these four years I have gotten a clearer image of what I want and how I want to do it. One of my goals is to develop, to move on. I think I was less aware of that in 1998 because I was at the beginning of a time of studying and I thought that I would be guided through (and by) it. But now I'm at the end and it's up to me to decide what I want to do and which way I will choose after school....
>
> At school there is a fixed developmental route for all students. Now I am at the start of a new part of my life, that I will fill in all by myself. There will be no teachers or school managers to interfere. (Eline, level-three-thinker, in 2004)

In this sense we feel that level three thinking is a prerequisite for the move to self-authorship (Kegan, 1994) and as such it is indeed *not* something to be sneezed at.

Across the Watershed (to level 4)

In this section we discuss those students who developed from reproductive learning to constructive learning and so have met the espoused goals of higher education. We will demonstrate that the students we have encountered in our study seem to move from reproductive learning to constructive learning with a longer or shorter stay at the highest level of reproductive learning, namely level 3 (see also the introduction of this chapter).

Moving from 2 to 4

Over the two semesters 27 students developed from learning-teaching conception 2, leaping across the watershed, to learning-teaching conception 4. We have selected four students from both semesters to illustrate this development. Jasper responded to the exit-questionnaire in 2003, and his entry-level was determined using the retrospective account of his view on learning in 1998.

> The first months at the Hotelschool were not dominated by learning or studying. In the case of an exam, I started one day before and then just hoped for a good outcome (that did not happen often!). Learning to me was cramming facts and practicing with old exams. No deeper thoughts came into it, let alone looking for connections. (Jasper, level-two-thinker in 1998)

Jasper realised he had changed his views on learning and teaching considerably, which he attributed in part to events other than studying at the Hotelschool

> As the years have gone by I certainly began to think differently about studying/learning. To some extent this is the result of a number of private

> events in the last five years that made me think differently about life, but also it is due to just getting older. (Jasper, level-four-thinker)

Jasper's observation almost literally echoes Reybold (2001), who remarked that "... other factors may stimulate epistemological change, including maturation or age and life experiences" (p. 414). His conception of learning in 2003 is clearly other than in 1998, and he described in an implicit way the development running through level 3,

> I personally feel that "learning by heart" becomes less and less important as you move through your studies. The ability to reproduce facts loses its value as seeing relationships becomes more important. The way of thinking plays a larger role than factual knowledge per se. Basic knowledge you need to have ready at hand, detailed knowledge can be looked up and be applicable as well. In order to train [my way of thinking] as my studies progress, it becomes more important to focus on developing my general knowledge, e.g. by reading journals such as the Economist, Newsweek, training myself in seeing connections. ...
>
> The area of "really" learning something becomes more grey as my studies progress. Because for me it's no longer about learning facts, but seeing relationships and through this the "big picture". (Jasper, level-four-thinker)

At this level, the role of the ideal teacher changes in a way that makes it more challenging and complicated to teach. Teachers are expected to be really interested in many aspects of their own subject, open-minded (and flexible), and they need to challenge the student *and themselves* in teaching, as Jasper wrote in response to the question about "a good assignment",

> An assignment where you are forced to dive into the current state of affairs and where you are pushed just that little bit further than just copying facts. By giving the student the opportunity to make connections and use his own creativity, the teacher is also stimulated to keep up and not be run over. (Jasper, level-four-thinker)

Georgina was a fellow student from the same semester (98-2). Her entry-level is also based on her retrospective account which was enhanced through several email follow-ups requesting elaboration on her entry-level thinking. From this email conversation (2001 through 2002) the following view could be reconstructed.

> In 98 I saw learning as something you had to do. I thought nothing "special" of going to higher education, everybody does it don't they? I also saw it primarily as learning for exams. ... In the beginning of my studies I found it pretty easy to pass an exam. Usually it was sufficient to learn some old exams and then I would pass. You could call this memorising.
>
> What I didn't find schoolish in the beginning was the co-operation with other students in groups. Everyone was so dependent on each other and my independence was severely tested. This was totally new to me. I do feel that

> in this first year you are thrown in at the deep end. I myself would have preferred to have had a little more preparation for Enterprising Learning. I also felt that some teachers really took the easy way out by saying, "Well, that's Enterprising Learning for you. You have to find your own information." ... A little more attention to explaining the purpose and the importance of Enterprising Learning in the first year would have helped. (Georgina, level-two-thinker in 1998)

Georgina proceeded to elaborate extensively on a number of experiences at the Hotelschool that had influenced her views on learning, teaching and *herself*. We present a selection of her remarks below.

> Working together ... is something I learned ceaselessly at the Hotelschool. Especially in the first year I had many negative experiences with teamwork. ... for instance not keeping to agreements, not meeting set deadlines, the combination of living and working together ... unfulfilled expectations, and I can go on for a while yet. This way I have learned much about my own way of working, and also how I can adapt and apply [this way of working] to achieve what I want. ... This way I learned to handle different ways of working and thinking....
>
> I was lucky to do the training electives. ... These have been very important to me because they helped me to prepare freshmen for the teamwork that is so dominant at the Hotelschool. I had the opportunity to teach these students. This helps you realise what you learned yourself. It was a real eye-opener to me.
>
> I learned to give and receive feedback. Especially in the beginning I found it very difficult to receive negative feedback. I saw this as a personal attack. I still find it difficult, but now I realise that you can learn the most from this type of feedback. (Georgina, level-four-thinker)

The combination of these (and other) experiences led Georgina to change her views on learning and teaching and by 2001/2002 she had come to see learning as,

> ... [meaning] something else. I see it more as developing myself. I notice that now I pick up things that I want to learn and I would like to know more about. ...
>
> I also find that I am far more independent ... which is I think the aim of Enterprising Learning. I feel that teacher guidance in phase 3 should stay as it is now ...
>
> I have learned the most from the final project. This project is rooted in reality. I found out how much information is needed to underpin a project and paint a realistic picture. I myself am responsible for the course of the project and the contacts with the principal. .. During my time at the Hotelschool I have acquired a lot of information about many subjects. Now I have completed these subjects, I can make connections and I see that these subjects flow together. (Georgina, level-four-thinker)

In response to an inquiry on what she meant with the reference to "teacher guidance in phase 3" (see chapter 8), she responded,

> What makes the guidance so good is the fact that I feel I am now more on an equal level with teachers. For instance that I can discuss particular issues with teachers and do not have to accept [what teachers say] anymore. I now have the opportunity to form and express my own opinion as long as it is supported by literature. ... Now I really see that you can learn in different ways. I notice for instance that now in my management internship, ... doing a presentation or training is something I "just" do. (Georgina, level-four-thinker)

Georgina's willingness to continue the email conversation is exemplified by her invitation to continue after the third email contact.

> Dcar Mr. van Rossum,
>
> Are you sure you don't have any further questions? I have to work [in night reception] all weekend so I have all the time in the world to answer more of them!
>
> I really hope my answers help you in your research.
>
> Kind regards,
> Georgina

And indeed about three months later she was more than happy to continue our conversation and added valuable information. Georgina's story is most informative because of the insight she gives us in the effect of various elements of Enterprising Learning and some subjects on the changing of her views on learning, teaching and herself. The third student we quote here, Hester, is a student of semester 97-2, who finished her studies before we started with email conversations. Hester's entry-level learning-teaching conception included almost all dominant aspects of the way of thinking at level 2.

> I knew I mastered the subject matter if I could retell what was in the book, if I knew the important definitions and concepts, and if I could do particular assignments/questions from the exercise book or textbook without making mistakes. What I wanted to achieve was getting a good grade. I always aimed for more than a pass and I usually succeeded.
>
> [In ideal teaching] the first 20 minutes or so is spent on explaining something or providing information, after which you are supposed to work with the information just provided yourself. This means to say that in all classes there is *some action*, not only having to hear longwinded and boring stories, because at a certain moment you concentration will be gone. If [teaching] is alternated with "do-things" classes are easier to live with and you learn more because you are paying more attention when teachers tell you something. A good teacher can explain well, knows the answers to your questions, or tells you where you can find them, ... (Hester, level-two-thinker in 1997, italics ours)

In particular in comparing her exit-teaching conception the development becomes clear. Hester also commented on the usefulness of group work and the emphasis on practical work at the Hotelschool, that had influenced her views on learning and teaching.

> I have learned not to work only on my own anymore. I've learned to accept the outcome of teamwork and not to try to put things right all by myself anymore. I do however, still work towards achieving an optimal group result. ...
>
> ... I did often miss theoretical depth at the Hotelschool. Perhaps a university education would fit me better, because I have this love for theory. I did learn in my time at the Hotelschool that practical thinking has its merits and advantages and I learned to combine the two methods of learning. Learning to me is gaining insight in - to me - still unknown matters.
>
> [Good] teaching invites students to think for themselves about the theory the teacher provided. ... [The ideal teacher] is a coach/counsellor while the students do assignments/discuss a particular subject. He/she is open to new/ other views/explanations of theory and stimulates students to think about the theory and to do something with it. ...
>
> [I really learned] during the final project. I see this project as the first real challenge outside my [first] external operational internship... A good assignment mirrors reality... (Hester, level-four-thinker)

Hester admitted she had learned a lot at the Hotelschool, implicitly indicating a move from memorising theory, through learning to apply it, towards combining these two ways of learning into learning to think for herself. Here we feel that again support is found for the assumption that students move to level-four-thinking only through level-three-thinking. At the same time she also felt insufficiently challenged by the depth of the Enterprising Learning curriculum as it was implemented at that time, and was considering further education at the university. The final student we quote here, Sara, made the move from level-two-thinker to level-four-thinker, through level-three-thinking more explicit.

> My attitude to learning has changed over the years that I was at the Hotelschool! First I thought I wasn't learning anything. Now, some years later, I realised that here at school you learn a different way of thinking, e.g. a critical helicopter view. You also learn to work in teams and solve problems independently. ... [In 1998] I saw learning as memorising knowledge. But until then I hadn't encountered any examples of where I could apply my knowledge in practice. When I did see that [I could apply my knowledge] I also saw that what you had learned could not always be applied in a standard way. But the idea behind it could. That made me look at things differently ... You come to the conclusion that there are no standard solutions to problems... [and] there are no standard problems with matching solutions. You cannot learn everything from books! (Sara, level-four-thinker)

Moving from 3 to 4

Of the five students who developed from learning-teaching conception 3 to 4, thereby – while moving only one stage upwards – crossing the difficult threshold between reproductive and constructive learning, we quote Eva. Eva's entry-level was categorised primarily based on her conception of good teaching

> The most important thing was that I understood the subject matter and so passed my exams …
>
> I learned the most from lessons where you worked together with the teacher by discussing or doing sums. A good teacher is sort of equal to the students and does not put himself above them, so students "want" to learn. (Eva, level-three-thinker in 1997)

While the usual focus of level 3, application, is not mentioned here, Eva was categorised as a level-three-thinker because of her need for more interaction (than a typical level-two-thinker, who is satisfied with the opportunity to ask questions) and for a more equal student-teacher relationship. This example shows as well that not all students mention all aspects of a way of knowing. Eva already emphasised understanding here, but as we have seen in chapter 1, understanding at level three focuses on reproduction and discussing what is learnt. Her responses to the exit-questionnaire in 2000 were more elaborate and contained far more references to the typical level-four-thinker way of thinking.

> I have really learned something when I see the relationships, understand the logic of it. When I understand the main line, or main idea and the related sub ideas I have learned something. …
>
> I (still) feel it is not really useful to learn complete definitions by heart (or stupid lists) because this doesn't help you see the relationships!! (Eva, level-four-thinker)

At level 4 students expect a different kind of interaction than at level 3, not merely an exchange of opinions in the form of discussions between teacher and students, but in an ideal class students are encouraged to think,

> … an ideal teacher tries to teach interactively. With this I mean that everybody thinks along and talks about what they think (about the subject under discussion) so that different viewpoints emerge. (Eva, level-four-thinker)

Eva felt that now and then she was inhibited in following her interests and her own way of thinking when working in a group.

> Sometimes I'm really interested in an assignment or project, but because of "pressure" from group members I'm not allowed to go into it as deeply as I would like to. (Eva, level-four-thinker)

Here we see one of the less discussed aspects of the move across the watershed, namely the change in type of motivation. Where in the first three levels, students are motivated by external goals (e.g. learning for parents, passing exams, future career), on the other side of the divide suddenly one's own interests become a driving force, motivation becomes intrinsic and the end product of your learning/work becomes something to be proud of.

> What I want to achieve [with learning] is that I get some peace in my head (as long as the subject interests me that is). Then I really want to understand everything about it, just for the sake of understanding!!
>
> ...
>
> [When] my interest has been aroused, then I will do my utmost best to make something really good. (Eva, level-four-thinker)

The main theme in Eva's thinking at the end of her studies is the strong tie between interest, intrinsic motivation and understanding, with understanding meaning getting the main idea and thinking logically. With her continuous search for understanding, driven by a personal need or interest, Eva is a real life example of the type of student Biggs typified as "a Susan" (Biggs, 2003 and chapter 11). Susans are students who more or less 'teach themselves' because as King and Kitchener (1994) phrased it they love to learn, seek new challenges voluntarily, take responsibility for their learning and enjoy intellectually stimulating environments.

Moving Beyond 4

In the current study there were only two students (both from semester 97-2) who developed beyond learning-teaching conception 4, namely Marius and Philip.[4] Both started out with learning-teaching conception 2, as Philip described,

> My favourite way of learning is to study the subject matter and then do an old exam or practice questions. Where I answer incorrectly I will go back and revise ... I would start by reading the entire subject matter through once, very lightly. Then go through [it] again, this time really digesting everything I had read.
>
> ...
>
> [A good teacher] presents the theory in an interesting manner. He also repeats the important things he has said during the lessons. (Philip, level-two-thinker in 1997)

Marius added to this view that at his private secondary school he was helped and supported with everything, and so also with learning, which he felt made learning easier and more fun. When contacted in 2002 (Marius) and 2003 (Philip), both young men had a pretty good idea of how they saw learning in 1997.

> In retrospect, learning in 1997 was fun and instructive, as we discussed over the phone. Private schooling – with only eight pupils per class and a teacher who really prepares you well for your final exams. Private schooling gives you the ultimate guidance from beginning to end, very little things you have to find out yourself. .... When I started at the Hotelschool it suddenly was totally different. Living in a dormitory, and having to organise everything yourself for the first time without the help you've had all you life from childhood upwards. Two to a room, sixteen to a house. (Marius, level-five-thinker in 2002)

Philip was not really sure of his exact views on learning and teaching in 1997, but he remembered that,

> ... I had a very black & white view on the world. I probably saw learning as something in the lines of the mastery of a body of knowledge as the way to prepare for life. In other words I saw the process of learning as being stagnant as opposed to dynamic. (Philip, level-six-thinker in 2003)

In his second year Marius started his operational internship in the U.K. where he had a great time until he heard his brother had been diagnosed with leukaemia, an event which according to Reybold (2001) may have contributed to his larger than average epistemological development.

> England was just super, I realised there that I am a real doer, later thinking also came into it, but then it was mainly seeing and doing. But besides the fun time I had, less pleasant things happened at home (in the Netherlands). My brother became ill, and this impacted me and my family a great deal. My bother was diagnosed with leukaemia in November 1998 and became mired in the hospital process, chemotherapy and other horrible things. ... I got a lot of support from school ... and I finished this internship which still gives me satisfaction. ....
>
> After my internship a lot happened .... the world turned on, but not for me. In 99 I did my practicals and some main subjects, but I don't know which ones. I do know I had to resit some of the main subjects. In December 99 my brother died, and after some months of doing nothing I returned to school, but I focused on small things mainly. Then I also did a second time around for the main subjects and finished up some old things. (Marius, level-five-thinker)

From his response to the learning conception question it became clear that Marius definitely had changed his view on learning and teaching by 2002, in becoming a level-five-thinker,

> Learning is broadening your perspective and becoming better in supporting your answers with arguments based on the knowledge you have. What I want to achieve with learning is acquiring sufficient knowledge to be able to argue my

> view points well, this means with (factual) knowledge. Something important I learned is being able to think logically … (Marius, level-five-thinker)

When asked (by return email) to elaborate on the phrase "Learning is broadening your perspective …" Marius replied,

> Through learning you begin to see things from different perspectives, from different points of view. That is what I mean with broadening your perspective!

His view on teaching had become very independence-oriented, a considerable change from his preference for the well cared-for environment of his private school time. His ideal teacher was his current "boss" at his management internship who

> … creates a very pleasant work atmosphere and lets me find out things for myself. When I have questions, I can always go to him. Especially the combination of good atmosphere and open communication are two factors which appeal to me and motivate me very much. (Marius, level-five-thinker)

This thirst for independence was also dominant in his view on a good assignment,

> To me, the final project is still a really good assignment. Looking for a project yourself, making contact yourself, posing the problem yourself and solving it yourself, with the option of asking the teacher or coach concerned questions. … The end product is a report that really represents your views... (Marius, level-five-thinker)

Marius' answers contained the major aspects of learning-teaching conception 5: i.e. the awareness of multiple perspectives, the emphasis on dialogue between teacher and student (boss and employee), and the need to be independent - finding your own way of (or approach to) handling problems and projects.

In 2003 Philip saw learning quite differently from his perception of stagnation he remembered from 1997.

> … I think good education is that which installs the skills necessary for life long learning. I am not too sure how to describe these skills but something in the line of critical thinking, quantitative reasoning, effective communication, ability to find needed information, the ability to work well with others. I think as well that the student-teacher relationship has to be equal. Perhaps even a business client relationship. I think teachers should also be engaged in the same process they are facilitating to develop in the students, namely continuous learning.
>
> The time period for which you are associated to the learning institute should change from the prescribed 4 years to life. (Philip, level-six-thinker)

As we saw above, Philip remembered his learning in 1997 as being "stagnant as opposed to dynamic". When asked to elaborate on that particular description, Philip started his reply with the following introduction or "explanation",

> I have to start by saying that this is definitely not a topic that allows one to shake the answers out of your sleeve. I am going to take the same approach as I did previously; just think and type and not ponder too much about sense and structure. I leave that up to you to decipher. The reason for this little explanation lies in the fact that when I think about the topic and questions you have asked me, my thought process just seems to snowball due to the topic's magnitude and being a perfectionist doesn't help either. I understand completely why you are writing a research paper on this. (Philip, level-six-thinker)

In an attempt to explain the difference between learning as a stagnant or a dynamic process, Philip found it difficult to find the right words.

> The following phrase has got something to do with what I think about it. A stagnant process is such when it is not synchronised with the speed of its external environment. …

He only found his voice about this matter when describing the ideal learning-teaching environment in response to a request to elaborate on the "business client relationship" between teacher and student.

> I think that if a student is dependent on the teacher or vice versa then this will create limits/barriers to the learning process. Namely the focus point tends to shift away from exploring the subject matter and towards interpersonal relationships etcetera. Possibly I am being a little too idealistic here. The ideal relationship is one where the teacher and student can be completely authentic with each other. Namely that here is nothing between them other than the intention to really learn/develop etcetera not to just get a grade or other motives. In this ideal relationship the role of teacher does not only lie with the person employed by the institution. This I think also supports dynamic learning; there is no fixed way things have to take place. Not like in the conventional means of education. The difference remains, at least should remain, that the teacher brings a greater supply of experience in learning. This is what allows him to be the facilitator. (Philip, level-six-thinker)

And elaborating on his view on dynamic learning Philip wrote,

> I believe the process [of learning] is infinite because time keeps on going, we as humans age both physically and mentally. As a result you are constantly adjusting that what you considered to be true. With true I do not mean what is right or, the other way around, what is false [or] wrong. But what works and does not work. I guess that's why they say: discovering the colour of truth. (Philip, level-six-thinker)

In this description we recognise all the important aspects of learning-teaching conception 6: i.e. the authentic relationship, the fact that learning and teaching are a two-way street, the irrelevance of teaching methods and the ever-changing nature of truth. In addition we see an alternative focus of teaching that we will discuss in more detail in chapter 11, namely a learning-teaching environment that is neither teacher-centred, nor student-centred but subject-centred (Palmer, 1998).

Lack of Development

As we have seen in Tables 7.1 and 7.2, some 15% of all students (97-2 and 98-2) fail to develop epistemologically. In particular the lack of development for level 2 (and perhaps also 3) could be seen as undesirable, as these students graduate with an insufficient level of epistemological sophistication. However, as we read through these essay-questionnaires and email conversations, we noticed subtle differences within the entrenched level-two-thinkers and level-three-thinkers. In this section we first present the responses of students who display no indication of epistemological growth at all. In the next section we discuss evidence for small – but perhaps significant – within-category developments indicating that epistemological growth is perhaps less stage like – and more continuous – than the models treated in this study suggest.

Entrenched level-two-thinkers

The first student we will quote here, Irene (98-2), came directly to the Hotelschool from pre-university secondary school. She thought that working in groups would definitely be different and was looking forward to it. However, she discovered that it did not fit well with her preferred way of learning, her view on knowledge and teaching.

> To me, learning consists of two things, knowledge and skills that you both need to master. At this time and at this school, I feel that I haven't learned much, and then I'm talking about knowledge. This is because we do a lot in groups and because the exams do not go that deeply. I found this a pity, especially right after I left secondary school and I still miss it a lot. I did learn lots of skills here ...[but] I have really learned something (at least that is how I really feel) if I have dived into the books to study certain subject matter. (Irene, level-two-thinker)

At the time we found it surprising that someone could seem to "choose" not to change even after being exposed continuously to group work focusing on applying knowledge in practice. In an attempt to check our first impression of lack of development, Irene was asked again by email if she felt she had changed at all. In response she wrote,

> I really haven't changed, I thought just briefly that working in groups would be good for me, but I realised quickly that I was wrong. ... I was young and wanted something [different]. Memorising and understanding in "the old fashioned way" worked perfectly for me. I still think about learning that way. I want it to be like it used to be, just a teacher in front of the class who explains the subject matter and if I have a question I want to be able to pose it

> so I can understand. ... All that looking for information yourself, just give me a couple of books to study ... and for the rest old fashioned lectures, and lots of them. Not too much group work, now and then is ok ... not all that independent learning if you please. (Irene, level-two-thinker)

It seems that Irene's disappointment in group work, especially the lack of depth that can be an initial result of team work, led her to look away from the possible challenge and advantages of learning to apply what knowledge you "learn" in a reproductive way. A certain disappointment with regard to the perceived challenges posed by higher education may also lie at the root of the lack of development observed in another student, Rosalie (97-2).

> My way of learning at the Hotelschool certainly changed over the years. At the start I learned long and hard, but that is less now. At first I was motivated to pass everything in one go. Then you notice that if you fail it's a pity, but you can easily resit in six weeks time. That's become my largest tripping-stone at school. Every time I think, "its not that important, I can do it again in six weeks time". ... Before, at secondary school you really had to pass or you would stay down. ... At secondary school it really gave me satisfaction to pass an exam, because then I had really learned a lot. ...
>
> Good teaching to me is teaching where students are not left completely free. With this I mean the new curriculum. [Sometimes subjects] were taught differently. You would get a fixed teacher to guide you on a weekly basis and who talked to you about your assignment only. This meeting was only for your own assignment and for your own group. It usually lasted about one hour, but in that time you could discuss everything and ask lots of questions. At that moment, you have the teacher's attention.(Rosalie, level-two-thinker)

Perhaps here, we have found an example of a student who may have indicated a more surface-level approach to learning if asked to evaluate the appropriateness of surface or deep level strategies to her own learning in a questionnaire. However, for now this remains speculation.

Entrenched level-three-thinkers

The second group of students to dig themselves deeper into their existing level of thinking is the group of students who entered the Hotelschool at level three and remained there. These level-three-thinkers fall into three sub-categories: firstly, entrenchment, which we will discuss here; secondly, subtle development, which we have called level-four-thinking-foreseen and which is discussed and illustrated in the section "No change?" below. The third theme that is actually dominant in this group is disenchantment with their studies and the Hotelschool. This latter group and their issues are discussed in the next chapter.

In a way, the reason for entrenchment for Cecile (98-2) echoes that of Irene above. Cecile found Enterprising Learning too much focused on application and practice, and too little on acquiring theoretical knowledge. In 1998 her idea of learning was a

> … large desk, tea and cookies, books on the table, closed door, music and then reading the text. Underlining and marking important things or jotting them down. … Six hours [of studying] a day was fine, it was my maximum concentration span... For languages [I would] practice texts, … for history and economics mostly doing questions and think about the subject matter. … I would also often learn with … friends around the table and then study. Discussing difficult things. Everybody has a different view on an issue. That's how you knew you really knew or understood it. (Cecile, level-three-thinker)

In 2001 she still saw learning as divided into theoretical knowledge and practical application,

> Learning is understanding and memorising something. I think there will always be a difference between people who understand and memorise by learning it by heart and those who understand and memorise by experiencing it in practice or in a "natural setting". … I feel the school is deficient with regard to the first way of learning: learning by heart. This to me is actually *real learning* and it's hardly required here. …
>
> I still think I never learned so much in such a short period of time as I did at secondary school. It's not that I didn't learn a lot here, just that I learned in a very different way and about completely different things. That is probably the result of the practical aspect of professional education. Everything but real theoretical knowledge I have learned here, and I'm convinced I learned a lot here. There is however a BUT.
>
> … By learning in groups all the time, you get the idea that you cannot work individually anymore. … The only individual learning you do is for exams. …
>
> [I would prefer] teaching in small groups (up to 15). This encourages discussions about issues. [For instance] the class of … started with a short theoretical introduction about the subject of the next assignment. Then we discussed the work of each group. We all had the same assignment, but each group developed its own view. Those were then discussed.
>
> … I feel a deep need for theory. Then I understand and remember it better. Theory alone would in many cases be sufficient for me. (Cecile, level-three-thinker, italics ours)

As Irene, Cecile felt the Hotelschool was too practical to her taste and therefore turned her eyes away from the opportunity to develop in a (possibly unexpected) way. Perhaps a "little more attention to explaining the purpose and the importance of Enterprising Learning in the first year" as suggested by Georgina above would have helped both Irene and Cecile to overcome their reluctance to change.

Entrenched level-four-thinkers

Only two students belonged to the group of entrenched level-four-thinkers. Joyce (97-2) was most eloquent in her critical view on Enterprising Learning. Again a certain measure of disappointment plays a role here, and we have seen similar forms of disappointment (disenchantment) in a previous study of student development in the old curriculum (van Rossum et al., 2002; see also Table 7.3 above). We will come back to the issue of disenchantment and add relevant new data from the current study in the next chapter.

Joyce started by describing the way she saw and experienced learning at secondary school.

> Really studying means to me that I have to put in effort to understand the subject matter. ... The last time I really studied was at my [pre-university] secondary school, in particular for subjects as physics, biology, chemistry and mathematics. I also did a semester of psychology at university during my third year at the Hotelschool. At my secondary school and for psychology I really needed to study. I had to make connections and cramming did not enter the picture at all. You had to understand what it was about, and the subject matter really needed to be made your own to see the various logical connections. (Joyce, level-four-thinker)

Her experience of learning at the Hotelschool did not meet her expectations.

> At the Hotelschool I never really studied. .. It is more like I look at the main points of the subject matter and take [what I have read] with me into the exam. ... At the Hotelschool I have had to cram definitions or subject matter into my head to pass the exam. ... As I said before, I don't feel I really have to study anymore. I am still pretty serious about looking at my notes, but I feel I have sort of unlearned real studying. ...
>
> Besides studying, learning also has a social meaning to me. Learning particular behaviours and the consequences of these behaviours. This [kind of learning] is more than amply provided at the Hotelschool. (Joyce, level-four-thinker)

Both students in this group were critical about the level and depth of theoretical knowledge and learning at the Hotelschool, but still remained fairly positive about the fact that they learned a lot about the interpersonal dimension of learning, as Soraya (98-2) said

> Personally I think that I learned a lot at the Hotelschool socially and that was confirmed during my internship. We have become real team players with attention for colleagues and we know how to give feedback in a clear and calm way. (Soraya, level-four-thinker)

No Change at All?

As mentioned above, the presence of students seemingly not developing to a higher level provided us with the opportunity to observe small within-level developments, indicating that the development described in epistemological development models may be even more gradual than frequently is found (*during* higher education).

Level-three-thinking-foreseen

A number of entrenched level-two-thinkers characterised their own learning as having changed since the start at the Hotelschool, while objectively speaking they remained firmly within the parameters of level-two-thinking. Looking more closely at their responses these students claimed to have become

- more (but vaguely) aware of the option of using what you have learned at some time in the future,
- more independent in their learning,
- more selective in deciding what to learn, and
- somewhat more confident about asking questions.

All these changes were observed without students changing their basic approach to and view on learning, nor changing their preference for (traditional) lectures. Below we quote two students to illustrate the changes observed between entry and exit-levels

In 1998 Pauline saw learning and teaching as,

> In the final year I … made summaries, and read them well. I made old exams... And I asked teachers many questions when I felt I couldn't do it alone. …
>
> I also liked classes where teachers "spoon-fed" you … so you knew what was really important and what you needed to know well. (Pauline, level-two-thinker)

In 2002 she felt her view on learning had changed and she described it as follows,

> After a while you learn that there are topics you see some future in. Topics you would like to know more about. … I mean topics that either have to do with your studies or with your general knowledge. For instance I would like to know more about history, while that used to be the first subject to drop in secondary education. …
>
> My ideal class is a lecture. I'm not a real studying type, but I pick things up quickly when they are told or explained. I like it when a teacher tells a story and leaves me free to make notes and lets me determine what is important and what not. I really hate it when you have to copy sheets the teacher has made. (Pauline, level-three-thinking-foreseen)

Our second student from this group, Tina (97-2), described her learning in 2001 as more selective than before.

> Even though I still make summaries, by hand (for else I don't feel I have really learned something if I haven't written it down myself), I have learned to split large amounts of subject matter into important and less important parts. So my summaries actually have become better. …
>
> An ideal teacher is someone who gives you the feeling that you cannot ask a stupid question…. Maybe because I was very anxious to fail, and I still find it difficult to ask questions in public, fearing to be seen as stupid. … Furthermore

> a teacher should try to treat students on an equal footing to lower the threshold for contact (from both sides) whenever lack of clarity occurs. (Tina, level-three–foreseen)

Based on these stories, we assume that if the vague awareness observed e.g. in Pauline's responses, in time becomes an acute awareness of the future usefulness of things learned, these students may move on to becoming full level-three-thinkers with the other aspects catching up as well.

Level-four-thinking-foreseen

In the current study we found only a few entrenched-level-three-thinker students responding in a somewhat a-typical level-three-thinker way in the exit questionnaire, which seemed to us to indicate a growing awareness of themes that are dominant in level 4. We quote Leon (97-2) who strongly rejected memorisation in preference of a reproductive type of application and understanding.

> I learn by reading through all the material to understand it … then I do assignments until I can do them quickly and without making mistakes. This method is beyond simple "cramming" … (Leon, level-three-thinker in 1997)

About four years later Leon described that, while he still learned in the same way, he had tried to improve on it since starting at the Hotelschool by paying more attention to learning. Looking closely at his responses the change is best observed in his exit teaching conception, with his learning conception not fundamentally different from that in August 1997. Below first we present his exit learning conception followed by his exit teaching conception.

> When a book seems to have a logical structure, I learn the chapters in sequence … For the learning itself I first read "quickly" through the chapter/book to get an idea of the relationships between the parts. Then I learn it in more detail so I understand the content as well as I can. …
>
> I learn the most by engaging in a pragmatic way with the content. The ideal teacher can explain the subject matter well. Furthermore he should indicate the relationships between the parts clearly and must be able to explain how the theory should be applied in practice. …
>
> [In a good assignment] not only the similarities between theory and practice are treated, but also the discrepancies. With this I mean that you don't only learn how to apply the theory in practice, but also when this is not possible or causes problems. (Leon, level-four-thinking-foreseen)

Even at the end of his studies, Leon was still a level-three-thinker in essence, because he expected the teacher (or the author of the textbook) to take the lead in sequencing the content and making connections. His role was 'merely' to understand the content as presented in a reproductive way. However, in the final section of this excerpt we feel that Leon showed that he had developed a budding awareness that simple or reproductive application of a model may lead to complications. This awareness is absent from the responses of typical level-three-thinkers, in particular when they have developed from learning-teaching conception 2. It may be a precursor of the typical level-four-thinking way of knowing where flexible applications of theory - e.g. adapting theory in the process of application - are a common phenomenon.

Methodological Issues

In this section we will discuss three issues that may have influenced the results of this study. Firstly there is some controversy to be expected regarding the use of retrospective descriptions to allocate students to epistemological categories. While the overwhelming body of literature in this field uses retrospection on (learning) experiences over the previous year, in our study we used a retrospective response covering at least 3, 5 years, and often a longer period.

Secondly, we discuss the issue of using written responses, and in particular the use we made of new technology (email) to elaborate on initial written responses. What are the advantages of written responses, and in particular the email conversations that students themselves indicated?

The third and final issue we treat in this chapter is a short exploration of other possible causes of changes in epistemology besides Enterprising Learning. A number of students in our study have indicated the curriculum of the Hotelschool as a major cause of their epistemological change, but some have named other influences, such as maturation, life experiences or other educational environments. In this exploration we will also pay specific attention to societal and cultural influences on epistemology.

Using Retrospection to Estimate Development

As described earlier in this chapter, the entry learning-teaching conception of each student was based on an entry-questionnaire response where possible. A substantial number of the students of semester 98-2 however was not included in the sample that was administered an entry-questionnaire in August 1998. For these students no other source of information about their entry level was available than their response to the retrospective question. Therefore, it is interesting to analyse the validity of such a question, especially when the period covered is so much longer than usual, namely several years.

In order to perform this analysis, it was fortunate that all students of both semesters were asked to remember their views on learning and teaching at their start at the Hotelschool, and to describe these views in retrospection. The phrasing of the retrospective question differed for the two semesters, see above. As said above, these retrospections would cover at least three and a half, and often more years. For this analysis we focus primarily on the students for which both an entry-questionnaire response as well as a retrospective description were available.

The three research questions here are:

1. To what extent did the retrospective description fit the original entry-level description?

2. What percentage of students failed to remember their views on learning and teaching of some years before?
3. What was the effect of these issues on the epistemological development pattern observed in this study?

In order to answer the first question, we focus on only those students of both semesters of whom both an entry questionnaire as well as an exit questionnaire was available. Of the 120 students of 97-2 and the 60 students of 98-2 who fulfilled this requirement, 12 students did not remember their view on learning at the start of their studies. These students would have been deleted from the analysis if they had not had a response to the entry-questionnaire. Of the remaining 168 students with both an entry and a retrospective response, some 19 students overestimated their entry level (11.3%), leading to underestimation of the development. Six students underestimated their entry level (3.6%), resulting in a smaller overestimation of development. Both those overestimating their entry level as those underestimating it, never differed by more than one level. In conclusion, about 85% of the students proved to be more than capable of describing their entry level correctly after at least 3.5 years. Where of semester 97-2, 82% of the students remembered their entry-level correctly, the score for 98-2 was slightly better (91% correct). Of course starting your studies may stand out in your memory more clearly than intermediate moments, especially since being admitted to the Hotelschool is preceded by a rather tough selection procedure. In addition this entry into a new school would stand out even more clearly if the teaching is quite different from what you were used to. Finally, the explicit reference to this moment in the retrospective question included in the exit-questionnaire for semester 98-2 was specifically aimed at helping students to remember more clearly.

To answer the second research question regarding the loss of data before analysis due to non-response to the retrospective question, we looked at those students in both semesters who did not provide any response to this question, not even after (repeated) reminders. As reported above, indeed a number of students had difficulty to remember their way of thinking about learning and/or teaching at the start of their studies at the Hotelschool, 5% of both 97-2 (6/120) and 98-2 (6/124) failed to provide a description of their entry-level, making a minimum expected loss of data of about 5% due to failure to remember probable.

In Tables 7.4 and 7.5 the epistemological developments of the two semesters are given as they would have been scored *using the students' own retrospective description of their entry level.* Here we look at our study as if we had no entry-questionnaire at our disposal, which gives us an understanding of what the effect of using a retrospective description would have been on the outcome of our study.

Underlying the analysis to answer the third research question is the comparison of Tables 7.1 and 7.4, both referring to semester 97-2. We focus primarily on semester 97-2 because this is the semester where all students were administered both an entry and exit questionnaire. Table 7.1 above described the results using both these questionnaires to independently allocate students to an entry and exit level. In Table 7.4, students of 97-2 were allocated using only their exit

Table 7.4 Epistemological development of semester 97-2 students using the retrospective question alone to allocate by entry-level

	1997 entry level based on retrospection							
exit	*1*	*2*	*3*	*4*	*5*	*6*	*exit*	*%*
1							0	0%
2	3	9					12	10%
3		68	16				84	70%
4		15	1				16	13%
5		1					1	1%
6			1				1	1%
entry	3	93	18	0	0	0	114	95%
%	3%	82%	16%	0%	0%	0%	100%	

Table 7.5 Epistemological development of semester 98-2 students using the retrospective question alone to allocate by entry-level

	1998 entry level based on retrospection							
exit	*1*	*2*	*3*	*4*	*5*	*6*	*exit*	*%*
1							0	0%
2		4					4	3%
3		80	19				99	80%
4		13	1	1			15	12%
5							0	0%
6							0	0%
cntry	0	97	20	1	0	0	118	95%
%	0%	82%	17%	1%	0%	0%	100%	

questionnaire, thus their entry-level is based on the retrospective learning conception question. Comparing Tables 7.1 and 7.4 then would provide insight into the effect of using only retrospective estimations of the entry level to determine epistemological development over multiple years. For semester 98-2 this analysis is not really possible, as for about half of the students there was no entry questionnaire.

The obvious difference between the Tables 7.1 and 7.2 and the two tables above is the discrepancy with regard to the number of students that have remained level-three-thinkers, the so-called "entrenched level-three-thinkers". Based on the entry-exit allocations of semester 97-2 (Table 7.1) one would expect about 3% of the students to be entrenched level-three-thinkers. When looking at Tables 7.4 and 7.5 one finds that using the retrospective entry-level (instead of the real entry-level where available) leads to between 14 to 16% (resp. 16/114 and 19/118) of the students being categorised as entrenched level-three-thinkers, while in fact a certain percentage of the students had developed from level 2 to level 3. In this regard it is also remarkable that the percentage of entrenched level-three-thinkers in the old curriculum, 11% - also allocated based on retrospection, see Table 7.3 above - is pretty similar to the percentages found for the two semesters analysed with retrospection here. Returning to semester 97-2, the overestimation of the percentage of entrenched level-three-thinkers with 11 percent points (16/114 in Table 7.4 - 3/120 in Table 7.1), is compensated almost entirely by the underestimation of the development from level-two-thinker to level-three-thinker (68/114 in Table 7.4 - 85/120 in Table 7.1).[5] On the other hand we have seen that in semester 97-2 there were also some students underestimating their entry-level, in total this overestimation of development was 3% for 97-2. For about half of semester 98-2 for which we had both questionnaire responses, we see a similar overestimation of entrenched level-three-thinkers, but no evidence of underestimation of their own entry-level.

In summary, these data lead us to conclude that using a retrospective question that spans multiple years to establish an entry level of epistemological development, in our study would have led to losing about 5% of the sample, due to non-remembering.

Secondly, 85% of our students were capable of remembering their entry level correctly after multiple years, while a more targeted question could even increase this percentage.

Thirdly, and perhaps more importantly, the use of retrospection alone could lead to underestimation of the epistemological development. In particular this refers to the underestimation of development from level 2 to 3 and to an (11%) overestimation of entrenched level-three-thinkers. On the other hand retrospection also led to a small percentage (3%) of overestimation of development in 97-2 (and none in 98-2). Taken together we would expect these two effects of using retrospection to result in an average *underestimation of development* of around 10%, with most of the discrepancies revolving around the development from level-two-thinker to level-three-thinker. We find this result not unexpected as these two levels seem to be fairly close together epistemologically (Samuelowicz and Bain, 2001 and Table 5.3, chapter 5). From a theoretical perspective we would expect something similar to occur for the shift from learning-teaching conception 4 to 5. However, such students are missing from this study.

Written Responses and Email Conversations

Already from the early beginnings of our research into students' thinking about learning and teaching, we have used written responses to open-ended questions as the basis of our analysis. The initial choice for this method was mostly pragmatic, it seemed to be a relatively low effort way to collect data and it fitted well with the objective to study larger samples from different disciplines. Over the decades we have not seen reasons to amend this procedure, as the written responses seemed to contain the essential information needed to develop a detailed developmental model regarding students' epistemological development. At no point did we need to stress anonymity of the questionnaire as students were aware that it was part of an academic research project and had no relationship to evaluation of their performance.

In the years at the Hotelschool, the essay questionnaires were presented to the students as a normal part of the school's effort to evaluate its performance, and samples of students were asked to fill in questionnaires on a regular basis. Again, no anonymity was guaranteed. Before the introduction of email, questionnaires usually remained one-off occasions, with only very limited recalls to students to add something to what they had written. Responses differed in length, from only a few lines, to more than two pages of closely written longhand. Over the years students began to submit typed out responses, such responses sometimes spanned several pages. All in all, although we were aware of the limitations of this method due to the lack of interaction and the only limited avenues open for elaboration, we remained convinced of the advantages of the data collection method with regard to effort and cost effectiveness.

With the school policy of providing all students with a school email address, we quickly realised the opportunity had arisen to introduce a measure of interaction into our now established essay-questionnaire methodology and so to remedy this particular shortcoming. As we have described above, from about 2001 onward students received the basic essay questionnaire by email, and responses were logged and read as they came in. During data collection one of the authors – namely the author known to the students as a teacher of the Hotelschool – was the principal researcher responsible for requests for elaboration and for the follow-up procedure. In these requests for elaboration, while sometimes phrasing was adapted to encourage responses, effort was made to avoid cueing to prevent eliciting biased responses. Elaboration-requests typically referred to a student's own words as much as possible followed by a straightforward request to elaborate if possible. We have described the procedure above and given examples in the section on the qualitative results.

During data collection we noticed that some students referred to the fact that answering these questions made them think more closely about the issue of learning and teaching. Something a number of them admitted to have never really done so before. Many indicated that they enjoyed the conversations, taking the rigorous follow-up procedure in the current study in their stride and expressing hope their contributions would help the study. Perry (1970) and Baxter Magolda (e.g. 2001) reported something similar where they described students telling them that during the year they had realised they needed to keep something in mind for the next interview, even looking forward to including it in the yearly conversation. Now and then students specifically referred to the added value of having to answer such unusual questions in writing, making them stop to think and ponder. We refer readers to the earlier sections of this chapter for examples (e.g. Iris, Georgina and Philip quoted earlier in this chapter). A further example is given by Charlotte (98-2) who developed from level-two-thinker to level-three-thinker and Maud quoted earlier in this chapter,

> I certainly have changed my way of thinking about learning over the years, but not consciously. *Only now that I stop to think about it to answer your questions I realise that I have changed.* I did realise at a certain moment that the more information I needed to store for an exam, the worse my results

> became. I started to concentrate on the most important parts, it seems I learned to filter information. … Also now I often realise that I have learned a lot from my experiences in the past years. (Charlotte, level-three-thinker, italics ours)

> I think a part of changing is unconscious, but a part is conscious too, because you learn that you have to adapt and look at things differently … But once you have changed, you don't even realise you have. Only when you start to think about it (because for instance you ask me about it for your study) you realise that you have changed. (Maud, level-three-thinker)

Next to these content or validity related considerations there are of course more economical ones. As many researchers know, data collection and preparing data for analysis (e.g. data entry) always have been considerable effort and cost intensive aspects of research. Doing face-to-face (or even telephone) interviews is time and labour intensive, as is preparing taped interviews for analysis through verbatim transcripts. By asking students to write down their responses, either at home (or elsewhere) in their own time, or in a group at a prescribed time, saves a lot of time and money. The use of email to increase the measure of interaction more towards a live conversation addresses we feel to a considerable extent the disadvantage of the one-off nature of the "old fashioned" essay approach, while retaining much of the economic and sample size advantages that led to the choice in the first place. In particular we feel that young people, who have grown up with computers and email, are more than willing to treat an email conversation in much the same way as a normal correspondence or conversation.

One essential requirement for this method of course is the access to email. In our study this was no obstacle, firstly the school provided an email address for all students. Secondly, in the Netherlands currently about 5.6 of the 7.9 million households are connected by broadband to internet. With on average 2.3 persons per household this would indicate 79% coverage of the current population, so access does not seem to be a problem in the Netherlands.[6] Thirdly, most of the students in our study worked/interned in high quality hotel and leisure environments, where email was and remains an essential part of the service. All this facilitated the ease with which we integrated this new technology into our data collection method. Even so, some students experienced difficulties in responding by email, for instance Willem, who was on an internship in China (see beginning of this chapter),

> Dear Mr. van Rossum,
>
> Again my apologies that it has taken so long to mail you back. It is not always easy to access email here [in Tianjin, China]. (Willem, level-three-thinker)

And even in a more western style society students ran into temporary email draughts

> Dear Mr. van Rossum,
>
> Due to a move of [the company] to the other side of the building we have not been able to access email or internet for a few weeks now. As it has been

> some time since I sent you my first responses, it seems high time to send you the second batch. (Christine, level-three-thinker, interning in South Africa using her own free email address)

A final suggestion we would like to put forward for consideration is the possible use of such learning conversations as a teaching tool. As students have commented on the impact of being asked about their learning (Perry, 1970; the current study) and their life experiences (e.g. Baxter Magolda, 2001), we feel that conversations about learning between teacher and students are an interesting avenue to explore. We would like to draw a parallel to Palmer's "good talk about (good) teaching" (1998, see chapter 11) and suggest adding "good talk about (real) learning" to a curriculum aimed at epistemological development.

Culture and Epistemological Development

There are discussions in the literature regarding the universal (cross-cultural) validity of the epistemological development models discussed and used in this study. For instance, Reybold (2001, 2002) felt that current epistemological research and theories over-emphasised cognition and cognitive processes and failed to take sufficient account of cultural aspects of knowing. Reybold stated that "we have not truly examined epistemology from a cultural perspective" (2001, p. 415) and that therefore "psychological inquiry is limited without attention to the cultural aspects of thinking and knowing" (2002, p. 538). In the current study, culture was not a specific issue that was included in the analysis. However, we discuss our position on the issue of culture in the final chapter in more detail in the section on the human condition, referencing many of the studies discussed throughout the current study.

The Hotelschool draws international students from all over the world and this enabled us to make a short excursion here. Talitha (97-2) is such an international student from Asia, who described her "culture shock" resulting from her move to Europe and afterwards from her confrontation with Enterprising Learning. In a separate correspondence, after her graduation Talitha described her development from a pre-Hotelschool level of perhaps level-one-thinking, through the entry-level of level-two-thinker and developing to level-three-thinker at the end of her studies. She linked her epistemological culture shock directly to her early experiences in Asia

> From cramming to knowing where to find it….
>
> I went to primary school in [Asia] till I was 10 which exposed me to the [traditional Asian] education system: I had to learn everything by heart, so it was very important to have a good memory. If you could reproduce everything, you were "intelligent". For a while, I kept this way of learning – if in a lesser degree – after coming to the Netherlands. When I came here I started in the second grade of primary school, because I spoke no Dutch. … Neither of my parents spoke Dutch either, and learning Dutch was difficult for me. My parents could never help me and from then on I had to find out everything myself. … Just as well I was really good at learning everything by heart, it really came in handy.

> After primary school I went to pre-vocational secondary school and successfully completed that. It was "easy" to reproduce knowledge. After this I tried one year of pre-professional secondary school, but that proved more difficult because it was less about reproducing knowledge than before.[7] Only at the next school, vocational ... education, I started to learn for the first time what it meant to "apply" knowledge instead of memorising it. For some subjects it was still mainly reproducing.
>
> The transition to the Hotelschool was *really big*, immediately I was confronted with Enterprising Learning. That was no picnic, you had to literally find out everything yourself, in particular you had to know where to find information, there was no spoon-feeding anymore. That really took some getting used to. Also the way teachers and students interacted [was different], teachers were more a listening ear instead of "God" who knew everything.
>
> I definitely feel that learning at the Hotelschool is more challenging than reproducing what is learned in class. I no longer know everything by heart, but I do know where to find it should I need it....
>
> [Now learning means to me] acquiring such broad knowledge that in the future I will be able to help my children with their learning issues. That was my main goal to study further. ... Now studying has an additional meaning. Still it is acquiring knowledge, but now my aim is to find a good job. And to have the knowledge to function well in this job.
>
> Studying to me means independence. I want to be completely financially independent. (Talitha, level-three-thinker in 2003, italics ours)

It is difficult to imagine the obstacles Talitha as a young child overcame, to find herself in a totally alien culture, not speaking the language and without very much support from grownups. She proved enterprising enough to graduate successfully from the Hotelschool and to continue into a promising career (as of 2008). We can do no less than admire her willpower and endurance. Secondly, we observe that Talitha displayed the same epistemological development as the majority of the other students, even though she originated from a fundamentally reproduction-oriented educational culture. It seems to us that any culture (in its traditional sense) can be interpreted as an external formula. And that traditionalist cultures can – in an environment that encourages independence (i.e. a different, perhaps educational culture) – be 'overcome' with sufficient effort.

Reybold (2001, 2002) observed something similar when she described women's epistemological development within a cross-cultural setting, studying 14 Malaysian women representing three different ethnic backgrounds common in Malaysia (Chinese, Malay and Indian). In an attempt to establish the influence of culture on epistemology, Reybold interviewed these women using a protocol based on Belenky et al. (1997) but adding questions about culture and tradition. Reybold "was not investigating Malaysian culture *per se,* but how these women perceive culture as a vehicle for knowing" (2002, p. 540). A main outcome of her study was that the women experienced epistemological development as "the redefinition of one's personal model of self in relation to one's cultural model of self, with the process of having three phases: (a) distinguishing a personal model of self from the cultural model of self, (b) negotiating conflict between the models of self, and (c) redefining the personal model of self .... Culture defines expected behavior and affect, constructing a template for each woman's sense of self, her cultural model of self. But each woman also noted how she incorporates personal perspectives into her sense of self, constructing a distinct personal model of self." (Reybold, 2001, p. 417). All women interviewed experienced a conflict between the cultural and the personal senses of self, and the approach to solving this conflict seemed to result in three distinct categories of "knowing".

Two women, those with the least formal education, were called Canonists. Canonists see truth as objectively observable, authority as absolute, and reasoning as based on trust and tradition, as do Absolutists (Baxter Magolda, 1992a). The two Canonists adopted the original cultural model of self, relying on the external formula of their culture/religion for decision making.

> The responsibilities of a woman are to take care of the family. Our Chinese, our woman always takes care of the house; she prepares the breakfast for the man. In fact, the Chinese people don't have [an] idea of equal. You [Reybold] have that idea, but we Chinese, we have to serve the man ... It is our Chinese way. (Janet; Reybold, 2002, p. 543)

The majority of the women were categorised as Consultants. These 10 women adapted their emerging personal models of self and negotiated "a shared authority between cultural expectations and personal desire. They justify their decisions based on personal experiences, but they often seek external evidence to *prove* their choices are right. These women prefer an interactive reasoning process .... [e.g.] they negotiate their lifestyle through some combination of family obligations, religious injunction, cultural expectation and personal desire" (Reybold, 2002, p. 544, italics ours). In the interaction between the two models of self (the personal and the external, cultural one) we recognise the interaction characteristic for our third learning-teaching conception, namely that between the self of the student and the external formula the teacher is to these students. Furthermore, Consultants use evidence not to support their opinions, but to prove the correctness of their own opinions. This and their gender-oriented empathy indicated to us their multiplist way of thinking (Perry, 1970) and their subjective way of knowing (Belenky et al., 1997).

> I do trust some expert opinion. In order to rely on it, it has to be proven. Otherwise, I will not rely on it. I listen to what they say, then I think for myself, 'Is this applicable? Is it right? Is this person giving me a wise opinion?' So I listen, but I don't always rely. It depends on what I think of a matter as well. (Geetha, Indian; Reybold, 2002, p. 544)

The third and final epistemological category Reybold found, the Architects, saw truth as political, authority as personal and evidence to be used to *support* arguments and personal decisions. These two women saw themselves as "authority and justify that authority based on their own experience, sometimes seeking evidence to support their decision-making, but not to prove it. Reasoning is a constructive process based on critical interpretation of diverse realities. These women describe themselves as 'global thinkers' ... [constructing their personal model of self] outside the boundaries of cultural expectations" (Reybold, 2002, p. 546). Noor described her position,

> In a society like Malaysia, it's very hard to push your ideas if you don't conform. There's a lot of resentment, also, when I speak, to conform. A lot of women are resentful because they realize I am not one of those who can be easily dictated, moulded to enter a certain area of discourse, what everyone else thinks. (Noor, Multi-ethnic; Reybold, 2002, p. 546)

The epistemological development[8] of the Consultants and Architects was nurtured by their families. Reybold saw family support of education for girls and women as the dominant factor associated with epistemological development, and this factor "is not addressed in the current literature on epistemological development ... [and it] is a *cultural* aspect of epistemological development because of the importance of family and relationships in Asian cultures" (Reybold, 2001, p. 425, italics ours). However, while we support the conclusion that culture is an important driving (or inhibiting) factor for epistemological development, we do not agree with Reybold that the influence of family is *not* a subject of research in epistemology. E.g. Belenky et al. (1997) discussed the role of family environments in the development in women's sense of voice. On the other hand, we would agree that considerably more attention to other factors than education (in their role of external formulas) is warranted. The importance of family support was described by Geetha,

> When I decided to go to a [local] university, my parent said, "No, you shouldn't study at a local university .... You will be studying in the Malaysian *context* again. You wouldn't have the experience of a foreign university, and we would like for you to have that. We think it would be good for you." (Geetha, Indian; Reybold, 2001, p. 420, italics ours)

Geetha's family obviously appreciated the added value of stepping out of the cultural context to get a better view on it. They seemed to have understood the issue of embeddedness: all of us are embedded in the external formula of our own culture, and only when you are able to "step out" of the culture, subject (i.e. the cultural self) becomes object, making reflection on it possible.

While the epistemological development was nurtured by family support, it was *challenged* by learning experiences and extended international opportunities, enabling a stepping out of one's own culture thereby fuelling the conflict between the cultural model of self and the emerging personal model of self. As Geetha said

> I'm not very conservative. I don't take many conservative ideas, and I think critically about them. Sometimes I talk about that to family members – that's a bit too modern for them. "This is because you went to study over there!" I have the strength to break the conservative ... For those of us who have the privilege of getting an education in another country, we are able to think critically. (Geetha, Indian; Reybold, 2001, p. 423)

From our research perspective we immediately wondered what Geetha, categorised as a Consultant and thus interpreted by us to be a multiplist thinker, meant by critical thinking. Considering our finding that many concepts considered self-evident in educational discourse (e.g. understanding, applying, independence etcetera) in fact are interpreted in various ways each consistent with a person's epistemological level of thinking, we looked for further evidence illuminating Geetha's way of knowing.

> Before going of to study, I was a very quiet person. I was always in a classroom situation where the teacher tells you everything and you do it. You sit down quietly and you listen to everything that is said. When we went [overseas], we had to get out of the shell of being quiet and shy. We had to talk, and the other people – the Australians – were like that. They talked a lot; they had their view of mind. It was not wrong for a girl to say what she thought; whereas in Malaysia, a girl shouldn't say what she thinks about certain things because it's socially not desirable. Now I have an opinion on most things, so I'm considered vocal. (Geetha, Indian; Reybold, 2002, p. 545)

Based on this evidence we concluded that probably Geetha was indeed a multiplist, with her interpretation of critical thinking referring to not always accepting other people's opinions but having one's own, and referring to the ability to "stand up on your own" (Reybold, 2002, p. 545) to voice it. Again we see, as we have before (e.g. chapter 5), it is not so much the words one uses that characterise a way of knowing, it is more the personal meaning one gives to them; not the words-as-said but the words-as-meant.

Finally, Reybold's work is interesting in a more general sense as well, because by describing these three types of women and these three "ways of knowing", Reybold, as did Kuhn (1991) and Kegan (1982, 1994) before her, has shown the relevance of personal epistemology in everyday life, everyday decision making and associated emotional responses. In this sense, Reybold spoke about a pragmatic epistemology, a "way of being". As personal epistemology is so often merely studied in an educational context, Reybold's work can be seen as an important contribution to this field of research, because, as Reybold stated,

> … ways of knowing also manifest themselves in the everyday lifeworld through mundane decisions and affect … the personal model of self is more than a mental construct or ideology; it produces behaviours and actions that correlate to ways of knowing. (Reybold, 2002, p. 547)

As a third, less exotic example of cultural influence shaping epistemology, it is interesting to contemplate whether (educational) cultures exist that underemphasise memorising and stress independent thinking. A possible candidate for such a culture could be the Montessori school culture. Beth (98-2) had attended Montessori type schools from pre-school upward. In coming to the Hotelschool she experienced a somewhat different (and opposite) kind of culture shock than Talitha.

> As I have attended Montessori schools all my life, the way of learning expected at the Hotelschool was definitely different from what I was used to. Especially the first year. Working in teams was nothing new to me, but the assessment method was more problematic. I really wasn't used to making notes during lectures, and the fact that the multiple choice exams were often based on these notes was really new to me.
>
> I would like to add that I'm not particularly good at multiple choice, but that it makes passing a lot easier for many students. I personally still prefer learning for understanding. Not cramming definitions but understanding what is said and being able to explain it in your own words. ... My *view* on learning hasn't really changed that much, I just adapted my *way* of learning. I learned to accept that at the Hotelschool cramming is sometimes necessary, because otherwise you will simply not pass some exams. (Beth, entrenched level-three-thinker, italics ours)

The fact that Montessori schooling as well as schooling based on the ideas of Helen Parkhurst, are fairly common in the Netherlands, might indicate that these school cultures are acceptable within the Dutch, predominantly traditional educational culture. One might wonder what would happen epistemologically if the dominant educational culture – from primary school upward – aimed at true independent thinking of students/pupils, and if teachers were enabled to function as facilitators of autonomous learning (or gardeners of the mind garden, see chapter 1). Currently there are some, sometimes controversial, experimental developments in Dutch secondary education. One such an example is given in a teachers union magazine, het Onderwijsblad [The Education Magazine], where the Discoveri school is described. At this school, which is a branch of a more traditional secondary school in the East of the Netherlands (Zwolle), pupils design their own curriculum – following their personal interest or passion – around a standard core curriculum. For instance Tamarinde, a girl of only thirteen but who talks almost like a seventeen-year-old when she says: "This is how I want to learn. Here I can follow my passions for dance and world languages" (het Onderwijsblad, p. 28). Her curriculum included Spanish, English, French and Dutch and she attended dance classes three times a week for lessons in modern dance. Stemming from her passion for dance, she developed an interest in her body and biology, and the latter subject was then included in her personal curriculum. In Tamarinde's words,

> This way you are much more motivated, because you really want to know it yourself, instead of because you have to. (het Onderwijsblad, June 2007, p. 28)

Originally the Discoveri concept included pupils' complete freedom to define what to learn and how to study, but it proved that they required a little bit more structure. One of the regular counsellors of Discoveri remarked about his pupils,

> Discoveri pupils are headstrong question posers. ... Curious children who are eager to learn, who want to do their own thing, want to *make their own way*. In traditional systems they are often just seen as difficult. (het Onderwijsblad, June 2007, p. 29, italics ours)

Pupils love it, but in the end, almost all pupils still want to get a more conventional diploma – e.g. by doing state exams – because they need it to enter further education or to get a job.

Other interesting work in regard to an alternative epistemological approach to learning is now going on at several universities in the Netherlands, where a multidisciplinary group of scientists is investigating the scientific, argumentative ability of very young children (ages 3 to 5).[9] As of 2010 a number of elementary schools will participate within this program Curious Minds (Talentenkracht in Dutch). It remains to be seen whether a truly different educational culture could circumvent the reproductive stages of current epistemological models. If indeed a culture is an external formula that shapes personal epistemology, it could be expected that a fairly traditional culture would lead to traditional thinking, as is prominent in our own study. On the other hand, it could well be expected that a sufficiently dominant, pervasive and 'progressive' culture might shape personal epistemology in a different way. Such a culture however would need to be society-inclusive, otherwise pragmatic considerations will always force schools and students to adapt to the dominant, less progressive culture in order to function in society.

Conclusions

In this chapter we have presented the views of many students on learning, teaching and their own epistemological development. These descriptions are based on their own stories, and we feel that indeed the epistemological journey they make progresses in a stepwise manner along a predetermined path. As Perry (1970) found before us, students move along the developmental path in different speeds, some turning away or coming to a (temporary?) standstill. The progress along this path from reproductive views on learning and knowing can be influenced by an activating curriculum. Comparing the epistemological development observed in a sample of students from the traditional curriculum to that of the 244 students included in the current study we can establish that the percentage of students who moved into a more complex view on learning and knowing more than doubled (85%) compared to the epistemological development found for students in the traditional curriculum (40%). Consequently, Enterprising Learning can be classified as considerably more successful in promoting epistemological development than a traditional knowledge-transfer oriented curriculum. Furthermore, the incidental cases of old-curriculum students experiencing only limited exposure to Enterprising Learning indicate at least anecdotal evidence that even short term exposure can lead to a noticeable change in epistemology.

On the down side, while 85% of the students moved at least one step up towards a more sophisticated epistemology, still 79% of the students exited the Hotelschool with learning-teaching conception 3: presumably an unsatisfactory level of epistemological sophistication for an institute of higher education, considering its espoused aim. However, that about four out of five students leave higher education with a primarily reproduction and application oriented view on learning and knowledge is not uncommon (e.g. Baxter Magolda, 1992a; Radloff, 2002). Further, considering the emphasis placed on application in Enterprising Learning, and the distribution of learning-teaching conceptions of the teachers involved (see chapter 9), perhaps this outcome was to be expected.

The comprehensive nature of the implementation of Enterprising Learning at the Hotelschool and the comments of students regarding the total immersion in this new learning culture, support our interpretation of a curriculum, and the underlying way of knowing, as an external formula (see chapter 3). Not only did this compulsory immersion change the way students viewed learning and knowing, it built up students' confidence that they were indeed able to meet the challenge. The majority of students were well aware that they were being forced to change their way of learning. Most of the students found this new approach exciting and grew comfortable with this new formula. Some experienced difficulties, which are described in more detail in chapter 8. Others felt that some aspects of the curriculum were inconsistent with their new learning approach and could be improved. These comments are also included in chapter 8.

Above we described developments in epistemology in detail, by quoting a number of typical students for each particular type of move. In addition, the large number of essays for learning-teaching conceptions 2 and 3 provided the opportunity to look at subtle changes more closely. Not with the aim of discovering new categories of description, but to explore the nature of the transitions. The current parsimonious model with only six categories covering the epistemological development through the first half of life, leaves the impression of rather abrupt shifts in ways of knowing. The data in this study however seem to point towards a much more gradual change. This is not contrary to the idea of clearly qualitatively distinct categories of description or ways of knowing. It only means that epistemological changes in people are more gradual than the quantum-leap impression the model may convey. As far as we know, there has not been much research done regarding the transitions between ways of knowing (or learning-teaching conceptions). Considering how difficult it is to arrive at clear descriptions of ways of knowing or learning-teaching conceptions, this may not be surprising. However, we feel that to improve teaching and the construction of developmental curricula such as Enterprising Learning, it is important to better understand the types of challenges and supports that will encourage epistemological development. Studying the subtle changes that precede and follow the immediate shift from one position to another may provide this additional insight.

Lack of even subtle epistemological development seems to be a source of students' discontent, even though it is not clear that students themselves had expected to change. At the same time, for the less epistemologically sophisticated students this lack of development seems to involve a form of active rejection of a new way of learning: students feel they are cheating when by learning less, they get better grades, or they feel that practical knowledge is not in the same league as theory. They long for a way of learning and teaching that is more familiar. We have dubbed this disappointment Nostalgia, and discuss it in more detail in the next chapter.

For the epistemologically more sophisticated students, lack of development leads to a different type of discontent: students find the courses too simple, too shallow and feel unfulfilled. Instead of wanting a familiar way of learning and teaching back, they long for something different, more challenging and often hang on in the hope of improvement after graduation. This discontent we have encountered before and have coined the name Disenchantment. We will discuss Disenchantment in the next chapter as well.

Regarding our data collection there has been some debate about the use of retrospective questions to measure development. In the current study we were able to examine the quality of responses to retrospective questions regarding views on learning that went back some 3 or more years. In much of the literature (e.g. Perry, 1970; Baxter Magolda, 1992a and later) the horizon for retrospective questioning is about one year. The issue is whether students are able to remember in much detail how they thought about and went about learning after such a long time. The current study seems to point towards the conclusion that the overwhelming majority of students were well able to recall the way they felt, thought and went about learning at the start of their studies. Only about 5% of the 244 students had absolutely no recollection of this. However, it proved that correct priming of the students, referring explicitly to the very beginning of their studies at the Hotelschool, improved recall. We feel that retrospective questioning can lead to acceptable results, providing the moment that triggers the recollection is exceptional enough. Entering a new environment, starting your student life, leaving home and living on campus, having passed a rigorous selection procedure: all this would seem to make the situation to be recalled sufficiently salient to lead to relatively robust results. On the other hand, even with relatively good quality recollection, one can expect at least 10% underestimating their own development, a finding partly compensated by perhaps 5% overestimating their epistemological development and thus resulting in a 5% underestimation overall. All in all, there is reason to be very careful in using retrospective questioning over long periods of time when not referring to a moment in time that stands out extremely clearly in the minds of the respondents.

A second issue we have encountered is our use of essays. As we have explained in chapter 2 and 7, the choice was initially pragmatic. In later years the results of our studies did not indicate to us the need to shift towards the more labour intensive and costly interview approach. Furthermore, in the current study in particular we have found that students themselves report on interesting by-products, a possibility that Marton and many others (e.g. Perry and Baxter Magolda) have commented on before. As we suspected, when asked to reflect on an issue many always found self evident, and subsequently to write down their thoughts, students realise that learning and knowing are much more complex than they had always assumed. They often commented on their own growing interest in the issue, that they were more than willing to expand on what they had written before in order to get things clearer in their own mind as well. We feel we have perhaps stumbled across a potentially powerful teaching tool for epistemological developmental education: the "good talk about good learning", to paraphrase Parker Palmer (1998 and chapter 11).

The final issue discussed shortly in this chapter is the influence of culture on epistemological development. In this chapter we have included only three examples that seem to indicate that culture, be it educational or more comprehensive, is an important influence on epistemological development. Not such an earth shattering conclusion, considering that the learning environment is in essence a culture all by itself. It would seem that an educational environment that is geared toward memory and reproduction of facts, leads to views on learning and knowing that are relatively unsophisticated. A curriculum that explicitly aims toward application and preparation for a successful career, such as Enterprising Learning, leads to a shift towards at least learning-teaching conception 3. The experience with elementary and secondary education geared towards more epistemologically sophisticated ways of learning and knowing, such as Montessori or Dalton education, seems to point towards the conclusion that epistemological development is less age-restricted than Piagetian approaches to epistemological and intellectual development have led us to expect. Indeed the first results of the Curious Minds (in Dutch, Talentenkracht) project in the Netherlands would seem to indicate that Piaget and many of his followers were somewhat pessimistic regarding young children's' abilities with regard to abstract or scientific and argumentative thinking.

The broader issue is of course whether the ways of knowing we have described here are indicative of the human condition, or typical only of the Western, Greek-Roman tradition of thinking, and whether our studies are an implicit form of cultural imperialism. In the final chapter of the current study we have summed up the disciplinary, respondent group, cultural and national background of the many, many, many studies we have included here to underpin our findings. We would refer our readers to that chapter to convince themselves, but it may be clear now that as we have stated earlier we feel that our model provides one possible window on a development that is more close to the *human condition* than to cultural imperialism. In this we agree with Csikszentmihalyi (1993).

NOTES

1 Due to administrative problems it was not possible to study the cohort 97-1.

2 It is unclear why this group of students with sophisticated entry conceptions is relatively large. As mentioned in chapter 6, the Hotelschool has a rigorous selection procedure for freshmen aimed at selecting the best students who are also highly motivated for the hospitality industry, and keeping a gender balance. It is possible that the selection process may have changed over the years between the old and the new curriculum, perhaps due to decreasing numbers of candidates. It could also be a result of changes in the quality of the "student supply", i.e. less students from pre-university secondary education (vwo) and more from pre-professional secondary education (havo).

3 Ian was an international student and we quote his original responses.

4 Philip was an international student and the quotes here are excerpts from his original English text.

5 We realise that adding and subtracting percentages in this way is not entirely correct, but we feel that as we are talking about shifts in distribution within the same sample, it is defendable here.

6 As of April 2008.

7 From a Dutch standpoint this pre-professional education is seen as fairly traditional and reproduction-oriented, which can also be derived from the epistemological entry level of the Hotelschool students in this study, many of these came directly from this type of education (havo).

[8] Of course, this is seen from a Western epistemological perspective, we – the current authors - are aware of our possible cultural bias here.

[9] The research programme Talentenkracht [Curious minds] is financed by the Dutch Ministry of Education and coordinated by the Dutch Platform Science&Technology. For more information see www.talentenkracht.nl or http://www.talentenkracht.nl/content/files/SITE1765/Brochure_CuriousMinds_eng. pdf

CHAPTER 8

ISSUES IN ENTERPRISING LEARNING

Learning to me has to incorporate some sense of a journey. I believe the process of learning has to feel almost like a story, it has to have a beginning, middle and an end. Naturally, every learning process has to involve an element of fact memorizing, remembering definitions of key terms and understanding of new terminology. However, I believe too much of my learning experience (so far), has been based on [these] aspects of learning. I am still waiting for a more dramatic middle and a much more fulfilling end to my story of learning!

(Lydia, level-three-thinker, 97–2)[1]

Frictions in Teaching and Learning

In earlier chapters we have seen that an amount of challenge and friction is conducive to learning, but too much friction would seem destructive to the learning (and teaching) experience. In the first section of this chapter we explicitly address what happens when students and teachers have widely different views on learning and good teaching, using the insights gained from our developmental model. We propose that a too large disagreement between students and teachers regarding their views on learning and good teaching leads to two different reactions that hinder learning and epistemological development: student disenchantment and disengagement on the one hand and nostalgia on the other.

Vermunt and Verloop (1999) already established that "learning and teaching activities are one another's mirror image and may be described in the same terms" (p. 265), that teaching and learning are intertwined, and that special attention should be paid to "the joint effects that teaching and learning may have upon one another" (p. 258). Also in the field of epistemology a similar observation was made by Lyons (1990) who claimed that students and teachers have interacting and interconnected epistemological perspectives. Lyons referred to this phenomenon as "nested epistemologies". These interconnections make it possible to

> ... examine the complex congruences and frictions occurring between students' learning activities and teachers' teaching activities in and outside of classroom situations. ... to identify learning tasks, situations, etcetera, that hinder or even impair [epistemological] development and [to] design learning tasks, materials and tests that stimulate [it]. (Vermunt and Verloop, 1999, p. 276)

In the first part of this chapter we look into this mutual influencing, in particular to the case where teachers' teaching strategies and students' learning strategies are not compatible. Where teachers' teaching strategies are compatible with students' learning strategies, Vermunt and Verloop talk about "congruence". When these strategies are not compatible, two (or perhaps three) types of friction may occur:

- Constructive friction: teachers' teaching strategies challenge students to "increase their skill in a learning or thinking strategy. [This friction] may be necessary to make students willing to change and to stimulate them to develop skill in the use of learning and thinking activities they are not inclined to use on their own" (Vermunt and Verloop, 1999, p. 270). We see similarities in this description to the concept of the holding environment proposed by Kegan (1994) and to Baxter Magolda's constructive-developmental pedagogy (1999, 2004, see also chapter 10);
- Destructive friction: on the one hand teachers may exert more control over student learning than students perceive necessary, or on the other teachers exert too little control over student learning, leaving students with the feeling of being pushed in at the deep end: either way "existing learning and thinking skills are not called upon or potential skills are not developed" (1999, p. 270). Consequently we feel there are two distinct types of destructive friction, which we have given different names and treat in different sections of this chapter:
  - **Disenchantment**: a destructive friction, where teacher over-control of learning may cause a *decrease in expression* of the students' available learning and thinking skills. We have called this type of destructive friction 'disenchantment' because students expressing it are severely disappointed and disillusioned about the in their eyes "overly school-like" approach to teaching. In our opinion these students do not lose their epistemologically more sophisticated thinking or learning skills, they just refrain from using them in the current educational situation. The first part of this chapter is dedicated to forms of disenchantment as we have found for the students in Enterprising Learning and also as described in a previous study about the old, more traditional curriculum (van Rossum et al., 2002);
  - **Nostalgia**: a destructive friction which can occur when students feel that teachers are shirking their responsibility for student learning, and feel abandoned and over-asked: they are 'in over their heads'. These students fail to understand the teachers' expectations and demands, and so they lack a holding environment providing them with clues. As a result they can develop a sort of nostalgia towards a more familiar traditional teaching approach as a refuge from current uncertainty. We discuss nostalgia in the second part of this chapter, see below.

The idea that these two types of destructive friction lead to different types of student reactions to the educational situation is not entirely unique, although we are unaware whether they are identified by distinct names in other studies. In fact we have found various empirical examples of either type, disenchantment and nostalgia, in studies by Baxter Magolda (e.g. 1999, 2001), Belenky et al. (1997), Kember (2001), Lindblom-Ylänne and Lonka (1999, 2000 and 2001) and Vermunt (2005). To illustrate the different tones of voice differentiating between disenchantment and nostalgia, we include a few of these examples here.

First a few examples of nostalgia. Maryann participated in a course winter biology which had as goal to teach students "to think like scientists", in short a university course developed with the aim to encourage level four thinking (self-authorship). For Maryann this proved a bit too much.

> Think like a scientist? No, the first part of the class absolutely not. It was just a straight lecture like any other class. ... All the thinking that is coming right now is at the very end. ... But I wish I had more concrete feedback, like am I completely wacko, are my ideas completely invalid? I mean it is good. ... he allowed me to come up with my own questions. But he is shooting them all down, so I don't know what to think. I do think that it was good at the very end that he made us think about stuff, but then he is not giving me anything. I have nothing to go by. He is just being very vague. He says you have to think about all the issues of your project; that is a statement he has made. What does he mean all the issues of my project? What *are* the issues of my project? (Maryann, Baxter Magolda and Buckley in Baxter Magolda, 1999, p. 119, italics ours)

Maryann's bewilderment speaks clearly from her last lines, she would give anything for a little more guidance, just to find out what the teacher really wants from her. A quote a little further in the chapter is somewhat more nostalgic in nature.

> I thought his lecturing was kind of confusing at some times. It was hard for me when he gave these big handouts for me to follow; it seems like he went very fast. It stresses me when teachers don't write on the board or don't write things down because they always go too fast for me. I always like for teachers to write it out rather than flipping slides because they always go too fast. (Maryann, Baxter Magolda and Buckley in Baxter Magolda, 1999, p. 127)

Kember (2001) also quoted a number of freshmen students participating in an interactive tutorial, who were pretty bewildered about the expectations of the teacher. We include one example who we feel echoed our student Sara in the paragraph on teachers and teaching in Enterprising Learning (see below).

> They (lecturers) expect us to know the topic and ask us about it. They expect us to ask questions, and they solve our queries. However, if we don't know the topic, we don't know how to ask questions ... My only question will be 'Would you start teaching from the beginning again?' Of course, they say 'No'. (Kember, 2001, p. 212)

Disenchantment is a well known phenomenon, with quite a few examples to be found in the student learning literature (see also chapter 10). We also include examples with regard to relationships outside the educational setting. First two examples from student learning literature.

Lindblom-Ylänne and Lonka quoted a 25-year-old female student with an in their terminology "dissonant study orchestration". We would say she was seriously disenchanted to the extent of doubting her chosen career.

> I'm enormously disappointed with this organisation, this has not suited me in any way. The way we learn and study has been very difficult for me, really. I could even say that this faculty hinders studying, this is the simple truth … We learn by heart, studying is very school-like. There aren't any discussions about interesting subjects after lectures … we don't go anywhere to talk about unclear things. There isn't any sense in the way they teach us … The study methods have been very difficult form me, enormously difficult … the content is not difficult, only the way we study. This system has been very difficult for me... There is this conflict ... if I had my own goals, I couldn't achieve them in this system because the conflict is huge... You're better to adapt to the system's goals, i.e. pass the exams and other things .. At least I haven't got the strength to wonder if I will become a good physician after learning this and this ... I buried my own goals a long time ago. (S4, Lindblom-Ylänne and Lonka, 1999, p. 13)

A second example comes from Kember (2001), with a female student who objected to a course focusing on lecturing and rote memorisation for exams. She found some relief for her disenchantment in interactive tutorials,

> I learned more in tutorials. The tutor will do exercises with us; or he will demonstrate how to do them. Lectures are so very boring that I almost fall asleep... There is lots of repetition in my [current] course and the diploma course... There are rarely new and interesting things in the course. I just attend the tutorials and do the laboratory work in order to finish my assignment … I need to remember lots of things for the examination only. It is useless and inapplicable. I hate to memorise them all again. I wonder why we can't be exempted. (Kember, 2001, p. 212–213)

We shall see similar responses in the sections on disenchantment and nostalgia below.

Disenchantment is not limited to the educational arena. In Belenky et al. (1997) we recognised a more personal form of disenchantment. Donna, who had spent seven years obtaining her bachelor's degree, felt her marriage could now be in serious trouble. Her husband had encouraged her to study, but he himself was not educated.

> We now view events that happen in our lives very differently. He reads them very straightforward, on a superficial kind of level. And I don't. I probe them. I read into them. He says he sees things in black and white and I see all kinds of shades of grays—all these gradations he doesn't see. That's been exacerbated by my education. I think it's a good thing. He thinks it's not so good. (Donna, Belenky et al., 1997, p. 147)

As in the examples within education, this relational type of disenchantment can lead to emotional distress, and a withdrawal into silence or anger (or both), as we see in Adele's description of her relationships with men,

> I feel like what ends up happening when the man does that enough, is that I begin not to want to even bother anymore. I begin withdrawing a lot, begin feeling angry most of the time. (Adele, Belenky et al., 1997, p. 148)

If we compare this last quote from Adele with the last sentences of the disenchanted medical student (S4) above, the similarity in response is striking.

When Worlds Collide: Disenchantment

Yerrick et al. (1998) reported a salient example of the antagonistic interactions that may result when students and teacher differ in their epistemological stance. In this study the teacher's positivist epistemology acted as a "subtle enemy to encouraging meaningful learning and constructivist views on the nature of [knowledge] and knowing" (Edmondson and Novak, 1993, p. 547). The positivist stance of the teacher in the study, Mr. Jones, was reflected in his reaction to the statement, "Scientific laws and theories exist independent of human existence. Scientists merely discover them",

> [Agree] Definitely, they [scientific laws] back up everything, friction … It's all Newton's laws. Basically it's an F = m.a deal. …
>
> … if we didn't know about friction, friction would still be there … when the guy [astronaut] gets up there for the first time he said, "Hey Newton's laws really do work!" (Mr. Jones, Yerrick et al., 1998, p. 630–631)

The fact that Mr. Jones confused the independent existence of the phenomenon friction with the theoretical postulation of Newton's law of friction, is essentially positivist. It is not that the phenomenon is dependent on our way of looking at it. Theory, even one working as well as Newton's, is an effort to explain the phenomenon, it is not the phenomenon itself. Such a theory can be replaced when a "better" explanation emerges – as Newton's theory replaced that of Aristotle – without the phenomenon itself disappearing or changing in any fundamental way. It is our understanding of the phenomenon that has been transformed and so transforms our perception of the phenomenon.

Not only was the teacher's epistemological perspective positivist, his teaching approach was, as could be expected (see chapter 1 and 4), an example of almost "complete teacher control" (Vermunt and Verloop, 1999, p. 269), as the following quote from Yerrick et al. illustrates.

> Mr. Jones: A couple of rules here I want to read to you about friction. In case you get into trouble about friction … And you know these. Friction acts parallel to the surfaces that are in contact and into which directions? …
> Students: Opposite …
> Mr. Jones: [Not waiting for students]
> Opposite directions. Okay. Does friction depend on the nature of the material? Yeah, whether I am sliding a book or sliding the

> ruler. It does depend on the material, doesn't it … Sliding friction is less than standing friction [pointing to the formula on the board]. Remember, if I push the book, it's hard to get it what …[pause less than 1 second] … started right? But what happens when you get it started? It slides okay doesn't it. So sliding friction is … it's harder to get it started. We did this a long time ago. Hard to get it started but then what happens … easy to slide. [Pause for 2 seconds]
> And if you remember this [formula on board], force equals mass times normal. What's true about friction. It's directly proportional to the normal. The normal is the force that he object is pushing down with … [another example lifting book]. So all you need to know is that frictional force is proportional to the normal. What's the rule about friction….?
>
> (Yerrick et al., 1998, p. 623/634)

The implicit messages about acceptable student behaviour, and the nature of knowledge and knowing in science that come across in this type of teaching are

- Students can/may only participate in limited interaction: "participation in classroom discourse is strictly bound to definitions, short answers [to direct questions of the teacher], and computations" (p. 622),
- Scientific concepts are seen as a set of proven facts, presented and explained by the teacher, and "each question serves to fit the final piece into a predetermined puzzle that represents [proven] physics knowledge about the world" (p. 623),
- Rehearsal is an important part of learning,
- Questions have only one correct answer,
- Speed is necessary to cover the content.

Mr. Jones ran "a tight ship" in his classroom, and as far as he could see this form of classroom management resulted in good relationships with students and students enjoying doing science.

> I have got my students trained … They need this … They feel successful ... I think they like it … They know what they need to do when they come in … And by the time they leave, students know exactly what they have done wrong on each item. … They need structure. They didn't do too well when we only had quizzes once in a while. They didn't keep up … We do thousands of 'em [computations] I am sure. (Mr. Jones, Yerrick et al., 1998, p. 635)

Mr. Jones put much value on his relationships with his students, "It is important that his students like physics and that they like him" (p. 639), but he judged his students mainly on their compliance with his style of classroom management.

> Kimberley? Oh she's great. She's smart and does her work. She's a real nice girl … How is Todd in terms of his work. I'd say someone like Todd is more talkative. Kimberly doesn't. She's quieter when she asks her

> questions. … Probably the smartest one is Todd. But as far as which one I like the best? …. [Kimberley] because I don't have to get on her as much. … …. I have to get on Todd to do his work. (Mr. Jones, Yerrick et al., 1998, p. 638–639)

So what was Mr. Jones' problem with Todd's learning behaviour, or perhaps a more fruitful question, what was Todd's problem with Mr. Jones' way of teaching? Todd seemed to have a quite different view on knowledge and knowing as was expressed in his response to the same positivist statement about the independent existence of scientific laws and theories as Mr. Jones answered above,

> [Disagree] It is difficult for humans to understand the complexities of nature, and thus we are forced to create laws and theories to arrive at a better understanding. For example, electrons. We don't know if they're actually there but we use them. I mean it works for us you know to make chemicals or whatever reactions and whether it actually works the way humans think, we'll never be sure unless maybe 20 years down the road we can find out. But for right now it works for us for the engineers and whatever… (Todd, Yerrick et al., 1998, p. 633)

Todd's more constructivist view spoke from his awareness that laws and theories are not "discovered" or found ready-made in nature, but constructed by humans in an effort to understand nature better. What was Todd's perception of teaching and learning in Mr. Jones' class?

> I guess each day we're presented with a new topic … and he starts by explaining the formula, giving us the laws … He's usually the one talking … he directs the class … there's not too much interaction. *We're just spectators …* (Todd, Yerrick et al., 1998, p. 638)

Todd's fundamentally different epistemological stance and his perception that no meaningful interaction was possible in Mr. Jones' class led to disengagement in the classroom and periods of problematic behaviour. A type of behaviour that Mr. Jones interpreted as "Todd's motivation problem", while Todd saw it as a fundamental difference of opinion about the nature of science and how to learn it. In discussing a particular incident in class, where Todd and a few of his classmates disturbed Mr. Jones' established classroom management procedure, Todd gave more insight into the nature (and source) of his disengagement.

> Interviewer: You take this kind of antagonistic role with Mr. Jones. … What was he playing with you or something?
>
> Todd: Well yeah, that was the whole point, you can't question anything he says. ….
>
> Interviewer: I just think it's interesting that you have this different opinion about the world and yet you don't voice it.
>
> Todd: We don't have that option. You can't. He boots everybody out. I'd like to graduate.
>
> Interviewer: Does he know that you disagree with him about the way you see science?

Todd: Not at all. You can't bring up another point because he will just ignore you and ridicule you.

Interviewer: So you are saying you don't see knowledge out in the worlds as the same as it is in here. Do you see that questions in the real world can be approached in the same way?

Todd: No. You need reasoning skills if you're an engineer or an architect of whatever. You can't just use formulas. You've got to be able to reason and come up with our own way to figure out whatever you're looking for. He doesn't necessarily test you on your comprehension of the subject. The materials he presents is more or less if you can do the algebra. A certain formula or something. He really emphasizes the formula. He figures that is what you're going to use if you go to engineering school and stuff that's what he stresses ....

Interviewer: So, do you ask questions that get at these differences? ...

Todd: I just don't do it at all. You can't bring up another point because he will just ridicule you. It's not like the real world because there's no interaction, no logic. If you ask a question he harasses you until you think you're stupid. And one time I just asked because I wanted to know [*how* we knew that] and he was like, "What are you stupid?"

(Yerrick et al., 1998, p. 642, italics ours)

In our study we would have identified Todd as a typical disenchanted student, whose disengagement was evoked by the fact that his epistemological perspective on science was more sophisticated than the perspective that was dominant in the classroom of Mr. Jones. That such disengagement is a common aspect of disenchantment can be seen in Max's description of some courses at the Hotelschool (within Enterprising Learning).

> A different critical view is immediately punished with a fail grade, or with feedback that goes little further than, "You obviously didn't understand it at all, because according to so-and-so it is like this and definitely not anything other. Go read the textbook again". At first it really irritated me and I tried to put up some resistance, but now I just do as I'm told: doing only what is required because that way you get a pass grade and eventually the desired diploma. (Max, level-three-thinker)[2]

As Edmondson and Novak said "there exists in education an enormous 'epistemological problem'... college level science courses show that they tend to exacerbate the problem, moving students toward more positivistic views. Furthermore, the synergism between learning approach (e.g. rote learning) and epistemological orientation (e.g. positivism) leads toward stabilization of learning strategies that are ineffective for understanding ... By emphasizing the active role of the knower in the construction of knowledge and encouraging students to reflect on their learning, educators invite students to move away from rote learning strategies and toward more meaningful ones" (Edmondson and Novak, 1993, p. 556–557). According to Edmondson and Novak, the *only* thing that educators need to do to redesign instruction in line with a more constructivist perspective is "to 'change their minds' about how teaching and learning can proceed" (p. 557). That changing educators' minds is not a simple task we have seen in chapter 5, and we make some suggestions on how to attempt to change their minds anyway in chapter 11.

Disenchantment in Enterprising Learning

Disengagement and the sensible strategy of 'keeping your head down until you have your diploma' that Todd and Max followed (see above) is echoed by Maurits, who admitted in his first lines to have reverted to lower level study strategies in order to just get through the exams.

> Honestly: [now at school] I think I have really learned something when I pass my exam with a little more than a minimum grade ... The incentive to really go for it is missing. During the first two semesters it was all new and very interesting. Now, three and a half years later, I've come to the conclusion that I only need to get enough pass grades with a minimum of effort. By nature I'm a very curious person who loves to see the "why" question answered, but that doesn't happen here in higher professional education. This prevents me from studying a subject as deeply as I would prefer. ... I know this is partly my own fault, but it is also due to the type of teaching we get. (Maurits, level-four-thinker)

Maurits was dissatisfied that he could not get his "why" questions answered, and here again we see a similarity to Todd's story. Maurits was considering to go to university after graduation, hoping he could satisfy his curiosity regarding "why things work the way they do" there. Soraya, also a level-four-thinker, was a little more critical about the level of subject matter knowledge and in particular the assessment system at the Hotelschool.

> I think everybody wonders at some time what he/she learned during their studies. And in practice it is evident that our subject knowledge is very basic. We learn about a lot of topics, so that we are able to look at subjects from different perspectives, what of course is positive. But, ask a Hotelschool student to do a serious market research, and chances are it will prove to be a pretty mediocre study because our subject knowledge is just not deep enough. ... I feel a lot more could be expected from students ... and their motivation could also be put to the test more. .... As far as I am concerned exams as they are currently could be abolished altogether, because they don't test students' mastery of subjects in any meaningful way. Exams say more about their cheating ability and the time students spend cramming old exams! (Soraya, level-four-thinker)

Even more explicitly disenchanted was Beatrice, who developed from level-two-thinker to level-three-thinker, but still was seriously upset about the quality of the teaching as she perceived it.

> Bringing it into practice is probably the most important issue as this is when it becomes obvious whether a person has totally comprehended the study

> material. ... The important thing about learning ... is that it is like riding a bike. If the comprehension and understanding is there then you will be able to use it the rest of your life and it will stick with you. Then I came to the Hotelschool ....
>
> .... unfortunately I was forced to change my way of studying when I came to the Hotelschool. For some reason, I feel like I have gone back to primary school where it does not matter if you are able to explain what you are talking about or use what you have learned. Here they want the students to simply show that you are able to "learn" things (by heart). They ask you to quote people, give exact definitions and give lists of things. That is how I have to study for my exams now, go through the book page by page, read through every handout and study each list that is given in order to be able to get a passing grade for an "important subject".
>
> I feel that the importance of a subject is lost and I can say for sure that I would still be able to answer questions from exams in high school without studying and not so easily answer exam questions from Hotelschool exams given in previous semesters. Why? .... It doesn't interest me. There is no structure in this way of learning so there is no "overall story", it then also speaks for itself that two days later all the study material has left my brain, and if I fail [the exam] I will have to start all over again. (Beatrice, level-three-thinker)[3]

Oddly enough, Beatrice had definitely developed, from a typical level-two-thinker (based on her entry- questionnaire) to a disgruntled level-three-thinker, but she seemed to have blocked her own old view on learning – in which memorisation was dominant – from her mind. Beatrice is one of the students whose retrospective account would have led to an underestimation of the developments, had we not had her entry-questionnaire. This blocking out of her earlier views on learning, seemed to have given her the idea she had not developed at all during her time at the Hotelschool, which may also underlie her disenchantment. Finally, we also found some students who were both disenchanted and displayed distinct nostalgia for more traditional teaching, such a student is Karel (level-three-thinker).

> At this moment learning at the Hotelschool means to me "learning and getting outa here". I only have to do two German letters and then I'm done. Nevertheless, I think it is absurd that you still have to memorise German (English, French) letters while you can simply take standard letters from the computer and adapt them. ... I feel a good assignment is any one of the internships. Then you learn that everything you have crammed into your head at school, you need to forget as soon as possible. ... They should make a choice in this "endless list" of subjects, so that subjects can become more tangible and real. (Karel, level-three-thinker)

After getting this off his chest, Karel proceeded to describe the way students and teachers should interact, in this voicing his nostalgia,

> In the name "Hotelschool" we see the word school, which is ironic because teachers here do not want to put in the effort to teach you something when you

> don't understand it. The words Enterprising Learning are used everywhere, and seem to mean "You go and find it all out yourself, from internet or in a book." Many a teacher hides behind this concept when they are too lazy or don't have the time or motivation to explain something to you. (Karel, level-three-thinker)

Karel did not display any signs of epistemological development over the years. If he realised this himself, this realisation may lie at the root of his disenchantment. On the other hand, his failure to develop could also be the result of a persistent nostalgia toward a more traditional teaching approach which prevented him to see the opportunities to develop at the Hotelschool.

Disenchantment before Enterprising Learning

In a previous study with students from the old, predominantly traditional curriculum at the Hotelschool The Hague, we also found numerous examples of disenchantment and nostalgia (van Rossum et al., 2002). As we have seen in chapter 7 (Table 7.3), 42 of these students did not show a change in learning-teaching conception over the years. Of these 42, 18 indicated that they had lost interest and had become disillusioned and angry with the school (disenchantment and nostalgia taken together). This means that in van Rossum et al. (2002) more students (some 26%) than in Enterprising Learning were either disenchanted or nostalgic: almost 17% of the Enterprising Learning students expressed either disenchantment or nostalgia. The fact that more than a quarter of the old-curriculum students had become seriously negative about their learning experience at the Hotelschool, can be seen as a belated support for the decision to reconsider the traditional way of teaching, changing it in the way indicated by the visitation committee in 1994 (see chapter 6), and developing Enterprising Learning.

Disenchanted and nostalgic students both expressed a decreased use of more sophisticated study strategies in favour of more surface level learning strategies. While disenchanted students felt the curriculum was too school-like, the nostalgic students indicated a preference for an even more traditional (school-like) teaching and learning environment. We will first present examples of disenchantment expressed by these old-curriculum students, examples of nostalgia will be given below in 'nostalgia before Enterprising Learning'.

Disenchantment, as we have seen above, occurs most often when students' existing more sophisticated (or deep level) learning and study strategies are not called upon by teachers, or are even usurped by teachers. Students then either protest, display "difficult behaviours" in class (see Todd in Yerrick et al., 1998) or refrain from using their existing abilities, conforming to the expected student role in learning (see Max above). Very often this means they display study behaviour appropriate to lower levels of epistemological development. Two level-four-thinkers who performed at level 2 are quoted below.

> Yes [I changed my way of studying]. I came from secondary school where I had always learned the main line. The Hotelschool is obviously much more detail oriented, small details are asked and old exams as well. I never used to learn like this.

> It's always learning at the last moment. Clearly filling up the short term memory and then getting to school. The scary thing is it works too. (Daniel, level-four-thinker, old-curriculum, van Rossum et al., 2002)
>
> [I changed] only in the way that I read less now, because I know which concepts to concentrate on and leave the B.S. ("bull shit" information) on the side. Old exams are a good guide on what the new exam will contain.
>
> My way of learning has become more specific and less analytical. For example: I can learn that there are 3 formulas to find the Break Even Point, but I wouldn't be too sure when to use which or if there's a better way to do it. (Rosanne, level-four-thinker, old-curriculum, van Rossum et al., 2002)

The level of discontent with the current situation becomes apparent when Rosanne gave her view on teaching at the Hotelschool. Her description was anecdotal and exaggeratedly negative

> (…) Good education is not only about blah-blah, then the teacher tests you, you get a grade (which is supposed to reflect what you learned…) and good luck if you passed. Most of the Hotelschool subjects operate under this principle. (Rosanne, level-four-thinker, old-curriculum, van Rossum et al., 2002)

A distinctly worrying outcome in the study with old-curriculum students was that all students with entry and exit level 5 (level-five-thinkers) in this study described a clearly negative development in study behaviour,

> My way of learning has indeed changed somewhat. At secondary school I was used to working through the whole subject matter and looking at it in an analytical way. I quickly noticed that here [at the Hotelschool] there just wasn't time to do this. Learning quickly became memorising and filling the short-term memory and afterwards finding out that you forget quickly as well. (John, level-five-thinker, old-curriculum, van Rossum et al., 2002)

A final quote given here is from Paula, a level-five-thinker who compared secondary Montessori education (promoting independent learning) with the current situation at the Hotelschool, again making her point through exaggeration.

> I went to a secondary school where I gradually learned to plan my own learning. I was very independent. I can still remember my first class at the Hotelschool. We were immediately informed that there would be an exam after 8 weeks and that we needed to study hard for this. We were given an overview of the literature and the topics to be treated. I felt it was only working through the literature and not doing exercises (active learning). I did not like at all that I could no longer plan when and what to study myself. I really needed to get used to this. During my career at the Hotelschool, most of my 'thinking for myself' faded away (...) (Paula, level-five-thinker, old-curriculum, van Rossum et al., 2002)

We have seen similar comments on changes in learning behaviour in the final section of the previous chapter, where Beth – also a Montessori trained student – discussed her experiences at the Hotelschool in an only slightly less disenchanted way.

Ships that Pass in the Night: Nostalgia

As we have said above, nostalgia is a phenomenon that occurs when students feel over-asked or simply fail to understand the demands of their current study environment. Their insecurity about what is expected from them, seems to invite a nostalgic wish for more familiar, traditional teaching and learning environments when their role was more clear. We have found examples of nostalgia in data regarding both curricula. First we discuss nostalgia in Enterprising Learning.

Nostalgia towards Traditional Teaching and Learning in Enterprising Learning

As we have said before, many students felt comfortable with doing assignments, interpreting Enterprising Learning as aimed at learning to apply theory in practice through frequent assignments, in particular cases and projects (see chapter 7). For quite a few on the other hand the call of the traditional approach to teaching and learning kept its allure.

> ... when I came to the Hotelschool, I thought I would have to study a lot. I saw myself sitting at my desk for hours. Reality proved to be different. ... Here it is mainly "doing a lot". A module ends with a final report and an exam. ... On the one hand this is fine. By writing all these reports you "learn" a lot automatically. Still I often felt that my need for knowledge was not really being satisfied. I'm the eager to learn type, I want to know everything and preferably a bit about everything. ... I satisfy my thirst for knowledge in other ways in my own free time by reading a lot and doing a lot of activities. (Mina, level-three-thinker)

Sometimes students changed sides with regard to group work and assignments, initially looking forward to a different way of learning, but ending up rather negative and rebellious about Enterprising Learning. Without an alternative perspective on more sophisticated approaches to learning, these students harked back to an approach they knew well and were successful in. Josephine is an example of this resentment.

> I feel learning is a combination of different elements, experiencing, reading, being taught, doing assignments (processing information) and looking for information yourself. For some people some approaches work better than others, everybody has their own study approach. For me it's more learning from books than looking for information for hours on internet so you can then put it in a report. ... Assignments and group work are something more for on the side, not an appropriate approach to get *all* the information. ...
>
> At the start of the Hotelschool I think I was more positive about working in groups. The idea of teamwork and learning about other people's views on issues seems fun. But after three and a half year I've more or less had it with these groups, it takes too much time and the added value is small, ...

> I feel, group assignments should help you process information and not, as it is now, consist of looking for information and doing something with it at the same time. … In principle I do agree with the basic idea behind "Enterprising Learning", but in reality it just didn't turn out that well. … I would be really happy with more exams and less group work.
>
> [Good teaching] to me is more "traditional" teaching: learning and exams, now and then a group assignment and submitting a report. (Josephine, level-three-thinker)

The nostalgia towards "traditional" teaching created tension between time spent on transmission-and-reception, and time spent on application-and-"doing" in Enterprising Learning. Occasionally students felt that they needed more transmission-and-reception time *first* before they could competently "do" anything.

> I think Enterprising Learning really is a good development in teaching, only it shouldn't be pushed so hard, then it defeats itself. It has to come gradually and not all at once just for the sake of it. … often it seems like everything is now completely turned around and everything is dumped in the student's lap. I think we should sit and listen to the teacher because we can learn from him/her, because he/she has the knowledge. Only after the transfer of knowledge Enterprising Learning can start. (Frank, level-three-thinker)
>
> … a good teacher teaches well by involving students in class … discussing with students and asking questions. I think a teacher should remain an instructor, sometimes in modern teaching he becomes too much a coach, I don't like that, a teacher is there to teach me something, and to motivate me to learn something and not only to be a coach. You need to be able to go to teachers with questions and they should give you the feeling they're there for you and not the other way around. (Helen, level-three-thinker)

From the final sentence in the quote of Helen we already get the impression that some teachers did not view their task in a way congruent with (or even tangential to) what students expected. Perhaps teachers act this way with the best of intentions, but there is evidence here that suggests that the message they are trying to get across does not register. Ann, participating in the same winter biology course as Maryann above, displays an almost classic case of nostalgia.

> I know [Chris, lecturer of winter biology] tried to play it off like there is still a lot of research, that it is a really new concept I guess, but still there is some stuff that is [fact]—like freezing cells. I understand what he was trying to do. He was trying to give examples to show what happened. But if he had just said cryoprotectants whatever, just said the point, I would believe him because he is the teacher. I don't need the proof. It's not like I'm going to argue with him about it. (Ann, Baxter Magolda, 1999, p. 3)

In particular the final sentence shows that Ann is missing the point of the course altogether. The whole purpose of the course was to get students "to think like scientists", in short to use evidence to build an argument towards a theoretical position that in turn could be argued about in class. Baxter Magolda's interpretation of what was happening in the classroom in this instance focused on Chris (the lecturer of the course) and Ann having diametrically opposed views on science. Where Chris viewed science as tentative knowledge, Ann was busy looking for the right (certain) answers. As Baxter Magolda described this interaction,

> Most likely, [Chris] is *unaware* of the view Ann holds about science ... and how it affects her learning in his course. Simultaneously, although Ann hears Chris describe cryobiology as an evolving field, her meaning-making system *has no room* for the idea the way Chris means it. ... This gap between instructor and student repeats itself daily across classrooms, disciplines, and institutions, making engaging students effectively in [meaningful] learning a major challenge. (Baxter Magolda, 1999, p. 3, italics ours)

We would like to characterise the essence of this miscommunication with the metaphor of ships passing in the night, neither aware of the destination of the other.

Nostalgia before Enterprising Learning

There was some evidence of nostalgia as well in the study of old-curriculum students although at that time we did not make this particular distinction. In this nostalgia, level-two-thinkers and level-three-thinkers indicated they had put in less effort and time into studying, putting "real learning" off to the last possible moment and increasing the use of other students' summaries and old exams. A typical example would be,

> Yes [my way of studying has changed]. Now I learn at the last possible moment. I used to learn everything well in advance and rehearse it the day before the exam. This way I 'retained' the subject matter longer, and I got better grades. (Bob, level-two-thinker, old-curriculum, van Rossum et al., 2002)

Not only did Bob's study behaviour deteriorate, but also his view on good teaching seemed to suffer from this negative development. Bob clearly preferred an even more traditional, stronger teacher-dominated teaching approach than typical for level-two-thinking: the teacher was made responsible for making the matter completely clear so 'learning' could take place.

> My ideal way of teaching is good lectures where everything is explained well and made clear. (...) Everything I hear I remember and this makes learning easier for me. I also find the lectures quite engaging. This is a pleasant way to master the subject, much nicer than working through boring books myself. (...) The ideal teacher to me is somebody who is good in his subject, gives clear lectures and clear assignments and above all is prepared to help the learning process when necessary. I feel the latter is most important. Especially, because at our school this hardly happens. *Almost nobody is there for you.* (Bob, level-two-thinker, old-curriculum, van Rossum et al., 2002, italics ours)

A very similar negative development was found for some level-three-thinkers. They also referred to postponing studying, putting in less effort etcetera. Belle put it most succinctly,

> I've had a wonderful time. The level of the lectures and subjects was a disappointment. I feel I haven't had to use all my brain at all. And I have unlearned how to learn!!! (Belle, level-three-thinker, old-curriculum, van Rossum et al., 2002)

The nostalgia is most clearly expressed in her preference for lectures and her dismissal of assignments as dominant means for learning, a very atypical attitude for the application-oriented level-three-thinkers for sure.

> Definitely lectures!! Of course assignments are useful, but not only assignments. Lectures are also very important. *I learn much more from lectures*. (Belle, level-three-thinker, old-curriculum, van Rossum et al., 2002, italics ours)

Enterprising Students: what else do they say?

Above we have discussed at length an important 'learning outcome' that can arise when students feel either insufficiently challenged or just the opposite, too severely challenged by the school curriculum. In these cases of destructive friction (Vermunt and Verloop, 1999), students feel bewildered and disoriented, often offering their disillusionment with the school and their studies in an angry tone, as we have seen above. Disenchantment as we have named this particular outcome of learning is not the only issue that students spontaneously weaved into the narratives of their school experiences. In the paragraphs below we will discuss and illustrate with quotes from students of both semesters several other issues that they brought forward with some regularity in their stories about learning and teaching within Enterprising Learning. These stories touched on many aspects of the teaching-learning process, and gave a more complete picture of the students' experiences in a relatively new and – to many of them – uncommon curriculum. Their comments were often submitted with the expressed aim to improve the experience of future students. The (sometimes overlapping) issues we will discuss here are

- Working in teams
- Assessment practices
- Teachers and teaching in Enterprising Learning
- Students and studying in Enterprising Learning
- Content matters
- Learning to select
- Breadth versus depth
- Influence of phase 3

Working in Teams

As we have seen in chapter 6, working in teams is a central and persistent feature of Enterprising Learning. For many of the students this was something they were not familiar with. On the whole, students were positive about working in groups, describing advantages such as the opportunity to hear other viewpoints on the subject matter (see chapter 7). The major objection students had was that in Enterprising Learning group work was compulsory and relentless.

> ... we have to work in groups all the time ... [which] makes it too easy to shirk certain tasks. Learning to work in groups is important, I agree, but because we do this all the time, some people start to fail to perform individually (I've seen this happen with a few students)... So, working in groups all the time I feel is not so good. I think it would be better to work in a group in one block and work individually in the next. (Niels, level-three-thinker)

> [Group work] "unlearns" you to work and learn individually. I think that it is a good thing to work in groups, but do we really have to do this all the time? (Frank, level-three-thinker)

Max and Leonie were both of the opinion that group work provided too little opportunity for assessment of individual performance, and they were concerned about 'free-riding'.

> I think that a teaching approach in which the teacher asks you to think about a topic and to make an assignment about it yourself and not in a group is more effective than dong everything in groups. Then the assignments are discussed in class, experiences and opinions are exchanged and the teacher makes you think further about what you have done. There just isn't only right or wrong, there are more roads to Rome and as long as you are doing the walking and the map reading yourself, you cannot hide behind someone else and the road is your own responsibility and not that of a group. I think education is a personal journey and not that of a group, every student is unique and here at school the individual is sacrificed too often for the collective. ... Bad students have too much power over good students at our school as the good students take the rap for the bad performances of others, because the whole group is responsible for the quality of the assignment. (Max, level-three-thinker)

> ... unfortunately there is only group work at this school and I feel one's abilities are tested for real when more individual assignments are carried out. [Then the] so-called 'free-riders' will be scanned rather quickly (...) and I feel an individual will learn more from it than he/she does currently. ... I feel the need to be tested on my own individual performance and only an exam is not enough at all. (Leonie, level-three-thinker)[4]

Many students besides these three mentioned that more variation in teaching approaches, mixing group work and individual work, would be more effective and motivating. It would also address the issue of free-riding as these students would be identified through their individual work.

Assessment Practices

A major aggravation mentioned by very many students was the perceived gap between what is learned by doing the assignments (namely to apply theory in practice) and the focus on theoretical detail that dominated the exams. In particular the focus on memorisation in many of the exams led them to interpret this as a fundamental contradiction within the system. The students quoted below expressed dissatisfaction at having to keep an "old way of learning alive", while all they wanted to do was move on.

> The Hotelschool, and the various cases we had to do, really helped me learn how to apply theory in practice. On the other hand school still made me learn stupid lists by heart because the assessment at exams was geared to (really small) details. I mean that during working on the assignments for 7 weeks, the theoretical framework of [a particular subject] slips into the background. But for the exam in front of you, you need to know all the details of a theory. I'm not talking about knowing the main lines and that you get questions to assess your understanding, but really checking if you remember the smallest details. .... [This] way of testing kept my old way of learning alive. The difference is that through cases you get more understanding. But this understanding was never assessed in the exams ... (Christine, level-three-thinker)

The issue of memorising as a tactic to pass exams was made even more explicit by the practice of cramming old exam responses. This practice was particularly successful as teachers often recycled questions over the year. Although students of course found this easy, they also felt dissatisfied as it failed to challenge them in a more constructive way

> I really don't like cramming thoughtlessly, although it is sometimes easier. That kind of learning is not too difficult for me, but I usually forget everything very quickly again. And in the end you really don't get very far this way ...
>
> I've told my parents that the Hotelschool has made me a lazy learner. I mean to say that it is really all made just too easy: using old exams with the same questions, and multiple choice testing. It can't really be ok that I can pass exams for higher professional education by just starting to learn the afternoon before? I'm really no "straight A" student, but I usually pass. This all sounds a bit conceited, but it isn't really. I do believe I did learn a lot at the Hotelschool, and that a lot has stayed with me. (Frank, level-three-thinker)
>
> At this school a great deal of exams are very, very predictable. Studying currently entails learning answers by heart instead of theory, as it gives us students the highest chance of success.
>
> For example the [main subject] exams in phase 2 are tested by multiple choice exams. 50 Questions to be exact. The [course] is repeated five times a year using one single textbook! Ideally that would mean 250 questions a year.

> By now, phase 2 exists longer than two years, but the teachers have not made the effort of coming up with 500 different questions. Therefore predictable questions! The best students are the ones with the best memories. I think that essays are the best way to test a person's knowledge. Not the current multiple choice memory game! (Edwin, level-three-thinker)[5]

Students expressed a keen willingness to be challenged more, and suggested alternative (and in their eyes more appropriate) forms of assessment. For instance, when asked to elaborate on what the opposite of the memory game was, Edwin said,

> The school should encourage students to develop their thoughts, combining theory with relevant up-to-date case studies. Therefore encourage students to write essays and value them. This may be *more work for students* and even more work for teachers, but it shows comprehension and isn't a memory game. (Edwin, level-three-thinker, italics ours)

Hans agreed with Edwin that assessment should be much more challenging and added the option of orals to the essay alternative.

> Speaking of study methods, I think open questions are much more useful, as is room for debate/discussion, and no multiple choice questions. ... many students learn for exams using old exams (fine), but if [teachers] use the same questions time and again, then I feel it's an opportunity missed. ...
>
> I really don't believe in MC-testing. I also don't believe in right and wrong. I'm more a person who is open to discussion. When you can answer a question with an explanation that shows that you understand and can apply it (whatever it may be), then I'm satisfied. MC-testing very often is vague and not unambiguous. There is always room for discussion. I used to write my explanations on how I reached my answer beside my mc-responses. I think oral exams are also very interesting in this sense. In orals it is easy to see if someone has really understood it or not. A teacher can ask further – or stop – when he feels the student shows understanding. (Hans, level-three-thinker)

There are a number of ways to address the dissatisfaction and frustration expressed by students about the perceived assessment procedure(s). If indeed a teacher's assessment approach is characterised by a dual aim, namely separate assessment of knowledge and application, making this clear at the onset of a course, block or semester will probably prevent a lot of confusion. If however the educational system is introduced as aiming for *one major goal*, for instance learning to apply theory in practice in the first phase of the Hotelschool, then ensuring more aligned assessment (Biggs, 1996, see chapter 11) would improve the achievement of this goal and prevent misunderstandings and frustration. As we will see in chapter 10, assessment is one of the most powerful tools teachers and educational institutes have to shape students' learning approaches and learning conceptions, and so it is very important to include aligned assessment protocols in the implementation of an innovative curriculum.

In the case of Enterprising Learning, with its espoused focus on activating students, more constructive learning and reflection, the question remains whether the ubiquitous use of multiple choice exams and recycling of questions was appropriate. We would like to put it even more strongly, one could wonder if there can exist an epistemological development-oriented curriculum for which these assessment practices would be appropriate? The final question we would like to pose here is whether it is appropriate for these practices to *dominate* in any curriculum at all (see also the final section of chapter 7)?

Teachers and Teaching in Enterprising Learning

> ... You need to be able to go to teachers with questions and they should give you the feeling they're there for you and not the other way around. (Helen, level-three-thinker)

As we have said before, from this final sentence in the quote of Helen (see nostalgia in Enterprising Learning above) we get the impression that some teachers did not view their task in a way congruent with what students expected. This is not necessarily a bad thing, as Palmer has said (1998, see also chapter 11), student dissatisfaction with a teacher may be a sign that real learning has taken place. On the other hand, sometimes students were rightfully angry about some teacher behaviours, as we will see below.

Students really do not seem to expect exceptionally strange things from their teachers. They usually only want to be supported while they learn how to handle things themselves. As Vermunt and Verloop said: "Going to school or university means almost by definition that students want their learning process to be teacher-regulated *to a certain degree*. On the other hand, there can be no learning if students are not capable or willing to employ any thinking activity" (1999, p. 269, italics ours). In Frank's words it almost sounds too commonplace to quote.

> Firstly, a teacher should act like someone who teaches, helping the students on their way by providing information. After this the student is expected to do something with the information. It is self-evident that not everything is presented on a platter and that a student does some research himself. But in the case that a student runs into trouble, and cannot seem to extract himself, the teacher should always be prepared to help him. The threshold to approach the teacher for this reason should always be perceived as low by the student. Therefore, a friendly and open relationship is essential. (Frank, level-three-thinker)

This may seem relatively traditional, but even in implementing an activating curriculum students need some mentoring: teachers who are willing and able to provide holding environments to assist them on their way and supporting their emerging independence. Of course there can be considerable debate on how long such support should be provided, but it seems some teachers felt that no transitional period was appropriate, hiding behind a skewed (or biased) perception of the aims of Enterprising Learning. Quite a number of students had "tall tales" about these teachers, some of these we quote below.

> For me the best way of teaching would be if the teacher would give an introductory lecture on the topic at the beginning of the module (…) and then [students] be sent off to do the assignments/projects individually or in groups and to have weekly sessions with the teachers to either receive feedback on the assignment made or help with a certain issue. This is exactly what the Hotelschool is trying to do, unfortunately the … teachers refuse to give out any information that could be beneficial to the student and they do not often say what is right and what is wrong, resulting in the student doing something without having a clue what. …
>
> From teachers I expect guidance. … they should be open to answer questions from students. And with answering questions I do not mean that they should say, "I don't know, why don't you look in the library?" This is what many teachers in school say when you come to them with a question. A good teacher should be able to tell whether or not the student with the question has done the necessary research and is still stuck or whether it is a student who is looking for an easy way out….
>
> A teacher should have an open attitude towards students, so that they do not feel intimidated to approach the teacher. When a student has a question about an issue, I feel the teacher should *either* answer the question *or* give a few good hints or questions that help the student further. I don't know how many times I went to a teacher with a question about for instance some theory I didn't understand and was sent on my way with the excuse, "This is really so simple, go and look it up in the library." I always felt that was really wrong. …. A good teacher should … be able to find the right balance between helping students [who really need it] and sending students [who are looking for an easy way out] on their way. Unfortunately this balance is missing at the Hotelschool. (Yvonne, level-three-thinker)[6]

Yvonne not only observed problematic teacher behaviour, but was able to diagnose the source as well. It would seem that teachers were unsure about the amount of help they were "permitted" to give to students within the activating curriculum that Enterprising Learning was supposed to be. They probably felt it was better to err on the side of caution, and provided less support than they might have in a more traditional curriculum. This to the considerable ire of the students as we see. Something similar seemed to have been going on in the minds of some teachers with regard to the amount of "real teaching" they felt they were allowed, as Timo described,

> Ideally, a teacher should be the first person to approach for all questions and problems. Enterprising Learning is a wonderful invention, but some teachers just seem to go overboard, by saying "I'm not allowed to teach anymore, so I'll just shut up and you can do the lesson…" It should be a game of give and

> take, with a thin line as a boundary. It could even vary from student to student, from subject to subject and from teacher to teacher. ... With the boundary I mean the interaction between student and teacher. What role should the teacher play with which student? I think you cannot define that at the outset, I mean to what point a teacher should be a "teacher" and from where he becomes a "coach". I think a teacher should evaluate this boundary on a case by case basis, and decide which student needs what approach. (Timo, level-four-thinker)

Here also, the student seemed to understand where the teacher's response was coming from, but also immediately diagnosed the missing competence, namely the lack of ability to decide when to change the role from "teacher" to "coach" and vice versa. Subsequently teachers failed to provide the support each individual student required. Sara expanded on Timo's observation that teachers expected students to "do the lesson" themselves.

> Ultimately ... I feel I did learn a lot. But I must say I've seriously criticised the [Enterprising Learning] system in the past, in particular the teaching method. ... I feel it happens pretty often that teachers expect you to have done a load of research before coming to the first class. If you hadn't, then the class was useless, because then it would be only one-way communication. Questions from the students were necessary, otherwise simply nothing would happen. In other words, I feel Enterprising Learning is taken a little too literally!! It is actually quite strange when a teacher tells you, "Well, I would love to teach, but sorry, I am not allowed to!" I've heard that many times!!! (Sara, level-four-thinker)

The multiple exclamation marks show the surprise and feeling of irony that Sara felt when confronted with teachers who seemed to refuse to "play their role". It would also seem that at least some teachers at the Hotelschool had a biased perception of Enterprising Learning, interpreting it as "dropping students in at the deep end" or as a curriculum based on a "sink or swim"-approach. It seems that students may have a solution to that particular teacher fallacy as well, as Yvonne suggested,

> The ideal teacher-students relationship is one of good communication. ... I feel that at the beginning of one's studies a teacher should stand above the students, but as one's studies progress, a teacher should come to stand beside each student. (Yvonne, level-three-thinker)

In fact, in the staff training for new teachers in Enterprising Learning (see chapter 9) such an approach (of changing student and teacher roles) was increasingly advocated over the years, with the aim of gradually decreasing the level of traditional teaching and assessment as students moved through the three phases of the curriculum at the Hotelschool (see chapter 6). In this way Enterprising Learning would better provide sufficient scaffolding (i.e. temporary holding environments) throughout the curriculum, while still providing the necessary epistemological challenges for students along their developmental track from level-two-thinker to level-four-thinker (see also chapter 6). One possible cause for the teachers' biased perception could be that the concept of Enterprising Learning itself evolved over time, growing from a rather static concept at the outset – with learning-teaching conception 4 simultaneously as the point of departure and destination (see chapter 6) – into a primarily dynamic and development-aimed concept from 2003 onwards – with students developing gradually from level-two-thinker to level-four-thinker (van Rossum and Hamer, 2004). In this light it is not so surprising that some teachers reacted (and behaved) the way they did.

On the other hand, the view on educational innovation that it limits the "allowed ways to teach" is not unique to Enterprising Learning. Although it is probably correct to say that most educational innovations are based on the assumption that "teaching" is no longer synonymous to "telling", we hope that there are not many that actually say "you are not allowed to tell your students what they need to know". Vermunt and Verloop (1999) observed that in higher education "[c]omplete teacher control or the total absence of teacher control rarely occur" (p. 269), and as far as we know educational innovators usually try to convince the more traditional teachers that a steady diet of only "teaching by telling" and "testing for reproduction" is not very effective in achieving the espoused goals of higher education. The main message then is *not* that teachers are not allowed to "tell" occasionally, but that in order for students to really learn, other methods should be used *as well* (see e.g. chapter 3 and 5). As such innovators on average do not limit the allowed ways to teach at all, on the contrary, they try to widen the range. Whatever approach is chosen, teaching (and learning) are in essence acts of communication and interpersonal interaction. As we have described it in previous chapters, learning and teaching are about the quality of the *meeting* (of minds). This brings us to the role the students saw for themselves in Enterprising Learning.

Students and Studying in Enterprising Learning

If, as Vermunt and Verloop justly observed, "there can be no learning if students are not capable or willing to employ any thinking activity." (1999, p. 269), it is worthwhile to explore how students perceived their own role in Enterprising Learning. In general, we saw that students agreed with the observation above, emphasising that students necessarily have an active role in learning.

> The whole idea of Enterprising Learning is ok, you are forced to find information about a topic yourself and to understand the topic (if you don't understand it, you can't really find good information about it). The role of the students is that he should be the one to come up with the information, to interpret it correctly and to use it in the report. (Victor, level-three-thinker)

> In an ideal class, students should know beforehand what part of the subject matter to prepare (or at least to have the option to prepare) so that students can get the maximum return on attending the class as well as on the expertise of the lecturer. (Mirjam, level-three-thinker)

> When Mr. B explains how to calculate X, and shows me how, I can do the calculations and even get a good result. Fine.

> [But] when Mr. B tells me that I have to calculate X and I have no clue whatsoever about X, I will have to rummage through the books to find out what it is, what it is for, and how to calculate it. This way I learn and understand it and I can probably use it in future as well. ….
>
> At the Hotelschool you make your own choices. I chose the Hotelschool myself and *I* am responsible for the things I do. When people around me says "Jeez, all that work, I really don't wanna do that" I've told them several times that they are doing it for themselves. And if they really don't want to do it, they shouldn't, and then they need to make a different choice. It's their life and they should make their own choices. … Anyway, the conclusion is that I know well that I'm in this for myself and not because I have to or others want me to. (Rens, level-three-thinker, italics ours)

Victor, Mirjam and Rens illustrate what it means to be an active student in Enterprising Learning. A role that expresses itself in having one's *own reasons* for studying, being prepared when attending lectures and group sessions, and being independent enough to find and work with information on one's own. Often, students criticised their fellow students when they failed to fulfil these requirements.

> Take for instance [support subject A]. I've helped a lot of groups with SPSS, because I noticed that many of my friends are not really capable of working with it. Each time I start with a group, I tell them that I'm not just going to do it for them, they need to sit with me and look over my shoulder [to learn to do it themselves], also to make sure they don't come back again just before the exam. Still, time and time again I see that in the end only a few students understand the program and can work with it. This means that a majority still is not able to work independently with this tool, while they passed the exam. So did they really learn something they can use later, I think not! (Victor, level-three-thinker)
>
> Students who attend classes for form's sake just to pick up something that way, should keep their mouth shut and their obstructing questions – that show they haven't prepared – should be ignored. … At school it sometimes feels like being back at secondary school…. (Mirjam, level-three-thinker)
>
> .. if students don't want to, then for me they shouldn't have to. It's their own choice, they pay enough for it. If they don't want to learn, then don't do it. Then just leave. By the way, I think that more students feel the same way, but only in the later years … (Rens, level-three-thinker)

In line with their independent stance with regard to learning, they also criticised teachers who wanted to exercise complete teacher control (Vermunt and Verloop, 1999), in particular when this occurred in the final stages of their studies.

> The role of the teacher is that he should be the one to put the student on the right path and then checks up on this path, and jumps in when it starts to go wrong. Unfortunately, what often happens now is that teachers want to have the report all their own way. … This may give a student the idea that the

> report is actually written for the teachers or the Hotelschool [and not for the principal]. (Victor, level-three-thinker)
>
> A teacher may steer when things go wrong. But he should not have the attitude "It's my way or the highway" and should realise that there are many roads to Rome. As long as the theory is applied correctly, a coach should not interfere. (Tom, level-three-thinker)
>
> It really should not be possible that teachers cling dogmatically to dated models of so-called guru's, these models are seen as the truth and students should stick to them and are not given the "freedom" to think independently. (Max, level-three-thinker)

Throughout our study we encountered many students who over the years had come to feel completely at home in Enterprising Learning, e.g. Tom,

> For me, problem-based learning is the ideal way of learning. In this way you have to focus only on that part of the theory that is applicable to the case on hand. There is no superfluous information that is not used in solving the case. This means that only the important information is discussed. ... I work best in groups. Everyone has their own view and their own way of applying, so various views on the use of a theory and the issue at hand are discussed. In this way I learn more. ... I prefer to work with a coach who keeps a close eye on projects and explains theories when necessary. Preferably all this happens *after* some contribution of my own, so that you are not "put" on the right track immediately, but you have to make some initial steps yourself. (Tom, level-three-thinker, italics ours)

On the other hand, some students "warned" us that the attitude of a number of students, perhaps including themselves, might not be appropriate to Enterprising Learning and as such could undermine the effectiveness of it.

> ... in my eyes the Enterprising Learning thing is a nice idea, but does not really function very well since most students in this school are still too young and wild to go with such a learning system... including myself possibly... I believe that the most effective way of getting students to study and understand stuff is still the old fashioned way with a strict teacher and tough classes. (Guido, level-three-thinker)[7]

Returning to the remark made above by Vermunt and Verloop (1999) with regard to the willingness or ability of students to employ thinking activity, we feel that sufficient evidence is present to ignore lack of ability as an obstacle to learning in this study. The willingness on the other hand may differ between students, but we feel a measure of mentored learning, introducing "young and wild" students to and supporting them in a more mature attitude towards their own (independent) learning, could easily remedy a possible lack of willingness, so that real learning can and will take place. Therefore, a more gradual introduction to problem-based learning (Enterprising Learning) would again seem to be a more fruitful approach to student epistemological development than a return to a traditional curriculum.

Content Matters

Some students felt that the information – the theories and examples provided at the Hotelschool – did not give a true picture of the full range of issues they might encounter in their career. As perceived by the students, the books and the teachers emphasised issues and solutions relevant to big businesses, large international hotel chains, multinational organisations, etcetera, and almost never were issues discussed that might commonly occur in smaller sized businesses. Rens, a son of a president of such a smaller business, shared his father's experiences with us to make his point.

> … I think that some, if not the majority, of the teachers are not objective and know primarily theory and not the real world. Of course a number of teachers come from the industry and some are still active in it, but it is very simple. I can explain: 95% of the marketing, management and other books used at school give a false image. This image is copied by teachers and that's why I call them subjective. The real world is not only as pictured in the books (and I now know this for a fact). Of course many models used and examples from "practice" can be recognised as occurring in large companies and multinationals.
>
> My views were formed by the real world and the (somewhat bitter) opinion of my father. I'll tell you about a talk we once had.
>
> Until recently, my father was the president of his own company, a company that built installations for gas stations, etcetera. We were in the car travelling to Amsterdam when I put my problem to him, "Dad, I don't understand why you have such problems with your personnel. It should be possible to motivate them and to make sure that they won't destroy the company?" His answer was elaborate, but I will give you the shortened version. "Personnel is the worst thing in the world" …. The people working for my father have different values. You can't just ask them to please just do their job. They stole from him and the person concerned was fired on the spot. The man started a legal procedure, when the judge told my father, "O well, Mr. Z, this man has worked 5 years for you and this is the first time something was stolen. You can reinstate him or pay him 50 thousand guilders". Reinstating was impossible because that would damage the work atmosphere, so the fine was paid. …… [A second workman] left the company to join the competition and took confidential information about clients with him. This case could not be proven legally. In the mean time it became clear that this latter man had also enriched himself in ways that could not bear the light of day, and that resulted in considerable financial damage to the company. My father's personnel ruined his company, with the occasional exception of a loyal employee of course.
>
> This look on reality, if also not completely representative, is completely ignored at the Hotelschool, so it seems. Talks about incentives and such are all good and fine when you are in the board of directors of [large company Y],

> but less relevant when you, as many students from the Hotelschool will probably do, start your own business that at the outset is considerably smaller than the 100 employees necessary for the financial space to pay for a HRM department and incentives for personnel.
>
> My advice: ask a guest speaker with some real experience (for the time being my father is keeping himself available).
>
> I feel that a little less rosy and subjective look on the business world can be expected from a Hotelschool teacher, but it doesn't happen at the moment. .... [Even in assignments] other, less positive (or even negative) issues would make a good base for an assignment. For instance an assignment to pull a sinking business out of the red, to make it back into a healthy enterprise, that kind of assignment I have definitely missed at the Hotelschool. (Rens, level-three-thinker)

A less personal story is that of Maarten, who felt that much of the theory students had to learn was included only to impress students with the importance of a subject, and not because it was particularly relevant at this point in time. Maarten wrote the response below not very long after 9/11.

> ... and when you really have to learn something .... it's very often pointless stuff coming out of the office of a teacher who just wants to prove how important his subject is. ... Education should move with the times. Current issues as the stock market, world economy, emerging economies and things like that are lacking completely. I think that is a pity. ... Include current affairs and interests into assignments. For instance include ... KLM or British Airways in assignments, or even stronger a company like Enron. Researching the pro's and con's of an extra swimming pool in a hotel with four of them already sounds a bit irrelevant [in comparison. On the other hand] there are enough small businesses that want to expand or market new products. Those are issues that are current and that you can learn from and be interested in because they are current. How are the large scale dismissals organised at KPN or ABN/Amro? (Maarten, level-three-thinker)

Where Rens looked for relevance closer to home in smaller businesses, Maarten was interested in the issues at both ends of the spectrum, including embezzlement, stock market crashes, emerging economies on the one hand and small and expanding businesses on the other hand. Both students would agree that to address these content matters, teachers should leave their safe and stuffy offices to make contact with the real world.

Learning to Select

In chapter 7 we encountered students who indicated that a major aspect of their new way of learning (in their development from level-two-thinker to level-three-thinker) was the ability to learn in a more selective way. Selection in those narratives referred to distinguishing between important and less important things, and then to either learn only the important things by heart, or to apply them in a case. This aspect of the development to level-three-thinker we had already found before in our study of the developments in the old curriculum (van Rossum et al., 2003). As in chapter 7, for these old-curriculum students the reason to apply selection was "the realisation that you do not need to know/memorise everything" (p. 93).

In this paragraph, selection is again an issue for students, but now it refers to selecting relevant information by quickly reading through *lots* of literature in order to find information to apply in a case or assignment.

> My way of learning certainly changed in a major way since I started at the Hotelschool. I can handle lots of literature much better, making distinctions between important and less important, learning now is more understanding and applying and less only knowing definitions. In the first phase I tried to learn everything, this is no longer possible and also not everything is relevant… (Odette, level-three-thinker)

> At the start of the Hotelschool you're pretty naïve. You think that everything is important and then try to cram everything into your head. Usually this is in vain because concentration is essential at such moments and I have a huge lack of that. Looking back it usually proved to be futile, so you realise at a certain moment that you only need to learn the essential parts of the subject matter. … This seems to be satisfactory for now, but it means a considerable change of learning style: more "efficient" is the key word here. … (Tom, level-three-thinker)

One approach to increase efficiency of the learning process could be to remove the search process by providing the basic information together with the assignment or case. Tom saw definite advantages to this approach.

> [Ideally] sufficient information is given and this makes endless seeking of information on internet superfluous and ensures you are into the subject matter real quickly. [Main subject C] always provides almost all the information you need for a case, so that the "scanning procedure" becomes unnecessary and interpretation becomes more important. (Tom, level-three-thinker)

Niels proposed an alternative way to increase the efficiency of the learning process by improving the ability of students to scan large amounts of texts, leaving more time for processing.

> At the Hotelschool they set you a sea of information out of which you need to fish the relevant information yourself … there was too much literature to learn everything by heart and that wasn't what they wanted you to do. … I feel that if they expect you to *scan* large amounts of literature on relevance, then they could consider to teach you how to do that. (Niels, level-three-thinker)

When asked to elaborate on the last sentence about scanning, Niels said,

> With the large amounts of text you need to read at the Hotelschool to do a case, a student is expected to be able to scan a text. I think not everybody is able to do that easily. I don't know how, but perhaps a text-scanning course could be given in the first year. (Niels, level-three-thinker)

It seems obvious that when students are expected to search relevant information for a case, and to do this in a short time, it can pose problems for those not accustomed to handling the really enormous amounts of information available, e.g. via internet searches. As most of the students in our study had not learned to scan for relevant information in secondary education, the Hotelschool could consider to offer an elective text-scanning course in the first phase for students who need it.

Breadth Versus Depth

The issue of breadth versus depth is a familiar one in as far that it refers to the choice made by an institute between offering a more general curriculum or a highly specialised one. In a general curriculum the aim is to "learn a bit about everything", leaving the deepening into specialist knowledge to a later moment in time. In this case graduates are very versatile and have a wide range of career opportunities. Although historically focusing on the hospitality industry, the Hotelschool seems to have become quite successful in this regard, with graduates working within the industry in a wide variety of jobs and all over the world, but many more (eventually) as successfully working outside it (see chapter 6).

A disadvantage of a more general curriculum is that there is always a proportion of the student population that might have had a different – perhaps a more business-oriented – education in mind when they came to the Hotelschool.

> The Hotelschool has not been able to contribute enough to what I feel is learning. The subject matter offered is, I feel, to light and superficial and that is a real pity. The students are not sufficiently challenged to delve deeply into the subject matter. (Max, level-three-thinker)

Max framed the issue without placing a blame outside his own expectations. Chiara on the other hand saw a role for teachers in discouraging superficiality and an emphasis on quantity.

> Now I learn things much more superficially, without thinking very deeply about the subject matter (I've usually already done that while doing the assignment) because I know I don't have to do that for the exam … I feel the set up of the assignments in phase 3 is good … Only personally, I feel that there should be more attention paid to [issues of] superficiality and quantity, and not only in phase 3. In the final phase quite a number of teachers fail you for this, while others praise you [for sheer quantity]. … I feel it would be an improvement if more attention is paid in the first years with regard to the trade-off between relevance and quantity: what is the relevance of a report and not how many pages is it. (Chiara, level-three-thinker)

Bas pulled the issue even wider, placing responsibility at the doorstep of teachers *and* fellow students together as both can contribute to a learning culture that – he felt – would serve the (hotel) industry better.

> When I started at the Hotelschool, I imagined that subjects would include the necessary theory, but more so would focus on relevant, practice related problems (...) I expected I would be forced and encouraged to think myself. This did happen to a certain extent, however, because of the mentality at the Hotelschool (caused by students as well as some teachers), this ambition is not always realised. Students often choose the easy way out (copying books [for assignments]). When teachers fail to counteract this the situation may arise that both parties resign themselves to it (it benefits the student to remain passive and the teacher sees the resulting average outcome as the maximum one). ... I think the level of the school could be higher by demanding more of individual students. ... Force students to think themselves and be creative, at least that will benefit them in the hospitality industry. (Bas, level-three-thinker)

As we said at the start of this paragraph, the trade-off between breadth and depth is a familiar problem for educational institutions everywhere, and not easily solved to the satisfaction of all parties concerned. So, what can the Hotelschool learn from the students who bring this issue up? The main thing is that the school should be very clear about its aims with regard to expected learning outcomes and career perspectives for graduates. Secondly, staff development could contribute to equipping teachers in such a way that they can support students better in attaining the espoused goals of the institute. Thirdly, clearer and unambiguous criteria for (designing and implementing) assessment of all types of student work can support teachers in expressing a united front with regard to the performance level(s) expected from students.

Influence of Phase 3

As it was in the old curriculum (see van Rossum et al., 2003), many students found the final phase of Enterprising Learning the most instructive. The final phase consisted of three main parts, strategic case(s), final project and management internship. Students started with two strategic cases (the Hotel and Restaurant case, later these merged into one case, MoSaC, Management of Strategy and Change, see chapter 6). They also performed a real research study for an outside client, this study is referred to as 'the final project' or 'graduation project'. This study was usually done by groups of three students. This phase was closed with a management internship, performed in the Netherlands or abroad. Of these three distinct parts within phase 3, students were most enthused about the graduation project, often referring to it as the major learning experience of their time at the Hotelschool.[8]

We could have quoted many students about the effect of the graduation project, but we chose three who build up the description of the effect this project had on their idea about themselves and their learning experience.

> Now we have started on our final project and we have been working on it for a few weeks now, I like the idea that it is our own project … and after three years at the Hotelschool we know exactly where to find which information. We can give it our own dimension and that is what I like until now. I mean that … my group can find a solution to the problem the principal has indicated and the solution [chosen is the one] my group feels is most effective. … we can set our own priorities, what is relevant to the project and what is not. It is *our* creation… (Leonie, level-three-thinker)
>
> Something I really learned a lot from is the final project. Five months of continuous working on a study [the results of which] the principal will actually use after this. That thought is really motivating. You're really working on something 'real' and it has to be really good.
>
> I did my project on building processes in hotels of a certain chain. I found this very educational, because here at the Hotelschool were are not really taught a lot about construction and everything around it (permits, laws, architect, contractor, etcetera)
>
> The guidance during the project I felt was really positive. The writing of the research plan and the guidance during this process gives you a good base. Then you do the research independently. I surely look back on this part as the most educational period in my studies. (Mina, level-three-thinker)

Mirjam is the most outspoken of the three students selected here, using a building metaphor to express her view on the purpose of the final project (and phase 3) in the Enterprising Learning curriculum,

> … in phase 3 I learned "differently" because it was expected that the formerly "crammed" subject matter was applied in a real-life case.
>
> What struck me in particular was that finally I started to see a relationship between everything I had learned in the previous years. What initially seemed to be a dull, tough and non-tangible mass, suddenly seemed to have a 'purpose'. It was funny to see that I had learned more than I had originally thought or that some of my grades had led me to expect.
>
> "Learning" no longer was: learning chapters 1 through 8 and chapters 13 through 15, readers and handouts by heart. But now it was formulating a research question (yourself !), planning a kind of thinking-route, and applying the knowledge you had. I think I would have taken in knowledge easier and quicker if I had seen the links between everything earlier. In retrospect I feel that during all the modules I learned how to build a house: one module would teach me how to make a roof, the next would teach me about wiring an plumbing, and a third would teach me about bricklaying, etcetera.
>
> However, while I was learning all this, it was not clear to me that I was learning about the "roof" or that this "roof" was supposed to go on top of a house. It may all sound a bit simple, but *during the final project I felt a light*

> *go on in my head. It actually startled me.* During phase 3 I noticed that probably half of my fellow students (some of them excellent roofers, some excellent carpenters) did not experience this "aha!" moment at all. Dear people, [O's model] with its remote, task and functional environment actually is nothing else than Marketing, …. what ever Mr. D says! Isn't it?
>
> Although of course I did learn a lot in phase 3 and my management internship, this kind of learning [in the final project] is completely different. It is not simply answering an exam question or choosing between three alternatives, because in real life you don't really need this type of knowledge when you can't see when which knowledge is relevant to getting a step closer to the solution of a bigger problem. Of course it is just as well that you graduate in groups of three. That means that if you are not very good at carpentry, but you know what you need to have built, you only have to make sure that you find an excellent carpenter. This all comes together neatly with the aim of a management study, but it also means that the personal qualities of various Hotelschool graduates may vary considerably. The first can be a people manager (but is not very practical in other ways), the second is exceptionally good in one area or another and perhaps the third was particularly good at hiding behind the qualities of the other members of the graduation group. (Mirjam, level-three-thinker, italics ours)

What then did students find so exceptional about this particular project? If we knew this, perhaps parts of the experience could be brought forward in the curriculum to encourage more speedy epistemological development and perhaps even encouraging larger developments, spanning more than one stage, than proved possible now.

Firstly, the realism: all students who mentioned this project, and many who discussed a good assignment, mentioned the excitement of working on a real or realistic project. The final project often was the first actual experience students had with real clients and a real (complex) problem waiting for a possible solution. Students felt strongly that they could not – in all honesty – just make up something to comply. In a sense the realisation that this project was "the real thing" reminds us of Gavin's thinking in describing the difference between college and life: "…before [at college] you always knew you could always just give up and go home. Now [after college] you can't give up and you can't go home. So you've got to kind of tough it out …" (Baxter Magolda, 2001, p. 285). Consequently, to encourage epistemological development the common distinction made between higher education and real life should perhaps be removed. In Baxter Magolda's words, "If college is going to prepare graduates for real life, college needs to become real life. That is to say, educators must create learning experiences that have substantive meaning for everyday life, require real responsibility on students' part, and that connect to students' internal self-evolution" (2001, p. 286). We feel that students' remarks quoted in the section on content matters point in the same direction, the motivating effect of realistic, complex and relevant problems. We rephrase our previous conclusion drawn there to include the students: teachers should leave their safe and stuffy offices *to help students* make contact with the real world (see also van Rossum et al., 2003, p. 96).

Secondly, the sense of ownership: the project was seen as students' personal responsibility and solutions to the problem at hand were seen as personal creations. This aspect is closely linked to realism as is pointed out above.

Thirdly, learning new things, seeing new opportunities: in the final project students often encountered issues and areas of expertise they had not explored before. For some students the final project was the missing link in deciding what kind of career to pursue (or to definitely not pursue).

Fourthly, the integrative aspect of the final project: as Mirjam's story illustrated, students often commented on the feeling of finally realising that there were actually relationships between the subjects and modules they had completed in previous years. For students who graduated at level three this was only a budding realisation, because they were not yet able to make these relationships themselves. But at least they suspected that there were indeed relationships, which of course is the first step towards constructing them themselves, and so the first step towards level four thinking and self-authorship (Kegan, 1994; Baxter Magolda, 2001). The latter two ways of knowing are commonly seen as the goals of higher education (see also chapter 10).

Conclusions

Where in the previous chapter we looked at the results of Enterprising Learning and *constructive* friction leading to learning, in this chapter we looked closer at the outcomes of *destructive* friction. When students' and teachers' epistemological outlook are too far apart, students can become seriously disaffected. Not that student dissatisfaction is always a bad thing, it may indicate true learning, but often it does not. We have identified two distinct types of student reactions to a too large a gap between teacher and student epistemology: disenchantment and nostalgia. Presenting evidence not only from our own respondent group, but also from studies by various other researchers, we feel we can state that both types, disenchantment and nostalgia, are not limited to educational environments.

Disenchantment is the term we use for the dissatisfaction that arises when students feel insufficiently challenged by the teacher. The students find the learning environment too schoolish, the teacher too controlling, that existing learning and thinking skills are not called upon and they often rebel. Rebellion expresses itself in various ways: antagonistic interactions (e.g. difficult behaviours or perceived motivational problems, Yerrick et al., 1998), disengagement expressed in emphasised extrinsic motivation by grades and diplomas (e.g. van Rossum et al., 2002; the current study), reverting to less sophisticated study strategies (e.g. van Rossum et al., 2002), and despair (e.g. Lindblom-Ylänne and Lonka, 1999; Kember, 2001).

Nostalgia is student dissatisfaction of a completely different kind. Nostalgia is not the result of feeling insufficiently challenged, but from feeling over-challenged and not knowing what to do about it. Nostalgic students realise that they do not truly understand what the teacher wants from them. This insecurity leads them to long for a learning-teaching environment in which their own role was clear and they knew what to expect from teachers, namely guidance and control. In the current study, nostalgic students often became less enamoured with group work and felt that all the "doing" interfered with learning (transmission and reception of knowledge). Some nostalgic students struggled on, others reverted to even less sophisticated views on and approaches to learning, placing all the responsibility for learning in the hands of the teacher. In the latter case students increasingly put in less effort into studying.

Regarding the incidence of disenchantment or nostalgia the comparison between the students of the old, traditional curriculum and Enterprising Learning leads to the conclusion that again Enterprising Learning has a better record. On the other hand, within the Enterprising Learning student group there were fewer students with sophisticated entry learning-teaching conceptions, which made in particular disenchantment less likely. Furthermore, considering that most students of the current study entered the Hotelschool with learning-teaching conception 2, and that Enterprising Learning was perceived (by most teachers, see chapter 9) to foster learning-teaching conception 3, the incidence of nostalgia may indicate that the introduction of Enterprising Learning can be improved upon by introducing more supports, especially in the first semesters, something students themselves suggested as well in the previous chapter.

Regarding the relentless group work in Enterprising Learning, students expressed concerns about the assessment of their individual performance. As has been observed in other instances of group work, free-riders are not only a concern of teachers, students are worried about them too. Students suggested some variation in teaching approaches by introducing a limited amount of individual work as well. The practice of assessment by group work was not their only issue with assessment at the Hotelschool. A major irritation was that the common type of assessment in exams did not conform with Enterprising Learning. Where Enterprising Learning focused on learning by application, exams were very often aimed at rote memorisation and reproduction of facts. Students felt that the exams were assessing the wrong thing: they felt the exams should have assessed whether they were able to apply what they had learned. This focus on factual and detailed reproduction led many students to employ study strategies they thought they could leave behind in Enterprising Learning, namely cramming and rote learning. Secondly, the teachers' habit of recycling questions – while it made cramming old exams a profitable approach – was the source of considerable dissatisfaction in students. Students expressed a keen willingness to be challenged more, and suggested assessment practices such as essays, exams with open questions, or oral exams, and the abolishment of multiple-choice exams. These students seem willing to put in more effort and don't seem to be looking for an obvious easy way out.

Talking about effort, students felt that on occasion teachers were not taking their role seriously and were not pulling their weight. Especially teachers who failed to provide support and much needed guidance while putting the blame on Enterprising Learning, were subject of scorn. Of course these students understood that they had to do a lot of work themselves, that becomes clear from their narratives, but they felt that when they really ran into a wall or dead-end, it was not right for a teacher to reply "I'd love to teach, but sorry, I am not allowed to..." (see Sara, level-four-thinker, above). Some students indicated that they understood where this idea came from: a failure of the teacher to know when to switch from teacher to coach. This issue is not uncommon. Traditional teachers confronted with an activating curriculum might truly not understand that there is another way of teaching than teaching-by-telling. They fail to perceive that while an activating curriculum aims to increase teaching-by-other-methods, it does not preclude some teaching-by-telling when that is necessary. It would seem that to improve Enterprising Learning, or any other activating or constructivist curriculum for that matter, teachers need to be educated regarding their role and be given time to develop in this role. We address the issue of staff development in chapter 11.

The students were not uncritical about their own role. They often expressed that being active in Enterprising Learning also meant developing their own reasons for learning, putting in effort (going to class, attending lectures and group sessions, looking for information themselves and working hard). Their move towards learning more independently made students increasingly reject too much teacher control. This attitude became to the fore most in the final stages of their studies. On the other hand, students observed that some of their colleagues were less diligent and they saw this as a danger to the success of Enterprising Learning.

The relevance of content was not always clear to students. Again not an uncommon finding, but one indicating that a little more attention to providing information on relevance may perhaps prevent demotivation. Especially students in the final phase remarked that if they had only known that all the separate courses and blocks indeed fitted together and were necessary to build their own house of professionalism, they would have paid more attention to them at the time. In a way, these students were hampered by a learning skill they had practiced to perfection in Enterprising Learning: learning to select what is relevant, useful, now – in a project – or in their future. They observed that while this skill is essential to Enterprising Learning, it perhaps made them disregard subjects and courses of which the relevance was not made sufficiently clear at the time.

Considering that the decision to introduce Enterprising Learning was based on the excellent evaluation of the final year of the old curriculum, it is surprising that these students still appreciated this phase more than the rest of their studies, and the graduation project in particular most of all. It was during the graduation project that they most often came to realise the connections between all that they had learned before. The students frequently commented on the feeling of ownership regarding the outcome of the project: it was something to be proud of, an achievement that had worth in the real world as well. As the project was commissioned by a real business client, students felt strongly they could not mess about or do a resit, reminding us of Gavin in Baxter Magolda's 2001 study who said that in the real world "you can't give up and you can't go home" (p. 285). In addition students felt that in doing the project, they learned so much in such a short time and it gave them a taste of the real life in the hospitality industry.

What can institutes learn from these outcomes? Firstly, that students are smart. They are involved with and interested in getting ahead, learning and improving themselves. There is no reason to expect that lack of ability or motivation are reasons for students to underperform in higher education. Secondly, institutes should be very clear about their aims with regard to expected learning outcomes and career perspectives for graduates. When institutes can design a curriculum where the barrier between college and career is less impenetrable, making it possible for students to experience and perhaps explore the professional world, it would seem that two birds can be felled with one stone: increased intrinsic motivation and higher quality learning outcomes. Thirdly, staff development could contribute to equipping teachers in such a way that they can support students better in attaining the espoused goals of the institute. Fourthly, assessment is too easily overlooked as an instrument to influence learning. Clearer and unambiguous criteria for (designing and implementing) assessment of all types of student work can support teachers in expressing a united front with regard to the performance level(s) expected from students. Such criteria of course should be aligned with the formulated goals of the institute's curriculum.

NOTES

1 Lydia is an international student and the quote is taken from her English language response.

2 In the remainder of this chapter we do not include the reference to the original semester of the student as the issues brought forward by the students quoted here are more or less equally valid for both semesters.

3 Beatrice is an international student and her excerpt is taken from her original response.

4 Leonie's exit questionnaire was written in English and the excerpt is taken from her original response.

5 Edwin is an international student and his responses are included in the original English.

6 Yvonne is an international student and her excerpt is taken from the original text.

7 Guido is an international student and the excerpt is taken from his original text.

8 It is important to note that a considerable number of the respondents had not finished their management internship yet at the time of answering the questionnaire and this could have influenced this outcome.

CHAPTER 9

TEACHER THINKING IN ENTERPRISING LEARNING

Does learning always have to have predictable outcomes?

(Mr. Grant, level-five-thinker, support subject teacher)

Teachers at the Hotelschool The Hague

At the Hotelschool teaching is organised in main subjects – all related to the focus of business management (e.g. finance, marketing, human resources) – and support subjects aimed at informing potential business managers about other areas that are important to their functioning in the hospitality industry (e.g. languages, quantitative research). In addition there are hospitality-related elective subjects, e.g. wine studies, conference management, consumer behaviour. And finally teachers participate in a number of internal and external practicals. Examples of internal practicals are the running of the Skotel (the school hotel) and various school restaurants. Examples of external practicals are the two major internships in hospitality organisations all around the world. Teachers from all these categories were included in the current study.

In this chapter we first describe the views on learning and good teaching expressed by a sample of the teachers at the Hotelschool. As we have seen in chapter 5, teachers' views on learning, knowledge and good teaching often influence their teaching practice, and through that the students' learning outcome. The purpose of this chapter is two-fold:

1. providing empirical evidence regarding the finding of chapter 5, that teacher thinking about learning and teaching is not different than student thinking and thus that the six-stage developmental model of learning-teaching conceptions based on students' narratives is equally applicable to allocate teachers' views on learning and good teaching;
2. supplying a possible explanation of the result regarding the effect of Enterprising Learning on students' epistemological development established in chapter 7.

The Introductory Course Enterprising Learning for New Teachers

At the onset of Enterprising Learning at the Hotelschool in 1997, as a matter of course an introductory training was set up to familiarise the then teachers with the aims of Enterprising Learning and the teaching approach required for a successful roll-out of the new curriculum. Following this first training, one of the authors was made co-responsible for a compulsory introductory course for all new personnel.[1]

The introductory course consisted of two four-hour sessions about a month apart. It focused on teachers discussing their views on learning and teaching, and the translation of these views to Enterprising Learning without actually providing teaching skills training. As such the course aimed at increasing awareness of teacher thinking and its effects on teaching, and less on teaching practice (see also chapter 11). As our learning-teaching conceptions model (van Rossum and Hamer, 2003, 2004) evolved over the years, the insights therein became increasingly an integral part of the course, providing the participating teachers with various alternative views on learning and teaching.

Courses were provided on a continual basis, several times per calendar year, with up to six participants per course. Each session required preparation by the participants: an essay on their thoughts regarding learning, good teaching, a good assignment and (in more recent years) assessment was required prior to the first session, and prior to the second session they were asked to prepare a lesson plan within Enterprising Learning based on their insights from the first session and their personal views. The examples presented in this chapter are almost all taken from these preparatory assignments. A few excerpts included originated from a separate essay-questionnaire for teachers on the issue of learning and (good) teaching. Some of the respondents are still employed at the Hotelschool, others have moved on to other careers or schools. As all new personnel since 1997 – with negligible exceptions – attended this course, and their learning-teaching conception was not a part of the original selection procedure, we assume that these essays give a faithful portrayal of the general teacher population of the Hotelschool. We cannot rule out that the specific hospitality focus of the school may attract a particular type of teacher. However, while the distribution of teachers' learning-teaching conceptions may prove to be context specific, we feel that the nature of each learning-teaching conception of teachers described below is more generally valid.

The (electronically) retrievable assignments for the introductory course were used to assess the distribution of views on learning and (good) teaching across the teaching corps over the years. Teachers were categorised using category descriptions similar to those used for students' learning and teaching conceptions. All in all we categorised 43 teachers from all sections. The analysis showed that about two-thirds of the teachers had a learning-teaching conception 3, about a quarter displayed level four thinking, and a minority of almost 10% had proceeded to relativist thinking (learning-teaching conception 5). These results are presented in Figure 9.1, where the categories on the x-axis refer to ways of thinking based on a combined categorisation of the teachers' learning and teaching conceptions.

Interrater reliability was 77%, slightly lower than found for the students (Cohen's Kappa was 0.74). In our experience teachers occasionally include certain terms and phrases, obscuring their less sophisticated conceptions with "big words" or disciplinary jargon. In other instances, not withstanding the assignment to describe one's own views on learning and teaching, narratives were constructed around literature read with only incidental references to personal views, making the reconstruction of the teacher's *own* learning-teaching conception almost a case of

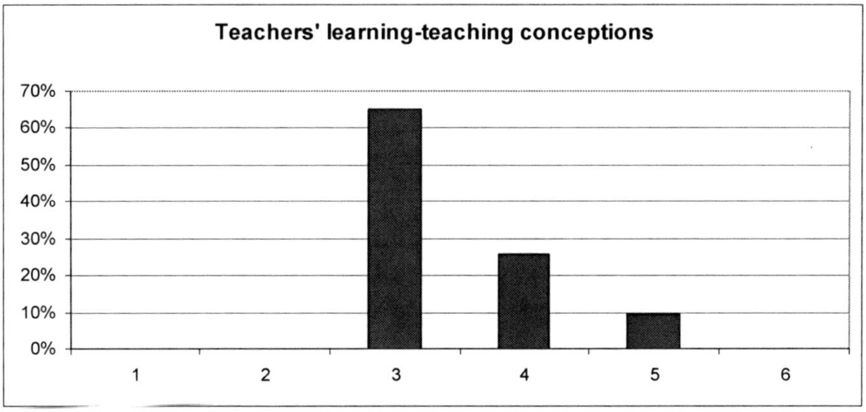

Figure 9.1. Teacher thinking at the Hotelschool The Hague during the study.

detective work. This made categorisation at times difficult. All differences were solved through subsequent rereading and discussion, following the same procedure used for the categorisation of student thinking described in chapter 7.

It would seem that here we found evidence that under certain circumstances responses used to construct categories of description may represent *more* socially constructed discourse and *less* personal experience or personal understanding (Säljö, 1994, 1997). In this case, the teachers could be assumed to be familiar with the disciplinary discourse on learning and teaching and so we needed to take into account that the respondents were able to use discourse, at times obscuring their personal understanding of the issues under discussion. In analysis, separating disciplinary discourse from personal utterances carries with it the danger of creating an additional interpretative layer, requiring researchers to underpin their categorisation more explicitly. It also requires judges to have extensive knowledge of the disciplinary discourse themselves. In interactive data collection it would seem preferable to include specific (non leading) probes aimed towards verbalisation of personal understandings in an attempt to break through the mist of disciplinary discourse (e.g. Säljö, 1994, 1997). On the other hand, the issue of responses mixing discourse and personal understanding underscores the need to interpret the data of each individual (be it an essay, interview or narrative) as a whole.

Teachers' Conceptions of Learning and Good Teaching

In the following paragraphs we use stories of teachers to illustrate the coherence in their way of knowing at each level found in this study, closing, as we did in chapter 1, with a short vignette or metaphor for each level of teacher thinking. For brevity sake we try to limit ourselves to three teachers per level, interweaving their stories to emphasise the issues they bring to the fore.

Teachers' Learning-Teaching Conception 3

At the Hotelschool this type of teacher thinking was clearly dominant, see Figure 9.1, and therefore we include an additional teacher here. [2] If we use the characteristics of level three student thinking to describe this level of teacher thinking, we would expect an emphasis on the application of knowledge in similar situations to those practiced in class, together with application foreseen later in life (e.g. career). Based on our own learning-teaching conception model we would further expect that these teachers emphasise the value of (teacher-dominated) interaction in the classroom and/or that they have a preference for shaping of student behaviour. Mr. Fox described in a most concise way the fundamentals of this level of teacher thinking.

> My desired end result when learning is that I should be able to use the knowledge in a similar situation, use it to evaluate or teach others to be able to do what I can do.
>
> The end result of good education should be that students are able to use the knowledge they have gathered. They are able to put into practice the theory they have learned and thus get the jobs they want. (Mr. Fox, level-three-thinker, main subject teacher)

And very appropriately for the hospitality industry he then proceeded to elaborate on his views using an example about cooking.

> Using a cookbook as an example, it contains recipes, pictures, articles, etcetera. When reading, these are registered by your brain. You may find these interesting and will most likely place them in your memory so that you can retrieve them again later on. Have you now learnt something? I think not! At this point only memories have been created and the passing on of information from the book to your brain has taken place. You find, you have reminders of what you have seen and a memory that you found them of interest.
>
> This does not mean, that you can now do something you could not do before or your skills have improved. Can you then learn to cook from a book? I think you can. If you only read the book, you are not applying the knowledge that is in the book (it will be no more than a memory). Actual learning takes place by applying knowledge you have read in the cookbook. When following the steps of a recipe, you undergo a series of experiences. You remember what you did, how it went, what went well and what did not. With every recipe that you do, you gain new experiences which give you either new insight or confirm what you learnt before. From your experiences you learn. (Mr. Fox, level-three-thinker, main subject teacher)

Our second teacher is interesting because she may represent proof of development in teacher thinking resulting from a move from traditional secondary education to problem-based higher education. In reflecting on her experience of teaching until recently, Ms. Stowe seemed to be describing her development from a level-two-thinker (mainly spoon-feeding students) struggling to become a level-three-thinker.

> Looking at my own theory [of teaching], I must admit that I am struggling to shrug off my ex-secondary school ideas of teaching. When I was a secondary school teacher, I think that I saw myself as a passer on of information. I hope that my lessons were humorous and I hoped that the children liked me and therefore were prepared to work for me because of this. I also worked hard – setting a good example was important, I thought. Therefore I always made sure that I had all the work marked by the next lesson so that I could give constructive feedback. I thought that this method worked at the time and place. My results were good (in exams) and I had a good relationship with the students.That was then.
>
> Now I am working in higher education. Although I think that some of the above principles still apply to teaching at all levels, there are some differences. I sometimes find it difficult not to spoon-feed the students. I give them answers instead of telling them to look it up themselves. ... My experience at the Hotelschool, in the [language] department, is that there is a progression in the learning process.
>
> The structure of the levels [in my subject] and what is expected of the students makes them progress in their way of learning. Putting their knowledge and skills into practice. They also assess each other, which is very revealing, because they are not always comfortable with the idea of criticising each other. The teacher can then leave the realms of pure language learning and talk about how to criticise someone in a constructive way etcetera. (Ms. Stowe, level-three-thinker, language teacher)

Ms. Taylor underwrote the importance of learning by applying, however she was somewhat concerned that all the time used for team work and independently searching for information would eat into the time that is needed to cover the basics. Her main objective in teaching seemed to be to cover the fundamentals in a traditional way first, and only then start applying and discussing once these fundamentals were mastered.

> Learning to me is increasing knowledge, skills... understanding the usefulness of the new knowledge before you start absorbing it helps, though sometimes you become aware only in retrospect that you have learned something.
>
> [...] when it has to do with skills – for example kitchen skills- I believe in the master/student model, where the student first can learn from watching examples, then under close supervision doing it for him/herself and only then doing it independently. For knowledge I believe in the value of the combination of reading/hearing/discussing/practicing and preferably in that order. Good education to me is at all times giving sufficient guidance and examples. Another important aspect to good education is the relation teacher – student. A teacher should have sufficient knowledge about the subject he/she is responsible for ... and [should be] willing to take students along in discussions. ...

> And to me, in a great many areas it is first important to get a very thorough understanding of the basics. Every subject has its own vocabulary and 'grammar'. Only when these grounds are covered to some extent in a structured and systematic way, you can start with applying this vocabulary and 'grammar' to more complex situations. Whether it is cooking, ICM or a language, if the fundaments are not solid, the buildings upon it will never stand solid either. And yet there is a major difference in how the fundamentals and the applications should be [taught]. The first strict, directive and straightforward, the latter with more room for initiative, insight and variation. (Ms. Taylor, level-three-thinker, main subject teacher)

She also felt strongly that – as the aim of the Hotelschool is not to train people only to be able to search for information – the time "wasted" on repeatedly making students search for information themselves could be better used to read, understand and apply knowledge that was provided through high-quality compulsory texts. As we have seen in chapter 7 and 8, many students at level three concur.

> … Personally I am worried about the whole trend towards competency-based orientation, because more often than not the step of creating a sound and solid foundation is skipped. 'Have your definitions straight before you start using the words.' ………
>
> The availability of material is another point of consideration. As long as 'search skills' are not one of the prime goals, I see added value of compulsory material, defined by the school, where all students get a common starting point, especially in this Internet age, where students otherwise get their info based upon what they accidentally stumble upon, again depending on their Internet search skills. In a number of situations I'd rather work with a number of high quality set texts, where the main effort of the students is directed towards applying. (Ms. Taylor, level-three-thinker, main subject teacher)

In our final story, by Ms. Smith, we see again a clear description of development in a teacher's views on learning and teaching, starting from her experiences as a pupil in (Dutch) secondary education. We feel this story is important because it gives support to the assumption central in this chapter (and in this study) that teachers are indeed "students grown up", and that teacher thinking is a direct continuation of student thinking. Ms. Smith described her own development from a traditional level-two-thinker pupil to a level-three-thinker student and becoming a level-three-thinker teacher.

> Secondary education gave me a pretty simple idea of when I had learnt something. Namely, you had learnt something sufficiently if you could reproduce the desired answers on tests, leading to a pass. At university I'm glad to say, this picture changed, only rote learning no longer led to pass marks, but you were pressured to apply the book knowledge on problems and to solve them. (Ms. Smith, level-three-thinker, support subject teacher)

In her first years as a university teacher she became acquainted with problem-based teaching, which influenced her views on learning and teaching even more.

> [In problem-based teaching] students are stimulated to actively collect information/knowledge independently and to process it … This teaching method influenced greatly my current views on learning and teaching. In this teaching method, learning is not only reproducing content, but also independently making the link between content and practice. In practice this means that students need to engage with a case. They need to look in literature individually for solutions for this particular case and then explain the theories they had found to their group members.
>
> … I feel that when someone really has learned something he should be able to apply this when confronted with a similar problem in practice. (Ms. Smith, level-three-thinker, support subject teacher)

Her experiences as a student and as a teacher are reflected in her current teaching practice. We see in the excerpt below that level three teachers feel that they have the responsibility to activate and motivate the student, and an important road to this end is indicating the future use of what is learned.

> Both the teacher and the student have an active role in learning. The teacher must ensure that the students become interested in the subject and want to know more, or should at the very least make clear to students why it is important to acquire particular knowledge or skills. Also it is the teacher's task to facilitate the learning process and to motivate the students. …
>
> A student is responsible him/herself for what he/she wants or does not want to learn. I think the more a student is actively engaged in acquiring new knowledge or skills, the better these will be retained.
>
> … A good assignment is an assignment that on the one hand prepares the student for an exam, while on the other hand it is also forward looking, and matches the real life practice the student will encounter in practicals and after graduation. (Ms. Smith, level-three-thinker, support subject teacher)

The distinction between passing an exam and applying knowledge necessarily led Ms. Smith to prefer two types of assessment.

> The assessment problem I prefer needs to be tailored to the level of the teaching objectives. In other words, a case problem or an open-ended question requiring application are meant for assessing a higher objective, and an explain-or-describe question is appropriate for a lower objective. (Ms. Smith, level-three-thinker, support subject teacher)

In an attempt to typify these teachers in a metaphor, we need to find an image that fits their preoccupation with reproductive application, shaping and control of the learning process. In all aspects we feel that the image of a Master-Apprentice relationship between teacher and student captures the most important aspects of this level of thinking. In this sense we have found the mirror-metaphor we used for the students - Rembrandt's apprentice - and so the teacher becomes "A Dutch Master" or "The Master Painter".

Teachers' Learning-Teaching Conception 4

In level-four teacher thinking, as in student thinking, learning to think for oneself, making connections, and seeing the big picture are the most prominent aspects. Application of knowledge is extended from 'applying in similar situations as practiced' to applying in new, unknown situations. Applications (of models and theories) become more flexible and immediate. Teaching then should aim at preparing students to open up to new ways of using known theories and models, making new combinations. An important requirement for learning at this level is acceptance of uncertainty. As Ms. Hunt described in her view on learning,

> One ... way of learning is pro-active learning. You want to learn something yourself. You are aware of it, start searching, make choices with a specific goal in mind. ... In this type of learning, uncertainty starts to play a more important role. You don't know exactly where learning will bring you, and during the search process you don't know if you're on the right track. ...
>
> *For this first assignment of the Enterprising Learning course you can also establish to what extent pro-active learning has taken place. Firstly, you can research, think about and compare your own experiences to find out what your own "views on learning and teaching" are. You make choices about what to write about and then you write it. In the mean time you also think about how you could use what you are learning right now in your own way of coaching students.*
>
> The older one gets, the more often one will use this type of learning. ... Now other aspects of learning also come into play, namely the extent of the learning outcome, the joy that was experienced during learning, and the measure in which that what is learned is applicable in other situations. These aspects reflect the quality of learning. ...
>
> Teaching should be aimed at the competencies that are necessary to be prepared for working (in the case of the Hotelschool) in the hospitality industry.
>
> Furthermore, it is important that teaching encourages you to think further. That you are stimulated to make connections and that it challenges you.
>
> *... in secondary school and at university I learned a way of thinking and a variety of "tricks", but if I'm really honest I learned the most when I was working and in contact with all kinds of people ... when I started working, I saw I needed to know more about a specific issue, I submerged myself in it and could apply it immediately.*(Ms. Hunt, level-four-thinker, main subject teacher, italics in the original)

The 'way of thinking' Ms. Hunt mentioned appeared in Mr. Curry's narrative as well where he described his views on learning and teaching.

> It's not only about remembering and understanding theoretical knowledge, but also about the attitude to engage actively with issues and problems. A few related concepts to mention here: independence and professionalism. Further, a students has really learned something when he/she can perform on another level of thinking. ...
>
> My aim is to make sure that students understand the theoretical knowledge of a subject and can – in principle - apply this in a work environment. It is not necessary that they apply only factual knowledge, I find it more important that they know how to use their theoretical knowledge to this end. I feel it is most important that they learn to engage with a problem independently and arrive at a well supported solution. My aim is to get students to titillate me for more information and knowledge. I try to reach that in phase 2 and hope to see it again in phase 3.
>
> ... a good assignment will result in a sound piece of research, showing analytical ability and providing students with occasions to develop new [business] opportunities. (Mr. Curry, level-four-thinker, main subject teacher)

In the third teacher's story, reflection on learning and on the role of experience in learning comes more to the fore. Ms. Pfeiffer increasingly put the needs and wants of students at the centre of the teaching-learning process.

> [One way of learning is] when I get new creative ideas while somebody else is presenting a certain subject or I'm reading a book: I learn to make new combinations.
>
> ... But the most important factor in the learning process is the student self. I believe that a person with an open attitude towards learning, who is eager to learn and not afraid to make mistakes, reflect on the experience and try again, will learn the most. So the challenge for a teacher is to create an environment in which as much students are encouraged as possible towards this attitude.

Besides reflection, integration is very important in her views on learning and teaching.

> [In good teaching] students are able to integrate [new knowledge/skills] with other things they have learned (see the big picture):
>
> students get the possibility (or are encouraged) to relate new things they learn to things they already knew/mastered, so they will see the big picture. This can be achieved for example by relating it to things they already experienced in practice, learned during other classes or read in the newspaper. Besides this analogies can be made [with] situations that look very different but can help you to find solutions for your own problem. (Ms. Pfeiffer, level-four-thinker, main subject teacher)[3]

In the narratives the teachers also discussed non-cognitive aspects of learning, as we have seen above in Ms. Hunt's story, where she mentioned the value of enjoyment in learning. In particular, Ms. Pfeiffer referred to the need for self-confidence building in teaching for students to grow.

> During and certainly at the end of the learning process students are not depending on the 'teacher' anymore to employ the new knowledge or skills they have learned. They have gained a certain confidence during the learning process enabling them to demonstrate the new knowledge and skills in new situations. To reach this goal students already have to practice this during the learning process, maybe starting with simple assignments [and moving toward] more complex ones. So they will gradually build this confidence. (Ms. Pfeiffer, level-four-thinker, main subject teacher)

Mr. Curry, in turn, shortly discussed the issue of pride and reciprocity in teaching and learning,

> In my view, good teaching challenges students and teachers. The student delivers work that he/she has learned a lot from and is proud of. And it works the other way around too, stimulating the teacher in turn. (Mr. Curry, level-four-thinker, main subject teacher)

Ms. Hunt also discussed the students' pride in the learning outcome achieved and characterised a good assignment as highly motivating,

> ... a good assignment makes you proud when you hand in the final product. You are proud of the performance level you have attained.
>
> ... a good assignment haunts you. Once you start working on it, you don't want to stop and you feel it is never really finished. (Ms. Hunt, level-four-thinker, main subject teacher)

All three teachers quoted here, experienced some problems with students' lack of intrinsic motivation and felt responsible for evoking this motivation by providing a good role model.

> For a teacher, being a role model is of utmost importance. A teacher who talks about his subject with little enthusiasm cannot expect his students to engage with gusto with the subject matter. It is important for a good teacher to feel that his work is a challenge.
>
> A teacher will need to perform a coaching role as well. However, there is the danger that the role of coach is not performed well, and that teaching (or coaching) is done routinely, without personal involvement or inspiration. A teacher's coaching role may, when frameworks are lacking, bog down in a lackadaisical attitude of the teacher, which is not conducive to creating an optimal learning environment for the students he should coach. Furthermore, he is not fulfilling the important function of role model in a good way. (Ms. Hunt, level-four-thinker, main subject teacher)

And it is precisely this type of lackadaisical teacher behaviour that students were complaining about in the previous chapter, where they quoted teachers shrugging off their responsibility to provide sufficient framing lectures and answer questions. As Ms. Hunt rightfully predicted, such teacher behaviour is extremely demotivating to students.

At this level, the teachers for the first time discussed the issue of different levels of thinking and performance as a possible obstacle to learning and teaching. This is a theme that will return at the next level of teacher thinking where level differences are experienced as a major problem, requiring an adjustment of teaching practice to accommodate these differences. At this level however, teachers are less deeply concerned with this issue, they expect that measures can be taken – for instance by providing teaching at various levels so that all students can learn – that "fix the problem". A humorous – and perhaps typically Dutch – example is given by Ms. Pfeiffer,

> [Good teaching] fits the starting knowledge/skills of the students also if students are on different levels.
>
> If there is a large gap between the current level of knowledge/skills and the desired level a person has to have at the start of a new learning process, the chances are high a person will not be stimulated to learn. Example: you have never seen a bicycle in your life and you have to learn to ride a bike backwards, sitting on the handlebars. If the learning process is only concentrated on moving from the saddle to the handlebars, but assumes you already know how to ride a bike, some students will not be able to reach the end goal. So the learning process in this example should start 'earlier' in the learning process, so students will first learn how to balance on the bike and ride on it normally [before proceeding to the handlebars].
>
> If students are on different starting levels a learning process should be developed in a way that students with a 'higher' starting level will be challenged from the beginning and have the opportunity to learn faster or learn more. (Ms. Pfeiffer, level-four-thinker, main subject teacher)

And finally, Ms. Hunt shared some thoughts on good assessment, criticising the use of reproduction-oriented assessment methods to "save time". Many students concur with her position (see previous chapter).

> The assessment must reflect what is learnt during the module. Therefore it is unacceptable that during seven weeks a module at the Hotelschool concentrates on applying [a concept/theory] and doing presentations, while in the eighth week students must study hard to pass a multiple choice test not assessing understanding but consisting of mainly factual questions and the recognising of concept definitions. This type of assessment is dangerous in the sense that students are encouraged to focus on ... reactive [and not on pro-active] learning. Students will also tend to forget what they learned pretty quickly. Finally it is unacceptable that assessment methods are chosen to match teachers' time restraints. (Ms. Hunt, level-four-thinker, main subject teacher)

In closing we feel we can characterise these teachers as the Inspired Detective, who shows his students how to "solve the case" through independently collecting evidence from various sources, and presenting a well supported theory not only about what happened but also about why. In this metaphor we again are able to match the one made for student thinking (see chapter 1).

Teachers' Learning-Teaching Conception 5

For teachers at this level of thinking the most important outcome of (their own) learning is an awareness of different perspectives on reality. In this sense, learning widens their horizon to include these other perspectives and an understanding of the consequences of these different perspectives. In this way knowledge at this level is inherently uncertain, and learning is flexible.

> The most flexible type of learning [to me is] using knowledge to develop new insights. To think of new areas of application, to adapt knowledge to new situations, to adapt theory, and the awareness that theory knows no absolute truth, and that learning is a form of renewal of the way one sees the world. (Mr. Altman, level-five-thinker, support subject teacher)

Another teacher in this category used the metaphor of glasses to describe the role of perspective in learning (see also Mark, in Baxter Magolda, 2001, p. 65)

> [Learning to me] means that … a *change* has taken place.
>
> I have experienced this myself in my studies. At university … I learned how to look at literary texts. How to arrive at an interpretation of a particular text. For instance, I learned that you can look at a text … from various totally different perspectives. It's just the pair of spectacles you use when reading a source text. You can look at a text from a 'psychological', 'emancipatory', 'sociological', or 'philosophical' viewpoint. Based on each viewpoint you can construct your interpretation. The interpretation may be presented in a 'paper', or defended in a oral examination. I learnt really a lot then. So to say, a change took place in me: I learned to look at literature in a different way. The big picture, the main lines and relationships in literature history came into focus for me in part through these lectures. (Mr. Hauer, level-five-thinker, language teacher)

The third teacher we quote here is Ms. Thomson who emphasised the dynamic nature of learning that leads to new ways of seeing and understanding.

> Learning is acquiring, processing, applying and developing knowledge. This leads to new insights, new ways of thinking and seeing. This makes you see the world from a different perspective which leads to a better understanding of the world. Eventually you arrive in the situation that you don't remember what the world looked like before you had this knowledge. … Learning, therefore, is a dynamic process: a building process. (Ms. Thomson, level-five-thinker, main subject teacher)

These three teachers had clear ideas about the teaching that would match their own learning, but they also described the difficulties they experienced in implementing their ideal way of teaching at the Hotelschool. They were all aware of the issue that students come into their classes with pre-existing ideas and values that may form obstacles to the type of learning and teaching they as teachers aspired to. Ms. Thomson, from her marketing background, formulated this as a 'marketing problem' involving knowing your target market.

> In marketing no strategy is implemented without looking at the target market: size and nature, needs and wants are researched and the strategy is adjusted accordingly.
>
> When I look at the students of the Hotelschool [I see students who are] ... cheerful, willing, relaxed, self-assured, eloquent, actively thinking along during classes, *but* easily distracted, 'strategically' studying ..., passive, not intrinsically motivated, not really interested in the subject but in the study points, not ambitious but settling for a pass, 'shrugging'.
>
> What I'm aiming for:
> - The teacher is coach, motivates, stimulates, is alert and interested in the student;
> - The learning environment is development-oriented and inspiring;
> - The teaching and assignments are interactive, differentiated, up-to-date, activating, applicable in practice, and team-work oriented;
> - Assessment is more holistic and should assess all aspects such as class participation, knowledge, team work, and application of knowledge.
>
> However, the current situation is that my goals are *not* translated into
> - the student who has become the director of his/her own education, who is active, problem solving, self-responsible and self-thinking.
>
> (Ms. Thomson, level-five-thinker, main subject teacher)

All the teachers in this category were very aware of the need to adjust teaching in a way that takes into account these pre-existing views and the entry level of thinking of the students (i.e. their "learning position"). And should one *not* take this into account, Mr. Altman foresaw tensions, frustration and (destructive) frictions.

> The estimate of the learning position of each [student] would need to be as unambiguous as possible. ... When the teachers' expectations far exceed the current student level, than a natural defensive reaction of the student towards the learning environment will occur, resulting in a student not attaining the learning goals (often not through his/her own fault), and growing uncertainty and frustration. (Mr. Altman, level-five-thinker, support subject teacher)

Some teachers had to struggle to overcome students' prejudices as well as their initial "learning positions". These may form an additional obstacle to learning. As Mr. Hauer formulated it,

> I see that many … students experience learning German as 'sensitive'. Many students need to overcome a threshold. This attitude is fed by their home background: "German grammar IS difficult", "For German you need to learn lots of lists by heart". …
>
> Many students come into the classroom for the first time with these images and feelings. These feelings and images toward my subject often determine the start situation. As teacher you need to be aware of these feelings/ images. …
>
> I've noticed that too many students do not take self-responsibility in learning seriously enough. In other words, they do not, or take too little responsibility. As a teacher, I sometimes tend to take too much responsibility onto myself for the [learning outcome]. …
>
> How can I put the responsibility more on the shoulders of the students? (Mr. Hauer, level-five-thinker, language teacher)

The roads to overcome the possible frictions and frustration can vary. Mr. Hauer chose to introduce self-responsibility and independence in a gradual way.

> In my approach I would like to take the ancient Chinese saying as point of departure: Do not give a hungry man fish, but give him a fishing-rod to fish with. The same goes for teaching. …
>
> As teacher you need to motivate your students to start working independently with what you have provided them with.
>
> Initially, in learning a foreign language, you are confronted with exercises that are still highly structured. … [To activate students] it would be preferable to use questions to put them on the right track. Through your way of posing questions you can steer students in a particular direction. The aim is to let the students find the right answer to an issue themselves. I sometimes find this pretty difficult.
>
> … only in an advanced stage usually the exercises become less 'structured' and will a student be capable of analysing the subject matter … more critically, and will a student be able to identify relationships with already learned concepts. Only then Enterprising Learning with its emphasis on self-responsibility can come to life. Then the student will be able to critically evaluate his/her own learning process with the knowledge and strategies learned (awareness). (Mr. Hauer, level-five-thinker, language teacher)

Ms. Thomson on the other hand, was considering adapting her teaching style towards one more tailored to the students' "learning position".

> … I ask myself if my definition of good teaching is tailored to the target audience: students of the Hotelschool, and their future work environment (where a much more strict hierarchy, hard work and less empowerment is common).

> Should I perhaps work much more like a coach of for instance a soccer team: letting students think along, but making the decisions and indicating the direction to go myself, assignment should then be sufficiently challenging, but unambiguous, groups are allocated by the 'coach', and when performance is below standard cussing is customary. A student with a reticent attitude, willing but not driven, studying strategically may require this and it may lead to better results. (Ms. Thomson, level-five-thinker, main subject teacher)

In discussing aspects of good assessment, Mr. Altman took into account the level of thinking of the students and the goals of Enterprising Learning, and adjusted his assessment method to match these.

> So presenting a real life situation and having students apply the appropriate knowledge .... to it. E.g. from [my subject], having students evaluate a newspaper article about a finished study with regard to the meaning of the results and the correctness of the conclusions drawn.

> .... [in some cases] not only assessment of theoretical knowledge and the application of this knowledge is required, but also of independently going through all stages of a research project, so that students are confronted with the incidental conflict between theory and practice, with learning to think ahead in order to 'prevent' possible problems, making them see the various relationships between different parts more clearly, so that true understanding will result. (Mr. Altman, level-five-thinker, support subject)

These teachers, which we would like to refer to as Thoughtful Opticians, have a clear view on their own ideal way of learning and teaching, i.e. based on gaining new perspectives and increasing learners' self-responsibility. However, before they can provide students with various types of spectacles with which to see the world in different ways, they feel the need to take the students' initial "learning position" into account in order to connect to them and through this connection guide them towards a more self-responsible way of learning and a more uncertainty-tolerant way of knowing.

So what does this mean for Teachers and Teaching at the Hotelschool?

The teachers' narratives quoted above show very clearly the distinct and qualitatively different ways in which at each level teachers see the teaching-learning process and environment. Level-three-thinkers focus on the reproductive application of knowledge and/or application foreseen, which for them is the main theme in teaching. Besides focusing on teaching students to think for themselves, level-four-thinkers frequently talk about non-cognitive aspects of learning, not only as means to facilitate learning, but as important outcomes of learning as well. Neither level-three-thinkers nor level-four-thinkers see major impediments to learning due to the gap between the starting level of the students and their own way of thinking.

Level-five-thinkers, on the other hand, worry a great deal about exactly this gap, their experience of "not connecting" in the way they feel necessary to attain the type of teaching they aspire to. The narratives in this chapter also show that it is possible to use a model derived from student thinking to describe teacher thinking.

Based on these results one might ask, "What is a good teacher in higher education?" As we will explain in chapter 11, the level of thinking or order of consciousness necessary for a teacher to be able to guide students to the espoused goals of higher education (see the next chapter) *must* lie on the constructive side of the watershed (see chapter 1 and 2). This means all teachers in higher education should be at least a level-four-thinker. As we have seen, this is currently not the case at the Hotelschool The Hague. The fact that the majority of teachers are level-three-thinkers might be one of the explanations for the large majority of students developing no further than level three. In chapter 11 we will discuss a number of approaches to staff development that are specifically aimed at – and have shown to be successful in – fostering teachers' epistemological development.

A Model of Teacher Thinking at the Hotelschool

Although only three types of teacher thinking were found in the current study, below, in Table 9.1 we have tried to summarise these results into a somewhat more complete model of teacher thinking. The various levels of teacher thinking proposed here are, of course, closely patterned on the levels of student thinking from our learning-teaching conception model described in chapter 1. This approach is the logical result of our assumption that individual teacher thinking is a direct continuation of student thinking and that therefore developments in teacher thinking are in essence identical to matching developments in student thinking.

The relationship established elsewhere (e.g. Kuhn, 1991) that participation in formal higher education is an important predictor of the level of epistemological development, makes it reasonable to expect exceedingly few, if any, teachers with very unsophisticated views on learning and teaching (level 1). This row in the table is therefore deleted, while retaining the numbering of the levels to be consistent with our model on student thinking. Our experience that many students enter higher education with a view on learning and teaching consistent with level two thinking, makes the existence of teachers who themselves function at level two probable. Indeed in the section on teachers' learning and teaching conception 3, two of the four teachers quoted described their own experiences at level two, one as a pupil and one as a teacher in secondary education. Such descriptions are not really rare and therefore we include the findings in the table below.

The highest level of teacher thinking we propose here, should match students' learning-teaching conception 6. However, we have found no evidence of such a teacher in the current study, and therefore this row of the table is (empirically) incomplete. However, in Hamer and van Rossum (2008) we have proposed a model of intellectual development across the life span, expanding the current learning-teaching conception model beyond level 6 thinking to include a new development focusing less on *learning to know* and more on *learning to be*

Table 9.1. A provisional (and incomplete) model of teacher thinking at the Hotelschool

	Student and teacher thinking		*Issues in teacher thinking*		
	Learning conception	*Teaching conception*	*Role of motivation*	*Teacher-student roles*	*Focus*
2	Memorising	Transmitting structured knowledge (acknowledging receiver)	Test oriented; facilitates learning	Teacher provides all information; students listen and may ask questions	Memorising
3	Reproductive understanding/ application or Application foreseen	Interacting and Shaping	Future oriented; facilitates learning	Teacher provides basic information, interacts and discusses with students	Applying (perhaps later on)
4	Understanding subject matter	Challenging to think for yourself / developing a way of thinking	Quality oriented; outcome of learning	Teacher poses questions/ problems and encourages students to think for themselves	The way of thinking within a discipline
5	Widening horizons	Dialogue teaching	Development oriented; outcome of learning	Dialogue	Awareness of multiple perspectives (relativism)
6	Growing self awareness	Mutual trust and authentic relationships: Caring	*Self oriented;* outcome of learning*	*Authenticity**	*Self-defining the self**

*) see Hamer and van Rossum (2008) and chapter 11

(see also chapter 1, and e.g. Chinen, 1985). In this model and also in chapter 11 of the current study we describe an example of a teacher functioning at level 6 and further propose the possibility of a seventh level of teacher thinking, both as exemplified by Parker Palmer (1998). We have used the insights from these three sources to complete level 6 in this table.

Conclusions

In this chapter we discussed empirical evidence of the similarity between teachers' views on learning and good teaching, and these views as expressed by students. In chapter 5 we have put forth persuasive arguments, based on a literature review, that teacher thinking is not different from student thinking: that teachers are nothing other than students grown-up. Examining the essays on learning and teaching from 43 teachers who worked at the Hotelschool during the implementation of Enterprising Learning we have found evidence for 4 distinct learning-teaching conceptions that match those of students, indicating that our six-stage developmental model of learning-teaching conceptions is applicable, one-on-one, to teacher thinking. The learning-teaching conceptions found here match levels 2 through 5, see Table 9.1 above.

Learning-teaching conception 2 was described by teachers while recalling how they learned and taught in secondary education. Main themes in this view on teaching were transference of knowledge, knowing is being able to reproduce knowledge at exams and tests, teaching includes pre-processing the subject matter, being stable and dependable and a good role model with regard to work-effort.

Teachers contrasted their old view and approach to the one they had now: learning-teaching conception 3. This view on learning and teaching was the most common in the sample of teachers, about two thirds of the teachers could be categorised as level-three-thinkers. These teachers indeed put a strong emphasis on being able to apply knowledge and procedures now and especially also later in the chosen profession. Students' putting their knowledge and skills into practice was seen as a definite progression, but at the same time teachers were worried about the time "wasted" on exercising competencies and skills such as searching for literature. The teachers' essays provided evidence that the exposure to a different, less traditional curriculum led to a change in the view on learning and good teaching, again indicating that teachers' epistemological development is susceptible to similar influences as that of students'.

About one quarter of the teachers viewed learning and teaching from across the watershed, learning-teaching conception 4. In this view learning involved making connections, being able to apply knowledge and theories to solve new and unfamiliar problems, acceptance of uncertainty, thinking in a particular way, learning to think for oneself, and the need to support solutions and arguments with evidence. At this level teachers for the first time refer to students' intrinsic motivation: their expectation that students engage with issues and problems, feel ownership of and pride in their own performance, etcetera. It is the teachers' job to provide an environment where students are not afraid to make mistakes, where they learn from these mistakes and try again, putting in effort towards reaching a solution and their own learning.

One in ten teachers at the Hotelschool during the current study viewed learning and teaching in a way that can only be characterised as relativist: learning as an awareness of other perspectives and of the effect that other perspectives may have on one's own perception of reality. Only these teachers mentioned explicitly that students may come into the classroom with their own perspective or conception of aspects of reality that could interfere with learning. This small group of teachers was aware of the need to take into account these pre-existing views to prevent frustration and misunderstandings, and they described the difficulties they experienced when trying to implement their own preferred way of teaching at the Hotelschool. The only possible way out was a gradual, perhaps even tailored introduction of more constructive learning and teaching.

So how can this knowledge help us understand the results found in chapter 7? From chapter 5 we have learned that the way teachers view learning and teaching, in short their level of epistemological development, affects the way they interpret their own role within an educational setting. In the same way as it does for students, teachers' way of knowing provides the framework of expectations regarding the students' role and appropriate learning outcomes. We have shown in chapter 1, that central concepts such as application or understanding are interpreted differently at the different levels of epistemological development, leading to widely differing interpretations of any educational innovation. The hierarchical nature of the epistemological development proposed here precludes that teachers fully understand the meaning of concepts as used in a more sophisticated approach to learning and teaching. In addition, it may prove unreasonable to expect teachers to be able to build bridges (or create holding environments) that lead to places they have never "been" themselves.

Under the circumstance that the majority of teachers providing Enterprising Learning were level-three-thinkers and usually teaching according to their maximum level of sophistication, it is not surprising that the majority of students seem to develop no further than they are challenged to. Level-three-thinkers focus on reproductive application of knowledge, now or in the future: an approach that is closely aligned to the most epistemologically naïve interpretation of Enterprising Learning. It is not surprising that Enterprising Learning was interpreted by the majority of the teachers and students to mean just this, with teachers able to create a bridge towards their own highest epistemological level, but not beyond. Indeed, the majority of students moved into level three. However, many more students than before Enterprising Learning changed their views on teaching and learning , indicating that a didactic and pedagogical approach in line with at least learning-teaching conception 3 can indeed speed up the epistemological development of students.

In principle further development was explicitly included within Enterprising Learning version 2 (and even more so in version 3 which is not evaluated here), but such development proved to depend on an epistemologically more sophisticated translation of the goals and aims of the curriculum. This means that to successfully implement any educational innovation aimed at a particular level of epistemological sophistication, it would seem crucial that teachers are supported to reach at least the level of epistemological sophistication central to this innovation. How to do this and the obstacles to overcome in staff development are the themes of chapter 11.

NOTES

1. The trainers for this course were Erik Jan van Rossum and ms. Ilse Würffel.
2. The assignments of Mr. Fox, Ms. Stowe and Ms. Taylor were written in English and the excerpts therefore are based on their original texts.
3. Ms. Pfeiffer's assignments were written in English and the excerpts therefore are based on her original texts.

CHAPTER 10

CHANGING TEACHING AND LEARNING

> *The sole direct path to enduring improvement in the methods of instruction and learning consists in centering upon the conditions which exact, promote, and test thinking. Thinking is the method of intelligent learning, of learning that employs and rewards mind.*
>
> *(Dewey, 1916, p. 153)*

In this chapter we will discuss the consequences of what we have learned in the chapters before for education, and higher education in particular. First we will try to establish what the agreed appropriate goal of higher education is, and what this means in relation to our model on student and teacher thinking. Many institutes profess to aim for excellence, but what does it mean to aim for excellence in higher education? Is higher education currently achieving its goal? Are the current levels of students' learning outcome sufficient to prepare our young people to deal with the growing complexity of society, let alone the possible increase in complexity in the coming decades? If not, how can we go about changing our current system to improve the record regarding reaching the goals that institutes and governments have set themselves? These are the questions addressed in this chapter.

As early as 1910, John Dewey gave a definition of *reasoned thinking* or reflective thought, where he described it as an "[active], persistent, and careful consideration of any belief or supposed form of knowledge in the light of the grounds that support it, and the further conclusions to which it tends."(1910/1997, p. 6). [1] In this 'definition' we recognise at minimum thinking that is consistent with level four as discussed at length in the early chapters of the current study. A feature of this level of thinking that Dewey discussed explicitly, and which has been somewhat under-emphasised in the epistemological models, is the ability to "suspend judgment" with regard to possible answers or solutions, until each potential answer or solution (i.e. ideas or hypotheses) has been formulated and fully thought through to arrive at its consequences (Dewey, 1910/1997, p. 74). Comparing various hypotheses and their consequences with the evidence results in what Dewey would call a considered judgement. The limiting characteristic of level four thinking lies in the context or discipline, this limit is present in Dewey's description of reflective thought, namely where he stated that a conclusion "'contains' the premises, thereby marking our sense of the inclusive and comprehensive unity in which the elements of reasoning are bound tightly together" (Dewey, 1910/1997, p. 81). It is this type of thinking that Dewey felt should be the (minimal) goal of education: "The disciplined, or logically trained, mind – the aim of the educative process—is the mind able to judge how far each of [the steps of reasoning] needs to be carried in any particular situation" (Dewey, 1910/1997, p. 78). In previous chapters we have seen that this is (still) not always the case, not even for higher education. So, the question here is now 'How to change teaching and learning to make this goal more attainable?', a goal Kember (1991, see below) associates with excellence.

In considering excellence in higher education, a second question that could be posed here is 'Is level four thinking sufficient as goal for higher education or should one, in the pursuit of excellence, aim even higher?' In a later section of this chapter, where we discuss views on wisdom (e.g. Labouvie-Vief, 1990 and Sternberg, 2003), we will try to answer this last question.

Does Higher Education Promote Reflective Thinking?

Introducing the thinking about how to change teaching and learning in higher education, we will first discuss some earlier work descendent from the school of 'student learning'. Gow and Kember (1990) considered the mission of higher education fostering students' ability to think for themselves within a given framework, for instance a specific discipline. They came to much the same conclusion as Dewey proposed, that the aim of higher education, or any education for that matter, should be *teaching to think*. Stated like this, higher education should encourage epistemological development towards *at least* the fourth order of consciousness (Kegan, 1994), Independent Knowing (Baxter Magolda, 1992a) and learning-teaching conception 4 (see chapter 1 and 3). However, Gow and Kember also concluded that this particular aim, teaching to think, is "invariably not directly or even indirectly tested" (1990, p. 308, see also Kember (1991 and below). In fact their study not only showed that higher education may not foster this level of thinking, it even painted a far more gloomy picture.

To study whether higher education indeed fostered epistemological development toward independent learning and thinking, about 1000 students, first and final year, filled in a Chinese version of the SPQ (Biggs, 1987) together with providing some personal details (e.g. age and gender). All students were from a Hong Kong institution of higher education. In our discussion we again only focus on the surface (rote learning) and deep level scales of the SPQ. Gow and Kember gave a specific meaning to deep level learning: "a student who adopts a deep approach has an intrinsic interest in the subject matter and so attempts to understand its underlying structure and meaning. We argue that there is more to being an independent learner than adopting a deep approach, but it is a precondition of independence" (1990, p. 308). In addition to these data, eight students were interviewed to supply depth to the quantitative findings. The questionnaire results portrayed a sombre situation with regard to learning to think in higher education: "... it is possible to visualise an image of the population employing a surface orientation less as the influence of their schooling declines. As they become older, and presumably more mature, their intrinsic interest in study tasks grows. With the passage of time, there seems to be a general tendency away from a surface orientation towards a deeper approach. *The exception to this tendency* appears to occur during the period of tertiary education.

The likelihood of a student adopting a deep orientation seems to *decline* as the student progresses through a course of study."[2] (Gow and Kember, 1990, p. 312–313, italics ours).

The reasoning why growing older seemed to be associated with more frequent use of a deep approach to learning (and knowing) lay in that "[m]ature students might have learnt to assess evidence, relate ideas and display a deep approach through the realistic tasks faced in their work and family environments" (1990, p. 313). Attempting to establish if the found decline in use of a deep approach associated with higher education was specific to the institute studied, Gow and Kember compared their results to literature, and to phenomenographic studies on learning in particular (e.g. Dahlgren, 1984). These latter studies showed repeatedly that students were able to pass examinations while entertaining serious misconceptions of crucial disciplinary concepts. All in all, the outcomes of the various studies brought Gow and Kember to the following grave conclusion,

> In neither the research reported in this article nor in the literature cited is it possible to discover any evidence that higher education was promoting the qualities of independent learning towards which they aspire. Indeed there is some evidence that students may become less likely to employ a deep approach as they progress through their course of tertiary study. It is, therefore, questionable whether typical higher education is succeeding in meeting the cited goals which are espoused by both government and lecturers. (Gow and Kember, 1990, p. 314–315)

The interviews were brought into play to explore some underlying factors that might have led to the somewhat disturbing outcome that higher education seemed to be fostering the exact opposite of its mission. Lining up the 'usual suspects', the factors that could be identified were

- extrinsic motivation: students studying more with the aim of obtaining a quailfication, than out of personal interest. This phenomenon was often associated with the current study not being the first choice of interest.

  > "My first choice was medicine but I did not get into Hong Kong University so I applied for Accountancy at the Polytechnic because it is practical" (p. 316).

- surface demands in assessment: assessment procedures, such as multiple choice or factual questions, may 'force' students towards a surface approach to learning.

  > "Understand? … I rather think there is not a lot to understand – mainly memorising. Memorising the terms, for example. What kind of injections, where to inject, the part of the body, the names… you also have to know the process for doing it. And you have to memorise these" (p. 317).

- perceived heavy workload: a perceived heavy workload leads to a surface approach to learning, because students haven't time to reflect on what is learned and how it is learned

  > "After class there is not enough time to study what has been taught. I know this is what I should do. But, there's not enough time to catch up because in

one lecture, the lecturer might cover two or three chapters. I have to prepare for my next class and not spend my time revising previous work. I have to forget about it while I prepare for the next week's work" (p. 317).

- didactic teaching style: teaching approaches focusing on transmission of content have an undesirable effect on students' learning approaches (see also chapter 5). Transmission was normal in Hong Kong.

  "In class, it's only very brief, very surface, superficial. It's like sticking stuff into your head or on your skin" (p. 318).

  Indeed, students mentioned that teaching in secondary education was less didactic, providing more opportunities for interaction, asking questions etcetera.

  "When I studied biology in school, you could ask a bit in class. Now in class there is no asking. We can ask questions before or after the class. School wasn't like that. If we didn't understand we could ask a question immediately" (p. 319).

  Students further observed that they were unsure about the value of transmission for their future as professionals.

  "They try to stuff us with information. Employers have complained that we are like robots, *lacking in independent thinking* and disinterested in the things happening around us" (p. 320, italics ours).

Based on this analysis, Gow and Kember proposed that in order to foster their own espoused aims, higher education needed to change drastically.

> Tertiary education must *challenge* students enough to develop their powers of independent reasoning. Teachers need to develop in their students an academic approach to their study, that is, and interest in what is learnt for its own sake and an active attempt to understand what is being studied. Teachers should be *concerned* with finding out how their students conceptualise the course materials they are studying and then focus on helping their students modify their unsophisticated conceptions…." (1990, p. 320, italics ours)

As Baxter Magolda (1999, 2004, and below) would phrase it, higher education needs to provide students with a balanced system of challenges and supports, creating a (series of) holding environment(s) bridging the gap(s) between adjacent levels of epistemological sophistication. The results of Gow and Kember (1990) clearly show that education that is characterised by transmission-oriented teaching, a heavy workload for students - while fostering extrinsic motivation by stressing qualifications and using assessments that focus on reproducing factual knowledge - is not very likely to provide the challenges and supports necessary for epistemological growth nor is it even likely to encourage deep approaches to learning.

In the background, there is always the question whether the epistemological models are typical for Western students only, and whether students from other cultures (e.g. Asian students) require a very different model, or only an adjusted version of the models discussed in this study. Volet et al. (1994) addressed this question explicitly, however, we find their other findings, referring to the longitudinal effect of higher education on students' approaches to learning, as – if not more – important for higher education. Using a reduced version of the SPQ, Volet et al. (1994) compared matched Australian and South-east Asian students at the beginning and the end of their first semester at a Western university in Australia. Using even this short-term longitudinal design, as Volet et al. did, is more appropriate to establishing real changes in epistemology or learning approaches due to education, than the more usual cross-sectional design used by e.g. Gow and Kember (1990). Volet et al. found, that during a 13-week introductory economics course, surface approaches to learning remained fairly stable and the use of a deep approach to learning decreased for students from both cultural groups. Volet et al. concluded, as Gow and Kember before them, that "[t]he effect of the course appeared to diminish both local and South-east Asian students' preferences for … deep approaches. While surface approach tended to remain static, it was more prominent at the end of the course due to the decline in the other [deep approach]" (1994, p. 314). Looking more closely at the nature of the course, we find this result hardly surprising: according to Volet et al. it was a course "that emphasised the acquisition of basic economics concepts and required their memorisation for examination purposes" (1994, p. 314).

Volet et al. had the aim to refute the "anecdotal claim that Asian students are inherently more inclined to be rote learners" (p. 304), because they felt this claim "is not supported by any serious empirical evidence" (p. 304). However, we feel that contrary to their goal, they established empirical evidence with regard to

- a difference in preferred study approach and
- a difference in perception of the nature of understanding

between Australian (Western) and Asian students. While these differences in our opinion, do not seem to necessitate revision of the existing epistemological models, the second difference in particular highlights a cultural difference that may influence the learning approach and the learning outcomes of Asian students in a Western educational system. Volet et al. (1994) found that while both groups of students refer to 'understanding concepts' as an important goal of their learning, the two groups differed in the interpretation of the nature of 'understanding' aspired.

> One difference appears, however, in the type of understanding that may be sought by South-east Asian students in comparison to local [Australian] students. The significant difference between the two groups … indicates that South-east Asian students' search for understanding may take place mainly at the level of the text, and thus may not involve, to the same extent as local students, attempts to relate the new information to previous or other knowledge or make sense of the new information in the light of personal or real-life experiences. (Volet et al., 1994, p. 316)

In this description of two types of 'understanding' we recognise two, mainly reproductive, interpretations of understanding characteristic for learning-teaching conception 2 and 3 respectively (see chapter 1, section on conceptions of understanding and applying, and van Rossum et al., 1985). We would like to stress that this difference does not reflect inherent or personality differences between students of different cultures. We feel it may reflect more the difference in educational practices in Western and Asian cultures, as Volet et al. agree,

> Students' accounts of their study in Singapore ... combined with tutors' observations indicate that the 'elaborative' approach to knowledge acquisition [i.e. relating what is learnt to e.g. real life] may not be encouraged in their home country." (1994, p. 316)

Volet et al.'s surprise about the 'puzzling' incongruity between the motives and strategies of local students, where the motive to pass examinations was associated with a preference for a strategy to relate what is learnt to real-life situations, is perhaps a consequence of Volet et al. not taking an explicit developmental point of view. In the developmental view, where descriptive categories of thinking form a hierarchy of inclusiveness, it is all too possible to combine level two motives with level three approaches, in particular because the combination is within the reproductive perspective. Their results might even be interpreted as evidence for a causality of change, namely that the learning strategy changes before the learning motive, influencing – over time – the motive to change accordingly. This might be an interesting hypothesis to test in future SPQ-research from a developmental perspective. A final remark on the results of this study is that the consolidation of Biggs' six-factor pattern observed in the latter measurement for local students, is consistent with findings regarding within-category development and increased between-category distinction of Vermunt's work with the ILS, see chapter 4. On the other hand, the dispersion pattern observed for the Asian students in the latter measurement may reflect the adaptation phase of their 'learning style' to the Western educational system.

Improving Higher Education Based on Student Learning Research

Having established, in the previous chapters and again with the two examples in the previous section, that higher education does not necessarily nor automatically lead to students who can think for themselves – independently (Baxter Magolda, 1992) or self-authored (Kegan, 1994) – using a deep approach to learn in a meaningful way, we now come to the question whether student learning researchers have viable suggestions towards changing higher education in such a way that the espoused goals become truly attainable. Kember (1991) reviewed literature on 'traditional' instructional design theories and 'modern' research into student learning to find "coherent instructional guidelines which might assist in producing more meaningful learning or encouraging students to employ a deep approach" (p. 291). While the daily reality of (higher) education had shown that most of the teaching practice still focused on transmission of content knowledge, Kember stressed that this failure to meet the agreed goals is not necessarily the result of a deliberate strategy: "Where goals have not been met it does not seem to have been because those who had to put them into practice disagreed with publicly stated aims. Rather that the teachers found it *difficult to put into practice* intentions which they themselves espoused" (Kember, 1991, p. 293, italics ours). Kember proceeded to list a set of instructional guidelines that seem to be important when teachers want to facilitate meaningful learning. These guidelines fall into two main categories, answering the questions '*What* should be taught?' and '*How* should it be taught?'

- Firstly, it is necessary to establish "what is to be covered by the course of instruction" (p. 294).

  A course should concentrate on the *key concepts* of a particular subject area as well as "ensuring that students have an appropriate understanding or conception of [these] key issues" (p. 294). Furthermore, students "need to be equipped with the fundamental skills of their discipline so that they can discover for themselves the information they need" (p. 294) and that they can apply this information "to solve novel problems" (p. 295).
- Secondly, there is the issue of the sequencing of content: 1) top-down, fundamental concepts first and details later, and 2) bottom-up, a knowledge base first and understanding and applying fundamental concepts later. While the bottom-up strategy seems to be familiar and fairly common in curriculum design, Kember cautioned that "[c]ourses which start by building knowledge base can also obscure the fundamental nature of a discipline, or fail to teach students the skills of practitioners in the subject area. Unless early conceptions of the nature of their discipline are explicitly challenged, students can cling to inappropriate views and corresponding approaches. For example, students might still believe that in history one remembers dates or in geography place names, while their teachers are concerned with objectives classified as analysis, synthesis and evaluation." (p. 296).
- Thirdly, there is the issue of linking the fundamental concepts of a discipline: "[f]or learning to be meaningful, students must not only have a genuine understanding of the most important concepts, but should also be able to relate one concept to another … or to their existing knowledge base" (p. 296). Structured overviews, tree diagrams, graphic organisers, mind maps, or graphic outlines are useful tools to promote meaningful learning, because "they involve students in actively constructing their own representations of content structures" (p. 297). Linking concepts using such tools for construction of meaning as described here, is, we feel, a typical learning-teaching conception 4 strategy.

Addressing the *how* it should be taught, Kember focused on remediating misconceptions, through the following steps

- *Diagnosis* of students' (mis)conceptions of key disciplinary concepts.

  This phase of exploration of students' conceptions and misconceptions is necessary, because research has proven that simply introducing new concepts and linking them is insufficient to "cause students to change deeply held conceptions" (p. 298) and thus such a teaching strategy will not lead automatically to real understanding. To uncover the deeply held (mis)conceptions of key concepts, teachers need to be able to ask 'good' questions: questions that reveal the students' deep-seated intuitive convictions about phenomena. As it is unrealistic to expect that there will exist (at any time in the future) an exhaustive list of all possible misconceptions students can hold in any discipline, it would seem unavoidable to train teachers in how to ask these questions. Kember discussed an example of such a training, expecting that such trainings would prove to be relatively familiar for many teachers as "it is a common practice for teachers to note mistaken ideas which arise in classroom discussion, or common mistakes in assignments. Parts of tutorials are often devoted to attempting to rectify the most frequent errors in the last assignment. The practice of looking for and trying to remedy common mistakes is therefore nothing novel to many teachers" (p. 300). In taking teaching a step further, by recognising the existence of students' alternative views, Kember requires teachers to function at least at an epistemological level consistent with learning-teaching conception 5, and Samuelowicz and Bain's levels of 'preventing misunderstandings' and 'negotiating understanding' (2001, see chapter 5). In many examples, in particular in chapter 5, we have discussed studies that have shown time and time again that teachers differ in their epistemological sophistication, and e.g. Hashweh (1996) has shown that epistemologically relatively unsophisticated teachers are far less able or inclined to look for misconceptions. We feel therefore, that Kember is grossly underestimating the problem here. Not only that, Kember seems to ignore the fact that teachers, especially novice teachers, themselves may suffer from various misconceptions or incomplete understandings of key concepts of their own discipline (see the narrative of Paul Walker in chapter 5), making diagnosis of student thinking an even more complex issue.

- *Challenging and changing* misconceptions may prove to be "a time-consuming process" (p. 301), especially when a range of students' misconceptions or incomplete understandings needs to be addressed. Not only is this process perhaps time consuming, it is also often 'tough going'. The difficulty inherent to challenging and changing deeply held intuitive beliefs is well described in the titles of publications such as "The Unnatural Nature of Science" (Wolpert, 1994) or "Historical Thinking and Other Unnatural Acts" (Wineburg, 2001). As Kegan (1994) says, letting go of intuitive beliefs is less like learning a new language, and more like unlearning one's own mother tongue. According to Kember, the most common strategy to challenge and remediate misconceptions is "extensive discussion sessions" (1991, p. 301) where students' intuitive beliefs are uncovered using probing questions in the context of carefully chosen, concept-related problems. To enhance meaningful learning it is necessary for teachers to assist students to develop more appropriate understandings "by combinations of challenge and support" (1991, p. 302). An approach that is clearly related to the work of Baxter Magolda on creating contexts for meaningful learning and learning partnerships (1999, 2004, discussed below).

Based on these issues, one can conclude that higher education could indeed lead to the espoused goal of delivering students capable of thinking independently (on a learning-teaching conception 4 level) when – and perhaps *only* when – the majority of teachers themselves is capable of functioning on a learning-teaching conception 5 (or perhaps 4) level. Kember suggests a way to enable teachers to diagnose, challenge and change students' misconceptions, collaborative action research, which "aims to bring about improvement in teaching practices through cycles of observation, reflection, planning and implementation" (1991, p. 303). We will return to this strategy in the next chapter Educating the Educators.

The Role of Assessment

Perhaps there are also easier – and organisationally less expensive – ways to change student learning in higher education. Strategies that are relatively easy to implement, and that can lead to a study approach more aligned to the espoused goals of higher education. In chapters 3 and 6, e.g. Phillips (1998, 2001) or the stories of the Hotelschool students, we have seen that the way students are assessed can make a large difference. Graham Gibbs (1999) discussed a number of cases showing the direct (and immediate) influence of assessment on student learning. According to Gibbs "[a]ssessment is the most powerful lever the teachers have to influence the way students respond to courses and behave as learners. … [it determines] how much effort they put in and what they allocated this effort to." (Gibbs, 1999, p. 41–42). It is precisely because assessment seems to have such a significant influence on student learning, that Gibbs stated that assessment "might as well be designed to have educationally sound and positive influences [on student learning] then leaving the consequences to chance." (p. 43). Of the six cases Gibbs discussed a few, in our opinion, focused primarily on the strategy 'putting students to work', resulting in dramatic improvements in pass rates. Although interesting in itself, these cases are less interesting in the framework of the current study as they do not explicitly address the quality of student learning. However, we will discuss one of these cases below – the case of the accountant – to illustrate how relatively small changes in assessment procedures can lead to considerable improvements in student learning. More in line with our focus, we will then follow this first case with a discussion of two cases that address the nature of the assessment questions – the cases of the philosopher of education and the Norwegian engineer.

The case of the accountant (Gibbs, 1999, p. 50). A traditional accountancy course, assessed by an end-of-course exam with questions on material covered in the lectures, had a very poor pass rate. It seemed that students were not studying regularly and were not receiving timely feedback on their performance during the course. The change in assessment procedure (and *not* in the assessment questions) focused on making students take shared responsibility for their own study behaviour.

> Students were formed into learning teams of four, allocated randomly. They were told that, although they would sit the exam on their own, they would be allocated the average mark of their team of four. Students were told of the positive impact of this method elsewhere and they approved of the change. Not trusting each other not to let others down, they all taught each other furiously, making sure that each of the other three in their group was completely on top of the content every week. Exam marks increased dramatically with *few* individual fail marks. (italics ours)

By making the re-sit mark part of the average group mark, the shared responsibility extended to the students having to do a re-sit exam.

> … the other students tutored the failed student through the re-sit, and almost all passed at the second attempt.

As there were no changes to lectures or exams themselves, Gibbs emphasised that this 'innovation' and change in pass rate was accomplished at zero cost. The next two cases focus less on 'putting students to work' and more on 'getting students to work differently'.

The case of the philosopher of education (Gibbs, 1999, p. 50–51). The end-of-course exam of a compulsory philosophy of education module for a teaching degree in further education, consisted of questions such as "Compare and contrast the philosophies of X and Y in relation to classroom practice Z". Not unexpected (to us), students had various – and very often less desired – ways of answering these questions.

> Students who had diligently attempted to memorize features of each philosopher they had covered in the course duly listed several features of each, the bright ones spotted a difference and the really bright ones understood a practical implication. …
>
> As it was possible to pass the course by memorizing some factual details, this is all most students did. In lectures and in their reading they tried to spot the facts they should note down about each philosopher for later use. Attempting to show understanding was dangerous in that they could be wrong – so they played safe with facts.

The solution implemented illustrated a major rule to follow in designing 'good' assessment: appropriate assessment leads to exactly those students' learning activities that are the objective of the teacher or course. So if the goal is that e.g. students must learn to think for themselves, one should design assessment that can only lead to a pass mark when students indeed think for themselves. This type of design is called constructive alignment (Biggs, 1996) and we will return to Biggs in the next chapter. In this module the new exam consisted of viewing a video of a teacher in a further education classroom practice. While the nature of the new exam questions remained unchanged year after year – requiring students to comment on the video and formulate advice for the teacher *from a philosophical point of view*, the content of the video was different each time. This relatively simple change had a striking effect on student learning behaviour.

> There was no way a student could prepare for such an exam by memorizing facts about philosophers. The only sensible way to prepare was to look at what went on in classrooms from a philosophical point of view and to discuss and tune up this point of view by using ideas gleaned from the lectures and the reading. Students took themselves off to observe classrooms, borrowed videos of classrooms, and sat and discussed what they had seen with other philosophy students.

The case of the Norwegian engineer (Gibbs, 1999, p. 51–52). A Norwegian engineering programme had similar problems, with students focusing on series of specialist subtopics as separate entities, and having exam questions closely related to the types of problems treated in class. This type of assessment is consistent with either learning-teaching conceptions 2 or 3, both on the reproductive side of the epistemological watershed. As expected, students proceeded to "memorize algorithms for predictable small-scale problems" and failed to learn "how to tackle unpredictable large-scale problems such as those they will encounter in work". This issue was addressed by changing the assessment, from a list of smaller problems to be solved to presenting "one very large, complex real-world problem".

> Instead of each problem being able to be tackled in about 10 or 20 minutes, they had all day and were not expected to finish – they were assessed on how much progress they had made. In addition, they could take into the exam *any kind of aid they liked* [like professional engineers would do in real life]. ... The result of such an exam is that students focus their revision and their preceding study ... on how to prepare for unpredictable real-world problems, just like a practising engineer. (italics ours)

The changed assessment in these latter two cases can be seen as examples of innovative assessment: in this case simulation of professional practice. McDowell and Sambell (1999) investigated students' perceptions of various forms of innovative assessment: e.g. self/peer assessment, group projects, open-book exams, simulated professional tasks, and oral/poster presentations. One of the advantages of innovative assessment is its emphasis on authenticity in the sense that assessment is based on tasks or activities that resemble those to be expected in professional life. Students' learning motivation, approaches and outcomes can be greatly improved by this kind of assessment, thus providing an opportunity for higher education to fulfil its mission. When confronted with authenticity students perceive such assessment as more relevant, more motivating and clearly more interesting than "jumping through assessment hoops" (McDowell and Sambell, 1999, p. 76).

> ... your abilities are actually far more important – your abilities to research, analyse, dissect an argument, your abilities to bring forward information out of a set of data. Those kind of analytical abilities I think are important in day-to-day life and they are going to come across far more in progressive assessment than they ever are in exams. (p. 76)

> I think the open-book exam helps you learn better, personally, because you sit there and actually read the stuff, rather than just sit there and commit it to memory ... I found myself questioning key concepts and ideas rather than hard facts about things. I was trying to understand the subject rather than memorise things. (p. 76)

In addition, innovative assessment can lead to changes in the teacher-student relationship, because students are given more responsibility for their learning.

> [During the group project] … We all try and figure it out for ourselves which I think is good. We don't feel that [the teacher]'s hanging around all the time looking over our shoulders. But you know where he is. (p. 77)

In these three quotations, it becomes clear that innovative assessment may in itself influence students' learning approaches towards a more deep, learning-teaching conception 4 approach. However, as usual there are some caveats here, encouraging students to change in response to unfamiliar assessment requirements is potentially more successful if the students feel supported by the teacher while meeting this new challenge. This support can be expressed in a number of ways:

- Showing consideration for students' workload as they may need more time to adjust to perform the new tasks;
- Maintaining motivation by interim guidance and feedback;
- The careful introduction of such new forms of assessment including explanation of student benefits, assessment criteria, marking and organisational procedures.

In essence, McDowell and Sambell proposed that introducing innovative assessment requires a balanced system of challenges and supports (see also Baxter Magolda, 2004, below), so that,

> [w]hen students are working on tasks which are not conventional, routine or the same for everyone, clear guidelines are needed as a safety net to ensure that students do not completely misunderstand what is expected. *Students are also better able to act independently and make their own decisions when they feel reasonably secure about the overall parameters for their work.* (p. 80, italics ours)

McDowell and Sambell asked themselves the question whether it is worthwhile to invest in innovative assessment in higher education. Based on their review of 13 cases, they concluded that it definitely is.

> [Innovative assessment] can give students a greater sense of *ownership* and personal involvement in the work and avoid the demotivating perception that hey are simply going through routine tasks which have been done by many students before them. *Collaboration* with fellow students rather than working in isolation can also help to maintain students' motivation and improve the quality of their learning as it opens up the possibilities for discussion, new ideas and varying approaches. (p. 81, italics ours)

This review shows that innovative assessment fosters behaviours or qualities in students that are typical for the more sophisticated epistemological levels of thinking and as such deserves *serious* consideration as a convenient lever "teachers have to influence the way students respond to courses and behave as learners" (Gibbs, 1999, p. 41). In addition the quote above has characteristics that are familiar for those of our readers now well acquainted with Kegan's concept of self-authorship. Baxter Magolda's concept of teaching and learning through 'learning partnerships' (2004) is intimately related to innovative assessment, with her emphasis on autonomy (ownership) and connection (collaboration).

What is Excellence in Higher Education?

If higher education is to foster 'excellence' in learning – the ability to think for oneself or the use of a deep approach to learning – it is in a better position to accomplish this when excellence in all its forms is more clearly defined. In 1983, Entwistle and Ramsden interviewed 57, mostly second-year students of various disciplines, selected to represent groups with extreme scores on subscales of the approaches to studying inventory (ASI). The semi-structured interviews focused on "students' approaches to academic tasks and their assessment strategies, and [provided] a detailed picture of students' perceptions of the contexts of learning in which they worked" (Entwistle and Ramsden, 1983, p. 132). From the analysis it soon became clear that a relatively simple dichotomy between deep and surface approaches to learning, see e.g. van Rossum and Schenk (1984), did not suffice to describe the complexity and richness of these interview data of students from a wide variety of disciplines and departments. Entwistle and Ramsden derived a set of six approaches, three mainly deep-learning oriented (D1-D3) and three clearly more surface-learning oriented (S1-S3), all quotes below are from Entwistle and Ramsden (1983).

- D1: Personal experience

  Personal experience refers to students interpreting knowledge as part of oneself and/or integrating the task with oneself.

  "I suppose I'm trying to imagine what he experiment is talking about, I think in a physical sense. Sort of get a picture of what it's about ... This one says an ultra-violet lamp emits one watt of power; it says calculate the energy falling on a square centimetre per second. I'm just thinking of the light and the way it spreads out, so therefore I know it's the inverse square law ..." (physics student, p. 138)

  "I'm very interested in social sciences generally. I find it very enlightening, very entertaining, very satisfying, to learn theories and then to observe them in reality. Casually, to say, 'Christ, look, it's happening, you know, the theory's there, that's what's going on,' and I think it adds so much, through the eyes of a sociologist or of a psychologist, and put a structure on what's going on." (psychology student, p. 142–143)

- D2: Relationships

  Relationships refers to students who see connections e.g. between material from different sources and/or with previously studied material.

  "You know a method of approach, so you find usually the thing simplifies itself greatly after you've removed a few of the non-essentials and put it into a logical form which relates to something you've done previously." (physics student, p. 139)

  "You read it, you see what it's about, and usually it's got, often it has some bearing on something else you've read before. It may confirm that or just add another side to it, of be completely different." (psychology student, p. 139)

– D3: Meaning

Meaning refers to students who think about the underlying structure and/or the intention of the whole task.

"You have to go through quite a few different designs to get to the right one … I'm sort of always thinking about what I can put in the conclusion when I'm writing the project… I'll try and show what I have achieved, well, understand, from the project." (engineering student, p. 139–140)

"It was a good chapter because it organised the readings that were to follow … which led me off to further articles, and at the end of it, making notes on the things I was reading, I had a great wad of it, which by that time, I had an idea of how my initial conception of the problem could be used to sort out all the information I'd now got. And it all sort of fitted together quite nicely. Because I think as I was writing I was thinking about how I was going to, how the final product was going to come about, and that sort of directed my reading in fact." (psychology student, p. 140)

Another three categories were necessary to describe the multiple aspects of the counterpart of the deep approach to learning.

– S1: Unrelatedness

Unrelatedness refers to treating each task, or parts of each task, as isolated phenomena, discrete and disconnected.

"I tend to give up on them. I tend to write very confused essays, because I have all these ideas going through my head, and I write them down, but I don't put them down in any particular logical sort of plan … I tend to do better in exams, because the confusion doesn't matter so much, as long as the relevant points are there … I don't seem to be able to link ideas together" (history student, p. 140)

"I don't exactly write down all the steps you should do. You should … write down those sort of things – this is the result, did it work or not? If it didn't, did something else do it? That's the best way of going about it. Well, I just sort of write down what I've done. Just do the calculations and work back from there. (engineering student, p. 140)

– S2: Memorisation

Memorisation refers to defining each task as a memory task.

"I hate to say it, but what you've got to do is have a list of the 'facts'. You write down ten important points and memorize those – then you'll do all right in the class test" (psychology student, p. 141)

"Formulae … just go in (to the examination) with as many formulae as possible, so you learn those parrot-fashion. And approaches to the way you work out problems, techniques involved in maths .. I seem to remember, just sort of one day or two." (engineering student, p. 141)

– S3: Unreflectiveness

Unreflectiveness refers to defining the task in an external way, with no intention to extract meaning from the material studied.

"You just go straight for the section which is relevant to that particular question … There'll be a topic in the book which the question comes under, and then you hunt through that section to see if they've got any … Hopefully, they'll have the exact question and you can copy it straight down without doing any work at all … Usually you have to hunt out he various related equations, then you just apply these to the problem. That's all, really." (physics student, p. 141)

"It's a bit confusing, (this subject) … I tend to rush through the books I'm reading for the essays, so I still don't really understand it when I've finished reading. And because there's such a lot of information I think you can oversimplify or go into too much detail. And I think I tend to oversimplify." (English student, p. 141)

From these quotes we can see that various types of surface learning are characterised by strategies and views common for students with reproductive learning conceptions or less sophisticated epistemological belief systems. The deep learning categories described here for the most part illustrate various aspects of learning-teaching conception 4, Independent Knowing or Self-authorship. Furthermore, the sample of students from various disciplines shows that deep and surface learning occur in all disciplines and contexts. Finally, these categories show the large gap between various surface learning strategies and the mirroring deep learning strategies: imagine the epistemological change necessary to move from a surface learning perspective across the watershed to constructive learning. Sometimes, when the world of the student and the world of teaching align, students suddenly see a new horizon. This is eloquently put by the following psychology student (Entwistle and Ramsden, 1983, p. 161).

I began to realize there, there was a structure in the things they were teaching us and it wasn't just a load of facts – that's only a recent, recent realization, perhaps only this term. I started to realize it when I realized that the English I'm doing form my free ninth, er, is very closely connected to psychology … the novelist seems to be very close to the psychologist, only he writes it in a creative – no, not creative – a more artistic form. And when I realized that those were so close I suddenly realized how interrelated all the topics in psychology were. And that's when I also read some articles on creativity; that's when I suddenly realized that putting your own pattern on it would probably make a better essay, and a more enjoyable essay. And the little anecdote is that I got an A for the first essay done in the new way – so I've carried on. I can see Perry [1970] as being fairly relevant and I think, I couldn't have seen him as being relevant until I'd got into some of the stages myself. So being taught about it in the first year didn't really help because I didn't understand wha, what they were teaching, or I thought, I mean, I knew the facts sort of but I didn't know what was really meant 'cos you can't understand

> there are two sides to an argument – if that's what you're understanding – until you see there are two sides to an argument .. I've become more interested in the subject, I think. I've begun to understand more of the subject, and perhaps, learned, learned things that, can apply in my everyday life more successfully. I mean things like my learning. I've learned perhaps, perhaps a better way of learning. (student 6)

Then again, sometimes the worlds do not align, they might even collide. When the student's world collides with that of the teacher, disenchantment with the educational system or process is the result, see the psychology student below (Entwistle and Ramsden, 1983, p. 172).

> I'm disappointed in some respects that it isn't what I expected it to be … All the time it's assessment, assessment, assessment. When I got a place here I thought, great, this is marvellous … I won't just be concentrating on … doing it for assessment. I'll be able to study … just time to sit back and think and talk about a subject, and read about it. No- it's all structured, you know. When I leave here I'll go straight back to my room and I'll say, "Right, what've we got to do next?"… It's good for individual teachers' images to get good marks out of their students on their courses. I don't think that is best achieved by following the academic philosophy of learning what you want to learn … You've got to enforce a strong, very strong and carefully organized structure upon your learning, which is directed, aimed directly at, the assessment that exists … I'm very disappointed … that I can't just, you know, go through and really have a think and really work things out. (student 7)

As we (and e.g. Perry, 1970) have stated before, crossing the watershed is not only difficult, it also requires courage, stamina and self confidence. While teachers may be aware of the need to challenge students to perform better, at a more sophisticated level of thinking, the teachers' support, scaffolding if you will, is necessary to underpin the student's emerging courage and self confidence to cross the divide and become responsible for his/her own learning. The extent of the courage needed, and the comfort that can be derived by having someone to go to – such as a supportive teacher – is described by an independent studies student:

> You have to take responsibility for the work yourself. You're not, you don't have the advantage of a pre-existing framework of suggested reading and suggested approaches in independent studies, so you have to be damn sure that you are interested enough and confident enough to see it through those times when you come to sort of minor crises, when you realise suddenly that it's all on your shoulders and you've got no one else to go to … It requires commitment and personal motivation. (Entwistle and Ramsden, 1983, p. 173)

But even when worlds align, not all students seem to able to find the motivation, the courage or self confidence to grow. While the relationship between surface-oriented teaching and surface-oriented learning is fairly straightforward (Entwistle and Ramsden, 1983, p. 189), again we find that providing meaning-oriented teaching does not automatically lead to meaning-oriented learning. "It seems that departments without good teaching and freedom in learning effectively act to prevent the development of meaning orientation in their students; departments which are positively evaluated encourage meaning orientation by providing the right conditions for it to grow – but it is *not* a necessary consequence" (Entwistle and Ramsden, 1983, p. 189, italics ours).

Of course, learning meaningfully is in itself not necessarily the goal of students in higher education. In fact many students choose to pursue higher education with a certain professional future in mind. In this sense, institutes of higher education should provide their graduates with at least some of the skills employers expect. What then do employers expect from graduates of higher education? According to Entwistle and Ramsden (1983), employers

> ... are not looking to [institutes of higher education] to supply specific technical skills: these are taught more effectively after graduation within the company. Employers are expecting degree courses to develop certain general qualities of mind, foremost of which seems to be the ability to think critically, objectively, flexibly and quickly, and to apply that thinking to a wide range of problem situations. (p. 215)

And in this sense the aims of institutes of higher education and the expectations of employers of their graduates might largely coincide. Until now we have assumed that excellence in higher education means the ability to "think well". However, as learning to think well is the espoused goal of most higher education institutes, maybe being able to think well should not be seen as constituting excellence. A graduate's ability to think well then is 'merely' achieving the espoused goal. In that case, *excellence in higher education* may require students not only being able to think well, but also to think wisely. Sternberg (2003) argued something similar in his discussion of an "expert student" and took it even further in discussing "good leadership" (2007).[3] At this point it would seem prudent to include a section illustrating some views on wisdom as an epistemological construct, as well as some thoughts on the teaching for wisdom.

Teaching for Wisdom

In Dawn's narrative – quoted in Chapter 3, comments on Baxter Magolda – Dawn appeared to discover 'wisdom' and 'creativity' at the sixth level of thinking. Dawn felt they were the successors of 'knowledge' and 'following others'. This discovery is consistent with the theory of *wisdom as integrated thought* proposed by Gisela Labouvie-Vief (1990). Labouvie-Vief's critique of many theories of intellectual development was that they are based

> ... on the assumption of the primacy of objective forms of knowing [providing] an incomplete and possibly distorted picture of the human mind. (Labouvie-Vief, 1990, p. 52)

Instead she proposed that,

> … a more complete picture of mental functioning ought to emancipate organismic forms of cognition as well … then, theories of thought need to be based on a duality of two modes of knowing that, although often in competition, ideally function in a dialogic relationship. In that dialogue, one mode provides experiential richness and fluidity, the other logical cohesion and stability. It is such smooth and relatively balanced dialogue between two modes that I define as *wisdom*". (Labouvie-Vief, 1990, p. 52–53, italics ours)

Labouvie-Vief had come to believe that "something akin to a single competence of wisdom" (1990, p. 78) may be an "ideal end state" (p. 79) of the process of (adult) intellectual development and she linked this end state to "the emergence of a certain worldview or broad epistemic structure" (p. 78). In addressing the issue of the age-relatedness of wisdom, Labouvie-Vief believed that wisdom and age should be decoupled and that wisdom as a way of thinking is rare even among adults.

Driven by the hope of constructing a theory of intellectual development "oriented by a normative view of transcendent ideals yet firmly grounded in the organic texture of life" (1990, p. 79), Labouvie-Vief distinguished two ways of knowing labelled by the ancient Greek terms *mythos* and *logos.* Mythos as defined by Labouvie-Vief refers to

> ... *speech, narrative, plot,* or *dialogue*... [in which] experience is holistic and based on a bond of close identification between the self and the object of thought. Thought and thinker, knower and known, are one single, indivisible unit, and it is from this bond that derives the meaning of an experience. The object of thought is not articulated separately from the motivational and organismic states of the thinker; rather the thinker's whole organism partakes in the articulation of the object and animates it with its own motives and intentions. (1990, p. 55–56)

And logos is seen as associated with "... *counting, reckoning, explanation, rule,* or *principle* and, finally, *reason*" (1990, p. 56) and epistemologically it refers to

> … that part of knowledge that is arguable and can be demonstrated and defined with precision and agreement. In *logos,* thinking, meaning is disembedded from a reality of flux and change and related to stable systems of categorization. The complexity of *mythos* is reduced, canalized into single modalities, contained in fixed meaning. Ideally, *logos* implies that knowledge can be rendered purely mechanical, computable, and deductively certain. (1990, p. 56)

In these two distinct ways of knowing we recognise subjective knowing as a form of *mythos* and procedural knowing (and even received knowing) as a form of *logos* (Belenky et al., 1997).

Labouvie-Vief saw Plato's work as the culmination of the historical process leading from *mythos* (mythical thinking) to *logos* (logical thinking).

> For Plato, the adult is no longer embedded in a concrete, organic, and participatory reality. Rather, the new reality is one defined by a new function, *psyche,* variously translated as *soul, mind,* or *spirit.* ... mental functioning is no longer identified with the organic and the mythic – with the senses, with actions, with poeticized accounts of reality. Rather it resides in our ability to step back from the purely sensory. ...
>
> ... the mind has become an autonomous agency. ... it also becomes less dependent on constant, concrete social monitoring. The new mind thus is more individuated and *self-authored.* (1990, p. 59, final italics ours)

The contrast to mythos becomes clear in e.g. Labouvie-Vief's description of Homeric hero's who show little evidence of self-consciousness and self-reflection, and lack "the mental types of regulation mastered by the modern adult: impulse delay and monitoring and self-ownership of action and feeling ..." (1990, p. 58).

> There is no language of a self different from its concrete actions and assets – a self as a permanent, persistent agent who authors its actions but is not identical with them. (p. 58)

Plato's singular emphasis on logos or rationality, led Labouvie-Vief to view his definition of wisdom as "extremely limited" (p. 60) especially when in the search for truths and laws of thinking, thinking is reduced to thinker-independent forms or procedures that ideally lead to

> ... a new form of decision making that was located purely in the realm of the abstract and the universal. In that realm, everybody could examine statements and be led to the same conclusion. The individuality of the thinker, then, no longer entered into the process of thinking. (p. 60)

This view of thinking as abstract, universal, and procedure driven, reminds us strongly of procedural knowing (Belenky et al., 1997; see Chapter 3) where form becomes more important than content.

According to Labouvie-Vief, the dominance of logos is not merely a historical phenomenon, but it has also influenced theory development regarding intellectual development until fairly recently. Furthermore, the logos-bias has limited the usefulness of a number of theories for the study of adult intellectual development. As an example Labouvie-Vief discussed Piaget's theory,

> ... even though for Piaget intellectual development emerges from an organic core, the mature adult is idealized almost purely in terms of *logos* processes, whereas *mythos* is devaluated as childish and immature. It does not, therefore, have its own line of development. (1990, p. 66)

Parallel to developments in philosophy in the twentieth century, Labouvie-Vief felt that more recent theories for (adult) intellectual development (e.g. Perry, 1970; Belenky, Clinchy, Goldberger and Tarule, 1997) seemed to have overcome this bias for logos. She proposed that these theories include more sophisticated stages of thinking that integrate mythos and logos, in short forms of wisdom. According to Labouvie-Vief,

> The goal of adulthood, therefore, ... consists of a balancing of *logos* [and mythos] as *mythos* is upgraded. ... ... a number of recent studies suggest that such a reintegration is organized by continued developments in the complexity of thought beyond those described by Piaget. (1990, p. 67)

In her model of adult intellectual development this goal is reached by moving through a sequence of three stages:

- the intrasystemic level within which the individual is able to "coordinate the elements that comprise a single abstract system" (p. 69). This level is we feel very similar to Perry's position 4b or our learning-teaching conception 4 (see Chapter 1);
- the intersystemic level where "multiple systems are acknowledged ... but these systems cannot yet be integrated and transformed reciprocally ... they still limit full openness of functioning." (p. 69). Here we recognise level five thinking or Perry's relativism and our own learning-teaching conception 5; and
- the integrated level where "historical change and contextual diversity are valued, resulting in an open flexibility tempered by responsibility and self-reflection. Self-chosen principles result in the potential for mature action and self-regulation." (p. 69).

Labouvie-Vief herself linked her model to the work of Clinchy and Zimmerman (1981 as mentioned in Labouvie-Vief, 1990) where sophisticated ways of knowing are coupled to "a new sense of self empowered with an awareness of [one's] own efficacy and responsibility as a thinker....(1990, p. 68). As we do ourselves, Labouvie-Vief placed the ability to come to *self-chosen* principles at this final, sixth level and not at the fourth level as Kegan (1994) seemed to propose in discussing self-authorship. In this Labouvie-Vief precedes and underpins our position that at level six the self-defining self is central. In addition, Labouvie-Vief placed the emergence of wisdom – the integration of *logos* and *mythos* – at this sixth level creating a link to Baxter Magolda's narrative of Dawn quoted before (Chapter 3). In Labouvie-Vief 's model we see a dynamic of differentiation from a single system (level 4) to multiple systems (level 5) followed by the integration of these systems in a 'human sized' self (level 6).

> The mature individual, ... realizes that the subjective and communal are a necessary part of one's endeavours to be objective. Still, they do not remain a goal in themselves. Rather, they become a vantage from which the individual searches for a new concept of objectivity- however, no longer one that is rooted in a "God's-eye view" of certainty but one that is more open, tentative, and human sized. ... the individual gradually gives up a definition of self in terms of abstract idealizations and elaborates one that reaffirms the significance of an organic ground: of the bodily, the figurative, and the mythic" (Labouvie-Vief, 1990, p. 72–73)

A similar attitude speaks from the response of one of Baxter Magolda's students, Mark, who once he had discovered the existence of multiple perspectives learnt to use his 'own pair of eyes'.

> I could read a text at [college] and say, "this is a feminist critique of this text," then whip on the other pair of glasses and say, "this is a Marxist critique of this text."...... I've gotten closer to understanding what my own pair of eyes internally and externally is seeing ... getting to what it means to be a human being with a soul. (Mark, age 30, Baxter Magolda, 2001, p. 37, quoted before in Chapter 3)

Labouvie-Vief further referred to a number of psycho-analytical theories in exploring her theory of wisdom and she found support for the embeddedness of *logos* (as ego) in more organismic self-processes: "... for Jung, the self is this more inclusive embedding and regulating process, and the major task ... is to give up the egoic idealized definition of self [level 4 thinking] and open oneself up to this broader organismic structure [level 6 thinking]" (1990, p. 74). Labouvie-Vief observed – as we have more recently (Hamer and van Rossum, 2008) – that there are only "scant data on what these mature forms [of adult thinking] may be" (p. 74) and suggested to make use of existing "writing[s] grounded in myth", "literature on personality changes during adulthood" or "individuals' biographical constructions" (p. 75–76). For instance by using myths and fairytales,

> ... tales featuring adults depict the search for wisdom rather than adventure, mastery of self rather than others, and rather than seeking personal victory and salvation, the self becomes oriented toward the "emancipation of the world. " (Labouvie-Vief, 1990, p. 75)

Or using biographical constructions,

> ... breaking out of conventional form constitutes a major crisis in the lives of artists as well as normal adults. Although not all adults are able to resolve this crisis in a positive manner, those who do may experience a surge of creative vitality and the evolution of a unique style which transcends personal and cultural experience and distills core patterns of the human experience ... A prime example is the painter Henri Matisse, who gave up painting during the last years of his life to create the works of his final maturity in a medium (paper cutouts) he had only taken op at around 60 years of age. (Labouvie-Vief, 1990, p. 76)

We find it interesting to note furthermore, that in one of her empirical studies Labouvie-Vief examined the qualitative differences in text processing and interpretation between younger (adolescents and college students) and more mature adults. Labouvie-Vief and her colleagues found similar text processing strategies to those we described in van Rossum and Schenk (1984). Interestingly, they found that "... the younger individual often reads text analytically, examining aspects of internal structure and keeping inferences to such intratextual processes. For the older adult, however, the interest of the text often lies ... rather in the fact that it signifies truths about the human condition. Hence inferencing is based on a symbolic processing style in which inner and psychological processes rather than purely logical ones are important" (Labouvie-Vief, 1990, p. 74). The mature adult learning outcome described here reminds us strongly of the SOLO-category 'extended abstract' (Collis and Biggs, 1979), a category indeed very rarely found in college students' interpretations of texts (van Rossum and Schenk, 1984).

Sternberg has a slightly different, but related take on wisdom. In Sternberg's earlier work, teaching for 'expertise' was interpreted in much the same way as discussed in the introduction of this chapter: excellence in thinking was formulated in a predominantly cognitive, analytical way consistent with learning-teaching conception 4 or reasoned thinking (Dewey, 1910/1977) as well as with Labouvie-Vief's assumption of *logos*-bias in many theories of intellectual development. Sternberg carried the argument of training expert students a little further, directly addressing the type of assessment necessary: "For starters, this means having students do tasks, or at least meaningful simulations, that experts do in the various disciplines. Second, it means teaching them *to think in ways experts do* when they perform these tasks." (2003, p. 5, italics ours). However, Sternberg is exceptional in his approach in the sense that in his earlier theory of Successful Intelligence, expert thinking is multidimensional. It not only included analytical thinking, but also creative and practical thinking, and even more, expert thinking also included memory. In Sternberg's own words,

> [Students] need creative thinking to generate ideas, analytical thinking to evaluate those ideas, and practical thinking to implement the ideas and convince others of their value. These kinds of thinking do not replace memory. Indeed, one cannot creatively go beyond what one knows, or analyze and apply what one knows if one does not know anything. (2003, p. 5)

In this description of expert thinking, we recognise a conception of learning or intelligence that can be formulated as a hierarchy of inclusiveness: expert thinking includes memory (learning conception 2), practical skills and generating one's own ideas (learning conception 3) and analytical or disciplinary thinking (learning conception 4). In another sense, one can see the development of expert thinking as a series of steps towards expanded awareness of the meaning of learning. In addressing the assessment of the four aspects of expert thinking mentioned, Sternberg (2003) contrasted the assessment of memory (e.g. multiple choice assessment) to that of the other three aspects (performance assessment). For each of these three aspects Sternberg gave specific examples on page 5:

- Analytical thinking : "encouraging students to analyze, critique, judge, compare and contrast, evaluate, and assess"
  History: Compare and contrast the respective natures of the American Revolution and the French Revolution.
- Creative thinking: "encouraging students to create, invent, discover, 'imagine if', 'suppose that' and predict"
  Literature: Create an alternative ending to the short story you just read.
- Practical thinking: "encouraging students to apply, use, put into practice, implement, employ and render practical what they know"
  Economics, Mathematics: Apply the formula for computing compound interest to a problem people are likely to face when planning for retirement.

Indeed, from these examples it becomes more clear that the skills or aspects Sternberg is referring to in his theory of Successful Intelligence, are related to the first four learning-teaching conceptions of our model (chapter 1). Sternberg tested the assumption of multiple dimensions in successful intelligence in a series of studies, and concluded that for attaining excellence, teaching (and assessment) based on this theory of Successful Intelligence is preferable to traditional, more memory-aimed teaching (and assessment). As Sternberg said "Becoming an expert physicist, composer, or teacher, for example, seems to require a blend of creative (generate ideas), analytical (evaluate the ideas) and practical thinking (make the ideas work and convince others of their worth) that goes substantially beyond deliberate practice…" (2003, p. 6).

However, confronted with the fact that "many of today's current leaders[4] are very intelligent and well educated, but foolish at the same time" (Sternberg, 2003, p. 7), Sternberg felt that his theory of Successful Intelligence did not seem sufficient to guarantee good leaders, good bosses, good teachers etcetera. In his analysis, even highly educated people (and experts) still may fall victim to a number of fallacies in thinking. Sternberg discussed five fallacies, of which we treat two, both of which in our opinion are most closely related to level four thinking: *the fallacy of omniscience* and *the fallacy of egocentrism.*

- *Omniscience* occurs "when people start to feel that they are not only experts in their fields, but also all-knowing about pretty much everything" (p.7)
- *Egocentrism* occurs "when people think the world centres around them. Other people come to be seen merely as tools in the attainment of personal goals, to be used and discarded as the egomaniac's needs change" (p. 7)

To counter these particular fallacies, which are characteristic for Sternberg's Successful Intelligence, for our learning-teaching conception 4 and even for Kegan's level four self-authorship, it is necessary for students to become 'wise' to the interests of others. Students need wisdom as the opposite of foolishness.

> [Wisdom] involves a balance between three kinds of interests: (a) intrapersonal (one's own), (b) interpersonal (other people's), and (c) extrapersonal (more than personal, such as institutional) interests, over the short- and long terms as (d) informed by values. *Thus wise people do not just look out for themselves.* They also take into account the interests of all for whom they have any responsibility. This means, in turn, that they have to *understand others' points of view* and what, from these points of view, they see as their desires or necessities. (p. 7, italics ours)

In this we recognise important elements of learning-teaching conception 5, however, in his Balance Theory of Wisdom Sternberg takes wisdom beyond the possibility of another obvious fallacy, namely 'sheer relativism'. We would liken this sheer relativism to the gamesmanship of Perry (1970) or the deconstructive relativism of Kegan (1994, and chapter 3). By carrying this concept of wisdom beyond relativism, he takes wisdom to level six thinking,

> .. if the knowledge is not used for a *common good* in a way that balances competing interests, then according to the balance theory, it is not used wisely[5] (p. 7)

In defining wisdom as a way of knowing beyond extreme confidence in one's own knowledge (or expertise, in short omniscience) as well as beyond the doubts of sheer relativism we feel Sternberg is describing a similar approach to wisdom as proposed by Meacham (1990). In exploring the possible loss of wisdom over the life span, Meacham described the essence of wisdom as "in knowing that one does not know, in the appreciation that knowledge is fallible, in the balance between knowing and doubting" (p. 201). In emphasising that wisdom should include the consideration of a common good, Sternberg's interpretation leads to the conclusion that wise people can make a positive difference in the world,

> ... wisdom provides a way to make important decisions and render important judgments. People who are wise do not make impulsive, mindless, or destructive decisions. ... wisdom represents an avenue to creating a better, more harmonious world. ... Finally, students are tomorrow's pillars of the community. We, as educators, need to teach a new generation to think rightly, soundly, and justly on behalf of their communities. (Sternberg, 2003, p. 7)

In this quote we recognise the social reform variant of learning conception 6, as found in van Rossum and Taylor (1987). On page 21 of this paper, van Rossum and Taylor sketched two possible (interconnected) foci of expanded awareness within this learning conception. On the one hand, at this level of thinking the learner focuses on a personal development towards harmony and happiness (we feel Labouvie-Vief's model is closer to this type of thinking), while the alternative focus is on understanding the social-cultural reality the learner is a part of as well as on changing and improving it (e.g. Freire, 2000, and Pratt, 1992). In the final sentences of Sternberg's quote above, he proposed that the true goal of excellent education should include teaching for wisdom: "... to teach children [students] not only to think well, but also wisely" (Sternberg, 2003, p. 7). In response to an interviewer asking the question 'How to teach students wisdom?', Sternberg listed several possible avenues: "By giving the good example yourself, by practicing dialectical and dialogical thinking, by learning to understand that what is true at one particular moment, may not prove true in the long run. And that other people have other perspectives that make sense to them. Something that the United States are remarkably bad at" (Sternberg in the NRC Handelsblad, Science and Education Supplement, 1 December 2007, p. 39, translation ours).

Sternberg proposed that no discipline need be excluded in the teaching for wisdom, nor that there is a minimum age requirement to start (see the final section of this chapter). Sternberg illustrated the former assertion with an example from American History: "students learn that the same people that the European Americans called settlers, some Native Americans called their equivalent of 'invaders'. The notion that Columbus 'discovered' America makes sense [only] in the context of a European-American perspective, but not in the context of a Native American perspective" (Sternberg, 2003, p. 8). Meacham also expressed a take on educating for wisdom, where he asked "How often does a teacher enter the classroom intending to challenge the students' beliefs, not merely so that false information might be replaced with presumably more valid information but so that the students might leave the class feeling less confident about their knowledge (and so more wise)?" (Meacham, 1990, p. 205). Sternberg put it even stronger: "Wisdom is not taught in schools. In general, it is not even discussed. ... many people will not see the value of teaching something that does not have as its primary focus the raising of conventional tests scores" (2003, p. 8). Wisdom, then, is in much the same situation as many other epistemologically sophisticated thinking skills, namely not being measured in conventional tests. In order to attain excellent education, instead of discarding teaching for wisdom, one could consider changing the tests in a way consistent with the section above on innovative assessment. Either way, Sternberg is clear about one thing,

> ...there is no easy path to wisdom or the teaching for wisdom – there never was, and probably never will be. ... an augmented conception of expertise takes into account wise *and* intelligent use of knowledge. The future of the world perhaps hinges on having experts who are wise as well as intelligent and knowledgeable. (Sternberg, 2003, p. 8)

While much can be said in favour of sowing the seeds of wisdom in students, for instance by emphasising the uncertainty of knowledge and simultaneously emphasising the need for choices, we feel some reluctance to embrace the position that education should instil a moral imperative in students to "do good". Such a curriculum hides within its folds the danger of yet another fallacy, that of the *visionary.* For before deciding what is for "the common good" wise people need to be aware of others in the same way as they are aware of themselves. We feel this requires even further epistemological development than level six thinking, at least the embracing of the other into the mindset of oneself (Parker, 1998 and the chapter Educating the educators, below). If institutes choose to teach for wisdom, it is essential that they also instil the awareness that "wisdom is characterized by the realization that one never has the final answer but that one must settle for a 'good' answer, one that *does the most good while doing the least harm...*" (Kitchener and Brenner, 1990, p. 221–222, italics ours).

Teaching for Excellence

In the above section we have tried to establish what defines excellence in higher education. We have come to the conclusion that what by some is labelled excellence, should actually be seen as the normal outcome of higher education, namely the ability to think well, critically and independently. The fact that graduates who display this ability are labelled excellent only proves that many institutes currently fail to reach their own espoused goals. Before advocating that higher education (or any education for that matter) should aim to teach for wisdom, we suggest that it should try to fully succeed in attaining the goals it has already set itself first. In the remainder of this chapter we make suggestions – helped by a number of other researchers in the field – on how higher education could foster epistemological development to (at least) level four. When institutes prove able to foster and encourage this development in many of their students, we call this phenomenon 'When Worlds Align' or constructive friction (Vermunt and Verloop, 1999): student epistemological development as a result of teaching using (a series of) appropriate holding environments. Teaching as When Worlds Align is the opposite of the situation When Worlds Collide, which we discussed in chapter 8.

Constructive-Developmental Pedagogy (Baxter Magolda)

Baxter Magolda (1999a) observed that when institutes of higher education tried to promote critical thinking and informed decision making, very often this resulted in teachers becoming the source of many students' dissatisfaction. In order to counter this miscommunication between students and teacher, she developed a constructive-developmental pedagogy aimed at better aligning the worlds of teacher and students in order to promote students' epistemological development toward self-authorship. In this approach self-authorship is seen as an epistemological point of view, and not as a skill much like critical thinking, "it is, rather, a way of making meaning of the world and oneself" (Baxter Magolda, 1999a, p. 6) or an order of consciousness (Kegan, 1994). In a way Baxter Magolda makes a similar distinction as we made (e.g. van Rossum and Schenk, 1984) between learning conception (epistemology) and study strategy or learning approach (set of skills). Self-authorship is seen by Baxter Magolda as a complex phenomenon, it is a constellation of coherent positions on three closely entwined dimensions of meaning making

- the cognitive dimension: the ability to construct knowledge in an uncertain world;
- the intrapersonal dimension: the ability to construct an internal identity separate from external influences; and
- the interpersonal dimension: the ability to engage in relationships without losing one's internally defined identity (sense of self).

Constructive-developmental pedagogy is seen as "a matter of creating the developmental conditions that allow [students] to generate their own ideas effectively, in essence to develop their minds, their voices and themselves" (1999a p. 7–8). In is interesting to note that in this line Baxter Magolda seems to echo Grow (1991) who described epistemological development as learning to learn, learning to see and learning to be. We feel that these three distinct areas of development refer to our learning conceptions 4, 5 and 6 respectively. In formulating the aim of constructive-developmental pedagogy in this way, we feel Baxter Magolda defined it as an appropriate approach to foster any development toward and within constructive views on learning and knowing. The pedagogy Baxter Magolda feels fits this model best requires that "teachers model the process of constructing knowledge *in their disciplines*, teach that process to students, and give students opportunities to practice and become proficient at it" (1999a, p. 9, italics ours). Reading this underlying pedagogy, we feel it is very similar to our own model's learning-teaching conception 4 idea of 'good' teaching. As such this pedagogy aims for level four thinking, and the current espoused goals of higher education. As Baxter Magolda refers regularly to the additional aim of fostering self-authorship – linking it directly to this type of teaching – the issue whether self-authorship is a way of knowing congruent with the fourth order of consciousness or that it is a process with a starting point at this (fourth) level of thinking remains unclear. This lack of clarity in turn leads to questions about the strengths and weaknesses of constructive-developmental pedagogy. We will attempt to bring more clarity at the end of this chapter.

Constructive-developmental pedagogy is based on three principles or 'supports' for good teaching (Baxter Magolda and King, 2004) that emerged from her longitudinal study into students' epistemological development during and after the college years. These principles form the *structure* of constructive-developmental pedagogy and are

- validating students as knowers: encouraging students to see themselves as capable of learning and knowing:

  "I appreciate instructors who try to get to know you on your level rather than trying to set up the hierarchical structure. The student is less intimidated. And although you know that your experience and your background and your knowledge of the subject are not what your instructor's are, you still feel that your opinions and your ideas are valid." (Gwen, Baxter Magolda, 1999, p. 66);

  "The professor encouraged us to critique theory. He made it comfortable to do this because he was down to earth. He gave us real-life examples to relate to. He played devil's advocate—I was initially intimidated because you're conditioned to accept the teacher's view. But he rewarded us for challenging him, and we learned more." (Tracy, Baxter Magolda, 1999a, p. 67);

- situating knowing (and learning) in students' own experience: drawing existing experiences into or creating experiences within the learning context:

  "One student [in the course on rural America] is from Japan. And when we talk about small towns and culture here, she talks about Japan. It makes you think about stuff a whole new different way. And what's funny is that I figured if you took a class on rural America, there would be more people in there from a small town. But it turns out that I'm the only one. There's a lot of stereotypes that everyone thinks about small towns, and I've been refuting them left and right. But then I have a lot of stereotypes about big cities. It's just interesting to see everyone's point of view (Alice, Baxter Magolda, 1999a, p. 69);

  "Our chemistry professor does things that help you relate. Talks about chemicals that curl hair, for example, or nitrates in red meat. He puts it into real life. Sometimes the information is just straight technical. It is hard to understand without ties to the real world." (Art, Baxter Magolda, 1999a, p. 68);

- learning as mutually constructing meaning: constructing knowledge that takes experience and evidence into account:

  "Our teacher is very open-minded. Someone will bring up something and she'll say, 'Oh, I never thought of that' or 'that's a good point'. Or someone will ask a question and she'll stay, 'I don't know.' Just honest, no pretenses. She also gives you blank paper with your multiple choice test so if you think a

> question is ambiguous you can explain yourself. She may give partial or full credit. It makes you feel like she cares what I have to say; she thinks that I have a brain and that I may not put the thing she wanted me to put, but at least I have my own reason for why I did it." (Marla, Baxter Magolda, 1999a, p. 71);
>
> " … When we have [exams] we sat down and discussed, depending on when would be a good break as far as what we're going to be studying and whether we did cases in classes. Do we want to do more than one team project? How do you feel? Do you really want to work on teamwork in this class? So a lot of that was a lot more flexible and it wasn't set for you right away … A lot more of your thinking is put into class." (Andrew, Baxter Magolda, 1999a, p. 72).

Baxter Magolda described a course (EDU 200) in which she felt her constructive-developmental pedagogy was applied. The semester long course for first- and second-year students aimed at "helping future teachers think [critically] about the complexities of education" (1999a, p. 167) by learning to "recognize, evaluate, and defend positions in educational discourse and learning to interpret, critique and judge educational practices in various contexts …" (1999a, p. 192). It was established at the outset of the course that the majority of the participating students were absolute or Transitional Knowers (80%). The main teaching approach in EDU 200 was the use of narrative (educational story telling) in three ways: 1) a "live" narrative in a weekly large group session, 2) related narrative readings, and 3) the heart of the course: interpreting and analysing the narratives (from 1 and 2) in small groups sessions and linking them to students' own educational experiences. Beside the learning goals and the teaching approach, a third epistemological challenge for students participating in this course lay in the content because it emphasised "multiple perspectives and critiques of education's purposes and practices." (p. 168).

In describing the outcomes of the course, Baxter Magolda acknowledged that the "world in which instructors wanted students to participate was a very different world from the one that many of the EDU 200 students inhabited" (p. 192–193). Offering such an "alien" learning environment to students – if not sufficiently introduced by building appropriate bridges to the new level of thinking – will, in our experience, prove too much a challenge for some, resulting in nostalgia. Indeed Baxter Magolda reported that many students complained about the vagueness of the content and the teaching approach, preferring more structure, more concrete information and practical ideas for teaching above "discussion of issues with no solutions" (p. 193), voicing nostalgia. The majority of students showed a similar epistemological stance at the end of the course as the Enterprising Learning students in our study at the end of their studies, namely learning-teaching conception 3, multiplicity or Transitional Knowing: meaning making as hearing and discussing one another's views,

> … I found that I was excited to learn about new approaches and to hear diverse opinions on subject. I think this course was wonderful because I got the chance to debate and listen to opinions I may not have heard before. (Baxter Magolda, 1999a, p. 193)

And as can be expected from the results of the pre-course measurement of the students' epistemological levels (see above) only a few students showed level four thinking at the end of the course.

> Some may have complained that they didn't know what the point of the course is, but I think they may be just a little too programmed for multiple choice tests and lecture-note-taking classes. And they missed the point. We leaned to think critically about a broad spectrum of philosophies and ideas, and that is valuable. (Baxter Magolda, 1999a, p. 194)

The discussion above may give the impression that most of the students were confirmed in their epistemological stance with which they entered the course, as the distribution of these three categories of evaluations of the course seemed to closely resemble the distribution of entry epistemological stances. A possible lack of major developmental shifts would not be unexpected, given the time frame (one semester) of the course. But what was the evidence of development that we found in Baxter Magolda's discussion of this example? For this we also made use of the description of the outcomes of this same course interpreted within the Learning Partnerships Model of Baxter Magolda and King (2004, see below). Cheryl is introduced as an example of students who seemed to have benefitted from the course epistemologically,

> I feel more like a part of this class. I feel less than the professor in a lecture where he is telling you his knowledge. I feel equal in this class because it is based on my experience. The students and teacher share experiences. I have something to contribute. I am usually quiet and don't speak in class. I feel like I can in here. (Cheryl, Baxter Magolda, 1999a, p. 196)

Cheryl's changed behaviour in class, going from pretty quiet to participating in discussions in class and offering her opinions, is identical to the move from learning-teaching conception 2 to 3. An epistemological development we have described in detail from a student's perspective in chapters 1, 7 and 8. In Elaine's response we see traces of a development towards evaluating opinions and a level-four like way of knowing. Elaine entered the course with a view on learning and knowing where her main interest was "in students explaining material to each other" (Baxter Magolda and King, 2004, p. 53). At the end of the course Elaine was open to the option of changing her opinions based on the shared experiences of others.

> Hearing opinions is important to deciding my own. I read, take my opinions, ideas that have been put forth, look further into it, compare to my ideas, and think about what we should do. I combine different things, get the main idea, compare it to my idea. I become a better person by changing my views as I learn about others' experiences. (Elaine, Baxter Magolda, 1999a, p. 197)

Elaine's openness to change her own opinion based on tales of experiences of others puts her beyond the purely multiplist level, but as she seems not to be evaluating the opinions on evidence, being more open to the existence of different opinions than to their validity, she probably has not yet entered the fourth order of consciousness (learning-teaching conception 4). We would say Elaine developed from level-two-thinker to level-four-thinking-foreseen (see chapter 7). According to Baxter Magolda there were a few students who felt that the "course content, discussions, encouragement to make their own decisions, and assignments had helped them process, think through, and make decisions about educational practice" (p. 198). So, perhaps a few students moved across the watershed to level four thinking. Quite an accomplishment within a half-year course. One of these students is Hugh, who developed from level-three-thinker (multiplist, valuing all opinions equally) to level-four-thinker.

> ...This class has helped me by giving me different ways of seeing things and thinking about things. My judgments will be my own; not other people who told you, you should think or do this. I appreciate this. I try to make decisions that say I've examined this situation and from past experience and what I've learned—what is the best way to handle this? (Hugh, Baxter Magolda, 1999a, p. 198)

From this discussion we may conclude that at least some students had developed epistemologically and attributed this to this specific course. An evaluation of the course by the teachers involved gave some additional insight into the nature of epistemological development: "students made progress on recognizing various positions but were *still hesitant* to make judgments about educational discourses and practices" (p. 200, italics ours). A description that indicates to us that the majority of students was still entrenched in a multiplist world – indicating success on the first goal – and had not developed toward level four thinking where evidence-based critique of educational purposes and practices would have been possible. The teachers themselves attributed this, to them somewhat disappointing, outcome to weaknesses in their own teaching approach: favouring participation (in discussion) and valuing students as knowers – and getting caught in the misconception that "letting students construct knowledge means letting them think anything" (p. 203). The solution lay in expanding the teaching approach,

> Both [teachers] remained committed to the goal of students' self-authorship but realized that they could balance guidance and structure with students' freedom to help students construct meaning in an informed way. (Baxter Magolda, 1999a, p. 203)

This realisation probably led to the expansion of constructive-developmental pedagogy into the Learning Partnerships Model (Baxter Magolda and King, 2004). In the Learning Partnerships Model the three teaching principles (supports) were augmented with three matching learning challenges, called key assumptions: "The *assumptions* modeled the expectation for self-authorship in each developmental dimension, challenging learners to move toward self-authorship. The *principles* offered the support necessary to do so" (Baxter Magolda and King, 2004, p. 41, italics ours). The three learning challenges assume

- knowledge as complex and socially constructed: aimed at establishing an internal belief system (epistemology dimension):

  "... There were a lot of things where there wasn't exactly a right answer. But you could come up with better answers and explain why you got to them. ...I like not always thinking there was one right answer because when you go out and try to deal with a lot of things, there isn't always one right answer. I think too much as an undergraduate we're taught to believe in black and white and there is no gray. And I think there's a lot more gray than there is black and white." (Andrew, Baxter Magolda and King, 2004, p. 44);

- self as central to constructing knowledge: aimed at establishing an internally defined identity (intrapersonal dimension):

  "I had a management class where we were in essence running a business. We ran a simulated airline. .. we had nine groups and nine airlines in the class and all of them chose different philosophies in how they wanted to run their business. ... In fact, the way our airline did it was different, the teachers said, than any other class had ever done. We just took a completely different approach, yet I was still successful." (Andrew, Baxter Magolda and King, 2004, p. 44);

- shared authority and expertise: aimed at establishing mutual relationships (interpersonal dimension):

  "In graduate school there was a lot more taking a position and defending it. ... [The teacher] even said in the grading of our report that he completely disagreed with it, but it was well argued and reasoned out, and he still gave us an A. I guess I kind of respected that aspect of–you know, 'We agree to disagree'." (Andrew, Baxter Magolda and King, 2004, p. 44);

Baxter Magolda's principles and assumptions are expected to lead to considerable more epistemological development in higher education than can be expected from more traditional teaching approaches. They will certainly transform educational practice but may require a considerable rearrangement of educational organisation and culture to succeed (Baxter Magolda and King, 2004, p. xxv). On the other hand, from the examples we have discussed (EDU 200 and winter biology, see also chapter 8) it becomes clear that sometimes students experience 'destructive friction' (see chapter 8) by not being welcomed at their side of the epistemological bridge. In Baxter Magolda and King (2004) more attention is given to both sides of the holding environment (e.g. Haynes, 2004) so implementation of our suggestion to plan for a series of 'bridges' to bring students to self-authorship is well underway, with King and Baxter Magolda (2004) providing a blueprint to developing a more stepwise approach to the Learning Partnerships Model.

Process-Oriented Teaching in Powerful Learning Environments (Vermunt)

Of the four learning styles or learning patterns Vermunt found in his studies (e.g. 1996, 1998, 2005) he considered stimulating the development of meaning-directed and application-directed learning (patterns) a major goal of (higher) education. Furthermore, this development should be situated within the context of (the teaching of) a specific domain or discipline. Thirdly, Vermunt felt students' self-regulation of learning is an important outcome of higher education, meaning that during their studies external regulation of learning (by teachers, books, assessment procedures etcetera) should be replaced by self-regulation. Finally, during the design of teaching-learning processes specific and explicit attention should be paid to the interplay between students' learning activities and teachers' teaching activities, in particular to avoid destructive friction (see also chapter 8) and to create constructive friction thereby promoting students' epistemological development.

Process-oriented teaching described in Vermunt and Verschaffel (2000) was developed to incorporate these four principles into one teaching model.

> It is an instructional model in which learners are taught to employ *suitable* learning and thinking activities to construct, change and utilize their knowledge of a particular subject domain. This type of teaching is called process-oriented teaching because it focuses on learners' processes of knowledge construction and utilization. The emphasis is on a gradual transfer of control over thinking and learning processes from the teacher and/or other instructional agents to students. (2000, p. 209, italics ours) …
>
> Process-oriented teaching is based on the interplay between self-regulation and external regulation of learning. This interplay may either give rise to congruence or to friction between learning and teaching strategies… (p. 210)

Process-oriented teaching is based on four general principles, that remain valid in all phases of the teaching-learning process:

– Focusing on (students') learning and thinking activities

  Vermunt discerned three types of activities, cognitive processing, affective and regulation activities (see also chapter 4). Cognitive processing activities are for instance looking for relations between parts of the subject matter or looking for applications. Affective activities can be motivating oneself or attributing learning outcomes to causal factors. Examples of regulation activities are monitoring the learning process or diagnosing possible causes of learning difficulties. In powerful learning environments (Vermunt, 2003), process-oriented teaching should focus on *high-quality learning*, i.e. higher order cognitive and meta-cognitive activities/skills. Regulation and affective issues are treated separately in the two paragraphs below.

– Gradual transfer of control over learning processes

  "Learning to learn … means the gradual transfer of learning functions [i.e. teaching/learning activities] from the teacher to the students, a gradual transition from external to internal regulation of learning" (Vermunt and Verschaffel, 2000, p. 214). This means that in powerful learning environments a person should experience *a succession of increasingly challenging learning environments* in which external regulation of the learning process gradually decreases and the role of the teacher "fades away" (Vermunt, 2003).

- Taking into account students' learning orientation

  Because students' learning orientations can influence their appraisal of learning situations, process-oriented teaching also focuses on students' personal goals and intentions: "The promotion of intrinsic orientations is the main aim ... the development of intrinsic orientations may be promoted by *stimulating affective activities*" (Vermunt and Verschaffel, 2000, p. 215, italics ours). The issue of 'making work into play' by enhancing personal involvement or personal relevance is also discussed below by Langer (1997). In powerful learning environments personal enjoyment can be enhanced by e.g. using increasingly complex real-life problems (Vermunt, 2003). The latter is very effective as we have seen in chapter 8, section on 'the influence of phase 3'.

- Developing students' mental model of learning

  Learning and thinking activities are not always triggered directly by teaching activities, they are also triggered indirectly through students' mental models of learning (learning conceptions) which determine the interpretation of the learning-teaching situation and so the learning and thinking activities students draw on. For students to be able to employ learning and thinking activities appropriate for the goals of higher education, it is important to develop students' mental models of learning in a more application- or meaning-directed direction. This development is encouraged by the articulation of and *reflection* on learning and thinking strategies students use themselves or that are used by their peers

  By dwelling on learning and thinking activities they had not thought of before, by comparing their own task approach, learning orientation, and learning conception with those of others, students gradually become more aware of their own and other possible learning and thinking activities ... This is especially important in ensuring the durability and generalization of learning and thinking strategies being taught. (Vermunt and Verschaffel, 2000, p. 215)

  We feel that, although Vermunt (2003) did not explicitly state so, students' reflection on learning and teaching should be formalised within a powerful learning environment, perhaps in the form of a periodical "good talk about (real) learning" (see chapter 7, methodological issues) among peers or with teachers/advisory staff. In the case of teacher-student talks, the list of teacher roles (see the next paragraph) is expanded to include that of *reflector* (Vermunt, 2007, p. 88)

Within process-oriented teaching, three phases are distinguished within the teaching-learning process, and each phase incorporates its own specific principles and teacher roles. Vermunt and Verloop (1999) acknowledged the complexity of the teacher's task in process-oriented teaching and in Vermunt and Verschaffel is was summarised as follows: "The role of the teacher is one of diagnostician, challenger, model, activator, monitor, [reflector,] and evaluator of students' learning and thinking strategies" (2000, p. 214). Vermunt (2007) was aware that not all teachers are equally up to this complex task description,

> … university staff [will] find it … difficult to adopt [these] very different roles …The [problem here is] not simply learning new skills, but fundamentally changing a mindset that previously involved regulating the study programme and controlling student activities working independently, to one which accepts an increasing level of student autonomy and collaborative learning. To call this change 'demanding' is to *understate* what is being expected; any such change will take *many years* to accomplish, but such changes are essential if we are to help students become self-regulated and self-motivated learners by the time they leave university. (Vermunt, 2007, p. 88, italics ours)

Phase 1: Tuning teaching strategies to learning strategies.

In this first phase preparatory steps are taken to ensure that the epistemological perspective underlying the learning environment is tailored to the epistemological perspective of the student (or students) in order to create congruence (at the very least, by matching epistemological perspectives), but preferably constructive friction (challenging students' epistemological perspective). It is of the utmost importance to avoid the occurrence of destructive friction (i.e. disenchantment or nostalgia, see chapter 8). The roles of the teacher in this phase are those of diagnostician and, in the case of constructive friction, challenger.

As *diagnostician* the teacher establishes "which learning and thinking activities students have mastered, how they think about learning and teaching, and what their learning orientations and personal goals are" (Vermunt and Verschaffel, 2000, p. 216). In the role of *challenger*, teachers use this initial information to define a constructive friction, namely in what *appropriate* way "to depart from students' existing learning and thinking strategies ….to make students realize that their present ways of learning and thinking no longer suffice" (Vermunt and Verschaffel, 2000, p. 216, 217). Seen this way, constructing a constructive friction looks rather similar to the creation of a holding environment (Kegan, 1994). For example, the diagnosis may show that

> in a particular domain … … students are not very good at translating … conceptual theories into practical applications ('concretizing/applying'). If it were, however, considered important for students to develop applicative skills, then process-oriented teaching would in this case be tailored to the development of concretizing/applying learning strategies. (Vermunt and Verschaffel, 2000, p. 216)

Destructive friction may occur when a teacher applies too much control over learning or thinking activities the students already master, for instance by extensively explaining relationships between parts of the subject matter when students have already shown they are capable of performing this independently. For example, the diagnosis may show that

> … students are quite skilled at discovering conceptual similarities and differences between various theories about a subject ('relating/structuring'). … a loose teacher control strategy would in this case be considered the best solution to avoid destructive friction, because students are capable of self-initiated usage of this activity. (Vermunt and Verschaffel, 2000, p. 216)

In chapter 8 we have given multiple examples of how students express destructive friction and these examples include disenchantment (too strong teacher control) as well as nostalgia (too weak teacher control). In the formulation of avoiding destructive friction by exerting loose control (above), Vermunt and Verschaffel created the possibility that initial congruence (matching levels of learning and teaching activities, and constant teacher control) may – over time – result in a new subtype of destructive friction, in this case perhaps 'boredom'. In a way, Vermunt (2003) described this phenomenon in a somewhat expanded version, where he discussed his work at the University of Maastricht. This university is well known for its innovative problem-based learning programme, which initially creates constructive friction for students. After a while, what once was a challenge has now become 'normal' for students, and the constructive friction has evolved into a congruence with students gradually getting "better in [the] skills that correspond to the degree of independence that is expected from them …" (Vermunt, 2003, p. 113). However, as the pattern of problem-based learning remained the same over the years, the challenge disappeared and "students seemed to get a bit bored with the system…" (Vermunt, 2003, p. 111). Here we see the essentially iterative nature of process-oriented teaching, new challenges need to be constructed on a continuous base.

Phase 2: Teaching learning functions

This second phase is the "actual learning phase, [where] learning [activities] that students do *not yet* sufficiently master are taught together with, and embedded in, the subject-matter domain." (Vermunt and Verschaffel, 2000, p. 212, italics ours). These insufficiently mastered learning activities (cognitive processing, affective and regulation) should not be taught in isolation, in Vermunt's model of learning patterns, in each pattern these three types form a unique epistemological ecology.

> Affective activities may hinder or promote the effective use of cognitive [processing] activities. Regulation activities do not take place in a vacuum, but are directed at the cognitive and affective processing of subject matter. Training isolated cognitive activities, without paying attention to their regulation, has proved to be hardly successful. … there is little sense in teaching students how to regulate cognitive activities that they do not master. (Vermunt and Verschaffel, 2000, p. 217)

We interpret this as meaning that in process-oriented teaching the learning activities that constitute a particular 'learning pattern' should be introduced more or less simultaneously in a constructive friction. In the words of Vermunt and Verschaffel,

> … process-oriented teaching is aimed at stimulating the development of meaning-directed and application-directed learning and discouraging undirected and reproductive-directed learning. (2000, p. 212)

If learning patterns are presented more or less "at once", it is even more important to understand the developmental sequence of such patterns, otherwise it is not unthinkable that one unwittingly creates considerable destructive friction. For instance, we feel this could happen when process-oriented teaching would aim at introducing a meaning-directed learning pattern in a constructive friction for a group of students with predominantly reproduction-directed learning patterns. In chapter 4 we have already discussed that learning activities within the application-directed learning pattern are very similar to those characteristic for our learning-teaching conception 3, placing the application-directed pattern *between* the reproduction and meaning-directed learning patterns. In our opinion, introducing those activities belonging to the application-directed learning pattern should precede the introduction of activities belonging to the meaning-directed pattern (which we feel is similar to learning-teaching conception 4).

In the role of *model learner*, the teacher demonstrates and explicitly discusses the learning activities that are to be taught in this phase. In the beginning of the learning process teachers

> … temporarily [take] over learning activities from students, the teacher's role is one of model learning and thinker, who demonstrates learning and thinking activities that are important for the subject domain. (Vermunt and Verschaffel, 2000, p. 218)

Then, having modelled the required learning and thinking activities, the role of the teacher gradual changes to *activator*, stimulating students to use these activities in carefully selected assignments (e.g. students inventing test questions). As the students work on these assignments, the teacher as external *monitor*, "provides students with feedback on the quality of their performance and of the underlying thinking activities, so that they may adjust the execution of these activities if necessary …" (Vermunt and Verschaffel, 2000, p. 218).

After successful activation and monitoring, the teacher must *fade out* his/her own role in the learning process so that students eventually become self-regulated in their use of their new learning and thinking skills. Vermunt and Verschaffel called this 'capitalizing on learning and thinking skills' and proposed that this should be made possible by providing sufficiently challenging (learning) environments that require employment of these new learning and thinking skills on a regular if not continuous basis. As the teacher's role fades out for one (or more) of the learning activities taught, he/she can 'fade in' (again) with regard to learning activities that have as yet not received sufficient attention, or have not been mastered yet.

At the end of the second phase, ideally, students have mastered sets of coherent learning and thinking activities (belonging to one learning pattern) which they can employ independently in increasingly complex (real-life) problems.

Phase 3: Assessing learning functions

In the concluding phase of the learning process, Vermunt and Verschaffel address the issue of aligned assessment, in the testing of the mastery of the learning and thinking activities that were the focus of the learning-teaching process. In the role of *evaluator* in process-oriented teaching, the teacher constructs tests in which

> .. the employment of thinking activities at which teaching is directed, should be awarded by a good test result. (Vermunt and Verschaffel, 2000, p. 219)

This view on assessment strongly resembles the notion of constructive alignment (Biggs, 1996, 2003) which we will discuss in the next chapter.

Vermunt's process-oriented teaching is a model that addresses in some detail the learning and thinking activities that should be the object of explicit teaching. It also addresses the nature of the varying roles teachers must be able to fulfil at different stages in the teaching-learning process. In our opinion, a drawback of this model is, as we have discussed above, the current absence of a clear developmental theory underlying the learning patterns and so defining the possible sequencing of constructive frictions.

Mindful Learning (Langer)

In the sections above we have discussed two approaches to changing teaching and learning that may imply rather substantial changes in current educational practices and perhaps in educational organisations as well. In this section we will discuss some findings that seem to indicate that perhaps quite interesting epistemological outcomes can be reached with surprisingly 'simple' measures. Measures that address what Langer (1997) called the "seven pervasive myths, or mindsets" (p. 2) of education that "make it hard to learn and in the process, make it hard to teach" (p. 7). The seven myths are all examples of how mindlessness in learning can have far reaching (negative) effects because they "stifle our creativity, silence our questions, and diminish our self-esteem" (p. 2). These three issues, creativity, questioning and self-esteem, we feel have close connections to the three dimensions of meaning making that according to Baxter Magolda are central to intellectual development (1999, see above). Langer's remedy for the stifling effects of these myths would lie in the emergence of 'mindfulness' in learning and teaching,

> A mindful approach to any activity has three characteristics: the continuous creation of new categories; openness to new information; and an implicit awareness of more than one perspective. (Langer, 1997, p. 4)

Langer observed, as others have done before, that views on the nature of learning function as lenses through which we perceive reality. In Langer's view, an essential ingredient to mindful learning is teaching students to notice new things about any body of information, to draw distinctions themselves: "Drawing distinctions allows one to see more sides of an issue or subject, which is more likely to result in greater interest" (p. 76). The concept of drawing distinctions returns in the discussion of the various myths below as will the issue of involvement with the material. We feel mindful learning and mindless learning represent (at least) two diametrically opposed views on the nature of learning and knowing, with mindfulness placed on the constructive side of the watershed.

Myth 1: the basics must be learned so well that they become second nature

The mindlessness of this myth lies in the fact that over-learned skills make people less sensitive to the context and situation at hand, and thus may lead to inappropriate or ineffective behaviours in (novel) situations. An example Langer gave relates to both student learning and teacher teaching

> One of the "basic skills" of teachers, and all lecturers, is the ability to take a large quantity of information and present it in bite-size pieces to students. For those of us who teach, reducing and organizing information becomes second nature. How often do we, so practiced in how to prepare information for a lecture, continue to present a prepared lesson without noticing that the class is no longer paying attention? Presenting all the prepared content too often overtakes the goal of teaching.
>
> For students, note-taking skills can be overlearned, practiced as second nature. Many of us have had the experience of turning to our notes and finding that we don't have the vaguest idea what they mean. (Langer, 1997, p. 12)

The mindlessness of over-learned skills and approaches – i.e. the unquestioning attitude of the 'second nature' – can be countered, Langer felt, by teaching skills and knowledge in a conditional way (*mindful teaching*), hereby increasing awareness of the value of doubt and uncertainty.

> Most of what we learn in school, at home, from television, and from non-fiction books we may mindlessly accept because it is given to us in an unconditional form. That is, the information is presented from a single perspective as though it is true, independent of context. It just *is*. Typically, no uncertainty is conveyed. (Langer, 1997, p. 17)

So how to go about teaching mindfully or conditionally? Langer gave a number of examples, of which we will discuss the use of 'conditional texts' in teaching, because it shows how traditional textbooks might be limiting learning and understanding. Langer described a study in which a standard financial text central to preparation for an important exam was rewritten "so that all statements originally expressed in absolute terms now conveyed a more conditional meaning" (p. 28). Below we present a small section of the original 12-page chapter text and the rewritten text.

Harvard undergraduate students were allocated at random to learning the standard text or the conditional one, and then were tested on factual knowledge and on creative use of the information. In addition they were asked about their perception of the material. The groups did not differ in factual knowledge of the material. However, the performance with regard to creative use of the information showed that the conditional (or mindful) group was more able to generate answers indicating a more flexible understanding of the studied material. In a way a conditional text may be validating students as knowers, much in the same way as Baxter Magolda suggested teachers do in her constructive-developmental pedagogy, namely by inviting students to think more about (and perhaps add to) the studied material.

Table 10.1. Example of a standard and a conditional text

Original text	*Rewritten text*
For local jurisdictions such as cities, the most common taxing power is on property. An *ad valorem* tax on the assessed value of real estate is the source of funds the local government uses to support its expenses and dept (GO bonds). School taxes are also charged at the local level.	For local jurisdictions, which could be counties and cities, the most common taxing power may be on property. An *ad valorem* tax on the assessed value of real estate is probably the source of funds the local government uses most often to support its expenses and dept (GO bonds). Of course, there are other ways a local jurisdiction can obtain money, one of which is through school taxes.

Source: Langer, 1997, p. 29

Myth 2: paying attention means staying focused on one thing at a time

Traditionally, paying attention is equalled – by teachers and students alike – to "holding the picture still" in your mind, while *mindful attention* would imply that attention is more easily given when the picture varies in the minds' eye.

> [Langer] polled twenty-five Harvard undergraduates, asking what it was that they did when they tried to pay attention. Twenty-one of them gave mindless strategies such as "Look at the professor"; "Write whatever is said". The others had slightly more mindful strategies but still with some residual attempt to fix attention (1997, p. 39)

Langer described the results of an experiment studying the influence of varying an object under attention. Adults travelling by train were asked to read short stories under five different experimental conditions. There were two mindful-reading conditions, one group was asked to vary three aspects of each story, the second group was asked to vary six aspects. Acts of variation could be reading the text from different perspectives, constructing different endings of the story read, etcetera. There were also two focused-reading conditions, one group was asked to focus on three aspects of each story and the other group was asked to focus on six aspects. In both focus conditions readers were stimulated to take in the information "as it was given" (p. 42). The control group was asked to read the stories without any specific instructions. The mindful-reading group remembered more about the stories, even though they had more to think about (and thus less time to keep each story "still in their mind"), and the more aspects they varied, the better their recall. Langer concluded that "varying the target of our attention, whether a visual object or an idea, apparently improves our memory of it" (p. 42). This means that increasing students' involvement with their study material (maybe promoting a more deep approach), through asking them to vary aspects of it (employing mindful attention), improves their recall, and perhaps their understanding too.

Myth 3: delaying gratification is important

This myth seems to be fundamental to learning-teaching conception 3, learning is an investment made, not always in an immediately pleasurable way, to ensure a more rewarding outcome in the (far) future. As Langer put it

> Delaying enjoyment makes sense if there are things that must be done *and* there is no evident way to enjoy doing them: Medical school is a killer, but that's what you have to do if you want to practice medicine; doing the laundry is boring, bit it's necessary if you want the kids to have clean clothes; if you're good now, you'll be rewarded in the hereafter. Is it true, though, that medical school, laundry, or being good have to feel like work? (Langer, 1997, p. 53)

Langer stated that almost any task can be made pleasurable by changing the attitude or mindset with which we enter the task. But she was equally aware that if one has held a particular mindset for a long time, for instance that doing laundry is odious, it may prove difficult to change it to a more mindful attitude. The real issue is that the perception (and enjoyment) of a task comes not from the activity itself, but from our own attitude toward it. If conceptions of learning can be seen as mindsets, moving from one mindset to another can change your attitude toward, and enjoyment of, learning. In this way mindful learning captures the motivational or affective aspect of learning. Learning for understanding and with intrinsic motivation would then seem more mindful (i.e. *mindful motivation*) than learning for reproduction and passing grades. In this sense mindful learning is linked to the affective dimension of Vermunt's learning patterns (Vermunt, 2005).

Again Langer had an appropriate experiment to prove her point. Participants in this experiment were asked to listen to or watch something they did not particularly like, for instance watching a football match or listening to classical or rap music. The two experimental groups were asked to either notice six or three (to them) *novel aspects* about each activity. Participants were free to choose their own aspects to focus on (Langer called this making 'their own distinctions' or noticing 'new things about any body of information', p. 75), these could be attention to the interactions between teammates, or identifying instruments, etcetera. In short participants in the mindful condition were asked to look or listen from personally chosen perspectives. The control group was asked to watch or listen without further instruction. In both mindful groups the liking of the activity increased, and it increased the most in the more mindful group (six aspects). Here, as with the myths above, the essential ingredient seemed to be involvement, or as Baxter Magolda would put it the validation of the individual as a knower.

> Involvement requires us actively to draw distinctions. .... Activities ... become enjoyable *only with involvement*. .... more often than not people expect to know whether they'll like [an activity] before they engage in it. Clearly, many more choices open up to us when we realize that we can take a more active role in determining our preferences. If we don't take this active role, then even play can feel like work. (Langer, 1997, p. 65, italics ours)

In phrasing mindfulness in this way, we feel Langer also built a bridge toward Baxter Magolda's self-authorship: the self becomes more active in defining preferences and making choices. Perhaps self-authorship can be viewed as a *mindful epistemology.*

Myth 4: rote memorisation is necessary in education

Everybody has the experience that (rote) memorisation of material can help to pass tests or exams, but memorisation in itself cannot help you to decide how to apply this knowledge in a novel context. Langer recalled a typical instance,

> ... "Battle of Hastings/1066". I have no idea what to do with that fact .... If someone else says, "the Battle of Hastings", I always blurt out, "1066", still expecting to get my A. Interestingly, there is no one event that constitutes "the Battle of Hastings". Historians have given one name to a collection of events, each of which could be seen from a collection of perspectives, as is true for most of what we take as "facts". (Langer, 1997, p. 70)

Information taken in by (rote) memorisation is usually considered as constituting of facts, because it is often presented without context or perspective, as a collection of facts that simply are. This presentation very often leads to *mindless processing* (i.e. memorisation). However, are facts really facts?

> Saying, for instance, that there were three reasons for the [American] Civil War omits both context and perspective. What did a fifty-year-old Southern white man think the reasons were? A fifty-year-old black? A young Northern woman? And so on. (Langer, 1997, p. 70–71)

Langer observed that in a number of subject areas, teaching for understanding is on its way to replace teaching for memorisation. However,

> These methods, all more effective than having students memorize material, are usually used sparingly and primarily with higher-level students even though virtually all students seem to be able to learn *without* memorizing. Too many students still suffer the hidden costs of learning in the more familiar manner." (Langer, 1997, p. 72, italics ours)

As Langer stated, and has proven with various experiments e.g. those discussed above, recall can be improved without reverting to (more) memorisation. Therefore the issue of content knowledge is not well served by memorisation, and would be better served by mindfulness in learning. While teachers can increase the relevance of material for students by linking it to students' interests and experiences, *mindful learning* is a way for students (themselves) to make material more meaningful and interesting. In this way mindful learning clearly has more ties to student self-regulation than to external regulation by teacher or textbook (Vermunt and Verloop, 1999). Student self-regulation therefore can be seen as a form of *mindful regulation.*

Langer described an experiment with secondary school pupils (ninth grade). Four experimental conditions were created by dividing the pupils into a mindful-learning group and a control (supposedly mindless-learning) group. In the mindful-learning group pupils were asked to make the material meaningful to themselves, in the control group pupils were asked "simply to learn the material" (p. 77). Then half of each group was told that they would be tested after the reading period, assuming that the expectation of assessment would lead to mindless processing in both half-groups. After the reading period all four groups were tested for recall and asked to write a creative essay based on the studied material. All four groups then were given homework, another reading under the same experimental conditions, and all were tested again on recall and creative writing about this second reading four days later. The half of the control group that learned in their usual way and expected a test, performed worst of all four groups; they recalled less and showed less improvement between tests. The pupils in the mindful-learning condition, on the other hand, showed "improvement in the intelligence and creativity of their essays" regardless of whether they expected to be tested or not (p. 78). Although this latter finding – that testing had no detrimental effect on the mindful approach to learning – was more or less unexpected but hopeful, even more interesting was perhaps the finding regarding differences between pupils in the mindful-learning group. About half of these pupils, although encouraged not to use memorisation to learn, persisted in using it as a learning strategy. When these pupils were compared to those who did follow the instruction to make the material more meaningful to themselves, the latter group outperformed the former on every measure: more recall, more creative essays, and more improvement between tests. Langer drew an optimistic conclusion from experiments like this one.

> Since memorizing is the standard approach students take to learning material, it is encouraging to see that after so many years of learning this way, so many of them are wiling to learn the material in a new way. Students in our studies not only made the material meaningful to themselves, but they used different perspectives and thus were introduced to the context-dependent nature of information. Approaching information in this way invites further distinction drawing, further interpretation. Because the information is not all tied up in a nice, neat package, there is reason to get involved with it. (Langer, 1997, p. 79)

Skipping two myths, 'forgetting is a problem' (we feel it is less relevant to this section) and the positivist idea that 'intelligence is knowing what's out there' (which we feel we have discussed in chapter 1) we proceed to the seventh myth because we feel it opens a window on the order of consciousness Langer used to describe mindful learning.

Myth 7: there are right and wrong answers

According to Langer, the object of education is often seen as achieving a particular (valued) outcome, without considering that desirability may be context dependent. In her view, attaining generally useful outcomes such as the ability to make inferences, or formulate hypotheses, or even mastering learning-to-learn skills are not sufficient to speak of mindful learning. In what way then does mindful learning transcend this outcome-oriented stance?

> When students are assessed [on these outcomes], they are not given an opportunity to choose their own objectives, nor are they allowed to explore processes that are outside the experts' repertoire of valued skills. (Langer, 1997, p. 123)

From this quote we observe that, as long as students are 'limited' to using preselected skills and procedures from the experts' world or discipline, they are firmly tied to at most level four thinking. The quote can be read as a rejection of the focus of our learning-teaching conception 4 – "the way they want us to think" – or of the goal of the winter biology course "to think like scientists" (Baxter Magolda, 1999a). As long as you remain within the rules and perspective of a particular context, decision making cannot be mindful. As Langer defined,

> Mindful decision making, as opposed to decision making passively based on data assembled by outside observers, is a process of active self-definition... our ability to view a situation from several perspectives may open a greater range of options. .... the flexibility to change perspectives can open up options that would otherwise remain hidden. When we systematically attempt to [objectively] narrow a choice, the perspective we most often neglect is our own experience. (1997, p. 125–126)

Mindful decision making may then overlap with Baxter Magolda's understanding of self-authorship.[6] Although Baxter Magolda recognised that self-authorship first expresses itself at level four thinking (as initial self-authorship), at this fourth level of thinking learners cannot yet reflect on the perspective underlying their beliefs and these beliefs are probably *not yet* "generated from an internal self-system either" (1999a, p. 56). This means, as Baxter Magolda said,

> Complex epistemological development, particularly Contextual Knowing, necessitates ... self-authorship. (1999a, p. 56)

So self-authorship – seen as a process of growth – is more closely linked to Contextual Knowing or in our view the fifth order of consciousness. Consequently mindful decision making and mindful learning are aspects of what Baxter Magolda would call mature self-authorship which in turn – in this more mature form – is an aspect of the fifth order of consciousness. We feel the quote below also illustrates the overlap between *mindful knowing* and constructed knowledge (Belenky et al., 1997) and can be seen as the balancing of reason and intuition, consistent with intersystemic level thinking (Labouvie-Vief, 1990).

> I have come to see things in my own way. I feel that everyone has something unique to say, but some people know how to develop it. Some people can go even further—they can go outside the given frames of reference. Most people have something to say inside given frames of reference. But then you take someone like Freud or Darwin—they are able to jump outside of the given to create a whole new frame of reference. ... They change everything for everyone. (Adele, Belenky et al., 1997, p. 133)

The theory of mindfulness insists on the awareness of uncertainty, because only when there is uncertainty personal choices are possible. Without uncertainty all decisions become an automatic following of rules, and the person or perspective of the decision maker has no influence on the outcome, reminding us of the views of Plato (Labouvie-Vief, 1990). However, where there is awareness of uncertainty, personal choices are not only possible, they become necessary and unavoidable. But not everybody will be immediately enthusiastic about mindfulness.

> One of the fears people may have of an educational system that creates a place for several perspectives [and uncertainty], is that nothing will remain stable, there will be nothing reliable on which they can lean for continuity. Yet we discover that by viewing the same information through several perspectives, we actually become more open to that information .... If we fail to explore several perspectives, we risk confusing the stability of our own mindset with the stability of the phenomenon itself. (Langer, 1997, p. 133)

In the rare example of teachers trying to infuse their teaching with uncertainty by exposing students to 'critical thinking' (e.g. by having students list the advantages and disadvantages of a theory or issue), in Langer's experience "such an exercise almost invariably falls short of the recognition that each potential benefit may also be a liability and that a disadvantage may become an advantage" (1997, p. 134).[7] What then is the advantage of mindful learning?

> When we are mindful, we recognise that every inadequate answer is adequate in another context. *In the perspective of every person lies a lens through which we may better understand ourselves.* If we respect students' abilities to define their own experiences, to generate their own hypotheses, and to discover new ways of categorizing the world, we might not be so quick to evaluate the adequacy of their answers. We might, instead, begin listening to their questions. Out of the questions of students come some of the most creative ideas and discoveries ...
>
> How can we know if we do not ask? Why should we ask if we are certain we know? All answers come out of the question. If we pay attention to our questions, we increase the power of mindful learning. (Langer, 1997, p. 135 and 139, italics ours)

Constructivist Teaching (Prawat)

Teaching for self-authorship, process-oriented teaching and mindful teaching all can be considered as proposals toward constructivist teaching. They all focus most explicitly on the students' epistemological development, and seem to assume that the teachers involved will – over time (Vermunt, 2007) – be able to perform as expected, meaning that teachers are able to teach in a way consistent with the aims and needs of constructivist teaching. However, as Prawat (1992) stated, teachers can be seen as major obstacles to the implementation of constructivist teaching because their views on learning and teaching very often are more in line with traditional (positivist) forms of teaching: "traditionally [teachers] are seen as 'tellers of truth who inculcate knowledge in students' ... Students play a relatively passive role: they are 'accumulators of material who listen, read and perform prescribed exercises'... " (Prawat, 1992, p. 356). These views on learning and teaching are fundamentally different from the views on learning and teaching underlying a constructivist teaching approach, in which students and their ways of meaning making are the focus of teaching. On the other hand, students' meaning making cannot replace the disciplinary knowledge to which the teacher must introduce them. As Baxter Magolda said, mutual construction of knowledge is not a "know-nothing learning process" (1999a, p. 20) and "validating students as knowers does not mean endorsing misunderstanding" (1999a, p. 28). To make teaching even more complex, in constructivist teaching disciplinary knowledge should not be presented as true and certain, but as tentative and the currently 'best approximation'.

> Epistemologically, the teacher educator must walk a fine line, arguing that science does turn up better ways of construing realty ... but this does not mean we are moving closer to "objective truth". New theories are not better because they correspond more closely to reality, but because they allow us to address a new and more vexing set of problems .... (Prawat, 1992, p. 356)

As Langer has showed, textbooks – with their frequent use of absolutist language – may make this balancing act more difficult than necessary.

As said above, Prawat felt that with regard to constructivist teaching the major change is the replacement of content as focus point with the students' own efforts to understand. Secondly, concurring with Vermunt (2007), Prawat acknowledged that constructivist teaching is more demanding: teachers who wish to pursue constructivist teaching "must work harder, concentrate more, and embrace larger pedagogical responsibilities than if they only assigned text chapters and seatwork" (Prawat, 1992, p. 357). Prawat is surely not alone in his assumption that teachers will need significant reasons to take this on. And reasons formulated by educational reformers only acquire substance after teachers have embraced a new, more constructivist mindset regarding learning and teaching. Prawat discussed four problematic beliefs (or myths) that constitute important aspects of a *traditional teacher*'s mindset. Each of these myths needs to be unmasked, an epistemological transformative process that will,

> require a great deal of discussion and reflection on the part of teachers. … and it is unlikely to occur without wholesale restructuring or reworking of the workplace. (1992, p. 389)

Myth 1: learners and subject content are separate and fixed entities

The first assumption underlying this myth is that learners can be described in terms of fixed, generic individual differences, e.g. IQ or any other trait descriptor, and teachers need to somehow adjust their teaching to these differences. This assumption is definitely alive and well in teacher thinking: "Interest in individual differences on the part of teachers .. appears to be holding steady and may actually be increasing, despite the fact that there is very little research base for much of what is included under this rubric" (Prawat, 1992, p. 362). This assumption results in that teachers focus more on *how* to present the content to students (the "Federal Express approach", 1992, p. 364), and much less on *what* content is presented. In constructivist approaches individual differences are not absent, on the contrary, only they refer to totally different issues, namely the diversity of students'

- understandings developed when engaging with a particular subject matter idea (e.g. in economics, the concept price);
- interpretations of context variables in the teaching-learning environment (e.g. desired level of interaction, assessment).

The second assumption underpinning this myth is that teachers feel that subject matter knowledge is fixed and handed down by authority. As one teacher Prawat interviewed said in explaining why she stuck to the textbook.

> I feel that, whoever all these authors are who came together to write this book, they must be whizzes at math, and therefore they know how to bring the level of math along in stages, within each concept. (1992, p. 365)

A we have seen in chapter 5, and Prawat echoed here, teachers with absolutist ideas about disciplinary content often teach in a traditional, transmission-oriented way. Constructivists see disciplinary knowledge quite differently, as evolving and tentative, and a discipline as a dynamic enterprise, leading to more *interactive* teaching approaches: "attentiveness to student cognition is one of the defining features of constructivist teaching" (Prawat, 1992, p. 367).

According to Prawat, either assumption is an obstacle to adopting an interactive, constructivist perspective on teaching, but the largest obstacle lies in the combined effect of these two underlying assumptions,

> [Constructivist teaching] requires a sophisticated understanding of students *and* of the content they are being asked to learn. Static views about either will serve as an impediment to this type of interactive [teaching]. (Prawat, 1992, p. 369)

Prawat described that in this interactive teaching, constructivist teachers need to construct holding environments more related to subject matter interpretations than to epistemological stances: creating bridges between a learner's current understanding of an important concept/subject matter idea and 'expert knowledge', consequently frequently settling for intermediate levels of understanding on the road to expertise.

Myth 2: naive constructivism – as long as students are active, learning takes place

Naive constructivism refers to the assumption that all types of student activity (i.e. all experiences) are sufficient to encourage learning, in short 'to experience is to learn'. There are reasons to doubt this assumption, as not every (enjoyable) learning experience is necessary an educational one in the sense that it adds to the student's subject-matter knowledge. As Prawat (1992) stated, to ensure learning, experiences should be "carefully selected and structured" (p. 370) so that a series of experiences form a road (or bridge) to deeper understanding of the subject matter, and underpin the construction of meaning congruent with current disciplinary knowledge,

> ... experiences are necessary, but they must contribute to the growth of subject-matter knowledge. Too often ... activities or experiences are not judged relative to this educative standard. There is little continuity from one activity to another or much of a sense of where an activity fits in the total scheme of things. (Prawat, 1992, p. 370)

Constructing such a series of experiences only leads to deeper understanding if there is time to reflect on and process the experiences, and to integrate them into "a fuller and richer and also more organized form, a form that gradually approximates that in which subject-matter is presented to the skilled, mature person" (Dewey, 1938/1997, p. 73–74).

To illustrate this, we take a marketing internship in higher education as an example. A naive constructivist conception of this internship would mean that any experience or activity that is vaguely connected to marketing will do. The assumption then is that the student is capable of distilling a 'new' understanding about marketing from these experiences, and in principle any understanding will do. This approach is in essence a "know-nothing learning process" (Baxter Magolda, 1999a, p. 20) and reminds us of the multiplist stance: any opinion is as good as another. A true constructivist approach to this internship would imply that the internship mentor together with the student, and perhaps the company as well, plans a series of experiences that will lead to a deeper understanding of one or more (pre-selected) aspects of marketing. It is also possible that this understanding is tailored to the context of the particular company in which the internship is completed.

Myth 3: learning is separate from understanding, application and problem solving

A common experience in education is that pupils and students are not able to apply the knowledge they have learnt to anything other than problems that are very similar to the exercises practiced in class. This transfer problem seems to be the result of traditional teaching, where teachers assume that students need to 'cover the basics' (i.e. memorise) before trying to apply or understand the subject matter. This idea of 'vertical transfer' (Prawat, 1992) assumes that "the mastery of simpler knowledge or skills (e.g. spelling and grammar) paves the way for the acquisition of more complex knowledge skills (e.g. complex writing)" (p. 373).

Constructivists look at transfer of knowledge in a very different way. Firstly, they feel that the transfer of knowledge is enhanced if the knowledge is "well learned" to begin with, where "well learned" refers not to memorising and disconnection, but to 'knowledge connectedness'

> … [which] is best done by building connections … The richness of the connections between elements of knowledge … directly affects the accessibility of any aspect of knowledge in a novel situation. (Prawat, 1992, p. 381)

Secondly, Prawat advocated not only to create cognitive structures around disciplinary content but to also focus on the 'big ideas' central to a discipline and have students construct their knowledge around these, thereby retaining the connection to context. In order to use the 'big ideas' as foci of knowledge construction, teachers must think more deeply about the *what* to teach, more than they are used to in a traditional approach.

> Ideas, being more substantive by nature, may be a more important resource for promoting thought than thinking skills per se. Ideas (e.g., the concept of photosynthesis in science, or the notion of additive composition in elementary school mathematics) can and often do serve as valuable lenses, directing our attention to important aspects of the environment that otherwise might go unnoticed. (Prawat, 1992, p. 378)

In using the big ideas as the heart of knowledge construction, Prawat is saying much the same thing as Kember (1991) when he talked about the key concepts of a discipline. Perhaps these big ideas are also more or less identical to the 'great things' of a discipline Palmer (1998) would prefer as the central issues in teaching (see the next chapter). Prawat expected this approach to be much more effective in creating expertise (highly connected, accessible and transferable knowledge).

> This model, powerful ideas *applied* to specific aspects of the environment, is much more likely to result in the acquisition of well-organized and highly transferable networks of knowledge … compared with the traditional model that is based on a clear delineation between different types of knowledge (i.e. lower order/higher order), and between learning and application contexts. (Prawat, 1992, p. 381–382, italics ours)

Myth 4: a curriculum is a fixed agenda consisting of preset means and predetermined ends

Traditionally, curricula are assumed to be closed systems characterised by a mechanistic view on education. The school is likened to an industrial plant, where students are raw material, teachers are process managers, and educational objectives are conceived as production goals. Prawat opposed this traditional linear view on curriculum ("a well defined course to be run", p. 384) to a view consistent with constructivism: "a multifaceted matrix to be explored" (p. 386) or a "network of big ideas" (p. 387). In a constructivist perspective a classroom is a place where teacher and students meet to explore in-depth core ideas of a discipline. In order to teach from a constructivist perspective.

> Teachers need to know where the teaching and learning process is headed, but not in the traditional sense of one topic following another. It is more important that teachers develop a global view, understanding the network of big ideas that helps define a domain of inquiry, and possible relationships among those ideas. (Prawat, 1992, p. 387)

Implementing such an idea-oriented curriculum

> ... places more of a burden on teachers. There is a greater need for experimentation and self-reflection ... In deciding which ideas from the discipline to emphasize, and how to situate those ideas in real-world phenomena, teachers must draw on several sources of knowledge, weighing not only what is most important for students to know from a disciplinary perspective, but also what students are best equipped to learn—and what they as teachers are best equipped to teach. (Prawat, 1992, p. 388)

This is a tall order to fill for any teacher, and it calls for serious thoughts (and research) on how to prepare current and new teachers for this burden. The issue of staff development aimed at constructivist teaching is discussed at length in the next chapter.

Conclusions

In this chapter we have established that there are two distinct aims that many agree upon that would be appropriate for higher education. The most common and least ambitious aim is to teach students *to think well*: this is to think logically, critically, independently, resulting in the ability to address unknown problems in a reasoned way (e.g. Dewey, 1910/1997; Gow and Kember, 1990; Vermunt, 2005). As Sternberg put it, to teach students how to think in ways experts do when they perform their tasks (Sternberg, 2003). In short the most commonly professed aim for higher education would be that all graduates are able to function on the level of the fourth order of consciousness, learning-teaching conception 4 and thus are self-authored (Kegan, 1994). Indeed this aim fits seamlessly with what future employers expect from graduates (Entwistle and Ramsden, 1983). One important feature of thinking well is often forgotten in the definition, and we feel the need to introduce it here anew: the ability to suspend judgment while seeking possible answers and solutions (Dewey, 1910/1997). This latter aspect is important in the sense that - if included more explicitly in the aims of higher education - it may help to prevent a particular fallacy Sternberg has commented upon: the fact that highly intelligent and well educated leaders are "foolish at the same time" (2003, p. 7) by feeling omniscient. Be that as it may, the consequence of the aim of teaching to think well is that if all graduates actually achieve learning-teaching conception 4 or self-authorship at the end of their studies, they have made the grade and should be seen as the norm. Anything less would indicate that higher education currently is not able to meet its own goals.

Some institutes profess to aim for excellence as well. Consequently this would mean they would aim to provide an education that not only teaches their graduates to think well, but that they are capable of something more sophisticated. So what could it mean to aim for excellence in higher education? There are several possibilities here of course. Following our developmental model institutes might be referring to graduation epistemology congruent with learning-teaching conception 5, relativism. Indeed in the later part of this chapter we feel that Ellen Langer for instance is describing an approach to learning and teaching, Mindful Learning, from this perspective (Langer 1997). Prawat (1992) may approach learning from this perspective as well, although in his proposals for constructivist teaching he formulates his suggestions all within a discipline, thereby placing it at level four thinking and self-authorship. Institutes that aim for excellence will have attained their goal when all of their graduates realise "that each way of knowing is a way of not knowing, that each discipline is itself an ideology offering the power of explanation but at the price of inevitably advantaging someone or something and disadvantaging someone or something else" (Kegan, 1994, p. 290). Such level 5 graduates would "have" a discipline or ideology and not "be had" by it.

Then there are those who would prefer that higher education aim for teaching students not only to think well *but also wisely* (e.g. Sternberg, 2003; Baxter Magolda, 2007, 2008). Well if that is the case, institutes would need to know more about wisdom and what thinking wisely means. We feel that to aim for thinking wisely would mean to upgrade the goal of higher education towards learning-teaching conception 6, a tall order considering the rarity of this type of thinking currently. As many researchers into wisdom have observed, wisdom as a way of thinking is rare even among adults (Sternberg, 1990). But what would it mean for teaching? It could mean that teaching should aim for fostering "integrated thought" where logic (logos) and affect (mythos) are integrated in a human sized self (Labouvie-Vief, 1990). It would mean fostering an epistemological development beyond the extreme confidence in one's own expertise (level 4) as well as beyond relativism (level 5), both epistemological hurdles of considerable durability. It would result in graduates who "do not make impulsive, mindless, or destructive decisions … [who] think rightly, soundly, and justly on behalf of their communities" (Sternberg, 2003). As Sternberg proposes it would entail teaching from paradox and with a constant dialectical perspective. We will describe this teaching approach in the next chapter in more detail, but we would like to add here that if institutes choose to teach for wisdom, it is essential that they also instil the awareness that "wisdom is characterized by the realization that one never has the final answer but that one must settle for a 'good' answer, one that does the most good while doing the least harm" (Kitchener and Bremmer, 1990, p. 221–222).

Well then, is higher education currently achieving its goal? Based on the many studies reviewed here and the outcome of our own (Hotelschool curriculum) study, the answer would seem simple, if perhaps depressing: from an epistemological standpoint, no it is not. Barring the occasional reported exceptions (e.g. Perry, 1970), usually higher education is not even attaining the least ambitious goal: teaching *all* their students to *think well* (e.g. Kegan, 1994; Kuhn, 1991; Baxter Magolda, 1992; Radoff, 2002). More worrying still, there are studies that seem to indicate that under certain circumstances higher education may even lead to *less* sophisticated study approaches and strategies, leading to worse outcomes than without higher education (Gow and Kember, 1990).

What are the characteristics of higher education that seem to hamper students learning to think? Gow and Kember list the most obvious, only one of which may perhaps be attributed to the student:

- if study choice is determined less by subject matter interest and more by the wish to obtain a qualification, perhaps even any qualification;
- assessment practices geared towards surface level study strategies, such as reproduction of facts and reproductive application;
- (perceived) heavy workload obstructing time to reflect on what is learned nor on how it is learned;
- didactic teaching styles, focusing on knowledge transfer, covering content and grades.

The current practice of higher education in many countries, cultures and disciplines, often leans towards precisely these characteristics. The issue of didactic teaching styles and its effect on student learning has been discussed at length in chapters 5, 8 and 9. We would like to add here that the current practice of mass-lectures to groups numbering 100 or considerably more, would not seem to diminish the deployment of didactic teaching styles and so we expect only contributes to lower than ideal learning outcomes.

Considering workload, many curricula that cover a lot of content and overload the student with work are based on the often erroneous assumption that understanding will come naturally once enough "basics" have been covered. Perhaps they are also based on the erroneous confusion of work overload with the requirement of putting in considerable effort towards becoming an expert (e.g. the 10,000 hour rule, see Gladwell, 2008). In any case, covering large amounts of content without sufficient time to digest and reflect upon what is really learnt, is hardly conducive of conceptual change learning or attaining real understanding.

More importantly though, we have consistently encountered a lack of attention, bordering on total disregard, for the role of assessment. Gibbs (1999) gives a small number of examples that seem to indicate that changing assessment practices is a powerful, and probably much underestimated tool to change learning and the quality of learning outcomes. In the current study as well, students themselves indicated that the traditional, reproduction oriented assessment practices were interpreted as a strong cue to keep on cramming and reproducing as the only way to pass. In the next chapter we will discuss an approach to curriculum design including assessment practice, used in staff development, that is equally relevant for improving the quality of student learning (Biggs, 2003, constructive alignment). Further, we would like to add here that in our experience assessment practices in secondary education need not be exempted here, nor any particular discipline.

Sternberg goes even further and suggests that teaching to think well and wisely, which can be aided by aligned assessment, has no minimum age requirement (Sternberg 2003).

Is the current level of learning outcome sufficient to prepare our young people to deal with the growing complexity of society, let alone the possible increase in complexity in the coming decades? Answering that depends on what role graduates are expected to play in society and what kind of society they are expected to play that role in. However, if in democratic society all adults are expected to be able to follow logical and reasoned arguments and to base their choices, political or otherwise, on evidence and reasoned thinking, we must now conclude that higher education is *not* preparing our young people for the current complexity of society, and so probably not for any future, more complex society. In truth, epistemologically higher education in western democratic society seems to be failing its students and society dismally. With more than three quarters of the general population persisting in at most multiplist thinking well into advanced adulthood, it would seem necessary to – at the very least – bring higher education, but preferably also secondary education, up to a level that students and pupils *learn to think well.* For the coming decade(s) we would settle for this to come true, before calling for education to teach students to think well, as well as wisely.

How then, can we go about changing our current system to improve the record regarding reaching the goals that institutes and governments set themselves? We have discussed four distinct approaches towards improving higher education in such a way that it will foster the development towards self-authorship or learning-teaching conception 4. Each of these four approaches to constructivist learning and teaching above all addressed important issues that can contribute to successful curriculum design for teaching and learning aimed at developing students toward level four thinking (or beyond). Each approach also has possible weaknesses that may undermine its power to change teaching and learning. For instance, a major weakness in all approaches discussed above is that none of them include a view on staff development to empower teachers to perform the complex composition of roles that seem to be required to implement constructivist teaching. This issue is the main focus of the next chapter of the current study, 'Educating the educators'. Below we attempt to point out important messages that emerge from these four approaches. What then are the aspects that would seem to be essential to a comprehensive model of constructivist teaching aimed at promoting e.g. self-authorship or meaning-directed learning?

In our opinion, any approach aimed at promoting epistemological growth should at the very least build on a developmental model of intellectual development that describes various stages of student thinking in a sequential order. Only with such a model is it possible to determine the probability of constructive or destructive friction occurring. In addition, if the goal of education lies more than one stage away from the students' (most common) entry levels, this model will provide clues on how to construct a series of constructive frictions encouraging epistemological transitions.

Secondly, as we have argued before and chapter 5 is rife with examples, such a model should not only focus on student learning, but also explicitly on teacher teaching (and learning). If teachers are expected to encourage epistemological growth, this implies that they themselves have experienced a similar transformation. It is unrealistic to expect positivist teachers to walk the epistemological tightrope Prawat described above, balancing the uncertainty of knowledge with the need to build trust in the disciplinary way of thinking. As it has proven difficult to change teacher thinking, this may mean that when an institute wants a speedy transformation of the curriculum toward constructivist teaching and learning, the epistemological perspective of new staff could become a selection criterion.

Thirdly, powerful learning environments need to remain challenging throughout the duration of the studies. As students grow epistemologically, what was challenging before becomes commonplace and 'boring' (if not destructive). The challenges can be of various natures, for instance increased challenge can be sought in more ill-structured real-life problems to solve, more complex skills to apply, and/or more depth and breadth in the 'big ideas' to explore. As Vermunt linked learning and thinking activities directly to learning domain-specific content, we would like to emphasise that a successful model should include thinking and learning skills (of students *and* teachers), as well as a thorough content analysis in terms of the fundamental ideas/concepts of a discipline.

Fourthly, following Langer, more research is necessary to explore the effectiveness of 'simple' changes in teaching material or teaching approaches. Is it really possible to encourage more meaning-directed learning with simple measures such as probabilistic texts or exercises to vary attention? Do they result in 'more connected knowledge' or do these measures mainly improve recall? What is the long-term effect of narrative teaching? What is the effect of such "tricks" on the views of teachers on their teaching practice? This issue is important, because it may prove possible to change teaching and learning without a major overhaul of the workplace or even a complete national educational system.

Finally, considerably more attention needs to be given to relatively low cost interventions with potentially large effects on attainment and learning outcome: in particular we would like to stress assessment practices. To improve the outcome of education towards a more sophisticated epistemology, it is unavoidable to include these goals in the assessment practices. If thinking well is the highest goal, exams should include at least some measurements regarding the quality of reasoned thought, the capability to solve novel or ill-structured problems such as encountered in professional practice. It is truly unacceptable that time and cost constraints (of teachers and government) now determine that assessment practices are chosen that actively undermine the necessary goal of higher education: to educate the students to think well.

NOTES

1 The original version of How we think was published in 1910. We are referring to the 1997 reprint.

2 The correlations, although statistically significant, were not large (p. 311).

3 On his acceptance of an honorary doctorate of the Tilburg University, an interview with Sternberg was published by the Dutch quality newspaper NRC Handelsblad, 1 December 2007.

4 We would like to add that persistent folly in leaders is not a recent invention, see e.g. Tuchman (1984).

5 While we would like to agree with Sternberg, history has shown repeatedly that 'the common good' is not so easy to define nor to establish beyond doubt. In addition, the phrase 'for the common good' of any community has in it the real danger of abuse of power. As the Romans put it, "Quis custodiet ipsos custodes?"

6 According to Kegan (1994), self-authorship is a way of meaning making consistent with the fourth order of consciousness.

7 In this particular formulation of the relativeness of right and wrong, we recognise a popular saying in the Netherlands that was coined by Johan Cruijff, formerly a world famous soccer player, trainer and perhaps an unrecognised philosopher as well ("Every disadvantage has its advantage"); he is nicknamed 'the Oracle' because of his ambigious sayings.

CHAPTER 11

EDUCATING THE EDUCATORS

> *Intellectual development is a journey requiring effort; it is not an inherent gift one does or does not possess. One chooses whether or not to embark on the journey and applies one's intelligence, among many other personal qualities to the journeying. Teachers must embark on that journey with reclaimed intrepidity and gusto if they are to meet their learners in genuine intellectual endeavour. If we want teachers to be educators, then we must educate them.*
>
> *(Hill, 2000, p. 50)*

In the previous chapter we have established that higher education aims to achieve at least level four thinking in her graduates, that is that ideally all graduates of higher education have crossed the divide from reproductive knowing to constructive knowing. Level four thinking is characterised by the ability to work well, using the established procedures, rules and assumptions generally accepted within a discipline or one system. Creativity within this way of knowing refers to novel ways of combining the disciplinary knowledge resulting in e.g. new insights, etcetera. This type of thinking has been extensively discussed in chapters 1 and 2. It is known as e.g. Independent Knowing (Baxter Magolda, 1992, 2001), procedural knowing (Belenky et al., 1997), modernism (Kegan, 1994) and Perry's position 4b (1970).

We have also established that to engage students in intellectual development, teachers need to have a fairly extensive repertoire of teaching strategies (e.g. chapter 5). To create tailored and sufficiently evocative challenges for students one may also expect teachers need to have relatively sophisticated views on knowledge, knowing, learning and teaching. In order to lead the students out (educate them) across the divide, teachers would need to have crossed it themselves. However, in chapter 5 we have illustrated that many teachers - perhaps even the majority of them – have so far failed to do so. In chapter 9 we have further made the case that teachers are able to support students to develop to their own level of thinking, but that it is unusual to say the least that they can lead students beyond their own. Furthermore it would seem that many teachers, despite their obvious disciplinary knowledge, remain fairly reproduction-oriented in their teaching and so encourage reproductive learning in their students. Therefore, imperative to improving (higher) education is the need to educate the educators towards sufficient epistemological sophistication. This conclusion immediately leads to three main questions here:

1. Can our model on student and teacher epistemology provide insights that can be used in designing staff development and teacher education?

2. What level of epistemological sophistication would prove sufficient to teach in higher education? and
3. What are viable routes towards educating our educators: should one concentrate merely on changing teachers' belief structures, or should one concentrate on improving teachers' teaching skills (repertoire etcetera) or will we find that it is necessary to address both (perhaps even simultaneously)?

A Teacher's Optimum Level of Epistemological Sophistication

As we have seen in chapter 5, the more epistemologically sophisticated teachers' views on knowledge and knowing are, the more versatile they prove to be in structuring the educational environment to create an epistemological stretch for their students, encouraging a steady development towards such sophistication in their students. We have also established that teachers need to know how to create a holding environment that is not asking too much of the students. An epistemological stretch should not 'overstretch' the students, the friction between the students' current way of thinking and the way of thinking required for the step upward should not become counter productive or a destructive friction (Vermunt and Verloop, 1999). Which teachers seem to be capable of this balancing act, which type of teacher is so finely attuned to the required steps that he/she seems able to create the required stepping stones that will provide a road toward increasing epistemological sophistication?

Should Teacher thinking be at the Highest Level of Current Epistemological Models?

If teachers need to be aware of different ways of knowing (or orders of consciousness) in order to be able to promote epistemological development in students, one could assume that teachers would need to be able to function at the highest level of epistemological sophistication themselves in order to recognise the intermediate steps towards this level, and so to know how to create each holding environment as necessary. If so, what type of teacher thinking are we talking about?

Teaching from the sixth order of consciousness/sixth learning-teaching conception

In 1998, Parker Palmer published a well known book on his thoughts about learning, teaching and ways of knowing, "The courage to teach". In this book he described the epistemological conditions necessary for (practicing) his view on good teaching. If we compare this view with our learning-teaching conception model, we feel that Palmer is an example of a teacher who functions on at least the sixth order of consciousness. As in our model growing self-awareness is central to the sixth learning conception, in Palmer's view our capacity for good teaching depends on our recognition of who we are, on the discovery of the (importance of the) self in teaching. Repeatedly Palmer referred to the necessity of authentic teaching, for instance in the phrases "We teach who we are" (p. 1) or "Who is the self that teaches?" (p. 7). In discussing the ups, but also the many downs of teaching, Palmer proposed three sources that add to the complexity of teaching, of which the first two, complexity of the subject and complexity of the students, are fairly well accepted as sources of "the tangles of teaching" (p. 2). His contribution is the recognition of a third source,

> But there is another reason for these complexities: we teach who we are.
>
> ... As I teach, I project the condition of my soul onto my students, my subject, and our way of being together. ... Viewed from this angle, teaching holds a mirror to the soul. If I am willing to look in that mirror and not run from what I see, I have a chance to gain self-knowledge—and knowing myself is as crucial to good teaching as knowing my students and my subject. ... When I do not know myself, I cannot know who my students are. I will see them through a glass darkly, in the shadows of my unexamined life—and when I cannot see them clearly, I cannot teach them well. When I do not know myself, I cannot know my subject—not at the deepest levels of embodied, personal meaning. I will know it only abstractly, from a distance, a congeries of concepts as far removed from the world as I am from personal truth. (Palmer, 1998, p. 2)

In Palmer's experience of asking students about their good teachers, one trait consistently comes to the fore

> ...good teachers share one trait: a strong sense of personal identity infuses their work. "Dr. A is really *there* when she teaches", a student tells me, or "Mr. B has such enthusiasm for his subject", or "You can tell that this is really Prof. C's life". (Palmer, 1998, p. 10)

Furthermore, Palmer felt that the consequence of his view of good teaching is that there is no one, single, "perfect" method of teaching, each teacher should seek the teaching approach that matches his/her selfhood. So, good teaching moves beyond the primacy of good techniques (as it does in our sixth teaching conception) to teaching true to the self.

> I began to look for a way to teach that was more integral to my own nature, a way that would have ... integrity for me ...
>
> Though I need sometimes to lecture and may even enjoy doing it, lecturing all the time simply bores me ...dialogical methods of teaching help keep me alive. ... That does not mean that lecturing is the wrong way to teach. It simply means that my identity ... is more fulfilled in dialogue. ...
>
> Here, I believe, is the proper and powerful role of technique: *as we learn more about who we are, we can learn techniques that reveal rather than conceal the personhood from which good teaching comes.* We no long need to use technique to mask the subjective self, as the culture of professionalism encourages us to do. Now we can use technique to manifest more fully the gift of self from which our best teaching comes. (Palmer, 1998, p. 23–24)

From our own perspective we would diagnose this standpoint as a clear example of the close links between one's way of knowing and view on knowledge, one's learning conception and teaching conception, forming an epistemological ecology resulting in a particular, coherent teaching approach. However, Palmer reminds us of the fact that his journey to selfhood was a long and ongoing endeavour, often proceeding at a slow pace.

To bring the difference between 'good' and 'bad' teaching into focus we will also quote Palmer on his (and his students') view on bad teaching. Bad teaching occurs when teachers distance themselves from their selfhood, when their words "float somewhere in front of their faces, like the balloon speech in cartoons" (1998, p. 11). Bad teaching results when we

> build a wall between inner truth and outer performance, and we play-act the teacher's part. Our words, spoken at remove from our hearts, become "the balloon speech in cartoons", and we become caricatures of ourselves. We distance ourselves from students and subjects to minimize the danger—forgetting that distance makes life more dangerous still by isolating the self. (Palmer, 1998, p. 17)

Here we recognise the "tumble into the shadow lands" and the distancing from the self Dawn spoke about (see chapter 3, comments on Baxter Magolda). The danger of losing oneself – and so the danger of bad teaching – is greater when teachers lose heart and can no longer hear their inner voice, when their self becomes divided because they need to function in a culture of (higher) education that idealises 'objectivism' as the main way of knowing. Palmer felt that objectivism reflected a "seemingly bloodless epistemology" (Palmer, 1987, p. 22) with serious consequences for education and society. In objectivism, knowers hold everything they know "at arm's length" (p. 22) distancing themselves from the world and creating

> a world "out there" of which we are only spectators and in which we *do not live*. (Palmer, 1987, p. 22, italics ours)

Secondly, everything (e.g. a discipline or students) that has now become object, one can

> ... chop ... up into pieces to see what makes it tick. You can dissect it, you can cut it apart, you can analyze it, even unto death. (p. 22)

And finally, in objectivism, we

> are now free with these dissected objects to move the pieces around, to reshape the world in an image more pleasing to us, ... this "power over the world" motif ... [results in us making] objects of each other and the world to be manipulated for our own private ends. (Palmer, 1987, p. 22)

See here the fundaments of the fallacies of level four thinking (or logos (Labouvie-Vief, 1990), and now also of objectivism), namely omniscience and egocentrism pointed out in the previous chapter (Sternberg, 2003). As an example of the distinctively odd consequences of this academic bias towards logos and against selfhood or subjectivity, Palmer recalled a student's reaction to his assigning a series of autobiographical sketches related to various course themes. This student came up to him and asked "In those autobiographical essays you asked us to write, is it OK to use the word 'I'?" (Palmer, 1998, p. 18). After affirming this, Palmer asked the student the reason for this question, who explained "I'm a history major ... and each time I use 'I' in a paper, they knock off half a grade" (p. 18). Palmer concluded that the academic bias against subjectivity makes teachers

> delude [their] students into thinking that *bad prose* can turn opinions into facts, and [teachers] alienate them from their own inner lives. (Palmer, 1998, p. 18, italics ours)

Another reason teachers often seem to prefer to teach (and learn) at some remove from their own hearts—and so to live a disconnected life—is what Palmer called the culture of fear in education. The separation between ourselves and our teaching seems to protect us against

> ... the fear of having a live encounter with alien "otherness", whether the other is a student, a colleague, a subject, or a self-dissenting voice within. We fear encounters in which the other is free to be itself, to speak its own truth, to tell us what we may not wish to hear. We want those encounters on our own terms, so that we can control their outcomes, so that they will not threaten our view of world and self. ...
>
> To avoid a live encounter with subjects of study, teachers and students alike can hide behind the pretense of objectivity: students can say, "Don't ask me to think about this stuff—just give me the facts", and faculty can say, "Here are the facts—don't think about them, just get them straight." To avoid a live encounter with ourselves, we can learn the art of self-alienation, of living a divided life. (Palmer, 1998, p. 37–38)

The way of knowing consistent with this sixth level of thinking, or sixth order of consciousness, would include the ability to deal with paradoxes, the ability to "embrace a view of the world in which opposites are joined" (Palmer, 1998, p. 66), in short the ability to think-the-world-together (and so balance e.g. logos and mythos, Labouvie-Vief, 1990) instead of thinking-it-apart as is common in objectivism. As Palmer said,

> Paradox is not only an abstract mode of knowing. It is a lens through which we can learn more about the selfhood from which good teaching comes (1998, p. 66)

In stating that paradoxical thinking is linked to the (examination of the) selfhood, Palmer placed this way of knowing firmly within the sixth order of consciousness, learning-teaching conception 6 or Internal Foundation. What then does all this mean for teaching? The approach to teaching and learning that follows logically from this way of knowing (or epistemology) is characterised by creating a learning-teaching space that is shaped by six paradoxes or paradoxical tensions. Such an ideal space should

- be both bounded and open:

  "If boundaries remind us that our journey has a destination, openness reminds us that there are many ways to reach that end" (Palmer, 1998, p. 75);

- be both hospitable and charged:

  "… a learning space must have features that help students deal with the dangers of an educational expedition: [e.g.] places to rest …[But if] students are to learn at the deepest levels, they must not feel so safe that they fall asleep … We only need fence the space, fill it with topics of significance, and refuse to let anyone evade or trivialize them." (p. 75);

- invite both the voice of the individual and that of the group:

  "If a space is to support learning, it must invite students to find their authentic voices … But [it] must be more than a forum for individual expression. It must also be a place in which the group's voice is gathered and amplified, so that the group can affirm, question, challenge, and correct the voice of the individual." (p. 75);

- honour both the (little) stories of the students, and the (big) stories of the discipline or tradition:

  "…there must be ample room for the … stories of personal experience … But .. the big stories of the disciplines must also be told in the learning space—stories that are universal in scope and archetypal in depth, that frame our personal tales and help us understand what they mean" (p. 76);

- both support solitude and surround it with the resources of community:

  "Learning demands solitude—not only in the sense that students need time alone to reflect and absorb but also in the deeper sense that the integrity of the student's inner self must be respected … if we expect the student to learn. Learning also demands community—a dialogical exchange in which our ignorance can be aired, our ideas tested, our biases challenged, and our knowledge expanded…." (p. 76); and

- welcome both silence and speech:

  "Words are not he sole medium of exchange in teaching and learning—we educate with silence as well. Silence gives us a chance to reflect on what we have said and heard, and silence itself can be a sort of speech…" (p. 77).

While Palmer stated very clearly that this approach to teaching, the principle of paradox, offers no algorithm or "teacher proof" recipe for good teaching, he also said that

> … if it fits who you are, [the principle of paradox] offers guidance *on any level* of education and with *any field* of study. (Palmer, 1998, p. 83, italics ours)

Teaching by the principle of paradox is not easy. Palmer warned us that

> We will not be able to teach in the power of paradox until we are willing to suffer the tension of opposites, until we understand that such suffering is neither to be avoided nor merely to be survived but must be actively embraced for the way it expands our own hearts. …
>
> By holding the tension of opposites, we hold the gateway to inquiry open, inviting students into a territory in which we all can learn.
>
> *How* to do this is not a question that can be answered, for it is done in the teacher's heart: holding the tension of opposites is about being, not doing. (Palmer, 1998, p. 85)

In this description of the suffering necessary to learn how to *be* a good teacher, we see an affirmation of our proposition that level six thinking may form the starting point of a new line of intellectual development, namely the line of 'learning to be' as opposed to 'learning to know' (see chapter 1 and Hamer and van Rossum, 2008).

A new epistemology?

If you, our reader, thought that this description of good teaching at this sixth order of consciousness is complex and daunting, you may also feel that this type of teacher and the related teaching as the aim of staff development in higher education is just taking it 'a little bit too far'. If so, we expect that you will find our following interpretation even more disturbing and perhaps unrealistic as a basis for staff development. In the second half of his book, we feel Palmer described a new (perhaps seventh) order of consciousness, a view by the way that Palmer himself does not seem to fully subscribe to. Where the sixth order of consciousness focuses on 'knowing the self' or learning to be yourself, and good teaching at this level is based on this self-knowledge, the seventh order of consciousness we propose here may focus on 'knowing in community'. This seventh way of knowing then, as before at the sixth level, shapes a new approach to (good) teaching.

> … we turn toward community—the kind of community that teaching and learning require, that can help renew and express the capacity for connectedness at the heart of authentic education. As we move from the teacher's inner life to community in education, it may seem that the subject is changing, but it is not. …
>
> Community cannot take root in a divided life. *Long before community assumes external shape and form, it must be present as seed in the undivided self: only as we are in communion with ourselves can we find community with others.* Community is an outward and visible sign of an inward and invisible grace, the flowing of personal identity and integrity into the world of relationships. (Palmer, 1998, p. 89–90, italics ours)

In recognising that knowing in community can only express itself *after* we know ourselves, we feel Palmer is describing a development in 'learning to be'. We have discussed this development in more detail in Hamer and van Rossum (2008). Palmer illustrates this way of knowing (or being) with a discussion of McClintock's genetics work,

> Of course, McClintock's science was distinguished by precise analytical thinking and impeccable data; one does not win a Nobel Prize without them. But data and logic and the distance they provide are only one pole of the paradox of great science. When McClintock, arguably the greatest biologist of our century, is asked to name the heart of her knowing, she invariably uses the language of relationship, of connectedness, of community. As one commentator puts it, McClintock "gained valuable knowledge by empathizing with her corn plants, submerging herself in their world and dissolving the boundary between object and observer". (Palmer, 1998, p. 55)

According to Palmer, McClintock's way of knowing is,

> ... a way of knowing and of living that has moved beyond fear of the other into respect for, even a need for, its otherness. ...
>
> This relational way of knowing—in which love takes away fear and co-creation replaces control—is a way of knowing that can help us reclaim the capacity for connectedness on which good teaching depends. (Palmer, 1998, p. 56)

To us this description of a way of knowing and its link to good teaching is the quintessence of this new order of consciousness, beyond the sixth level of thinking (see chapter 1 and Hamer and van Rossum, 2008), because it is also linked to a new epistemology: "*reality is a web of communal relationships, and we can know reality only by being in community with it.*" (Palmer, 1998, p. 95). This epistemology culminates in Palmer's conception of good teaching (at level seven)—a community of truth:

> *...to teach is to create a space in which the community of truth is practiced* (1998, p. 90, 95 and 120) ...
>
> ... that I need to spend less time filling the space with data and my own thoughts and more time opening a space where students can have a conversation with the subject and with each other ... (1998, p. 120)

The community of truth assumes that community is reality's essential form and for us to know reality demands being in community with it ourselves. In such a community, knower and known are joined in an image of knowing that,

> ... embraces both the great web of being on which all things depend and the fact that our knowing of those things is helped, not hindered, by our being enmeshed in that web. It is an image that lifts up not only our visible connections to human forms of being—with their opportunities for intimacy,

> civility, and accountability—but our invisible connections to nonhuman forms as well. It is a model of community capacious enough to carry the educational mission of knowing, teaching, and learning. (Palmer, 1998, p. 99)

The shift in the role of the teacher from 'nurturer of the young' to mediator for the community of truth is mirrored in the move from an emphasis on creativity (level six, see Dawn's narrative in chapter two) to generativity and hospitality in teaching (level seven). For Palmer, generativity is the opposite of stagnation in adult intellectual development,

> It is a lovely and exact word because it suggests two related dimensions of a healthy adult identity. On the one hand, it suggests *creativity*, the ongoing possibility that no matter our age, we can help co-create the world. On the other hand, it suggests the endless emergence of the *generations,* with its implied imperative that the elders look back toward the young and help them find a future that the elders will not see. Put these two images together, and generativity becomes "creativity in the service of the young"—a way in which the elders serve not only the young but also their own well-being. …
>
> [And Palmer adds] … I hope never to lose … the fear I feel when I am not in life-giving communion with the young. I hope never to encounter an alienated student sitting in the back row of a class and act as if he or she did not exist … (1998, p. 49)
>
> Good teaching is an act of hospitality toward the young, and hospitality is always and act that benefits the host even more than the guest. … By offering hospitality, one participates in the endless reweaving of a social fabric on which all can depend—thus the gift of sustenance for the guest becomes a gift of hope for the host. *It is that way in teaching as well: the teacher's hospitality to the student results in a world more hospitable to the teacher.* (Palmer, 1998, p. 50, italics ours)

So good teaching here is not merely a set of techniques, it is also – and more importantly – a meeting of minds, a co-creation of reality and an act of human hospitality. A remarkable feature of this new approach to teaching – the community of truth – is that it is neither teacher nor student centred, two poles of teaching that recur in all we have read and written about above. The community of truth is in fact *subject centred.* Palmer chose 'subject centeredness' because he felt that "*a subject is available for relationship; and object is not*" (p. 102). What then are these subjects that are central to this community of truth? Palmer defined these subjects as

> … the great things that call us together—the things that call us to know, to teach, to learn. …
>
> By *great things,* I mean the subjects around which the circle of seekers has always gathered—not the disciplines that study these subjects, not the texts that talk about them, not the theories that explain them, but the things themselves.

> I mean the genes and ecosystems of biology, the symbols and referents of philosophy and theology, the archetypes of betrayal and forgiveness and loving and loss that are the stuff of literature. I mean the artifacts and lineages of anthropology, the materials of engineering with their limits and potentials, the logic of systems in management, the shapes and colors of music and art, the novelties and patterns of history, the elusive idea of justice under law. (Palmer, 1998, p. 107)

> … at the center of our attention is a subject that continually calls us deeper into its secret, a subject that refuses to be reduced to our conclusions about it. (p. 105)

The communal and co-creative aspect of learning, teaching, and knowing, and Palmer's corresponding interpretation of truth, conflict, and science in a community of truth, speaks clearly from a number of paragraphs quoted below in our attempt to fill in more clearly the character sketch of this seventh order of consciousness.

– Good teaching becomes *weaving* or *dancing together*

  "Good teachers possess a capacity for connectedness. They are able to weave a complex web of connections among themselves, their subjects, and their students so that students can learn to weave a world for themselves. The methods used by these weavers vary widely ... The connections made by good teachers are held not in their methods but in their hearts—meaning *heart* in its ancient sense, as the place where intellect and emotion and spirit and will converge in the human self." (1998, p. 11)

  "… my gift as a teacher is the ability to dance with my students, to co-create with them a context in which all of us can teach and learn, and …this gift works as long as I stay open and trusting and hopeful about who my students are." (1998, p. 72)

– Good teachers invite the unspoken voices, they *hear people to speech*

  "… one of the great tasks [of a teacher] in our time is to 'hear people to speech' ... A good teacher is one who can listen to those voices even before they are spoken—so that someday they can speak with truth and confidence. What does it mean to listen to a voice before it has spoken? It means making space for the other, being aware of the other, paying attention to the other, honoring the other. … It means entering empathetically into the student's world so that he or she perceives you as someone who has the promise of being able to hear another person's truth." (1998, p. 46)

– Truth becomes an *eternal conversation* about great things

  "I understand truth as the passionate and disciplined process of inquiry and dialogue itself, as the dynamic conversation of a community that keeps testing old conclusions and coming into new ones." (p. 104)

- Knowledge advances through *conflict*

  "... the community of truth advances our knowledge through conflict, not competition. .... Conflict is the dynamic by which we test ideas in the open, in a communal effort to stretch each other and make better sense of the world." (p. 103)

- Science emerges only from *intimacy* between knower and the known

  "No scientist knows the world merely by holding it at arm's length ... Science requires an engagement with the world, a live encounter between the knower and the known. That encounter has moments of distance, but it would not be an encounter without moments of intimacy as well." (p. 54)

The discussion of McClintock's scientific work is a perfect example of this latter issue and the position stated here can be taken as a natural evolution in the merging of logos and mythos as proposed by Labouvie-Vief (1990). After this rather esoteric and theoretical treatment of teaching at this level, we can imagine our readers would appreciate some "straight talking" about what all this really means to teaching, the skills teachers need, and how it fits in our discussion of staff development.

Teaching from the Seventh Order of Consciousness

Which approach to teaching follows naturally from the conception of good teaching as creating a space in which the community of truth can be practiced? Palmer introduced the concept of 'teaching from the microcosm', an approach that reconciles the demands of creating a space for a community of truth and those of the familiar approach known as 'covering the field'. His approach to this paradox was

> Rather than use that space to tell my students everything practitioners know about the subject ... I ... bring them into the circle of practice in that field, into its version of the community of truth. To do so, I can present small but critical samples of the data of the field to help students understand how a practitioner in this field generates data, checks and corrects data, thinks about data, uses and applies data, and shares data with others.
>
> That is, I can teach *more with less*, simultaneously creating space and honoring the stuff in question. (Palmer, 1998, p. 122, italics ours)

How precisely did Palmer defend this assumption that you can teach more with less? He felt this is possible because

> ... every discipline has a gestalt, an internal logic, a patterned way of relating to the great things at its core. ...
>
> ... so profound that every *critical* piece of it contains the information necessary to reconstruct the whole ... (Palmer, 1998, p. 122–123, italics ours)

So the assertion that you can teach more with less, *only* holds if you know what things to select, namely preferably only the critical, or great, things of a discipline. Through these great things then the discipline can be reconstructed, much like any part of a hologram contains the information on the whole. On reflection, this approach to teaching seems to be less revolutionary than Palmer's underlying epistemological perspective discussed above. We feel it displays many similarities to Kember's key concepts as the cornerstones of the content of good teaching (Kember, 1991, see also the previous chapter). The language may differ, but the purpose and aims of the proposed versions of good teaching seem to be identical. And in a sense the concept of community of truth in turn shows much resemblance to the community of learners as proposed by e.g. Beishuizen (2004). Such a community of learners is described in Palmer's example of a curriculum reform in a medical school. In this reformed medical school the role of the mentor became

> ... to guide a collective inquiry into the "great thing"—the patient and the question of illness and health—that has been placed at the center of the student's attention. (Palmer, 1998, p. 125)

In this way mentors shift the focus of the students away from learning theory and covering the field towards the real aim of their study, namely learning to *heal.* In this approach the circle of students around each patient functions as a community of truth (and learning) – a living centre or hub – where students

> ... move out to other educational settings for insights not available at the hub—to the library for independent research, to lecture halls for systematic data on various topics, and to seminars, workshops, and labs for practice in the use of particular skills. But wherever they go, they always return to the hub with new facts and theories that help them understand the patient and the problem. (Palmer, 1998, p. 126)

In fact, in this example we see again that good teaching is defined less by technique, and more by focusing on the essence of what one needs to teach, the great things of a field, and by focusing on the self that teaches (and learns). So good teaching is not only about what can be seen from the outside, it is also about what cannot be seen directly, about what lives inside the teacher and the students. Perhaps in analogy to the phrase, 'you teach who you are' (Palmer, 1998) we could add here the phrase 'you learn who you are'. In this Palmer confirms our position in chapter 5, that the difference between average and good teaching is less about the method itself, and more about the *method-as-meant.*

However, in teaching from the microcosm teachers need to possess certain skills necessary to keep the learning space open and so *not* to fill it with their own knowledge. These skills are, we feel, as important to good teaching as the related conceptions of learning and teaching we usually focus on. Palmer listed four important categories of skills for teaching from the microcosm:

– Skills related to preparing a learning space

  Defining the course "in a way more engaging than engorging ....allowing [students] to encounter the subject, each other and themselves. ...

> [Providing e.g.] readings with substance ... most often found in primary texts ... [Thus the teacher] must be well acquainted with the literature of [his/her] field." (Palmer, 1998, p. 133)

– Skills related to using and protecting a learning space

  Asking good questions: questions that open the space and do not prematurely close the possibility of dialogue (e.g. "What did the textbook have to say about concepts and indicators in Chapter Four?"), but not so open that students lose themselves in "a trackless wasteland" . (Palmer, 1998, p. 133)

– Skills related to deflecting answers, comments and connecting students in dialogue

  Deflecting comments and questions addressed to the teacher, bouncing them back to the students: "... this deflecting involves a challenge to [the teacher's] soul: [he/she] must learn how to trust that the community has the resources necessary to deal with the issue at hand." (Palmer, 1998, p. 134)

– Skills related to lifting up and reframing what students say

  Creating "benchmarks of how far we have come [in our dialogue] and how far we have to go toward whatever we are trying to learn" so revealing "a trajectory of inquiry that can both confirm what we know and take us somewhere new." Through "attentive listening" a teacher can make "students full participants in this miniature version of the community of truth." (Palmer, 1998, p. 134–135)

Palmer seems to hold the same position we do: that views on learning and teaching (such as our conceptions) and teaching skills are two sides of the same coin. So as Palmer, we feel that both the conceptions and the skills of teachers should be addressed in any approach of staff development (see below). As Palmer summarised, by

> reconstructing the dynamics of teaching and learning in the community of truth, I remind myself that teaching this way involves much more than going with the flow. I must hone certain skills and learn others as I go to make a space for this kind of education to happen. (Palmer, 1998, p. 135)

Implications for Staff Development: Good talk about Good Teaching

For teachers who wish to become better teachers – want to grow in their profession – Palmer proposed two major sources of learning and nourishment: teachers should turn "to the inner ground from which good teaching comes and to the community of fellow teachers from whom we can learn more about ourselves and our craft" (1998, p. 141). However, Palmer felt the problem with this approach is that the culture of education fosters separation more than dialogue: "Academic culture builds barriers between colleagues even higher and wider than those between [teachers] and [their] students" (Palmer, 1998, p. 142). Teaching is "perhaps the most privatized of all the public professions", for "When we walk into our workplace, the classroom, we close the door on our colleagues" (p. 142). A price that teachers have to pay for this privacy of practice is

> … evaluation practices that are distanced, demoralizing, and even disreputable. Lacking firsthand information about each other's work, we allow the artifacts of the student survey to replace the facts that can be known only in person. (1998, p. 142)

The alternative could be "Good talk about good teaching" (Palmer, 1998, p. 144). Palmer's ideas on staff development and professional growth can be summarised as *being there*, observing each other teach, talking to each other about teaching, asking real questions and giving real answers. Palmer felt that the "growth of any craft depends on shared practice and honest dialogue among the people who do it … teaching has evolved very slowly because of its privatization. … Good talk about good teaching is what we need—to enhance both our professional practice and the selfhood from which it comes" (Palmer, 1998, p. 144).

Having a good talk about teaching amounts to much more than any old good talk. Palmer was clear on one issue, talking about techniques alone does not constitute a 'good talk about teaching among colleagues'. For a good talk, colleagues should address *topics* that take them "beyond technique and into the fundamental issues of teaching" (Palmer, 1998, p. 144) using *ground rules* that keep them from defeating themselves before the talk deepens to these real issues, perhaps even the *great things* of teaching and learning. To enter such talks requires *leadership* that invites colleagues to join and carry on the conversation. Two topics seem to be communal to Palmer, discussing critical moments in teaching and learning, and "exploring metaphors and images of who we are when we are teaching at our best" (1998, p. 147).

Palmer saw a critical moment in much the same way that Hashweh (1996) saw critical incidents when he used these in his research to see how teachers cope with such moments in teaching. A critical moment is as Palmer said "one in which a learning opportunity for students will open up, or shut down—depending, in part, on how the teacher handles it" (p. 145). Addressing critical moments Palmer himself saw as a relatively simple door to open, suitable to faculty workshops, inviting teachers to share practices. Using the aid of a horizontal timeline, Palmer invited the participants to name the critical moments they experienced throughout e.g. a course. Such critical moments include for instance "the first graded exercise that reveals how few of your students understand the subject" (p. 146) or erroneous answers clearly based on misconceptions about the fundamentals of a discipline (see Hashweh, 1996, and chapter 5), or even when something unexpected happens that could require a teacher to deviate from the original plan (e.g. Jean ignoring the thunderstorm, Martens, 1992, see chapter 5). Once the collegial discussion on these critical moments ensues something extraordinary can happen, "faculty talk openly about events that have perplexed and defeated them, as well as those they have managed with ease. That is, they do what we must do if we are to help each other grow as teachers: speak openly and honestly about our struggles as well as our successes" (Palmer, 1998, p. 146). The next step in this exercise would be the clustering of related moments and teachers forming a small group around a cluster of moments that interest them. The purpose of such a circle is "*not* to critique each other's pedagogy but to speak honestly from our own experience and listen openly while others do the same" (p. 147, italics ours). According to Palmer, such workshops can lead to professional growth, when teachers learn about themselves and good teaching.

> As we listen to each other's stories, we are often reflecting silently on our own identity and integrity as teachers. When person A speaks, I realize that the method that works for him would not work for me, for it is not grounded in who I am. But as I listen to person B, I realize that the method she uses is one I would like to learn, for it feels integral to my nature. (Palmer, 1998, p. 147)

Here, Palmer painted a clear and magnificent image, but we need to realise it is done by a master. When a master painter creates a picture, one could think that it just seems too easy. And indeed this conclusion is correct, it just *seems* that way. It is in fact not easy to create the atmosphere necessary for this 'good talk about good teaching', and the faculty advisor leading this community of truth needs to possess the same skills that any teacher would need to create this type of community. Most prominently, he or she needs to be able to create a learning space, without filling it himself/herself.

We already discussed the often unrecognised power of metaphors in teaching and learning in chapter 5, in particular in relation to the work of Judith Yero (2002). Palmer also used this topic of conversation in faculty workshops, asking participants to answer the question, "When I am teaching at my best, I am like a _______" (p. 148). The idea here is that the metaphor a teacher uses "offers some clues to [his/her] identity and integrity as a teacher" (p. 148), and so clues to the place where according to Palmer, good teaching comes from. With Yero's admonition in mind, it is worthwhile to remember that it is not really the metaphor that matters, but the *metaphor-as-meant*. This means that insight into the place where good teaching comes from lies in the elaboration of the metaphor and not in the literal wording of it. Using metaphors can be interpreted as unlocking the *mythos* aspect of teaching and knowing (Labouvie-Vief, 1990). Taking Palmer as an example, he used the metaphor of a sheepdog as the basis of his conception of good teaching. Many years ago, Palmer began to see himself as a hard working Border collie with the following four main characteristics: providing a safe place for the sheep [the students] to graze [learn], holding the flock together, keeping predators out, and regularly moving the flock forward to new pastures. Over the years and based on this image Palmer developed his current conception of good teaching, namely creating a space in which the community of truth is practiced. Palmer's acknowledgement that his interpretation of the sheepdog had changed over the years, might imply that Palmer's original conception of good teaching might have been somewhat more teacher-directed than teaching from the microcosm and the community of truth can bear. Furthermore this story proves that again it is not the literal image of the sheepdog that provides all the clues, but it is the way in which the teacher feels the sheepdog should behave in keeping the sheep safe: what kind of sheepdog are we talking about?

Additionally, Palmer suggested that once the metaphor is understood fully, teachers can take heart from their metaphors when teaching is hard. When all else seems to fail, teachers can fall back on their metaphors and the guidance they give them in everyday practice.

As we have stated above, having a 'good talk about good teaching' obviously requires following the ground rules for real dialogue and can only thrive under good leadership.

> Good talk about good teaching can take many forms and involve many conversation partners—and it can transform teaching and learning. But it will happen *only* if leaders expect it, invite it, and provide hospitable space for the conversation to occur. Leaders who work this way understand that good leadership sometimes takes the form of teaching. They lead from the same model we have been exploring for teaching itself, creating a space centered on *the great thing* called teaching and learning around which a community of truth can gather. (Palmer, 1998, p. 160, italics ours)

What is the Minimum Level of Teacher thinking required to meet the Aims of Higher Education?

The (most frequently) aspired end level of higher education is consistent with learning-teaching conception 4, Independent Knowing, procedural knowing, and modernism (see the previous chapter). However many teachers at various levels in the educational system themselves have not reached this level of thinking (see for this mainly chapter 5). It is improbable that they are able to create an epistemological stretch inviting students beyond their own level of thinking, and it certainly would seem impossible for them to lead students towards the levels of thinking Palmer described. These teachers lack the epistemological sophistication to "teach from the most truthful places in the landscape of self and world, ... to invite students to discover, explore, and inhabit those places in the living of their own lives" (Palmer, 1998, p. 183).

What then is the most important epistemological evolution that teachers need to 'suffer' before they can aspire to invite their students to grow towards the (espoused) aims of higher education? It would seem unavoidable that all teachers in higher education at least should function at learning-teaching conception 4 level. This is not a simple condition, for we have repeatedly seen, most prominently in chapter five, that crossing the watershed (see chapters one, three and four) is probably the most difficult epistemological transition to make. The thinking at levels 3 and 4 can in many senses be seen as diametrically opposite, despite that they are adjacent stages in many models of epistemological development. Considering this, and the fact that for many the ideas of teaching as 'weaving webs of connectedness' or 'teaching from the microcosm' would seem to refer to approaches to teaching that are unrealistic, beyond the goals of higher education or even simply impossible to implement, below we propose a considerably less esoteric (and more down to earth) approach to staff development in order to ensure that teaching staff may attain the level of epistemological sophistication essential to effective higher education.

Approaches to Staff Development

Teaching from Constructive Alignment

The examples of Gibbs, described in the previous chapter, are but a few proving that the goals teachers say they have with their course are not always reflected in the teaching/learning activities implemented in the course, nor in the types of assessment used. In such cases students will often choose to find out what the teacher wants, and give it to him/her. Consequently, if assessment focuses on reproduction, no matter the high blown goals of the teacher, students will also focus on reproduction. Similarly, if the teaching/learning activities chosen do not reflect the professed need for more sophisticated thinking skills, but e.g. focus on reproductive application, students are more than capable of picking up this cue and responding appropriately. Not only is this student behaviour contrary to the espoused aims of (higher) education, sometimes while responding to the cues students become seriously disillusioned about their studies. We have discussed this phenomenon, disenchantment, extensively in chapter 8.

Biggs (1996, 2003) introduced the concept of constructive alignment in order to line up the teaching/learning activities and the types of assessment used to the espoused goals of teaching. Biggs gave some examples of teaching based on constructive alignment. A good example is for instance the approach of problem-based learning (PBL) as commonly implemented in medical education and which is often assumed appropriate for professional education: "PBL is alignment itself. If the aim is to become a doctor, then the best way of doing so is being a doctor – under appropriate guidance and safeguards. If the aim is to apply biology to solving biological problems, then solving biological problems is the main [teaching/learning activity]. The objectives stipulate the problems to be solved, the main [teaching/learning activity] is solving them, and the assessment is seeing how well they have been solved" (Biggs, 2003, p. 232). In more general terms, according to Biggs PBL is an approach that is based on the following argument,

> To practice as a particular professional requires solving problems that belong to that profession. Thus, professional skill is the goal; professional practice comprises the [teaching/learning activities], professional skill is what is assessed (amongst other things). It is distinguished from apprenticeship in that it is theory-based: it is not just a matter of performing the skills in an uninformed manner. … the student is required to base decisions in knowledge, to hypothesize, to justify, to evaluate and to reformulate, all of which are the kinds of cognitive activity that are required in professional practice." (Biggs, 2003, p. 240)

In this description we can recognise (again) the espoused aim of higher education, namely the ability to think critically, at least to be able to do so within one's discipline, i.e. level four thinking. As such constructive alignment would seem to be a fruitful approach to curriculum development as well as everyday teaching in higher education. However, Biggs also gave two examples of poor alignment, misalignment or non-alignment in PBL, thus proving that a PBL-curriculum in itself need not necessarily be constructively aligned.

> In an otherwise fine problem-based learning (PBL) course at a particular university, one tutor completely wrecked the process. The aim in PBL is for students to pose questions and to follow up plausible answers to a given problem. This they do by reference to theory, past experience, similar cases, etcetera, asking questions and testing possible answers in discussion. In this particular case, the tutor replied to every question put to her, all-knowing and sneering: "That's for me to know, and for you to find out." So the students in the group gave up asking questions, and PBL acquired a bad name. So did the tutor. (Biggs, 2003, p. 77–78)

> An equally devastating effect was achieved in another case when the course coordinator decided to retain the traditional final-year examination, leaving the students unsure whether their conclusions drawn from case study work would be relevant to the final exam. They were not. Not surprisingly, performance was low and the course evaluation of PBL was unfavourable … (Biggs, 2003, p. 239)

These examples show that constructively aligned teaching is vulnerable, not only to the epistemological sophistication of the teachers involved, but also to the epistemological sophistication of the institute's assessment culture (or policy).

Constructive alignment is not only a seemingly simple and logical concept regarding the consistency of teaching, it is also grounded in a particular epistemological perspective or conception of learning. This epistemology is known as constructivism which emphasises that the learner and his/her activities are central in the creation/construction of knowledge and meaning (Biggs, 1996). Like Palmer, Biggs rejected 'objectivism' in which teaching is "a matter of transmitting … knowledge, learning or receiving it accurately, storing it, and using it appropriately. This view comprised the espoused theory of teaching for many years, and when one looks at much current practice, it is still the dominant theory-in-use." (Biggs, 1996, p. 347–348). Furthermore, in Biggs's opinion this persistence of objectivism in higher education is frequently the 'logical' result of changed circumstances: "With several hundred in a class, what can you reasonably do but teach by mass-lecture, and assess by multiple-choice and machine-marking?" (2003, p. 2)

Looking for the implications of constructivism for good teaching, Biggs used the examples of two types of students – the Susans and Roberts in higher education – to illustrate the need for a more aligned and purposeful approach to the development of academic (thinking) skills. Examples of these skills are e.g. 'thinking like a mathematician', 'performances of understanding' (e.g. acting differently and thoughtfully in novel contexts), and 'appreciating relationships', all of which we recognise as aspects of learning-teaching conception 4. The academically committed students, like the Susans, characteristically use high level activities such as theorising, applying and relating more or less spontaneously to attain a disciplinary 'way of thinking'.

> So when [a Susan] learns she goes about it in an 'academic' way. She comes to the lecture with sound, relevant background knowledge and possibly some question she wants answering. In the lecture she finds an answer to her pre-formed question; it forms the keystone for a particular arch of knowledge she is constructing. Or it may not be the answer she is looking for, and she speculates, wondering why it isn't. In either event, she reflects on the personal significance of what she is learning. Students like Susan ... virtually teach themselves, with little help from us. (Biggs, 2003, p. 3)

The often more qualification-driven Roberts need more support to reach a similar level of academic engagement and learning outcome.

> [A Robert] is at university not out of a driving curiosity about a particular subject or a burning ambition to excel in a particular profession, but to obtain a qualification for a decent job. ... He is less committed than Susan, possibly not as bright, academically speaking, and has a less developed background of relevant knowledge; he comes to the lecture with few questions. He wants only to put in sufficient effort to pass. *Robert hears the lecturer say the same words as Susan heard, but he doesn't see a keystone, just another brick to be recorded in his lecture notes.* He believes that if he can record enough of these bricks and can remember them on cue, he'll keep out of trouble come exam time. (Biggs, 2003, p. 3, italics ours)

Underlying this example is Biggs's view that "Good teaching is getting most students to use the higher cognitive level processes [e.g. relating, applying and theorising] that the more academic students use spontaneously" (Biggs, 2003, p. 5). Furthermore good teaching implies promoting a deep approach to learning, while avoiding those factors that encourage a surface approach to learning (see also the previous chapter). Under this approach to good teaching Biggs felt that the "presence of a surface approach is thus a signal that something is out of kilter in our teaching or in our assessment methods ..." (Biggs, 2003, p. 15). A deep approach to learning is fostered in an environment where teaching focuses on the structure of the subject, on active learning by questioning and presenting problems, on building on students' previous knowledge, and on confronting misconceptions. In such an environment assessment should focus on structure (not on discrete facts), on depth of knowledge, in short on what Biggs called the target performances of understanding (1996, p. 356). This means assessment should not focus on the type of knowledge typically assessed with short-answer and multiple-choice tests, and so should refrain from focusing students on the somewhat bizarre epistemology of primarily remembering or recognising correct answers (Biggs, 1996, p. 357).

Biggs's approach to good teaching comes from the realisation that there are different ways of thinking about teaching. Biggs distinguished three distinct levels of thinking. The first level is very similar to the 'transmission of information model' of teaching, where all activities are formulated from the teachers' perspective and failure to learn is attributed to aspects of the students (e.g. lack of motivation, etcetera). We would characterise this level as learning-teaching conception 2 and Biggs called it "a *blame-the-student* theory of teaching" (Biggs, 2003, p. 22). Staff development here would logically focus on enlarging and updating the teacher's professional content knowledge, facilitating covering the course content. The second level is still very teacher centred, focusing primarily on what the teacher does to successfully transmit concepts and understandings to the students. The teacher needs to have a variety of teaching skills at his/her disposal to ensure that learning takes place. Contrary to the previous level, here lack of learning is the teacher's fault, and as such it is a *blame-the-teacher* theory of teaching. This theory of teaching is usually accompanied by a traditional view on staff development, focusing on 'how-to-do' and 'tips and tricks' courses. Both these ways of thinking about teaching Biggs did not see as ways leading to good teaching. In Biggs' eyes, good teaching required a third way of thinking about teaching, focusing on what the student does. At this level of thinking all parts of teaching and learning form an interactive system (the 3P model of teaching and learning, Biggs, 2003, p. 18), and thus Biggs called this third way of thinking about teaching the first 'systemic' level. Here teaching is seen as facilitating learning and is very similar to our fourth learning-teaching conception: it implies a view of teaching that is *not just* about facts and concepts to be covered and understood, but *also* about what *kind of understanding* is expected, what *kind of teaching/learning activities* promote this expected kind of understanding, and finally what *kind of assessment* measures this understanding. In order to construct good teaching based on the way of thinking of this level, Biggs (2003) proposed that three key questions need to be answered:

- How does one define those appropriate levels of understanding?
- What must students do to reach these levels of understanding?
- How does one know (and assess) that the students have indeed attained these levels of understanding?

By following these three questions one can construct an aligned curriculum or course. However, alignment in itself says nothing about the nature of what is being aligned nor about the level of thinking/learning that is the outcome of this alignment. To fit this concept of alignment to constructive student learning, Biggs linked the epistemology of constructivism to these three key questions: in constructive alignment, all three questions need to be answered from a constructivist learning perspective. The strength of constructive alignment lies in its consistency and focus on constructivist learning, as Biggs said,

> It is easy to see why [constructive] alignment should work … …
>
> All components in the system address the same agenda and support each other. The students are 'entrapped' in this web of consistency, optimizing the

likelihood that they will engage the appropriate learning activities, but paradoxically leaving them free to construct their knowledge their way. …

Constructive alignment makes the students do the real work, the teacher simply acts as broker between the student and a learning environment that supports the appropriate learning activities (Biggs, 2003, p. 27)

Thus, constructive alignment leads to teaching "as a balanced system in which all components support each other, as they do in any ecosystem…. Each of these components should work towards the common end, *deep learning*" (Biggs, 2003, p. 26, italics ours).

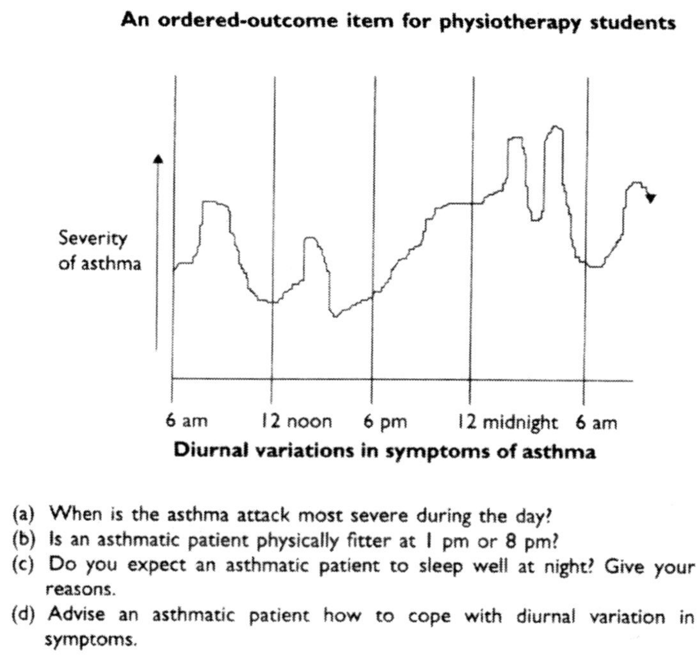

Figure 11.1. Assessment example of levels of understanding.

Source: Biggs, 2003, p. 183

As said above, constructive alignment is based on answering the three key questions, where the first question would need to result in the formulation of a hierarchy of performances of understanding that represent the range of desired outcomes – from excellent to pass – and thus define the range for assessment. All performances that are below the pass level result in a fail score. Biggs (2003) included an almost self-explanatory example of assessment using a hierarchy of performances of understanding within one single exam question about the diurnal variations in symptoms of asthma. In this example, the sub-questions reflect the range from minimum performance of understanding (i.e. being able to read a graph correctly), to the maximum desired performance (using the information in the graph and caring skills to advise the patient on ways to cope with this variation in daily life). We include the example in Figure 11.1.

Of course the range of understanding can vary by course, depending on the objectives of a course. This means one can choose to formulate less complex performances of understanding (for instance in introductory courses) or to increase the desired complexity of understanding (in advanced courses).

Interestingly enough, Entwistle (2007) noted that the 'teaching for understanding' approach – on which Biggs's notion of constructive alignment is partly based – which also focuses on defining performances of understanding indicative of the depth of learning, makes use of

- *generative topics:* important, focal disciplinary issues or concepts, and
- *throughlines:* helping students see the purpose of their courses and the connections between various (generative) topics.

In our opinion Entwistle is describing here very similar things as Palmer where he discussed the *great things* of a discipline and *trajectories of inquiry* (Palmer, 1998).

Reflective Practice and Action Research

As said before constructive alignment is flexible, it can be used on various levels and for various purposes. It is not only a way to construct a curriculum or course for students, Biggs has also used this principle in developing courses for staff development (Biggs, 1996) and later also as a framework to encourage teachers to reflect on their teaching practice (Biggs, 2003). In his 1996 article Biggs discussed a psychology course for in-service primary and secondary teachers at the University of Hong Kong. The main purpose of the course was not increasing content knowledge of psychology, but "to get [the teachers] to think about teaching and learning and to enact classroom decision-making, in a way enriched by psychological knowledge" (1996, p. 352). Biggs described how he applied the three key questions to construct this course.

In accordance with the principle of constructive alignment, Biggs formulated a **hierarchy of performances of understanding**, indicating the range of performances from 'most desirable' (in this case e.g. that students are able to use the course content in order to *reflect* on their own teaching, to *understand* the meaning of psychological theory or concepts for their own teaching, and to *improve* their teaching practice) to 'unsatisfactory' (e.g. fundamental misunderstandings). These performance levels 'defined' the grading system, but of course the main objective of the course was for as many students as possible to attain the highest level of understanding. Furthermore, the highest performances of understanding, and in particular the verbs used in describing this understanding, directed the choice of teaching/learning activities appropriate to the aims of the course.

In choosing the **teaching/learning activities** to use, Biggs concentrated on activities that increased the probability that students were 'forced' to show the desired performance of understanding. So, if one of the main aims is *reflection* on one's own teaching, then the course must include an activity that encourages reflection, for instance using a diary "to record critical learning related incidents and to reflect upon them" (Biggs, 1996, p. 355). However, to *understand* the meaning of theory for one's own teaching an activity such as answering self-addressed questions on content would seem appropriate (e.g. What is the main point I learned today?). It would seem that the students' daily teaching practice was used as the teaching/learning activity aimed at applying what they had learned and *improving* their own teaching.

To assure continued alignment, the **assessment practice** chosen required the same careful consideration as the choice of teaching/learning activities and should again match the verbs used in the most desired performance of understanding. However, to ensure that one could grade each student consistent with their attained level of understanding, Biggs felt that this particular course required a portfolio assessment, providing the students (in-service teachers) with the opportunity to display their understandings in a variety of ways. The portfolio included the diary, in order to assess the level of personal *reflection*. The self-addressed questions (included in the diary) addressed the issue of personal *understanding* of the content. To assess the extent to which the course had indeed changed (and *improved*) the teacher's practice, the portfolio included evidence from their daily teaching practice such as e.g. lesson plans, assessments by their own students, etcetera.

This aligned course resulted in almost 80% of the students attaining very high levels of understanding and demonstrating that the course had *changed* their everyday practice. Biggs concluded that,

> There may be many reasons why this happened, but the most obvious is that they were required to do so by the design of the unit: the objectives defined the performances, the teaching methods elicited them and the assessment tasks both confirmed (and no doubt motivated) those performances. (1996, p. 359)

In 2003 Biggs introduced the notions of 'the reflective teacher' and 'reflective practice', indicating that staff development aimed at changing (and improving) teaching implies more than providing teachers with "a whole new bag of teaching tricks" (p. 5). Both notions are closely related: "Through reflective practice, [reflective] teachers can ... create an improved teaching environment suited to their own context" (p.1).

In what way can a teacher reflect on problems in practice in order to improve his/her teaching practice, to attain good teaching in the sense that deep learning is promoted while factors supporting surface learning are eliminated? Biggs proposed a four step programme to reflective practice:

- Defining the problem

> In defining the problem the reflective teacher should focus on what *the student is doing* (using Biggs's third level theory of teaching): "So the first step is to *reflect* on the problem, using the constructive alignment theory ... which

addresses both students' learning behaviour, and the design of [one's] teaching. Examine [the] problem in these terms, hypothesize as to the possible reasons for it and possible solutions." (Biggs, 2003, p. 253, italics ours).

- Implementing a change

  Reading and experience (one's own or that of e.g. colleagues) can give pointers towards possible solutions. A possible solution strategy should then be translated into a tailored way of handling the problem, i.e. one or more chosen actions.

- Monitoring the change

  Proceeding from the existing situation, through the set of chosen actions to encourage more deep learning, it is necessary to establish any possible change in student behaviour over time. This ideally requires a before and at least one after measurement of student approaches to learning.

- Fine-tuning

  When there is minimal change, no change or change in the opposite direction, it is time to reconsider the chosen actions. This may require a fresh look at the (original) problem or a closer look at the student behaviour. If on the other hand matters did improve, that is that deep learning behaviour is increasing, fine-tuning may result in speeding up the process, by e.g. changing the chosen action somewhat, etcetera.

Reflective practice often requires multiple loopings through the four steps listed here. Within reflective practice Biggs saw a role for a 'critical friend' supporting the teacher in reflection on and changing of his/her teaching practice. A number of people around a reflective teacher could take on this role, e.g. colleagues (perhaps in the same faculty) or teaching developers. However, such a critical friend should not 'take over' the reflection process, an important role of the critical friend is to be a mirror for the teacher: it is the teacher's teaching that is the focus and "The critical friend should *not* tell you what to do, because that shuts down the reflection process" (Biggs, 2003, p. 254, italics ours). If the critical friend oversteps the mirroring role – for instance by inserting personal experience or expertise – he/she appropriates the teacher's problem and makes it his/her own. Kember expressed the same concern in his discussion of the role of critical friend in staff development: "The role of the facilitator … becomes one of helping instructors to achieve *their* declared goals. … the facilitator becomes a critical friend helping the insider to make wise judgements in the process of educational transformation" (Kember, 1991, p. 304, italics ours). Reflective practice as a practitioner initiated course towards professionalisation is also known by another name, concern-driven pedagogy (concerngestuurde didactiek, Vermunt, 2006). In this approach also experienced problematic issues are examined and discussed in small groups of teachers as a form of intervision. Colleagues may observe each other's practice and provide feedback when new practices are introduced.

A second issue that is important for the use of the critical friend is the issue of confidentiality. The relationship between teacher and critical friend should be based on trust, and any implementation of this approach should refrain from using information from reflective practice to enter personnel files, etcetera. This means that it is incredibly important that the critical friend approach is not used as an assessment tool for management.

From the discussion above it is easy to see that engaging in reflective practice as a means to professional development can be formally encouraged within 'action research' or 'action learning' (Kember, 2000). Biggs saw action research and action learning – as a means for professional development of teachers – as the more durable option,

> ... action research is being systematic about changing your teaching, and making sure the changes are in the right direction; that your students are now learning better than they used to. The target of action learning is the teaching of the individual teacher herself or himself. The 'learning' in action learning refers not only to student learning, or even to learning about teaching, but to learning about *oneself as a teacher*, and learning how to use reflection to become a better teacher. Learning new techniques for teaching is like the fish that provides a meal today; reflective practice is the net that provides meals for the rest of your life. (Biggs, 2003, p. 7)

Action research is the approach used by Kember (1991) and he described a number of collaborative staff development projects in higher education. These projects were aimed at improving teaching practice that encouraged students towards more meaningful (and deep) learning. One of these projects we feel is most relevant here, namely the project of the Optometry department at the Hong Kong Polytechnic. The members of Optometry collaborated with a critical friend in changing their practice, introducing more active and student-centred forms of student learning (Kember and Gow, 1992). In this case students formed groups and each group was asked (as a part of the course) to present a section of the subject in whatever form they chose. It is interesting to note, given the results described below, that the Optometry staff perceived these students to be "highly reliant upon didactic teaching methods and student resistance was perceived as the major barrier to innovation" (Kember, 1991, p. 306). The majority of the students rated this type of teaching as more meaningful (i.e. applying knowledge and independent learning) than lecturing. Kember concluded that

> The positive reactions of the students are an indication of the success of the student group for presenting parts of the course. ... [suggesting] that small-scale action research projects are viable as a method of implementing more meaningful learning. (1991, p. 306)

Kember's examples in his 1991 paper showed that firstly, small projects may have relatively large results with regard to promoting deep learning. Secondly, that teachers often seem to misperceive the capability and willingness of students to adapt (enthusiastic) to change. And thirdly, that a (respectful) partnership between content experts (the teachers) and developers (the critical friends) can work.

Kember and Gow (1992) stated that at that time there was little evidence of action research as a staff development strategy for improving teaching and learning in higher education. This statement was true in particular when employing the definition of action research of Carr and Kemmis (1986, p. 165–166).

> It can be argued that three conditions are individually necessary and jointly sufficient for action research to be said to exist: firstly, a project takes as its subject-matter a social practice, regarding it as a form of strategic action susceptible of improvement; secondly, the project proceeds through a spiral of cycles of planning, acting, observing and reflecting, with each of these activities being systematically and self-critically implemented and interrelated; thirdly, the project involves those responsible for the practice in each of the moments of the activity, widening participation in the project gradually to include others affected by the practice, and maintaining collaborative control of the process.

As Kember and Gow proposed, teaching is such a social practice that can be changed by collaborative action, ultimately affecting student learning. They, like Biggs (2003), particularly stressed that the initiation of their action research projects should always proceed 'without dictating', it should be a *respectful collaboration.*

> To avoid the genesis of technical action research, in which the investigation is of issues suggested by the facilitators, we have insisted that projects we support are derived from the concerns and suggested changes of participants. (Kember and Gow, 1992, p. 301)

Kember and Gow described a vast variety of action research projects implemented at the Hong Kong Polytechnic (including the Optometry course described above). One should note as well, that despite this considerable variety of projects, the main goal of each project was to improve teaching and student learning through – respectfully collaborative – staff and course development. Furthermore, often their decision to support various projects was based more on the enthusiasm of the participants than on a "purist interpretation of the nature of action research" (1992, p. 305). Regarding the effectiveness of this approach, Kember and Gow said,

> Our, so far subjective, impression is that action research projects have great potential. ... [However, we] would certainly not suggest action research be adopted at the expense of all other staff development activities as we have found that it does not have universal appeal ... some lecturers ... do participate in other staff development activities, probably preferring *more passive forms* which do not involve in on-going commitments. Many probably avoid any involvement at all. (1992, p. 308, italics ours)

In anticipation of the final section of this chapter, we would like to note here that Kember and Gow seem to be using the social practice of teaching as an entry point towards creating a reflective stance in the participating teachers and affecting the teachers' epistemological growth. In action research, the critical friend plays an important role in the birth of the reflective teacher, but his/her role is more like that of a midwife at a natural birth than that of the gynaecologist performing a caesarean.

Another researcher who, over the years, has come to support action research as a viable means for staff development is Graham Gibbs. Initially Gibbs' work as a staff developer was primarily pragmatic (1998) and based on the assumption that advising teachers about new ways of handling teaching problems would prove sufficient to help them improve their teaching. However, later Gibbs came to the realisation that although his advice did improve teaching in some (usually quantitative) ways, often it had not helped teachers understand their own teaching, nor had it helped them to understand their students' learning better. Gibbs concluded that because this initial approach lacked a theoretical framework, it often remained unclear to teachers why certain techniques gave particular results and so this approach seldom challenged teachers' (implicit) conceptions of teaching and learning. Gibbs came to this insight in part because he frequently encountered teachers with considerably different views on teaching and learning than those fundamental to a new method or technique Gibbs was introducing. Gibbs has a way with words describing these "aha erlebnisse".

> It is a common experience of staff developers to, from time to time, encounter almost total intransigence from some individuals in the middle of workshops. After a period of apparent open-mindedness and interest, participants suddenly dig their heels in and stop you dead in your tracks. … … Participants start every sentence with 'yes but …' and engage in all kinds of extraordinary defensive mechanisms. … I have gradually learnt to recognize that what has usually happened is that *I have tripped over a fundamental underlying conception of teaching and learning* which is challenged by the conception implicit in the methods being discussed. These fundamentals may involve the notion of a fixed corpus of knowledge which must be covered, the belief that students require some kind of mastery of a body of knowledge before anything else can be tackled, or the conviction that students are incapable of making any appropriate decisions about what or how to study because they are not yet subject experts. … Staff development runs up against these notions, and the conceptions of teaching and learning which underlie them, all the time, and cannot make much headway without tackling them. The problem is *how*. (Gibbs, 1998, p. 27–28, first italics ours)

This quote shows not only that teachers have implicit ideas about teaching and learning, but also that such – often epistemologically less sophisticated – ideas seriously hamper the implementation and effectiveness of epistemologically more sophisticated teaching methods and course designs. Not only are epistemologically less sophisticated teachers "in no position to make appropriate decisions about what directions to innovate in or how to implement innovations effectively" (Gibbs, 1998, p. 29), but also that "Without a more sophisticated conception of good teaching or good learning, lecturers will often be in no position to understand why things have gone wrong or even to notice that things have gone wrong" (p. 29). Therefore, to change practice effectively staff development needs to address the teachers' unsophisticated implicit theories of teaching and learning. Gibbs proposed a particular approach to action research, where teachers/lecturers research their own practice using literature from student learning research as a framework facilitating reflection on their practice. By focusing on student learning research (e.g. literature on deep and surface approaches to learning) teachers (may) become aware of various theories of learning, leading in time to reflection on their own implicit theories and preconceptions regarding good teaching and good learning. A similar approach was used in the teacher training for Enterprising Learning at the Hotelschool The Hague. In Gibbs' experience, without the theoretical framework from student learning research teachers tend to become locked in their own implicit conceptions of teaching and learning, obstructing reflection and change. Gibbs' approach to action research proved that "it was possible to shift students from a surface to a deep approach and to improve the quality of learning outcomes in a variety of contexts and through a variety of innovations, and to identify under what circumstances and through what mechanisms these beneficial changes were possible" (1998, p. 31). However unfortunately for our exposé on staff development, Gibbs failed to mention the effects of this action research approach on the teachers' own conceptions of good teaching and good learning.

The approaches discussed above, Biggs's constructive alignment and the concept of reflective practice, as well as Kember's and Gibbs' approaches to action research come together in the research of Gordon and Debus (2002). They focused on pre-service, early childhood teacher education students (undergraduate level). Gordon and Debus formulated three conditions aimed at improving the educational programme of these students, and designed towards increasing their use of deep approaches to learning while simultaneously – meeting Biggs' definition of good teaching – decreasing their use of surface approaches to learning.

- Interventions in the presage and process stages of Biggs' 3P model of teaching and learning (Biggs, 2003, p. 18–19):
  - in the presage stage (before learning takes place), Gordon and Debus communicated to the students in various ways the intention of modifications made to the programme, the assumption here was that this would influence the students' perception of the learning environment in the sense that in this new environment deep learning would be the appropriate behaviour.
  - in the process stage (during learning), the interventions were aimed at changing the teaching practice in the programme, such interventions included e.g. the introduction of co-operative, problem-based learning methods, and of assessment techniques that involved 'student exposition' such as essays and written reports.
- Constructive alignment throughout the whole programme was created by the logical coherence between the presage and process interventions.
- These interventions were accompanied by an embedded action research methodology: core members of the teaching team were involved in all stages of the programme changes, "The researcher, and the lecturing staff, believed that if the contextual [programme] modifications, their purpose, and the students' current approaches were not made explicit, then many students might not perceive that the opportunity for change was available, or indeed necessary" (Gordon and Debus, 2002, p. 493).

It remains unclear to us whether the lecturers involved all possessed sufficiently sophisticated views on teaching and learning to pull this off, neither is it clear to us, if not, how the lecturers' views on learning and teaching were affected by the embedded action research design. And, finally no information was given on how within this programme any possible developments in lecturers' views on teaching and learning were monitored. However, the fact that some teachers felt ethically compelled to introduce new teaching practices in final-year courses of the traditional programme (see below) perhaps may be interpreted as an indication that at least some teachers may have experienced conceptual change. Perhaps the design chosen by the researchers also included a type of subterfuge that Gibbs (1998) used, namely focusing teachers on student learning research in order to change their own thinking on teaching and learning circuitously, but we cannot be sure.

The effects of this new programme were measured longitudinally by comparing the responses of students belonging to a cohort before the modifications were implemented (cohort 1, the traditional programme) to the responses of a cohort following the modified programme (cohort 2, about 50% of the programme had been modified to encourage more deep level learning). For our current review we only discuss the responses of these two cohorts to a modified version of Biggs' SPQ (1987, see chapter 4) administered in three waves, at the beginning of the first and second years and at the end of the final third year. Both cohorts began their course with high levels of reported surface level learning, and both displayed clearly lower levels of reported deep level learning, a finding that was not surprising as Gordon and Debus stated that "students typically enter the first year of university using predominantly surface approaches, especially when they have progressed directly from their final year of secondary education" (2002, p. 503). Almost 25 years ago we made the identical observation, using almost the same words (van Rossum and Schenk, 1984). By the end of the third year, the two cohorts differed significantly in the pattern of their use of surface and deep level learning. Cohort 1 students (traditional programme) reported only a slight decrease in surface level learning, and a small increase in deep level learning, closing the gap between these two approaches to learning: "they completed their course with approximately equal reliance on deep and surface approaches" (Gordon and Debus, 2002, p. 494). The students in the modified programme (cohort 2) showed a substantial decrease in the use of surface level learning, and because they reported a greater use of deep level learning, this resulted in "a predominant use of deep approaches" (2002, p. 494) in this cohort at the end of the programme: "The pattern of learning approach development observed with cohort 2 was in the direction sought by the … study, for both surface and deep approaches, and was significantly different from the pattern displayed by the students in cohort 1" (Gordon and Debus, 2002, p. 496).

It is interesting to note that Gordon and Debus observed a possible contamination of the traditional programme with aspects of the modified programme. This contamination occurred because teachers active in the modified programme, felt ethically compelled to implement some successful modifications in courses of the traditional programme. Something similar occurred in our own research on Enterprising

Learning (see chapter 8), where we observed students of the previous (traditional) curriculum who followed some courses of the new curriculum, and submitted comments on the differences between the old and Enterprising Learning curriculum and the impact it might have had on their thinking (van Rossum, Würffel and Hamer, 2002). This contamination (both in our own research and in the study by Gordon and Debus) could imply that the effect of the old (traditional) curriculum may have been slightly overestimated.

Narrative Inquiry in Practice: An 'Alternative' Approach to Staff Development

Narrative inquiry (Lyons and LaBoskey, 2002a) can be seen as a form of 'practitioner action research' that can have a powerful influence on teachers' professional development and it reflects a (research) approach that complements our own 'way of knowing' well.

> Narrative as a way of knowing in teaching needs to be linked to existing research on epistemology, for example, that described by William Perry (1970) and Mary Belenky and her colleagues [1997]. Recently Blythe Clinchy … has explicitly examined the narrative elements of research on ways of knowing. (Lyons and LaBoskey, 2002b, p. 22)

In their introduction Lyons and LaBoskey (2002a) discussed how, in the early nineteen-nineties, the search for alternative ways of teacher assessment led them to using teaching portfolios. These portfolios contained "evidence of their learning about teaching, their students' learning, and their development and performance as beginning professionals" (p. 1) student-teachers were required to collect during their study and the first years of their professional lives. This portfolio approach to assessment led to two discoveries

- the *usefulness of portfolio practices* to support (novice) teachers' engagement in reflective inquiry into their own teaching practice, indicating a possible use as an instrument in staff development and, more important to this section,
- the *significance of the use of narrative* in teaching portfolios and other teaching practices: "[Lyons and LaBoskey] came to see that narrative was not simply storytelling, but could be *a mode of inquiry*, a way of knowing, knowing about teaching." (2002a, p. 1, italics ours), and they "began to see that teachers' conversations about teaching or learning, essential to portfolio making, were in fact narratives that captured discourses of meaning and interpretation. Conversations became texts to examine and hold up to scrutiny for teachers themselves." (2002a, p. 2)

This narrative way of knowing to us, seems to draw on a *mythos* type of epistemology (see Labouvie-Vief, 1990) and formed for Lyons and LaBoskey the basis for a new 'scholarship of teaching': "a view of knowledge that … could foster attention to 'practical competence'; support teachers to claim the legitimacy of their own investigations; and generate a knowledge of practice, complementary to other research yet testably valid …" (2002a, p. 2). It is interesting to note that here Lyons and LaBoskey attempt an upgrading of mythos to redress the balance between mythos and logos as Labouvie-Vief suggested as necessary to develop integrated thought (see chapter 10). Currently, as Lyons and LaBoskey stated, narrative has become an important mode of inquiry in education,

> ... attention to narrative, long focused on its ancient role as a likely medium for carrying a message, something to be conveyed and learned, now shifted to it as a means to capture the situatedness, the contexts, and the complexities of human action in teaching and learning. Narrative was more than a story, a teller, or a text. (2002a, p. 3)

However, narratives alone, undertaken for personal reasons or in the framework of a portfolio, do not always lead to epistemological growth or even critical reflection. Indeed, as Vermunt emphasised, how portfolios are used by teacher trainers and in particular the way the trainers provide feedback on the content is often more important than the use itself. The use of narratives in professional and epistemological development lies in the interaction between "reflection on the learning experience and the learning experience itself" (Vermunt, 2006, p 13, translation ours).

In the first chapter of their book, Lyons and LaBoskey (2002b) presented the narratives of two teachers 'storying' their (classroom) experiences and their knowledge of teaching. In their opinion these narratives can serve as *exemplars*, i.e. models of inquiry other teachers can apply in their own settings, and also they can serve as *objects available for validation* as trustworthy by a relevant research community. Validation is used here in the more fundamental sense of attributing a value to something (and not in the quantitative, methodological sense), i.e. does the exemplar describe something recognisable, is it referring to something experienced as 'real' by others? At the same time, these two narratives showed that narrative practice, narrative inquiry, in short 'knowing through story' can

- increase teachers' knowledge of their teaching practice,
- help teachers to reflect on and rethink their craft, and – ultimately –
- change the way teachers actually teach, and consequently
- teach teachers to teach.

Lyons and LaBoskey (2002b) discerned 'real' narrative practices, which are defined as "intentional, reflective human actions, socially and contextually situated, in which teachers with their students, other colleagues, or researchers, interrogate their teaching practices to construct the meaning and interpretation of some compelling or puzzling aspect of teaching and learning through the production of narratives that lead to understanding, changed practices, and new hypotheses." (p. 21). Real narrative practice (or inquiry) is characterised as

- more than 'telling a story', it is a way of knowing;
- situated in a particular context, and usually collaborative in nature;
- interrogating puzzling aspects of learning and teaching and improving the knowledge of teaching;
- involving the personal and professional identities of those engaged in it; and
- involving the construction of meaning.

To illustrate the use of such exemplars for staff development and the improvement of teaching practice, we will now discuss the experience of Rebecca Akin (2002) with narrative practice. Akin herself attributed the development in her understanding of teaching to "the purposeful articulation of the dilemmas, experiences and situations in which I have found myself over my novice teaching years" (p. 63). She started writing about events in her classroom and school site in her third year as a teacher in an urban public school. Akin began this practice to sustain herself in a to her oppressive professional environment where "the most essential players, the students and teachers, are often mere shadows for others to define as they will … often without actually having *seen* the student or teacher to whom the shadow belongs" (p. 65, italics ours). Furthermore, she was uncomfortable with the fact that "what brief time is allowed for talk is always either taken up by faculty meetings, where the agenda is dominated by the administrator, or staff development, which as the name implies is typically a training involving 'experts' from outside coming in to teach specific, predetermined strategies. *Time to do the necessary work of thinking, reflecting, evaluating, and modifying our own work is simply not provided*" (p. 65, italics ours).

Akin's original conception of teaching – as a novice teacher – was influenced by the 'grand narrative of teaching'. In this conception, within the school organisation the teacher is a passive recipient of information (e.g. about the school and common practice), but in the classroom the teacher reigns supreme. Teaching in this conception is seen as methodological and purposeful and behaviour is "objectively identifiable, predictable, rational, linear, and consistent" (p. 69) and as such this conception can be seen as a Platonian (i.e. logos-dominated and objectivist) interpretation of teaching, where the person of the teacher is written out of the image of teaching, and teaching is made 'mechanical'. As Akin described it, she was able 'to write herself back into the text of teaching' through her writing, leading to a reconceptualisation of teaching and of herself as a learner,

> … through this writing I put myself back into text of teaching in a meaningful role, as one of learner and engaged participant. I gain an important sense of *ownership* over my work, an increased ability to focus and a stronger, more confident sense of myself as being in control of my teaching and learning. I've come now to a place where I understand that reimagining myself as capable in light of the uncertainty I experience daily, seeing my struggles framed as part of the work of an inherently complex profession, valuing my perspective in a professional culture whose very structure discourages deep thought and reflection, and liberating myself from the isolation that is fed by a fear of being exposed are all essential for engaging in the difficult work of sustaining myself intellectually and emotionally as a teacher. (Akin, 2002, p. 74)

Where Akin started her professional life as a teacher with a rather traditional and objectivist view on teaching and learning, her current conception of learning shows us how far she has come since then,

> As a teacher I've given a considerable amount of thought to the nature of learning and knowledge. I've come to hold a fairly standard constructivist view of learning, where I believe numerous and varied learning opportunities are essential to the individual's ability to develop knowledge. Implicit in my understanding of learning is the conceptualization of knowledge as fluid—the idea that knowing is a way of being and interacting with the world, rather than the possession of information imposed from a particular source. Above and beyond achievement of district standards, what I most hope to provide for my students is the opportunity to become powerfully in control of their learning, to use critical thinking skills, intuition, inquiry, and communication with others to continually reevaluate and expand their understanding of the world around them and their place within it. Such learning, I believe, is at the core of living and engaged and responsible life. (p. 66)

In our opinion such a considerable intellectual development, i.e. from probably learning-teaching conception 2 across the watershed to a position where she formulated one of the most complete examples of learning-teaching conception 6 we have ever seen, is exceptional in such a short period and clearly indicates the power of 'the storying of experience' as an instrument for staff development and personal growth.

Considering the fact that Akin came to this strategy of writing to escape a to her intolerable situation, and that if she hadn't found this way to cope, she felt she would have 'succumbed' intellectually and emotionally, we come back to the famous adage accredited to Aldous Huxley,

> Experience is not what happens to you, it's what you *do* with what happens to you.

Not only can narrative practice contribute to personal growth and improvement of teaching practice, when practiced in small groups of colleagues it can also function to redress the isolation and dependency teachers experience in their professional life. As Freidus (2002) concluded, within schools teachers tend to become isolated and dependent on outsiders' opinions and information about teaching. In her narrative research she found that conversations within focus groups can

> ... encourage and support teachers to share and reflect upon the stories of their own practice ..., [and] hearing and sharing stories appears to have enabled [these teachers] to 'get beyond their own mess', nurture new habits of mind, and engage meaningfully in the tasks at hand. ...
>
> As teachers shared stories, they began to understand the thinking and caring behind the teaching of colleagues whose classroom practice frequently looked quite different from their own. With this understanding, they could begin to see these teachers as *supports* rather than barriers to their own efforts to help students learn. (Freidus, 2002, p. 169, italics ours)

In addition to personal growth, teachers begin to see themselves as part of a community of learners, exchanging instructional strategies and enriching their personal repertoire. In this more collaborative setting of narrative practice we see clear similarities (in approach and purpose) with Palmer's 'good talk about good teaching'.

Development of Conceptions, Practice or Skills?

One might say that until now we have focused too much on (changing) teachers' ways of thinking or teachers' orders of consciousness as a point of departure for staff development. However, in this section we will first take our position even further, as we agree with Gibbs (1998, see above) that when teachers have a relatively less sophisticated conception of teaching and learning, they are in no position to understand or implement teaching methods or course designs based on more sophisticated conceptions of learning. One could also formulate this issue slightly differently: if it is the case that learners approach learning tasks in a surface level way because of their limited understanding of learning (van Rossum and Schenk, 1984), would then not the same be true for teachers? If conceptions are like lenses, through which we view reality (see chapter 1), would glasses with too weak prescription lenses not prevent us from seeing clearly? Thus one might ask whether it would also be true that teachers' "unsophisticated conception of teaching and learning prevents them from teaching more effectively?" (Gibbs, 1998, p. 24). In this section we look at an innovative approach to staff development based on views very similar to our own (Ho, 2000; Ho et al., 2001). But to balance the sheet, we will look at authors that disagree with us to some degree (Eley, 2006; Devlin, 2006).

In 2000, Angela Ho reported a conceptual change approach to staff development which was based on the assumption that *only* through changing teachers' conceptions on teaching and learning (towards a more sophisticated level) a genuine improvement in teachers occurs, and consequently *only then* can any genuine improvement of teaching practice and student learning occur. As Ho said "giving teachers 'teaching recipes' is not adequate to develop them into independent, flexible decision makers about teaching" (2000, p. 30) and so we need methods "which can bring about fundamental changes towards teaching excellence in tertiary teachers ..." (Ho et al., 2001, p. 144). Ho's conceptual change programme consisted of four three-hour sessions each a week apart. The programme, implemented in April 1995, was offered to twelve voluntary participants, all teachers at the Hong Kong Polytechnic University. In each session one or more activities were planned, each activity representing one of four "potent elements" (Ho et al., 2001, p. 146):

- a self-awareness process: activities aimed at teachers' self-reflection clarifying their current espoused conception of teaching and their current teaching practice (theory-in-use);
- exposure to alternative conceptions and to good teaching practices related to these conceptions: providing teachers with alternatives to aspire to, i.e. models for improvement;
- a confrontation process: discussion of possible inadequacies in, or inconsistencies between, teachers' current conception of teaching and their current teaching practice;

- building commitment: encouraging teachers to engage in changing practice, e.g. "to put into practice the conception of teaching which they would aspire to for self-development" (Ho et al., 2001, p. 147) or to discuss "in small groups how to manipulate [features of their current teaching practice] to reduce a surface approach and to foster a deep approach" (Ho, 2000, p. 39).

With regard to these elements, Ho recognised that in the practice of such a conceptual change programme they "will be to a large extent intertwined" (p. 35). Therefore, the list above does not give a fixed sequence of implementation, but should be interpreted as a listing of essential ingredients, the measure of each to be determined by the logic of the moment and as appropriate to the situation. In addition, Ho stressed that the programme as implemented was based on the collaborative inquiry of participants, "Through sharing of ideas and collaborative problem solving, it was hoped that participants could further consolidate the changes that they proposed to carry out" (Ho, 2000, p. 40).

In 2001, Ho et al. reported a comprehensive evaluation of the effectiveness of this conceptual change programme to staff development. The three levels of programme impact that were evaluated were the impact on 1) teachers' conception of teaching (or the change therein), 2) students' perceptions of teachers' teaching practice, and 3) students' reported approaches to learning . The first effect was measured with three interviews for immediate and long term effects, the other effects were measured using pre- and post-questionnaires and comparing cohorts. In addition the evaluation design included a control group of teachers who had registered for the course, but had not participated, and their students. Of the twelve participating teachers, three came to the programme with relatively sophisticated conceptions of teaching. As such these teachers were not exemplary of the target clients of the staff development programme and therefore these teachers were excluded from 'the effective sample' (Ho et al., 2001, p. 156). Using the dimensions and scoring procedures that borrowed heavily from Samuelowicz and Bain (1992, see chapter 5), a panel of educational professionals allocated the nine teachers to three 'change groups'

- the 'Yes' change group (n=2): changes in teachers' conceptions of teaching were considered significant enough to expect changes in students' perceptions of teaching practices and in their reported approaches to learning;
- the 'Unsure' change group (n=4): the changes in teachers' conceptions of teaching were noticeable, but smaller than in the first group, so while changes in students' perceptions of teaching practice and approaches to learning were anticipated, they could not be guaranteed; and
- the 'No' change group (n=3): only minor or no changes in teaching conceptions were found, and so little to no changes were expected to occur in students' perceptions of teaching practice or in their learning approaches.

This categorisation led Ho et al. to conclude that in two-thirds of the participants conceptual change had occurred, "though the degree of improvement varied among the six changed subjects: two of them … demonstrated impressive changes, while the other four … showed moderate changes" (Ho et al., 2001, p. 156). For each 'change group' the results of changes in student perceptions and learning approaches were compared to the control group.

For the 'Yes' change group, the results showed a significant and extensive improvement of students' perceptions of their teaching, and that student learning in the post-programme courses was significantly improved, e.g. these teachers had become more able to induce deep learning and less likely to induce surface learning in their students after completing the programme.

In the 'Unsure' group the students' perceptions of teaching practice showed significant, but moderate improvement, but only one of the teachers in this group was found able to encourage in any significant way students' deep approaches to learning.

In the case of the 'No' change group indeed hardly any to no change at all was found in students' perceptions of teaching practice, and the same held for students' approaches to learning.

Overall, for all six teachers who experienced conceptual change, significant changes in perceived teaching practice were established, but only three of these teachers were able to influence students' approaches to learning in the desired direction. Based on these outcomes, Ho et al. concluded that such a short conceptual-change oriented programme could be considered a promising alternative to existing staff development approaches. Not only this, but they also concluded that changing conceptions of teaching is a prerequisite to changing teaching practice. However, they also noted that there remains some uncertainty about the causal direction between changes in conceptions and changes in practice, emphasising that in fact these effects might (also) be in the opposite direction,

> … the literature lacks empirical evidence that *development* in conceptions of teaching will accordingly and promptly bring about improvement in teaching practice. The issue of *transition* between a change in conceptions of teaching to a change in teaching practices has not been studied in a systematic way previously … Contemporary research only informs us of the static relationship between existing conceptions and teaching practice, but lacks findings relating to the dynamics of the way changes in teaching conceptions are transferred to changes in teaching practices and at what rate. (Ho et al., 2001, p. 164–165)

We would like to add here, that while from an objectivist point of view the causal direction could prove to be interesting, from an epistemological ecology standpoint the point becomes more or less irrelevant, by definition any substantial change will ultimately lead to a new balance regardless of its origin in the system. The question about speed of change on the other hand is relevant whatever standpoint is taken.

A more fundamental issue, namely whether there is any causal relationship at all between teachers' teaching conceptions and their teaching practice was the focus of a study by Eley (2006). Eley criticised firstly the assumption underlying Ho et al. (2001) that higher education teachers' teaching practice was consciously formed by their beliefs about and conceptions of teaching, and secondly, he criticised the assumption that to change teaching practice one must change these fundamental beliefs and conceptions first. In his attempt to answer the question 'what sort of concept is a teaching conception?', Eley reviewed a number of studies showing relationships between teachers' conceptions of teaching and teachers' approaches to teaching (see e.g. chapter 5). In his opinion while these studies might indicate that it could be the case that conceptions of teaching are evoked when teachers make decisions while e.g. planning specific teaching activities – and consequently that these conceptions play a direct and functional role in actual teaching practice – he posed the question, 'but might it be less than that?'. Eley felt that what had actually been demonstrated in all these studies was

> ... a relationship between verbal responses to two classes of general, open questions. It is not a relationship between conscious, articulated conceptions that might reside as cognitive tools in the minds of teachers, and detailed day-to-day teacher planning and actions. We presently do not have evidence that conceptions of teaching constitute a direct functional influence on specific teaching actions. It still remains that conceptions of teaching might be outcomes from *post hoc* reflections on experiences, *and only that.* (Eley, 2006, p. 194, final italics ours)

In his own research Eley tried to establish whether conceptions of teaching indeed are used as a *conscious tool for decision making* in planning what to do in a specific upcoming teaching episode. The assumption underlying his research design was that,

> If ... conceptions of teaching are actual functional influences on the detail of teaching decisions, then one might expect observable vestiges of such influences in these teachers' recollections. On the other hand, if conceptions of teaching are instead outcomes in an independent class of activities, that being reflection on past experiences, such vestiges need not be observed at all. (2006, p. 195)

Hereby assuming that all tertiary teachers are *consciously aware* of the theory of teaching conceptions and use it as a tool in their daily practice. In a way this is much like assuming that acrobats are physiologists and know Newtonian physics and *must* always use this knowledge *consciously* to perform well.

Eley interviewed 29 teachers of first and second year undergraduate university courses in a variety of disciplines. In these interviews the teachers were asked to recall and describe "how they prepared what they eventually did in a recent class" (2006, p. 196). The teaching and learning issues considered during planning and subsequent teaching as expressed in the interviews led to the development of six categories used to characterise the teachers' planning and teaching.

- Sensitivity to existing student knowledge

  Do teachers say that they take into account e.g. students' background or pre-existing knowledge in (the planning of) teaching?

- Prompting student engagement

  "[Does] the teacher deliberately or consciously prompt student active engagement in some manner?" (2006, p. 199)

- Awareness of student thinking during teaching

  Do teachers intentionally consider "the cognitive reactions that the students might be experiencing in response to the teaching episode?" (p. 199)

- Student thinking as a basis for planning

  Do teachers make references to "expected student thinking or mental processing peculiar to the teaching topic" in the planning of a teaching episode? (p. 200)

- Introspection as source of models of student thinking

  Do teachers "explicitly introspect on [their] *own* thinking ... as a basis for intuiting likely student thinking?" (p. 200)

- *Explicit use of teaching conceptions in decision making*

  Do teachers mention anything "that would indicate that general, 'theory-like' conceptions of learning or teaching were consciously and deliberately evoked" (p. 201) either in preparation of, or during a teaching episode.

  As we feel that this category is the central issue in his study, we include one example as illustration.

  My general philosophy is that it is more effective to concentrate on a small area and explain it well, and show the logic behind that area, in depth. ... ... so I pick an example that I think is quite instructive, concentrate on it, and really focus in on what's going on. (Eley, 2006, p. 201)

The teachers' teaching was characterised by the presence of these activities or lack thereof, using the ratings 'clearly present', 'apparently present', 'not evident', and – in the case of the latter category – also 'present as post hoc reflection'. This rating thus did not include an indication regarding *the quality* of the scored issue (or activity). The results showed that the events described by the first four categories, and to a somewhat lesser extent also those described by the fifth category, were very much part of the teachers' planning and teaching practices. However, the events that would be described by the sixth category were mentioned only occasionally in the interview protocols.

> Both raters agreed that 18 of the teachers gave no indication at all that anything interpretable as a conception of teaching had been *consciously* used in the planning thinking. A further six teachers were identified as possibly indicating such conceptions, but both raters agreed that none had described these conceptions as being part of their planning processes. Only five of the 29 teachers in the sample indicated that some sort of articulated conception of teaching might have been an explicit component in planning decisions. ... the findings here do not support such conceptions being *consciously* evoked as a necessary reference point or guide in making detailed planning decisions related to any specific teaching episode. (Eley, 2006, p. 204, italics ours)

So, if teachers' conceptions of teaching were not functionally involved in the detail of teacher thinking and practice, as Eley stated as the result of his study, what then was the role of such conceptions? Eley felt that conceptions of teaching might better be interpreted as

> outcomes from teachers' reflective activities. From time to time teachers might simply think back over recent and specific teaching experiences, consider how effective the practices might have been, or what outcomes might have been observed, and maybe speculate on how things might be varied in some future context .... Occasionally teachers might recognise 'customary patterns' in their teaching. Sometimes, perhaps in response to collegial conversations, such recognised patterns might be articulated in the form of an internally consistent general view. ... [here,] conceptions of teaching are seen as entities that can exist independently of detailed planning and teaching activities. (Eley, 2006, p. 209–210)

In this conclusion we read Eley's acknowledgment that there may be teachers that come to theory formation about their own teaching, but that many do not. On the basis of most of the research presented in the current study we cannot but agree. That teachers indeed very often are not actively aware of their thinking regarding teaching and learning is very eloquently put by Mr. Grant, one of the teachers of the Hotelschool who participated in a staff development course aimed at increasing awareness of implicit theories/views on teaching and learning. For Grant, only after direct confrontation while writing a required essay regarding his views on learning and teaching, he realised,

> The more I think about [teaching and learning] and write this paper, the more I realise how little I know about the subject... or rather, the more I realise how much there is for me to learn about it! (Mr. Grant, support subject teacher, see chapter 9)

The whole issue underpinning our current study is the fact that many teachers and students approach teaching and learning as something self-evident, and not as something one needs or even could seriously reflect upon. The second issue presented here, seeing things that work, and opposing those to things that don't, is not the same as theory formation. According to Wolpert knowing what works and what does not is the essence of technology. However, knowing why something works in a certain way and not in another is the essence of science (Wolpert, 1994). To understand *why* something works for one teacher or group of students, and *not* for another must clearly involve theory development, either by the teachers themselves or by educational researchers.

So then, what is the essence of our theory development about teaching? In almost all of our review and research until now, we have assumed that in the way people look at learning and teaching, one can find a certain pattern. A pattern which we, and many others discussed above, have developed a theoretical framework upon. Such a theoretical framework therefore is something that is put onto the reality we observe, much like a sketch on tracing paper that lies on top of the picture of reality. Such a sketch has two main characteristics, 1) it reduces the amount of detail as all models do, and 2) it is not really a part of reality and therefore anything in reality is not necessarily aware of this model's existence. Anything within the picture we have traced over in forming our model, functions anyway regardless of our model. Much like a bird is able to fly and soar without knowledge of the theory of aerodynamics. Or to use a more human example, the issue of speech. One does not need to know the theory of a language syntax or semantics consciously to be able to speak and communicate. It is somewhat the same with learning and teaching conceptions, with orders of consciousness and ways of knowing. Teachers and students would surely function in the way they do even without our theoretical model. These teachers and students have perfectly functioning (implicit) models of teaching and learning in their heads already, commonly based on their own educational experiences and they use these, usually without engaging in much reflection, to form their approaches to teaching and learning. As such, Kegan (1994) would say these teachers and students are 'had by their models', they *do not* have them. And as Kegan would expect, these teachers (and students) *cannot* and therefore *do not* consciously discuss or refer to these unconsidered internal models. So far there need not be any problem for the teachers and students, but perhaps there might be considerable problems for Eley's interpretation of his study.

The issue of the functional role of teaching conceptions only then becomes a problem for teachers (and students) when they are confronted with educational innovations that are based on models *different from their own.* And in particular this proves a problem if these innovations are based on *more* sophisticated views on knowledge and knowing. Then we may need theory to increase teachers' (and students') awareness of their (limited) implicit models and the discrepancies between these implicit models and those underlying the innovation. The function of models such as our own (or the other models described in chapters 3 through 5) is to make reflection on what you are doing possible. As such our study is a typical example of explaining a seemingly natural phenomenon (i.e. learning and teaching as self-evident) using an 'unnatural' phenomenon (see Wolpert, 1994), i.e. a considered theory of the different ways in which teachers and students see learning and teaching.

Finally, looking at the task used to tap into any (implicit or explicit) theory with regard to teaching or learning, one might wonder whether this type of task is the most appropriate one for teachers to evoke their conceptions of teaching. In recalling and describing how one prepared for a recent teaching episode, a teacher could start by explaining the situation in clear terms, so framing the thoughts towards the observable and concrete and away from the implicit and hidden. The interviewers took great care not to introduce any prompts towards 'a broader reflective discussion'. Teachers are more than capable to pick up this cue and perform accordingly.

Coming back to Eley's study, his suggestions for staff development based on the results are most interesting. Stating clearly at the outset, approaches such as Ho's conceptual change programme are not ones Eley would prefer. In his opinion a more skill-oriented approach would be more appropriate. Staff development should focus more on teaching teachers best practices for various teaching situations.

> If we want a teacher to behave in specific, more 'student oriented' ways in a particular context, then we need to arrange for that teacher to practise those specific ways in that particular context. (p. 211)

This approach seems a return to the traditional approach to staff development and assumes that teaching expertise or being an excellent teacher means that teachers have mastered and have available a rich repertoire of context-specific teaching practices or skills which "enable proficient, rapid and adaptive responses to a wide variety of teaching situations (p. 212) ... [and that] If we concentrate on developing rich repertoires of teaching practices, maybe conceptions of teaching are entities that then follow, and thus more sensibly serve as possible indicators of the existence of those repertoires" (p. 213). We find the proposal to use rather 'elusive' things as teaching conceptions as indicators for rather obvious things such as a range of observable (changed) teaching practices, somewhat odd – to say the least – and his suggestion therefore a rather construed way to keep the theoretical concepts (e.g. teaching conceptions) in the picture.

Perhaps a better example of a **skills modification approach** to staff development, without bothering with such elusive things as teaching conceptions, would be a study which the second author of the current study was involved in. In this study (Hamer, 2010), eight schools participated in offering a teacher training course to all the science and math teachers of one ninth grade class (see Appendix, 3 havo). The teacher training focused on training teachers in observable teaching behaviours such as giving positive feedback, making connections between subject matter and everyday life or professional practice, organising group work, explaining well, etcetera. Each teacher chose three behaviours to work on out of a list of ten. Teachers then participated in 4 or 5 afternoon sessions in collaborative discussion of and training in their own chosen behaviours. The training did not address teacher beliefs at all in any way. Pupils were included in the design in various ways. Firstly, all pupils were informed at the start that their teachers were going to participate in this training in order to improve their teaching and increase the quality and enjoyment for the pupils. Secondly, in each school the teacher trainer included pupils in the training scheme, either by asking pupils (ages 14 to 16) to volunteer for one or more training sessions with the teachers, or to act as pupil-pal ('leerlingmaatje' in Dutch) for one of their own teachers. Effects were mostly measured qualitatively, but the study included a before and after inventory measurement of pupils' perception of teaching practices regarding the behaviours included in the training. Positive feedback and connecting school science and math to everyday life/professional practice were chosen most often by teachers as behaviours to work on. Pupils responded with increased self-confidence and an increase in the choice for a science profile (see Appendix). As an unexpected by-product the qualitative evaluation showed that teachers were very pleasantly surprised that these teenagers – often perceived as lazy and uninterested in science and math – could become so involved and committed to a training of their teachers that they would actually give up free afternoons, while other pupils were happy to discuss teaching practice with their teachers constructively and at length. Pupils on the other hand, remarked that they came to see their teachers as real people who actually cared about how their pupils experienced their classes enhancing their appreciation as well as their self-confidence in their science performance. This study did not focus on, nor assess changes in pupils' learning strategies or learning outcome.

In Eley's opinion, Hativa (2002) supported his rather radical reversal of current views on staff development towards the traditional. As Eley described, in Hativa's study two law professors received personal consultation to improve (some of) their problematic classroom behaviours in order to increase teaching effectiveness. Eley concluded that Hativa's study showed

> ...clear improvement on all the pre-treatment problem behaviours targeted by the interventions. But interestingly, the results also showed sympathetic shifts in expressed beliefs and attitudes that aligned with those treated behaviours, even though the strong emphasis in the interventions had clearly been on practising modifications to specific teaching behaviours. (Eley, 2006, p. 212)

However, the question is whether Hativa herself would agree with this interpretation of her study. In her own description of the intervention study (Hativa, 2002) and in another contribution with Goodyear in the same book (Hativa and Goodyear, 2002) she repeatedly emphasised her preference for a more comprehensive approach to staff development, stronger even, she felt "that the focus must be on conceptions and approaches, rather than 'mere' behaviours" (Hativa and Goodyear, 2002, p. 357). In this particular study (Hativa, 2002), she used personal consultation to address three obstacles to good teaching, 1) teacher characteristics and aptitudes, 2) pedagogical knowledge and 3) *teacher thinking, perceptions and beliefs about instruction and students*. In the description of the consultation, she seemed to have focused especially on factors 1 and 3 (2002, p. 311). Hativa stated very clearly that while "most instructional development programs solely address the promotion of pedagogical knowledge by enhancing knowledge of teaching techniques, [a body of] literature suggests that unless all other factors in the three categories [listed] are addressed, efforts to improve instruction are doomed to fail" (Hativa, 2002, p. 293). This seems to us in direct contradiction to Eley's interpretation of her research and her position on staff development. Furthermore, Eley seems to take a idiosyncratic position in the body of research in the field because as Hativa and Goodyear concluded,

> All the authors[1] agree that instructional development programs should address not only mastering teaching skills and techniques but also deeper aspects that contribute to good teaching – such as beliefs about knowledge, learning and teaching. Without attention to these deeper issues, new teaching methods are almost certain to fail. (2002, p. 353)

Now we return to Biggs, who asked the question that seems to be central to much of the thinking about staff development, "Does enduring change in a teacher's approach to teaching come about by *thinking* differently about teaching, ... or by *acting* differently...?" (2003, p. 255). There are champions for both approaches, with Guskey (1986) and Eley (2006) as advocates for the 'behaviour-first' approach – which seems to hinge on the reduction of cognitive dissonance, and a host of researchers mentioned above in an note (and throughout our review in this book) as advocates for the 'beliefs-adjustment-necessary' approach. And Devlin can be seen as taking an intermediate critical position towards the main stream 'beliefs-adjustment-necessary' approach (Devlin, 2006). Like Hativa, Biggs came to the conclusion that to improve teachers' teaching practice, it works both ways (Biggs, 2003, p. 256).

> How do you get people to stop smoking? Do you try to persuade them that smoking is not a good idea? Or do you hang 'No Smoking' signs everywhere? So, how do you get teachers to teach better? By convincing them that [more sophisticated] theories are better than [more traditional] theories of teaching? Or by making them members of a [Problem-Based Learning] team, thus requiring them to teach in a different way. You do both. (Biggs, 2003, p. 259–260)

And here we are again, the complex real world increasingly consists not of either/or answers, but both/and answers. In our view the issue is actually not both/and, but all-three/and/and: you need to learn the *skills* to implement a particular *practice* or technique, but you need the right type of *conceptions* about teaching and learning to pull it off.

Furthermore, agreeing with Biggs as well as Palmer, for staff development to be effective, it requires good leadership.

> Quality enhancement of teaching is a collective responsibility that goes beyond the individual. Both believing and practising a [more sophisticated] approach to teaching is easier where colleagues also believe and teach in that way, and where the [teaching] environment supports [sophisticated] teaching and rewards good teachers for being innovative and reflective. Everybody is in this together…. (Biggs, 2003, p. 260)

Finally, in closing this study into student and teacher thinking, we feel that the approach of addressing multiple aspects of teaching in order to attain durable change is consistent with our epistemological ecology concept. In biology as well as in education, ecologies are notoriously resistant to change, with a dynamic returning to much the same balance after small, limited or short-term disturbances. To perturb an ecology sufficiently to cause a considerable change of structure—a new balance, a higher order of consciousness, in short an expanded awareness—it is necessary to put pressure on as many aspects of the current ecology for as long as possible, while providing a supportive (holding) environment conducive of change in the desired direction.

Conclusions

As we have established before in chapters 5 and 9, epistemologically more sophisticated teachers are better able to tailor their teaching towards epistemological development. If the aim of higher education is to encourage epistemological development to at least level 4 thinking, then the logical question is, 'What level of epistemological sophistication would prove sufficient to teach in higher education?' and 'What would teaching from these ways of knowing look like in higher education?' Which teachers are capable of creating the series of stepping stones (holding environments) that will encourage all students to proceed along the daunting road of epistemological development?

In the chapters 7 through 9 we have seen that to promote development towards learning-teaching conception 3, it is sufficient that all teachers function at least at this level of epistemological sophistication. Therefore, for higher education to attain its espoused goals – teaching students to think for themselves – it would seem sufficient to ensure that all teachers are capable of fourth order of consciousness thinking. However if an institute aims toward excellence, it would seem necessary for teachers to employ an even more sophisticated way of knowing and teaching so that they can build the series of bridges perhaps beyond self-authorship or learning-teaching conception 4. In this chapter we discussed two approaches to learning and teaching that are clearly epistemologically more sophisticated than self-authorship, level 4 thinking: the sixth learning-teaching conception leading to 'authentic teaching from the paradox', and a possible seventh learning-teaching conception resulting in 'teaching from the microcosm' in a community of truth.

As we have described before (chapters 1 and 3), the sixth learning-teaching conception is characterised by growing awareness of the role of the self in knowing, in creating knowledge and in learning. A second aspect was the focus on the authentic self of the teacher and that instruction methods or techniques became unimportant and uninteresting. In the sixth order of consciousness one learns from another authentic person, who cares for the students as much as for his or her area of expertise. Such teachers infuse their identity in their teaching, *they teach who they are* (Palmer, 1998). Central in the sixth order of consciousness is the ability not only to hold two opposites in mind (level 5 thinking, Relativism, see chapter 3 in the section on Kegan), but to embrace these opposites because they both contain essential elements of the world. In Palmer's words, "Paradox is not only an abstract way of knowing. It is a lens through which we can learn more about the selfhood from which good teaching comes" (1998, p. 66). Authentic teaching from the paradox is based on at least 6 paradoxical tensions (see before). This list of paradoxes show great overlap with the type of teaching Baxter Magolda would call a Learning Partnership (2004) and it would seem that authentic teaching from paradox is essentially fully student-centred.

In Hamer and van Rossum (2008) we described in more depth the characteristics of a possible seventh learning-teaching conception. Central to this way of knowing was the focus on not only knowing the self, but also embracing the other or otherness without reservation and recognising that knowing the other enriches the self. Knowing within this way of knowing can only exist in a community because, "reality is a web of communal relationships, and we can know really only by being in community with it" (Palmer, 1998, p. 95). When teaching necessarily is undertaken as a community of truth, then hospitality in learning is essential and teacher (the host) and learners examine issues of knowing and truth together: a community of truth is *subject centred.* Teaching in a community of truth means focusing on the "great things" of learning or disciplines. In gathering around "the great things" and co-creating knowledge and understanding of these great things, covering large amounts of content is impossible and unnecessary. In a community of truth you can *teach more with less*: this is to teach from the microcosm. However, you can only teach more with less, if you know exactly what things to select as subject in the community of truth. You need to know what things constitute the critical, crucial aspects of a discipline: the so called great things of a discipline. Through these *great things* and the *avenues of inquiry* employed in the community of truth, one can then actively reconstruct the discipline itself together. In this description we recognise Entwistle's Teaching for Understanding approach (2007), where the great things are important, focal disciplinary issues or concepts (generative topics) and the avenues of inquiry are the throughlines. In teaching from the microcosm again, as with teaching from paradox, the method of instruction is irrelevant, but teachers need specific skills to create a community of truth. These skills are very similar to the skills necessary to perform a good phenomenographic interview and include the famous bracketing skills. To create a community of truth and to teach from the microcosm, teachers need to be very knowledgeable of their field of study, but must be able to create an open learning space and not fill it with their own knowledge. They need to bracket their knowledge, without falling into the trap of constructing a "know-nothing" situation. In short they need to mentor, but not lead; to ask, but not prime; to tell, but not lecture and to listen empathically as students discover the core of the discipline and of learning itself.

In chapter 5 (and 9) we have seen that many teachers in higher education do not (yet) function at a level of epistemological sophistication sufficient to empower their students to attain learning-teaching conception 4 thinking, let alone beyond. What are viable routes towards educating our educators? In this chapter we have introduced eight (or perhaps nine) approaches to staff development, all of which can be used to promote teachers' epistemological development to level 4 thinking or beyond:

1. a "good talk about good teaching" (Palmer, 1998) induced either by
   a. exploring personal metaphors in teaching (Palmer, 1998; see chapter 5 e.g. Yero, 2002; Martinez et al., 2001) or
   b. a community of truth around critical moments in teaching (Palmer, 1998);
2. constructive alignment (Biggs, 2003);
3. reflective practice (Biggs, 2003) or concern-driven pedagogy (Vermunt, 2006);
4. action research (e.g. Kember, 1991);
5. a combined action research approach, (Gordon and Debus, 2002);
6. narrative inquiry (Lyons and LaBoskey, 2002a);
7. conceptual change approach (Ho, 2000, 2001), and
8. skills modification approach (Eley, 2006; Hamer, 2010).

A **good talk about good teaching** can be framed as a dialogue or as a community of truth where colleagues observe each other, talk about teaching, asking real questions and giving real answers, addressing topics that take teachers "beyond technique and into the fundamental issues of teaching" (Palmer, 1998, p. 144). Palmer suggests two avenues of inquiry to reach a good talk about good teaching: the exploration of personal metaphors of teaching and a workshop examining critical moments in teaching.

Exploring personal metaphors as a window onto personal views on teaching and learning was already introduced in chapter 5 (Yero, 2002). As Yero stressed in that chapter, Palmer stresses here that in exploring personal metaphors it is not so much focusing on the metaphor itself, but on the meaning given to the metaphor—on the personal story underlying the metaphor. It is a way to unlock the mythos aspect of teaching and knowing. In exploring the metaphor, a teacher can examine his or her underlying assumptions about teaching, learning, their expectations of students and views on their own role in teaching and learning. It is more than possible that a teacher uses the same metaphor over the years, but attributes distinctly different meanings to it over time that tell about the epistemological development the teacher has experienced. It is not the metaphor that is important, but the metaphor-as-meant (see chapter 5). A colleague or mentor may take on the role of critical friend, mirroring what is uncovered in the inquiry process and opening new areas of inquiry. In Palmer's experience, a metaphor need not only be used for staff development, it can when examined to explore the underlying meaning, give teachers heart to continue to develop and enjoy their craft.

Discussing **critical moments in teaching** is an approach often used by Palmer in workshops aimed at encouraging a 'good talk about good teaching'. In such a workshop teachers discuss the timeline of a course and name critical moments within a class or course where a learning fork exists: an opportunity for students to open up to learning or to shut down. Such critical moments include for instance the first graded test revealing low subject understanding, or an unexpected opportunity to address something not planned but relevant to the course discipline and of immediate interest to students (Martens, 1992, see chapter 5). All teachers have experienced these moments, either by realising they missed an opportunity to open students up, or by experiencing a renewed student energy when such opportunities are taken advantage of. The next step in such a workshop might be to cluster related critical moments and the formation of smaller groups interested in the inquiry of this type of critical moment. In the discussion that can follow, the workshop mediator must employ all the skills of the teacher in a community of truth as listed above. The discussion must not evolve into a critique of each other's pedagogy, but should evolve into an open and truthful exchange of personal experience in an empathic atmosphere. It requires leadership to keep the inquiry into these critical moments on the track of a community of learners, while the mediator must have the ability to create a learning space without filling it himself.

In teaching from **constructive alignment** the issue is to ensure that all aspects of the teaching-learning process are aligned and support the development of a constructivist approach to learning. As Biggs (2003) describes, constructive alignment refers to the alignment of objectives, learning and teaching activities and assessment practices. So if "the aim is to apply biology to solving biological problems (objective), then solving biological problems is the main teaching and learning activity ... and the assessment is seeing how well they have been solved" (Biggs, 2003, p. 232).

The approach seems almost to logical to require in detail discussion, but it seems it is necessary to explicate all decisive moments in the process of designing a constructively aligned class, course or curriculum, because only all too often in particular assessment practices send a diametrically opposed message to the students, who are only too able to respond to this unexamined cue. Constuctive alignment focuses not only on *what* the student must know, but also on what kind of understanding is expected (*how* the student knows) and what kind of *activities* will support this kind of knowing as well as what type of *assessment* is appropriate to monitor and evaluate the *how* of knowing as well as the *what*.

It is possible to use constructive alignment for introductory courses as well as advanced courses or, as suggested now, for staff development. The method says nothing about what is being aligned nor about the level of thinking that is necessarily the outcome of the aligned course. To implement this methodology in a variety of situations resulting in a variety of learning outcomes, it only requires to define an appropriate hierarchy of performances of understanding and going through the other steps with equal reflection and attention to the aims of a course or curriculum. In traditional education, the aims of the curriculum are often *not consistently* applied to the teaching-learning activities nor to assessment practices, conveying a message about learning and knowing undermining the espoused aims. Constructive alignment aims to address this by explicitly examining all aspects of the course or curriculum in order to form a united, and inescapable learning experience. As with all more constructivist educational innovations, constructive alignment is vulnerable, not only to the epistemological sophistication of the teacher implementing it, but also to the institutional assessment policy and organisational environment. It flourishes best where institute and colleagues are convinced of the efficacy of the approach and committed to implementing it in full.

Reflective practice or concern-driven pedagogy is an approach to staff development where teachers themselves identify an issue in student behaviour that is undesirable, and reflect on whether there is something in their own teaching practice that may contribute to the expression of this behaviour. Identification of the possible contributing teaching practice offers pointers towards change. Again a colleague or teaching developer could assist the teacher in identifying the aspect of the teaching practice that may need amending, not by offering solutions or personal experience, but by mirroring the teacher's own inquiry. This first step of course implies the formulation of the desired change in student behaviour, perhaps even in a hierarchy of desired performances. The second step of reflective practice is implementing a possible change in teaching practice. In the third step, the effects of this change need to be carefully monitored, and a teacher would need to think about how to monitor (or assess) the change in student behaviour *before* implementation, as the teacher is required to do in implementing constructive alignment. The outcomes of the monitoring in turn will most probably lead to further refinements (the fourth step), each of which again ideally should run through the first three steps: identification of the problem and hypothesising possible changes in teaching practice, implementing these changes, and careful monitoring. Adverse outcomes lead to reconsideration of the initial hypothesis, to a new path of inquiry and new adjustment of the teaching practice. Too small changes in the desired direction are reason to seek options to reinforce the change. Of course to be successful a teacher must feel free to be truthful about unexamined assumptions in his or her teaching practice and to experiment without fear of repercussions. This means reflective practice must take place in confidence and the process nor the outcomes may be used in any sense for institutional evaluation purposes.

Where in reflective practice, reflection leads to changes in practice, in **action research** the road can be reverse, with changes in practice leading to reflection on what constitutes better teaching and learning in both teachers and students. Action research often rests on a collaboration between teaching staff, teaching developers and students with the aim of improving the quality of teaching. Teachers (as experts), teaching developers (as critical friends) and students are all involved in implementing new forms of teaching. Students are asked to participate in the changed teaching practice. Many action research projects are small, but often have relatively large results, Teachers are often surprised by the willingness of students to try something new and the students' excited reactions. Consciously using action research as a staff development tool is not common, and usually no measurements of changes in teaching conceptions are included. However, there are indications that, at least occasionally, teachers changed their perceptions of students and of a good teaching practice, which in turn led to changes in their views on teaching. Gibbs (1998) proposed action research as a possible alternative and perhaps roundabout way to staff development: reflecting on and changing perceived student learning and teaching practice is much less threatening to teachers than reflecting on their own implicit views on learning and teaching. By having teachers' collaboration in implementing clearly new teaching and learning activities in order to improve student learning, these teachers see that students are different, more involved in learning, than they thought. It may open teachers up to the awareness of different perceptions of and views on learning and teaching, making it easier for them to contemplate changing their own perception of students and of good teaching. The guidance of teacher developers is essential to overcome the problems that epistemologically less sophisticated teachers may have in fully understanding and implementing teaching activities aimed at improving the quality of student learning (usually towards deep level learning).

Gordon and Debus (2002) present an approach to staff development as a **combination** of reflective practice, constructive alignment and action research for which we suggest the name **reflective-practice action research**. Here, as in reflective practice, the teachers are actively involved in researching and designing a new teaching practice. However, contrary to the usual practice in action research, students are consciously and explicitly included in the research design by not only informing them of the changed practices, but also informing them of the intent of the changed teaching practices (Hamer, 2010). In Gordon and Debus' 2002 study the idea of involving students was that it would reinforce the effect of the teaching practices alone. The programme was designed making use of constructive alignment, to ensure that all aspects were logically consistent and transmitting the same message to the students as was conveyed to them during the introduction of the study. In action research it is not uncommon that interventions or changes in teaching practice evolve during the study. Such course corrections during the study are symptoms of the iterative cycle present in reflective practice and as in reflective practice it means that teachers and teaching developers work together throughout the cycle of changes necessary to reach the desired goal: high quality student learning.

The next approach to staff development discussed in this chapter is **narrative inquiry,** and it can be seen as another example of action research, namely **practitioner action research.** Narrative inquiry grew out of an attempt at an alternative approach to teacher assessment: teaching portfolios (Lyons and LaBoskey, 2002a). Building a portfolio proved to be a useful tool that supported (novice) teachers' reflection and inquiry into their own teaching practice. On the other hand, writing narratives – rounded stories that elucidated teachers' thoughts and their approach to issues they experienced as problematic to their own teaching – proved a mode of inquiry leading to epistemological development. Studying narratives enabled the study of teachers' individual meanings and interpretations. Like exploring personal metaphors, narratives seem to unlock the mythos aspect of epistemology and thus can provide insight into unexamined aspects of teachers' views on learning, knowing and teaching. Writing personal narratives increases teachers' knowledge of their teaching practice, it helps them reflect on and rethink their craft. This close and personal examination of one's own assumptions and prejudices may in turn lead to more consciously engaged changes in epistemology and actual teaching practices. Narrative inquiry can be collaborative, and in that way it may lead to something as 'a good talk about good teaching' (Lyons and LaBoskey, 2002b). It can also be undertaken more as a personal quest for clarity and growth (Akin, 2002).

The approaches to staff development discussed above, all include elements where practice and epistemology are confronted. In working towards a good talk about good teaching Palmer uses metaphors or a time line of a course to examine the interplay between teacher beliefs about learning and teaching and teaching practice. Biggs assumes that teachers and developers using constructive alignment are at least capable of thinking about teaching from a constructive standpoint, so from a particular epistemological level of sophistication. In constructive alignment beliefs are essential to the design of a constructive curriculum. In reflective practice, reflecting on teaching practice and resultant student behaviours are directly linked in an ongoing cycle of development and improvement. Action research is of course tightly linked with the issue of teaching practice, it is often through changes in teaching practice that teachers experience a change in their own views on good teaching and student learning. All approaches described above, if undertaken in collaboration with colleagues, not only promote epistemological growth towards a constructivist level that is necessary to lead out (educate) the students towards epistemological equality and the attainment of the goals of higher education, they encourage teachers to see themselves as part of a community of learners, exchanging important and relevant experiences, enriching their repertoire and craftsmanship.

The approaches above assume that examination of practice and beliefs both is essential. There are approaches that prefer to focus on changing either practice/skills or beliefs assuming that change in the one will result in change in the other. Ho (2000, Ho et al., 2001) is a representative of the latter school of thought. She designed a **conceptual change approach** to staff development that is designed to address, almost in isolation, the teaching conceptions of teaching staff. In a small number of relatively short sessions, Ho addressed the teachers' current espoused conceptions of teaching and the nature of current teaching practice. She then exposed teachers to alternative conceptions of good teaching and arranged a constructive confrontation between teachers' teaching conception and teaching practice, rounding the course off with building commitment towards a more sophisticated teaching conception. In Ho's experience such an approach can indeed lead to conceptual change regarding teachers' views on good teaching, leading to observable changes in their teaching practice. Although not all changes were equally large, for all teachers who experienced conceptual change, teaching practice changed as well.

An example of the advocates for a **skills modification approach** is Eley (2006). Eley based his argument on the finding that teachers do not consciously employ teaching conceptions when designing a lesson or course. However, contrary to what Eley thinks, this does not necessarily mean that teaching conceptions are irrelevant to teaching practice. Be that as it may, the question remains whether addressing skills only may indeed lead to changes in teacher beliefs. While Eley's study fails to make this clear, the second author of the current study was involved in a action research study in the Netherlands (Hamer, 2010) that seems to point towards the possibility that focusing only on improving didactic skills can indeed change at the very least pupils' and teachers' perception of each other in a positive way.

NOTES

1 Among these authors are such well known and respected educational researchers as Noel Entwistle, David Kember, Elaine Martin, Ference Marton, Michael Prosser, Paul Ramsden and Keith Trigwell to name but a few.

CHAPTER 12

EPILOGUE

We might ... begin listening to ... questions. Out of the questions... come some of the most creative ideas and discoveries ...

How can we know if we do not ask? Why should we ask if we are certain we know? All answers come out of the question. If we pay attention to our questions, we increase the power of mindful learning.

(Langer, 1997)

Our Approach and Theory Development

Our work is best interpreted as developmental phenomenography (Bowden, 2000, see also chapter 2): our focus is less on elaborating the theoretical knowledge base with regard to the range of *ways of knowing*. Our primary outlook is more pragmatic and practical: e.g. by putting our theoretical model (chapter 1) to use in designing a more activating curriculum (see chapter 6) in order to improve the quality of student learning in higher education (chapters 7 and 8). By establishing that the model based on student thinking is equally applicable to teacher thinking (chapters 5 and 9), it is possible to shed light on how teachers can be better prepared to implement constructivist or activating teaching in higher education (chapters 10 and 11). Furthermore, outside the educational arena, we have experienced that our model can shed new light on instances where communication breaks down although objectively all parties are talking the same language. For us the development captured partially in our model is "real" in a very practical sense, and we hope to have made a convincing and compelling argument that

1. phenomenography, as a qualitative, scientific approach, leads to a valid description of ways of knowing, perhaps better referred to as orders of consciousness (Kegan, 1994) because then the focus on the cognitive is de-emphasised and the affective is given its proper place, which is more in keeping with the complex nature of these ways of knowing (Hazel et al., 1997);
2. our learning-teaching conception model is only one window (of many originating outside phenomenography) onto a general and more fundamental development in human thinking; and
3. this more general intellectual development in human thinking is of broad interest because of its implications for the quality of (higher) education, but particularly for the functioning of democratic society.

In our opinion the current study includes more than sufficient evidence that our learning-teaching conception model describes an intellectual development where each new way of knowing is a more complex way of making sense of reality (chapters 1, 3, 4 and 5). Furthermore, the stages are hierarchically inclusive, meaning that anyone functioning at a more complex way of knowing has access to all strategies, views and behaviours characteristic of earlier stages. From our data collected since the nineteen-eighties (approx. 650 respondents including teachers) we conclude that not all students or teachers develop at the same speed, nor do all students or teachers complete all six stages. From various studies discussed here one can even conclude that a considerable proportion of the general population remains entrenched in reproductive or traditional ways of knowing and thus is not well equipped to function in a complex society.

As we have seen in chapter 1, the distribution of ways of knowing forms a somewhat squat pyramid. This finding is confirmed in various studies for the student population (e.g. Baxter Magolda, 1992; Radloff, 2002; Marra et al., 2000), but also for the general population of Western societies (e.g. Kuhn, 1991; Kegan, 1994). Based on these findings we expect that the pyramid is particularly plump at the base, with approximately 75% of the mass forming a reproductive base of levels 1 through 3. Research shows that even the least sophisticated ways of knowing, absolutism and dualism, can persist into advanced adulthood (e.g. Kuhn, 1991; Weinstock and Cronin, 2003). Even after higher education, a large proportion of graduates may still perform in a level-three-thinker way (e.g. chapter 1 and 7; Baxter Magolda, 1992; Radloff, 2002). The next layer of the pyramid is much smaller, with about 20% of the mass representing learning-teaching conception 4, or the proportion of the populace competent in scientific thought (e.g. Kuhn and Weinstock, 2002; Richardson, 2007 in press). The two highest learning-teaching conceptions found seem to be very rare (see chapter 1 and e.g. Kegan in Debold, 2002), forming a short tapering antenna, with only less than 4% representing level 5 thinking and only slightly more than 1% representing learning-teaching conception 6 (e.g. Kuhn and Weinstock, 2002; Weinstock and Cronin, 2003). The distribution of ways of knowing for the proportion of the population that has participated in higher education may be slightly less squat (e.g. Perry, 1970): occasional evidence shows that about half of higher education graduates may reach level four thinking or higher eventually (e.g. Kuhn, 1991; Kegan, 1994; Pavelich and Moore, 1996; Wise et al., 2004), while the first conception seems to be very rare (e.g. Belenky et al., 1997; Perry, 1970). However, even in this subpopulation learning-teaching conception 6 seems to be extremely rare, although one might expect it to be more common in samples including a greater proportion of adult, mature or even elderly respondents (e.g. Marton et al., 1993; Tornstam, 2005). Indeed, in Baxter Magolda's ongoing longitudinal study the occurrence of very complex ways of knowing in her participant group increases (Baxter Magolda, 2009).

Developmental phenomenography – as we have applied it in the current study: using our model to design curricula or teacher training with the aim of improving teaching and learning – is also an example of the practical use of phenomenography as an evaluation tool. In this we follow Micari et al. (2007) who stated that

> Phenomenography is appropriate when evaluators seek to move beyond measuring performance to measuring *development* in understanding or conception: *how* people think…. (p. 472, italics ours) …
>
> … the phenomenographic approach is not a substitute for basic assessment of learner performance. Educators can hardly be expected to do their jobs without some indication of *what* learners know. Rather, the phenomenographic approach offers insights that would remain hidden if only traditional assessment methods were used—it helps educators understand not just *what* their learners know but also *how* they know it …..
>
> Traditional measures of learner performance can provide critical information about the content of learners' knowledge. … To be truly accountable for high-quality education requires understanding how, and not just what, learners know. A program evaluation model that enables educators to assess how their interventions help change the way learners think, and not only what they know, will help move us closer to a system of education that produces individuals who are not simply learners but who also have the capacity to become excellent lifelong thinkers. (Micari et al., 2007, p. 474, italics ours)

In this, Micari et al. agree with us, that without phenomenographic measurement of (developments in students') epistemology, institutes of higher education lack an indispensable tool to assess whether they are attaining their goals. If the aim is to change student thinking, one should also assess the changes in student thinking that may or may not occur during their studies. Currently, most educational institutes assess performance or *what* people know, and not *how* they know. We propose that policy makers (i.e. government) and institutes use our study to acquaint themselves with the benefits of this additional evaluation approach to the improvement of the quality of higher education.

Above we have said that our model is real in a practical sense, but of course the reality of this model, as with all other theoretical models, is something other than actually constituting reality. The whole issue underpinning our current study is the fact that many teachers and students approach teaching and learning as something self-evident, and not as something one needs to examine. Our model or developmental theory of epistemology in learning and teaching is something more than a mere listing of things that seem to work, and things that don't seem to work. We have examined what students and teachers say about learning and teaching in order to provide a theory that helps to understand *why* something works for one teacher or group of students, and *not* for another. Such an attempt must clearly involve a scientific approach and theory development.

So then, what is the essence of our theory development about learning and teaching? In almost all research reviewed and presented here, we have found that in the way people look at learning and teaching, one can find a certain pattern. A pattern which we, and many others discussed above, have developed a theoretical framework upon. Such a theoretical framework therefore is something that is put onto the reality we observe. Above in chapter 11 we have likened it to a sketch on tracing paper that lies on top of the picture of reality. Such a sketch has two main characteristics, 1) it reduces the amount of detail as all models do, and 2) it is not really a part of reality and therefore anything in reality need not necessarily be aware of this model's existence. Anything within the picture we have traced over in forming our model, functions anyway regardless of our model. Much like a bird is able to fly and soar without knowledge of the theory of aerodynamics. Or to use a more human example, the issue of speech. One does not need to know the theory of a language syntax or semantics consciously to be able to speak and communicate. It is somewhat the same with learning and teaching conceptions, with orders of consciousness and ways of knowing. Teachers and students would surely function in the way they do even without our theoretical model. These teachers and students have perfectly functioning (implicit) models of teaching and learning in their heads already, commonly based on their own educational experiences and they use these, usually without engaging in much reflection, to form their approaches to teaching and learning. As such, Kegan (1994) would say these teachers and students are 'had by their models', they *do not* have them. And as Kegan would expect, these teachers (and students) *cannot* and therefore *do not* consciously discuss or refer to these unconsidered an unexamined internal models.

The issue of the functional role of learning and teaching conceptions only then becomes a problem for students and teachers when they are confronted with educational innovations that are based on models *different from their own*. And in particular this proves to be a problem when these innovations are based on *more* sophisticated views on knowledge and knowing. Then we may need theory to increase teachers' and students' awareness of their (limited) implicit models and the discrepancies between these implicit models and those underlying the innovations. The function of models such as our own (or the other models described in chapters 3 through 5) is to make reflection on what you are doing possible. As such our study is a typical example of explaining a seemingly natural phenomenon (i.e. learning and teaching as self-evident) using an 'unnatural' phenomenon (see Wolpert, 1994), i.e. a considered theory of the different ways in which teachers and students see learning and teaching.

The Research Questions

As announced in chapter 2, below we will discuss our research questions in general terms, referring back to the chapters for details.

Convergence of Outcomes

Based on chapters 3 through 5 we feel that our learning-teaching conception model gives a accurate approximation of how people think about learning and teaching and how their thinking develops. Not only that, it has captured at least one aspect of a more general intellectual development with far reaching consequences not only within the learning and teaching environment of higher education, but also for a good functioning of a complex democratic society. Furthermore, we feel that this general intellectual development is a naturally occurring one (Csikszentmihalyi, 1993), and one that is crucial to the proper functioning in a complex society including many groups, competing interests and value systems (Kegan, 1994). It might even be crucial to the survival of our planet (Csikszentmihalyi, 1993). It is a development that can be accelerated by formal (higher) education that focuses on systemic thinking, different perspectives or paradoxes. The development can sometimes be greatly accelerated by formal education (see Perry, 1970) or life's turns and twists. However, it can also be arrested for long periods of time in 'traditional cultures', e.g. strongly traditional education, focusing on lectures, memorisation and reproduction.

Through studying related epistemological models, we have come to the conclusion that the general intellectual development we feel is captured in our learning-teaching model, as in these other models, refers not to a development of *what* you know, but *the way* you know and *how* this influences the perception of reality. Furthermore this development runs through a stepwise increasing of complexity of thinking, where one regularly *revisits* familiar issues perceiving them from this increased level of complexity in *the way* one knows. In particular, the concept of orders of consciousness has led us to a deeper understanding of the qualitatively different ways of knowing underlying each learning-teaching conception, as well as understanding of possible dynamics of the development, namely the 'stepping out of embeddedness' and viewing that what was once subject as an object available for reflection (Kegan, 1994). Our understanding of the meaning and the structure of in particular the more rare conceptions (1 and 6) was greatly improved by the study of these various epistemological models (see chapters 3 and 4). Finally including two models from outside the educational context helped us to understand the everyday significance of these qualitatively different ways of knowing.

Epistemological Ecology

Our review of qualitative and quantitative approaches to student learning led us to the conclusion that the general intellectual development we refer to above takes place as a series of qualitatively different constellations of views on many, many different aspects of cognition and affect, and behaviours. Furthermore these constellations are fairly robust, leading us to propose the metaphor of an Epistemological Ecology. This metaphor holds in itself understanding of

- the threshold that seems to be necessary to overcome when moving from one ecology to another: Kegan refers to the 'disturbing of the self ' as a major source of anxiety and insecurity, on occasion hampering development. Natural ecologies are robust because of many feedback loops and self-correcting balances. Epistemological ecologies seem equally capable of reasserting themselves when insufficiently disturbed;
- the results of many studies indicating all kinds of different effective, partially effective or non-effective interventions. As in a natural ecology, there seem to be many ways to influence the existing balance (including e.g. the views on

learning and teaching), and the issue of causality is not always clear (Nieminen et al., 2004);

- the conclusion that comprehensive and long-term interventions will prove to be more successful than single-type or one-off interventions; and
- the expectation that fragile ecologies will be more prone to sudden shifts.

As we have suggested above (chapter 4), to stimulate epistemological change, it is probably necessary to confront students with a prolonged comprehensive and concerted learning environment that provides students with time and support to change their initial naive epistemological perspectives and to cope with the more complex requirements of this environment (Kember, 2001). Furthermore, we have reason to believe that exposing teachers to a comprehensive and concerted learning-teaching environment geared towards a more complex way of knowing, will eventually, if sufficiently supported by staff development efforts and peer intervision, influence their own views on learning and teaching (chapters 5, 9 and 11) towards more complexity.

Teachers are Students Grown Up

If it is true that, while a large body of evidence exists regarding student learning, much less is known about teacher learning (Vermunt, 2006), this study may provide a way to get around this dearth of knowledge by supplying the community of researchers of teacher learning with a "ready-to-wear" theoretical framework. In chapters 5 and 9 we presented evidence that teachers are indeed nothing other than students grown up, meaning that they view learning and teaching in essentially the same ways as students. It is true that teachers – in part because of their participation in higher education and their greater life experience – on average are further along the epistemological development we have sketched above, but still there are many teachers who view learning and teaching from a profoundly reproductive perspective (mainly learning-teaching conception 3). When not addressed in teacher training this reproductive view may perpetuate itself through generations of teachers who have failed to experience epistemological growth towards constructivism in higher education. Each generation of these fundamentally reproduction oriented teachers in turn instilling the same reproductive way of knowing in their students and thereby undermining the purpose of education: teaching people to think for themselves, to evaluate evidence and to be capable of formulating an informed opinion. This means that in particular in teacher education it is important to address the more philosophical issues regarding the nature of disciplinary knowledge and theory-laden observation, as well as addressing beliefs about truth, learning, motivation, effort, talent, etcetera. We would suggest to pay particular attention to this in teacher education for the natural and applied sciences (e.g. physics, mathematics, law, accounting, business administration) as it may, at least initially, go against the grain of existing and future teachers. Not only will this make a start towards breaking the chain of perpetuation of reproductive epistemology, it will help teachers implement future more constructivist educational innovations more successfully.

Regarding the relationship between teacher epistemology and their teaching practice, we must conclude that it is not simple nor symmetrical. Where epistemologically naïve teachers are constrained to reproduction-oriented teaching practices by their epistemological beliefs, constructivist teachers have many more options and strategies in teaching open to them, making them in principle more versatile and effective. But constructivist teachers also experience many obstacles to teach in accordance with their convictions. These obstacles can be clustered into three groups, individual (e.g. inexperience), organisational (e.g. school or departmental culture), and societal (e.g. parents' expectations, government regulations). This would seem to result in (secondary and higher) education that is predominantly traditional, positivist and reproduction-oriented in nature and so does not provide pupils and students with the necessary capabilities to function well in a modern society: they are truly *In over their heads* (Kegan 1994).

Epistemological Development in Enterprising Learning

When we compared the epistemological development of students of the old traditional curriculum with that of students exposed to Enterprising Learning, it was clear that of the students exposed to Enterprising Learning, the percentage that moved into a more complex view on learning and knowing was much higher than that found for students in the traditional curriculum. Consequently, Enterprising Learning can be classified as considerably more successful in promoting epistemological development than a traditional knowledge-transfer oriented curriculum. However, while by far most (85%) of the students developed at least one step up towards a more sophisticated epistemology, still 79% of the students exited the Hotelschool with learning-teaching conception 3: presumably an unsatisfactory level of epistemological sophistication for an institute of higher education, considering its espoused aim. That about four out of five students leave higher education with a primarily reproduction and application oriented view on learning and knowledge is not uncommon (e.g. Baxter Magolda, 1992; Radloff, 2002).

Further, considering the emphasis placed on application in Enterprising Learning, and under the circumstance that the majority of teachers providing Enterprising Learning were level-three-thinkers and presumably were teaching according to their maximum level of sophistication, it is not surprising that the majority of students seem to develop no further than third level thinking. Level-three-thinkers focus on reproductive application of knowledge, now or in the future: an approach that is closely aligned to the most epistemologically naïve interpretation of Enterprising Learning. It would seem that Enterprising Learning was interpreted by the majority of the teachers and students to mean just this, with teachers able to create a bridge towards their own highest epistemological level, but not beyond. Indeed, the majority of students moved into level three thinking. However, many more students than before Enterprising Learning changed their views on teaching and learning, indicating that a didactic and pedagogical approach in line with at least learning-teaching conception 3 can indeed speed up the epistemological development of students.

In principle further development was explicitly included within Enterprising Learning version 2 (see chapter 6), but such development proved to depend on an epistemologically more sophisticated translation of the goals and aims of the curriculum. This means that to successfully implement any educational innovation aimed at a particular level of epistemological sophistication, it would seem critical that teachers are supported to reach at least the level of epistemological sophistication central to this innovation.

Student Dissatisfaction: Disenchantment and Nostalgia

Not all students were satisfied with Enterprising Learning, two types of dissatisfaction in particular seemed to spring from epistemological mismatches between students and teachers. We have called these two distinctly different types of dissatisfaction Disenchantment and Nostalgia.

Disenchantment is the term we used for the dissatisfaction that arises when students feel insufficiently challenged by the teacher or curriculum. Most often it arises with the more epistemologically sophisticated students, in particular when students' views are more sophisticated than those of the teacher or those expressed in the teaching-learning environment. These students often find the learning environment too schoolish and the teacher too controlling. They experience that existing learning and thinking skills are not called upon and they often rebel. Rebellion expresses itself in various ways: antagonistic interactions (e.g. difficult behaviours or perceived motivational problems, Yerrick et al., 1998), disengagement expressed in emphasised extrinsic motivation by grades and diplomas (e.g. van Rossum et al., 2002; the current study), reverting to less sophisticated study strategies (e.g. van Rossum et al., 2002), and despair (e.g. Lindblom-Ylänne and Lonka, 1999; Kember, 2001). Disenchanted students long for something different, more challenging and often hang on in the hope of improvement after graduation.

Nostalgia is student dissatisfaction of a completely different kind. Nostalgia is not the result of feeling insufficiently challenged, but from feeling over-asked and not knowing what to do about it. At the same time, for the less epistemologically sophisticated students this type of dissatisfaction seems to involve a form of active rejection of a new way of learning: students feel they are cheating when by learning less, they get better grades, or they feel that practical knowledge is not in the same league as theory. Nostalgic students realise that they do not truly understand what the teacher wants from them. This insecurity leads them to long for a learning-teaching environment in which their own role was clear and they knew what to expect from teachers, namely guidance and control. In the current study, nostalgic students often became less enamoured with group work and felt that all the "doing" interfered with "real learning" (transmission and reception of knowledge). Some nostalgic students struggled on, others reverted to even less sophisticated views on and approaches to learning, placing all the responsibility for learning in the hands of the teacher. In the latter case students increasingly put in less effort into studying.

Regarding the incidence of disenchantment or nostalgia the comparison between the students of the old, traditional curriculum and Enterprising Learning leads to the conclusion that again Enterprising Learning has a better record. On the other hand, within the Enterprising Learning student group there were fewer students with sophisticated entry learning-teaching conceptions, which made in particular disenchantment less likely. Furthermore, considering that most students of the current study entered the Hotelschool with learning-teaching conception 2, and that Enterprising Learning was perceived (by most teachers, see chapter 9) to foster learning-teaching conception 3, the incidence of nostalgia may indicate that the introduction of Enterprising Learning can be improved upon by introducing more supports, especially in the first semesters, something students themselves suggested as well.

Changing Higher Education

Regarding the use of our model in higher education, we feel that Perry (1970) has formulated the aims of higher (liberal) education quite adequately:

1. learning to think: being able to argue and use evidence to come to an informed conclusion or decision (learning-teaching conception 4, self-authoring);
2. recognising relativism and context: comparing perspectives within oneself or between people, cultures, etcetera (relativism, learning-teaching conception 5, self-transforming);
3. taking a personal stand: defining your position, with respect for others and their choices (learning-teaching conception 6, self-defining; Hamer and van Rossum, 2010).

Sternberg (2003) expanded the range of possible aims for higher education to include not only to teach students to think well, but to think wisely, meaning that graduates would

4. not make impulsive, mindless, or destructive decisions.. [but who] think rightly, soundly and justly on behalf of their communities (self-transcending, Csikszentmihalyi, 1993).

Most common for higher education is to formulate aims based on the first bullet point given here: the equivalent of level four thinking or self-authorship (Kegan, 1994) and reasoned thinking (Dewey, 1910/1997). This would mean that an institute of higher education needs to succeed in educating all their graduates to at least level four thinking. Additionally, excellent higher education then must mean that all graduates must be capable of something more sophisticated than reasoned thinking. It would mean that the aims of higher education include one or more of the bullet points 2, 3 or 4 above. Either way, higher education would be fulfilling its aims if, and only if, all graduates are capable of fourth order of consciousness thinking. Considering that in most Western countries absolutist, dualist and multiplist thinking are common in the general population, and not uncommon even among the highly educated, together with indications that the situation is not much better in other countries and regions across the globe, it would seem an inevitable conclusion that in an epistemological sense **higher education currently is failing** its students and society. Barring occasional reported exceptions (e.g. Perry, 1970), higher education in general is *not* preparing its graduates for the complexity of current democratic society; a conclusion we share with Kegan (1994) and Sternberg (e.g. 1990, 2003). It is not even releasing graduates onto the labour market that meet expectations of employers. The question remains then, why higher education is mostly unaware of this poor record? Presumably because it focuses on *what* graduates know and mostly neglects to assess *how* graduates know.

What are the **characteristics of a system** that would promote epistemological development towards at least reasoned thinking? In what way can our developmental model of learning-teaching conceptions help to design such an educational approach? Firstly, let us emphasise that we do not necessarily advocate any major systematic overhauls. Systems as they are can mostly stay as they are, only the focus needs to change from knowing *what* students know, to including knowing *how* students know as well. Central to our point is that to attain the most modest goal in higher education, teaching to think well, "only" the teaching and learning approach of teachers as well as organisations needs to change. In most cases students will follow these changes if supported as well as challenged sufficiently. And it is in exactly this respect that our model can provide a theoretical fundament to construct education aimed at epistemological development.

In chapter 1, 3 through 5 we have sketched a developmental path along which teachers can guide students (and pupils) in a stepwise manner. The stages on the epistemological highway are hierarchically inclusive, implying that capabilities of earlier, less complex *ways of knowing* not only remain available (to use as a strategy) as development progresses, but that mastering a less sophisticated way of knowing is essential to understanding the next stage. Skipping a level of complexity, a stage, therefore seems undesirable, which means that if education is used to promote development, it needs to be in an **evolutionary** fashion (e.g. a stepwise introduction of increased complexity) and not a revolutionary fashion (e.g. a shock treatment). In many countries that would necessitate a curriculum geared towards at least three epistemological levels:

- dualism (as the most common student entry level after formal secondary education, learning-teaching conception 2),
- multiplism and professional application (learning-teaching conception 3),
- culminating in reasoned thinking (Dewey, 1910/1997), learning-teaching conception 4, procedural knowing (Belenky et al., 1997) or modernism (Kegan, 1994).

The amalgamated model described in table 3.6 above provides ample diagnostic pointers to define epistemological entry and exit levels for each stage in a developmental pedagogy. Depending on the entry level epistemology, a curriculum and teachers would need to **create a slope towards increasing complexity**, not based on random mutations (as in biological evolution) but on the conscious and deliberate creation of challenges that engage learners in an ongoing journey across epistemological stages. In our opinion, any approach aimed at promoting epistemological growth should at the very least build on a developmental model of intellectual development that describes various stages of student thinking in a sequential order. Only with such a model is it possible to determine the probability of constructive or destructive friction occurring. In addition, if the goal of education lies more than one stage away from the students' (most common) entry levels, this model will provide clues on how to construct a series of constructive frictions/holding environments encouraging epistemological transitions.

As Vermunt stated, "The success or failure of educational reform is defined by the teachers who implement it" (2006, p. 9, translation ours). To successfully implement a developmental constructivist curriculum, teachers need to be well acquainted with the particulars of each stage themselves to be able to create the bridge, the supports and the challenges necessary to invite learners of all ages to cross over into the unknown and daunting reality of increased uncertainty. This means that to successfully implement a constructivist curriculum, it is necessary to include the **teachers' epistemology** in planning the curriculum and allocating teachers to particular phases in the curriculum. If teachers are expected to encourage epistemological growth, this implies that they themselves have experienced a similar transformation. It is unrealistic to expect positivist teachers to walk the epistemological tightrope Prawat described in chapter 10, balancing the uncertainty of knowledge with the need to build trust in the disciplinary way of thinking. As it has proven difficult to change teacher thinking, this may mean that when an institute wants a speedy transformation of the curriculum towards constructivist teaching and learning, not only subject expertise then must be a criterion for placement of teachers in higher education, but *epistemological sophistication* must become a criterion too.

Furthermore, we propose to eliminate from developmental pedagogy the term independent learning associated with constructivist learning and which has been overwhelmingly misunderstood. Independent learning carries with it the impression of student self-sufficiency often interpreted to mean that constructivist learning welcomes students who do *not* ask questions, who require *less* teaching from teachers as students – as independent learners - are expected to teach themselves. Contrary to common belief, teaching a constructivist curriculum requires more effort and deeper disciplinary knowledge from teachers, while 'independent' students should not be left to their own devices and be perceived as solely responsible for their learning. Constructivist teaching in fact means *teaching more,* requiring fundamental and deep understanding of the subject matter, students who are unafraid of asking questions, and requiring *not* less but a different kind of teacher-student interaction. We propose to substitute this apparently misleading term with **mentored learning**, a term addressing the active role of both teacher and student in learning. Mentored learning indeed encapsulates a third important aspect of a developmental constructivist curriculum as well; the need for creating not only challenges, but providing supports as well. Because changing *the way* you know means disturbing the self (Kegan, 1994) it should be introduced in a teaching-learning environment characterised by sufficient supports (to overcome anxiety) and appropriate challenges (to evoke change; Baxter Magolda, 2004), preferably distributed throughout the curriculum (e.g. Marra and Palmer, 2004).

In order to improve the record of higher education regarding attaining its own aims, we need to address the obstacles that currently prevent large scale implementation of a developmental constructivist curriculum. Firstly we need to invest heavily in **staff development** in higher education, but also in secondary and perhaps even elementary education, in order to equip teachers for the daunting task of changing their teaching practice to encourage epistemological growth (see below). Staff development is essential as in particular a reproduction-oriented teacher will teach in a reproduction-oriented way, regardless of materials or organisational culture. If anything, chapter 5 proved that there is no such thing as a teacher-proof constructivist book or software tool, which cuts off other possible avenues of changing teaching practice besides staff development.

Secondly, we need to look much closer at the **hidden reproduction-oriented messages** now conveyed in e.g. teaching practices, teaching materials and assessment practices, and which are reinforced by society and government requirements: learning and teaching need to assess not only *what* graduates know, but also *how* graduates know. However, we must be careful to emphasise that the how of knowing is not independent of the what, while addressing simultaneously the misconception that knowing a lot (i.e. covering all of the basics) is an absolute requirement for, and automatically leads to, a new, more complex *way of knowing.*

Thirdly, powerful learning environments need to remain **challenging throughout** the duration of the studies. As students grow epistemologically, what was challenging before becomes commonplace and 'boring' (if not destructive). The challenges can be of various natures, for instance increased challenge can be sought in more ill-structured real-life problems to solve, more complex skills to apply, and/or more depth and breadth in the 'big ideas' to explore. As Vermunt linked learning and thinking activities directly to learning domain-specific content, we would like to emphasise that a successful model should include thinking and learning skills (of students *and* teachers), as well as a thorough content analysis in terms of the fundamental ideas/concepts of a discipline.

Fourthly, considerably more attention needs to be given to relatively low cost interventions with potentially large effects on attainment and quality of learning outcome: in particular we would like to stress **assessment practices and the nature of teaching materials**. To improve the outcome of education towards a more sophisticated epistemology, it is unavoidable to explicitly include these goals in teaching materials and assessment practices. To counter the misconception of certainty of knowledge, teaching materials and teaching practices need to emphasise that what is included in the study text is not necessarily absolute or definitive. Study texts of a more probabilistic nature may open up students and pupils to the option of further, more independent thought. If thinking well is the highest goal, encouraging students (and pupils) to think should be central in teaching and exams should include at least some measurements regarding the quality of reasoned thought, the capability to solve novel or ill-structured problems such as encountered in professional life. It is simply unacceptable that lack of attention for the how of knowing, as well as perhaps time and cost constraints (of teachers and government), lead to a choice for assessment practices that actively undermine the goal of higher education: to educate the students to think well.

And finally, we suggest that a developmental constructivist curriculum includes a new tool which was found as a by-product of student reflection in the studies described in chapters 1, 3, 7 and 8: the **good talk about good learning**. Students themselves reported that the development of their own thinking was initiated and fuelled by the researchers' request to describe their assumptions and expectations about learning and teaching. They often commented on their own growing interest in the issue, that they were more than willing to expand on what they had discussed before in order to get things clearer in their own mind as well. It would seem that *mentored reflection*, putting again its own requirements on teachers, is a potentially powerful teaching tool for an epistemological developmental pedagogy.

Educating the Educators

As we have stated before, in chapter 5, variables that increase the likelihood of traditional, positivist teaching practices are first and foremost the epistemological beliefs or teaching conceptions of the teachers. If these are traditional and positivist, then teaching practice will be so too. So this would seem to indicate that first and foremost we need to **address the epistemological belief structures** of teachers, changing them towards a constructivist structure in order to change their teaching practice towards a developmental constructivist pedagogy. In chapter 11 at least 8 methods to address staff development are described, all aimed at changing teachers' belief structures and mostly linking belief structures directly to teaching practice:

1) a good talk about good teaching (Palmer, 1998) induced either by
   a) exploring personal metaphors in teaching (Palmer, 1998; see chapter 5 e.g. Yero, 2002; Martinez et al., 2001) or
   b) a community of truth around critical moments in teaching (Palmer, 1998);
2) constructive alignment (Biggs, 2003);
3) reflective practice (Biggs, 2003) and concern driven pedagogy (Vermunt, 2006);
4) action research (e.g. Kember, 1991);
5) a combined action research approach, (Gordon and Debus, 2002);
6) narrative inquiry (Lyons and LaBoskey, 2002a); and
7) conceptual change approach (Ho, 2000, 2001).

For details on these approaches and the results, see chapter 11.

Furthermore, we need to address various obstacles to the acceptance of the **need to change current teaching practice**. Of these obstacles, most importantly seems to be that we need to convince teachers, parents, institutes, departments and governments that traditional reproduction-oriented teaching is not the type of teaching we need in (higher) education. It is imperative that all parties reach a consensus that complete and utter teacher control of the teaching-learning process is not the road to reasoned thinking and that covering the basics does not necessarily result in the type of thinking necessary to function well in modern democratic society. If teachers, institutes and (local and national) governments are convinced of this, implementing a developmental constructivist pedagogy will not be hampered by misunderstandings and subtle sabotage. To convince all parties concerned of this, it is necessary to show that constructivist learning and teaching is in fact more demanding than traditional teaching. That traditional teaching is not better than constructivist teaching, but that it is in fact taking the easy way out as well as ignoring the real goal of (higher) education, namely preparing our young people for the complex and demanding reality of modern (or even postmodern) society. As we have said before, constructivist teaching is a "tough kind of love." A love, perhaps, that teachers and educational policy makers themselves need to experience first, before they can bestow it on the students.

Thirdly, we need to emphasise here that constructivist beliefs, while clearly very relevant and necessary, *cannot and do not* replace **subject expertise**. An often mentioned obstacle teachers mention regarding their ability and inclination to teach from a constructivist standpoint is lack of confidence in their own subject expertise and self-efficacy. This means that to implement a developmental constructivist pedagogy it is necessary to only employ those teachers who feel sufficiently expert in the field of study they are asked to teach. It cannot be else than detrimental to the implementation of a developmental constructivist curriculum to put insufficiently expert teachers in a position that they feel the need to follow the syllabus faithfully because they simply are not familiar enough themselves with the subject matter. When this happens, such teachers cannot be expected to understand the misconceptions and incorrect prior knowledge students enter the classroom with. And as such it is unreasonable to expect them to be able to employ sufficient flexibility to adequately give form and function to developmental constructivist pedagogy.

Fourthly, in educating our educators we need to include the **mentoring of novice teachers**. An important obstacle mentioned by novice teachers to teaching in accordance with their constructivist beliefs is lack of experience with classroom management. This would mean that novice teachers need adequate support during the first phase of their career. We suggest that novice teachers start out with a smaller teaching task (less hours/courses than the maximum), to create time for them to reflect on classroom management, and to acquire sufficient experience of how to handle the multitude of management issues before burdening them with a standard teaching appointment.[1] Furthermore, supporting novice teachers towards the implementation of a developmental constructivist pedagogy would of course necessitate mentoring by experienced constructivist teachers. Emphasising again the dire need for a concerted and comprehensive effort towards staff development in higher (and secondary) education; an effort aimed at moving our entire teaching staff towards a *constructivist way of knowing.*

Finally, focusing on beliefs is not the whole message. In order to implement a developmental constructivist pedagogy, teachers need a **training in** those **skills** that are assumed to be available to teachers within such a pedagogy. For instance, it may be important to believe that addressing misconceptions is important in reaching conceptual change, however, it is a particular skill to be able to recognise such misconceptions in the classroom or perhaps even to provoke them in order to address them explicitly. A second skill necessary to constructivist teaching is the teacher's ability to create a space for discussion and dialogue about subject knowledge without filling it with his/her own expertise. How to prevent posing questions becoming a reproduction-oriented quiz or a "filling in the blanks"-exercise, is another underestimated skill. As we have said above, belief systems do not replace subject expertise. Now we add that they *do not* replace (relevant constructivist) teaching skills either. Educating our educators therefore is not an either/or issue, it is in fact an "and… , and… , and ..."-issue.

The Human Condition?

As we have indicated above, we feel that our learning-teaching conception model accesses a general, naturally occurring process of intellectual development (Csikszentmihalyi, 1993), open to anyone with the inclination to examine their life, the way they know and learn and who they are. In chapter 1 we have discussed possible dynamics underlying this development: the stepping out of embeddedness where what was once subject becomes object and thus available for critical reflection. In Hamer and van Rossum (2008 and 2010) we have explored the possible remainder of this intellectual development, the steps of which constitute not the development in 'learning to know' (as in learning-teaching conceptions 1 through 5), but in 'learning to be' following another tier of 5 steps, starting from learning-teaching conception 6 as described in the current study to an order of consciousness where "the self has become entirely identified with the world. It would be the recognition essentially of the oneness of the universe" (Kegan in Debold, 2002, p. 147). In this final stage, foreseen and described by Kegan, there is no subject at all. Here one would not look "out on the world from any vantage point that is apart from it. You're then taking the world's perspective" (Kegan in Debold, 2002, p. 147). In chapter 1 we would call this the viewpoint of a level-ten-thinker and it is what Csikszentmihalyi and Rathunde would describe as "a systemic ecological consciousness" (1990, p. 32).

We feel that the *nature* of this development in 'learning to know' or even 'learning to be' is independent of culture, discipline or gender. However, the speed and frequency with which people move through various stages may be influenced by just these factors. Below we discuss arguments underpinning our, for some controversial, position in more detail.

Culture. Considering that research discussed in this study shows that a similar development can be found in populations all across the globe, it seems this development is not idiosyncratic to Western culture. Mugler and Landbeck (1997), looking specifically at higher education students in the culturally and linguistically very diverse South Pacific region (Melanesia, Polynesia and Micronesia), agree with this conclusion stating

> The conclusion from studies in different countries is that the conceptions of learning described originally for Western countries are recognisable elsewhere. (p. 230) …
>
> There is also an uncanny similarity between quotes by students from other studies and ours, which suggests the similarities of learning experiences in different cultures and accounts for the recurrence of the same categories of description …. (p. 233) …
>
> … some approaches to study and conceptions of learning have many features in common across cultures, reflecting the universality of some cognitive processes…. (p. 236)

Indeed Boulton-Lewis et al. (2000a, 2000b, 2001 and 2004) also concluded that the learning conceptions, learning orientations and learning approaches of indigenous Australian university students did not differ in significant ways from those of other university students. Moreover, they proposed measures to improve student learning, that would fit seamlessly into any university context (Boulton-Lewis et al., 2004, p. 108–109).

> we have not identified any striking differences in the ways of going about learning between these students and other similar groups of students with comparative educational backgrounds when entering university …
>
> … these students would have had a more enjoyable and successful university experience if they had been helped more to develop their strategies for learning. Such assistance might have been useful for them to alter their ways of studying so that they matched more closely to their conceptions and to those strategies required for effective formal learning at university.

If culturally defined at all, the universal intellectual development may perhaps be idiosyncratic to similarities in the *educational culture* in countries with *formal* education systems (on occasion imported from the West, e.g. Mugler and Landbeck, 1997, p. 237). The studies reviewed here and which all seem to point towards a universal development less dependent on *ethnical culture*, are based on samples from Europe (e.g. Dutch, British, Spanish, Scandinavian), the Middle East (e.g. Israeli, Palestinian), Asia (e.g. Malaysian, mainland, Taiwanese and Hong-Kong Chinese, Indian, Indonesian, Vietnamese), various ethnic groups within the US (e.g. European, African, Native and Hispanic), the Commonwealth (e.g. Australian, including indigenous, and Canadian), and the South Pacific region. The only large groups of countries (and cultures) that seem to be missing in this review are continental Africa and the Southern and Middle America's. Although, e.g. Boulton-Lewis et al. (2004) refer to a studies with Nigerian and South African students and Mugler and Landbeck (1997) refer to studies from South America, all resulting in recognisable learning conceptions. Not only can we speak of the universality of some cognitive processes or conceptions, there is reason to believe that even more specific characteristics of this development are more universal than one might expect. For instance, Mugler and Landbeck, list the following

- the dominance of reproductive learning conceptions and study approaches, learning conception 3 being by far the most common;
- adverse learning environments leading to surface-level learning, e.g. traditional transmission-mode teaching, heavy workload, reproduction-oriented assessment;
- beginning university students' initial lack of deep-level learning skills and the difficulty experienced by higher education to develop these skills in students.

Boulton-Lewis et al. (2000b, 2004) on the other hand, found that a large number of their indigenous Australian students had dissonant conceptions and strategies, perhaps indicating that ethnic culture may lead to the persistence of particular (surface level) strategies that are no longer in line with students' developed conceptions of learning. To establish whether the intellectual development is indeed specific for developed cultures with a *formal educational system*, studying the epistemology of samples from groups with no *formal* educational system (perhaps native South American indians, Papua etcetera) may prove interesting. The question could be whether these groups with cultures much closer to nature, often characterised by mystic influences and informal learning experiences, express similar or distinctly different views on reality not captured in any of the models discussed in this study. To propose hypotheses for this research, we expect that these cultures may use different words or different ways to describe the same ways of knowing while the distribution of these ways of knowing in these populations may differ as well.

In chapter 7 we have explicitly looked at formal educational cultures. It would seem that an educational environment that is geared toward memory and reproduction of facts, leads to views on learning and knowing that are relatively unsophisticated. A curriculum that explicitly aims towards application and preparation for a successful career, such as Enterprising Learning, leads to a shift towards at least learning-teaching conception 3. The experience with elementary and secondary education geared towards more epistemologically sophisticated ways of learning and knowing, such as Montessori or Dalton education, seems to point towards the conclusion that epistemological development is less age-restricted than Piagetian approaches to epistemological and intellectual development have led us to expect. Indeed the first results of the Curious Minds (in Dutch, Talentenkracht) project in the Netherlands would seem to indicate that Piaget and many of his followers were somewhat pessimistic regarding young children's abilities with regard to abstract or scientific and argumentative thinking.

The broader issue remains whether the ways of knowing we have described here are indicative of the human condition, or typical only of the Western, Greek-Roman tradition of thinking, and especially whether our studies are an implicit form of cultural imperialism. This would imply that in Western culture the development of more complex ways of knowing is seen as advantageous and something to revere. In that case, wise and sophisticated thinkers would be greatly honoured. However, in our search for examples of wise people, we have come across a number of instances that seem to indicate that in the Western world as well, such ways of thinking are mostly not appreciated nor valued by the majority. We need only call to mind the fact that Socrates was forced to kill himself, that Spinoza wrote his philosophical works in the guise of a treatise on mathematics to prevent accusations of atheism and heresy (Hamer and van Rossum, 2008) or even more recently that Sternberg who attempted to develop education for wisdom experienced opposition with consequences for his career. In the Western culture the phenomenon of guru, acceptable in many Eastern countries, is not one easily accepted and sophisticated thinkers are seen as (often unnecessarily) making things more complex than they are. This leads us to conclude again that the development that we, and many others in the current study, describe is one uniquely and universally human. Furthermore, the fact that higher, more complex ways of knowing are so extremely rare in all cultures we have looked at, only underlines that all cultures are rife with obstacles and fears obstructing this natural development.

Age and Disciplines. Not only are many cultures sampled, the reviewed research contains many ages and different student populations as well: ages range between 14 to 73, with a large oversampling of the group in higher or advanced education (18 to 30 years). Educational cultures studied cover the full range from secondary or high school to post graduate, again with a large oversampling of college and university college students and including occasional samples from Ivy-league institutes, higher professional education, community colleges and distance education. In addition pre-service and student-teachers as well as teachers in various levels of education have been studied, from nursery upward to academic. In all these age groups and contexts recognisable learning and teaching conceptions are found, be it in varying frequencies.

Finally the epistemology of students and teachers from a wide range of disciplines has been object of study. Disciplines discussed in studies reviewed in the current study include science (including the natural sciences, pharmacy, mathematics, architecture, engineering), arts and humanities (e.g. history, literature and writing, philosophy), law, medicine, business and hotel administration, accounting, economics and the social sciences (e.g. psychology, pedagogy). In chapters 4 and 5 it proved difficult to untangle the issues of disciplinary culture versus teaching practice (e.g. Vermunt, see chapter 4). For instance physics and mathematics are often taught from a positivist epistemology, focusing on scientific knowledge as an accumulation of certain facts and formulas representing reality. Teachers of these disciplines tend to ignore the tentative nature of scientific theory until very late in education, if addressed at all and thereby maintain a myth of, if not simple knowledge, at least a body of certain and irrefutable knowledge. Social sciences and humanities on the other hand, lacking the exact reproducibility of the sciences, need to address the tentative nature of knowledge much more explicitly even at an introductory level. This difference in instructionally induced myth-maintenance may be at the core of the view that epistemological beliefs are domain or context specific. In our opinion on the other hand, it would seem that it is not the discipline itself that shapes the epistemological belief structure attributed to it, but the *discipline-as-experienced* or even perhaps the discipline-as-presented. Indeed there are branches of and schools of thought in social science that try very hard to present themselves as empiricist and positivist (see chapter 2).

Gender. As many of the studies reviewed here - and our studies in particular - were mixed gendered we feel that one cannot honestly continue to dismiss many studies into conceptions of learning or ways of knowing as irrelevant to female epistemological development because they describe only male approaches to (or conceptions of) learning and knowing: a critique expressed explicitly by feminist researchers such as Hazel, Conrad and Martin (1997). Hazel et al. feel, as Belenky et al. (1997) did earlier regarding epistemology, that "Women's voices seem to be missing" in phenomenographic research (1997, p. 217). Perhaps they have a valid point where they assume that connected knowing is more frequently found for women and that separate knowing is more common in men, a point that was partially confirmed by Belenky et al. (1997) and Baxter Magolda (1992). However, as Belenky et al. found both voices in an all female respondent group, and Baxter Magolda consciously sought but failed to find evidence of gender differences in ways of knowing in a mixed respondent group, it would seem that connected and separate knowing are voices available to men and women alike. Although it might be that these different tones of voice are gender related, a term Baxter Magolda used to indicate that within each way of knowing there were subtle gender trends. In particular she found that in the less sophisticated ways of knowing forms of connected knowing were more common in women, but they were not exclusive to the female way of knowing (1992). In Baxter Magolda's later work, as in ours, the affective aspects of learning and knowing, another possibly blind spot of phenomenography as described by Hazel et al. (1997), have become increasingly central. In particular Baxter Magolda's disentanglement of three dimensions, epistemology, interpersonal relations and intrapersonal relations (e.g. 2004; 2007) reflects this growing attention to affect. Regarding our own work and the inclusion of affective aspects of learning and knowing, we can refer to the concept of the epistemological ecology (chapter 4), where aspects such as motivation, confidence, identity development, interpersonal relations etcetera, are seen as equally important as the more cognitive aspects such as conceptions of learning—in particular the first five conceptions.

Regarding our research since the 1980s we can further add to the incomplete review of phenomenographic studies presented by Hazel et al. (1997) who refer to only one "rare study indeed [an earlier version of Marton et al., 1993]—two of the principal researchers were women and most of the subjects were mature-age female students ... Conceptions of learning, which had been studied in many male dominated fields and with groups of male subjects, received a notable addition of a higher conception: 'changing as a person'. For this to have happened, a link had to be made explicitly to the broader lives of the participants and *women of insight* had to express and detect the idea of changing as a person" (p. 214, italics ours). Hazel et al. clearly overlooked the footnote on page 292 of this paper accrediting the discovery of the sixth learning conception to two researchers, van Rossum (male) and Taylor (female) as early as 1987 (!). And even earlier, Erik van Rossum and Simone Schenk (1984) in their much referred to paper, explicitly mentioned their mixed gender respondent group (female dominated, p. 75), discussing in detail attempts at discovering gender differences (p. 78–79). This goes to show that the study by Beaty, Dall'Alba and Marton was not so rare as Hazel et al. make it out to be, and that mixed gender groups were studied from the very early beginnings of the phenomenographic research tradition. Also, we expect that Säljö's seminal learning conception study (1979a) included a fair percentage of women in the respondent group.

As for the need for a female eye to discover the sixth learning conception implied by Hazel et al., we would like to express once again (see chapter 1) that this initial discovery was based on a mixed gender respondent group of Arts students, and was pointed out to the research group by one of its male members, Rien Deijkers. Rien was at that time very much interested in Zen and recognised a distinctly different voice in an extremely small set of responses that until then we had struggled with to include in our learning conception model. Finally, we would like to complete this refutation by pointing out that the current authors have always worked with mixed gender subject groups, accessing mostly disciplines where female students are common if not dominant, and have always worked in mixed gender research groups. All publications by van Rossum, barring one or two single authored ones, were co-authored by at least one female researcher. Even so, we have not found any evidence of gender determined voices, but acknowledge that women and men may use different tones of voice depending on the circumstances. In our opinion, both tones of voice are appropriate and essential to learning and knowing, good teaching and to true understanding. Clearly at least in our own work, women and their voices have always claimed their rightful place in the outcome space.

In addition, very little quantitative evidence was found for gender differences: women seem more aware of the effort aspect of learning and show a small preference for co-operative learning. It is still possible that gender differences are more pronounced in the less sophisticated ways of knowing, a conclusion that is supported by Baxter Magolda as well, where she comments on male and female approaches to learning becoming less different as students move towards increased epistemological sophistication (1992). In chapter 3, we even suggested that Silence (learning-teaching conception 1) may have two, gender related but not gender specific, faces; absolute obedience (most common for women) and violence (not uncommon in men). Then again, violence in Silence may lie at the root of child-abuse by women. It would seem that perhaps the two tones of voice discerned in Procedural Knowing (learning-teaching conception 4: connected and separate knowing) are the last vestiges of gender related differences in ways of knowing. However, to establish this, more study is necessary to link the less sophisticated epistemological positions to gender related behaviours or views. This issue clearly requires more specific study.

New Avenues of Research

Silence

In many studies this first order of consciousness is not described in depth, probably for the same reason that the sixth order of consciousness probably is not well defined yet: its relative rareness in the usual groups studied. Some researchers even fail to make the distinction between the first two orders of consciousness at all. Belenky et al.'s (1997) inclusion of women who could describe this almost selfless epistemological point of view can be seen as a major contribution to epistemology. Their in-depth description of Silence in particular helped us to understand the non-reflective stance we had noticed before in learning-teaching conception 1. The essential lack of ego-awareness—a retreat into nothingness that goes so far as to "erase" the self—and the lack of any timeline, a future, it all paints a grim picture of existence indeed. In our opinion, Silence is not an epistemological way of knowing or strategy unique to women. Considering the hierarchical inclusiveness of each epistemological position, it is only logical to postulate that silence – at least as a strategy and often in a less severe form – is not at all uncommon in women nor men. Furthermore in chapter 3, we postulated that silence may have two faces: absolute obedience and power play or violence. Understanding silence and the circumstances that help counter it may prove useful as a theoretical framework for further research into victims of abuse, violence or war.

Learning to be: Higher Orders of Consciousness

On the other hand, still relatively little is now known regarding the nature of the possibly even higher orders of consciousness: beyond 5 (Relativism). As we have said before this is partly due to the extreme rareness of these higher orders of consciousness in the groups studied traditionally for student and teacher thinking. In Hamer and van Rossum (2008) we postulated in more detail that the epistemological development (learning-teaching conceptions 1 through 5, Learning to know) is followed by an existential development which we have dubbed *Learning to be*. The first conception of being would then be the sixth learning-teaching conception, or sixth order of consciousness. At this level of thinking one lives one's own convictions (Baxter Magolda, 2008) and it is characterised by a self-defining self (Hamer and van Rossum, 2010): there is an awareness of the central role of the self in meaning making.

In chapter 1 we have shortly described the possible dynamics that would lead to a second tier of five existential orders of consciousness, culminating in a felt oneness with the universe, where nothing is subject anymore, all is object and one takes the world's perspective (Kegan in Debold, 2002). In order to study these higher orders of consciousness we need to look at alternative sources of data. One approach could be including considerably more mature respondents, people with a large amount of life experience or subjects who are considered wise and have had time to contemplate complex issues (and the meaning of life). We would propose to include (conceptions of) wisdom explicitly as one possible focus for such research, as wisdom emerged in our highest learning-teaching conception, as well as in Baxter Magolda's Internal Foundation (2007) as a new theme guiding introspection and action. Furthermore, we suggest to link the current epistemological models to research into adult development, gerontology (e.g. gerotranscendence), and perhaps even into philosophy and elder tales. Alternative sources may also include biographic and narrative material portraying the lives of wise and exceptional people or their writings themselves (e.g. Gandhi, de Spinoza, Castaneda, Krishnamurti). Other sources could include interviewing living writers and theorists such as Parker Palmer or Mihaly Csikszentmihalyi. A final suggestion regarding possible subjects of study would be to include exceptionally original and creative artists (living or dead).

Such research would not only require an open attitude to new sources of data, it would put particular requirements on the researchers as well. As until now each order of consciousness is characterised by a particular and unique way of meaning making, we expect that higher orders of consciousness will also be characterised by "their own language." As it has proven already difficult to recognise and understand the more sophisticated ways on meaning making (ways of knowing) of the first tier, we have provided a possible theoretical framework to detect and recognise even more sophisticated ways of meaning making (Hamer and van Rossum, 2008, see also chapter 1).

Transitions

After suggesting further research into the outer edges of our own model, we feel that also more study is required into the nature of the transitions between stages. The major emphasis in epistemological research has been on changes from one position to the next (e.g. Baxter Magolda, 1992; Marton et al., 1993). In studies descendent from the Perry scheme (1970) , as well as those relying on the subject-object interview (Kegan, 1994), a coding system is employed that recognises that an earlier stage can linger on while a new stage is in development. Such codes for instance look like 3, 4, 4 meaning that the student in question is mainly a level-four-thinker, but still has some active characteristics of Multiplicity. This type of coding implies a much more gradual and subtle type of change between positions. Although we do not usually describe such responses in detail, in the current study we have paid particular attention to the small but seemingly significant changes within stages, see chapter 7. Our purpose was to shed some light on the dynamics of change, the transitional phenomena, and perhaps so help understand how to better evoke epistemological development.

As far as we know, there has not been much research done regarding the transitions between ways of knowing (or learning-teaching conceptions). Although there are some studies that discuss detailed categories of description within for instance the range of reproductive positions (e.g. White, 2000), we feel that much more study is needed. What are crucial experiences and pivotal moments in the learning-teaching experience that bring a particular move about? Are the crucial moments and drivers the same for all crossings or can we identify specific moments and drivers for each transitional move. In particular we would appreciate more insight into the crossing of the watershed. We feel that to improve teaching and the construction of developmental curricula such as for instance Enterprising Learning, it is important to better understand the types of challenges and supports that will encourage epistemological development through a series of tailored holding environments.

Further Research of the Epistemological Ecology

We introduced the concept of an epistemological ecology in chapter 4 because we felt that much research was looking at epistemological development from a too simple vantage point, sometimes even focusing on only one or two, usually cognitive, dimensions. In Baxter Magolda's work the interplay between several qualitatively different dimensions is explicitly described, leading to our own closer examination of the dimensions in our own model. However, also in our work, obvious and important elements driving and defining the learning-teaching experience are not included. Such elements belong for instance to the affective dimension (e.g. motivation, self-confidence, emotions) or to a dimension covering such things as beliefs about effort in learning, the nature of general ability and specific talents, etcetera. Not only was much research "too simple", it often contained (rather automated or mechanistic) assumptions about directionality of influence between different beliefs or dimensions, with sometimes contradicting outcomes. Lastly, the existing studies also often expected that a specific intervention, often small scale and short in duration, should lead to a permanent change in a way of knowing. From such a reductionist and Newtonian approach it would indeed be difficult to understand the robustness and self-correcting nature of ways of knowing.

For example, let's look at a typical freshman student entering higher education directly following secondary education. Such a student sees knowledge in a particular way, usually dualist; has particular interpersonal expectations of the teacher (transmission of knowledge); is motivated by grades and diplomas; often feels obligated towards parents to do well; has a limited sense of an independent identity apart from family, friends and social group; may feel insecure about his/her capabilities regarding studying and coping with university life, to name but a few. Is it really reasonable to expect that an intervention aimed at a study strategy or study process (e.g. one course with constructivist teaching) will unbalance this whole constellation of beliefs enough? This question led us to propose a more complex approach to designing interventions. The epistemological ecology is a metaphor that we hope will increase the explicit use of multiple-targeted and prolonged interventions, in order to perturb a relatively stable ecology and to circumvent the self-correcting nature of it.

However, still not enough is known about the complexity of an epistemological ecology: we do not know enough about all the species involved (dimensions), and the nature of all their needs and wants (interactions between dimensions). More research is necessary to identify the dimensions, their interplay and the way how to induce imbalances in an ecology to promote intellectual development. Because of the inherent complexity we expect that a concerted approach will include the interactions within relatively "simple" structures first. This is an excellent approach, as long as all studies aim towards integration of knowledge in the end. Our own research, and many studies described above, can be seen as the fundament of such a concerted and comprehensive international effort. Our study emphasises in particular the cognitive (epistemological) and interpersonal (teacher-student relationship) dimensions and the way they move together. In keeping with our attempt at convergence of outcomes validity (see chapter 2), we advocate more interaction between quantitative and qualitative research efforts, as both are necessary to define the range of and approach to the necessary studies.

Low Cost Interventions

Although epistemological development is a complex issue, probably requiring investment in time and money, we feel that this is not a reason to leave it at that. Are there 'smart' and preferably low cost interventions possible that can break through the current deadlock of the perpetuation of reproductive ways of knowing? We feel that below we discuss three very promising options.

Variation in perspectives. An interesting, and almost incredibly simple approach to improving the quality of learning could be the application of mindful-learning experiments (Langer, 1997) in realistic learning-teaching environments in higher education. Langer's experiments (see chapter 10) are based on the assumption that variation increases involvement, and so improves the quality of learning outcomes. In Langer's approach the variation refers to requiring students to actively engage with study material, for instance by changing perspectives. Changing (disciplinary) perspectives is also the variation approach chosen by Cherry (2005) to encourage out-of-the-box thinking within the learning experience. By changing perspectives in assignments or about study material, students become more aware of having taken numerous aspects of their default perspective for granted. In this way, by stepping out of the default perspective, students' creativity may be accessed more readily. Looking at the world from a different perspective can be a (self-)disturbing but positive experience and therefore may encourage development and change. To our knowledge this area is a relatively new and uncharted territory in educational research and educational innovation would benefit from more evidence regarding the epistemological effects of variation in perspectives.

Probabilistic study texts. Another, relatively easy to implement intervention, based on the mindful-learning approach explored by Langer (1997), is the use of probabilistic study text. Usually study texts present the scientific knowledge base of a discipline as certain, unchanging and definitive. In studying, students then interpret these texts to constitute the whole of the disciplinary knowledge, without any options for them to expand upon the knowledge given in the text. In an epistemological sense, students are not encouraged to think of other examples or to question what is presented, in short an active student engagement with the material is not perceived as relevant or desired. Langer experimented with simple textual changes, substituting all "epistemologically closed" phrasing with more probabilistic phrasing, leading again to more active involvement with the study text (for details see chapter 10). We would like to see much more research done in real life study situations to build up the body of knowledge regarding the effects of probabilistic study texts on the quality of student learning and thinking.

Assessment practices. As we have observed before, in current educational practice it would seem that assessment practices are underestimated as a tool to influence student learning and thinking. Many teachers in higher (and secondary) education are unaware of the hidden curriculum behind assessment practices; that students are more than able to pick up the hidden message underlying assessment practices. The hidden message behind multiple choice examination is that recognition, reproduction, fragmented knowledge and luck constitute a good quality learning outcome (see also chapter 8). In chapters 10 and 11 we have discussed studies that demonstrated that changing assessment practices to match the professed goals of a course or of higher education leads to large changes in the quality of student learning against relatively low costs. We feel that in the effort to improve the quality of student learning in higher education more evidence regarding the effects of more and new constructivist assessment practices is necessary.

All three of these avenues of research into low cost interventions have in common that they pressure students to look at reality from a different vantage point than they are familiar with. Changing perspectives – or variation – is a central theme in *The university of learning* (Bowden and Marton, 1998), which according to Cherry,

> poses—and wrestles with—that striking and practical question ...: how do we prepare others (and ourselves, for that matter) for situations that are highly variable and novel and that do not neatly match up with the boundaries that we try to maintain between discipline or knowledge areas? (Cherry, 2005, p. 312)

In short, these three low cost approaches are examples of quickly implementable and presumably viable ways for higher education to prepare students for practice in the age of complexity.

NOTES

[1] In the Netherlands currently a full-time teaching job is 29 classroom hours a week in secondary education. In higher education the size of a teaching task depends on departmental or institutional commitments.

REFERENCES

Akin, R. (2002). Out of despair: Reconceptualizing teaching through narrative practice. In N. Lyons & V. K. LaBoskey (Eds.), *Narrative inquiry in practice* (pp. 63–75). New York: Teachers College Press.

Åkerlind, G. S. (2003). Growing and developing as a university teacher, variation in meaning. *Studies in Higher Education, 28*(4), 375–390.

Åkerlind, G. S. (2004). A new dimension to understanding university teaching. *Teaching in higher education, 9*(3), 363–375.

Åkerlind, G. S. (2005). Variation and commonality in phenomenographic research methods. *Higher Education Research and Development, 24*(4), 321–334.

Ashworth, P., & Lucas, U. (2000). Achieving empathy and engagement: A practical approach to the design, conduct and reporting of phenomenographic research. *Studies in Higher Education, 25*, 295–308.

Baxter Magolda, M. B. (1992a). *Knowing and reasoning in college*. San Francisco: Jossey-Bass.

Baxter Magolda, M. B. (1992b). Students' epistemologies and academic experiences: Implications for pedagogy. *The Review of Higher Education, 15*(3), 265–287.

Baxter Magolda, M. B. (1999a). *Creating contexts for learning and self-Authorship*. Nashville: Vanderbilt University Press.

Baxter Magolda, M. B. (1999b). The evolution of epistemology: Refining contextual knowing at twentysomething. *Journal of College Student Development, 40*(4), 333–344.

Baxter Magolda, M. B. (2001). *Making their own way*. Sterling, Virginia: Stylus Publishing.

Baxter Magolda, M. B. (2004). Learning partnerships model – a framework for promoting self-authorship. In M. Baxter Magolda & P. M. King (Eds.), *Learning partnerships* (pp. 37–62). Sterling, Virginia: Stylus.

Baxter Magolda, M. B. (2004a). Evolution of a constructivist conceptualization of epistemological reflection. *Educational Psychologist, 39*(1), 31–42.

Baxter Magolda, M. B. (2007 in press). *Transforming knowledge to wisdom: Promoting self-authorship in college*. Paper presented at the AERA national meeting, April 2007.

Baxter Magolda, M. B. (2008). The evolution of self-authorship. In M. S. Khine (Ed.), *Knowing, knowledge and beliefs: Epistemological studies across diverse cultures* (pp. 45–64). New York: Springer.

Baxter Magolda, M. B. (2009). *Autoring your life*. Sterling, Virginia: Stylus Publishing.

Baxter Magolda, M. B., & King, P. M. (2004). *Learning partnerships*. Sterling, Virginia: Stylus.

Beah, I. (2007). *A long way gone – Memoirs of a boy soldier*. New York: Farrar, Strauss and Giroux.

Beaty, E., Dall'Alba, G., & Marton, F. (1997). The personal experience of learning in higher education: Changing views and enduring perspectives. In P. Sutherland (Ed.), *Adult learning:A reader* (pp. 150–165). London: Kogan Page.

Beers, S. E. (1988). Epistemological assumptions and college teaching: Interactions in the college classroom. *Journal of Research and Development in Education, 21*(4), 87–94.

Beishuizen, J. J. (2004). *De vrolijke wetenschap*. Amsterdam: Papyrus Press.

Belenky, M. F., Clinchy, B. M., Goldberger, N. R., & Tarule, J. M. (1986/1997). *Women's ways of knowing: The development of self, voice and mind*. New York: Basic Books.

Bendixen, L.D. (2002). A Process Model of Epistemic Belief Change. In B. K. Hofer & P. R. Pintrich (Eds.), *Personal epistemology* (pp. 191–208). Mahwah, NJ: Lawrence Erlbaum Ass.

Biggs, J. B. (1979). Individual differences in study processes and the quality of learning outcomes. *Higher Education, 8*, 381–394.

Biggs, J. B. (1987). *Student approaches to learning and studying*. Hawthorne, Victoria (Australia): Australian Council for Educational Research.

Biggs, J. B. (1996). Enhancing teaching through constructive alignment. *Higher Education, 32*, 347–364.

REFERENCES

Biggs, J. B. (1999). *Teaching for quality learning at university: What the student does*. Buckingham: SRHE and Open University Press.

Biggs, J. B. (2003). *Teaching for quality learning at university: What the student does* (2nd ed.). Berkshire: SRHE and Open University Press.

Biggs, J., Kember, D., & Leung, D. Y. P. (2001). The revised two-factor study process questionnaire: R-SPQ-2F. *British Journal of Educational Psychology, 71*, 133–149.

Bignold, D. (2006). Schooled and tooled. *Caterer and Hotelkeeper*, August, 23–25.

Bowden, J. A. (2000). The nature of phenomenographic research. In J. A. Bowden & E. Walsh (Eds.), *Phenomenography* (pp. 1–18). Melbourne: RMIT Publishing.

Bowden, J. A., & Green, P. J. (in press a). Relationality and the myth of objectivity in research involving human participants. In J. Higgs, N. Cherry, R. Macklin, & R. Ajjawi (Eds.), *Researching practice: A discourse on methodologies*. The Netherlands: Sense Publishers.

Bowden, J. A., & Green, P. J. (in press b). The voice of the researched in qualitative research: Relationality and rigour. In J. Higgs, N. Cherry, R. Macklin, & R. Ajjawi (Eds.), *Researching practice: A discourse on methodologies*. The Netherlands: Sense Publishers.

Bowden, J. A., & Marton, F. (1998). *The university of learning: Beyond quality and competence in higher education*. London: Kogan Page.

Bowden, J. A., & Walsh, E. (2000). *Phenomenography*. Melbourne: RMIT Publishing.

Boulton-Lewis, G. M., Wilss, L. A., & Lewis, D. C. (2001). Changes in conceptions of learning for indigenous Australian university students. *British Journal of Educational Psychology, 71*, 327–341.

Boulton-Lewis, G. M., Marton, F., Lewis, D. C., & Wilss, L. A. (2000a). Aboriginal and Torres Strait Islander university students' conceptions of formal learning and experiences of informal learning. *Higher Education, 39*, 469–488.

Boulton-Lewis, G. M., Marton, F., Lewis, D. C., & Wilss, L. A. (2000b). Learning in formal and informal contexts: Conceptions and strategies of Aboriginal and Torres Strait Islanders university students. *Learning and Instruction, 10*, 393–414.

Boulton-Lewis, G. M., Marton, F., Lewis, D. C., & Wilss, L. A. (2004). A longitudinal study of learning for a group of indigenous Australian university students: Dissonant conceptions and strategies. *Higher Education, 47*, 91–112.

Bråten, I., & Strømsø, H. I. (2004). Epistemological beliefs and implicit theories of intelligence as predictors of achievement goals. *Contemporary Educational Psychology*, 371–388.

Bråten, I., & Strømsø, H. I. (2005). The relationship between epistemological beliefs, implicit theories of intelligence, and self-regulated learning among Norwegian postsecondary students. *British Journal of Educational Psychology, 75*, 539–565.

Brickhouse, N. W. (1989). The teaching of the philosophy of science in secondary classrooms: Case studies of teachers personal theories. *International Journal of Science Education, 11*(4), 437–449.

Brickhouse, N. W. (1990). Teachers' beliefs about the nature of science and their relationship to classroom practice. *Journal of Teacher Education, 41*(3), 53–62.

Brownlee, J., Purdie, N., & Boulton-Lewis, G. (2001). Epistemological beliefs in pre-service teacher education students. *Higher Education Research and Development, 20*(3), 281–291.

Buelens, H., Clement, M., & Clarebout, G. (2002). University assistants' conceptions of knowledge, learning and instruction. *Research in Education, 67*, 44–57.

Cano, F., & Cardelle-Elawar, M. (2004). An integrated analysis of secondary school students' conceptions and beliefs about learning. *European Journal of Psychology of Education, 29*(2), 167–187.

Cantwell, R. H., & Scevak, J. J. (2004). Engaging university learning: The experiences of students entering university via recognition of prior industrial experience. *Higher Education Research & Development, 23*(2), 131–145.

Carr, W., & Kemmis, S. (1986). *Becoming critical: Education, knowledge and action research*. Brighton, Sussex: Falmer Press.

Chan, K. (2003). Hong Kong teacher education students' epistemological beliefs and approaches to learning. *Research in Education, 69*, 36–50.

Chênevert, R. J., & van Muyden, J. (2001). Module audit Hotelschool Den Haag. Internal report Hotelschool The Hague.

Chênevert, R. J., van Hest, P. B., & van Rossum, E. J. (1993). *A glance in the mirror -self evaluation report Hotelschool The Hague*. Den Haag: Hotelschool The Hague.

Chênevert, R. J., Würffel, I. I., van Rossum, E. J., & van der Horst, A. (2000). *The measure taken – self evaluation report Hotelschool The Hague*. Den Haag: Hotelschool The Hague.

Cherry, N. L. (2005). Preparing for practice in the age of complexity. *Higher Education Research & Development, 24*(4), 309–320.

Chinen, A. B. (1985). Fairy tales and transpersonal development in later life. *The Journal of Transpersonal Psychology, 17*(2), 99–122.

Collis, K. F., & Biggs, J. B. (1979). *Classroom examples of conginitive development phenomena: The SOLO taxonomy*. Final report, Educational Research and Development Committee, Woden, A.C.T.

Csikszentmihalyi, M. (1993). *The evolving self – a psychology for the third millenium*. New York: HarperCollins Publishers.

Csikszentmihalyi, M., & Rathunde, K. (1990). The psychology of wisdom: An evolutionary interpretation. In R. J. Sternberg (Ed.), *Wisdom, its nature, origins and developments* (pp. 25–51). Cambridge, UK: Cambridge University Press.

Dahl, T. I., Bals, M., & Turi, A. L. (2005). Are students' beliefs about knowledge and learning associated with their reported use of learning strategies? *British Journal of Educational Psychology, 75*, 257–273.

Dahlgren, L.-O. (1984). Outcomes of learning. In F. Marton, D. Hounsell, & N. Entwistle (Eds.), *The experience of learning* (pp. 19–35). Edinburgh: Scottish Academic Press.

Debold, E. (2002). Epistemology, fourth order consciousness, and the subject-object relationship. *What is enlightenment?* Fall-Winter 2002, 143–154.

Demastes, S. S., Good, R. G., & Peebles, P. (1995). Students' conceptual ecologies and the process of conceptual change in evolution. *Cience Education, 79*(6), 637–666.

Devlin, M. (2006). Challenging accepted wisdom about he place of conceptions of teaching in university teaching improvement. *International Journal of Teaching and Learning in Higher Education, 18*(2), 112–119.

Dewey, J. (1910/1997). *How we think*. [Unabridged 1910 version] Mineola, New York: Dover Publications, Inc.

Dewey, J. (1916). *Democracy and education*. New York: The Free Press.

Dewey, J. (1938/1997). *Experience and education*. New York: Touchstone.

Doblaev, L. P. (1984). *Studieteksten lezen en begrijpen [Reading and Understanding Study Text]*. Apeldoorn: Van Walraven.

Duell, O. K., & Schommer-Aikins, M. (2001). Measures of people's beliefs about knowledge and learning. *Educational Psychology Review, 13*(4), 419–447.

Dweck, C. S. (2002). Beliefs that make smart people dumb. In R. J. Sternberg (Ed.), *Why smart people can be so stupid*. New Haven, CT: Yale University Press.

Dweck, C. S., & Bempechat, J. (1983). Children's theories of intelligence: Implications for learning. In S. Paris, G. Olson, & H. Stevenson (Eds.), *Learning and motivation in children*. Hillsdale, NJ: Erlbaum.

Edmondson, K. M. & Novak, J. D. (1993). The interplay of scientific epistemological views, learning strategies, and attitudes of college students. *Journal of Research in Science Teaching, 30*(6), 547–559.

Eley, M. G. (2006). Teachers' conceptions of teaching, and the making of specific decisions in planning to teach. *Higher Education, 51*, 191–214.

Entwistle, N. J. (1997). Introduction: Phenomenography in higher education. *Higher Education Research & Development, 16*, 127–134.

Entwistle, N. J. (2007). Research into student learning and university teaching. In N. J. Entwistle & P. Tomlinson (Eds.), *Student learning and university teaching* (pp. 1–18). Monograph Series II of the British Journal of Educational Psychology, Number 4.

Entwistle, N. J., & Ramsden, P. (1983). *Understanding student learning*. New York: Nichols.

REFERENCES

Entwistle, N. J., & Walker, P. (2000). Strategic alertness and expanded awareness within sophisticated conceptions of teaching. *Instructional Science*, *28*, 335–361.

Entwistle, N. J., & McCune, V. (2004). The conceptual bases of study strategy inventories. *Educational Psychology Review*, *16*(4), 325–345.

Entwistle, N. J., McCune, V., & Walker, P. (2001). Conceptions, styles and approaches within higher education: Analytic abstractions and everyday experience. In R. J. Sternberg & L. Zhang (Eds.), *Perspectives on thinking, learning, and cognitive styles* (pp. 103–136). Mahwah, NJ: Lawrence Erlbaum Associates.

Fitzgerald, J., & Cunningham, J. W. (2002). Mapping basic issues for identifying epistemological outlooks. In B. K. Hofer & P. R. Pintrich (Eds.), *Personal epistemology* (pp. 209–228). Mahwah, NJ: Lawrence Erlbaum Ass.

Fox, D. (1983). Personal theories of teaching. *Studies in Higher Education*, *8*(2). 151–163.

Freidus, H. (2002). Narrative research in teacher education: New questions, new practices. In N. Lyons & V. K. LaBoskey (Eds.), *Narrative inquiry in practice* (pp. 160–172). New York: Teachers College Press.

Freire, P. (2000). *Pedagogy of the oppressed.* (30th ed.). New York: Continuum.

García Duncan, T., & McKeachie, W. J. (2005). The making of the motivated strategies for learning questionnaire. *Educational Psychologist*, *40*(2), 117–128.

Garrett-Ingram, C. (1997). *Something to believe in: The relationship between epistemological beliefs and study strategies.* Paper presented at the AERA, March 1997, Chicago.

Gibbs, G. (1998). Changing lecturers' conceptions of teaching and learning through action research. In A. Brew (Ed.), *Directions in staff development* (pp. 21–35). Buckingham: SRHE and Open University Press.

Gibbs, G. (1999). Using assessment strategically to change the way students learn. In S. Brown & A. Glaser (Eds.), *Assessment matters in higher education* (pp. 41–53). Buckinham: Open University Press.

Gladwell, M. (2008). *Outliers – The story of success.* New York: Little, Brown and Company.

Gomes, P. (2004). *Tropenkind [Child of the Tropics].* The Hague: Van Stockum.

Gordon, C., & Debus, R. (2002). Developing deep learning approaches and personal teaching efficacy within a preservice teacher education context. *British Journal of Educational Psychology*, *72*, 483–511.

Gow, L., & Kember, D. (1990). Does higher education promote independent learning? *Higher Education*, *19*, 307–322.

Gow, L., & Kember, D. (1993). Conceptions of teaching and their relationship to student learning. *British Journal of Educational Psychology*, *63*, 20–33.

Grow, G. (1977). *What is a teacher?* Retrieved September 6, 2006, from http://www.longleaf.net/grow/eacher.html

Guskey, T. R. (1986). Staff development and the process of teacher change. *Educational Researcher*, *15*(5), 5–12.

Hamer, R. (2010). *Tien didactische aandachtspunten voor bètavakken op de havo.* [Ten teaching behaviours of interest for science and math in secondary education]. Research Series of the National Platform Science & Technology. The Hague: Platform Bèta Techniek.

Hamer, R., & Van Rossum, E. J. (2008). *Learning to be: Conceptions of being. Beyond relativism and postmodernism.* Paper presented at the International Conference on Self-Authorship, May 2008, Riva San Vitale, Switzerland.

Hamer, R., & Van Rossum, E. J. (2010). Linking learning conceptions to self-Authorship and beyond. In M. B. Baxter Magolda, E. G. Creamer, & P. S. Meszaros (Eds.), *Development and assessment of self-Authorship.* Stirling, VA: Stylus

Hashweh, M. Z. (1996). Effects of science teachers' epistemological beliefs in teaching. *Journal of Research in Science Teaching*, *33*(1), 47–63.

Hativa, N. (2002). Becoming a better teacher: A case of changing the pedagogical knowledge and beliefs of law professors. In N. Hativa & P. Goodyear (Eds.), *Teacher thinking, beliefs and knowledge in higher education* (pp. 289–319). Dordrecht, The Netherlands: Kluwer Academic Publishers.

Hativa, N., & Goodyear, P. (2002). Research on teacher thinking, beliefs, and knowledge in higher education: Foundations, status and prospects. In N. Hativa & P. Goodyear (Eds.), *Teacher thinking, beliefs and knowledge in higher education* (pp. 335–359). Dordrecht, The Netherlands: Kluwer Academic Publishers.

Haynes, C. (2004). Promoting self-authorship through an interdisciplinary writing curriculum. In M. Baxter Magolda & P. M. King (Eds.), *Learning partnerships*. Sterling, Virginia: Stylus.

Hazel, E. Conrad, L., & Martin, E. (1997). Exploring gender and phenomenography. *Higher Education Research & Development, 16*(2), 213–266.

HBO-raad. (1994). *Profession: Hospitality – report of the visitation committee for hotel management schools in the Netherlands*. Kelpen: Drukkerij Tonnaer.

HBO-raad. (2000). *Hospitality management in the new millennium*. Report by the visiting and accreditation committee for hotel management schools in the Netherlands. Den Haag: Lifoka.

Hill, L. (2000). What does it take to change minds? Intellectual development of preservice teachers. *Journal of Teacher Education, 51*(1), 50–62.

Ho, A. (2000). A conceptual change approach to staff development: A model for programme design. *The International Journal for Academic Development, 5*(1), 30–41.

Ho, A., Watkins, D., & Kelly, M. (2001). The conceptual change approach to improving teaching and learning: An evaluation of a Hong Kong staff development programme. *Higher Education, 42*, 143–169.

Hofer, B. K. (1999). Instructional context in the college mathematics classroom: Epistemological beliefs and student motivation. *Journal of Staff, Program & Organization Development, 16*(7), 73–82.

Hofer, B. K. (2000). Dimensionality and disciplinary differences in personal epistemology. *Contemporary Educational Psychology, 25*, 378–405.

Hofer, B. K. (2001). Personal epistemology research: Implications for learning and teaching. *Journal of Educational Psychology Review, 13*(4), 353–383.

Hofer, B. K. (2002a). Personal epistemology as a psychological and educational construct: An introduction. In B. K. Hofer, & P. R. Pintrich (Eds.), *Personal epistemology* (pp. 3–14). Mahwah, NJ: Lawrence Erlbaum Ass.

Hofer, B. K. (2002b). Epistemological world views of teachers: From beliefs to practice. *Issues in Education, 2*(8), 167–173.

Hofer, B. K. (2004). Exploring the dimensions of personal epistemology in differing classroom contexts: Student interpretations during the first year of college. *Contemporary Educational Psychology, 29*, 129–163.

Hofer, B. K., & Pintrich, P. R. (1997). The development of epistemological theories: Beliefs about knowledge and knowing and their relation to learning. *Review of Educational Research, 67*(1), 88–140.

Hofer, B. K., & Pintrich, P. R. (2002). *Personal epistemology*. Mahwah, NJ: Lawrence Erlbaum Ass.

Hotelschool The Hague. (2000). *Study guide 2000/2001*. Den Haag: Hotelschool The Hague.

Hotelschool The Hague. (2004). *75 Jarig Jubileum hotelschool Den Haag [75th Anniversary Hotelschool The Hague]*. Den Haag: Onkenhout.

Hotelschool The Hague. (2005). *Weekbericht [Weekly News]*. 23.

Huxley, A. (1972, quoted in Kegan 1982). Visionary experience. In J. White (Ed.), *The highest state of consciousness*. New York: Archer.

Jehng, J.-C. J., Johnson, S. D., & Anderson, R. C. (1993). Schooling and students' epistemological beliefs about learning. *Contemporary Educational Psychology, 18*, 23–35.

Kang, N.-H., & Wallace, C. (2004). Secondary science teachers' use of laboratory activities: Linking epistemological beliefs, goals and practices. *Science Teacher Education, 89*. 140–165. Published online 19 November 2004 in Wiley InterScience (www.interscience.wiley.com)

Kardash, C. M., & Howell, K. L. (2000). Effects of epistemological beliefs and topic-specific beliefs on undergraduates' cognitive and strategic processing of dual-positional text. *Journal of Educational Psychology, 92*(3), 524–535.

REFERENCES

Kardash, C. M., & Scholes, R. J. (1996). Effects of preexisting beliefs, epistemological beliefs, and need for cognition on interpretation of controversial issues. *Journal of Educational Psychology, 88*(2), 260–271.

Kegan, R. (1982). *The evolving self – problem and process in human development.* Cambridge, MA: Harvard University Press.

Kegan, R. (1994). *In over our Heads.* The mental demands of modern life. Cambridge, MA: Harvard University Press.

Kember, D. (1991). Instructional design for meaningful learning. *Instructional Science, 20*, 289–319.

Kember, D. (1997). A reconceptualisation of the research into university academics' conceptions of teaching. *Learning and Instruction, 7*(3), 255–275.

Kember, D. (2000). *Action learning and action research.* London: Kogan Page.

Kember, D. (2001). Beliefs about knowledge and the process of teaching and learning as a factor in adjusting to study in higher education. *Studies in Higher Education, 26*(2), 205–221.

Kember, D., & Gow, L. (1992). Action research as a form of staff development in higher education. *Higher Education, 23*, 297–310.

Kember, D., & Kwan, K.-P. (2000). Lecturers' approaches to teaching and their relationship to conceptions of good teaching. *Instructional Science, 28*, 469–490.

King, P. M., & Baxter Magolda, M. B. (2004). Creating learning partnerships in higher education. In M. Baxter Magolda & P. M. King (Eds.), *Learning partnerships.* Sterling, Virginia: Stylus.

King, P. M., & Kitchener, K. S. (1994). *Developing reflective judgment.* San Fransisco: Jossey-Bass Publishers.

Kitchener, K. S. (1983). Cognition, metacognition, and epistemic cognition. A three-level model of cognitive processing. *Human Development, 26*, 222–232.

Kitchener, K. S., & Brenner, H. G. (1990). Wisdom and reflective judgment: Knowing in the face of uncertainty. In R. J. Sternberg (Ed.), *Wisdom, its nature, origins and developments* (pp. 212–229). Cambridge, UK: Cambridge University Press.

Kuhn, D. (1991). *The skills of argument.* Cambridge, UK: Cambridge University Press.

Kuhn, D. (2001). How do people know? *Psychological Science, 12*(1), 1–8.

Kuhn, D. (2005). *Education for thinking.* Cambridge, MA: Harvard University Press.

Kuhn, D., & Weinstock, M. (2002). What is epistemological thinking and why does it matter? In B. K. Hofer & P. R. Pintrich (Eds.), *Personal epistemology* (pp. 121–144). Mahwah, NJ: Lawrence Erlbaum Ass.

Kuhn, D., Cheney, R., & Weinstock, M. (2000). The development of epistemological understanding. *Cognitive Development, 15*, 309–328.

Kurfiss, J. (1977). Sequentiality and structure in a cognitive model of college student development. *Developmental Psychology, 13*(6), 565–571.

Labouvie-Vief, G. (1990). Wisdom as integrated thought: Historical and developmental perspectives. In R. J. Sternberg (Ed.), *Wisdom, its nature, origins and developments* (pp. 52–83). Cambridge, UK: Cambridge University Press.

Langer, E. J. (1997). *The power of mindful learning.* Cambridge, MA: Da Capo Press.

Larsson, S. (1983). Paradoxes in teaching. *Instructional Science, 12*, 355–365.

Leadbeater, B. (1986). The resolution of relativism in adult thinking: Subjective, objective or conceptual? *Human Development, 29*, 291–300.

Lederman, N. G. (1999). Teachers' understanding of the nature of science and classroom practice: Factors that facilitate of impede the relationship. *Journal of Research in Science Teaching, 36*(8). 916–929.

Lindblom-Ylänne, S., & Lonka, K. (1999). Individual ways of interacting with the learning environment – are they related to study success? *Learning and Instruction, 9*, 1–18.

Lindblom-Ylänne, S., & Lonka, K. (2000). Dissonant study orchestrations of high-achieving university students. *European Journal of Psychology of Education, 15*(1), 19–32.

Lindblom-Ylänne, S., & Lonka, K. (2001). Students' perceptions of assessment practices in a traditional medical curriculum. *Advances in Health Sciences Education, 6*, 121–140.

Linder, C. J. (1992). Is teacher-reflected epistemology a source of conceptual difficulty in physics? *International Journal of Science Education, 14*(1), 111–121.
Lonka, K., & Lindblom-Ylänne, S. (1996). Epistemologies, conceptions of learning and study practices in medicine and psychology. *Higher Education, 31*, 5–24.
Lotter, C., Harwood, W. S., & Bonner, J. J. (2007). The influence of core teaching conceptions on teachers' use of inquiry teaching practices. *Journal of Research in Science Teaching*. Published online in Wiley InterScience (www.interscience.wiley.com)
Lyons, N. (1990). Dilemmas of knowing: Ethical and epistemological dimensions of teachers' work and development. *Harvard Educational Review, 60*(2), 159–180.
Lyons, N., & LaBoskey, V. K. (2002a). *Narrative inquiry in practice*. New York: Teachers College Press.
Lyons, N., & LaBoskey, V. K. (2002b). Why narrative inquiry or exemplars for a scholership of teaching? In N. Lyons & V. K. LaBoskey (Eds.), *Narrative inquiry in practice* (pp. 11–27). New York: Teachers College Press.
Maor, D., & Taylor, P. C. (1995). Teacher epistemology and scientific inquiry in computerized classroom environments. *Journal of Research in Science Teaching, 32*(8), 839–354.
Marchese, T. J. (1998). The new conversations about learning. Insights from neuroscience and anthropology, cognitive science and workplace studies. *New horizons for learning*. Document available from http://www.newhorizons.org/lilfelong/higher_ed/marchese.htm (21 October 2007).
Marra, R., & Palmer, B. (2004). Encouraging intellectual growth: Senior college student profiles. *Journal of Adult Development, 11*(2), 111–122.
Marra, R., Palmer, B., & Litzinger, T. A. (2000). The effects of a first-year engineering design course on student intellectual development as measured by the Perry scheme. *Journal of Engineering Education*, 39–44.
Martens, M. L. (1992). Inhibitors to implementing a problem-solving approach to teaching elementary science: Case study of a teacher in change. *School Science and Mathematics, 92*(3), 150–156.
Martinez, M. A., Sauleda, N., & Huber, G. L. (2001). Mataphors as blueprints of thinking about teaching and learning. *Teaching and Teacher Education, 17*, 965–977.
Marton, F. (1981). Phenomenography: Describing conceptions of the world around us. *Instructional Science, 10*, 177–200.
Marton, F. (1986). Phenomenography—A research approach to investigating different understandings of reality. *Journal of Thought 3*(21), 28–49.
Marton, F., & Booth, S. (1997). *Learning and awareness*. Mahwah, NJ: Lawrence Erlbaum.
Marton, F., & Säljö, R. (1984). Approaches to learning. In F. Marton, D. Hounsell, & N. Entwistle (Eds.), *The experience of learning* (pp. 36–55). Edinburgh: Scottish Academic Press.
Marton, F., Dall'Alba, G., & Beaty, E. (1993). Conceptions of learning. *International Journal of Educational Research, 19*(3), 277–300.
Marton, F., Hounsell, D., & Entwistle, N. (1984). *The experience of learning*. Edinburgh: Scottish Academic Press.
Marton, F., Hounsell, D., & Entwistle, N. (1997). *The experience of learning* (2nd ed.). Edinburgh: Scottish Academic Press.
Mason, L., & Boscolo, P. (2004). Role of epistemological understanding and interest in interpreting a controversy and in topic-specific belief change. *Contemporary Educational Psychology, 29*, 103–128.
McDowell, L., & Sambell, K. (1999). The experience of innovative assessment: Student perspectives. In S. Brown & A. Glaser (Eds.), *Assessment matters in higher education.* (pp. 71–82). Buckinham: Open University Press.
McKeachie, W. J. (1995). Learning styles can become learning strategies. *The National Teaching & Learning Forum, 4*(6), 1–4.
McVicker Clinchy, B. (2002). Revisting women's ways of knowing. In B. K. Hofer & P. R. Pintrich (Eds.), *Personal epistemology* (pp. 63–87). Mahwah, NJ: Lawrence Erlbaum Ass.
Meacham, J. A. (1990). The loss of wisdom. In R. J. Sternberg (Ed.), *Wisdom, its nature, origins and developments* (pp. 181–211). Cambridge, UK: Cambridge University Press.
Menthowski, M. and Associates. (2000). *Learning that Lasts*. San Francisco: Jossey-Bass.

REFERENCES

Micari, M., Light, G., Calkins, S., & Streitwieser, B. (2007). Assessment beyond performance: Phenomenography in educational evaluation. *American Journal of Evaluation, 28*(4), 458–476.

Moore, W. S. (1988). Current issues in the assessment of the Perry scheme. *The Georgia Journal of College State Affairs*, 11–14.

Moore, W. S. (2002). Understanding learning in a postmodern world± reconsidering the Perry scheme of ethical and intellectual development. In B. K. Hofer & P. R. Pintrich (Eds.), *Personal epistemology* (pp. 15–36). Mahwah, NJ: Lawrence Erlbaum Ass.

Morgan, A., & Beatty, L. (1997). The world of the learner. In F. Marton, D. Hounsell, & N Entwistle (Eds.), *The experience of learning* (pp. 217–237). Edinburgh: Scottish Academic Press.

Morgan, A., Gibbs, G., & Taylor, E. (1981), *What do open university students initially understand about learning?* Study Methods Group Report No. 8. Institute of Educational Technology, Open University, Milton Keynes.

Mugler, F., & Landbeck, R. (1997). Learning in the South Pacific and phenomenography across cultures. *Higher Education Research & Development, 16*(2), 227–239.

Nelson, C. (1999). On the persistence of unicorns: The trade-off between content and critical thinking revisited. In B. A. Pescosolido & R. Aminzade (Eds.). *The social worlds of higher education* (pp. 168–184). London: Pine Forge Press.

Nieminen, J., Lindblom-Ylänne, S., & Lonka, K. (2004). The development of study orientations and study success in students of pharmacy. *Instructional Science, 32*, 387–417.

Pajares, M. F. (1992). Teachers' beliefs and educational research: Cleaning up a messy construct. *Review of Educational Research, 62*(3). 307–332.

Palmer, P. J. (1987). Community, conflict and ways of knowing, *Change*, Sept/Oct., 20–25.

Palmer, P. J. (1998). *The courage to teach.* San Francisco: Jossey-Bass.

Paulsen, M. B., & Feldman, K. A. (1999a). Student motivation and epistemological beliefs. *New Directions for Teaching and Learning, 78*, 17–25.

Paulsen, M. B., & Feldman, K. A. (1999b). Epistemological beliefs and self-regulated learning. *Journal of Staff, Program & Organization Development, 16*(2), 83–91.

Paulsen, M. B., & Feldman, K. A. (2005). The conditional and interaction effects of epistemological beliefs on the self-regulated learning of college students: Motivational strategies. *Research in Higher Education, 46*(7), 731–768.

Paulsen, M. B., & Feldman, K. A. (2007 in press). The conditional and interaction effects of epistemological beliefs on the self-regulated learning of college students: Cognitive and behavioral strategies. *Research in Higher Education.*

Pavelich, M. J., & Moore, W. S. (1996). Measuring the effect of experiential education using the Perry model. *Journal of Engineering Education*, 287–292.

Perry, W. G. (1970). *Forms of intellectual and ethical development in the college years: A scheme.* New York: Holt, Rinehart & Winston.

Perry, W. G. (1981). Cognitive and ethical growth: The making of meaning. In A. W. Chickering & Associates (Eds.), *The modern American college* (pp. 76–116). San Francisco: Jossey-Bass.

Perry, W. G. (1986). Book reviews – The experience of learning. *Harvard Educational Review, 56*(2), 187–194.

Perry, W. G. (1988). Different worlds in the same classroom. In P. Ramsden (Ed.), *Improving learning – new perspectives* (pp. 145–161). London: Kogan Page.

Phillips, F. (1998). Accounting students' beliefs about nowledge: Associating performance with underlying belief dimensions. *Issues in Accounting Education, 13*(1), 113–126.

Phillips, F. (2001). A research note on accounting students' epistemological beliefs, study strategies, and unstructured problem-solving performance. *Issues in accounting education, 16*(1), 21–39.

Pinker, S. (1997). *How the mind works.* London: Penguin Books.

Pinker, S. (2002). *The blank slate.* London: Penguin Books.

Pratt; D. D. (1992). Conceptions of teaching. *Adult Education Quarterly, 42*(4), 203–220.

Prawat, R. S. (1992). Teachers' beliefs about teaching and learning: A constructivist perspective. *American Journal of Education, May*, 354–395.

Prosser, M., & Trigwell, K. (1999). *Understanding learning and teaching: The experience of higher education*. Buckingham: SRHE/Open University Press.

Prosser, M., Trigwell, K., & Taylor, P. (1994). A phenomenographic study of academics' conceptions of science learning and teaching. *Learning and Instruction, 4*, 217–232.

Qian, G., & Alvermann, D. (1995). Role of epistemological beliefs and learned helplessness in secondary school students' learning science concepts from text. *Journal of Educational Psychology, 87*(2), 282–292.

Qian, G., & Alvermann, D. E. (2000). Relationship between epistemological beliefs and conceptual change learning. *Reading & Writing Quarterly, 16*, 59–74.

Qian, G., & Pan, J. (2002). A comparison of epistemological beliefs and learning from science text between American and Chinese high school students. In B. K. Hofer & P. R. Pintrich (Eds.), *Personal epistemology* (pp. 365–385). Mahwah, NJ: Lawrence Erlbaum Ass.

Quinlan, K. M. (1999). Commonalities and controversy in context: a study of academic historians' educational beliefs. *Teaching and Teacher Education, 15*, 447–463.

Quinlan, K. M. (2002). Scholarly dimensions of academics' beliefs about engineering education. *Teachers and Teaching: theory and practice, 8*(1), 41–64.

Radloff, A. (2002). Learning to teach: Changes in technical college teachers' beliefs about learning and teaching over a two year teacher education program. In N. Hativa & P. Goodyear (Eds.), *Teacher thinking, beliefs and knowledge in higher education* (pp. 265–287). Dordrecht, The Netherlands: Kluwer Academic Publishers.

Reuland, R. J., Bos, R. A., de Vries, A. C., van Rossum, E. J., & Würffel, I. I. (1997). *Code of practice*. Internal report Hotelschool The Hague.

Reybold, L. E. (2001). Encouraging the transformation of personal epistemology. *Qualitative Studies in Education, 14*(3), 413–428.

Reybold, L. E. (2002). Pragmatic epistemology: ways of knowing as way of being. *International Journal of Lifelong Education, 21*(6), 537–550.

Richardson, J. T. E. (2000). *Researching student learning: Approaches to studying in campus-based and distance education*. Buckingham: SRHE and Open University Press.

Richardson, J. T. E. (2005). Students' approaches to learning and teachers' approaches to teaching in higher education. *Educational Psychology, 25*(6). 673–680.

Richardson, J. T. E. (2007 in press). Mental models of learning in distance education. *British Journal of Educational Psychology*.

Rodríguez, L., & Cano, F. (2006). The epistemological beliefs, learning approaches and study orchestrations of university students. *Studies in Higher Education, 31*(5), 617–636.

Rodríguez, L., & Cano, F. (2007 in press). The learning approaches and epistemological beliefs of university students: A cross-sectional and longitudinal study. *Studies in Higher Education, 32*(5), 647–667.

Rozendaal, J. S., de Brabander, C. J., & Minnaert, A. (2001). *Boundaries and dimensionality of epistemological beliefs*. Paper presented at the 9th Bi-annual Conference of the European Association for Research on Learning and Instruction, Fribourg, Switzerland.

Ryan, M. P. (1984a). Conceptions of prose coherence: Individual differences in epistemological standards. *Journal of Educational Psychology, 76*(6), 1226–1238.

Ryan, M. P. (1984b). Monitoring text comprehension: Individual differences in epistemological standards. *Journal of Educational Psychology, 76*(2), 248–258.

Säljö, R. (1979a). *Learning in the learner's perspective. I: Some common sense conceptions*. Reports from the Institute of Education, University of Göteborg, Mölndal, No. 76.

Säljö, R. (1979b). Learning about learning. *Higher Education, 8*, 443–451.

Säljö, R. (1979c). *Learning in the learner's perspective. II: Differences in awareness*. Reports from the Institute of Education, University of Göteborg, Mölndal, No. 77.

Säljö, R. (1994). Minding action; conceiving of the world versus participating in cultural practices. *Nordisk Pedagogik, 14*(2), 71–80.

Säljö, R. (1997). Talk as data and practice – a critical look at phenomenographic inquiry and the appeal to experience. *Higher Education Research & Development, 16*, 173–190.

Samuelowicz, K., & Bain, J. D. (1992). Conceptions of teaching held by academic teachers. *Higher Education, 24*, 93–111.
Samuelowicz, K., & Bain, J. D. (2001). Revisiting academics' beliefs about teaching and learning. *Higher Education, 41*, 299–325.
Samuelowicz, K., & Bain, J. D. (2002). Identifying academics' orientations to assessment practice. *Higher Education, 43*, 173–201.
Sandberg, J. (1997). Are phenomenographic results reliable? *Higher Education Research & Development, 16*, 203–212.
Schoenfeld, A. H. (1988). When good teaching leads to bad results: the disasters of "well-taught" mathematics courses. *Educational Psychologist, 23*(2), 145–166.
Schoenfeld, A. H. (1996). In fostering communities of inquiry, must it matter that the teacher knows "the answer"? *For the Learning of Mathematics, 16*(3), 11–16.
Schommer, M. (1990). Effects of beliefs about the nature of knowledge on comprehension. *Journal of Educational Psychology, 82*(3), 498–504.
Schommer, M. (1993). Comparisons of beliefs about the nature of knowledge and learning among postsecondary students. *Research in Higher Education, 34*(3), 355–370.
Schommer, M. (1994). An emerging conceptualization of epistemological beliefs and their role in learning. In R. Garner & P. A. Alexander (Eds.), *Beliefs about text and instruction with text* (pp. 25–40). Hillsdale: Lawrence Erlbaum Associates.
Schommer, M. (1998). The influence of age and education on epistemological beliefs. *British Journal of Educational Psychology, 68*, 551–561.
Schommer, M., & Walker, K. (1995). Are epistemological beliefs similar across domains? *Journal of Educational Psychology, 87*(3), 424–432.
Schommer, M., Calvert, C., Gariglietti, G., & Bajaj, A. (1997). The development of epistemological beliefs among secondary students: A longitudinal study. *Journal of Educational Psychology, 89*(1), 37–40.
Schommer, M., Crouse, A., & Rhodes, N. (1992). Epistemological beliefs and mathematical text comprehension: Believing it is simple does not make it so. *Journal of Educational Psychology, 84*(4), 435–443.
Schommer-Aikins, M. (2002). An evolving theoretical framework for an epistemological belief system. In B. K. Hofer & P. R. Pintrich (Eds.). *Personal epistemology* (pp. 103–118). Mahwah, NJ: Lawrence Erlbaum Ass.
Schommer-Aikins, M. (2004). Explaining the epistemological belief system: Introducing the embedded systemic model and coordinated research approach. *Educational Psychologist, 39*(1), 19–29.
Schommer-Aikins, M., & Hutter, R. (2002). Epistemological beliefs and thinking about everyday controversial issues. *The Journal of Psychology, 136*(1), 5–20.
Schommer-Aikins, M., Duell, O. K., & Barker, S. (2002). Epistemological beliefs across domains using Biglan's classification of academic disciplines. *Research in Higher Education, 44*(3), 347–366.
Schraw, G., & Olafson, L. (2002). Teachers' epistemological world views and educational practices. *Issues in Education, 8*(2), 99–148.
Schraw, G., Dunkle, M. E., & Bendixen, L. D. (1995). Cognitive process in well-defined and ill-defined problem solving. *Applied Cognitive Psychology, 9*, 523–538.
Schreiber, J. B., & Shinn, D. (2003). Epistemological beliefs of community college students and their learning processes. *Community College Journal of Research and Practice, 27*, 699–709.
Sheppard, C., & Gilbert, J. (1991). Course design, teaching method and student epistemology. *Higher Education, 22*, 229–249.
Sinatra, G. M., & Kardash, C. M. (2004). Teacher candidates' epistemological beliefs, dispositions, and views on teaching as persuasion. *Contemporary Educational Psychology, 29*, 483–498.
Stephenson, B. W., & Hunt, C. (1977). Intellectual and ethical development: A dualistic curriculum intervention for college students. *The Counseling Psychologist, 6*(4), 39–42.
Sternberg, R. J. (2003). What is an "Expert Student"? *Educational Researcher, 32*(8), 5–9.
Sternberg, R. J. (2007). Interview in the NRC handelsblad, science and education supplement, 1 December 2007, p. 39.

Stipek, D. J., Givvin, K. B., Salmon, J. M., & MacGyvers, V. L. (2001). Teachers' beliefs and practices related to mathematics instruction. *Teaching and Teacher Education, 17*, 213–226.

Taylor, I. P., & van Rossum, E. J. (1986). *De relatie tussen visies op leren en intelligentie [The relationship between views on learning and intelligence].* Internal report. Tilburg: Tilburg University.

Tornstam, L. (2005). *Gerotranscendence*. New York: Springer Publishing Company.

Treffers, A., ter Heege, H., & Dekkers, A. (1982). Het stomste vak van de wereld (deel 2). [The most stupid subject in the world – part 2]. *Willem Bartjens, 1*(2), 81–88.

Trigwell, K., & Prosser, M. (1996). Changing approaches to teaching: A relational perspective. *Studies in Higher Education, 21*(3). 275–284.

Trigwell, K., Prosser, M., & Taylor, P. (1994). Qualitative differences in approaches to teaching first year university science. *Higher Education, 27*, 75–84.

Trigwell, K., Prosser, M., and Waterhouse, F. (1999). Relations between teachers' approaches to teaching and students' approaches to learning. *Higher Education, 37*, 57–70.

Tsai, C.-C. (1998). An analysis of scientific epistemological beliefs and learning orientations of Taiwanese eighth graders. *Science Education, 82*(4), 480–485.

Tsai, C.-C. (1999). "Laboratory exercises help me memorize the scientific truths": A study of eighth graders' scientific epistemological views and learning in laboratory activities. *Science Education, 83*(6), 654–674.

Tsai, C.-C. (2002). Nested epistemologies: science teachers' beliefs of teaching, learning and science. *International Journal of Science Education, 24*(8), 771–783.

Tsai, C.-C. (2007). Teachers' scientific epistemological views: The coherence with instruction and students' views. *Science Education, 91*, 222–243. Published online 19 september 2006 in Wiley InterScience (www.interscience.wiley.com)

Tuchman, B. (1984). *The march of folly - from troy to Vietnam*. London: Sphere Books Ltd.

Van de Sande, J. P. (1999). *Gedragsobservatie [Behavioural observation]*. Groningen: Wolters-Noordhoff.

Van Hest, B., van Rossum, E. J., Thijssen, T., van Muyden, J., & Reuland, R. (1998). *Curriculum Hotelschool Den Haag 1998*. Internal report Hotelschool The Hague.

Van Rossum, E. J. (1988). Insight into Understanding. In R. Säljö (Ed.), *The written world* (pp. 195–208). Berlin Heidelberg: Springer-Verlag.

Van Rossum, E. J., & Hamer, R. (1985). *Learning: qualitative differences between novices and experts.* Paper presented at the 11th International Conference on Improving University Teaching, Utrecht, The Netherlands.

Van Rossum, E. J., & Hamer, R. (2004). Learning and teaching: A model of linked continua of conceptions. In C. Rust (Ed.), *Improving student learning – theory, research and scholarship* (pp. 121–133). Proceedings of the 2003 11th International Symposium Improving Student Learning.

Van Rossum, E. J., & Hamer, R. (2008). *Learning to know. Self-authorship: A state or developmental process?* Paper presented at the International Conference on Self-Authorship, May 2008, Riva San Vitale, Switzerland.

Van Rossum, E. J., & Schenk, S. M. (1984). The relationship between learning conception, study strategy and learning outcome. *British Journal of Educational Psychology, 54*, 73–83.

Van Rossum, E. J., & Taylor, I. P. (1987). *The relationship between conceptions of learning and good teaching: A scheme of cognitive development.* Paper presented at the Annual Meeting of the American Educational Research Association, April 1987, Washington DC, U.S.A.

Van Rossum, E. J., & Würffel, I. I. (1995). Onderwijsvernieuwing op de Hotelschool Den Haag [Educational innovation at the Hotelschool The Hague]. Internal report Hotelschool The Hague.

Van Rossum, E. J., Deijkers, R., & Hamer, R. (1984). Aanpassen of stimuleren. – over Kunst en Kunde. [Adaptation or Stimulation – about Art and Ability]. *Onderzoek van Onderwijs, 13*(4), 41–44.

Van Rossum, E. J., Deijkers, R., & Hamer, R. (1985). Students' learning conceptions and their interpretation of significant educational concepts. *Higher Education, 14*, 617–641.

van Rossum, E. J., Hamer, R., & Würffel, I. (2003). Students' learning conceptions: Relationships with teaching conceptions and developments. In H. Oost & S. Wils (Eds.), *Kennis Ontwikkelen – 22e Landelijke Dag Studievaardigheden.* Utrecht: IVLOS, University Utrecht.

Van Rossum, E. J., Würffel, I., & Hamer, R., (2002). *Development of students' learning conceptions in higher vocational [professional] education and their relation to teaching conceptions.* Paper presented at 22nd Landelijke Dag Studievaardigheden (LDS), April 2002, Utrecht, The Netherlands.

van Rossum, E. J., Wurffel, I. I., & Hofma, B. (2004a). *Entrepreneurial learning revived.* Internal report Hotelschool The Hague.

van Rossum, E. J., Wurffel, I. I., & Hofma, B. (2004b). *Ondernemend leren: ijkpunten per fase [Enterprising Learning: elaborated criteria per phase].* Internal report Hotelschool The Hague.

Vermetten, Y. J., Vermunt, J. D., & Lodewijks, H. G. (1999a). Consistency and variability of learning strategies in different university courses. *Higher Education, 37*, 1–21.

Vermetten, Y. J., Vermunt, J. D., & Lodewijks, H. G. (1999b). A longitudinal perspective on learning strategies in higher education – different view-poinst towards development. *British Journal of Educational Psychology, 69*(2), 221–242.

Vermetten, Y. J., Vermunt, J. D., & Lodewijks, H. G. (2002). Powerful learning environments? How university students differ in their response to instructional measures. *Learning and Instruction, 12*, 263–284.

Vermunt, J. D. (1996). Metacognitive, cognitive and affective aspects of learning styles and strategies: A phenomenographic analysis. *Higher Education, 31*, 25–50.

Vermunt, J. D. (1998). The regulation of constructive learning processes. *British Journal of Educational Psychology, 68*, 149–171.

Vermunt, J. D. (2003). The power of learning environments and the quality of student learning. In E. De Corte, L. Verschaffel, N. Entwistle, & J. van Merriënboer (Eds.), *Powerful learning environments.* Amsterdam: Pergamon.

Vermunt, J. D. (2005). Relations between student learning patterns and personal and contextual factors and academic performance. *Higher Education, 49*, 205–234.

Vermunt, J. D. (2006). *Docent van deze tijd: Leren en laten leren. [Teacher in our time: Learn and let learn].* Inaugural speech at the acceptance of the chair "Didactiek van het doceren en van het opleiden van docenten". Utrecht University, 24 March 2006.

Vermunt, J. D. (2007). The power of teaching-learning environments to influence student learning. In N. Entwistle & P. Tomlinson (Eds.), Student learning and university teaching. *British Journal of Educational Psychology*, Monograph Series II, 4.

Vermunt, J. D., & Verloop, N. (1999) Congruence and friction between learning and teaching. *Learning and Instruction, 9*, 257–280.

Vermunt, J. D., & Vermetten, Y. J. (2004). Patterns in student learning: Relationships between learning strategies, conceptions of learning, and learning orientations. *Educational Psychology Review, 16*(4), 359–384.

Vermunt, J. D., & Verschaffel, L. (2000). Process-oriented teaching. In R.-J. Simons, J. van der Linden, and T. Duffy (Eds.), *New learning.* Dordrecht, The Netherlands: Kluwer Academic Publishers.

Volet, S. E., Renshaw, P. D., & Tietzel, K. (1994). A short-term lon gitudinal investigation of cross-cultural differences in study approaches using Biggs' SPQ questionnaire. *British Journal of Educational Psychology, 64*. 301–318.

Weinstock, M., & Cronin, M. A. (2003). The everyday production of knowledge: Individual differences in epistemological understanding and juror-reasoning skill. *Applied Cognitive Psychology, 17*, 161–181.

White, B. C. (2000). Pre-service teachers' epistemology viewed through perspectives on problematic classroom situations. *Journal of Education for Teaching, 26*(3), 279–305.

Widick, C. (1977). The Perry scheme: A foundation for developmental practice. *The Counseling Psychologist, 6*(4), 35–38.

Widick, C., Knefelkamp, L. L., & Parker, C. A. (1975). The counselor as a developmental instructor. *Counselor Education and Supervision*, 286–296.

Wineburg, S. (2001). *Historical thinking and other unnatural acts.* Philadelphia: Temple University Press.

Wise, J. C., Lee, S. H., Litzinger, T., Marra, R. M., & Palmer, B. (2004). A Report on a Four-Year Longitudinal Study of Intellectual Development of Engineering Undergraduates. *Journal of Adult Development, 11*(2), 103–110.

Wolpert, L. (1994). *The unnatural nature of science – Why science does not make (common) sense*. Cambridge, MA: Harvard University Press.
Wood, K. (2000). The experience of learning to teach: changing student teachers' ways of understanding teaching. *Journal of Curriculum Studies*, *32*(1). 75–93.
Wood, P., & Kardash, C. (2002). Critical elements in the design and analysis of studies of epistemology. In B. K. Hofer, & P. R. Pintrich (Eds.), *Personal epistemology* (pp. 231–260). Mahwah, NJ: Lawrence Erlbaum Ass.
Yero, J. L. (2002). *Teaching in mind – How teacher thinking shapes education*. Hamilton, Montana: MindFlight Publishing.
Yerrick, R. K., Pedersen, J. E., & Arnason, J. (1998). "We're just spectators": A case study of science teaching, epistemology, and classroom management, *Science Education*, *82*(6), 619–648.
Zuidweg, M. (2003). Dus dit is de universiteit [So this is university]. *HBO-Journaal*, *5*(25), 28–30.

APPENDIX

The Dutch Educational System

This study was performed within the Dutch educational system, however, the audience will certainly include scholars from other nations. We have regularly encountered difficulties in establishing exactly which age group and what type of education was the object of study in the literature. To clarify the issue regarding our own study we include a description of the Dutch system, the one most familiar to us.

Formal, compulsory education in the Netherlands starts at 5, with most children entering elementary or primary education at age 4. Primary school consists of 8 schoolyears, from 4 to about 12 years of age. At the end of primary school, pupils usually undergo a national aptitude test and are recommended towards one of three types of secondary education, two are more theoretical and general in nature, the third is geared towards vocational education. As compulsory education lasts until 16, all children continue for at least another 4 years of secondary education.

The general secondary education consists of pre-university education (6 years, from 12 through 18, gymnasium (classic school) or vwo/atheneum) geared towards academic higher education, and pre-professional education (5 years, from 12 through 17, havo, comparable with GCSE or standard high school) geared towards further higher education of a more practical or applied nature (hbo).

Vocational education consists of a lower cycle (4 years, from 12 through 16, vmbo) with various school types varying in the amount of practical or theoretical education, and an upper cycle (4 years, from 16 through 20, mbo). While it is possible to leave formal education after the lower cycle vmbo, it is not considered a sufficient diploma for a continued career.

An integral part of the Dutch system is the option to 'stack' or accumulate school diplomas. Stacking schooltypes is an essential aspect in providing optimal education to all. It is possible to start secondary education in the theoretical vocational stream (vmbo-tl), and proceed after successful graduation through havo and vwo, entering each in the pre-exam year with the option of entering academic university at 20. An alternative route would be formed by stacking a more practical type vmbo, then mbo followed by a professional bachelor's degree (hbo) or after a successful first-year hbo entering academic bachelor education. These stacking routes are indicated by the horizontal arrows in figure A.1 below.

Characteristic for the Dutch system is that in secondary education all pupils are required to make a choice regarding subject orientation around 15 years of age. The subject orientations, streams or learning paths consist of

- Science and Technology (advanced math, sciences); Technology (vocational stream)
- Science and Health (math, chemistry and biology); Healthcare (vocational stream)
- Economics and Society (math and economics); Economics (vocational stream)
- Culture and Society (elementary math, languages)

– Agriculture (vocational stream)

Higher education is currently organised around two types of universities. The general universities providing mostly academic courses, with a bachelor's degree after 3 years, and master degree courses that can take up 1 to 2 years depending on the discipline. Currently general universities usually offer applied, educational and research oriented master courses. The Dutch higher professional education has recently consolidated into Universities of Applied Sciences (in Dutch, Hogescholen) which provide higher education of a more practical and applied nature. The Hotelschool The Hague is one of the Hogescholen in the Netherlands (see gray area in Figure A). The bachelor's courses at Applied Universities are four years, and master degrees can be obtained in two years. Applied Universities also offer 2-year Associate Degree courses to graduates of vocational education (mbo).

Doctorate degrees are available only from general universities at this time and require an additional research effort. Doctorate degrees can be earned within the university context or outside of it.

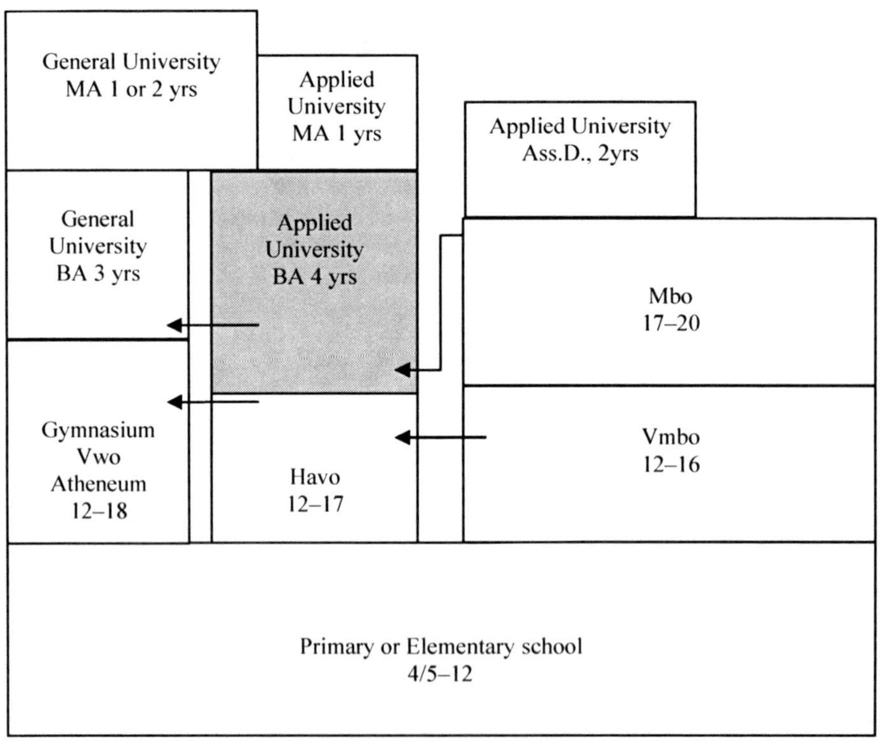

Figure A. The dutch educational system.

AUTHOR INDEX

SUBJECT INDEX

Q

R

S

Lightning Source UK Ltd.
Milton Keynes UK
17 May 2010

154310UK00001B/3/P

9 789460 912511